T
A

AFRICAN PROCONSULS: European governors in Africa, ed. by L. H. Gann and Peter Duignan. Free Press, 1978. 548p ill map index 78-57054. 29.95 ISBN 0-02-911190-0. C.I.P.

Very little has been done to study the literally thousands of individuals who have served as governors of European overseas territories in modern times. A comprehensive list of such individuals does exist (cf. D. P. Henige, *Colonial governors from the fifteenth century to the present,* CHOICE, Mar. 1971), but only the most famous or infamous have been investigated (e.g., Wingate, Lugard, and Graziani). This handsome volume deals with some of the famous (Faidherbe, Gallieni, Lugard), as well as some whose reputations are known but whose biographies are not (Binger, Eboué, Delavignette, Andrew Cohen, Ryckmans) and some whose names are relatively unfamiliar (Hugh Clifford, Coryndon, Rutten, Norten de Matos, Schnee). Gann and Duignan of the Hoover Institution, well known for their *Colonialism in Africa, 1870–1960* (CHOICE, Jul.-Aug. 1970), have approached the topic with this collection of essays on 15 European governors in Africa, written by scholarly Africanists. France, Britain, Belgium, Portugal, and Germany are represented; Italy and Spain are not. Each national section is preceded by a general essay. The lengthy essays on French governors (by William B. Cohen) and British governors (by

Continued

AFRICAN PROCONSULS

A.H.M. Kirk-Greene) are particularly useful; those on Portugal (D Wheeler) and on Belgium and Germany (Gann) are relatively brief. Level upper-division undergraduate and graduate.

African Proconsuls

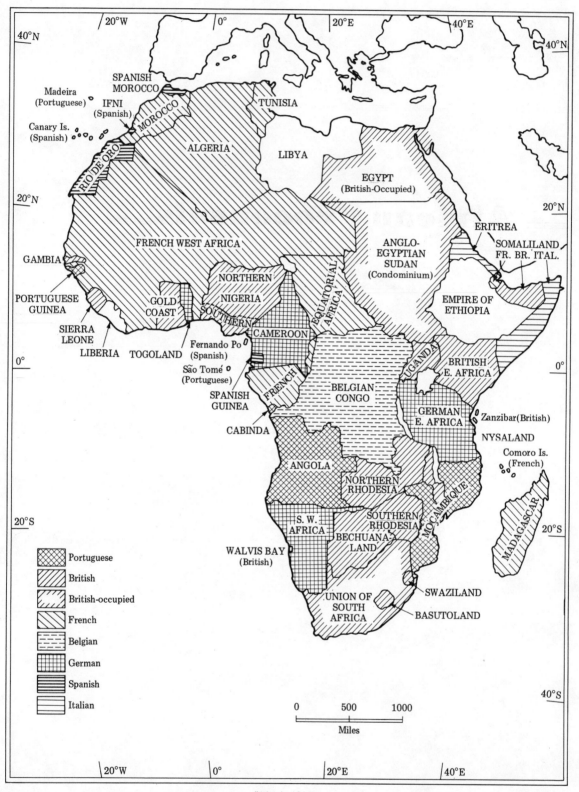

Africa in 1914

African Proconsuls

European Governors in Africa

L. H. Gann and
Peter Duignan, Editors

226728

THE FREE PRESS
A Division of Macmillan Publishing Co., Inc.
NEW YORK

Collier Macmillan Publishers
LONDON

and

HOOVER INSTITUTION

STANFORD, CALIFORNIA

The Free Press
A Division of Macmillan Publishing Co., Inc.
866 Third Avenue, New York, N.Y. 10022

Collier Macmillan Canada, Ltd.

Library of Congress Catalog Card Number: 78-57054

Printed in the United States of America

printing number
1 2 3 4 5 6 7 8 9 10

Library of Congress Cataloging in Publication Data

Main entry under title:

African proconsuls.

    "Published under the auspices of the Hoover Institu-
tion."
    1. Africa--Politics and government. 2. Colonial
administrators--Africa--Biography. 3. Europe--Colonies
--Africa--Administration. I. Gann, Lewis H.
II. Duignan, Peter.
JQ1875.A1A35   325'.31'0922 [B]   78-57054
ISBN 0-02-911190-0

Contents

France

Great Britain

Belgium

Portugal

Contents

Germany

Contributors

Adiele Eberachukwu Afigbo, professor of history, head of the Department of History and Archaeology, and dean, Faculty of Arts, University of Nigeria, Nsukka. Author of *The Warrant Chiefs: Indirect Rule in Southeastern Nigeria, 1891–1929* and other studies on West African history.

Leland Conley Barrows, associate professor of African and European history at Voorhees College. Now preparing a study on Faidherbe.

Henri Brunschwig, director, Ecole des hautes études en sciences sociales. Author of numerous works on imperialism in Africa, including *Mythes et realités de l'impérialisme colonial français, 1871–1914* and *L'Avènement de l'Afrique noire du 19ᵉ siècle à nos jours*.

William B. Cohen, associate professor of history, Indiana University, Bloomington. Author of *Rulers of Empire: The French Colonial Service in Africa*.

Bruce Fetter, associate professor of history, University of Wisconsin at Milwaukee. Author of *The Creation of Elisabethville, 1910–1940* and editor of *Urbanism Past and Present*.

Peter Duignan, Director of African and Middle East Studies and Senior Fellow, Hoover Institution. Co-author of *The Rulers of German Africa* and co-editor of *Colonialism in Africa* and other books on colonialism.

John E. Flint, professor of Commonwealth history, Dalhousie University. Author of *Cecil Rhodes* and other works on European imperialism; co-editor of *The Cambridge History of Africa*.

Harry A. Gailey, professor of history and coordinator of African studies, San Jose State College. Author of the standard *A History of The Gambia* and a number of other books related to African history.

L. H. Gann, Senior Fellow, Hoover Institution. Co-author of *The Rulers of British Africa, 1870–1914*, co-editor of *Colonialism in Africa* and other books on African history.

G. Wesley Johnson, Jr., professor of history, University of California at Santa Barbara. Author of *The Emergence of Black Politics in Senegal* and other studies of francophone Africa.

Anthony H. M. Kirk-Greene, Fellow of St. Antony's College, Oxford University; a former British administrator. Author of numerous studies on British colonial history; now preparing a history of the British colonial service.

Virgil L. Matthew, Jr., professor of history, California State University at Fresno. Now preparing a study of Gallieni.

William Bunnell Norton, professor of history (emeritus) and research associate, African Studies Center, Boston University.

Ronald Robinson, fellow of Balliol College and Beit Professor of History of the British Commonwealth, Oxford. Co-author of the seminal study *Africa and Victorians: The Official Mind of Imperialism* and of other studies.

Woodruff D. Smith, associate professor of history, University of Texas at San Antonio. Author of *The German Colonial Empire.*

Brian Weinstein, professor of political science, Howard University. Author of *Eboué,* the standard biography of Governor-general Eboué, and of works on the politics of language.

Douglas L. Wheeler, professor of history, University of New Hampshire, Durham. Co-author of *Angola* and of *Republican Portugal: A Political History, 1910–1926.*

Preface

Modern African historians have not set much store by full-scale biographies, least of all biographical studies of former colonialists. Instead, scholars have tended to place greater emphasis on factors concerned with state building, nation-building, and the mobilization of resources and of men. This book attempts to restore the balance. It presents portraits of French, Belgian, Portuguese, German, and British empire builders; it also attempts to cover colonialism in all its various stages. In addition, there are a number of chapters that discuss the wider problems of governorship in the former British, French, German, and Portuguese colonies.

The portraits of the various governors follow a broadly similar outline. Our contributors describe the governors' background, education, and early career and place them in their social, political, and national setting. The different authors devote considerable attention to the governors' official careers and conclude with assessments of their postcolonial activity. Given the disparate nature of the material available and the disparate nature of colonial governance at different periods of time, under different European flags, we have not attempted to impose rigid uniformity. The chapters in this volume are meant to be historical essays in their own right not standardized entries for a historical encyclopedia. But there is a connecting thread. The proconsuls who are our subjects served at different times and in different places; they faced an extraordinary variety of administrative and political problems. They were all servants of alien regimes; they were also among the unwitting state builders of modern Africa. In A.E. Afigbo's words, they were "men of two continents"—political architects as well as agents of destruction.

Our labor has been lightened by the scholarship and also by the patience displayed by our contributors in the face of administrative delays. In addition, we should like to express our thanks to the Director of the Hoover Institution and to the Earhard Foundation for their generosity, in supporting the Hoover Institution's "Builders of Empire" project, of which this volume forms a part.

 **Introduction**

COLONIAL governors were an extraordinarily diverse group. At first sight, no single category of professional men seems more heterogeneous than the chief colonial executives who presided over the European colonies in sub-Saharan Africa from the so-called Age of the New Imperialism to decolonization. They held a variety of titles—governor-general, high commissioner general, high commissioner, governor, chief commissioner, administrator, lieutenant governor. The total number of officeholders who ruled a designated territory or a group of territories during this period exceeded 800. To be exact, between the start of the Berlin conference in 1884 and the year in which Zambia and Malawi attained their independence, 1964, there were 333 French officials, 293 British, 142 Portuguese, 27 German, and 26 Belgian.

This array of governors differed from each other in every conceivable respect—in manner, in appearance, in physical size. Sir Robert Coryndon, for instance, looked like a hero straight out of Kipling—a commanding presence, tall, broad-shouldered, and physically strong; he could lift a pony on a bet or bend a half crown piece for the amusement of his friends. Sir Gordon Guggisberg was a giant. On the other hand, Sir Harry Johnston, a former art student, was a rotund, little man, as unlike the conventional picture of the empire builder as could be imagined. Lord Frederick Lugard's smallness of stature likewise contrasted oddly with his military manner and aspirations.

In terms of personal qualities, governors had little in common. Eduard von Liebert of German East Africa possessed in full the authoritarian personality so beloved by the Frankfurt school of sociologists. He grew up under his grandfather's stern and patriarchal guidance. At the age of eleven he was sent to a Prussian cadet school, where life was harsh and where the youngest and weakest were beaten without mercy by their more athletic peers. Liebert joined his regiment at sixteen as an ensign, and from then onward the regiment was his home, his family, his fatherland, his all. The emperor's friends were his friends; the emperor's

1

enemies were his enemies. He hated the Jews; he hated the Liberals; he hated the Social Democrats. He joined the Nazi party long before Hitler seized power, at a time when members of Liebert's social class still accounted membership in such a plebeian group as a social disqualification. But men like Liebert were the exception. Heinrich Schnee, son of a German provincial judge of liberal leanings, had a happy childhood. There was nothing in his personality that remotely resembled Liebert's ruthlessness. Robert Delavignette had a marvelous youth: his early life was not socially restricted; he was inspired by two most unusual schoolteachers; his parents were reasonable and kind. Like many other governors, Delavignette became a "solid and obstinate liberal."

Governors were equally diverse in their politics. There was a contingent of unrepentant Tories. They included men like Sir Francis Chaplin, journalist, mine manager, South African parliamentarian, and administrator of Southern Rhodesia under the British South Africa Company. Chaplin was a Tory of Tories, one of the foremost representatives of the "high mining" school in pre–World War I South African politics. He stood for mining capitalism and the imperial connection. Chaplin would have no truck with white workers; indeed, within his own lifetime, his position as a right-wing Unionist became archaic. But Chaplin was by no means typical of colonial governors. A substantial number veered to the left of center. Delavignette was a left-wing Catholic married to an outspoke Socialist. José Norton de Matos turned into a convinced opponent of the Salazar dictatorship. Louis Faidherbe, a French soldier and governor, offended conservatives in the French army by his admiration for Léon Gambetta and for Gambetta's determination in 1871 to conduct a people's war against the invading German army. Louis Gustave Binger, like most of his colleagues, was a Republican, well regarded by French anticlericals. Schnee, in Germany, was a National Liberal with a reformist bent. Julius von Zech, his compatriot, was an adherent of the Center party. Félix Eboué, a black West Indian, owed his gubernatorial post to his Masonic connections and to the Popular Front government set up in 1936; soon afterward he became a champion of de Gaulle.

Their geographic origins do not lend themselves to rigid classification. A substantial proportion of British governors came from the gentry and were linked by education, social connections, and personal preference to London and the home counties. The "Celtic fringe" did not go unrepresented but played in no way as important a part as did southeastern England. The British administrators maintained close links to the Anglican church, the older universities, and gentlemen's clubs. They took pride in a common love of open-air pursuits and in their respect for form. Thus, they achieved a remarkably cohesive ethos. Gentlemen on the whole trusted one another—and with good reason. Personal corruption among British governors and judges was almost unknown. Tensions between civilian and military officers were less than among continental colonials. There was more social cohesion within the various ranks of the British governing stratum than within those of its continental counterparts. Junior clerks in the upper division of the colonial office one day might head the ministry; assistant district commissioners one day might reside in Government House. They were gentlemen by definition. The very system in government offices whereby junior officials minuted documents before sending them to their seniors for further comment reflected in some measure the social cohesion of the British administrative elite.

British governors occupied a peculiarly favored position within metropolitan society. When Britain acquired its new African empire, its financial and economic stake in the area was small. But it had at least a long-standing tradition of overseas service, and such service in the dependencies carried with it a good deal of prestige. Colonial governance was an occupation fit for gentlemen. British governors on the whole were more highly placed socially and better remunerated financially than their confrères on the continent. During the heyday of empire, British governors formed part of the British ruling group—the most homogeneous ruling stratum in Europe—or were easily assimilated into it. They therefore looked upon themselves as gentlemen rather than bureaucratic or military specialists. As gentlemen, they prized the virtues of the amateur, virtues that their education was designed to enhance. Unlike their counterparts in continental bureaucracies, they had not been trained exclusively in legal and administrative studies; instead, they had taken degrees in a variety of subjects, commonly literary or classical. Most British governors had been molded by the public schools, where members of the financial aristocracy rubbed shoulders with sons of landowners and where a classical education was prized beyond all. Those who had not gone to public schools had at least attended good grammar schools shaped to a greater or lesser extent by the public school ethos. A high proportion attended Oxford or Cambridge or a great military institution like Sandhurst. Later in life they joined distinguished clubs where they once more mingled on terms of social equality with merchants, bankers, senior civil servants, and military officers.

The administrative cadres on the continent were not as tightly knit as the British. In Germany a good number of colonial dignitaries were nobles from the more backward rural areas—East Prussia, Pomerania, Bavaria, and so forth. The industrial cities of the Ruhr or trading communities like Hamburg and Bremen, for whose collective benefit the colonial empire had supposedly been built, went unrepresented. The French recruited a considerable number of their colonial officials from peripheral regions like Alsace, Corsica, and Algeria. The Portuguese relied heavily on northern Portugal as an area of recruitment. The Belgians drew many of their administrators from the Ardennes—a French-speaking, poverty-stricken region but one well supplied with schools. In addition, the Belgian establishment had a strong urban orientation; Brussels played a relatively larger part in furnishing senior officers than did Paris or Berlin. But every rule had its exception, and every exception its subexception, so that sociologists cannot easily establish all-embracing rules with regard to gubernatorial provenance.

For all the differences, there were nevertheless distinctive uniformities. European colonization in Africa was primarily a middle-class achievement. The majority of governors came from the middle layers of society. Exceptions included Joaquim Mousinho de Albuquerque and Ayres d' Ornellas, who were aristocrats of most distinguished families. Adolf Friedrich, Duke of Mecklenburg, ranked high in the *Almanac de Gotha*; Albrecht Freiherr von Rechenberg traced his lineage from the Silesian *Uradel*, more ancient than many a ruling dynasty of European states. Such men, however, were the exception, although the German colonial administration employed a larger number of noblemen as governors than any other nation at the time. But men like Eugen von Zimmerer or Hans Georg von Doering, though well connected and *hoffähig* (fit to be presented at court), were essentially middle-class in taste and connections.

The average British governor—like the average German or Belgian or Portuguese senior administrator—was the son of a civil servant, a military officer, or a professional man. The British colonial service also had a strong link to the ministry, a tie of a kind not possible in Catholic countries with a celibate priesthood. Out of ninety-five twentieth-century governors whose social origins were investigated by Colin Hughes and I. F. Nicolson,[1] no fewer than thirty-four were the sons of Anglican clergymen. Direct links with the instruments of production or with finance were rare. The same was true in France and Germany. Manufacturers and bankers were less likely to send their sons into the colonial service than were professional men or civil servants. Again, there were exceptions: Wilhelm Solf, a well-known German governor, later German secretary of state for the colonies, was the son of a prosperous Berlin industrialist. By and large, however, the classes for whose benefit the empires were supposedly being built did not administer the newly won possessions.

Professionally, many governors had been trained as soldiers—Binger, Lugard, Mousinho de Albuquerque, and von Zech. Others had started life in the navy; the Portuguese especially were apt to advance sailors into high positions. There were physicians—men like Jean Bayol in France or Sir James Maxwell in Great Britain; there were engineers like Guggisberg; there were lawyers, artists, policemen, and representatives of a host of other occupations. In their personal tastes, some governors rarely opened a book; others were not only avid readers but were also copious and competent writers. Portuguese governors often had a flair for literary expression. So did many British governors, who with their classical educations were better able to express themselves than their French colleagues—apt to be trained in law and administration rather than in literature. Sir Ronald Storr's *Orientations* figured in the catalog of the Readers' Union. Sir Charles Eliot was a writer of merit and a fine linguist; his *Turkey in Europe* still ranks as a minor classic. A substantial number of governors with scholarly inclinations made their reputation as linguists (Binger, Johnston, and Eliot), and some were students of ethnography, and one of crown jewels.

For the most able or the most fortunate members of the colonial administration, the colonies were an open frontier that facilitated social promotion. Sir Edward Twining, a failed district officer, became a successful governor and, later, a peer. Lord Lugard, a humble subaltern, also rose to the peerage. So did Theophile Wahis, a onetime soldier who had earned his king's favor in the Belgian Congo. France, with its revolutionary tradition of *la carrière ouverte aux talents*, was more likely to give a chance to a poor boy than either Germany or Great Britain. A career like that of Binger, who advanced from a private in the army to national fame as soldier, explorer, scholar, and governor, would have been unthinkable in the Reich. Binger's experience was not exceptional. Of the pre-1900 French colonial governors investigated by William Cohen (see p. 19), nearly half had no academic training beyond primary school; educational achievement was much more important after the turn of the century. Nevertheless, governors of lowly social origin rarely came from the peasantry or the working class. They were apt to be sons of petty officials, noncommissioned officers, or small tradesmen. Whatever their nationality, the bulk of European governors thus were bourgeois in origin.

The criteria that entered a governor's promotion differed widely. Membership in an establishment religion was an advantage. Most German governors were Lutheran; most British governors were members of the Anglican church. Other French governors, like Eboué, benefited from membership in Masonic orders and from a reputation for republicanism and anticlericalism. In the eyes of the Belgian Catholic bourgeoisie, the early Congo Free State administration was never quite respectable; the Congolese service initially had an anticlerical flavor. An increasing number of Catholics from provincial, middle-class families entered the service after the *reprise* of 1908, so that most Belgian governors adhered to the Church of Rome. German governors were expected to be *kaisertreu*, and a regular—or at least a reserve officer's—commission was almost a sine qua non for advancement; but Catholics like Count von Zech and Freiherr von Rechenberg—members of the Center party and men with irreproachable connections—were still able to secure high offices. Political or religious patronage was less important for British governors. Given a decent respect for the opinions of others, a gentleman might profess any creed—or none. Sir Matthew Nathan was a Jew, Sir Hugh Clifford a Catholic, and Sir James Maxwell a Calvinist: all of them gained distinction under the Union Jack.

Factionalism was more evident on the continent than it was in Great Britain. France, Belgium, and Portugal were rent by quarrels between clericals and anticlericals. In Franch and Portugal, there was also a sharp cleavage between republicans and opponents of the republican system. These divisions affected a governor's promotion prospects as they did not in England; they might also plague his professional life in minor ways. The upper ranks of the bureaucracy were also structurally divided. The French and Belgian administrations, for instance, maintained rigidly separate corps, each with a tradition and an ethos of its own. Within the French bureaucracy, the *inspecteurs d'état* formed an elite, many of whose members advanced to high positions. The *inspecteurs* had no counterpart in Great Britain; their role was to assure administrative centralization, to investigate abuses, and to weed out wrongdoers. They operated in a system in which trust was less apt to be taken for granted; they were heirs to an ancient centralizing tradition derived from monarchical governance and to the quarrels and mistrust that divided French society after 1789.

Despite their middle-class backgrounds, governors were apt to affect courtly ceremonial. They were concerned to an extraordinary extent with the pomp and circumstance of high office. Whatever his social origins, a governor stood at the head of local colonial society. He combined executive leadership with ceremonial primacy, like an eighteenth-century monarch. Medals, orders, gun salutes, splendid receptions, and intense preoccupation with the formalities of social precedence helped to make colonial rule visible. An impressive ceremonial and a magnificent Government House were meant to overawe the indigenous people at a time when the physical power of the colonial state machinery was weak—much weaker than the physical power of the state apparatus in the metropolis. Honors and decorations also served to supplement the colonial official's financial income with psychic rewards, as well as with visible badges bearing witness to the recipient's achievements and position in society. Again, British governors profited the most. A British governor normally obtained a knighthood; he became a member of the gentry ex officio; a governor-general invariably was raised to the peerage. Continental governors, on the other hand, were more apt to be regarded as members of a purely bureaucratic elite. A German governor was not eligible for a patent of nobility unless he had distinguished himself as a soldier. The French and Portuguese republics naturally had no aristocratic titles at their disposal, though advancement into the Legion of Honor served a comparable purpose.

The financial fortunes of governors upon retirement were diverse. Chaplin ended up with a string of directorships in the South African mining companies; Lord Lugard became a director of Barclay's Bank after he left office; Ernest Roume, a great Frenchman, went to Le Nickel Compagnie; Gabriel-Louis Angoulvant, a compatriot, to the Compagnie générale des colonies. As Cohen points out, however, French governors with a subsequent record of financial involvement had not necessarily favored commercial companies while in office; governors who had supported free enterprise in their colonies did not necessarily pick up directorships on retirement (p. 19). The great majority of all governors, moreover, retired in modest circumstances. Some died in relative poverty, like Schnee; others left their families in a position of near deprivation—like Albert Dolisie, a Frenchman, whose friends had to help his widow by obtaining a tobacco license for her.

Generalizations on the place of retired governors in this history of their respective countries are difficult to formulate. They became high metropolitan officials, diplomats, scholars, or propagandists. Norton de Matos was appointed as a cabinet minister and played a major part in propelling Portugal into World War I. Bayol was elected to the French Senate, where he sat on the democratic left. Faidherbe helped save his country's military honor during the final stage of the Franco-German war of 1870–1871. Hubert Deschamps occupied the first chair of African history at the Sorbonne and became a successful man of letters. Many colonial dignitaries combined several roles in their lifetime. Binger served in turn as soldier and explorer, as governor, and then as a high-ranking civil servant in the French colonial ministry. William Ponty successively made his name as conqueror, administrator, and scholar. Delavignette started as a *roi de la brousse*; he ended as a scholar of international renown—and also as a bitter critic of French methods designed to quell the Algerian rising. Lord Lugard, after retiring from the governor-generalship of Nigeria, acquired further laurels as a theoretician of colonial government. His reputation was enhanced by the lucky chance of finding a biographer in Margery Perham, who was able to use a vast array of written records in her research. Other governors were not so fortunate. Count von Zech, a model ruler in every respect, left no papers; his very name remains unknown to all but a tiny number of specialists.

The colonial governorships contained their share of failures and misfits. But, as a rule, these officials were men well above average ability. They had arrived at the top of their professional career—commonly by merit and ability displayed under trying circumstances. Their achievements were considerable. They were the unacknowledged state builders of modern Africa. The newly independent republics that now cover the African map are, for the most part, of colonial provenance. They owe their boundaries, their modern administrative systems, the foundations of their modern economy, their modern social services and their modern transport system, and—above all—the language of modern government and of modern cultural intercourse to the colonial rulers—among whom the governors occupied a key position.

In Germany, France, and Belgium alike, colonial enterprise was more marginal in relation to the national economy as a whole than in Great Britain. In Belgium, for example, Leopold II had been forced to persuade a reluctant bourgeoisie to back the Congo enterprise, which had begun as the king's personal undertaking. Bismarck soon lost interest in the colonies; few Germans wanted to settle there, and anxious German parents—such as those of Schnee and of Theodor Seitz—warned their sons not to enter colonial service. The French Parti colonial was a small group that gained influence only when it managed to enlist in its support the popular forces of French nationalism. Until at least the 1920s, the French colonial ministry remained one of the least sought after cabinet posts. The ministry itself achieved a level of incompetence and disorganization rivaled by no other government department, and the colonial administration enjoyed correspondingly low prestige. Except for a minority of dedicated men, it was apt initially to attract the least able French officials, those who found it most difficult to make a career in the metropole.

The main ambition of most colonial governors from France and from Portugal was to spend as little time in the colonies as they could. As a result—at least until the 1920s—French colonies changed governors with breathtaking rapidity. Not surprisingly, both French and Portuguese colonies suffered more from high-level corruption than did British or German dependencies. There were no British or German equivalents for men like Governor Alfred-Louis Woelfel, the first commissioner of the Togo mandate, who was involved in land speculation, or for Governor Frédéric-Charles Hesling of Upper Volta, who pushed cotton growing to benefit his relatives. The French position improved only after World War I, when educational standards rose rapidly within the ranks of the colonial elite and when high-level corruption was largely eliminated.

Whatever their nationality, colonial governors shouldered broadly similar tasks. The colonial powers exercised only nominal control over the vast areas that they claimed in the earliest stage of colonialism. The first representative of metropolitan power was often a consular officer who resided at a coastal settlement. His military resources were negligible; at best, he might call upon occasional support from a visiting cruiser or gunboat. He was not expected to rule; his task was to assist local merchants, to adjudicate between aggrieved traders, and to provide information to the home government. He depended essentially on the goodwill of African potentates and relied—above all—on his diplomatic skill.

This indirect influence gave way to conquest. Military occupation often was a long drawn out affair. Governors were faced with an all-pervasive scarcity of men, money, and means. They conquered great territories with armies of battalion size. They ruled provinces as large as kingdoms with staffs fit to run a parish council. Their fiefs were devoid of railways, bridges, modern port facilities, survey departments, agricultural services, repair shops, electric power, modern schools, hospitals, research facilities, and such; the very towns and essentials of modern life had to be built from the start.

Empire building in the early days principally attracted professional soldiers, experienced in commanding men in action, fitted by training and personality to wage campaigns—but often educated in special skills like cartography, military engineering, or the art of exploration. Early German governors, for instance, were primarily military officers. King Leopold of Belgium drew his most faithful supporters from the army. French and Portuguese governors were mainly naval and military men from diverse social backgrounds. The pioneering period of empire building afforded opportunities in addition to a variety of civilians not subject to promotion in routine-bound bureaucracies. There were adventurous physicians turned explorers; there were consular officials; there were big-game hunters; and former police sergeants with a flair for government.

The pioneers ruled in an intensely personal fashion. The metropolitan organization was weak; restraints imposed by the home governments often were feeble. Governors were frontiersmen; they were concerned, above all, with conquest. But their ability actually to control the territories under their nominal sway was strictly circumscribed. A French colony in its early stage thus was correctly described as a *fédération des cercles* in which the governor was little influenced by Paris and the commandants often snapped their fingers at the occupant of Government House. The central machinery at the governor's disposal was extremely simple. Business was conducted through a chief secretary or a *Kanzler* or a *secrétaire général*, assisted by a few senior officials including the head of the military establishment.

The second stage came with the end of pacification. The soldier gave way to the civilian, the man of action to the bureaucrat, the amateur without academic rank to the credentialed specialist. The change occurred at different times, in different places; the rate of transformation varied strikingly from territory to territory and from province to province. But there were certain regularities. The development of civil government went with vast improvements in communications both within territories and between the metropoles and the colonial peripheries. Steamships, railways, and telegraphs—followed by trucks, bulldozers, and finally radio and aircraft—changed the nature of government. The heads of outlying districts became more responsive to gubernatorial decrees; the governors could be controlled more easily by their home governments. Reform commonly entailed economic change. The local revenue of the colonies no longer depended on precolonial commodities like ivory, wild rubber, and gold dust—goods that had been produced with a small outlay of capital and often by coerced labor. Instead, the colonies began to furnish the world market with bulky crops like cocoa, coffee, and cotton. Mineral-rich territories started exporting zinc, copper, and industrial diamonds—raw materials of a kind that could not have been produced or transported in large quantities with the technology available to precolonial societies.

Under the new dispensation, the colonial rulers attempted to attract more metropolitan capital so as to improve their "undeveloped estates." There was talk of reform, promoted for both economic and humanitarian ends, from the beginning of the present century by great colonial secretaries like Joseph Chamberlain in Great Britain, Bernhard Dernburg in Germany, and Jules Renkin in Belgium. These men and their disciples were convinced that profits, efficiency in government, and African well-being went together. Ministerial organization in the metropole improved. "Scientific colonialism" on the spot was represented by men like Governor-general Roume, a brilliant intellectual, who also floated the first development loan for French West Africa, promoted railway building, and reformed the bureaucracy.

The place of governors in the economic development of the colonies deserves a book to itself. Their activities showed immense variation. Transient potentates who stayed only for a year or so in a French colony were plentiful; their part in economic decisionmaking was obviously small. But there were many others who stayed long enough to make their influence felt. Conventional Marxist historiography sees the latter as mere agents of certain bourgeois pressure groups. This approach, however, ignores the element of choice that was open to them—the voluntarist element that went into the determination of policy at a time when the conquered colonies seemed almost a tabula rasa to the uninitiated, when local pressure groups were insignificant, and when a gubernatorial decision might have far-reaching consequences for the future.

A governor who knew his own mind often had several alternatives open to him. There were, for instance, the pro-settler governors. Liebert was determined to encourage the enterprise of small white farmers in German East Africa. His successors—especially von Rechenberg and Schnee—did not share Liebert's enthusiasm for petty white entrepreneurs. Von Rechenberg thought primarily in terms of developing the country through African cultivators; Schnee believed that the government should aim at a compromise solution that would provide a place for peasant and planter alike. In Kenya, Eliot played a major part in shifting economic policy. When he arrived, Kenya was regarded as an appendage of Zanzibar, of little value except as a stepping-stone to Uganda. But Eliot was convinced that the Kenyan highlands might develop into another California or another New Zealand, where Europeans would become rooted in the land. He amended the land regulations so as to make settlement more attractive to white colonists. He encouraged European settlement in a variety of other ways. The economic configuration of colonial Kenya probably owed more to Eliot's predilections than to those of any other individual.

Partialities and prejudices of individual governors played an equally important role in determining economic controversies between the rival merits of plantation agriculture and peasant farming. In 1923, for instance, a famous confrontation took place between Lord Leverhulme, the British soap and margarine magnate, and Governor Clifford of Nigeria. Leverhulme argued that the British colonies had been founded for the purpose of encouraging British commerce. Clifford considered this "a monstrous and mischievous heresy." He argued that the people of Nigeria should "retain their independence." Leverhulme never succeeded in obtaining any territorial concessions in British West Africa, and he shifted his operations to the Belgian Congo.

The construction of colonial infrastructures was greatly influenced by the governors. In German East Africa the Northern railway had been built with a view to promoting European plantation agriculture, but such plantations did not generate sufficient traffic to pay for the railway's construction. The success of the Uganda railway proved to von Rechenberg, however, that Africans could multiply their crops and pay more taxes than ever before if transport were provided for their produce. Von Rechenberg was convinced that the necessary traffic would come from Unyamwezi—the core of German East Africa, a well-populated region in the interior—as well as from Rwanda and Burundi, two densely settled interior regions. Railway building would reduce African unrest by making the cultivators more prosperous; it would also have strategic advantages in facilitating the rapid movement of soldiers in the event of new African risings comparable to the Maji-Maji outbreaks in the southern part of German East Africa. In 1907 von Rechenberg proposed that a railway be build from Dar es Salaam (on the coast) to Tabora (in the interior); on its completion in 1911, he suggested that the railway be extended to Lake Tanganyika. The construction of a line from Tabora to Rwanda was being prepared when war came in 1914.

Pre–World War I governors like von Rechenberg had thought primarily in terms of individual improvement schemes. These might center on the provision of railways or on the elimination of disease—a theme stressed by men like Robert Codrington in Northern Rhodesia. The postwar years saw the start of development plans envisaging wider objectives. When Guggisberg arrived at the Gold Coast in 1919, he carefully outlined a ten-year development plan. Its object was "the general progress of the people of the Gold Coast towards a higher state of civilization"; its keystone was to be education. Since schools were costly, government revenue must increase. Like von Rechenberg, Guggisberg argued that this could be done by improving the transportation and communication systems, thereby opening new areas to trade and reducing freight rates for both imported and exported goods. His plan called for an expenditure of £24 million, a large sum for the time. The postwar depression forced Guggisberg to reduce his expenditure to just over £16 million, yet he managed to carry out the major part of his plan. There were no natural harbors in the Gold Coast so in 1928 Sir Gordon began to build an artificial harbor at Takoradi. He laid out plans for Achimota College, initiated a drive for better roads, built the country's first modern hospital, and devised a scheme for training Africans to serve in responsible government positions. Guggisberg therefore foreshadowed development planning, with its belief in state intervention and its wider social objectives, which came to characterize the last decades of colonial rule after World War II.

These colonial rulers tried to link two separate strands of policy. They wished to promote economic development. They also started to speak in terms of a "dual mandate," of "trusteeship," of *Fürsorge*, of *moralisation*—terms that began to gain wide currency from the first decade of the present century and that served to legitimize the new period of bourgeois reform. Theoreticians of colonial rule increasingly looked upon Africans as "economic men," as cultivators or as wage workers capable of responding to the economic incentives of a market economy—rather than as idle heathens who should be coerced for their own and their employers' good.

Notions of government differed considerably over time and from one territory to the next. By and large, however, the colonial rulers considered their task done if they protected the security of person and property, raised revenue, and ran essential services like transport. Development was to be left in the main to the private enterprise of merchants and mine owners in the economic field and to missionaries in the spiritual sphere. The bureaucracies at the disposal of governors remained strictly limited. A few years before the outbreak of World War I, the Gold Coast —a country as large as the state of Oregon—was still run by only 91 British civil officials and about 100 British military and police officers.

During the heyday of colonialism, the governor played a decisive role in administration. Within every colonial establishment he headed a strictly hierarchical organization, bound by precedent. Governors were far from being autocratic rulers. Their powers were rigidly controlled by law and restricted by the pervasive weakness of colonial state machinery. As an example, between 1911 and 1950 British military power in Northern Rhodesia—a territory larger than Great Britain, Germany, and the Low Countries put together—consisted of a weak infantry battalion of 800 African soldiers commanded by a handful of British officers. The Colonial Office liked governors who ruled in a pacific manner. The use of violence, entailing military expenditure, unfavorable comments in the local and overseas press, Parliamentary debates, and public commission of enquiry reports, was apt to blacken an official's reputation. Colonial governance, moreover, was relatively stable for a time. A colonial governor—unlike a Latin American dictator—could not be displaced by a putsch or a coup d'état; the traditional type of Africa resistance largely disappeared, and the new political forms of resistance and modern guerrilla movements—based on political more than tribal affiliation—had not yet developed into a powerful force. Unlike European tyrants such as Hitler or Stalin, a colonial governor could neither "mobilize" the masses nor "liquidate" his enemies. There were commotions. There was unrest, such as the riots that broke out in the Northern Rhodesian copper belt in both 1935 and 1940. The bloodshed involved in the two riots, however deplorable, was on a small scale (23 African miners lost their lives). Yet the riots produced a vast body of reports, debates, questions, and memoranda inquiring into the deficiencies of British rule. Official apprehension contributed to the creation of a social science research organization, the Rhodes-Livingstone Institute (now the Institute for Social Research at the University of Zambia), with a marked left-of-center political orientation. There was a sense of social concern and of moral outrage. Subsequent historians then built a massive superstructure of learned works based on official and semiofficial publications that would never have seen the light of day under less humanitarian regimes. (In 1964, after Zambia had obtained independence, over 700 people were killed in incidents occasioned by the suppression of the dissident Lumpa Church. The destruction of the Lumpa Church, however, did not make the international headlines, and failed to enter academic consciousness.) Compared to precolonial rule by warlike conquerors like the Bemba and the Ngoni, for example, governance under the Union Jack was mild. Contrasted with postcolonial potentates like Idi Amin in Uganda, or Jean-Bedel Bokassa in the Central African Empire, or Macias Nguema in Guinea, leaders like Sir Andrew Cohen—rightly portrayed by Ronald Robinson as a liberal, high-minded, and highly cultured official (see pp. 353-64)—were men of peace. We are therefore unable to share A. E. Afigbo's assessment that colonialism created "one of the most illiberal regimes of modern times," run by men "perhaps more amenable to psychoanalysis than to conventional historical investigation" (see pp. 531-34).

We agree, on the other hand, with Afigbo's strictures regarding the unrepresentative nature of colonial governance and the colonial penchant for government by conspicuous display. The colonial powers were determined to impress their subjects. Among their European colleagues, British governors generally held both the most powerful and the most dignified position. The governor was appointed by his sovereign on the recommendation of the secretary of state after consultation with the prime minister. He was the monarch's representative; in theory, at any rate, all power and responsibility rested with him. His pay was high—sometimes higher than the British prime minister's. He initiated policies, shared in their making and implementation. He supervised the work of all colonial departments. He headed the executive council—a kind of cabinet. He acted as president of the local legislature. He alone communicated with the secretary of state for the colonies. He usually held the title of commander in chief. His actual stay in the colonies was five years, much longer than his Portuguese or French confrères. If he were a man of strong character, his personality might permeate the entire administration. He might not have time to enforce his policies down to the provincial or the district level, but he did enjoy a good deal of de facto independence from the colonial office. Metropolitan authorities usually hesitated to meddle with the man on the spot regarding matters on which local administrators were better informed than their London colleagues. There was a good deal of informal give-and-take between imperial and local authorities, strengthened by the discrete ties of public school, church, clubs, and associations like the Royal Empire Society. As long as a governor did not occasion a public scandal, a parliamentary crisis, or a financial deficit, his position was secure.

In the British possessions, unlike those of all other colonial powers, day-to-day legislation regulating the normal work of government originated in local legislative bodies composed of both "official" members—mostly top-ranking bureaucrats—and "nonofficial" members. The nonofficials at first represented special interests and, in the later stages of colonialism, an electorate that gradually widened. In the initial phase of colonial rule, the governor acted more or less as his own prime minister. Toward the end of the colonial era, the governor became a constitutional monarch; power then was exercised by a ministry composed of parliamentarians able to command a majority in the chamber. In running the colony, the governor was assisted by the chief secretary (sometimes known as colonial secretary), who headed the local civil service. His office, the secretariat, was the nerve center and memory of government, the connecting link between the central administration and the outlying districts as well as between the central departments of government.

Belgium and imperial Germany were constitutionally almost as stable as Great Britain. Under Belgian and German auspices, colonial governors held a position similar to that of their British colleagues. Governors from Belgium, Germany, France, and Portugal all possessed limited powers of legislation. The Belgians and Germans also held tenure for extended periods; they exercised a great deal of influence on the day-to-day administration of their territories. Unlike British governors, however, they had to put up with interference from the metropolitan legislature on budgetary matters. Yet a British governor placed, say, under the Kaiser's flag would have found conditions broadly similar. A *Kanzler* or *Erster Referent* took the place of the chief secretary; the *Referenten* in the capital corresponded to heads of department under the Union Jack. Foreign ceremonial, though perhaps abstruse and elaborate, would not have struck a British incumbent as ridiculous.

French possessions were run on somewhat different lines. Through administrative rationalization French Africa was divided into two federations: French West Africa (1904) and French Equatorial Africa (1910). Each federation was headed by a governor-general who supervised the work of the territorial governors. In theory, the system was highly centralized. In practice, governors and governors-general enjoyed a great deal of independence. Governors-general in many ways resembled British governors. They alone might correspond with the minister of colonies; they controlled the military establishment. They supervised the civilian administration except for finance and justice, which enjoyed a certain autonomy. They commonly initiated policy. Unlike the British, however, they were subject to inquisitions held by *inspecteurs d'état* directly answerable to the ministry of colonies. The French gubernatorial corps was much more politicized than its British equivalent. Governors changed with bewildering rapidity; the effective power of the office was therefore much diminished. Hence, the local bureaucracy, including the governor's cabinet and various bureaus dealing with specialized issues like economy and finance, assumed an importance unknown in the British system.

The colonial governments that went down to dissolution during the 1950s and 1960s differed considerably from those of an earlier era. After World War II, the task of defending and administering the colonies no longer seemed as prestigious as during the heyday of colonialism. Careers in great corporations, in academia, and in newly emergent service professions became increasingly attractive. Colonial governance lost its air of romance. The olden day *roi de la brousse* had been a petty sovereign; under the new dispensation, the district commissioner or police commissioner became a bureaucrat hedged in regulations and bound by social concerns.

In the 1920s, for example, a Rhodesian police officer assigned to a lonely outstation had been a man of great local consequence. Four decades later he had lost much of his independence: he was subject to orders transmitted from Salisbury by telephone; he was in constant communication with the capital by helicopter, automobile, or truck. Even the charms of an open-air existence had diminished. The land was fenced in. Big-game hunting had become almost a sport of the past. If he were a sports enthusiast, he would find the capital better equipped with playing fields, swimming pools, and tennis courts than was his outpost. The very nature of his work had changed. Government had become more complex, more bureaucratic, and more publicity oriented. "Unrest" had grown more widespread and was better publicized abroad. Administrators were expected to be experts in "social problems" if not in counterinsurgency.

In the more advanced territories, there were also far-reaching economic changes. The more developed regions crossed the threshhold of industrialization, first represented by light industry, agricultural processing plants, and manufacturing designed to support such basic industries as mining. Governments took an increasingly active part in colonial economies; the Southern Rhodesian iron and steel industry, for example, owed a great deal to government intervention during World War II. Methods of production grew more complex and more specialized than they had been in the past. Employers now needed an experienced and stable labor force—not unskilled hands of the kind needed to run backwoods enterprises. There was a call for social reform. There was a new concern with urban problems. The more advanced colonial governments began to seek the advice of social scientists—whose recommendations then were normally ignored. Theoreticians of colonial government now thought of Africans as customers rather than as mere producers. Experts in labor relations no longer worried about the accustomed labor shortages but about unemployment.

At the same time, colonial government became a complex affair. The governor and district commissioners had to collaborate with a growing number of experts within the administration; they also were forced increasingly to contend with

African politicians skilled in the arts of propaganda and party management. The old type of proconsul—like Johnston of Nyasaland, whose regime could be fairly described as "one of benevolent autocracy tempered only by financial stringency" —died out. The typical governor now was more of a moderator and a politician than a policymaker.

In times of emergency—internal or external—there were reversions to the older pattern. Pierre Ryckmans, governor-general of the Belgian Congo during World War II, was a viceroy in the true sense. Belgium had been occupied, as in World War I; the Belgian government was in exile. Belgian power, such as it was, derived largely from the Congo. Ryckmans, a cultured liberal and a highly literate lawyer—author of a book entitled characteristically *Dominer pour servir*—was suddenly elevated to a position of major importance.

Decolonization, whether achieved by peaceful or by warlike means, placed special emphasis on the governor's personal ability. But now he required skills very different from those of his predecessors. In the 1920s, for instance, a British governor rarely had to worry about public opinion at home, much less about what foreigners said abroad. Colonial matters were debated in a half empty House of Commons. Governors in the 1950s and 1960s worked in the glare of world opinion as represented or manipulated by radio and television commentators, newspaper editors, clergymen, professors, U.N. diplomats, and salaried philanthropists. Governors operated in circumstances wherein colonial rule appeared to be illegitimate by its very nature, quite irrespective of its performance. Colonial governance had to change in style as well as in substance.

The Portuguese tried to hold on to the bitter end. Portuguese colonial government in its final stages reverted to its military antecedent; military commanders placed in charge of entire territories—men like Kaúlza de Arriaga and Antonio de Spínola—resembled the viceroys of old. In the end, the junior Portuguese officers, tired of a never ending war, accomplished what the guerrillas had been unable to achieve; the army overthrew the Lisbon regime and dismantled the colonial empire.

The British and French, however, had preferred to decolonize by negotiation. At the Gold Coast, for example, Governor Sir Charles Arden-Clarke played a decisive role in effecting a pacific transfer of power to African control; his skills were those of a politician, negotiator, and broker rather than those of an old-time administrator.

The objectives of the decolonizing governor were strikingly different from those of his predecessor. Whether he was liberal in outlook like Arden-Clarke or a committed Marxist like Rear admiral Rosa Coutinho, president of the local military junta during the tail end of Portuguese rule in Angola, the decolonizing governor headed an administration of transition. His task was dual in nature. He was expected to dismantle the imperial structure but also to assure the departing metropolitan power some residual influence in the newly independent country. Influence might be of many kinds—economic, political, or even ideological—but Portuguese Communists were as anxious as British Tories to play some part in shaping the African successor states in their own image. The decolonizing governor, in certain respects, oddly resembled the consul of the 1870s, the diplomatic broker in the coastal settlement who had relied primarily upon indirect means of exerting power.

The colonial governors reflected the changing functions and foci of the metropolitan societies from which they had sprung. They were also agents of change in their own right—conquerors, administrators, development planners, diplomats, and scholars. Their part in the development of Africa has been neglected of late, as scholars have tried to right the balance of African historiography by tilting their attention from imperial to Afrocentric studies. But the building of a railway, the construction of a mine, the application of scientific research to African problems, and the creation of archives are as much part of African as of imperial history, though they may have been initiated by immigrant whites. The states of modern Africa are colonial—not precolonial—products; so are the medical, educational, and scientific services that sustain them and the African elites who exercise postcolonial dominance. The colonial governors were themselves more than the servants of empire. They were also the unwitting state builders of a new Africa.

We therefore see no reason to diverge from the views expressed in an earlier book entitled *Burden of Empire*.[2] We argued—as did Marx and Engels well over a century ago in the respective contexts of India and Algeria—that the Western colonizers were conquerors with a difference. The representatives of the "New Imperialism" radically diverged from Zulu, Ndebele, Tutsi, or Swahili invaders of earlier times. The Western empire builders, wittingly or unwittingly, brought to Africa methods of production, scientific knowledge, and philosophies of governance qualitatively different from those available to African chiefs and warlords of previous generations. Railways, deep-level mining, veterinary laboratories, geological surveys, printing presses, agronomy, medical science, modern methods of administration, schools, hospitals, research institutions—in short, the whole complex of Western arts, sciences, and governance—initially traveled to Africa in the imperial baggage train. The very criteria against which the Western record in Africa later came to be judged—democracy, the rule of law, and the rights of man—would have been incomprehensible to African rulers like Msidi and Lobengula whom the Western imperialists displaced.

These conclusions would not have shocked Marx or Engels who, in certain respects, had more in common with Kipling than with self-styled Marxists of a later generation. But these conclusions are no longer popular today. No academic laurels are won by defending them. Colonialism instead has acquired an almost Satanic quality, yet one oddly fused with irrelevance. As Afigbo puts it in his concluding essay, "the political and administrative structures that obtained for most of the colonial past can be described largely as irrelevant from the point of view of the subsequent political and administrative structures of African states."[3] Colonialism, as he sees it, created a tradition of ruthless repression, a monstrous regime of European adventurers," a monstrous drama: in which Africans were subjected to defeat, humiliation, and exploitation. "The governors described in this volume were distinguished by aberrant personalities; they and their regimes are more amenable to psychoanalysis than to conventional historical investigation."

Our own interpretation is very different. Afigbo undervalues the links that tie colonial to post-colonial Africa. The African independence movements used the languages of their Western opponents, English, French, and Portuguese; they also used Western concepts. They did not try to recreate ancient empires like Ghana,

Songhay, Oyo, Jokun, and such like. Neither did they restore the work of pre-colonial African conquerors like Mansa Musa, Askia Muhammad, Shaka, Usman Dan Fodio, and other ancient rulers mentioned by Afigbo. On the contrary, what he calls, "the monstrous regiment of European adventurers," the Lugards, the Cecil Rhodes, the Faidherbes, the Bingers, the Albuquerques, have as good a claim to be regarded as the state builders of modern Africa as the African nationalists who later took over from the colonial regimes.

European colonialism, as we are well aware, had its seamy side. Africans will not soon forget the brutalities of King Leopold's "Red Rubber" regime in the Congo, or the ruthlessness with which the Germans suppressed the Herero of Namibia. These methods, however, did not characterize the colonial regimes as a whole; overall they ceased to disfigure the pages of Africa's history after World War I. For all their respective deficiencies, the worst of the governors described in these pages never stooped to the crimes committed by post-colonial regimes in countries as diverse as Burundi, Uganda, Equatorial Guinea, and the Central African Empire. Governor Binger compares favorably with emperor Bokassa; Sir Andrew Cohen shines by comparison with field marshal Idi Amin. And the historical record is clear—few profited directly or indirectly from their posts. Money could not have been their goal; none died wealthy but many died poor.

Given the role of Western colonial enterprise in Africa, the composition, character, and effects of colonial rule therefore raise some of the most significant questions that can be posed regarding modern Africa. The future of Africa's rulers remains linked to the proconsuls of the African past.

Notes to Introduction

1. Colin Hughes and I. F. Nicolson, "A provenance of proconsuls: British colonial governors, 1900–1960," *Journal of Imperial and Commonwealth History* (1977, v. IV, no. 1, 1975, p. 77–106.)
2. L. H. Gann and Peter Duignan, *Burden of Empire: An appraisal of Western colonialism in Africa south of the Sahara.* (Stanford, Hoover Institution, 1971), see also Peter Duignan and L. H. Gann, eds. *The Economics of colonialism* (*Colonialism in Africa*, v. 4, Cambridge, 1975).
3. See p. 528.

France

The French Governors

William B. Cohen

FRENCH colonization in the New World began in the seventeenth century under the ancien régime. In establishing their overseas administration, the French, relying on a centralizing tradition, used a metropolitan model. Each region of overseas France, just as each province in France proper, was ruled by a governor who was in charge mainly of military and security affairs and had to share his powers with the intendant in charge of judicial and financial affairs. Their powers were interrelated, and there was often conflict between the two. The existence of both offices was seen as the best means for Paris to keep informed of what was going on in France's distant possessions, thus thwarting their independence, since dissatisfied intendants and governors would inform the capital of a rival's malfeasance. Because of their military functions, most governors were military officers, often men of the minor nobility; the intendants came from the bourgeoisie or at best the nobility of the robe. The office of governor overseas under the ancien régime was frequently a relatively humble occupation. Governor Pouancey of Saint-Domingue (later Haiti) had to demand in 1681 that he be supplied with two garrisons of twenty-five men each since "it is to lower the office of governor to force him personally to arrest a thief, a traitor, or a drunk."[1] The title of governor did not always give its holder the prestige and authority that should have gone with the office. In 1717 outraged settlers in Martinique forcibly sent the colony's governor back to France. Nor did the office of governor assure the holder of much luxury; he was often housed modestly. Chevalier Boufflers, who served as commandant of Senegal (this office did not rate the title of governor until 1828), described his residence on the isle of Gorée as "the poorest, the dirtiest, and the most degraded of all buildings."[2]

Officials chosen for such positions were not always the best men France had to offer. In the case of Boufflers, he was an unusually sensitive and intelligent individual; he had gone overseas in order to earn enough money to reestablish his fi-

nances so that he could support the beautiful Countess Sabran, whom he had secretly married. But of many other officials it was probably true, as Choiseul wrote
of the officials he had sent to Guiana:

> I have chosen subjects to govern who have thrown me into terribly misleading
> paths; some were greedy, others despotic, ignorant and unreasonable. One such . . .
> whom I thought had a super intelligence is nothing but a fool and a dangerous fool.
> . . . M. Turgot [brother of Minister Turgot] is crazy and dishonest at the same
> time.[3]

Although in part these complaints were intended to shift the blame for the disastrous colonization policies that Choiseul had attempted in Guiana to the overseas
officials, they do ring a note of truth, however.

The Development of the Office

After the ancien régime was overthrown the overseas administration was made
more efficient and rational in its operations—just as was the government in
France. Power was no longer shared between governor and intendant. The latter
post had been abolished and the governor, like the Napoleonic prefect, concentrated authority in his own hands.

Algeria, a military conquest, was administered by the ministry of war and had
army officers as governors. The remaining territories were administered by naval
officers. That seemed natural; the colonies were seen as part of French maritime
trade and they were administered by the minister of marine and colonies. Few civilians were interested in colonial posts. The colonies were considered unhealthy
and not particularly prestigious assignments. Naval officers were accustomed to
obey orders and would accept a posting to a colony; they went because they were
ordered to do so and because they knew their term of service would be short.

In the thirty-eight years following the recovery of Senegal from England in
1817, thirty-three governors served, nineteen of them between 1839 and 1854,
when Faidherbe was appointed. With the exception of three—two army officers
and one lawyer—all were naval officers. Their administrations were not always
the best. Habits and ambitions learned in the navy could not easily be shed on dry
land. Some were impatient with their assignment; Lecoupé, a marine officer appointed governor in Senegal, complained in 1820 that he had been "called by the
king to fill a post that had nothing to do with the career I have chosen."[4] In
Guadeloupe complaints were frequent about one particular naval officer serving
as governor, of whom it was said, "during the two years he is serving here he continues to think himself aboard his ship."[5]

In black Africa the only colony with a governor was Senegal, which until the
1860s was but a collection of scattered forts. The other minor posts such as those of
the Ivory Coast, Dahomey, and Gabon were headed by a commandant.

French territorial expansion in the 1880s resulted in a more structured administration. To begin with, all conquests inland from Senegal eastward and southward down the Guinea coast were placed under the authority of Senegal. But this
was too large an area to administer and was therefore subdivided. In 1882 a sepa-

rate colony of the Rivières-du-Sud (present-day Guinea) was created; as conquest spread further south the territory came to include Dahomey and the Ivory Coast. Rivières-du-Sud was split into three colonies in 1893—Guinea, Ivory Coast, and Benin—each with a lieutenant governor, so-called because these officials were subordinate to the governor of Senegal, whom they had to keep informed.[6] The Sudan region was at first under military rule and its superior commandant was nominally subordinate to Senegal; but in 1892 the region was placed under a lieutenant governor, signifying more independence. The region continued to grow as a result of continued wars of conquest. After 1904 known as Upper Senegal—Niger, it was split in the early 1920s into Sudan, Niger, and Upper Volta, each with a lieutenant governor.

To the south the same process was occurring in Equatorial Africa. Gabon here filled the role Senegal had played in West Africa; it was the base from which further expansion occurred. With the acquisition of the Congo the post of commissioner general was created for that colony and for Gabon, which now had its own lieutenant governor. Expansion northward led to the establishment of the colony Ubangi-Shari-Chad, which in 1906 was split into Ubangi-Shari and Chad.

These colonies were joined into federations because of the French experience in Asia. Distant from Paris by many thousands of miles, the colonial governors of Cochin China, Annam, Cambodia, and Tonkin resented the attempts of Paris to impose centralized administration, and the ministry of marine and colonies found these administrators hard to control. A solution was found to this dilemma in 1887 with the establishment of the federation of Indochina headed by a governor-general. He represented Paris, and his mission was to mediate between the metropole's desire for central control and that of the local governors for more or less unimpeded power. In part Indochina served as a model for Africa, but there were local exigencies that forced the establishment there of the government-general.

The territorial boundaries of some African colonies were uncertain and in the war that several colonies had to wage against Samory—the Mandinké (Mandingo) warrior and state builder—their activities tended to lack coordination; it even happened that a governor would invade the neighboring colony. The most notorious example of this occurred in 1894 when Governor Lamothe of Senegal invaded Fouta Djallon, placed under the authority of the governor of Guinea, and did so without consulting a third governor also very affected by the campaign against Samory: the governor of the Sudan. Friction between the governors developed to such an extent that the minister of marine and colonies was to say in 1895, "frontier violations which sometimes occur in Europe never cause as complicated and heated correspondence as that which occurred between the neighboring three governors."[7] To coordinate the military campaign against Samory and to prevent future border conflicts between the colonies, the minister appointed in 1895 a governor-general of Afrique occidentale française (French West Africa) to govern Senegal and at the same time oversee the military activities of the neighboring colonies. The governors surrendered to him their military powers; they had to send their political correspondence to Paris through him, but otherwise his role was reduced to a superintendent capacity. The appointment to this post of a colonial inspector general, Jean Chaudié, underscored the supervisory nature of this role.

The inspectorate founded in 1887 served as the *missi dominici* of the ministry, making sure that ministry regulations were followed throughout the empire. Inspectors were carefully selected, recruited only after a tough competitive examination. Their prestigious status as an elite corps derived from the stringent selection procedures and their renown as independent men. Humanitarians often were attracted to the service, and they tended to be on the lookout for the interests of the French treasury and the rights of the colonial peoples. Whereas London sent men of high qualifications out as governors and administrators of the British colonies and did not feel it necessary to control their actions, Paris never trusted its colonial officials to the same degree. And this was not necessarily a reflection on the quality of men who served in the French overseas empire but rather reflected the continued concern of the French central administration for full control over its agents be they in the metropole or abroad. Chaudié's real authority thus came from his office as inspector not from his role as governor-general.

The position of governor-general grew in importance when the office was separated in 1902 from that of governor of Senegal and the governor-general's capital was moved to Dakar. To build the necessary roads, railways, and harbors in the conquered regions, a common plan of development needed to be worked out and some common source of funding established. By a decree of 1904 the government-general was given considerable power by henceforth having the benefit of receiving all the trade revenue collected; it also could borrow money and it paid for justice, customs, education, and, most important, public works throughout the federation. The new governor-general, Ernest Roume, was a forceful man who increasingly brought the colonies under control and attempted to assert Dakar's right to close supervision of the entire federation.[8] French West Africa served as a model for Equatorial Africa. Beginning in 1886 the commissioner of Congo and its dependencies administered the Congo and supervised the lieutenant governors under his authority. Then in 1903 a separate lieutenant governor was appointed for the Middle Congo and the commissioner's sole function now became a supervisory one over the lieutenant governors under him. In 1908 the title of commissioner general was changed to governor-general and the federation in 1910 was rechristened Afrique équatoriale française (French Equatorial Africa). The government-general of Madagascar did not signify the federation of several colonies; rather, the person governing the island had the title of governor-general because of the size and importance of the colony.

By the 1920s, when various territorial shifts had ended, the federation of French West Africa consisted of Dahomey, Guinea, Ivory Coast, Mauritania, Niger, Senegal, Sudan, and Upper Volta; Equatorial Africa embraced Chad, Congo, Gabon, and Ubangi.

The Powers of the Governor

The authority of the governors-general and governors was formally spelled out. The governors-general were the representatives of the ministry of colonies in the federations. On important matters they had exclusive right to correspond with the minister of colonies, and they coordinated orders from Paris for the entire federation. The governor-general had full military authority over his federation although he could not lead troops into battle. He had all civilian officials under his orders except for finance and justice, which enjoyed a degree of autonomy. He could appoint and dismiss all employees of the government-general; this included not only his staff in the federal capital but also members of the federation corps such as the teaching corps, customs services, public works, railroads, finances, medicine, police, and prisons. He had under his authority officials who were members of corps appointed and recruited by Paris, notably the corps of governors and the corps of colonial administrators. Although these officials were not recruited by the governor-general, he could influence their careers by recommendations he made to the ministry in quarterly personnel reports. The minister decided what colony a governor would occupy, and administrators were put at the disposal of the governor-general; he in turn would assign them to an individual governor, who then would appoint the administrator to a district.[9]

On paper, the system was highly centralized. But in reality it did not work that way. Distances and a claim to local expertise made the governor-general almost independent of Paris, whereas the governor was little controlled by his superior in Dakar or Brazzaville. The complaint made by Doumergue, minister of colonies in 1902, might well have been made at any time until World War II: he lamented that his subordinates overseas kept him insufficiently informed, making it impossible for him to give accurate information in Paris.[10] The governor-general was supposed to promulgate laws passed in Paris in order to make them effective in his federation. Often he failed to do so and even carried out policies diametrically opposed to the regulations coming from Paris. An inspection of French Equatorial Africa in 1911 revealed that most of the revenue collected in that federation lacked legal standing and the customs collected went against the international treaties signed by France on trade in the Congo basin.[11]

The federations thus maintained considerable independence. Instead of following policy dictated by Paris, they usually initiated it themselves. Deschamps, who served as governor in 1939 and in the years preceding had served also in the government-general secretariat in Tananarive, explained that the ministry most often served as a rubber stamp by enacting into instructions suggestions it received from its overseas representatives. The texts emanating from Paris, he wrote, "had nearly always been proposed by the governors. The offices [in Paris only] modified them to fit legal provisions, to avoid economic or parliamentary sanctions, or simply to show who was master."[12]

With the exception of two or three, none of the ministers had had previous overseas experience and therefore did not feel capable of interfering in the activities of colonial administrators. The staff in Paris also lacked previous overseas posting; after 1930, when some overseas officials were brought to the ministry, it was nearly a matter of course that they were not assigned to deal with the colony in which they had served for fear they would be too partial.[13]

True, the ministry had the general inspectorate available to it to oversee the ways in which the rules and regulations of the empire were adhered to by overseas officers. But the empire was large, and the few inspectors available had to examine everything from finances to roads. They were usually good at ferreting out financial mismanagement but not always at noting other administrative errors. Thus, the French administration in the Congo had to become a national scandal in 1904 before the ministry apparently realized that something was wrong. Only large-scale revolts of the kind that broke out during World War I in the Sudan finally alerted Paris to the destructiveness of wartime recruitment and forced labor.

The inspectorate could never create the centralized system totally accountable to Paris that was desired. Inspectors on mission often behaved imperiously, not hesitating to give local officials a dressing down. It was ten years later that Delavignette heard from old hands in the Sudan of the angry rebuke that Inspector general Méray gave Governor Clozel in 1915 as they held a yelling match on the palace balcony in regard to the expense of the building's construction.[14] But after making officials nervous, the inspectors quickly departed; in 1919 the minister of colonies noted that there was very little follow-up on their suggestions and reports.[15] Inspectors could only investigate on the spot and report to the ministry in Paris; they did not have the power to replace officials or to make decisions.

At times the minister recalled a governor-general in order to consult with him, but there was no systematic method for such encounters. The first conference of governors and governors-general was held in Paris in 1935 and then mainly to plan for the economic recovery of the colonies, which, like France, had suffered from the economic depression.

Centralization of control increased after World War II, however. As a result of political reforms, each territory sent deputies to Paris; the governments often had such slim majorities that, fearing a loss of support, they had actively to solicit the support of the African deputies. The particular complaints of a deputy about a governor had to be heard. Faster communications meant that Paris could inspect the overseas territories with greater dispatch, and cabinet ministers and the president of the republic went on tours of the empire. The new manner in which political personalities from France were able to make direct, on-the-spot policy was not always in France's interest. Georges Chaffard convincingly demonstrated that it was de Gaulle's personal visit to Conakry in 1958 that led to a worsening of relations between France and the leader of the Guinea government, Sékou Touré. The French governor, Mauberna, used to the exaggerated rhetoric of Touré, would have been able to maintain close relations with Guinea and perhaps even to assure that in 1958 Guinea would have voted for membership in the Community. De Gaulle's visit to Conakry made the "no" vote a certainty, and personally piqued by what they felt had been mutual rudeness, both de Gaulle and Touré hardened their positions toward each other.[16]

In addition to the personal visit, improved means of communication also tended to diminish the authority of the governor and to concentrate power in Paris. There was the telegraph—but also the telephone. Seeing the instrument that directly linked Governor-general Chauvet of French Equatorial Africa to Paris, Deschamps on a visit to Brazzaville in 1955 exclaimed to Chauvet, "My poor friend, the profession is finished."[17]

Before World War II the governor-general's control over his governors varied a lot. Sometimes, as a result of close friendship and bonds of loyalty, a governor made valiant efforts to carry out the policies of his superior. Examples would be Chavanne's rule of the Congo under Brazza's governor-generalship and Clozel's of Upper Senegal–Niger under the governor-generalship of Ponty. At other times, though, governors could easily ignore the government-general; it was far away. Only the governors of Senegal and Mauritania, both of whom were located in Saint-Louis, Senegal, were under the close scrutiny of the governor-general in Dakar, distant only a few hours by train or car. Examples of the meddling in Senegalese affairs by the governor-general of French West Africa are legion. But that was not the case, for instance, of the governor of Niger or of Upper Volta.

Although the government-general did not have inspectors until World War II, it did exercise important control over individual colonies. Medical, education, and public works services all depended on Dakar and Brazzaville. The assigning of colonial administrators to a colony was decided by the government-general (but the governor determined the exact post the administrator would occupy in the colony; he supervised them and expressed his opinion on their contributions in quarterly personnel reports). The budget for each colony had to be approved by the government-general, and it gave grants of money to each colony. Thus, there were powers available to it, but they were not always exercised in a coordinated manner by the federal capitals. Hence, in 1933 the governor-general discovered that there was a "lack of coherence in building road systems. Every colony has built roads and track to its borders without considering whether the neighboring colony was disposed to extending them. From this sometimes there result roads that lead nowhere or at least roads without continuity."[18]

All the governors of a federation convened annually for the council of the government-general, an advisory body to the governor-general. But policy was rarely made here, and the council met mainly because it was supposed to; its only function was to pass on the budget of each colony. The possibility of an occasional all-governors' conference to discuss mutual problems was never discussed; in 1933 Governor-general Brévié was to present such an idea as an original one that evidently had not been tried before.[19] The main control that the governor-general exercised over his governors was the recall power; Paris would usually recall a governor when the governor-general insisted. But otherwise there was considerable freedom of maneuver for each governor. In a circular in 1934 the governor-general was to complain to his governors of their "manifest intention to leave the governor-general in ignorance."[20] And this complaint came from as forceful and experienced a governor-general as Brévié.

The governor usually viewed the secretariat of the government-general in a hostile manner, thinking of its multifarious offices as overly involved with red tape and divorced from colonial realities. That was true also of the individual colonial administrators and their relationship to each colonial capital and its governor before 1945. To the many stories told of the independence of the commandant, Deschamps's memoirs add a new one. When a whale was washed ashore, he telegraphed Tananarive for instructions. The answer was so complicated that Deschamps decided to ignore it, cabling back that the whale had been devoured by sharks in the meantime and had decomposed.[21] In effect, the governor was so busy with his bureaucratic tasks in the capital that he rarely had time to oversee the work of the commandants.

Over the years an elaborate bureaucracy sprang up in the colonial capitals. There was the governor's cabinet, which included his closest collaborators; a bureau of political and administrative affairs; a bureau of economic affairs; and a bureau of finances. The daily work of the administration was supervised by the secretary-general, who usually served as acting governor in the latter's absence. Until World War I there was a separate corps of the secretariat from which the secretary-general and his subordinates came; thereafter they were members of the corps of colonial administrators called to serve in the capital for various periods. The staff directly depending on the governor and his secretary-general was quite large. In 1916 in Senegal the staff numbered fifty-two; if one added those services such as education—located in Saint-Louis but really a local service of the government-general although also supervised by the governor—there would be roughly another fifty people in Saint-Louis. In Guinea the governor's staff numbered forty-five officials and, again, approximately the same number of other officials less directly dependent on the governor but still under his jurisdiction.[22]

The supervision of these officials and the increasing bureaucratic tasks of collecting material demanded by either Dakar or Paris kept the governors busy at their desks in the capital. The governor of Dahomey noted in 1933 that since the establishment of the French administration the paperwork of administering the colony had tripled or quadrupled.[23] Finding himself increasingly tied to headquarters, the governor could rarely go on tour. His visits were of short duration; as André Gide, who visited Equatorial Africa in 1925, noted:

> When a governor goes on tour his subordinates usually present reports containing the facts they think most likely to please him. Those that I have to place before him are of a kind I fear that may never come to his notice; and the voices that might inform him of them will be carefully stifled.[24]

The size of a colony made effective inspection and supervision a near impossible task. When Eboué became governor of Chad he went on tour; it took him seventeen days to reach the northernmost areas of the colony. Bad roads made visits long and very tiresome: "The trip was more of an athletic event than an administrative tour."[25] A formal mechanism was instituted in 1906 for supervising the local districts, called *cercles*, when an *inspection des affaires administratives* was established for each colony. But the person appointed inspector—there was one to a colony—was usually one of the oldest and most senior men. His infirmities often prevented him from actively supervising the *cercles*, and as late as 1937 this inspection system was declared a failure.[26] Some governors had particular programs they favored, leaning heavily on their subordinates to carry them out. Thus, Governor Lamblin of Ubangi decreed that all houses were to be built according to specifications issued in Bangui. This was evidently done and Gide, in traveling, said that he could tell when he had left Ubangi for the huts were "much less fine, less clean, and actually sordid."[27] But if Lamblin had control in architectural matters, it did not mean that he was fully cognizant of everything that went on in the colony—as Gide amply documented.

In general, it was difficult for the governor to exercise absolute supervision of the many *cercles* and subdivisions making up each colony. A colonial inspector wrote of the Ivory Coast that the colony "now resembles a kind of federation of *cercles*, which their commandants rule as masters according to their inspiration."[28] As in the case of the relationship between governors and governors-general, the best way of assuring a total adherence to the governor of the individual commandant ruling the district was by appointing men who felt special bonds of affection and loyalty toward him. When Deschamps became governor of the Ivory Coast in 1941 he was able to have the governor-general put at his disposal five administrators who had been his classmates at the Ecole coloniale, several of whom were Socialists like himself.[29] He appointed them to head different *cercles* in the colony. This insured control over the commandants and gave the colony the strong imprint of the governor, but even here this method did not always succeed. Acts of brutality occurred of which Governor Deschamps was uninformed.

After World War II there was a change in the relationship between the center and the periphery. Improvement in communications and the instituting of representative political bodies at the government-general and the territorial levels (in addition to giving each territory representation in Paris) encouraged governors-general and governors to maintain closer control over their subordinates.

Recruitment

As the colonial administration matured regular channels of promoting people to governorships developed. But in the beginning no set pattern existed for the appointment of civilian governors. One of the most common means, of course, was to put men in charge of the colony that they had helped to explore and acquire for France; this was the case with the appointment of Brazza as commissioner general of the Congo in 1886 and of some of the officials put under his command as governors of individual colonies—Ballay in Gabon in 1886, Chavanne in 1889 as governor of the Congo. After they had served for a few years as district administrators, other explorers who had come to the Congo with Brazza also took over as governors: Dolisie in the Congo in 1894 and Liotard as high commissioner of the Ubangi in 1894. Bayol shaped the territory of Guinea and became its first governor in 1883 after exploring and signing treaties for France with local chiefs, and Binger, having acquired the Ivory Coast for the metropole, in 1893 was appointed first governor of that colony. Archinard, who had been the main mover in the military conquest of the Sudan, became its first lieutenant governor in 1892; other military men who had also played an important role, such as de Trentinian, succeeded him.

These men knew the regions over which they were given control. Brazza had started off as an explorer of the Congo ten years prior to his appointment as commissioner general there; Binger had been on various expeditions in West Africa for eleven years prior to his appointment to head the Ivory Coast. Explorer-governors had often begun their careers as medical men: Bayol and Ballay had first gone overseas as naval physicians serving as expedition doctors; Liotard had been a pharmacist. Others were military men—Brazza had gone on his first expedition to the Congo as a naval ensign, Dolisie as a second lieutenant in the infantry. Although businessmen were appointed to individual posts, none was appointed to a governorship.

Men with no prolonged overseas experience at times were sent to take over important posts. Chaudié, who was an inspector general, was appointed governor-general of French West Africa in 1895. He had some experience of overseas matters, having gone on missions of inspection, but he had not lived in French West Africa for any prolonged time. And Roume, appointed to the same post in 1902, had never been overseas; but in Paris he had headed the Indochina section of the ministry of colonies and was familiar with colonial matters. Governor Bertin, appointed to head the Ivory Coast in 1896, had been bureau chief in the ministry of colonies.

A common source of African governors in these early years were men who had proven themselves in the older French possessions—in small colonies such as the French Antilles, in the French possessions on the Indian subcontinent, and in the

Pacific. The governor of Senegal in 1888, Clément-Thomas, had previously served as governor of New Caledonia, and his successor, Lamothe, had served as governor of Saint Pierre and Miquelon. Grodet had served as governor of Martinique and French Guiana prior to becoming governor of the Sudan.

The most usual source of African governors in the early years, however, was the close administrative aides of the governors, the men who usually ran the secretariat of the colony. Mouttet had served as director of the interior (the early title for secretary-general) of both Guadeloupe and Senegal prior to becoming governor of the Ivory Coast in 1896; Pascal had served as secretary-general of the Ivory Coast and Dahomey before becoming governor in 1900 of the latter colony. Lemaire was secretary-general of the Ivory Coast and Madagascar prior to 1899, when he was appointed governor of the Congo. Cousturier did his apprenticeship for governor of Guinea (1891) as secretary-general in Gabon. As secretaries-general they had learned the administrative tasks involved in running a colony and often had occasion to serve as acting governor; they, also had acquired knowledge about African matters. Some governors, of course, had merely acquired certain bureaucratic virtues, having gained knowledge of colonial affairs prior to reaching Africa. For instance, Martineau, prior to his appointment as governor of Somali in 1899, had been director of the interior of New Caledonia; Roberdeau had served briefly in Senegal, but more important he had headed the secretariat in Saint Pierre and Miquelon, Guadeloupe, and Guiana before his appointment in 1896 as governor of the Ivory Coast.

Already at this early date one pattern originated that was to be maintained throughout French rule; namely, the surest route to being appointed governor was to serve in the secretariat, preferably as secretary-general of the colony. Service in that post developed bureaucratic expertise and the habit of forming an overall colonial view, which was thought necessary for a governor. The secretary's proximity to the governor and his chance of serving in his stead during the latter's absences gave the colony's governor an opportunity to evaluate his secretary's potential, and Paris often accepted these evaluations. Rare were the times, however, that a secretary-general would take over as governor of the same colony he had headed. The example of Pascal's becoming governor of Dahomey in 1900 after he had been its secretary-general is unusual.

In spite of the recent acquisition of empire in Africa, the French made an impressive effort from early on to appoint men with some sort of colonial experience. But such experience in the early years did not mean formal training, so that one could be quite young when one first went overseas. Binger, with no education to speak of, went to West Africa in the rank of private soldier at the age of 26; eleven years later he was governor. Lagarde, after being secretary to the governor of Cochin China at 22, found himself governor of Somaliland five years later. True, it was a small and insignificant outstation of the French empire on the horn of eastern Africa, but a governorship was a governorship. Lagarde was the youngest man ever appointed governor. As the empire matured the ministry could ask a longer apprenticeship from its men before their appointment. The increased emphasis on long experience and formal education meant an advance in the governors' age. The average age for those appointed prior to 1900 was 40; for those appointed between 1900 and 1920, 44.7; and for 1920–1940, 49. A dramatic demonstration of this difference is to note that whereas the youngest governor ap-

pointed prior to 1900 was Lagarde at 27, for the period 1900–1920 it would be
Van Vollenhoven at age 30. Between the two world wars it would be Rapenne,
who in 1938 became governor of Niger at age 37, closely followed by Deschamps
in Somaliland, who was 38 the same year.

Although more selective in later years than at the beginning of the empire, the
ministry in Paris initially was considerably more careful in picking governors than
colonial administrators, the men who functioned at the district level. Having decided that men who were already in the colonies would be used as governors,
however, the ministry was not able to recruit a group that was particularly distinguished in its education. Of the governors appointed before 1900, a third had a
degree from an institution of higher education such as a law degree or a diploma
from Saint-Cyr, the military academy; a fifth had the *baccalauréat* degree indicating successful completion of training at the *lycée*; and the remainder—nearly
half—seem to have had no formal training beyond primary school. This roughly
parallels the education of the men being recruited into the corps of colonial administrators. Since men were appointed as governors later in life than as administrators, the educational level of the governors still indicates some sort of elite selection, for they were better educated than the cohort group from which they
were selected.[30]

With time, as the colonial administration recruited men of some education,
these were nearly invariably selected later as governors. Higher education was
valued, and men who were trained had a greater chance of being promoted to
governor than others within the colonial service. Those appointed after 1900
usually had already served in the colonial bureaucracy some fifteen to twenty
years. Looking at persons appointed between 1900 and 1914 and comparing their
education with that of men who entered the colonial service fifteen to twenty
years earlier, one notices how formal education grew in importance as a criterion
for appointment. Thus, whereas nearly half of the colonial administrators entering the service between 1887 and 1900 had less than a secondary school education,
only fifteen percent of the governors fell into this category; a quarter of the administrators entering before 1900 had a university degree or diploma from an institution of higher learning, yet two-thirds of the governors appointed prior to
1914 had such degrees. The best training for service in the corps of colonial administrators was attendance at the Ecole coloniale. Prior to 1900 about seven percent of the corps came from the school; but of the governors appointed between
1900 and 1914 sixteen percent were graduates of the Ecole, among the most distinguished being Angoulvant as governor of Ivory Coast and Van Vollenhoven as
governor of Guinea.

The way in which education helped serve for promotion can be seen in the
ages at which men of differing educational backgrounds were appointed to their
first governorship. The average age of the Ecole coloniale graduate appointed as
governor prior to 1914 was thirty-eight compared to the average age of men with
other educational backgrounds, which was forty-four. Another way this difference can be seen is by looking at the median age of appointment. For graduates of
the Ecole coloniale appointed to their first governorship prior to 1914 it was
thirty-five; for men with other higher education it was forty-three; and for those
with education less than the secondary level it was forty-five. Looking at the fre-
quency of age of the governors, an even greater discrepancy may be noted.

Whereas none of the Ecole coloniale graduates appointed to their first governor-ship before 1914 had reached the age of fifty, a third of those with other forms of higher education and forty percent of those with no education were in their fifties before being appointed as governor.

The French emphasis on having educated men as governors never, however, led to a mandarinate system. Thus, some graduates of the Ecole coloniale who had been brilliant in school were not promoted; others who had done quite poorly were appointed as governors. Van Vollenhoven before World War I and Deschamps in the 1930s became governors and they had graduated at the head of their class at the Ecole coloniale; but others such as Eboué were close to the bottom.[31]

We do not have adequate information on the social class of the governors, but given the system of French higher education, which was heavily class-bound, it is safe to assume that they were recruited from at least the middle levels of the bourgeoisie. There were, of course, notable exceptions. Gentil, who was a graduate of the Ecole navale, was the son of a modest commercial employee earning only 1,800 francs a year—that would be close to the poverty line; a manual worker earned over 2,000. After World War I the same selective mechanisms continued favoring the Ecole coloniale graduate. Whereas approximately fifteen percent of those entering the corps prior to 1914 came from the school, over a third of the governors appointed in the interwar period were graduates. Men with higher educational qualifications than their colleagues were chosen.

There were many reasons in addition to a prejudice in favor of the man considered cultured and hence capable of leadership. Although many governors at some time had served as a *cercle* commandant prior to their appointment, very few went directly from commandant to governor. Usually intervening between the two posts was service in the secretariat of a colony or in Paris at the ministry, and sometimes both. Ecole coloniale graduates and a large number of university graduates in general had legal training and were thus considered particularly qualified for administrative tasks such as those needed in the secretariat; once there, they acquired the experience and the contacts that opened the road to a governorship. The governors would spot a *cercle* commandant considered unusually capable and bring him to the capital to serve; thus was he launched on his career. In the 1930s this program was institutionalized when the brightest young administrators were brought to Paris for a stint in the ministry; there it was thought they would develop the outlook that would make them capable governors. Deschamps, for instance, was called from Madagascar to serve in Paris for a couple of years; he then returned to Madagascar and later was appointed governor of Somaliland. Paris had had time to take measure of the man. Henri d'Arboussier seems to have been the exception; he served all his career as a bush administrator and, with no experience in either a colonial capital or Paris, was appointed governor. But significantly, in spite of his great abilities as a *cercle* commandant—he was one of the most brilliant of the pre–World War I era—he was given rather insignificant posts: resident commissioner of the New Hebrides and of New Caledonia.

Service in both the colonial capital and Paris was the best means of being noticed and receiving a gubernatorial appointment; if a choice had to be made between the two, Paris was more important. The three youngest men in the different eras of French colonial administration before World War II had had long stays in the French capital prior to their appointments. Lagarde had gone out to Cochin China but had returned to Paris to serve the undersecretary of colonies as personal secretary. Van Vollenhoven, upon graduating from the Ecole coloniale, took his first position in the ministry, served there for two years, and then, at twenty-eight, was posted to Senegal as secretary-general; from there to governor of Guinea was a short step. Rapenne served in Paris for many years, rising in the central bureaucracy prior to his posting to Niger in 1938.

Patronage

Given the distances that separated the overseas territories from Paris, one of the best ways of insuring discipline seemed to be to appoint men who would be loyal to the minister and his program because they shared his political outlook and knew they had been appointed as a result of patronage. Such links could develop from service at the ministry. Political influence was important, too. Grodet, appointed governor of the Sudan and later commissioner general of the Congo, was a singularly incapable man; his successive appointments led one biographer to speculate that only political influence explains his advancement.[32] This suspicion may be confirmed by his later political career: he was to serve as deputy from French Guiana. Some officials had close political ties to influential members of the Colonial party in Parliament, which seems to have helped their career. This was the case with Antonetti. His stepfather was an official in Algeria and had an excellent relationship with the head of the French Colonial party, the deputy from Algeria, Eugène Etienne, who apparently intervened several times on Antonetti's behalf. Antonetti had a brilliant career as governor of Upper Senegal, Niger, Ivory Coast, and between 1924 and 1934 as governor-general of French West Africa. When Delafosse sought a governorship during World War I, it was through Etienne and Lucien Hubert, family friends, that he hoped to attain the appointment. Although Delafosse's superior in Dakar was opposed to such a promotion, the politicians' influence prevailed in the end and Delafosse was given a governorship.[33] Van Vollenhoven, when he was appointed governor-general of French West Africa in 1917, had had the political support of two influential parliamentarians: Lebrun and Clémentel, two former ministers of colonies.[34]

Before World War II there were few politicians who served as governors of African colonies; but Indochina was a different matter. A posting there was prestigious and was considered an honorable consolation prize for an also-ran or for someone Paris wanted out of the country. Bert in the 1880s and Sarraut in the 1910s served as governors-general of Indochina. The only deputy who served as governor in Africa before 1945 was the Radical Socialist Victor Augagneur, who went to Madagascar as governor-general in 1905. After returning to France to serve again in Parliament and as a cabinet minister, he went back overseas in 1920 as governor-general of French Equatorial Africa. But Augagneur was an unusual individual who joined to his leftist political program an authoritarian outlook that suited a proconsul.

Political links seem to have been important if not in achieving governorships at least in securing promotions. Membership in the freemasonry was considered a sign of political reliability and many men who reached the pinnacle of success as governors-general were Freemasons. In the Third Republic such membership was the sign of having "advanced ideas," meaning especially anticlericalism and commitment to the republic. Freemasons could be found at all levels of the administration. The ministry of colonies in Paris had many Freemasons on its staff and they tended to help along the careers of officials overseas who were fellow Masons. The director of personnel in the 1920s, Gaston Joseph, was a Freemason; in fact most of the bureau chiefs in the Paris ministry belonged to one order or another of the Masons. When Delavignette, a Catholic, became director of political affairs in 1947 he was, he claimed, the first non-Freemason ever to occupy that post.[35]

Freemasons had their own network of contacts and friendships. Finding his acting governor in Ubangi hostile to freemasonry and "advanced ideas" in general, Félix Eboué—then an administrator—signaled to his friends in Paris to contact the minister of colonies, Louis Perrier, a brother Mason, to prevent the titularization of the acting governor. The latter was not named governor.[36] Membership in the freemasonry was secret, but many officials did not hide it; Governor-general Ponty had carved on his tombstone the three dots in a pyramid symbolic of the freemasonry. Colonial gossips were relatively well informed on these matters; according to Delavignette, of the eight governors-general of French West Africa between 1908 and 1940, six were Freemasons.[37] In the other colonies freemasonry was also important; in French Equatorial Africa governors-general Augagneur, Reste, and Eboué were Masons.

One of the largest transfers of governors in Africa occurred as a result of the Popular Front's coming to power in 1936. Of the sixteen colonies in black Africa, eleven received new governors in 1936. The minister of colonies, Marius Moutet, a Socialist, decided to attempt overseas reforms, and one way he did so was by appointing new governors. Unlike postwar ministers, who did not hesitate to appoint as governors men without any previous foreign experience, Moutet appointed men who already were overseas. He promoted the Socialist governor Coppet to be governor-general of French West Africa; nevertheless he also promoted to governorships many colonial administrators who were not Socialists but, because of having received a promotion from Moutet, would presumably prove loyal—among them Lefebvre, who went as governor to Senegal, Court, who went to Niger, and Mondon to Ivory Coast. In other cases, men who already were governors were given new assignments: Blacher was appointed to Guinea and Masson de Saint-Félix to Ubangi. Promotion to the post of governor or reassignment would remind the appointees of their dependence upon Paris and make reforms easier to impose. Thus, a political change in Paris had a dramatic effect on gubernatorial appointments. Such changes were not necessarily bad, and political considerations here tended to facilitate reform overseas.

Sheer political patronage based on the spoils system, however, also existed, becoming increasingly common after World War II. The war itself politicized governorships. Because their loyalty to Vichy was suspect, governors were replaced during World War II, and those colonies that were under the authority of the Free French also replaced the politically questionable. Nearly every governor appointed after 1945 had won some resistance medal. Few of the colonial administrators were purged after the war for collaboration, but for governors it was considered an inexcusable crime. Governors-general Boisson, Cayla, and Annet were tried for treason, and many governors were dismissed from the service. The gover-

norships after the war—as, incidentally, most of the positions of responsibility in
the French bureaucracy—now were retained by former resistance workers. Some
of them had accomplished heroic feats such as Messmer in North Africa and Indochina, others had less dramatic records—for instance, service in the colonial administration in French Equatorial Africa during World War II, which, under the
leadership of Governor-general Eboué, had rallied to the Free French. Reliance
on Freemason or resistance credentials demonstrated the continuing importance
of political fealties.

In colonies that had well-developed local politics—Senegal was the only one in
Africa before World War II—opposition of a deputy could prevent a governor
from being posted to that colony or could hurry his departure. By his membership
in freemasonry and the Radical party, the Senegalese deputy Blaise Diagne maintained close political contacts in Paris; his goodwill was also necessary to recruit
black troops during World War I. The political influence of Diagne was such in
the colonial administration that Angoulvant, appointed governor-general of
French Equatorial Africa, was to rejoice, "Think of it, in [Equatorial Africa]
there is no deputy, not even a white one."[38]

Colonies with deputies, except for Senegal, were the "old colonies" such as the
Antilles, Réunion, New Caledonia, and the Indian possessions; the men appointed
governors there had to enjoy the support and confidence of local politicians in
order to serve effectively. Eboué was named governor of Martinique and then
Guadeloupe as a result of the support given to his candidacy by political groups
and personalities alternately having good and bad relations with whichever minister of colonies happened to be in power.[39]

Politics became even more important in the selection of governors after World
War II. The unstable political coalitions of the Fourth Republic made it necessary
to distribute cabinet and junior cabinet posts to members of various parties in
order to insure parliamentary support for the coalition governments. To extend its
fragile support, the government proffered governorships to men with known political memberships. To bolster the tripartite governments—made up of the Socialists, the Communists, and the Catholic MRP—of the early Fourth Republic,
the empire was carved up into political fiefs: the Ivory Coast was administered by
personnel with Communist leanings, Senegal by Socialists, and Upper Volta by
MRP governors. When the Communists left, tripartism included the Radical
party, which also enjoyed the division of spoils. In 1948 three new governors-
general were appointed: Béchard, a Socialist deputy, was made governor-general
of West Africa; Chévigné, an MRP deputy, governor-general of Madagascar; and
Cornut-Gentille, a Radical, became governor-general of Equatorial Africa.[40]
After World War II, when political rights were extended to the inhabitants of
other colonies, political pressures were also exercised by local politicians. When
Houphouet-Boigny of the Ivory Coast came to a political agreement with the
French government to abandon his program of opposition both in the territory
and in Paris, he was able to effect the recall of Governor Péchoux, who had carried out a lengthy program of repression against Houphouet and his Parti démocratique de la Côte d'Ivoire.[41]

The intrusion of politics in the selection of governors may not have been as unseemly as it appears for the role of the governor was often political in nature.
Before World War II he already played a semipolitical role in having to juggle the

interests of various regions, in trying to strike a balance between the interests of the trading houses and those of the African populations, and in arbitrating the inevitable feuds between various administrative services. After the war, of course, his role became increasingly political. He had an elected territorial assembly with which he had to work; it passed on the colonial budget and finally in 1957 it acquired full legislative powers and he had to share his authority with the elected African executive branch. The governor needed to maintain cordial relations with the local politicians to exercise effective control over the territory.

Often the territories were viewed as rotten boroughs, as a means of creating additional political support for the government in power in Paris or at least for political parties the governor favored. In 1946, when the National Assembly failed to elect the president of the republic on the first ballot, the Socialist minister of overseas France, Marius Moutet, had the overseas parliamentarians flown into Paris and they broke the deadlock by helping to elect the Socialist Vincent Auriol president. It was when Houphouet-Boigny promised to dissociate his political party from the Communist party and henceforth support the Union Démocratque et Socialiste de la Résistance (UDSR), the political party of the minister of overseas France, François Mitterrand, that the administrative harassment of the Rassemblement Démocratique Africain (RDA) ceased. The overseas administration was heavily politicized; often governors functioned as electoral agents, much as the nineteenth-century French prefect, who in metropolitan France was expected to insure that the election in his department was favorable to the party in power.

Many governors became heavily involved in local political squabbles and deliberately fostered politicians' careers or even the fortunes of whole parties. The governors were not beyond bribery, and journalist Georges Chaffard has claimed that in 1958, in order to win a "yes" vote on membership in the short-lived Communauté Française (a loose confederal arrangement), governors transferred large sums of money to the main political parties in their colonies. In every colony but Guinea they succeeded. Of course it was not just money; rather a whole network of fine political contacts was necessary for success. In Senegal the governor and the governor-general had been able to cultivate the main religious leaders of the territory and win them over to a "yes" vote in 1958. In Niger the governor was able to split the opposition.[42] It turned out, of course, that this election did little to stop the oncoming independence and by 1960 all the African territories except Somali were free. But during these two years the role of the governor was especially political as he prepared for the devolution of empire. Close collaboration with the African leaders allowed for peaceful transition and independence came without too large a shock. Only in Guinea were the bonds of empire abruptly broken. In the postwar period, British governors strictly adhered to the notion that as civil servants they were to be politically neutral and refrain from any partisanship. But this was not the case with French governors. They were following a tradition that had been adopted even among higher civil servants in France proper, who increasingly played a semipolitical role in the Fourth Republic. This tradition continued into the Fifth Republic in which it became even more difficult to draw a convenient line between politicians and civil servants.[43]

The political skills and acumen that the governors needed after World War II led to a lessened emphasis on recruiting officials with a long colonial career. Rather, men often were chosen who, in France, had shown political skill. More frequently than before World War II, governors were chosen not from members of the corps of colonial administrators but rather from men foreign to it. For example, not a single governor-general of French West Africa between 1946 and 1958 had ever served as a colonial administrator. Barthe, who had served between 1946 and 1948 came closest—he had been a colonial inspector; Béchard (1948–1951) had been undersecretary of armaments and a Socialist deputy; Cornut-Gentille (1951–1956) was a prefect; Cusin (1956–1958) had been member of the Indochina Bank and the Cour des comptes. Such appointments, however, probably allowed for greater flexibility of the colonial administration; these men infused into the administration a new spirit. They played the role the French sociologist Michel Crozier has called "authoritarian reform figures." Like the castes of higher civil servants making up the *grand corps* in France, these political appointees overseas tended to play the role of brokers between the civil service and the local political parties.[44]

The increasingly political nature of the governor's office after World War I is evident in the subsequent careers of former governors. Far more than before the war, governors entered national politics after overseas service. Before World War I Governor-general Augagneur, after his tenure in Madagascar, had become a cabinet minister (but he had been a deputy prior to his appointment to the governor-generalship). The only other governors prior to World War I who entered national politics subsequent to their governorship were Bayol, governor of Rivières-du-Sud (1883–1889), who was elected in 1903 to the French Senate, sitting on the democratic left, and Grodet, governor of Sudan (1893–1895), elected in 1910 to the National Assembly as deputy from Guiana under the party label Independent Socialist.

The Personality of the Governor

Though the heads of colonial federations and colonies were constrained prior to 1945 by the great independence that their subordinates enjoyed and after the war by the careful supervision that they received from their superiors, governors-general and governors were never mere figureheads. They were important men who helped shape the spirit and direction of the territories they ruled. Their attitudes were often molded by personal convictions that had developed as a result of their experiences overseas. Governor-general Ponty's African policies were strongly influenced by his experiences as an administrator in the Sudan. As Jacques Lombard has written, the Sudanese experience gave French officials the impression of the African chief as a "fanatic warrior, tyrannizing the populations around him and dominating them by force."[45] Ponty's membership in the Radical party and his anticlericalism also help explain his hostility to traditional African rule.

In his style of administration Gallieni in Madagascar drew on the principles of governing that he developed during military expeditions in the Sudan and Indochina. Gallieni emphasized the decentralization of power and the granting of initiative to local French administrators. His native policy, *la politique des races*, assumed that indigenous peoples were to be ruled by chiefs from their own ethnic group; a large number of traditional chiefdoms had been dismantled because the Hovas had gained ascendency over much of the island. Brévié had been an administrator in Niger, where native authorities were still strong, and he had closely studied Islamic institutions in West Africa. When he became governor-general in the 1930s he was to show respect for and sensitivity to traditional rule and was to try to rebuild the native authorities, which, under pressure from the French, had been considerably weakened.

Political affiliations and even his profession before becoming governor had an impact on a man's overseas career. Augagneur was a Radical and an anticlerical and had been a medical doctor. When he became governor-general of Madagascar in 1905 he instituted a violent anticlerical campaign, which the missionaries in the island were to feel; he also showed a great concern for health questions, helping to organize a medical service.[46]

The temperament and human attributes of each governor also helped color his administration. De Coppet, the Popular Front governor-general of French West Africa, invited young African students for lunch in the government-general's palace in 1936; it was the first time this had been done, and the educated African elites greeted it as a signal honor to them. De Coppet also insisted on the attendance of all governors at Moslem high holiday celebrations, thus showing French respect for the single largest indigenous religious group in West Africa. After World War II, Governor Orselli of the Ivory Coast attempted to break the social segregation of black and white in the colony and invited Africans to social functions at the gubernatorial palace. One of his successors, Messmer, also valiantly tried to fight the pernicious segregationist policies of the white settlers in Abidjan and sponsored an interracial social club, the Cercle d'amitié.[47] In the Sudan Governor Louveau in the early 1950s, on his own initiative, without waiting for appropriations from Dakar, established a school in Bamako for public works professionals. Such acts helped considerably to define the quality of Franco-African relations.

The effectiveness of governors was in part circumscribed by their limited stays in a colony. The French administration put little value on permanence; the moving around of governors and other officials was seen as a way of preserving effective control from the center and preventing the governor from developing too much of a local bias. With the passage of time the average stay of the governor went down; between 1900 and 1919 it was 3.0 years, in the interwar years 2.7, and in the dozen years of the Fourth Republic (1946–1958) it was 2.0. There, of course, were exceptions: thus, in the years 1900–1919 the average length of stay in Gabon and Chad was 2.0; for the Sudan, Somaliland, and the Ivory Coast, 4.8; in the interwar period the governor's term in Gabon and Niger was 1.8 years on the average; for Sudan and Madagascar it was 5 years. During the Fourth Republic, Senegal, Mauritania, and Ivory Coast had governors stay an average of 1.5 years; Madagascar and Sudan enjoyed average terms of 3 years.

These stays are calculated on the basis of formal appointments of governors but do not signify that the officials actually spent their terms entirely in the colony. Governors absent for consultation, vacation, or sick leave kept the title of governor, being replaced only temporarily by an acting governor. If the long term of service of Governor Lamblin at first seems impressive—he was officially governor of Ubangi-Shari from December 1921 to October 1928—it is less so when one realizes that of the seven years he was absent for a total of three. Governor-general Antonetti, officially governor-general of French Equatorial Africa from

1924 to 1934, was in France a total of forty months on vacation, consultation, or sick leave.

The rapid turnover of governors made it very difficulat for them to leave a personal mark on a colony. Although Gallieni's energy and abilities had much to do with the impact he had on Madagascar, his ten-year tenure in that colony, three times the average term of French governors contemporaneously serving elsewhere, undoubtedly contributed to his effectiveness.

Table 1.   Average Stay of African Governors and Governors-general

Area	1900–1919	1920–1950	1946–1958
French Equatorial Africa	3.1	3.3	2.0
French West Africa	3.1	5.0	3.0
Cameroons	—	2.5	1.7
Chad	1.9	2.5	2.0
Congo	2.7	2.2	1.5
Dahomey	2.7	2.5	2.0
Gabon	1.9	1.8	2.0
Guinea	2.7	4.0	1.7
Ivory Coast	3.8	2.5	1.5
Madagascar	2.7	5.0	3.0
Mauritania	2.7	2.8	1.5
Niger	—	1.8	2.4
Senegal	3.1	2.8	1.5
Sudan	3.8	2.8	2.0
Togo	—	2.8	2.0
Ubangi	2.7	2.5	2.0
Upper Volta	—	3.0[1]	2.4

[1]Upper Volta had no governors between 1932 and 1947; the averages for 1920–1940 are calculated for the years 1920–1932.

In the movement of governors certain patterns developed. As a rule, governors in a West African colony would later be moved to another colony in the same federation. French West Africa was considered more prestigious than Equatorial Africa, and it would have been slightly demeaning for a governor serving in the former to be transferred in the same capacity to the latter. This did not apply to the governor-generalship of Equatorial Africa, however, which did attract governors from West Africa: of the fifteen governors-general of Equatorial Africa in the fifty years during which the post existed, seven had previously served in French West Africa. Governors in West Africa in fact had a better chance to be promoted to governor-general of Equatorial Africa than did governors in Equatorial Africa. Only one governor-general of this federation, Eboué, had served as governor within Equatorial Africa prior to his advancement. In contrast, some of the most promising governors began their careers in West Africa and were then transferred to Equatorial Africa: de Coppet, for instance, served in Chad before going to Dahomey and then becoming governor-general of French West Africa. The hierarchical relationship between the two federation may also be gauged by noting that three governors-general of West Africa previously had been governors-general of

Equatorial Africa, their posting to Dakar being a promotion. But not a single governor-general of French West Africa subsequently served as governor-general in
Brazzaville.

The status of Madagascar is less clear. Merlin, after serving in French West
Africa, transferred to Madagascar in 1917, then went to Equatorial Africa in
1919. Augagneur served in Madagascar, returned to France for several years, and
went to Equatorial Africa in 1920. De Coppet went to Madagascar in 1939 after
serving as governor-general in West Africa. On the whole it seems safe to say that
Madagascar and West Africa were on a par.

Some colonies seem to have served as testing grounds for governors. Between
1880 and 1940 the average of all colonies receiving a man on his first overseas
gubernatorial posting was sixty-three percent. In French Equatorial Africa Chad
received eighty-seven percent of initial postings, the Congo eighty-three percent,
and seventy-six percent for Gabon. Similar percentages did not apply to colonies
in West Africa: Niger, with seventy-seven percent, was the only colony in this federation exceeding seventy percent. Some colonies seem usually to have been given
men with previous experience as governors: in Cameroon, sixty-seven percent of
the governors had had earlier appointments; in both Dahomey and Guinea the
figure was fifty-six percent.

Table 2.   Previous Gubernatorial Experience, 1880–1940

Cameroons	67[1]	Mauritania	50
Chad	13	Niger	23
Congo	17	Senegal	40
Dahomey	56	Sudan	30
Gabon	24	Togo	25
Guinea	56	Ubangi	34
Ivory Coast	47	Upper Volta	34

[1]Expressed as a percentage of the governors for each colony.

Residencies, Rewards, and Emoluments

Saint-Louis had been the center for Senegal and, initially, all of French West
Africa. As new colonies were established, each territory acquired its own colonial
capital to house the governor and his staff; but in the early days it was possible to
do without a cumbersome central bureaucracy. Victor Liotard, commissioner for
Ubangi in the 1890s, was able to explore the area and still administer it from
wherever his camp might be. He traveled with his files and thus could "decide on
affairs in the area he was visiting and those of which he was informed from other
regions."[48] And his superior, Brazza, commissioner of the Congo, was able to absent himself for two years from the capital; he, too, was on exploration trips.[49]

But bureaucratic burdens soon tied the governor down to his capital, the latter
developing into an urban center, often charmingly laid out. Governors competed
with each other in building splendid capitals. Bangui, on the river of the same
name, was a lovely city whose architecture was reminiscent of that in southern
France; it took the place of Liotard's tent. Conakry, the capital of Guinea, was

unusually elaborate for the size of its population and available financial resources. A colonial inspector wrote critically, "The plan of the city was conceived with a certain exaggeration; the avenues and boulevards stretch for 48 kilometers, this for a population of 8,000." But in the end even he was moved by Conakry's charm: "These defaults are compensated in part by the seductive general impression of the city."[50]

The construction of avenues and public buildings constituted a heavy drain on the budget of each colony in the early years. The capital of the Ivory Coast, Bingerville, was estimated to cost 1.5–1.8 million francs. In the Sudan, Governor Ponty built an elaborate administrative city on the plateau of Koulouba above Bamako overlooking the Niger river, evidently under the assumption that the plateau would be healthier than the valley. Koulouba, including its plush governor's palace, was estimated to have cost 5 million francs, a sum equal to the entire income of the colony during 1905–1909, the years of the city's building. And this does not include nonremunerated services such as heavy levies of forced labor and foodstuffs from surrounding villages to help feed the laborers.[51] Koulouba served as a model for the Upper Volta when it became a colony in 1919; the new governor, Hesling, set up the administrative offices in Ouagadougou, also on a slight hill (which he called "Koulouba"). With forced labor he built within six months eleven administrative buildings to house the new capital.[52] Because it was so sparsely populated and had few funds, Mauritania did not have a capital; its governor resided in Saint-Louis, Senegal. To affirm his rule Governor Gaden made frequent tours of Mauritania, and his return by camel was a common sight in the Saint-Louis of the 1920s. Only after independence was the capital city, Nouakchott, established.

The locations chosen for capitals were often important trade centers whose populations expanded as commerce grew. In addition, the civil servants—white and black—required a host of new services so that the expansion of government in itself stimulated urban expansion. Ouagadougou, which at the turn of the century had 5,000 inhabitants, in 1926 had 12,000; Bamako in 1888 had 800; in 1907, 6,000; in 1920, 15,000; Dakar in 1904 had 23,500; in 1921, 32,500; and fifteen years later, 92,600.[53]

In these growing urban centers, the French presence was symbolized by the palace. Yet the early gubernatorial residencies were not elaborate. In the Sudan in 1893, Governor Grodet found himself housed in three barely furnished rooms, the main furniture being eight chairs; a split barrel served as a bathtub.[54] Even later some residencies were still very humble. When he took over as governor of Chad in 1938, Eboué found the "palace" to be a two-story cement building with cracked walls; the first floor consisted of two large rooms, the second of two bedrooms and a bath. It had no electricity and the water had to be pumped up into the bathroom each day. The furniture lacked in elegance, being locally made.[55] Delavignette arriving in the Cameroons in 1946 described his palace as "nothing but a great cabin, the roof of which is threatening to collapse."[56]

Palaces therefore varied; that of the governor-general in Dakar was deliberately imposing to impress what were considered the sophisticated inhabitants of Dakar. Governor-general Roume spent 3 million francs to build his residence on the plateau of Cap Vert overlooking the Atlantic. The palace in Ivory Coast also overlooked the ocean but was impractical; although the building had a beautiful balcony, which dominated the lagoon, Governor Deschamps, who served in Abidjan in 1941, wrote that he found the rooms "gigantic, dark, and lacking air." One day, just after he and his guests left the dining room, the room's ceiling fell in; two enormous wooden columns had collapsed from termite damage.[57] In the Sudan, in line with his generally elaborate schemes for Koulouba, Governor Ponty's imposing palace, with its magnificent view of the Niger River, was sixty-two meters long, fifteen meters wide, and thirteen meters high—more imposing than the palace of the governor-general in Dakar, noted a colonial inspector:

> It is sumptuous, even too sumptuous. . . . On the first floor the palace has a large dining room joined to a salon and billiard room, three offices, a guards' room, a waiting room, a pantry, and a linen room. On the second floor are three bedrooms, three baths, and a small living room. An interior gallery connects to a magnificent terrace as long as the building and forty meters wide . . . from where one has a view of the entire Niger valley.[58]

The palace and the administrative city were seen as striking ways of revealing the French presence. In his person the governor represented this power, and he was provided with a stately uniform, as spelled out by the regulations of 1905:

Jacket: navy blue with gold embroidery, and triple rows of embroidery on the collar.
Pants: navy blue with a gold or white stripe.
Hat: general's model embroidered with gold, a cockade, and a white plume.
Belt: gold or white silk.
Sword.[59]

Palace guards were issued special uniforms, again to emphasize the pomp of the gubernatorial office. Servants filled the palace grounds. In 1946 the palace in Duala had a butler, a cook, five "boys," countless scullery hands, gardeners, and a chauffeur. They enjoyed a special sense of importance by serving the governor, and sometimes it was they who imposed ceremony upon their employer. Delavignette, as high commissioner of the Cameroons, invited a cardinal to lunch and was asked to make the meal simple, some boiled eggs and fresh fruit. He gave his butler the order but was disobeyed. The two were served the eggs and fruit, but as they rose from the table the butler burst in to ask them to wait; he returned in triumph with a succession of plates of fish, roast meat, salad, cheeses, desserts, and wines. The butler had decided that the "cardinal must dine like a prince . . . and that I owed it to myself as high commissioner to have a table worthy of my status," wrote Delavignette about this incident.[60]

The French government recognized the distinction of the office of governor by awarding its holders various honors, the most common being the Legion of Honor. This Napoleonic award was deeply sought after in France and granted to men of distinction in all walks of life, including outstanding actors, writers, and businessmen. To have reached middle age without having received the Legion of Honor was thought of as a slight, hence Gide's quip that every Frenchman over fifty has the Legion of Honor and gonorrhea. A man usually had had a distinguished career before being named governor and therefore already was a chevalier of the Legion; once he occupied his post he would be "promoted" to officer and finally commander of the Legion.

Individual colonies also bestowed medals. Ivory Coast had the order of Benin; Somali, the Nichan el Anwar. Such medals were, as a matter of course, awarded the governor by the minister of colonies. Governors visiting from other colonies would award their host a medal for his hospitality. When Governor Deschamps hosted the governor-general of Indochina, he was given the medal of the Million Elephants and the White Parasol, and the empress of Annam bestowed upon him the Dragon of Annam.[61] A governor who had established a school or in other ways shown his solicitude for education would often receive the Medal of Public Instruction given by that ministry in Paris, and the ministry of agriculture would award the Mérite agricole.

There was no lack of medals to bedeck a governor's chest, and some seem to have made a real art of acquiring them. Governor Grodet in the 1890s somehow was able to get himself awarded, among other medals, the Spanish Order of Merit of the Navy and the Officer Cross of Orange Nassau.[62] Although several times offered the Legion of Honor, Deschamps writes that he turned it down, feeling that it would be improper to accept such an award since he had been in charge of its distribution while in Paris. But when he became governor of Somali, he found himself painfully outranked by other officials bedecked in splendid medals—especially the Italian consul—and he wired Paris to grant him the right to wear the Nichan el Anwar.[63]

A civilian corps of governors was established in 1887 to help supervise the running of a growing empire. There were five classes of governorship with pay commensurate to class. Colonial assignment depended on how a colony was ranked, its classification reflecting the colony's importance to Paris. Such a system of posting governors limited the ministry's choice of personnel and in 1893, although ranks were retained for salary and promotion purposes, the classification of colonies was eliminated. Now a governor first class could serve in one colony, only to be succeeded by a governor fourth class. And a governor could be promoted in rank without having to leave the colony.[64]

In 1900 the corps of governors was limited to three ranks and it would remain that way. The salary of a governor first class in 1903 was 30,000 francs; that of second class, 25,000; and that of governor third class, 20,000. The governor-general earned twice as much as the governor first class; his salary was 60,000 francs. The governor first class earned twice as much, and the governor-general nearly four times as much, as the most senior official in the corps of colonial administrators who staffed the French districts, the *cercle* commandants.[65] The same ratio was maintained in 1920; but by 1930, in the face of massive inflation and budgetary constraints, the salary of the governor-general and governor had declined in relation to each other and to that of the highest paid colonial administrators. The governor-general earned 150,000 francs; the governor first class, 125,000 francs; and the senior administrator, 67,000 francs.[66]

These salaries compared favorably with those in the metropole. Although the lower ranks of the overseas administration did not compare well with the army at home, governorships did. The lowest rank governor earned as much as a general; governors-general earned three times as much. Throughout the colonial era governors' salaries were close to those paid the highest members of the metropolitan civil service, the directors general of the ministries. Though they performed some of the same tasks as the prefects and were regarded by Paris as a special form of overseas prefect, the overseas governors were paid less; for example, in 1914 the prefect of the Seine earned 50,000 francs and the prefect of the Paris police 40,000, as compared to between 20,000 and 30,000 francs for the governor. The governor-general, on the other hand, with his 60,000 francs, was earning more than the prefects. Governors were thus relatively well paid but were by no means the highest paid civil servants, as was the case with British governors, who tended to receive the very highest salaries granted by the English government. In 1914 the governor-general of Nigeria received £7,500 annually, the secretary of state for colonies received £5,000, and the chief of the imperial general staff received £3,000.[67]

Emolument additional to salary was in costs of representation, which helped defray the official expenses involved in presiding over a colony. In 1888 the governor of Senegal received 15,000 francs yearly for representation costs. In 1921 the governors-general received 216,000 francs; the governors received between 30,000 and 45,000 francs a year.[68] These funds allowed the governors to carry on a relatively extensive social role as head of the colony. They were nearly always hosts to visiting dignitaries and officials of various sorts and were expected to entertain lavishly. In the Cameroons, Governor Delavignette on Joan of Arc Day had 400 visitors at the palace; in one afternoon they consumed ten cases of champagne, five cases of whiskey, and uncounted cases of beer and soft drinks.[69] Such social duties quickly exhausted the representation costs and undoubtedly also absorbed some of the governors' salaries.

The salaries do not seem to have made anyone rich. The expenses of maintaining a home in the colonies as well as in France and of educating their children in boarding schools in the metropole absorbed much of the governors' income. When Governor Dolisie of the Congo died in 1899, his family was left penniless and his former superiors and political friends had to try to obtain for his widow a tobacco license.[70] Even after he was named governor, Eboué seems to have continued to be plagued by financial problems. In general, however, the salary allowed for a comfortable existence and seems to have been a financial attraction even to individuals not within the colonial service. A recent biographer of Victor Augagneur claims that the salary and other emoluments, which totaled as much as 100,000 francs, help explain why this Radical Socialist mayor and deputy was willing to resign the mayoralty of Lyon to become governor-general of Madagascar in 1905.[71]

After retirement from active service some governors, because of the experience they had acquired overseas, were appointed to lucrative posts in the business world. Of the governors-general, Roume went to Le Nickel Compagnie and the board of directors of the Suez Canal; Angoulvant, to the Compagnie générale des colonies; Governor Merlin joined the Banque française de l'Afrique and Governor Bobichon the Banque coloniale d'études (he also held interest in cotton companies in French Equatorial Africa).[72] After World War II former governors also occupied significant posts in the business world. The possibilities of occupying such positions made the colonial officials potentially receptive to pressure from the business community. However, not all governors subsequently appointed to the boards of companies had favored business interests while in office; whereas those who had done favors to firms were not necessarily rewarded with commercial jobs upon retirement.

Social Life

Unfortunately we know very little about the social life of the governors or their day-to-day work because they did not write their memoirs like some of their British counterparts. The first one to be published was in 1975—Hubert Deschamps's *Roi de la brousse*—and of the twenty years he served overseas only four were in the capacity of governor. While British governors have published over twenty memoirs, the French have not been as willing to write of their overseas experiences. This reticence is curious. The memoir is nearly as popular in France as in England. Politicians, generals, and metropolitan civil servants write their memoirs.

French colonial officials shunned such a tradition probably because they were trained in law and the legal outlook hindered the development of a literary tradition. British officials, educated in the classics, had a far richer literary culture, which permitted them to write with greater ease—and probably also made them more prone than their French counterparts to see their careers as heroic and fascinating, worthy of being told to their contemporaries. Significantly, the one memoir writer, Deschamps, was not trained solely in law but also had had a liberal arts university education. There was, moreover, less interest in colonial questions in France than in Britain, a lack of interest that discouraged French overseas officials from committing their memories to paper. The market for colonial books was thus limited, and publishers did not leap at the opportunity to publish colonial memoirs. Historians, therefore, have to rely almost exclusively on official files in reconstructing the social milieu of the governors.

The main function of the governor was as the representative of the republic in his colony. This often meant a ceremonial role; it was he who laid the wreath on the unknown soldier's tomb, who gave speeches on July 14. He was the head of the European community in the colony and played an important social function in giving dinners, attending banquets, and generally providing for the social life of the European community.

The wives of governors frequently set the social tone. Governor-general Ponty late in life married an actress from a visiting troupe that came to perform in Dakar. Several of his subordinates followed suit and also wedded members of that troupe. Although Ponty married the leading actress, his marriage still reveals a social egalitarianism of which his British colleagues would not have been capable. Before World War I the actress was regarded as a desirable sex object but hardly a suitable marriage partner for a man of prestige and power like a governor-general. But that did not hinder Ponty and his aides in their choice of wives. Madame Ponty was a consummate performer and set off a long series of skirmishes for rank and precedence among her former colleagues from the troupe, much to the amusement of everyone except the governor-general. Indeed, Robert Randau, writing under the pseudonym of Arnaud in his novel *Le Chef de porte-plume*, savagely satirized the Dakar of pre–World War I.

Getting along with the governor-general's wife was important. Arriving in Dakar in late 1915, Madame Delafosse endangered her husband's chances of being promoted to governor by responding coolly toward the insistence of Madame Clozel, the governor-general's wife, on a close friendship—colonial gossip said the latter was a lesbian.[73] Some of the governors' wives behaved in bizarre ways. Madame Ponty had a carriage of which she was so fond that when she went on leave she would take the carriage wheels with her to France to insure that no one would ride in it while she was gone. Madame Clozel also considered such action.[74] Yet the latter, in France during World War I, selflessly devoted herself to nursing wounded soldiers.[75]

Governors' wives played an important role supervising the domestic functioning of the palace. Their value was most obvious when they were not there. Delavignette, who went to the Cameroons without his wife, found that he could not keep track of his cook's expenditures. "In six days 130 eggs! Admittedly small eggs and all of them were not fresh. But 130 eggs for one omelette and a few cakes, that's a lot. . . . In three weeks, four jars of jam have been consumed, but I can't remember having eaten any," he wrote his wife.[76] In addition to their domestic duties, the wives filled other roles. We know very little about their lives; unlike their British counterparts, none wrote memoirs. And, probably unfairly, only the most outrageous examples of their behavior have been recorded. Some by their contacts and relations seem to have played a role in promoting their husbands' careers, but in general they were of secondary importance.

Pettiness was not limited to the circle of official wives. The men, too, got involved in intricate struggles for precedence and protocol. In 1846 the officials surrounding Governor Ollivier in Senegal drove that desperate man to suicide by their constant bickering.[77] A little over half a century later the governor of Gabon was ill-tempered and overly harsh with his subordinates because he felt slighted when a younger man was appointed acting governor-general of French Equatorial Africa. He actually refused to obey the latter's orders.[78] As the colonial societies became larger some of this pettiness disappeared; often it was less the reflection of the personalities involved than a reaction to the boredom that prevailed in the small, restricted, European colonial milieu.

The improvement of communications with France and the increasing comforts that became available in the colonies, especially in their capitals, made it possible for the governors to bring their families with them. In the bush, however, before the 1930s French district administrators still had African female companions. In a governor's palace the last time a permanent African mistress had been installed was in the mid-nineteenth century with the governorship of Faidherbe. He had married *à la mode du pays* and—although not his wife according to Napoleonic law—his companion received the honors of a governor's spouse. They had several children. The administrator d'Arboussier was legally married to a Fulani woman from a distinguished family. One wonders why d'Arboussier, who was an experienced African administrator—he spoke several languages and knew much of West Africa from personal experience—was not given a post as governor in West Africa. He and his family went to New Hebrides and New Caledonia, where he served as governor. Was he refused an African post because it was thought his wife's connections might make him partial to a particular ethnic or religious group? It is unlikely that her color would have deterred the administration from appointing d'Arboussier, however. Before World War II there were two black West Indians who became governor: Eboué went to Chad in 1938 and was governor-general of French Equatorial Africa in 1940; Blacher served in the interwar years in Dahomey, Niger, and Guinea.

Retirement

After World War II it became more of a pattern for former governors to seek national political offices, revealing the essential political proclivities of their office. Lapie, after serving in Chad during World War II, became a prominent Socialist deputy, who in 1950–1951 was minister of education and in 1956–1958 was vice-president of the National Assembly: Cornut-Gentille, governor-general of Equatorial Africa in 1947–1951 and of West Africa in 1951–1956, served as French representative to the United Nations Security Council (Algeria was then in the forefront of debates in the international organization) and then as ambassador to Argentina before being called back to Paris to become de Gaulle's minister of overseas France. Bourges, governor-general of Equatorial Africa (1958–1960), was a Gaullist deputy, a junior cabinet officer under de Gaulle and Pompidou; President Giscard d'Estaing appointed him minister of defense. Messmer, governor of Ivory Coast and Cameroons and governor-general of Equatorial Africa (1958) and West Africa (1959–1960), held the highest political position of a former governor: minister of defense under de Gaulle and Pompidou's prime minister. At Pompidou's death Messmer considered running for president.

After serving overseas ex-governors also entered nonpolitical careers. Some went into private business. Some began distinguished scholarly careers; Deschamps occupied the first chair in modern African history at the Sorbonne and wrote prolifically on subjects related to overseas history and Madagascar. Jore, who had been governor of Senegal in the 1920s, forty years later was writing about the history of the French presence in that colony; in spite of his advanced age, he remained an active member of the Société française d'histoire d'outre-mer. Durand, who served in the same colony in the 1940s, retired and became a novelist; he lists his current profession as *homme de lettres*. Delavignette served at the ministry of overseas France after his tenure in the Cameroons and then taught at the colonial training school, the Ecole nationale de la France d'outre-mer. He also continued to write about colonial questions.

Other governors who served at the very end of the colonial era had the pleasure of being ambassadors to the newly emancipated colonies. In 1962 the ambassadors to Niger and Gabon were its former governors. This was quite different from the British, who, though in some cases integrating onetime colonial governors in the foreign service, never sent them as ambassadors to their former colonies. Even more unusual, some French ex-governors were appointed as ambassadors to France from the African states; this was the case with Ramadier, former governor of Guinea, Cameroons, and Niger, who was named by Mali as its first ambassador, Délégué général, to Paris, and Mauberna, the last governor of Guinea, who was Niger's first ambassador to France.

A Balance Sheet

In the colonies they had ruled, many governors left behind concrete memorials of their efforts. Even after independence their names still are affixed to street signs. The largest avenue in the center of Dakar is Avenue William Ponty; Faidherbe rates a wide street, and the early nineteenth-century Governor Blanchot has a smaller side street in a neighborhood of fading reputation. Not only men long since dead but even ex-governors who were still alive were paid tribute by the independent states. In 1964 the Ivory Coast invited on an official visit Governor Latrille, who had valiantly stood up for the Africans against the white planters between 1943 and 1947. Latrille was feted for his sense of courage and devotion, and one of the most important streets was named Boulevard André Latrille. Such appreciation for the work of former governors was not limited to regimes that were notably pro-Western and continued to maintain close ties with France. Thus, in 1961 Sékou Touré invited the last French governor, Mauberna, to attend the congress of the Parti démocratique de Guinée; to large applause, Touré declared: "If today in a formerly colonized country, now independent, a former colonial governor is acclaimed by all those whom he had to rule, it is incontestably because M. Mauberna has left nothing but good memories in Guinea."[79] And in independent Mali, President Modibo Keita drove through the streets of Bamako with a former governor, Louveau, rendering him homage for his brilliant services as the head of the former colony.

The governors themselves have in different ways judged their efforts overseas. Reste, who served in the 1920s and 1930s as governor in Africa, painted in brilliant colors the accomplishments of his fellow governors and other French officials in Africa: "We gave enlightenment to these men who lived in poverty amongst riches they ignored. Until our arrival they had not participated in the common tasks that mankind has been pursuing for millennia, the work of progress."[80] Governor Deschamps, twenty years his junior, a man who had imbibed Schopenhauer and Nietzsche in addition to the classics of the Enlightenment, set up maybe a more balanced view of the accomplishments of the governors and their men. He listed on the positive side the establishment of a *pax francese* throughout the empire, protection of the indigenous people from exploitation, economic development, an opening up of the colonial peoples to the rest of the world, and a spread of Western culture and education, which introduced the colonial peoples to modern technology and also laid the foundations for unity in states that most often were multilingual and multiethnic. Deschamps, after making this listing, adds:

> All of this was never accomplished consciously or perfectly. I can well recognize what was missing and what could have been accomplished. But such shortcomings came from a general policy or lack thereof [in Paris]. We did our best with the means put at our disposal. And what we left behind was not without use. . . .
>
> In the short run our colonization may have been oppressive here and there (less as a result of what we did than as the result of economic exploitation, and it was far less oppressive than certain governments in Europe and elsewhere); in the long run colonization was part of the march toward world unity.[81]

The governors had all the varying foibles of men. Some were cruel and insensitive. Gentil in the Congo at the beginning of the century promoted his subordinates on the basis of the amount of taxes they collected. This led to wide-scale abuses, which he condoned. Governor-general Antonetti of French Equatorial Africa pushed a ruthless program of rail building, which decimated countless villages and killed thousands. Some governors were corrupt and venal. Governor Woelfel of Togo, the first French commissioner in the mandate, was involved in land speculation; Governor Hesling of the Upper Volta pushed cotton growing, which benefited relatives associated with European commercial houses but pauperized the African populations.[82]

Others were humane and principled, often taking the defense of the African. To use but a few examples after World War II: Governor Latrille in the Ivory Coast defended the rights of the Africans against the settlers; in the Cameroons, Delavignette upheld the political equality of the black legislators with the white ones. Governor-general Barthes lucidly spoke out at the governors meeting of 1947 in behalf of extending to Africans all the economic, political, and social rights of Frenchmen regardless of the cost to France of such a policy.[83]

By their administration the governors introduced into the colonies a certain sense of commonality that has become the basis of the national feeling in the successor states. Although at times it has been hard for the central governments to uphold the unity of the state, their ambition has always been to maintain the territorial confines of the former colony. The territorial shape of present-day African states is thus one of the legacies of the colonial governors. On the debit side, the governor acted as an unfortunate model for African political leaders. Copying him they often resorted to elaborate and expensive ceremony. They also tried, as did their European predecessors, to establish over the country a rigorous central control, which often stifled initiative and self-expression.

In his summing up of the contributions of the governors, Deschamps emphasized their role as economic modernizers. They certainly played a role, but it should be noted that until World War II the French administration—bereft of funds—did little more than erect the most rudimentary infrastructure for some of the colonies. In education remarkably little was accomplished, especially for a nation that prided itself on its culture and *mission civilisatrice*. Most of the remarkable and lasting economic accomplishments in French Africa occurred in the last fifteen years of colonialism with the institution of the economic development program FIDES. Economic development in Africa and the spread of Western education and technological knowledge were very uneven in the colonial period, creating social and ethnic tensions that persist.

It is by no means certain that colonial rule was necessary to the economic development that has occurred in Africa.[84] It is possible that European trade and technology would have penetrated more successfully without colonial rule. If European techniques and values had not been identified with foreign conquest, Africans might more eagerly have embraced them. In the manner of the Japanese they might have readily adapted the Western technology they thought useful for their own society. All of this is possibly true, but it did not happen that way. Rather, it was under the colonial impact that the most important social and economic transformations occurred. Although the governors were not alone in effecting these changes, they played their role and share responsibility for the accomplishments and shortcomings of twentieth-century Africa.

Notes

1. In Pierre Vaissière, "Origines de la colonisation à Saint-Domingue," *Revue des questions historiques* 79, n.s. (January–April 1906):485 note.

2. In Léonce Jore, *Les Etablissements français sur la côte occidentale d'Afrique de 1758 à 1809* (Paris, 1964), p. 86.

3. In John R. Singh, "French Foreign Policy, 1763–1778, with Special Reference to the Caribbean" (Ph.D. diss., University of Oklahoma, 1972), p.164.

4. In Pierre Gentil, "Soldats du Sénégal" (unpublished paper, available at the French *Archives nationales, Section outre-mer* (hereinafter cited ANSOM).

5. In Josette Fallope-Lara, "La Guadeloupe entre 1848 et 1900" (unpublished *thèse de 3ème cycle*, Faculté des lettres et sciences humaines, Paris, n.d.).

6. Decree of 1 August 1889, *Bulletin officiel des colonies* (hereinafter cited *BOC*) (1889):806–811; decree of 10 March 1893, *BOC* (1893):209–210.

7. In Colin W. Newbury, "The Formation of the Government General of French West Africa," *Journal of African History* 1 (1960):115.

8. Ibid:111–128; Cakpo Vodouhe, "La Création de l'Afrique occidentale française, 1895–1904" (unpublished *thèse de 3ème cycle*, Faculté des lettres et sciences humaines, Paris, 1973–1974).

9. Pierre Charmeil, *Les Gouverneurs généraux des colonies françaises: Leurs pouvoirs et leurs attributions* (Paris, 1922).

10. Circular of minister to governors-general, governors, and the commissioner general of the Congo, 6 September 1902, *BOC* (1902):905–906.

11. Inspector general Frézouls to minister, Brazzaville, 19 April 1911, Inspections des colonies, Rapports d'ensemble, Archives de la Service d'inspection de la France d'outre-mer (hereinafter cited ASIFOM).

12. Hubert Deschamps, *Roi de la brousse: Mémoires d'autres mondes* (Paris, 1975), p. 128.

13. Anon., *Réalités coloniales* (Paris, 1934), pp. 176–177.

14. Interview with Robert Delavignette, July 1975.

15. Circular, Henry Simon, colonial minister, Paris, 3 February 1919, Affaires politiques 2553/9, ANSOM.

16. Georges Chaffard, *Les Carnets secrets de la décolonisation* (Paris, 1967), 2:165–268.

17. Deschamps, *Roi de la brousse*, p. 324.

18. Letter, governor-general to minister, 10 February 1933, 18G141, *Archives de l'Afrique occidentale française* (hereinafter cited AAOF).

19. Ibid.

20. Circular, 14 September 1934, 18G56/17, AAOF.

21. Deschamps, *Roi de la brousse*, p. 122.

22. *Annuaire de gouvernement général de l'Afrique occidentale française, 1915–1916* (Paris, 1916).

23. Lieutenant governor of Dahomey to governor-general, 29 May 1933, Porto-Novo, 18G67/17, AAOF.

24. André Gide, *Travels in the Congo* [and] *Return from Chad*, trans. Dorothy Bussy (New York, 1937), pp. 57–58.

25. Brian Weinstein, *Eboué* (New York, 1972), pp. 216–217.

26. Governor-general to governors, 6 January 1937, 8G54/17, AAOF.

27. Gide, *Travels*, p. 50.

28. 1931 report, 4G34, AAOF.

29. Deschamps, *Roi de la brousse*, p. 237.

30. On the education of the members of the corps of colonial administrators see W. B. Cohen, *Rulers of Empire: The French Colonial Service in Africa* (Stanford, 1971), pp. 34–35.

31. Weinstein, *Eboué*, pp. 26–27.

32. Marcel Blanchard, "Administrateurs d'Afrique noire," *Revue d'histoire des colonies* 9 (1953): 411–420.

33. Louise Delafosse, "Comment prit fin la carrière coloniale de Maurice Delafosse," *Revue française d'histoire d'outre-mer* 61 (1974):94–97, 101–102.

34. Ibid., p. 92.

35. Delavignette interview, July 1975.

36. Weinstein, *Eboué*, p. 111.

37. Freemasonry also had its adherents in the officer corps of the *Armée coloniale* and especially in the Republican and anticlerically inclined *infanterie de marine*.

38. Delafosse, "Comment prit fin," p. 99.

39. Weinstein, *Eboué*, p. 115.

40. Philip Williams, *Politics in Postwar France* (London, 1954), p. 388; Aristide R. Zolberg, *One-Party Government in the Ivory Coast* (Princeton, 1964), p. 97.

41. Ruth Schachter Morgenthau, *Political Parties in French-speaking West Africa* (Oxford, 1964), p. 101.

42. Chaffard, *Carnets secrets*, 2:289.

43. Ezra N. Suleiman, *Politics, Power, and Bureaucracy in France: The Administrative Elite* (Princeton, 1974).

44. Michel Crozier, *The Bureaucratic Phenomenon* (Chicago, 1964), pp. 197–198.

45. Jacques Lombard, *Autorités traditionnelles et pouvoirs européens en Afrique noire* (Paris, 1967), p. 106.

46. Charles Richard, "Le gouvernement général de Victor Augagneur à Madagascar, 1905–1910" (unpublished *thèse de 3ème cycle*, Faculté des lettres et sciences humaines, Paris, 1974), pp. 300, 330.

47. Morgenthau, *Political Parties*, pp. 186, 204.

48. Anne Claude de Mazières, "Victor Liotard et la pénétration française dans le Haut-Oubangui" (unpublished *thèse de 3ème cycle*, Ecole pratique des hautes études, 1975), p. 135.

49. Général de Chambrun, *Brazza* (Paris, 1930), p. 186.

50. Inspector general Phérivong to minister, Dakar, 31 May 1911, Rapports d'ensemble, ASIFOM.

51. On Bingerville, Inspector of colonies Lapaly to minister, Bingerville, 31 January 1908; on Koulouba, Inspector general Maurice Méray to minister of colonies, Koulouba, 4 March 1910, Rapports d'ensemble, ASIFOM.

52. Elliott P. Skinner, *The Transformation of Ouagadougou* (Princeton, 1974), p. 29; idem, *The Mossi of Upper Volta* (Stanford, 1964), p. 161.

53. Skinner, *Transformation*, p. 33; Claude Meillassoux, *Urbanization of an African Community* (Seattle, 1968), pp. 3–10; Sérigne Lamine Diop, "La Situation Démographique et son évolution," in M. Sankalé, L. V. Thomas, and P. Fougeyrolles, eds., *Dakar en devenir* (Dakar, 1968), p. 80.

54. Blanchard, "Administrateurs d'Afrique noire," p. 413.

55. Weinstein, *Eboué*, p. 216.

56. Delavignette to his wife Annie, Duala, 17 March 1946, Delavignette Archives.

57. Deschamps, *Roi de la brousse*, p. 245.

58. Inspector general Maurice Méray to minister of colonies, Koulouba, 4 March 1910, Rapports d'ensemble, ASIFOM.

59. Decree of 10 October 1905, *BOC* (1905):1086–1087.

60. Robert Delavignette, "L'Offrande de l'étranger: Mémoires d'une Afrique française" (unpublished memoirs, 1975), pp. 368–371.

61. Deschamps, *Roi de la brousse*, p. 205.

62. Blanchard, "Administrateurs d'Afrique noire," p. 413.

63. Deschamps, *Roi de la brousse*, p. 205.

64. Decree of 5 September 1887, *BOC* (1887):653–654; decree of 2 February 1890, *BOC* (1890):245–248; decree of 14 March 1893, *BOC* (1893):215–216.

65. The amounts cited here are the colonial salaries; there was a base salary, 15,000, for a governor first class and he received an additional 15,000 francs as a colonial supplement. Decree of 4 July 1896, *Journal officiel, lois et décrets* (1896):4361; Alfred Viénot, *Personnel des gouverneurs, des secrétaires généraux* (Paris, 1913), p.3.

66. Decree of 10 July 1920, *BOC* (1920):1931–1947; decree of 21 July 1921, *BOC* (1921):1311–1314; decree of 29 August 1930, *BOC* (1930):1547–1550.

67. Henri Montarnel, *Les Salaires, l'inflation, et les charges* (Paris, 1925); pp. 27–30; Roger Grégoire, *The French Civil Service* (Brussels, n.d.), pp. 261–265; Paul Carcelle and Georges Mas, "Les Traitements et la situation financière," *Revue administrative* 7 (January-February 1949):19; L. H. Gann and Peter Duignan, *The Rulers of British Africa, 1870–1914* (Stanford, 1978).

68. *Annuaire colonial* (Paris, 1888), p. 21; Charmeil, *Les gouverneurs généraux*, p. 28.

69. Delavignette to his wife, Duala, 13 May 1946, Delavignette Archives.

70. Blanchard, "Administrateurs d'Afrique noire," p. 392.

71. Richard, "Gouvernement général de Victor Augagneur," p. 55.

72. Jean Suret-Canale, *Afrique noire, occidentale et centrale*, vol. 2: *L'Ere coloniale, 1900–1945* (Paris, 1964), 396.

73. This is discreetly handled by Delafosse, "Comment prit fin," pp. 80–81.

74. Ibid., p. 88.

75. Ibid., p. 91.

76. Delavignette to wife, Duala, 7 April 1946, Delavignette Archives.

77. P. Marty, "Le Suicide d'un gouverneur de Sénégal (1846)," *Revue d'histoire coloniale française* 8 (1920):129–144.

78. Inspector general Frézouls to minister, Brazzaville, 15 March 1911, Rapports d'ensemble, ASIFOM.

79. Quoted in Chaffard, *Carnets secrets*, 2:268.

80. F. J. Reste, "Grands Corps et grands commis de la France d'outre-mer," *Revue des deux mondes* (15 March 1959):334.

81. Deschamps, *Roi de la brousse*, pp. 350–352.

82. Hesling's actions led to an inspection and eventual recall.

83. "Conférence impériale," February 1947, copy of minutes in Delavignette Archives.

84. That the economic trends that we have come to associate with colonialism had already begun before imperial conquest is convincingly demonstrated by Anthony G. Hopkins, *An Economic History of West Africa* (London, 1973), chaps. 3–4.

Louis Léon César Faidherbe (1818–1889)

Leland C. Barrows[1]

Louis Léon César Faidherbe (1818–1889) is classed along with Bugeaud, Gallieni, and Lyautey as one of the outstanding architects of the French colonial empire. His legendary reputation rests almost entirely on his accomplishments during his two terms as governor of Senegal (1854–1861, 1863–1865). The duration of his service as governor, his tenacity in carrying out what was in fact a very limited plan although it seemed spectacular in light of his predecessor's accomplishments, and the precedents that he set earned him an exaggerated reputation as the veritable founder of French West Africa. He also became known as an Africanist from his published writings in history, anthropology, and linguistics. The major role he held in the Franco-Prussian war as commander in chief of the Provincial Army of the North was secondary to the Senegalese career, which established his national position.

Background, Education, and Early Military Career

Faidherbe was a graduate of France's elite Ecole polytechnique; yet his family origins and early background were modest.[2] Born in the industrial town of Lille not far from the Belgian frontier, he was the fifth and youngest child of hosier Louis Joseph César Faidherbe and Sophie Monnier Faidherbe. Faidherbe's father, a sergeant major in the revolutionary and Napoleonic armies, had been imprisoned during the Hundred Days for having expressed anti-Bonapartist sentiments. Freed when Louis XVIII returned to power, his national guard company awarded him a ceremonial sword. André Demaison's claim that this may have influenced Faid-

51

herbe's supposed anti-Bonapartist, republican sympathies seems doubtful inasmuch as the senior Faidherbe died when his son was a child. But the episode may have stimulated Faidherbe to engage in some political opportunism to advance his career.

Faidherbe's mother managed to support the family and to keep the business afloat. Her youngest son began in primary school to display a talent for drawing and mathematics. Recommendations by his teachers and appeals by his mother to several local politicians won him a full scholarship to a preparatory school at Douai and a half-scholarship to the Ecole polytechnique in Paris, which he entered in November 1838.

In later years Faidherbe's personality would be disciplined, unsmiling, and aloof. The experience of having been a poor boy at Polytechnique may have disillusioned him and contributed to his later reputation for coldness; or perhaps it was bitterness at the gambling debts incurred while on garrison duty at Metz and Belfort (he had great difficulty paying them off).[3] The school's reputation for liberal republicanism and Saint-Simonism undoubtedly had its influence. That many of its graduates became civilian entrepreneurs in business and industry may have facilitated Faidherbe's dealings with such persons in Senegal and Algeria. But in 1838, when the tall, blond adolescent entered Polytechnique, he tended to be a hell-raiser, a good caricaturist—some of his drawings survive—and a composer of bawdy songs for the guitar.[4] His grades suffered. He placed near the botton of his class at graduation in 1842 and only nineteen out of twenty-three in the entrance examination for the engineer corps. His performance at the Ecole d'application for engineers at Metz was little better. But by becoming an engineer he gained admission to an arme savante, which allowed him a greater degree of intellectual curiosity and creativity than was the usual case in the French army officer corps of the period.

Algerian and Colonial Assignments

As a colonial officer Faidherbe only made a strong impact on Senegal; but his actions and attitudes while governor were profoundly influenced by his earlier assignments in Algeria (May 1844–June 1846) and Guadeloupe (March 1848–September 1849). It was not only the exotic that prompted him to request Algerian and colonial assignments but the combat pay and chances for rapid promotion that came with the former, the double pay with the latter, and the extra allowances for both. Faidherbe could pay off his gambling debts and help with his aging mother's support. The assignment to Algeria in 1844 served as an escape mechanism, on outlet for his frustrations, and a stimulus to develop his talents.

He was first sent to the Third Company of Engineers at Mostaganem, and shortly after the Sidi-Brahim disaster of September 1845 he transferred to the engineering staff. At both posts his primary duty was to assist in the opening of trails and roads to connect the coastal garrisons with major interior settlements. He seems not to have taken part in much combat although the roads were intended for military use and his province saw the terminal French struggle against Abd el-Kader and Bou-Maza.

The five surviving letters written to his mother during this period indicate that although he was captivated by Algeria, his attitude was contradictory toward its peoples and cultures. In one case he compared the "majesty and dignity" of the "poorest Arab" of Mostaganem to the "deformed, . . . awkward, . . . gauche, . . . crude, ridiculously dressed, . . . ignoble, . . . and badly built " French peasant or worker from his home district.[5] But he supported the aims of the French military and the means used to accomplish these aims. In this and a later letter he praised Islam for being a great world religion and for forbidding the consumption of alcohol, but he predicted that the advance of French civilization would make alcoholics of the Algerians.[6] It was the start of his ambivalence toward Islam— positive when he was not in a position of responsibility and could be objective, negative when in power and confronted not only with Islamic state builders but also with the mass appeal of Islam as a religious and cultural system distinct from that of France.

Faidherbe took a dim veiw of the poor Spanish and Maltese settlers of Mostaganem, but he considered that wealthy colonists with capital to invest would lead to the future prosperity of Algeria. Though conscious of the differences between French aims in Algeria and in Senegal, he would retain this view while serving in Senegal. He never developed the anticivilian, anti–big business attitudes that characterized Marshal Bugeaud, the most famous French governor of Algeria, but tended more to resemble fellow-Polytechnicien Lamoricière, who was serving at the time as commandant of Oran province.

Much to his disappointment and despite his promotion to captain second class, the completion in June 1846 of the tasks undertaken by the engineers in Oran province sent Faidherbe back to Belfort and then to Lille. Fortunately, the influence of two generals, Charron and Négrier, brought him an assignment to Guadeloupe to fill a last-minute opening there in the engineer corps.

Part of the Faidherbe legend is that he became an ardent republican and negrophile while stationed in Guadeloupe because he was caught up in the events of 1848, particularly the final emancipation of slaves in the French colonies. He and a handful of other radical whites, so the story goes, so annoyed the planters by campaigning for the election as deputy for Guadeloupe of the emancipator, Victor Schoelcher, that they convinced the governor to have Faidherbe recalled. Nothing in the available records points to this scenario. Faidherbe had to leave Guadeloupe because he had the least seniority of the engineer officers there at a time when metropolitan authorities initiated a reduction in personnel. After his second tour of duty in Algeria he would have been reassigned to Guadeloupe in 1852 had he not, at the last moment, been designated for Senegal.[7] His performance was acceptable; inspection certificates for 1848 and 1849 indicate that his superiors thought highly of him.

What may have given rise to the myth that Faidherbe was forced out of Guadeloupe is the notation on his 1848 certificate that he was "attracted to exaggerated socialism—easily impassioned by radical opinion [and] should be directed into reasonable channels by good advice." The same certificate also commented that Faidherbe was studying geology, natural history, and several foreign languages on his own but that he needed to "be more consistent" in these studies and to "give them a positive aim."[8] His interest in the blacks of Guadeloupe led to his later request for assignment to Senegal, as acknowledged in the draft of a letter to Jomard, president of the Geographical Society of Paris, a later version of which was published in the society's bulletin in February 1854.

During his second assignment in Algeria (December 1849–June 1852) Faidherbe led a fairly sedentary existence as director of the engineers in the isolated, newly occupied oasis settlement of Bou-Saada, where he built the fort. With the support of General Bosquet—also a Polytechnique graduate, an engineer, and the commandant of Mostaganem during Faidherbe's earlier Algerian assignment—he also took active part in the Kabylie campaigns of 1851 and 1852, fighting under General Saint-Arnaud, commander in chief of the expedition, who recommended him for the Legion of Honor. Faidherbe received the decoration—his first—in April 1852.

In an effort to open a road through the Djurjura mountains to connect Bougie (Bejaia) with Algiers, Faidherbe was attached to the column that was trapped by a blizzard fifty kilometers west of Bougie in February 1852. The men panicked and, despite their officers' efforts, fled back to Bougie, 150 dying of exposure. Faidherbe collapsed from fatigue and survived only because he was carried part of the way by two troopers. The exerience has been blamed for his chronic arthritis, but nothing in his writings indicates that he suffered any ill effects. After a few weeks of rest in Bougie, Faidherbe proceeded with construction of the mountain road. He returned to France in June 1852 on a four-month furlough, which was cut short in August by his sudden assignment to head the engineer corps at Saint-Louis du Senegal.

Proconsul and Soldier in West Africa, 1852–1865

Faidherbe arrived in Saint-Louis just as the French government decided to make radical changes in the system of economic and political linkages that until then had characterized French relations with the Senegalese polities. In 1852 French authority in Senegal was confined to a series of miniscule *comptoirs* (trading stations) the two principal ones being Saint-Louis on N'Dar island sixteen kilometers from the mouth of the Senegal river, and Gorée, a rocky island two kilometers east of the southern point of Cape Verde.

The French administrative apparatus of Senegal and its dependencies always appeared more substantial on paper than was the case in reality. Administration and local government in Saint-Louis combined the characteristics of municipal government in France and the system of naval command and administration that one might find in a small base or on a ship at sea. A royal ordinance of 1840 had spelled out the powers of the local colonial administration and had given the governor much theoretical power. One who was skillful could increase these powers by taking advantage of the slow communications between Senegal and France and the fact that he was the principal vehicle of communication with his superiors in Paris. The governor was advised by a privy council consisting of the heads of administrative services: an *ordonnateur*, or head of the interior administration, a secretary, a treasurer-comptroller, and the head of the judicial service, plus two appointed unofficial notables. Of the departments represented, only that of the judicial service was well developed. It consisted of several judges and two courts at Saint-Louis and at Gorée, respectively. The *ordonnateur's* staff included himself and one clerk. Gorée, except for a brief four years of complete separation from the government of Senegal, was ruled by the governor but allowed a separate executive council and budget.

Faidherbe worked through the command structure of the small French force placed at his disposal. Outlying posts like Bakel remained under martial law. The usual effectives of the colony were three companies of marine infantry, a squadron of *spahis*, two batteries of artillery, a subsection of engineers, the native companies and *tirailleurs sénégalais* created by Faidherbe in 1857, and special levies, which from time to time were lent to the Senegalese government. Faidherbe could draw up to forty officers at any one time for military and administrative assignments in Saint-Louis or in the hinterland posts.

The truly sovereign powers in the areas were African polities like the Trarza, Brakna, and Idaw 'Aish Mauritanian confederations on the right bank of the river; the Tukulor (Toucouleur) *almamate* of Fouta-Toro, which dominated 600 kilometers of the left bank of the middle Senegal valley; Cayor, a powerful Woloff kingdom that stretched from the Senegal river opposite Saint-Louis to the edge of Cape Verde, 200 kilometers south; and Walo, a smaller and weaker Woloff kingdom that occupied most of the delta of the Senegal river, extending northeast of Saint-Louis to Dagana, 100 kilometers away.

Based at Saint-Louis, which they had occupied in 1659, the French exploited the trade possibilities of the river. As far as Podor in western Fouta-Toro it was navigable all year, and seasonally to Bakel, site of a major French fort; to Sénoudébou, site of a smaller fort of the Falémé river, a tributary of the Senegal; and to Médine, a pro-French village in Khasso near the Félou falls. Gorée—the second *comptoir*—was a trading center for Cape Verde, the *petite côte* extending from Rufisque to the Saloum estuary and giving access to the Serrer kingdoms of Sine and Saloum; for the Casamance river, which the French penetrated as far inland as the Songrougrou junction and the post of Sédhiou; and for the Rivières-du-Sud of what became French Guinea.

Trade was conducted very much on African terms. The gum trade in particular (gum constituted the major French import from Saint-Louis) was highly regulated both by the Mauritanian rulers in whose territories most of the crop was grown and by the French colonial government in Saint-Louis in favor of the city's small African and mulatto merchants. During almost the entire period of Faidherbe's governorships the Senegal river, and hence Saint-Louis, continued to derive most of its export wealth from gum. (The value of peanuts exported from Saint-Louis—most of them coming from Cayor—never exceeded that of gum; in 1860, for instance, the gum exported was valued at 1,875,261.50 francs in comparison to 444,828.50 francs for the value of peanuts.).

Peanuts grew better in the Senegalese polities like Cayor and Baol on the plain lying between the Senegal river and the Gambia than they did in the polities of the Middle and Upper Senegal, and peanut oil had become an essential ingredient in the manufacture of French blue marble soap as well as an increasingly popular cooking oil. The growing importance of the crop contributed to French decisions to involve themselves more closely in the southern area. This explains the French hostility to the *thièdos* (the warrior class), whom they accused of interfering with the expansion of this new produce. Some African rulers, fearing the effects that a cash crop economy would have on their free peasantry, indeed encouraged the *thièdos* to plunder the tillers. This in turn caused the peasants to seek help from Islamic reformers like Maba-Diakhou, under whose rule—and as orthodox Moslems—they might by allowed to respond fully to this new market stimulus.

The development of trade had encouraged the rise of a substantial class of Afro-European merchants, partly gallicized, profoundly interested in inland commerce. Until Faidherbe's appointment relations between the African states of the interior and Saint-Louis had almost always been the exclusive preserve of the municipal governments of Saint-Louis and Gorée.Not only did the local mulatto mayors have close cultural ties—and in some cases family ties—with the hinterland rulers, but their stability in office was much greater than that of the French governors. (During the period from 1817 to Faidherbe's governorship there had been seventeen governors or, if interims and divided assignments are counted, thirty-seven shifts in gubernatorial power in as many years. During the same period Saint-Louis had five mayors.)

The merchants, white and black, helped to shape the political future of Senegal. Prodded by various groups and individuals—the wholesalers led by the Maurel and Prom Company, a former governor of Senegal Bouët-Willaumez, and an interministerial commision formed in 1850 to make recommendations for the future development of the French colonies—the naval ministry formulated a series of specific instructions that it gave first to Captain Auguste Protet, governor since 1850, and then to Faidherbe himself. They were supplemented by two long petitions, dated December 8, 1851, and February 11, 1854, which were signed by major Saint-Louis wholesalers and notables and were the basis of nearly everything that Faidherbe would accomplish while serving as governor of Senegal.[9]

Initially, the plan of 1854 applied only to the Senegal valley. It called for the colonial government:

1. to suppress the three Mauritanian controlled, seasonal, gum trading *escales* of the lower river with several fortified, French controlled trading posts, two of which—at Richard-Toll and Dagana—already existed and the third—at Podor—was to be built;
2. to allow French controlled African villages to form around these posts, where wholesalers could open trading branches to buy and sell any products year-round;
3. to reduce progressively and then end all *coutumes* (trade and land occupancy taxes paid by the French government or by private parties to African rulers), those remaining during transition to be calculated according to a percentage of the value of the annual trade with a given polity;
4. to suppress all navigation tolls (also called *coutumes*) along the Senegal river, particularly the major one at Saldé-Tébékhout in central Fouta-Toro;
5. to require that the Senegalese rulers recognize the French as the proprietors of the Senegal river;
6. to institute what the French called free trade—indicating trade freed of all African imposed taxes and other restrictions;
7. to free the left bank of the Senegal river by force if necessary from all Mauritanian political control and to end the practice of some Mauritanian clans of raiding the sedentary left bank black populations.

This was the blueprint for French control of a major inland waterway that happened, incidentally, to be the only reliable dry season source of fresh water for many of the peoples living along its banks. A few steam gunboats would easily intimidate the villages on the Senegal and its navigable tributaries. Landing parties would carry the destruction a few kilometers inland on both sides. The same tactics would eventually be applied to the coast and to the Saloum, the Casamance, the Rivières-du-Sud, albeit on a much reduced scale during Faidherbe's era.

The expanding peanut culture in the inland areas south of the Senegal river in Cayor and in Baol would stimulate Faidherbe and others to attempt to adapt this plan to dry land in an effort to halt what they considered the depredations of the *thièdos*, Woloff crown soldiers of servile origin accused of interfering with the agricultural activities of the peasantry. The land based campaigns that this adaptation required involved the French in unanticipated complications.

No sooner had he arrived in 1852 as director of the Saint-Louis engineers than Faidherbe threw himself into action. He visited the whole French sphere, traveled to Grand Bassam and Gabon with Captain Baudin, commandant of the French West African naval squadron, where he took part in a punitive raid against the Jack-Jacks near Grand Bassam, built a fort at nearby Dabou, and supervised major repairs and improvements in the fort at Libreville, Gabon. In a study of possible public works projects for Senegal he made several important recommendations including one for the French occupation and fortification of Dakar and another for the construction of a bridge to link Sor island, opposite Saint-Louis, to the Cayor mainland. He later recommended that the French occupy Gandiole, a salt producing center and a major Cayor peanut exporting point at the mouth of the Senegal river opposite the bar. He began to study African languages and history and to write for publication. His private papers indicate that he was fascinated by the middle and upper Niger valley. "It would be shameful," he wrote, "for France, mistress of Senegal and Algeria . . . to leave to other nations the trade of the Sudan."[10]

At the end of 1854 a series of events brought Faidherbe to the governorship. The Bordeaux based wholesalers of Saint-Louis became increasingly disillusioned with Protet, who was overly cautious and slow in executing his orders. Their complaints drew the attention of the naval minister, Théodore Ducos, a native of Bordeaux. The expeditions that Protet undertook between March and May 1854, first to reoccupy and to fortify Podor and then to punish the major Tukulor settlement of Dialmath in Dimar, were unsatisfactory. At Podor he failed to declare an immediate end to the *coutumes* and *escales*. The attack on Dialmath, even though it was classed as a French victory, resulted in 175 French casualties—too high for a mere colonial campaign, thought Ducos.[11] Under heavy criticism from both Ducos and the Saint-Louis wholesalers, Portet requested his recall by the end of July 1854.

Some of the wholesalers had meanwhile decided to propose Faidherbe as governor. Hilaire and Marc Maurel were initially impressed by him because, like Bouët-Willaumez, he had served in Algeria and he argued publicly that the French should make use of Algerian tactics and energy in combating the Mauritanians. In the Dialmath expedition Faidherbe had rallied that French forces as they were being repulsed by the village's defenders.[12] Faidherbe in 1854 published illustrated accounts of both expeditions in *L'Illustration journal universel* of June

and July 1854. By chance, his account of the Dialmath affair—one that emphasized his own role—appeared in the July 10, 1854, issue of the *Moniteur universel*,
rather than Protet's; General Fitte de Soucy, commander in chief of the engineer
corps, had had it published without Faidherbe's knowledge to give publicity to
the engineers.

It may have been Hilaire Maurel of the Maurel and Prom Company who proposed Faidherbe for the governorship on June 19 in a personal interview with
Ducos in Paris. In August he and eighteen other powerful Bordeaux merchants
presented the minister with a long, signed petition requesting the appointment.[13]
So that in rank Faidherbe would be equal to the *capitaines de vaisseaux* who
usually governed Senegal, Ducos rewarded him for his valor at Dialmath by having him promoted to major in advance of his actual seniority. An imperial decree
of November 1, 1854, raised Faidherbe to the governorship.

Since a second imperial decree of the same date detached Gorée and its dependencies to the south from the jurisdiction of Saint-Louis, during the first four
years of his governorship Faidherbe concentrated on the Senegal river valley. His
preliminary instructions, while cautioning that his nomination "was not the beginning or the continuation of a bellicose era," authorized him to back up his authority with force.[14] As an Algerian veteran, he was convinced that most of the
Senegalese polities would have to be defeated militarily at least once before they
would agree to the new French terms, so he made use of this authorization. He
took on the Trarza Mauritanians, Fouta-Toro, and supporters of El-Hadj Omar,
being careful to make hostilities with the Trarzas grow out of his enforcement of
treaties that previously had been ignored. With the second group he claimed self-
defense as a result of difficulties created by Protet's forceful reoccupation of Podor
and other long-standing differences between the French and the Fouta-Toro
almamate.

The coincidental arrival of the Tukulor Islamic reformer and state builder, El-
Hadj Omar Tall was a boon to Faidherbe. Omar's resemblance to leaders such as
those whom the French had already encountered in Algeria served to bolster support for him from the metropolitan government. The threat that he posed to the
traditional rulers of Fouta-Toro, Guidimakha, Khasso, Bondou, and others led
them to make accommodations with Faidherbe since the limited nature of the
governor's plan seemed to be less menacing than the social revolution presaged by
Omar's domination.

In January 1855 Faidherbe burned the Tukulor settlement of Bokol in Dimar,
one of two of the Fouta-Toro provinces easily accessible by boat during the dry
season. His objective, however, was the Trarzas—particularly those who habitually spent the dry season in Walo—in order to end their domination of this polity
and to impose the new trading regulations on them and on the Braknas. Except
during the rainy season, when Faidherbe sent most of his forces upstream to combat the Omarians and Fouta-Toro, he made the Mauritanians his first priority. To
get them out of Walo on the left bank and to eliminate the pro-Trarza ruling lineage in this polity, he annexed it to the colony after it had been invaded and gutted.
He initially had doubts about this annexation but had failed to find a compliant
ruler from a rival lineage to whom he could offer the throne. Walo would serve as
a model for future French annexations in West Africa. Faidherbe continued a war
of attrition against the Mauritanians, killing their cattle, denying them access to

the Senegal river, and launching raids short distances inland. He also attempted to pit their ruling clans one against the other, and the religious and gum selling groups—the *marabouts*—against the warriors. The Idaw 'Aish emirate, however, remained at peace and even allied itself with the French against the Omarians; their ruler Bakar, for political, religious, and social reasons feared Omar more than he did Faidherbe.[15]

Peace with the Mauritanians finally came in the spring of 1858 in the form of a compromise settlement. The Trarzas and the Braknas as well as the Idaw 'Aish agreed to abandon all political claims to the left bank and to trade their gum only at the French posts on French terms. The French, in turn, agreed to respect the strict independence of the Mauritanians and to pay to the rulers of the three principal emirates a duty of three to four percent of the value of gum exported from their territories.

By 1859, after heavy fighting, Faidherbe was able to make similar settlements with left bank polities although the situation was complicated by local leadership crises that arose as a result of the Omarian movement. The French made peace treaties with friendly leaders in the various riverine polities. They did not guarantee *coutumes* by treaty to any of them but made it clear that cooperative leaders would be offered presents paid for by a well-endowed fund set up for the purpose. They required the rulers of the Fouta-Toro provinces of Dimar and Toro in the west and Damga in the east to agree to their separation from the *almamate*. A pro-French *almamy*, Mohamadou-Birane-Wane, tacitly accepted this separation. Similar settlements were made with the polities of Guidimakha, Gadiaga, Khasso, and Bondou and with some of the chieftancies of Bambouk. With French aid two leaders—Bokar-Saâda of Bondou and Sambala of Khasso—eventually built strong anti-Omarian followings in their two polities despite the popular appeal of the Omarian ideology and pro-Omarian rival leaders in both cases.

By opening forts at Médine in Khasso at the foot of the Félou falls in 1855, Matam in Damga in 1857, and Saldé in central Fouta-Toro in 1859 and by strengthening Bakel and Sénoudébou, the French authorities were able to intervene more directly in the affairs of the left bank societies than in those of the right bank settlements. But the situation in the mid-Senegal valley remained ambiguous. Traditional leaders, particularly in Fouta-Toro, had been intimidated rather than conquered and would be the source of much instability in the future.

Faidherbe did not wish to destroy the Omarian empire but simply to prevent it from incorporating the Senegal valley polities east of Bafoulabé and to block Omar's Tijjani ideology from permeating the Woloff and Serrer peoples of western Senegal. He fought some major campaigns against Omarian forces, one of which—the relief of the siege of Médine in July 1857 and the battles that followed it—has been made an epic in colonial hagiography. When French forces in November 1859 destroyed Guémou, the last Omarian stronghold in the French sphere, Faidherbe authorized the commandant of Bakel to make peace overtures to Thièrno-Moussa, Omar's governor of Kaarta and Diombokho. The result was the agreement of 1860, which guaranteed the independence of the Omarian empire east of Bafoulabé, regulated the relations between the two spheres until 1880, and provided for the Mage-Quintin expedition of 1864–1866.

Having imposed the basic plan on the Senegal valley by the summer of 1858, Faidherbe began to lobby seriously for the return to his jurisdiction of Gorée and its dependencies. His aim was to "organize" Cayor "a little"[16] and to impose treaties of the sort made in the Senegal valley on Cayor—which linked Saint-Louis to Cape Verde and Gorée—and on the principal riverine and coastal polities to the south, all of which formed a vast area wherein the peanut culture was making great headway. By February 1859 Prince Jerome Bonaparte, the head of the experimental combined ministry of Algeria and the colonies (in existence from June 24, 1858, to November 24, 1860), had acceded to Faidherbe's request.

Faidherbe had given greater substance to French claims to Cape Verde and the so-called *petite-côte* by marching 800 men from Dakar—annexed by Protet in 1857 while serving as commandant of the French West African naval squadron—to Rufisque, Portudal, Joal, and then inland to Fatick in Sine, where they defeated the Sine army. Along the way he imposed new commercial regulations on Rufisque and punished a few African officials accused of having molested French traders. When it was over, the rulers of Sine, Saloum, and Baol had signed treaties recognizing French predominance in the area and agreeing not to interfere with trade. Small blockhouses were constructed at Rufisque, Portudal, and Joal along the coast and a larger fort was built at Kaolack in Saloum.

Concerning Cayor, Faidherbe planned to build a telegraph line along its coast linking Saint-Louis and Gorée and to place three small forts at equal distances along the route. These forts were to be supplied from the sea and would serve as bases from which military expeditions could move inland if necessary to intimidate the *damel* of Cayor and the *thièdos*. *Damel* Biraima would be invited to sign a treaty embodying these provisions and new commercial arrangement. But weak and alcoholic though he was, he refused to sign despite considerable prodding by Faidherbe's agents. After Biraima's death in January 1860, however, Faidherbe claimed that he had made a deathbed declaration in favor of the treaty, and he attempted to have it honored by the next *damel*, Macodou. The latter's refusal led Faidherbe to request permission of the new naval and colonial minister, Chasseloup-Laubat, to open hostilities against Cayor to enforce provisions of a treaty that probably did not exist.

The coast of Cayor proved unsatisfactory for successful amphibious operations and the coastal route only skirted the populated heartland of Cayor, from which it was separated by a belt of sand dunes, so Faidherbe was forced to fight a land campaign against a powerful foe and to settle for inconclusive results. Failing to win over Macoudou after three invasions in the spring of 1861, he finally installed a rival *damel*, Madiodio, from a collateral but rival lineage, and annexed to the colonial territory the peripheral provinces of Ndiambour in the north and Diander in the south (he had seized Gandiole and its salt pans earlier). But Madiodio was incapable of resisting Macoudou's partisans, based initially in Baol, and those of Lat-Dior, onetime contenders for Biraima's succession.

A semblance of peace returned to Cayor during Jauréguiberry's administration (1861–1863). He allowed Lat-Dior to supplant Madiodio on condition that he honor the treaty to which Madiodio had agreed, a condition that was accepted; but when Faidherbe returned to Saint-Louis in 1863 he drove Lat-Dior out without justification and reimposed Madiodio. This action only increased the turmoil in Cayor. Madiodio remained as incompetent as ever. In March 1865, before leaving Saint-Louis for good, Faidherbe ousted Madiodio, whom he retired on a small pension, and declared what was left of independent Cayor annexed and broken into seven cantons.

By then Cayor was beset with famine, and the export of peanuts had dropped considerably. Although it remained peaceful for the next few years while recovering from this devastation, it did not return to normal until 1870, when Governor Vallière disannexed it and allowed Lat-Dior to reascend the throne. The invasion of Cayor was clearly Faidherbe's greatest failure in Senegal.

The French were less active south of Cayor even though the engineer officer Pinet-Laprade—commandant of Gorée after 1859 and Faidherbe's successor in 1865—increased French pressure in the Casamance river area, where the French had two posts, Carabane and Sédhiou, and in the Rivières-du-Sud of Guinea. They threatened war against Maba-Diakhou, a disciple of El-Hadj Omar's, who had attempted since 1861 to construct an Islamic state on the model of his master's empire among the Mandingo and the Serrer between Cayor and the Gambia river. As long as Maba did not directly attack their posts or their subjects, the French were initially disposed to leave him alone. Pinet-Laprade argued that if Maba's *marabout* army freed the area of *thièdo* depredations, peanut culture would be stimulated. But Jauréguiberry and then Faidherbe grew alarmed when it seemed that Maba was supporting Macoudou before he died in 1863 and then Lat-Dior after Faidherbe dethroned him. In 1862 Maba and Macoudou jointly made an unsuccessful attack against the French post at Kaolack.

In October 1864 Faidherbe finally reached a compromise with Maba. He recognized his authority south of the Saloum estuary on the conditions that he allow free trade between his subjects and the French and that he respect the independence of Cayor, Djoloff, Baol, and Sine. It settled the question of Maba as far as Faidherbe was concerned, but serious hostilities broke out between Maba's forces and the French during Pinet-Laprade's governorship (1865–1869). They did not end until Maba was defeated—not by the French army but by the traditional army of Sine at the battle of Somb in July 1867.

Because Faidherbe's budget as well as his political and military objectives were limited, his forces were small. In 1855 his regular effectives were made up of three companies of marine infantry, a squadron of *spahis*, one company of artillery, a detachment of sappers headed by a few engineer officers, two companies of African troops, and some 700 volunteers from Saint-Louis. The local fleet numbered seven steam launches and a small assortment of other craft. With these Faidherbe developed an effective system of amphibious warfare. Its range was greatest during the rainy season, when the boats could make maximum use of the inland waterways of the region.

Faidherbe worked to increase his limited number of troops. He encouraged the African population of the enclaves, particularly of Saint-Louis, to volunteer for service by promising them a generous share of any booty they might take. He used traditional intertribal rivalries to obtain volunteers from one group when fighting its traditional enemies. His most important manpower innovation was the founding of the *tirailleurs sénégalais* in 1857. The French had employed African auxiliaries in their West African posts almost since their arrival, and Faidherbe's achievement was to create in Senegal an African force akin to the *tirailleurs undigènes* of Algeria.

Unlike the already existing *compagnies indigènes*, the *tirailleurs sénégalais* consisted of free volunteers relatively well paid, allowed a special discipline and special rations consisting of traditional African foods. They were provided with a comfortable and colorful uniform similar to that of their Algerian counterparts, which included baggy pants but eliminated the tight collar of the regulation French army uniform that the earlier African troops had hated. Each *tirailleur* was armed with the sort of double-barreled shotgun that previously had been used only as a gift in dealing with powerful African potentates. What Faidherbe created, using an Algerian pattern and Senegalese material, was an elite African contingent for the French army—the governor's *thièdos*. Despite the misgivings of the naval minister, Admiral Hamelin, Faidherbe had formed two companies of *tirailleurs* by June 1858. Their number was raised to five in 1859, six in 1860, and eight in 1867.

But to Faidherbe the importance of these troops was not great. Without them he completed pacification of the Senegal valley and undertook such expeditions as the two raids on Lake Kayar in the Trarza zone in 1856 and 1857 and the battles following the relief of Médine in 1857. Although he used them in the conquests of Cayor, he placed more importance on the loan of three companies of *tirailleurs indigènes* from Algeria. They had both propaganda and military value in Cayor,[17] and their use in 1861 marked the first time that native Algerian troops were deployed in French possessions other than Algeria.

When he later evaluated his role as governor of Senegal, Faidherbe gave the *tirailleurs sénégalais* little importance. In none of his published writings, not even in *Le Sénégal, la France dans l'Afrique occidentale* (1889), did he describe how or why he created them. In his pamphlet *Base d'un projet de réorganisation d'une armée nationale,* which he wrote in 1871 at the close of the Franco-Prussian war, he excluded the colonial and Algerian native troops from any role in France's metropolitan defenses and recommended the use of "special forces" solely to maintain order in each colony. He even recommended that the marine infantry be integrated into the regular army.

Jauréguiberry, however, who had severely criticized the *tirailleurs sénégalais* while he was governor of Senegal and had refrained from using them in his massive Fouta-Toro campaign of January and February 1863, predicted before he left office that they would become an intercolonial fighting force.[18] When serving many years later as minister of the navy he ordered the expansion of the *tirailleurs sénégalais* and their development along these lines. Had he foreseen their use in Europe he would have rivaled General Charles Mangin as a black army theoretician.

Much of Faidherbe's success as governor of Senegal was the result of the good relations that he cultivated with powerful wholesalers in Saint-Louis. He particularly followed the advice of Marc Maurel of Maurel and Prom. Less than a month after his first inauguration in 1854 he had the company granted choice lots for their trading depots and stores at Podor and at Dagana and allowed it to do business all year. He favored a proposal made by Marc Maurel to end most *pacte colonial* restrictions on the foreign trade of Saint-Louis and contributed to a reform of the local customs tariffs—also desired by Maurel and Prom—that went into effect in 1866.

Faidherbe continued to favor the cultivation of export crops, especially peanuts. Saint-Louis continued to rely primarily on gum exports. But the total value of peanuts exported from other parts of Senegambia, including Rivières-du-Sud, was much higher than that of gum from Senegal. The value of gum exports fell while that of peanuts continued to rise. Another trade aspect came up in November 1859, when Faidherbe agreed to a suggestion made by the Bordeaux chamber of commerce that French shippers be allowed to import rice from any source into Senegal. "If the blacks," he declared, "are content with growing and eating millet, it does not help our trade. There is every advantage for us to have them grow peanuts, *béraf*, and cotton...instead of millet and then [for us] to sell them rice imported from India in French ships."[19] Responding to ministerial promptings, Faidherbe also attempted to encourage the growing both of indigo and of cotton for export, the latter staple showing some promise during the period of the Union blockade of the Confederacy in the United States. But neither crop had any long-term commercial success.

A more serious failure resulted from Faidherbe's attempt between 1858 and 1860 to occupy the gold-bearing area of Bambouk and to attempt heavy mining operations there. He had argued in 1856 in a report addressed to Admiral Hamelin that the area had "the richest gold mines in the world not yet exploited."[20] But two years of effort and considerable expense produced only insignificant quantities of marketable gold. The bitterness that the fiasco engendered between Faidherbe and Hamelin's successor, Chasseloup-Laubat, may have contributed to Faidherbe's sudden decision to resign in 1861.

Faidherbe tried to prevent the wars that he fought with the Senegambian polities from interfering with business. Except for a brief, government imposed boycott for propaganda purposes during the off-season of 1856, gum could always be traded at Podor if the *marabouts* themselves could get there with their supplies. When Faidherbe later decided to invade Cayor, he attempted with less success to schedule his campaigns to avoid interfering with the peanut harvests.

Faidherbe's support in the business community was hardly unanimous. Many of the *traitants* and their leaders—Justin Devès and Durand-Valantin, the ex-deputy—were bitterly opposed to him. Several wholesalers—Lacoste, Chaumet, and Merle—were never more than lukewarm supporters, and his enemies often made common cause with jealous naval officers in attempts to have him recalled. But each time friends stood by him, intervened with the ministry in his behalf, and prevailed.

The wholesalers gave Faidherbe poor advice when they urged him to replace the 2 percent tax on gum imported into Saint-Louis from the hinterland with a general head tax of three francs a year per adult, which the colonial government attempted to collect in certain areas of Senegal as of January 1, 1862. The price that gum could fetch in France was still falling, and the wholesalers claimed that even a 2 percent reduction in the total tax of 21.5 percent that it generated would save the gum trade from ruin. Faidherbe refused to consider reducing the duty paid the Mauritanian rulers since it was the cornerstone of his compromise with them, but he agreed that a head tax charged to the annexed population would be a good substitute as well as a visible sign of their submission to France.[21] He thought that the money could be more easily extracted from the supposedly submissive and annexed left bank populations. However, a few of the populations in question resisted it violently—those of Dimar and Toro and those of Diander in Cayor—feeling that they had never agreed to pay a tax to French authorities. It contributed to the anti-French outbreak in Fouta-Toro that Jauréguiberry suppressed only with difficulty.

It should be pointed out in all fairness to both governors, however, that Stéphan, the *ordonnateur* (chief administrative officer), rather than Faidherbe, drew up the actual tax ordinance, completing it after Faidherbe had ended his first term and designating its starting date as January 1, 1862. Jauréguiberry, who arrived in December 1861, thus was forced to begin the tax's collection before he could master the intricacies of Faidherbe's treaty system and judge which of the Senegambian polities were or were not taxable. The bitterest irony of this head tax, however, was that even after it went into effect Chasseloup-Laubat insisted that the colonial government continue to collect the two percent tax on gum brought into Saint-Louis. The local budget could not do without it.

Administrative and Educational Innovator

Although Faidherbe has been credited with developing administration and education in Senegal, his contributions in this domain were small, not very systematic, but in keeping with the limited nature of the plan that he was following. When he took over the governorship in 1854 he found that there was very little legal distinction made in enclaves between those persons who could be called citizens and those who could be called subjects; nor could a distinction be made between permanent residents and transients among the African population of Saint-Louis. The directorate of exterior affairs, founded in 1845 to centralize relations between Saint-Louis and the hinterland polities, was practically nonfunctional. No system for administering annexed territories existed because there were none to administer under French rule other than the few tiny French enclaves. Last, Faidherbe found that the educational system was geared to offer primary instruction to children of the Christian population of Saint-Louis, white and mulatto, but not to the Moslem black majority.

Faidherbe started to attack these problems by borrowing methods and terminology from his Algerian experience; he usually gave his solutions very little substance, however, particulary concerning the hinterland. His first measures were to wrest control of the relations between Saint-Louis and the hinterland from the mulatto *habitant* dominated municipal government. He strenghtened the directorate of exterior affairs, confiding it to Louis-Alexandre Flize, one of his most talented officers, who held the position during both of Faidherbe's governorships. He then removed the mulatto mayor, Jean Derneville, replacing him with the white merchant Héricé and then with Blaise Dumont, a totally loyal *habitant* businessman.

A greater problem lay in the fact that Islam was the religion of the majority of the Saint-Louis population and that many of these Moslems were attracted to El-Hadj Omar's Tijjani brotherhood. Faidherbe, who in his official capacity always distrusted Islam, recognized that he could not hope to suppress it. But he could favor and regulate the more conservative and traditional Qadiri variety. In November 1855 he expelled all Tijjani *marabouts* from Saint-Louis. In the next two years he formulated regulations by which the colonial government would examine and certify teaching *marabouts* who wished to practice in Saint-Louis. He required Moslems to register births, deaths, and marriages with the French civil authorities. Finally, he coaxed the ministry into authorizing him to open a Moslem court in Saint-Louis, limited to cases involving marriage, divorce, and inheritance: voluntary for Moslems who wished to be judged by Malaki law. The French court system retained primary jurisdiction in all other civil and all criminal cases and appellate jurisdiction as far as the Moslem court was concerned.

Faidherbe sugarcoated these innovations by making members of a francophile elite responsible for their functioning. He appointed a Moslem vice-mayor whom he made responsible for the registration of Moslems with the French civil authorities. He appointed the colonial government's chief interpreter and *tamsir* (head of the Moslem community), Hamat N'Diaye Anne, as *qadi* of the Moslem court. He and another Moslem notable served on the examining board created to certify *marabouts.*

At the same time, Faidherbe tried to create institutions that would introduce the Moslems to secular French culture. He required the *marabouts* to send their students to a lay evening school, founded in 1857 to teach French and arithmetic. In the next several years he opened similar schools at Bakel, Dagana, and Podor. He also founded the more famous Ecole des otages (renamed in 1861 the Ecole des fils de chefs et des interprètes) to teach French and arithmetic to the student pledges whom African potentates left in Saint-Louis. Faidherbe's aim was to begin the creation of a francophile elite in the interior. The school closed in 1870, but the idea was picked up again and expanded after 1886, when Gallieni became the superior commandant of the Upper Senegal–Niger territory.

Similarly, when Faidherbe founded the *Moniteur du Sénégal* and the *Annuaire du Sénégal,* he insisted that they both be written almost completely in French and not bilingually, as was the practice in Algeria. Few people in Senegal, he explained to the minister, could actually read Arabic. "It would be infinitely better that the newspaper be translated [to the masses] by those who know French rather than by those who know Arabic, for we must beware of the latter."[22]

Faidherbe's approach to governing African territory was to interfere as little as possible. His usual method was to intimidate traditional rulers into acceding to fairly limited demands and to force some of the polities to accept new pro-French rulers if the previous ones proved intractable. His approach had defects. It tended to create great pressures in the polities, which weakened their structures of government and led to the anarchy he wished to avoid. In some societies it led to anti-French outbreaks when his departures from Senegal were interpreted as a lessening of French pressure. Also, his administrative methods and terminology gave the impression that the Senegalese hinterland was closer to being fully conquered than it really was. When Faidherbe annexed whole blocks of territory other than the villages around French forts, as in the case of Cayor, he did so as a last resort, after failure of his halfway measures.

The directorate of exterior affairs underwent several name changes, which implied that it did more than oversee French relations with the independent polities of Senegal and supervise the administration of annexed Walo. In 1857 Faidherbe renamed it the directorate of native affairs. Jauréguiberry attempted at the end of 1861 to add to this body and create a combined directorate of interior and native affairs. Upon his return in 1863 Faidherbe renamed the bureau once again, this time calling it the directorate of political affairs, like its counterpart in Algeria. But the directorate was not a *bureau arabe* even though many Saint-Louis residents referred to it informally by that name. Except when he was sent on a mission into the interior, the director had little specific authority over the French *arrondissement* and post commandants since both tended to correspond directly with the governor.

Between 1856 and 1859 Faidherbe designated three major territorial units for Senegal and it dependencies, which he called *arrondissements:* Saint-Louis, Bakel, and Gorée, each named after their administrative centers and including lesser French posts. But he did not define the functions and responsibilities of *arrondissement* and post commandants. He merely gave new appointees specific written orders upon their departure from Saint-Louis. Faidherbe was also vague regarding peacetime relations between *arrondissement* and post commandants and independent African rulers, but he allowed the commandants a great deal of authority over French citizens and visitors within their jurisdictions.

The fate of Walo in 1855 is the textbook example of how an African polity could be conquered, annexed by France, broken into artificially created cantons—called *cercles* prior to 1863—each administered by a French appointed warrant chief (*chef de canton*) who might or might not be qualified to rule. In 1859 Faidherbe even wrote a constitution for Walo in the two languages of Woloff and French, which spelled out the power of the warrant chiefs and their relationship to the French superior commandant of Walo, who at that time was also the commandant of Dagana.

His annexations of territories other than African villages around French posts were often more nominal than real—good examples being the cases of Dimar and Toro. When Jauréguiberry took over the government of Senegal, he discovered—much to his consternation—that nothing available in writing in Saint-Louis, except for an obscure footnote on page 278 of the 1861 *Annuaire du Sénégal*, proved that Toro had ever been annexed. Cayor, even annexed, remained relatively unorganized.

The plan that Faidherbe was attempting to follow did not require systematic conquest or annexation of all the African territories of Senegal. As far as he was concerned, Senegal was not to be a new Algeria. When he wrote in 1859 that "Senegal should be nothing more than a subdivision of Algeria,"[23] he meant that, with the dissolution of the short-lived ministry of Algeria and the colonies, Senegal should not be returned to the jurisdiction of the naval ministry but to that of the war ministry, which was also responsible for governing Algeria. He was reflecting an antinavy view shared by many persons in Saint-Louis. As Marc Maurel wrote, "Such an annexation . . . would rid us completely of the navy . . . and permit us to pick up crumbs from an always well-garnished table."[24] Faidherbe's request that Senegal be given a director of the interior was intended as a way of relieving the *ordonnateur*, or chief administrative officer—usually of a naval vessel—of responsibilities for the small civil population of Saint-Louis and the other enclaves that were not really his.

Jauréguiberry, a trained naval administrator shocked by the discrepancies between theory and fact that he discovered in Faidherbe's administrative system, resolved to "break with the administrative past . . . [as Faidherbe] had broken with the political and military past."[25] To increase centralized control by Saint-Louis, he created seven *arrondissements* from Faidherbe's three, and he proposed to create a structured and combined directorate of the interior and of native affairs. He spelled out in detail the responsibilities and powers of *arrondissement* and post commandants, as well as responsibilities of representatives of the director of the interior and native affairs in the various *arrondissement* centers. Jauréguiberry traced lines of authority from the governor's office through the directorate to the *arrondissement* and post commandants. He did not elaborate on how the unannexed African polities were to fit into this administrative structure, but the implication was that they would be annexed as soon as feasible. He further proposed the creation of consultative commissions in the administrative centers of each *arrondissement* to be made up of official and unofficial members authorized to deliberate on all questions of local interest except political ones. Last, he proposed the reestablishment of the general council (*conseil général*) that had been abolished in 1848.

Chasseloup-Laubat, the naval minister, approved most of these proposals; but again, as he had done earlier with Faidherbe, he turned down the request that he authorize the establishment of a bureau of the interior, citing as justification the added expense involved. He refused even to consider reestablishment of the general council—the idea was too liberal for the Second Empire. But the other proposals soon went into effect.

When Faidherbe returned to Senegal in 1863, he retained many of Jauréguiberry's innvoations. However, he again reduced the number of *arrondissements* to three and diminished Jauréguiberry's centralizing tendencies, particularly as they concerned the directorate of native affairs. At this point Faidherbe completed the transfer to Senegal of the Algerian administrative terminology. Large subdivisions of the three *arrondissements* became twelve *cercles*, six of them corresponding to six of Jauréguiberry's seven *arrondissements*. The subdivisions within Walo that had been called *cercles* since 1855 were now called cantons, and Walo as a whole became part of the *cercle* of Saint-Louis. The directorate was renamed to become directorate of political affairs. But, now as before, most of the Senegalese polities remained either independent or only nominally annexed but intimidated. Faidherbe's system continued to lack substance and to depend more on the presence of its creator than on administrative structure for its smooth operation.

Faidherbe undertook a number of projects to improve material conditions in Saint-Louis as well as in the other enclaves. He ordered the refurbishing or the construction of a number of the town's public buildings, the paving of a number of its streets, the clearing of a quay that encircled the island, and the erection of the first public latrines. He planned the system by which fresh water would be piped into Saint-Louis from the Lampsar creek, a delta channel of the Senegal river; this project would be completed by Governor Brière de L'Isle after 1877. Faidherbe had the narrow branch of the Senegal river bridged in 1856 to connect Saint-Louis with Guet-N'Dar on the Langue de Barbarie—the long, narrow sand spit, which separates Saint-Louis from the Atlantic Ocean. He obtained permission to bridge the main branch of the Senegal river with a pontoon bridge completed in 1865.

Faidherbe had little to do, however, with the development of port facilities at Dakar even though he had recommended in 1853 that the French occupy this town and had surveyed the site for the Mamelles lighthouse, whose beacon would shine for the first time in 1864. The decision to build first one and then two breakwater piers was made in Fance as an effort to force the new navigation company—The Messageries impériales, which connected Bordeaux and Marseilles to South American ports—to have its ships stop for coaling on French territory rather than in the Portuguese Cape Verde islands. The layout of the port, the grid plan for the town of Dakar, and the supervision of the construction were all the work of Pinet-Laprade, commandant of Gorée after 1859.

Although Faidherbe never denied the strategic importance of Dakar, like his mentors in the Maurel and Prom company he never believed that it would have much future as a commercial center. Morale in the business community had begun to suffer because Jauréguiberry not only favored moving the capital of the colony to Dakar but also because he favored Pinet-Laprade's pet scheme to forbid commercial transactions at Rufisque and to force the traders established there to move their operations to Dakar, twenty-two kilometers west. To restore public confidence in Saint-Louis, Faidherbe sponsored the publication of an article in the *Moniteur du Sénégal* that stated that Saint-Louis would always be the largest city in the colony even if Dakar became the capital.[26] As late as 1889, several years after the opening of the Dakar–Saint-Louis railway, Faidherbe was still claiming that Saint-Louis was a viable seaport despite the bar at the river's mouth. One major Bordeaux company, he wrote—no doubt Maurel and Prom—dispatched six ships a year from Bordeaux directly to the upper river and back, hence bypassing the railway altogether.

The official weekly newspaper, the *Moniteur du Sénégal* (called the *Feuille officielle du Sénégal et dépendances* from January 1860 to June 1864), which Faidherbe founded in 1856, and the *Annuaire du Sénégal*, which he founded in 1858, were two of his most significant creations. They resulted from orders given to Protet to found a government printing press in Saint-Louis and to begin publication of these official organs. Under Faidherbe's editorship, both published more than official notices and documents. He and some of his talented subordinates—Flize, Azan, and Pinet-Laprade—contributed articles on African history, anthropology, and linguistics. In addition, they both reproduced material like that appearing in French and Algerian newspapers and are valuable sources for the study of the period.

While Faidherbe was serving as governor, his attitude toward the various Senegalese people was ambivalent as it had been earlier in Algeria toward the Arabs and Berbers. He was ruthless or benevolent toward them, depending upon their degree of receptiveness to his policies. He always distrusted Islam, even when practiced by pro-French peoples or individuals, and remained unimpressed in the cases of the Woloff and the Serrer populations by the opposition of Islamic reformers like Maba-Diakhou to the *thièdos*.

Faidherbe's methods of warfare were violent; he was a strong practitioner of the *razzia*. But he devoted a percentage of the sales of the booty taken in *razzias* to help finance the founding of a social club in Saint-Louis aimed at promoting interracial understanding.[27] Having destroyed the commercial privileges of the mulatto elite in Saint-Louis, he then tried to assimilate them to the Europeans by very direct methods. He favored interracial liaisons, and in 1885 was angered when the apostolic prefect of Saint-Louis, the Abbé Barbier, forbade the upper class, young mulatto women of Saint-Louis to attend a ball given in honor of the emperor, to which all his officers had been invited. Liaisons between European men and pure-blooded African women he saw as a means of increasing the links between Europeans and Africans. They also increased the number of mulattoes. Faidherbe himself had one and possibly two children by his Sarakholé mistress, Dionkounda Siadibi.[28]

Toward slaves, Faidherbe's attitude was more practical than humanitarian. He avoided applying provisions of the emancipation decree of 1848 in areas that he brought under French control, particularly the villages adjacent to French posts. On the subject of slave ownership he conveniently adopted the distinction made by Carrère, the judicial service head, between French citizens and subject. In 1855 Faidherbe promulgated an *arrêté* that permitted French citizens in all the enclaves except Saint-Louis and Gorée to hire captives from their African masters for use as laborers.[29] In 1857 he issued an *arrêté* that codified a practice in which he had engaged since the beginning of his governorship to the effect that only those captives from African polities at odds with the French would be automatically freed upon setting foot on French soil; captives from friendly polities would be expelled as "undesirable vagabonds."[30] He permitted Pinet-Laprade to make use of captive labor in the construction at Dakar.[31]

There appears to be no truth to the legend that Faidherbe threatened in November 1857 to resign the governorship in protest over the possibility that as part of his government contract of March 1857 the Marseilles merchant Victor Régis might be permitted to recruit for contract labor for the West Indies as far north as Senegal. In the section of *Le Sénégal, la France dans l'Afrique occidentale* that discusses this issue, the letter of resignation that Faidherbe quotes does not mention this question at all nor did the minister's reply, which he does not quote.[32] Régis's base of operations being on the Ivory and Dahomey coasts, he had little desire to recruit in Senegambia. Faidherbe's threat to resign, it seems apparent, was motivated by a desire to obtain renewed ministerial support for his continued struggle against the Trarzas and for his plan to create the *tirailleurs sénégalais.*

A difficult question to answer about Faidherbe's two governorships is how far east he really wished to expand French rule. It is evident from his writings, private and published, that he was fascinated by the mid-Niger basin. When the Third Republic began to expand inland from the headwaters of the Senegal river to the mid-Niger, the protagonists of the advance—Governor Brière de L'Isle, Captain Gallieni, Borgnis-Desbordes, and others—claimed that they were following Faidherbe's policy, claims he did not deny even though he criticized the violence of their campaigns against Ahmadou and other African rulers. On the contrary, he maintained that he had always favored peaceful penetration of the area in cooperation with local African rulers.[33] This assertion was only partially true.

As early as 1856 Faidherbe had recommended that the French government recognize the sovereignty of El-Hadj Omar east of Bafoulabé. In 1858 he suggested that exploration missions penetrate the upper and middle Niger regions not only from the upper Senegal but also from the mouth of the Niger river. Not to do so, he argued in reference to the latter scheme, would be "an unpardonable political error."[34] Nothing immediately came of either suggestion although Faidherbe obtained permission to sponsor several exploratory missions of a more limited nature into areas bordering Senegal, such as southern Mauritania and Fouta Djallon.

In 1863 Faidherbe returned to Senegal with a comprehensive plan to send an emissary to Ségou, Omar's new capital, to negotiate a treaty that would allow the French to open a trail connecting Médine with Bamako along which would be placed three fortified trading posts at strategic points. The two emissaries, Mage and Quintin, who departed for Ségou in 1864 on what would be an epochal journey, accomplished little before Faidherbe's final departure from Senegal in May 1865. He claimed that he wanted only a peaceful penetration of Omar's empire, wherein the latter's sovereignty would be respected. But if indeed Faidherbe really had such a hope it was naive; had he proceeded with the construction of these posts they would have led to the same conflicts as had the posts and the telegraph line in Cayor.

Except for his participation in the Franco-Prussian war and his continued scholarly endeavors, Faidherbe's later career was not spectacular—probably a result of his deteriorating health and a resulting decline in what could be called his political acuity. Each time he resigned from the governorship of Senegal, he claimed poor health as justification and requested new assignment in Algeria. In 1861 he served as commandant of the subdivision of Sidi-Bel-Abbès from September of that year to May 1863. After his second resignation, a period of leave, and a struggle with the war ministry, he was named commandant of the subdivision of Annaba (Bône), beginning in February 1867; and he served intermittently as interim commandant of the province of Constantine from 1869 until November 1870.

But Faidherbe clearly disliked not being the chief in Algeria. In a letter to General Frossard—head of the emperor's military household, with whom he had been corresponding regularly since 1856—he threatened to resign from the army if he were not soon promoted from colonel to brigadier general.[35] Frossard replied soothingly, encouraging Faidherbe to take advantage of the navy's dissatisfaction with Jauréguiberry to obtain reappointment as governor of Senegal. But Faidherbe would not consider returning to Senegal without the rank of brigadier general. He received both the promotion and the assignment.

Leaving Senegal the second time in May 1865, Faidherbe spent a very long sick leave in Algeria. But when the war ministry wished to transfer him to a subdivision in Corsica, he claimed that the climate would aggravate his chronic bronchitis—a specious argument considering the similarities between the climates of Corsica and of northern Algeria—and refused. André Demaison claims that the real reason for this refusal was that Faidherbe did not wish to serve the Second Empire in domestic assignments. In this instance he knew that the government needed to fill all its general officers' posts on the island in order to use the army to enforce the conscription law, which was particularly unpopular in Corsica. As a result of this issue Marshal Randon, then war minister, almost forced Faidherbe into retirement at forty-eight, but he relented and finally permitted him to accept the available assignment in Algeria.

Within two years, however, Faidherbe began to ask for more. In frank letters to Marshal Niel, Randon's successor in the war ministry, he requested promotion to divisional general and assignment to head the divisional command of Constantine province should the incumbent, General Périgot, whom he had previously replaced on an interim basis, resign because of his own ill health.[36] Again Faidherbe threatened to retire if his request were denied. Niel reminded him that he was not the only ambitious brigadier general in the French army but urged him in no circumstances to retire.[37]

Faidherbe was not opposed, at least openly, to the Second Empire. He cultivated the friendship of members of the imperial entourage like General Frossard, Prince Jérome, and several others. Their letters indicate that Napoleon III thought highly of Faidherbe though they had never met. That he could quibble about his assignments, even refusing one, indicates that he was held in official favor.

During his stints at Annaba and Constantine, Faidherbe got along well with the white colonists—and this at a time when the *régime du sabre* in Algeria was under civilian attack. In early 1870 he served as president of the court-martial of several *bureau arabe* officers and the commandant of the *cercle* of Tebessa in eastern Algeria. They were accused of complicity in the April 1869 murder by local *qadis* of members of a caravan approaching the Tunisian border from Tebessa in eastern Algeria. The episode, which became known as the *affaire de l'oued-Mahouine*, rivaled the *affaire Doineau* of 1856 in stimulating the antimilitary sentiments of many settlers and their liberal supporters in France. The trial was complicated in that the defense counsel was the radical lawyer and politician Jules Favre, a major spokesman for the antimilitary, anti–*bureaux-arabes* groups in France. Paradoxically, in winning acquittal for the officers, Favre increased the unpopularity of the system in general by transferring the blame for what had happened to the entire military government in Algeria. Both military and civilian authorities praised Faidherbe for his impartiality during the trial. Colas, the new radical deputy from Constantine, wrote to the minister of war in April 1871 that Faidherbe had "the unanimous confidence of the army and population" and requested that he be appointed to head the division of Constantine. Faidherbe's return would cause the province, at that time wracked by the revolt in the Kabylie, to "return to order."[38]

Commanding General of the Army of the North

Faidherbe was on leave in Lille when the Franco-Prussian war began. Much to his annoyance Marshal Leboeuf, the new war minister, ordered him back to Algeria to serve once more as commandant of the subdivision of Annaba (Bône) rather than acceding to his request for a metropolitan command, believing that Faidherbe's talents would be better used to keep order in Algeria, from which most metropolitan troops were being withdrawn. With the fall of the Second Empire Faidherbe offered his services to the government of national defense. He made such a good impression on Léon Gambetta when the two men met at Tours on November 28, 1870 that Gambetta offered him command of the Army of the North headquartered at Lille. Faidherbe assumed this command in early December.

The Army of the North consisted basically of the Twenty-second and Twenty-third Infanty Corps and was one of several provincial armies created by the new government to continue the war after the surrender at Sedan and the beginning of the sieges of Metz and Paris. Testelin was its creator, a veteran of the 1848 revolution, whom Gambetta named special commissioner for defense in the four northernmost departments. When Faidherbe took over, this army consisted of 17,000 poorly trained regular troops and several thousand irregular *gardes mobiles*. To these were added escaped officers and men from the armies of Sedan and Metz. By January Faidherbe could claim 35,000 regular troops, "half of whom fight seriously."[39] His two military objectives were to keep the Prussians out of northeastern France and to help the Army of Paris break out. He succeeded in the first objective but, except for tying down some 25,000 Prussians who might have been better used elsewhere, he failed in the second.

The Army of the North earlier had fought valiantly at Villers-Bretonneux but had not succeeded in driving the Prussians from Amiens. Faidherbe's first engagement, recapturing the fortress of Ham, was a success; but he failed to take La Fère to the east, which would have facilitated communications with Rheims, a major

Prussian communications center. Turning west to relieve Amiens, on December 23 he met the forces of General Manteuffel at Pont Noyelles, near the junction of the Hallue and the Somme rivers. His troops made good use of their *chassepots* and *mitrailleuses* and even slept on the battlefield that night—a proof of victory— but the next day retired to Arras in exhaustion.

Faidherbe then went to the relief of Péronne, south of Arras, the remaining fortress in French hands along a strategic route linking Amiens with Rheims. The Prussians had surrounded it on December 27. The fort itself could easily withstand a long siege, but when the Prussians trained their artillery on the town rather than on the fort itself, the townspeople began to pressure its commandant to surrender. Faidherbe told them to stand firm.

To reach Péronne meant dislodging the Prussian Eighth Corps, commanded by General von Goeben, from Bapaume. Faidherbe's troops managed to occupy the suburbs of Bapaume on three sides and even forced most of the Prussian troops to evacuate; yet they never occupied the town themselves. Michael Howard writes that Faidherbe tragically misjudged the real weakness of the Prussian position. Faidherbe later asserted in his *Campagne de l'armée du Nord* (1871) that he did not complete the operation at Bapaume because he had forced the bulk of the Prussian troops to withdraw and that occupation would have necessitated destroy- ing what was, after all, a French town.[40] According to Demaison, "Faidherbe . . . an engineer officer [was] above all a builder. Had he been an infantryman, an ar- tilleryman, or a cavalry officer, he would have slept in Bapaume [that night] even if it were half destroyed."[41] His troops retreated north to Arras during the evening of January 3 and Péronne—despairing of relief, its discouraged commandant pressed by the town's citizens—surrendered six days later, its defenses still intact. Its fall negated any value that Faidherbe's effort at Bapaume might have had.

Faidherbe's final action in the war was to lead a diversion that was to move either toward the Oise or toward Paris, whichever would tie down the Prussian soldiers while General Trochu in Paris made a final attempt to break the siege. An attempt to trick the Prussians into thinking that he was moving west toward Amiens and Paris when in reality he was moving east failed because the Prussian general, Von Goeben, guessed his strategy and forced him to give battle at Saint- Quentin. The result was hardly a French success. Faidherbe lost 15,000 men either as casualties or as prisoners—half his army. The other half, however, made an orderly retreat to the north on January 19 taking most of the army's artillery pieces with it, a retreat so well executed that Von Goeben did not realize what was happening and failed to order pursuit until a day later. Faidherbe's men had escaped, but they did not again take the field.

Given its lack of training, the Army of the North fought well but not very deci- sively. But it did provide the French with a little honor in a war with otherwise dismal consequences.

Public Offices

When Faidherbe relinquished command of the Army of the North in March 1871, he was physically and psychologically spent and wanted nothing more than a long rest and a chance to get back to his writings. But the local republican leaders in

Lille, particularly Testelin and Warin—editor of the influential *Echo du Nord*—
hoped to use his fame as a war hero to bring him into politics on their side. They
first sponsored Faidherbe for election to the municipal council of Lille and then to
the general council of the department of the Nord, elections he easily won. Then
they decided to have him elected to the National Assembly. But when elected
spontaneously by the department of the Somme in February, Faidherbe refused to
serve because he was still in active command of his army. Only after being elected
by three departments in July did he agree to represent the Nord.

Success in politics was a crowning achievement for such contemporaries of his
as Admiral Jauréguiberry, who would serve two terms as minister of the navy and
colonies, and General Farre, Faidherbe's immediate subordinate in the Army of
the North, who became minister of war in 1879. Faidherbe's political career was
marred by a combination of poor health, little sustained interest, too rigid a personality, and lack of political acumen—at least in this arena. He left his campaign
for the deputyship to the editor of the *Echo du Nord*.

While still in the military, Faidherbe's political position on several issues conflicted with the emerging French conservatism. He continued to support Léon
Gambetta, and he opposed the tendency of the National Assembly to consider itself constituent. His enemies accused him of having tacitly favored the Paris Commune because he did not offer his services personally to Thiers when the latter
decided to crush the Commune by force. Indeed, when Thiers summoned Faidherbe to Versailles in March 1871 to discuss ways by which the remnants of the Army of the North could support the Army of Versailles, Faidherbe, pleading poor
health, only went as far as Saint-Denis; he sent his aide-de-camp on to Versailles.
His enemies forgot that he had earlier made plans to use the Army of the North to
occupy Lille should the local radicals there get out of hand.[42]

Once elected to the National Assembly, Faidherbe annoyed supporters of both
Gambetta and Thiers by not immediately taking his seat after election; instead, he
took a two-week cure at Aix-les-Bains. And after having sat for less than three
weeks, he suddenly resigned to protest passage of the Vitet bill, which confirmed
the constituent powers of the Assembly. Although he would eventually draw
closer to Thiers, the immediate result of Faidherbe's resignation was that he was
not included in either the Changarnier commission, created to evaluate government promotions, or the commission formed to draft a new conscription law. In
the case of promotions, Faidherbe strongly believed that those officers and men
who had fought throughout the whole Franco-Prussian war should be properly rewarded, have their promotions confirmed, and be given seniority over those who
had been captured at the start and had never returned to active service. The
Changarnier commission disagreed, being particularly reluctant to reward officers who had fled German captivity because they had violated their word of
honor that they would not attempt to escape. Faidherbe, who had not granted
promotions frivolously, defended his men in writing and in person before the commission, and convinced the members to confirm the ranks and seniority of his
principal subordinates.

Like the majority of the commission on conscription at the beginning of its
deliberations, Faidherbe favored a short-term conscript army. All able-bodied
young men, he believed, should be required to serve. He would exempt only those
preparing to teach or to serve as clergymen in the recognized churches. He would

not exempt married men, but he favored imposing a special tax on bachelors over the age of twenty-five to help defray the cost of supporting the wives and families of needy married draftees—and incidentally to encourage marriage. As the debates dragged on, however, the majority of the commission agreed with Thiers and several others that a professional army that relied on a relatively small number of long-term draftees was best for France. The law of 1873 fell far short of Faidherbe's ideal. The 1905 law would come much closer.

Within a month of his resignation from the National Assembly, Faidherbe sought from Thiers a military desk job—all that he was now physically fit for— and funds to undertake a short research mission in Egypt. He obtained the latter thanks to his old friend, J. Lambrecht, an industrialist from Lille who served as minister of the interior from July 1871 until his death in October. The desk job was granted when Faidherbe returned from Egypt; in October 1872 he was appointed to the Commission centrale des chemins de fer until its dissolution in 1878, when he became a member of its successor, the Conseil supérieur des voies de communication. Faidherbe's dossier shows, however, that these appointments were honorary—a means for him to retain his full salary, which he desperately needed to pay for his medical treatments.[43] Faidherbe had wanted to be on the Conseil des fortifications. Although Thiers seemed to favor the idea, his war minister, General Cissey, argued that since Faidherbe had not held an engineering command since 1854 his knowledge of military engineering would be out-of-date.[44]

Faidherbe's public career did not end even after paralysis confined him to a wheelchair in 1874. In 1879 he was elected to the French Senate from Lille, again sponsored by the *Echo du Nord*; and in 1880 Charles de Freycinet, formerly the war delegate in the government of national defense and now prime minister, named him grand chancellor of the Legion of Honor. Faidherbe was not very active as a senator, but he did take part in the debates on French expansion into the Sudan. He advised Admiral Jauréguiberry, minister of he navy in 1879 and 1880, on the projected railway to run from Kayes to Bafoulabé and eventually .to Bamako and in 1883 and 1886 argued strongly against abandonment of the project. As grand chancellor he supervised a major reform in the Legion's finances and democratized the three boarding schools operated by the Legion for the daughters of legionnaires.

The Scholar

Faidherbe developed eclectic intellectual interests that included African history, linguistics, anthropology, and what could be called public relations. He began taking notes during his first Algerian assignment and publishing articles after he reached Senegal, the first ones being four descriptive essays for the popular *L'Illustration journal universel* on the French possessions in Senegal, the Ivory Coast, and Gabon. He then turned to more serious scholarship with "Les Berbères et les arabes des bords du Sénégal" in 1854 and "Populations noires des bassins du Sénégal et du haut Niger" in 1856, both published in the *Bulletin de la Société de géographie de Paris*. He became quite close to Jomard, editor of this journal and president of the society, with whom he corresponded. It was Jomard who urged

Faidherbe to submit to the Volney competitition of the French Institute of 1856 a study that he had witten about the Berber dialect spoken in the Senegal valley. This entry won honorable mention and was published in 1877 as *Le Zénaga des tribus sénégalaises: Contribution à l'étude de la langue berbère.* Between 1860 and 1887 Faidherbe published eight other short studies and vocabulary phrase lists of Woloff, Serrer, Sarakholé, Poular, Arabic, and Berber.

The bulk of Faidherbe's writings had the practical aim of publicizing his activities, particularly in Senegal. He also wrote a book, two pamphlets, and an extended letter to the editor of the *Moniteur de l'armée* in which he defended the performance of the Army of the North during the Franco-Prussian war and the role of its commander in chief.

His writing about North Africa and about Senegalese anthropology, history, and linguistics indicate that like Sir Harry Johnston he undertook some scholarly activities for the sake of scholarship. As far as Senegal was concerned, however, he believed that knowledge of local history and anthropology had practical applications. It helped him, for instance, to implement policies of divide and reign. Linguistics, he believed, enabled a colonizer to avoid "the difficulties of all sorts that can arise in the relations of a civilized people with an uncivilized people when they cannot understand each other."[45] But he also recognized in a very modern way that comparative linguistics was a valuable tool for studying African history.[46] He continued to subscribe to what is now called the Hamitic thesis as far as Foulbé origins were concerned, yet he recognized that certain similarities between Poular, Woloff, and Serrer suggested a common origin for the three languages and the three peoples who spoke them.[47] He was only a step away from the modern understanding of the relationships among the speakers of the West Atlantic languages group.

Faidherbe's final years in Algeria (1865–1870) were particularly fruitful for his scholarly activities. He became honorary president of the Academy of Hippo, a learned society founded by local colonists of Annaba. And he went on numerous archeological expeditions to such sites as Roknia, Bou-Merzoug, Oued-Berd, and Tebessa in search of prehistoric remains and grave markings, dolmens, and ancient Numidian inscriptions. Several writings emerged from his research: *Mémoires sur les éléphants carthaginois* (1867), *Voyage des cinq nasamons d'Hérodote dans l'intérieur de la Lybie* (1867), *Recherches anthropologiques sur les tombeaux mégalithiques de Roknia* (1868), *Collection complète des inscriptions numidiques* (1870), *Inscriptions numidiques: Réponse à M. le docteur Judas* (1871), *Les Dolmens d'Afrique* (1873), *Epigraphie phénicienne* (1873), and others of lesser importance.

His works reflect the author's first-rate powers of empirical observation and the influence of scholars such as Renan, Topinard, and Paul Broca, with whom he corresponded frequently. He applied the terminology and the cephalic measurements of Paul Broca to prehistoric skulls that he unearthed and even ventured suggestions as to how one of Broca's craniometers could be improved. He used the concepts and terminology of race that had been developed by Gobineau and popularized by others, especially Renan.

Faidherbe developed a strong interest in the popular Nordic hypothesis. But even though he tended to glorify the achievements of the dolichocephalic, tall, blond man, "la dernière fixée dans la série du perfectionnement progressif des êtres vivants que nous enseigne le transformisme,"[48] and to categorize humanity into inferior and superior races, he was made uneasy both by the impossibility of rigidly classifying races according to physical criteria and by the ease with which blacks, when given the chance, could acquire a European, middle-class culture.[49]

The only writings of Faidherbe's generally remembered today are those dealing with the history of French rule in Senegal, particularly his last work—the 501-page compendium *Le Sénégal, la France dans l'Afrique occidentale* (1889). This work is informative but hard to evaluate because it recapitulates other works by Faidherbe such as his fascicle sequence *Le Soudan français*, published between 1881 and 1885, "Journal des opérations de guerre au Sénégal," which appeared in the *Annuaire du Sénégal* in 1861, and *Annales sénégalaises de 1854 à 1885 suivies des traités passés avec les indigènes*, published by the naval ministry in 1885 with no specific author listed. it also quotes from a letter that Emile Maurel, the son of Hilaire, wrote Faidherbe in which he had argued in favor of the upper Senegal route to the mid-Niger. The same passage had appeared earlier in the second fascicle of *Le Soudan français* in 1883.

In 1885 Faidherbe admitted that arthritis had so crippled his hands that he could barely write. He could dictate, assuming that he was still lucid; but one of the obituary notices that appeared at his death in 1889 suggested that he had not been so in recent months—just when *Le Sénégal* was published. In the preface of the book Faidherbe acknowledged that he had been helped in its compilation by his son-in-law, Captain Brosselard-Faidherbe, and by two of his aides—Captain Bizard and above all Captain Ancelle, himself the author of an anthology on European explorers in West Africa.

Conclusion

Faidherbe's African reputation rests on his role as governor of Senegal for nearly nine years and on his efforts and those of his associates to create what might be called a Faidherbe legend. In person and by reputation he influenced the next generation of colonial proconsuls, men like Brière de L'Isle and Gallieni, who continued the push into the interior after 1879. Both men corresponded with Faidherbe, visited him when they were in France, and generally claimed to be following in his footsteps—claims that he and his heirs did not discourage.

Faidherbe's role in the Franco-Prussian war was honorable. He kept the Germans at bay in his sector, and along with General Chanzy and Admiral Jauréguiberry proved that at least some soldiers trained in colonial warfare could also fight effectively against fellow Europeans. The *tirailleurs sénégalais*, which he founded, were expanded by his successors and used in conquering the rest of France's African empire. They played an important role in the *revanche* when it came.

As an Africanist, Faidherbe in a sense inaugurated France's scientific study of its tropical African colonies. In addition to publications of a practical nature, propaganda, and self-justification, he produced several works of theoretical scholarship in linguistics and anthropology. His achievement in this respect is all the more signficant in that the French army at the time offered a poor intellectual environment. Indeed, many of the senior officers who held major commands in Algeria or powerful positions in the war ministry in Paris were frankly anti-intellectual. As a colonial scholar-administrator Faidherbe prefigured men like Paul Marty and Maurice Delafosse.

As an innovator in colonial affairs and as a conqueror, Faidherbe was not as distinguished as Bugeaud, Gallieni, and Lyautey. In Senegal, however, he synthesized and brought to fruition ideas for the development of French domination, a few of which went back as far as the seventeenth century. He raised the level of efficiency in the old mercantilistic system for exploiting the resources of the navigable waterways of Senegambia and their hinterlands. He introduced into this West African trading colony more modern and vigorous practices of military conquest, repression, and direct rule developed by the French army in Algeria. Finally, he created the nucleus of a comprehensive system of colonial administration that others would expand.

Notes

1. I wish to express my gratitude to the French Colonial Historical Society and to the Hoover Institution for the award of a grant in 1975. I would also like to express my appreciation to Dr. Lester Brown, president of Voorhees College, and to Dr. Kariuki Karei, former chairman of the Social Science Division of Voorhees College, and to Mrs. Mary Small, reference librarian at the college, for their invaluable cooperation.

2. Reconstructing Faidherbe's early years and the personal side of his active life is difficult because he wrote no real reminiscences other than several quasi-official accounts of French expansion in Senegal many years after he had quit the governorship. Most of his private papers, including what must have been a voluminous correspondence carried on with his mother until her death in 1856, were lost by his heirs. A few items, the Ogé-Lamoitié Papers, have remained in the hands of Madame Denise Lamoitié of Paris, Faidherbe's great-granddaughter, who kindly permitted me to consult them. These materials and the information available in Faidherbe's two personal dossiers constituted by the war and naval ministries permit a rudimentary reconstruction of the unoffical side of Faidherbe life and career.

3. Inspection certificate, 1845, Faidherbe personal dossier, War Ministry, Archives historiques de l'armée (Vincennes); André Demaison, "Faidherbe," in *Les Grandes Figures coloniales* (Paris, 1932), p. 8.

4. Inspection certificate, 1840, Faidherbe personal dossier, War Ministry; Georges Hardy, "Faidherbe" in *Collection les grands coloniaux* (Paris, 1947), pp. 11–14; interview with Professor Lucien Genêt of the Lycée Louis-le-Grand, Paris, 19 June 1968.

5. Faidherbe to his mother, Sophie Monnier Faidherbe, June 1844, Ogé-Lamoitié Papers.

6. Faidherbe to his mother, Sophie Monnier Faidherbe, June 1844 and n.d. (incomplete), Ogé-Lamoitié Papers.

7. Faidherbe to naval minister, 29 January 1849, 17 October 1849; governor of Guadeloupe to naval minister, 31 August 1849; war minister to naval minister, 31 May 1852, all in Faidherbe personal dossier, Naval Ministry, Archives nationales de France (Paris); General Delgrave to war minister, 29 June 1852, Faidherbe personal dossier, War Ministry.

8. Inspection certificate, 20 October 1848, Faidherbe personal dossier, War Ministry.

9. Bouët-Willaumez to naval minister, 6 November 1844, Sénégal VII 10c; naval minister to Protet, 4 and 5 January 1853; 14 December 1853, 5 and 21 January 1854, Sénégal I 37c, 39b, 40c; naval minister to Faidherbe, 8 December 1854, Sénégal I 41a, all quoted in Christian Schéfer, *Instructions générales données de 1763 à 1870 aux gouverneurs et ordonnateurs des établissements français en Afrique occidentale* (Paris, 1927), 1:166–172, 216–229, 239–246, 265–273; naval minister to Vèrand, 3 November 1853, Sénégal I 38b, Archives nationales, Section d'outre-mer (Paris) (hereinafter cited ANSOM); naval minister to Protet, 18 May 1854, 27 July 1854, Sénégal I 40c, ANSOM;

Georges Hardy, *La Mise en valeur du Sénégal de 1817 à 1854* (Paris, 1921), pp. 341–342; "Pétition addressée à monsieur le gouverneur du Sénégal," 8 December 1851, attached to Protet to naval minister, 16 May 1852, Sénégal XIII 1a, ANSOM; *Deuxième Pétition adressée à M. le gouverneur du Sénégal* (Bordeaux, 1854). For a description of how Faidherbe's instructions were formulated see Leland Conley Barrows, "The Merchants and General Faidherbe: Aspects of French Expansion in Senegal in the 1850s" *Revue française d'histoire d'outre-mer* 51, no. 223 (1974):238–246, 249–259.

10. Ogé-Lamoitié Papers.

11. Marc Maurel to Auxcousteaux, 19 and 22 April 1854, 19 May 1854, 3 and 30 June 1854; Marc Maurel to Hilaire Maurel, 11 and 14 April 1854, 17 May 1854, 3 June 1854, all in Maurel and Prom Papers; collective letter signed by Maurel and Prom and four other Bordeaux companies to the minister of the navy, 1 June 1854; Hilaire Maurel to Mestro, 12 and 17 June 1854, 25 July 1854, all in Sénégal IV 17d, ANSOM.

12. Marc Maurel to Auxcousteaux, 19 May 1854, 3 and 30 June 1854, Maurel and Prom Papers; Faidherbe to Colonel Roux, 10 September 1854, Faidherbe personal dossier, Naval Ministry.

13. Petition to naval minister, 28 August 1854, Sénégal IV 17d, ANSOM.

14. Naval minister to Faidherbe, 9 November 1854, Sénégal I 40c, ANSOM, quoted in Schéfer, *Instructions*, pp. 256–258.

15. Marc Maurel to Hilaire Maurel (Saint-Louis), 9 and 11 May 1855, Maurel and Prom Papers; Faidherbe to naval minister, 27 July 1855; deliberations of the executive council, 20 October 1857, all in Sénégal VII 26bis, ANSOM.

16. Faidherbe, "Mémoire sur la colonie du Sénégal," 1 October 1858, Sénégal I 45a, ANSOM.

17. Faidherbe to colonial minister, 13 April 1860, Sénégal I 46a, ANSOM; Louis Léon César Faidherbe, *Le Sénégal, la France dans l'Afrique occidentale* (Paris, 1889), pp. 261–266.

18. Jauréguiberry to MMC, 26 December 1862, Sénégal I 48b, ANSOM; Jauréguiberry, "Notes sur l'organisation militaire et administrative du Sénégal et dépendances," Sénégal VII 13c, ANSOM.

19. Deliberations of the executive council, 29 November 1859, Sénégal VII 26bis ANSOM.

20. Faidherbe, "Mémoire sur la colonie du Sénégal," 5 August 1856, Sénégal I 43d, ANSOM.

21. Deliberations of the executive council, 11 October 1859, Sénégal VII 26bis, ANSOM.

22. Faidherbe to naval minister, 25 December 1855, Sénégal I 41b, ANSOM.

23. Faidherbe to colonial minister, 14 October 1859, Sénégal I 46a, ANSOM.

24. Marc Maurel to Monsieur Pierre, 20 October 1860, Maurel and Prom Papers.

25. Jauréguiberry to MMC, 17 December 1861, Sénégal I 48 b, ANSOM.

26. *Moniteur du Sénégal*, 22 September 1863.

27. Faidherbe to naval minister, 1 April 1857, Sénégal XI 3a, ANSOM: Naval Minister to Faidherbe, 22 May 1857, Sénégal XI 3b, ANSOM.

28. Genêt interview, Demaison, "Faidherbe," p. 125; superior of the Holy Ghost Fathers to naval minister, 28 October 1855, Sénégal X 4ter, ANSOM; naval minister to Faidherbe, 16 November 1855, Sénégal VIII 17d, ANSOM; Archives nationales du Sénégal (Dakar), 1B67.

29. François Renault, "L'Abolition de l'esclavage au Sénégal: L'Attitude de l'administration, 1848–1905," *Revue française d'histoire d'outre-mer* 63, no. 210, pt. 1 (1971):10.

30. Ibid., p. 11.

31. Faidherbe to Pinet-Laprade, 22 February 1865, quoted in Jacques Charpy, *La Fondation de Dakar (1845–1857–1869)*, no. 1: *Collection des documents inédits pour servir à l'histoire de l'Afrique occidentale française* (Paris, 1958), p. 350; see also Renault, "L'Abolition," p. 14.

32. Faidherbe, *Le Sénégal*, p. 386; Faidherbe to Hamelin, 15 November 1857; Hamelin to Faidherbe, 19 February 1858, all in Faidherbe personal dossier, Naval Ministry.

33. Louis Léon César Faidherbe, *Le Soudan français*, fascicle 4: *Pénétration au Niger* (Lille, 1886), pp. 5–7, 13.

34. Faidherbe, "Mémoire sur la colonie du Sénégal," October 1858, Sénégal I 45a, ANSOM.

35. Frossard to Faidherbe, 3 February 1863, Ogé-Lamoitié Papers.

36. Marshal Niel to Faidherbe, 19 April 1869, Ogé-Lamoitié Papers; Faidherbe to Marshal Niel, 27 April 1869, Faidherbe personal dossier, War Ministry.

37. Marshal Niel to Faidherbe, 27 April 1869, Ogé-Lamoitié Papers.

38. Colas to war minister, 14 April 1871, Faidherbe personal dossier, War Ministry.

39. Quoted in Michael Howard, *The Franco-Prussian War: The German Invasion of France, 1870–1871* (London, 1961), p. 392.

40. Louis Léon César Faidherbe, *Campagne de L'armée du Nord* (Paris, 1871), pp. 45–46.

41. Demaison, "Faidherbe," pp. 230–231.

42. Daniel Foucaut, "Le Rôle politique du Général Faidherbe dans le Nord" (thesis, Diplôme d'études supérieures, University of Lille, 1967), pp. 29–30.

43. "Note sur la situation du Général Faidherbe," 13 February 1879, Faidherbe personal dossier, War Ministry.

44. Chabaud de La Haune to Faidherbe, 30 August 1872, Ogé-Lamoitié Papers.

45. Louis Léon César Faidherbe, *Langues sénégalaises: Wolof, Arabe-Hassania, Soninké, Sérère: Notions grammaticales, vocabulaires, et phrases* (Paris, 1887), p. 1.

46. Faidherbe, *Notice sur la colonie du Sénégal* (Paris, 1859), p. 23.

47. Faidherbe, *Notice sur les travaux du général Faidherbe* (Paris, n.d.), p. 14.

48. Faidherbe, "Collection complète des inscriptions numidiques (libyques)," *Extrait des mémoires de la Société des sciences, de l'agriculture, et des arts de Lille* 8, no. 8 (1870):30.

49. Ibid., pp. 26–29; Faidherbe, *Les Dolmens d'Afrique* (Paris, 1873), pp. 419–420.

Joseph Simon Gallieni (1849-1916)

Virgil L. Matthew, Jr.

MARSHAL Gallieni's long and varied career was primarily that of an empire builder in the late nineteenth and the early twentieth century, although he is probably best known as the military governor of Paris and the hero of the Marne in 1914. Starting his career as a second lieutenant in the Franco-Prussian war, Gallieni entered the colonial service soon after his release as a prisoner of war; his first overseas post was on the island of Réunion. Subsequent colonial duty included West Africa, Martinique, Indochina, and reached its climax in Madagascar, where he served as governor-general from 1896 to 1905. This tall, spare, bushy-eyebrowed, and mustachioed leader spent the last eleven years of his life in France as commander of armies and as a member of the supreme war council. Recalled to active duty as military governor of Paris at the beginning of World War I, Gallieni's alert, restless, ascetic, and bespectacled figure presented a striking contrast to his portly and placid fellow meridional Joffre. Gallieni's last service for France was as minister of war, a position from which he resigned for reasons of health shortly before his death.

During his colonial career Gallieni put forth a number of concepts that were important not only for those areas he commanded, but also in the development of French colonial thought—particularly through the application of these concepts by his disciples, the most famous of whom was Hubert Lyautey. Gallieni was an administrator who favored the idea of association, which called for collaboration and cooperation between the French and the native peoples. Two other policies are even more directly associated with him, namely, the *tâche d'huile*, or "oil spot," and *la politique des races*. The oil spot technique was a means of pacifying an ever broader area around a center of control by making use of the native peoples. Gallieni employed this technique in West Africa and Indochina and perfected it in Madagascar. *La politique des races*, also perfected in Madagascar, called for commonsense administration adjusted to the conditions and the needs of the particular region and its people.

Early Life, 1849–1876

Joseph Simon Gallieni was born at Saint-Béat, just north of the Spanish border, on April 24, 1849, the son of Gaëtan Gallieni and Françoise Perissé. His father, who left Lombardy to avoid service in the Austrian army, had enlisted in the French army, serving from 1829 until his retirement in 1860. It was while he was in command of a frontier garrison that he met and married Françoise Perissé and, after his retirement, he returned to Saint-Béat to become a winegrower and local magistrate under the Second Empire and the Third Republic. Joseph was thus a product of sturdy mountaineer, provincial, and military traditions associated with austere morality, hard work, sense of duty, and intense patriotism.

At the age of eleven Gallieni left home to attend the Prytanée de La Flèche, a military school for the sons of soldiers, in preparation for Saint-Cyr. The distance from home and the difficulties and expense of travel meant that the young Gallieni was removed from his family except for the long vacation during the month of October and that the instructors took the place of his parents. These professors tended to be Voltairean rationalists, often critical of the Second Empire, and they influenced their young student not only in his development of a rigid self-discipline but also in his attitude toward religion and politics. It was also here that Gallieni formed a number of lifelong friendships with fellow students who, though sons of soldiers, did not follow a military career. Many schoolmates later entered the theater, the arts, and literature, which may account in part for Gallieni's wide circle of nonmilitary friends.[1]

In 1868 he graduated from La Flèche and entered Saint-Cyr. An indication of Gallieni's sentiments at the age of nineteen is given by his entrance composition, which was an attack on the ancien régime, especially the period of Louis XV, and a glorification of the patriotism of the revolution. Gallieni was known throughout his career as a republican general, in contrast to many of his monarchist colleagues. When he served on the supreme war council between 1908 and 1914, he was one of only two or three members labeled "republicans."[2]

A hard-working student at both La Flèche and Saint-Cyr—ranked about in the middle of his classes at both schools—Gallieni chose the colonial infantry, or marines, while at Saint-Cyr. Although love of adventure and, after the Franco-Prussian war, a desire to escape from the humiliation of defeat are the usual reasons given for his choice, the fact that Gallieni was a *métis*—Italian and Catalan, republican in sympathy, and not at the top of his class—146th in a class of 275—may have had some influence on his choice of the marines, the least highly regarded of the services.

When the "class of Suez" was assigned to duty on July 14, 1870, Gallieni joined the Third Marine Division as a second lieutenant, and it was in this capacity that he took part in the battle of Sedan, assigned to the so-called Blue Division fighting at Bazeilles against the Bavarians. His regiment held off the enemy for an entire day with such intensity that, when they were finally forced to surrender, the Bavarians threatened reprisals and were deterred only by one of their own officers. Slightly injured, Gallieni claimed that he and his nineteen comrades, all that remained of the regiment, were not a part of the surrender of Sedan.[3] His letters to his family at this period have a sort of "all is lost save honor" quality about them, and he had the painful satisfaction of being received by General von der Tann and congratulated along with his commanding officer, Major Lambert.

As a prisoner, Gallieni was detained at the fortress of Magdeburg and then, after the armistice, was allowed to reside in Neuburg, Bavaria, with the family of a professor. During this period of almost seven months, he set to work studying the German people, their customs and history, a mode of dealing with foreign settings that he adhered to in his colonial career. He also learned German and eventually was able to speak and write the language fluently. This interest in languages is shown by the daily journal he kept between the years 1876 and 1879, written in German, English, Italian, and even some Latin, entitled *Erinnerungen of My Life di Ragazzo*. He later learned Spanish, and added African and Asian languages during his tours of duty on those continents. Gallieni admired the German people, whom he considered "as good if not superior" to the French and more law-abiding. In this period he was very critical of French politicians and journalists, Napoleon III, and the lack of organization in the French army; and his republicanism was again revealed by his delight at the proclamation of the Third Republic.[4]

In March 1871 Gallieni was released to return to France and was reassigned to the marines at Rochefort-sur-Mer, but he was looking forward to service overseas, and in April 1872 he departed for the island of Réunion, where he remained until June 1875. It was while he was on this assignment that he was advanced to the rank of lieutenant in April 1873. Réunion was not an exciting station, but it gave Gallieni time for study and his first contact with the tropics. He also had his first indirect contact with Madagascar since French settlers and missionaries sometimes came to Réunion, especially during periods of trouble on the greater island. But eager for a more active life, Gallieni was able to get a transfer to the *tirailleurs sénégalais* and returned to France in 1875. After the usual period of rest and service at home, he departed for Dakar in December 1876.

During this stay in France Gallieni began his remarkable daily journal. This record was undoubtedly useful for the perfection of his knowledge of languages and for the organization of his thoughts on various subjects. It reveals the wide range of interests of the young lieutenant—German history, military organization, African geography, music, and poetry—alongside lighter, personal passages. The journal shows Gallieni to have been a warm and friendly young officer, quite in contrast to his deliberately cold and austere manner, a pose enhanced by his physique, which gave him the appearance of a figure from El Greco.[5] A fellow officer who served with Gallieni at this time described his colleague as complex, meditative, withdrawn, serious, and reserved, but with fits of gaiety, unhappy at social gatherings, an untiring worker whose government duties were not enough and who used his free time to study all subjects especially military topics and languages.

West Africa, 1877–1881

The new assignment in Senegal was not immediately demanding or interesting and may explain Gallieni's journal notations in which he speculated on the possibility of leaving the army for the consular service, where his knowledge of languages would be useful.[6] Illness, such as yellow fever and shingles, did not improve the situation, but Gallieni's spirits and career were about to take a turn for the better. In April 1878 he was promoted to the rank of captain, but, more important, he came to the attention of the governor of Senegal, Louis Brière de L'Isle, a colonial activist who wanted to complete the expansionist projects envisioned by Louis Faidherbe during his terms as governor in 1854–1861 and 1863–1865.

Brière de L'Isle's plans called not only for the control of trade between Senegal and the Niger but also for the construction of a railway, which required territorial command of the area ruled by the Sultan Ahmadou of the Tukulor empire. This task was to be given to Gallieni, who was appointed political director of Senegal in January 1879 and in August was sent on a political and topographical mission to the upper Senegal, where French control ended at Médine, a place that Faidherbe had saved from a Tukulor attack in 1857. This first mission was a reconnaissance to establish good relations with the tribes opposed to the Tukulors and to found a post at Bafoulabé. At this period many Frenchmen, including Gallieni, believed that it was necessary to move quickly in order to prevent the British from taking over the Sudan commercially and politically. The French were also faced with the problem of the Tukulor empire—whether to cooperate with it or to encourage its enemies and sow discord among its vassals. In his own account Gallieni shifts from one policy to the other, but his reports show that his original aim was opposition to the Tukulors.[7]

By 1880 the railway project was moving forward and it was necessary to take action. In February of that year, about a week after the Gallieni expedition to the Niger left Saint-Louis, Admiral Jean Jauréguiberry, minister of the navy, laid before the French Chamber of Deputies a proposal for a railway from Dakar to the Niger.[8] The survey of the route thus became one of the major objectives of the expedition; but other duties included gaining permission for the construction of forts at Fangala and Kita, and the signing of protectorate treaties with the local tribes. Various treaties were signed with local chiefs culminating in the treaty of Kita, April 25, 1880, which placed considerable emphasis upon commercial operations. Celebration of the signing included native dancing, which the young and somewhat puritanical captain found indecent.

The next step on the way to Ségou, the capital of Sultan Ahmadou, was Bamako on the Niger, and Gallieni chose the more direct but dangerous route through hostile Bambara country. At Dio the mission—which consisted of 5 French officers, 160 native troops, and over 300 pack animals—was ambushed and suffered serious losses, including most of its baggage with the gifts intended for the sultan. Under such conditions Gallieni might have been expected to retreat, but he decided to continue. He believed retreat whould have an adverse effect, especially in those areas in which the French had recently come as protectors.

The reception of the mission by Ahmadou was perhaps more scornful than hostile. Gallieni's position was weak and the Tukulor sultan had reason to distrust the French, who were cooperating with his enemies and building forts while attempting to reach an agreement with him. Instead of allowing the mission to enter Ségou, it was stopped a few miles away at the village of Nango in June 1880 and kept waiting there for the next ten months. Despite Gallieni's repeated complaints and promises of military assistance, the French were held as virtual captives in uncomfortable and unhealthy conditions. Not until late in October did Ahmadou begin negotiations through his minister, Seydou Djeylia, and on November 3 the treaty of Nango was signed. Both sides gained and lost by the agreement. The French got a protectorate to forestall what they believed was a British threat, as well as commercial and navigation rights; the Tukulors got arms for use against their African opponents. Gallieni was pleased with the results of his diplomacy but the treaty was never ratified by the French government because of the arms agreement, although discrepancies between the French and Arabic texts was the reason given.[9]

The conclusion of the treaty did not end the ordeal for Gallieni and his group, who continued to be detained at Nango until March 1881. During this period the French engaged in a show of strength to maintain their prestige and avenge the ambush at Dio. This action was carried out by a career artilleryman who had previously served in Indochina, lieutenant colonel Gustave Borgnis-Desbordes, the superior commander of the Upper Senegal, and might have led to reprisals against the Frenchmen at Nango, but Ahmadou wanted to avoid open conflict with France. Actually, Borgnis-Desbordes's arrival at Kita to begin the construction of a fort and his destruction of the village of Goubanko gave heart to the "captives," and Gallieni's letters to Ahmadou, after hearing this news, take on a much firmer tone. There was also a note of desperation about Gallieni's action as he feared the angry sultan might attack; but on March 10 the latter sent the signed treaty, along with horses and supplies, and the Frenchmen were finally able to depart from Nango on March 21, 1881.[10]

Brière de L'Isle was unstinting in his praise, and Gallieni was promoted to the rank of major and awarded the Cross of the Legion of Honor, but the mission to Ségou could hardly be regarded as a success. However, it was followed by an uneasy, ten-year truce; it opened up the route to the Niger; it arranged treaties with the native chiefs; and it surveyed the route of the future railway to the Niger.

The African climate and the rigors of the virtual captivity at Nango forced Gallieni to take a long rest—two years in France and three years in Martinique. He returned to France in June 1881 and the following summer, August 1882, the recently promoted major was married to Marthe Savelli, a member of a Corsican family. As a result of this marriage, Gallieni became master of a Provençal farmhouse near Saint-Raphaël, La Gabelle, which was to be the Gallienis' home in France for the rest of their lives. The assignment to Martinique, from April 1883 to May 1886, offered an opportunity to write a book on his recent African experiences, *Voyage au Soudan français*, and to complete his reports on the topography of the Niger. Gallieni was always firm in the belief that he and others engaged in colonial service should publish accounts of their actions as quickly as possible in order to encourage French interest in the empire.

West Africa, 1886–1888

By the late 1880s French imperial interest seemed to be in a state of decline. The Ferry ministry had been brought down over events in Tonkin, and the Boulanger episode had renewed interest in Alsace-Lorraine. However, French advances continued and the period from 1885 to 1889, especially in Africa, has been called "the loaded pause."[11] The Berlin conference of 1884 had set the ground rules for the scramble for Africa, where the French were involved with all the old problems— tribal conflicts, Moslem chiefs, difficulties with Great Britain, extension of the area of French control, and completion of the railway. Between 1880 and 1886 Borgnis-Desbordes and his successors had expanded the area of French control and had come into contact with new and powerful Moslem leaders. The most important of these was Samory, who caused trouble for the French for sixteen years, between 1882, when Borgnis-Desbordes collided with him on the Niger, and his capture in 1898. The other major threat came from the religious leader, or *marabout*, Mahmadu Lamine.

This was the situation in the Sudan when Gallieni returned to France in 1886 to be promoted to lieutenant colonel; soon afterward he was summoned from Saint-Raphaël to Paris by the undersecretary of state for the colonies, Jean de La Porte. Together with Faidherbe, Brière de L'Isle, now deputy inspector general of the marine infantry, and Borgnis-Desbordes, now the colonial department's Sudanese expert, La Porte arranged for Gallieni to be named the new commandant of the French Sudan. Borgnis-Desbordes even drafted the instructions, which called for a "firm, prudent, and peaceful" policy, dealing first with the rebellion of Mahmadu Lamine and then with the rehabilitation of the forts and the resumption of the railway construction.[12]

The lieutenant colonel who arrived at Dakar in October 1886 was much more mature and experienced than the young captain of five years earlier, and during his term as commandant he was able to initiate a policy of pacification that was the beginning of his famous oil spot technique, used later in Tonkin and Madagascar. Gallieni's twofold task was both diplomatic and military, negotiating where possible and using force where necessary. The military task consisted of the consolidation and pacification of those areas already taken, sometimes recklessly, by his predecessors. The more fruitful diplomatic task consisted of the extension of French influence in the neighboring states of the Upper Niger. In all this Gallieni's major concerns were the growth of trade, which was possible only under peaceful conditions, and the provision of effective protection for those who accepted French rule.

The first step was the preparation of an expedition against Mahmadu Lamine, who had embarked upon an independent career as a religious leader against Ahmadou and had taken up his position at Diana between the Senegal and Gambia rivers. Lamine was a former disciple of Umar, the founder of the Tukulor empire, and an unsuccessful claimant to his temporal rule. But before moving against this rebel leader, it was necessary to assure the neutrality of Ahmadou and Samory by initiating negotiations, which, even if unsuccessful, could give the French valuable time. Gallieni wrote a friendly letter and sent gifts to Ahmadou, manifesting his desire to live in peace. As for Samory, he sent an embassy under Captain Etienne Péroz to renegotiate the treaty of March 1886, which had made concessions to the African leader that the French no longer wanted to continue. Among other things, Gallieni regarded French control of the entire left bank of the Niger as essential for the development of commerce and for the diversion of the trade of the empire of Samory to French and away from English territories.[13]

The first attack against Mahmadu Lamine resulted in the destruction of his fortified village of Diana in November–December 1886; but Lamine was able to escape and the final reckoning with this African leader did not come until the following year.[14] However, Gallieni immediately began arranging treaties with the local chieftains, who accepted French protection and agreed to send their sons to French schools. Faidherbe had founded the Ecole des otages at Saint-Louis, which produced the first educated native administrators for Senegal, and Gallieni imitated Faidherbe's policy in the Sudan since he regarded schools as one of the most important means of extending French civilization and influence. These treaties also show Gallieni's primary interest in economic considerations and the belief that he was in a race with the English.[15] His concern with trade did not imply ruthless exploitation of the natives. He was a convinced imperialist—though a humanistic one—who regarded Africa as potentially vital to the future of France. But he did not view Africans with racial arrogance and he had a high opinion of many of those with whom he worked, especially those who were loyal to the interests of France.[16] Gallieni's later policy of races, which took the interests of the natives into consideration, was, as we have seen, one of his major achievements. Nevertheless, his first concern was the interests of France, and native rulers and institutions that stood in the way were to be eliminated.

While these events were taking place, Captain Péroz was successful in his mission to Samory, who, with some reluctance, accepted the new French demands. These included abandonment by Samory of the left bank of the Niger, acceptance of a French protectorate, and agreement to the construction of a French fort at Siguiri, at the junction of the Niger and Tinkisso rivers. This agreement of March–April 1887 had the effect of extending French control of the Upper Niger as far as Liberia and Sierra Leone.[17] Shortly after this event one more adversary was disposed of—permanently—with the capture of Soybu, the son of Mahmadu Lamine, who had directed the siege of Bakel the previous year. Soybu had put up a stubborn fight when taken and Gallieni indicated he would have liked to grant him a pardon, but any act of clemency would have been regarded as a sign of weakness. A court-martial returned a verdict of guilty and Gallieni ordered him shot (Soybu is reported to have given thanks for being allowed to die like a soldier).

A new agreement was also reached with Ahmadou, the sultan of Ségou, in May 1887. Like Samory, Ahmadou needed French arms against his African adversaries, and he offered even less objection to the French demands. By the treaty of Gouri the states of the sultan were placed under French protection and opened to French traders, who were also authorized to navigate the Niger and its tributaries. As with the treaty with Samory, this agreement was only temporary so far as Gallieni was concerned. He had no reason to trust the Tukulors and he regarded such agreements as a means of forestalling the spread of British influence but in no way limiting his own freedom of action.

In addition to military campaigns and diplomatic negotiations, Gallieni also directed his attention toward the rebuilding and improvement of the areas under his control. Expeditions were sent into previously unknown territory, new routes were surveyed and roads built, and railway construction was resumed. The Upper Niger was also divided into six *cercles* for better protection and administration. Along with the establishment of *écoles des otages* ("schools for hostages") Gallieni also established *villages de liberté* ("freedom villages") to provide refuges for displaced natives, mostly former slaves, who were either unable or unwilling to return to their old tribal organizations. Whether these villages were simply friendly bases for the French, a means of fighting the slave trade, a part of the oil spot technique, which—like the *cercles*—was a method of providing centers from which French influence could spread, or simply an attempt to assure a ready supply of laborers for public works is a subject of controversy.[18] With these considerable accomplishments behind him and with the approach of the rainy season, Gallieni was able to take a leave of absence in France between June and November 1887.

Upon his return to West Africa he resumed the unfinished business of Mahmadu Lamine, launching a second campaign against this religious leader, who had regained much of his strength and was attacking areas nominally under French protection. Although Lamine had made offers of submission, Gallieni regarded these as ruses and was determined to deal with him once and for all. With his usual care and skill, Gallieni prepared for Lamine's destruction, something he believed was necessary not only to bring peace to the region but also to remove any possible native threat to the route to the Niger and the construction of the fort at Siguiri. The second campaign against Mahmadu Lamine, under the leadership of Captain Fortin, assisted by African allies, resulted in the capture of Lamine's stronghold at Tubakuta. Although Lamine escaped, he was wounded and captured by an African rival and died while being taken to the French. The death of the *marabout* produced the desired effect and the chiefs signed treaties accepting French suzerainty in December 1887.[19]

While the final expedition against Lamine was taking place, Gallieni was busy organizing the move to Siguiri and the construction of a fort, an undertaking that also involved the construction of roads, bridges, and telegraph lines. Since Samory had forced the people to evacuate when he withdrew from the left bank of the Niger, Gallieni had to make every effort to convince them that the French had come to stay. Although not immediately successful in getting the people to return, he was encouraged by the appearance of Moslem traders and expressed the hope that Siguiri would replace the English posts in Sierra Leone.

Still an ardent expansionist, Gallieni wanted to increase the area of French influence and trade even further and he sent out several missions, especially into Fouta Djallon, which later became part of French Guinea. Gallieni sought to secure the western region against possible British expansion, as well as to extend French authority and commerce northeastward to the middle Niger, to Timbuktu, and to the areas within the great loop of the river. Once again, the presumed threat of British—or even German—interest in the region served as a spur to the French. At the time, Gallieni regarded the area bounded by Saint-Louis, Timbuktu, Siguiri, and Benty as a valuable commercial domain, and by launching a second gunboat on the river he made France mistress of the Upper Niger.[20]

It was on this tour of duty in the Sudan that Gallieni came into his own as a colonial leader, having formulated his own ideas concerning the methods the French should use in order to expand, pacify, and develop their colonial empire. During his first assignment in West Africa he had been under the intellectual influence of Governor Brière de L'Isle, but in the Sudan he became a leader and a man of initiative. He also developed some definite ideas concerning the role of France in West Africa, which were, unfortunately, not followed by his successor as commandant of the Sudan, Major Louis Archinard.[21]

The last chapter of Gallieni's book on his experience in the Sudan, *Deux Campagnes au Soudan français, 1886–1888*, gives a careful evaluation of the French position and the potential for the future. It is also an attack on the policies of Archinard. Gallieni noted that the question of the French Sudan was closely related to the overall African situation, especially in connection with the various agreements with Germany, Portugal, and Great Britain. As a result of the agreements, missions of exploration, and treaties with native rulers, the limits of French control had been expanded in all directions, and objectives needed to be reconsidered in this new light. He admitted his error in attempting to expand northward toward Timbuktu. The French had been mistaken about the value of the upper Senegal and Niger and he now considered the regions of Fouta Djallon and Rivières-du-Sud, or French Guinea, as the most important for future development. These areas had large populations, resources, and access to the sea. He had also changed his attitude toward Ahmadou and the Tukulors, and he now believed that the veneer of civilization given by Islam made them the best customers for French goods. He opposed any further military action against the Tukulors or even against Samory since this would serve only to decrease the population of an already underpopulated area. Although Gallieni recognized that administration by the military was necessary until the economy had developed sufficiently, he recommended that Europeans be replaced wherever possible by Africans trained in French schools and also that the military forces should be reduced—or at least the number of European soldiers.

Perhaps Gallieni's most striking change was in his opinion of the railway, which he now considered of little value. Even if extended to the Niger, it would not link up with either a great navigable river such as the Mississippi or the Amazon or an important commercial route such as the Loire or the Rhine; perhaps worst of all, the Niger flowed into British territory. The area had little commerce—even Timbuktu was only a market for salt and slaves—and France should avoid the acquisition of large areas simply for "map coloring" and should confine itself to coasts and navigable rivers. French efforts and money should be used for the building of roads and schools since this was the best means of assisting the local people to develop commercially. Gallieni's recommendation that old, expensive, useless forts be abandoned and that new ones of native materials be located to create centers of influence was a forerunner of his oil spot technique, and his proposal that further penetration be carried out in part by indigenous peoples was a beginning of his policy of races.[22]

Many of the same ideas were expressed in the report of a departmental commission (1889–1890) on future French policy in the Sudan. This commission, on which Gallieni represented the military, was established by the undersecretary of state for the colonies, Eugène Etienne, who was convinced of the need for a reexamination of objectives. It was Gallieni who had encouraged Etienne to convene this body, and its report of January 1890 reflected the views of the commandant. It called for an end to military conquest, major cuts in European troops and their replacement by Africans, and evacuation or reduction of forts and posts and it opposed extension of the railway. Gallieni also submitted a special report calling for the occupation of Fouta Djallon. Unfortunately, only a few minor recommendations were carried out. Any change of policy in the Sudan required the cooperation of the commandant, and Major Archinard's views were diametrically opposed to those of his predecessor.

Archinard was determined to destroy—not to collaborate with—the Moslem states, and the results were war against both Ahmadou and Samory, greatly increased expenditures, and the destruction of any possiblity of economic development. He was the protégé of Borgnis-Desbordes, who was now military advisor to the colonial department, and they were the victors in this struggle. In spite of efforts by Etienne to name Gallieni, it was Archinard who was reappointed to the position of lieutenant governor of the French Sudan in 1892.

Gallieni returned to France in July 1888 after transferring his office to Archinard and spent the next four years at home until he sailed for Tonkin in 1892. During this period he not only completed a book on his second tour of duty in West Africa and served on the colonial department commission in 1889–1890 but also continued his military studies at the Ecole de guerre; Gallieni received the staff's special congratulations and a commendation, along with his certification. This rare citation came in spite of the attitude of the metropolitan army toward colonial officers.[23] While at the Ecole de guerre Gallieni frequented the Latin Quarter and came into contact with various literary and artistic groups. Among those he met were Pierre Gheusi, later director of the Opéra comique and a member of Gallieni's staff during his term as military governor of Paris (1914–1915), and Maurice Barrès, the nationalist writer, who described Gallieni as "an Italian, a schemer" because of his ability to confound his opponents.[24]

Indochina, 1892–1896

In March 1891 Gallieni was promoted to the rank of colonel and given command of the Sixth Marine Regiment at Brest, from which he was assigned as chief of staff of the colonial army corps at Paris. By this time he was eager to return to overseas duty, and reports from Indochina encouraged him to become a tonkinois as well as a former soudanais.[25] Perhaps his failure to be reappointed to the Sudan in place of Archinard, or his opposition to the policies of the military in that region, encouraged him to seek a new arena. At any rate, he sailed for Tonkin in September 1892.

Although the Ferry cabinet had fallen in 1885 over the attempt to control Tonkin, the French had remained. The result was several years of expensive fighting against the so-called Black Flags, or "pirates"—guerrillas under local warlords whom the French regarded, rightly or wrongly, as agents of Chinese arms and policy. Unquestionably, they were aided by elements in China and it was not until the border was secured that their resistance to French occupation was controlled. It was this protracted conflict that Gallieni lived with from 1892 until 1896. One possible advantage to France of this long struggle was that it provided a laboratory for the rising school of colonial administrators. It was in Tonkin that Gallieni perfected his policy of races in pacifying and organizing the border provinces. This period in his career was also a decisive factor in the elaboration of his techniques of colonial warfare, which he later put to good use in Madagascar.

Gallieni was "aided by a staff of brilliant officers—if they outranked him, he inspired them, if they were subordinates, he taught them."[26] The most famous of these subordinates was Major Hubert Lyautey, who at the age of forty had left the metropolitan army for service in the colonies. Lyautey found his career in colonial administration serving under Gallieni, whom he admired both as a man and as an administrator, and he told his mentor: "I regard myself as the apostle of your ideas, the flag bearer of your method."[27] The two men were attracted to each other immediately and became lifelong friends and associates. They both disliked bureaucratic red tape, and one of the first "lessons" Gallieni gave to Lyautey on this subject was to take away the latest service manual and similar works the latter had brought from France so that he would not even be tempted to look at them, saying "it is on the spot, in handling men and things that you learn your job."[28] Gallieni noted that he was careful not to tell Hanoi the full extent of his plans and to describe his "most daring and revolutionary acts" as "mere rectifications of parishes"; yet he also said that one should "violate all the stifling rules" and not be afraid to speak out through books, newspapers, and in public even at the risk of loss of promotion and career.[29]

    Gallieni was able to get so much from his subordinates because he chose the man he felt capable of doing the job and then left him a free hand to carry out the assigned task—at least this was the case with men such as Lyautey. He drove his men, but he left the initiative to them and he was open to suggestions. Lyautey noted with amazement that he once saw Gallieni send an order by telegram "at the suggestion of a mere sergeant."[30] When Gallieni named Lyautey as his chief of staff during a major military operation against the "pirates" in 1895, he made it clear that he did not want to hear about problems, that his only concern was results. He believed that Lyautey could perform the task, but if not he would drop him "like a hot potato," that where the service was concerned he had no sentiment.[31] It was also Gallieni's habit to avoid discussion of an operation once it was under way and to divert himself with a book on philosophy or an English novel. As he explained to Lyautey, the leaders understand the orders and, if they do not, nothing more can be done. Above all, messengers should never be sent as they would cause confusion and useless trouble and probably would not arrive in time.

    In 1891 Jean de Lanessan had been named governor-general of Indochina and he brought with him a new policy of dealing with the Black Flags. This included division of the area of Tonkin along the Chinese border into four military zones headed by commanders with full military and civil authority to destroy the rebels and to pacify and organize the country. Gallieni was assigned to the relatively quiet First Military Territory between Hanoi and the Chinese frontier, and here he put his methods into operation. They included fortification of the frontier, sealing off the Black Flags and preventing them from crossing back and forth from China, and enlistment of the villagers by supplying them with rifles and ammunition, under careful supervision, so that they could provide their own protection against the guerrillas. This was a part of the larger system he developed, known as "progressive occupation," which put forth the idea that it was not enough to defeat the enemy, that the military commander must look forward to the organization of the country in cooperation with the local population. Lyautey defined progressive occupation by saying that "military occupation consists less in military operation than in an organization on the march."[32]

    Gallieni was able to give wider application to these ideas and methods when he was named commander of the Second Military Territory. The situation here was much less settled than in the First Territory and initially more military action was required. Although progressive occupation called for the avoidance of the use of military columns whenever possible, Gallieni was willing to take such action where necessary, as in the reduction of the guerrilla stronghold of Lung Lat. His policy of providing arms for the villagers also paid off in this engagement, as it was they who fatally wounded the guerrilla chief.[33]

Progressive occupation required men capable of dealing with all types of problems, civilian as well as military. Once the necessary military action had ended, in fact, the duties of his soldiers became essentially civilian in nature, and Gallieni wanted the collaboration of the men as well as the officers in this work.[34] He was proud to note that, as in the Sudan under him and in Algeria under Marshal Bugeaud, the commanders of sectors and posts had made themselves into engineers and architects, and the legionnaires, colonial infantry, and native sharpshooters had become bricklayers, carpenters, and blacksmiths—an example of the ability and ingenuity of soldiers when given a job to do. Gallieni believed that it was desirable to have soldiers perform useful tasks as supervisors of construction, teachers, and skilled workers. Unlike many other military men, he did not believe that such work, with its consequent abandonment of the drill field, was prejudicial to military discipline. In fact, he believed that by providing the soldier with interesting work his concern for the colony increased, even to the extent of settlement in the country after the end of his term of service. He regarded the soldier as the precursor and collaborator of the colonist, not as a conqueror with no consideration for the future. At times Gallieni felt moments of envy for his civilian colleagues but then he concluded that he liked the excitement of the unexpected and the dangers of his task—the challenge of being the first to bring European civilization to other peoples. It was the lot of the military to prepare the way for civilian authority.

By the time his command was scheduled to end in the summer of 1895, Gallieni was becoming more and more restive under the increasing demands to adhere to bureaucratic regulations. At one time, when he saved provisions worth a million francs by taxing gambling houses to get funds that were not forthcoming from the administrative center at Hanoi, he was informed that it would have been better to have lost the stores rather than to have saved them by "irregular methods." Governor-general Léon Rousseau, at least originally, was much less sympathetic to Gallieni's methods than Lanessan had been and there was increasing control from Hanoi; but Gallieni remained until the early part of 1896 in order to lead one more military operation against a powerful guerrilla chief. By the time of his departure, however, he was deeply concerned about the continuation of the system he had established and which had met with such success.[35]

He returned from Tonkin with his *politique des races* developed, the policy that he was to apply most successfully in Madagascar. This program included three major points:

1. The administrative organization of a country must be perfectly in accord with the nature of the country, of its inhabitants, and of the aim that one has in mind.
2. All administrative organization must go along with the country in its natural development.
3. Political action must be combined with the use of force, and the former is the much more important.[36]

Political action was, for Gallieni, primarily an ethnographic problem because it consisted of the recognition and the profitable employment of the local usable elements—the people, the workers—and the neutralization, if necessary the destruction, of the nonusable elements—the rebellious or unsubdued chiefs whose prestige must be destroyed and whose forces must be annihilated. As for the use of force, he noted that the purpose of all forward movement is the effective occupation of the conquered territory and that these actions must be joined as soon as possible to economic action. The purpose of the conquest is to restore peace; to assure the social needs of the populace by the establishment of markets, dispensaries, infirmaries, and schools; and to improve the economy by opening channels of communication and transport and by creating outlets for the products of the country.

Madagascar, 1896–1899

When he returned to France in 1896, Gallieni had reason to expect a long leave with his family at Saint-Raphaël after three and a half years in Indochina. However, in April the new colonial minister, André Lebon, summoned him to compliment him on his work in Tonkin and to discuss the current situation in Madagascar. Lebon knew of Gallieni's success in West Africa and Indochina. Lebon also had news of Gallieni from his friends and advisors in various imperialist and colonial organizations, such as the Union coloniale and the Comité de l'Afrique française, and from those who had received glowing letters in his praise from Major Lyautey.[37] A few days later Lebon offered Gallieni the command of the Madagascar corps of occupation with full civil and military authority. It was an offer that Gallieni felt he could not refuse although he was aware of the difficulties. Not only was the situation in Madagascar disturbing, but the political situation in France was anything but stable. During the time Gallieni had been in Indochina (1892–1896) there had been ten governments, and the colonial office, which had been separated from the navy only in 1894, had Lebon as its fifth minister. This was disturbing to a man who believed that no work was possible without continuity of action and unity of views. This was also the period of the Panama scandal, the assassination of President Carnot by an anarchist, and the beginning of the Dreyfus affair.

France had a long interest in Madagascar dating back to the days of Richelieu and Louis XIV. Though the French never relinquished their claims, they were of no practical importance until they were willing to support them by force, and there was little reason to do so until France knew something of the prize. This was not revealed until the explorations of Alfred Grandidier between 1865 and 1870. During the course of the nineteenth century the situation was complicated by the appearance of English and other missionaries, especially those of the London Missionary Society. It was not until the 1880s, however, that the Franco-Malagasy conflict became serious, leading to a war (1883–1885) that resulted in the establishment of a French protectorate in 1885. The treaty saved the faces of both sides since the French recognized the Merina kingdom of Madagascar, which controlled, directly or indirectly, about two-thirds of the island.

However, the fall of the Ferry government implied a ban on further colonial ventures and the Malagasy construed the treaty as a victory. The Merina were not content to leave well enough alone and the next decade was one of conflict involving the French, English, and Malagasy. In 1894 the French sent Charles Le Myre de Vilers to establish a real protectorate, but after his forced withdrawal from the capital the next steps were an ultimatum and war. In 1895 General Jacques Duchesne led an expeditionary force that finally succeeded in taking Tananarive after seven months. But the chief enemies of the French were the terrain, problems of supply, and disease.

Although Queen Ranavalona III was forced to accept a treaty giving France possession of the island in January 1896, this did not meet the problem because it continued the fiction that the Merina kingdom and Madagascar were synonymous. The result was that almost immediately after the conquest practically the whole island was in a state of anarchy, with rebels rising up against the Merina or the French or both. Conditions were made worse by the conflict between General Emile Voyron, the successor to Duchesne, and the new resident general, Hippolyte Laroche. The latter was a cultivated, Protestant freethinker whose only colonial service had been a short term in Algeria, whereas Voyron was an old colonial soldier, undiplomatic, intensely Catholic, and unsympathetic to the Third Republic. All these factors, plus the change of ministries in 1895–1896, contributed to the initial failure in Madagascar.

The situation was further complicated by the argument over the method to be used in handling the latest French acquisition. After 1890 the anticolonial spirit in France had begun to lessen but there was division among the colonialists. There were those who still held to the old policy of annexation and assimilation even though assimilation had failed in Indochina. At the other extreme were those who favored the newer idea of the protectorate as exemplified in Tunisia, and there was a third school that held that annexation did not necessarily imply assimilation. Out of this third school developed the new policy of "association," which was to be best exemplified by Gallieni in Madagascar. As a result of this conflict, Madagascar became a kind of "touchstone of colonial policy."[38] At the moment, the French ministry and Parliament were generally opposed to assimilation, and in view of the recent success in Tonkin it was only natural that association be applied in Madagascar. Diplomatic disputes, as well as internal difficulties on the island, served to encourage the French government to declare Madagascar a colony rather than a protectorate in August 1896.[39] Having adopted this new policy, the next step was to find an experienced man who was both an able soldier and a skilled administrator. The choice for Lebon was obviously limited, but the selection of Gallieni proved to be most fortunate for both France and Madagascar.

Although he was familiar with military events that had been taking place on the island, Gallieni admitted that he had little knowledge of other aspects and he sought advice from Alfred Grandidier, the great explorer and authority on Madagascar. Characteristically, while seeking advice from experts, Gallieni had no interest in cluttering up his mind with official reports and refused the enormous dossiers offered by the minister, saying he preferred to await his arrival at the scene before judging the situation and deciding upon the measures to be taken.[40]

In July 1896 Gallieni was named commander of the French troops in Madagascar and the following month he was advanced to rank of brigadier general and departed for his new assignment, arriving in Tananarive on September 16. Although his first instructions were limited to military powers, Gallieni insisted that all powers—military, political, and administrative—must be combined to be effective. After the usual bureaucratic delays, this concentration of powers was effected and Gallieni was now free to take the action he deemed necessary.[41] At the time he arrived, all of Imerina was in revolt except the area around Tananarive, communication to the coast was precarious, villages were depopulated, and commerce was paralyzed.[42] The situation called for immediate military action and the application of the oil spot technique by the establishment of military *cercles*. The policy of races had to wait until some semblance of order had been achieved. Imerina was divided into four *cercles*, with all military and civil authority concentrated in the commander of the *cercle*, who was responsible only to Gallieni.

Popular resistance against French occupation had broken out at the end of the rainy season in March 1896 and spread throughout the island. Not only were the Merina in revolt, but resistance movements developed among the tribes wholly or partially independent of the Merina monarchy. Since Gallieni believed that opposition to the French conquest was mainly Merina resistance led by members of the old ruling class with the royal court and the queen as the rallying point, he began a policy of appeal to the various tribes, especially those that had been vassals of the Merina. But first he moved against the obstacle of the Merina monarchy. He insisted that Queen Ranavalona III, as a French subject, call upon him when he took over the powers of resident general, and he "twisted the knife" by asking his pro-Malagasy predecessor, Laroche, to convey the message. He replaced the Merina flag with the French tricolor and informed the queen that she was now merely "Queen of Imerina" rather than "Queen of Madagascar."[43]

When the resistance continued, Gallieni moved against the royal officials. The prime minister was forced to resign, and the minister of the interior and an uncle of the queen were condemned and shot, an action that Gallieni later regretted. Events surrounding the national-religious ceremony of the Festival of the Bath, November 20, 1896, convinced Gallieni that the queen must go, but he was not yet ready to move. By February 1897 he was ready, and the queen was suddenly informed that she would depart for Réunion within six hours. Gallieni's interpretation of the action was that he had "invited the queen to resign her functions and at her request [had] authorized her departure to the island of Réunion." This fait accompli raised a storm of protest in Parliament, but Gallieni received the support of the cabinet even though Lebon had advised against hasty action.[44] Gallieni explained his high-handedness by saying that difficulties of communication did not permit instructions on every decision and that all his acts were guided by three principles essential for the establishment of French control: destruction of the prestige and authority of the Merina, replacement of English influence by French, and development of commerce. The final and most telling argument was that the exile of the queen had been successful.

Destruction of the monarchy had removed the only national symbol from the revolt and had also answered the question of Merina hegemony, but the state of anarchy was still serious. The insurrection might have been suppressed by a massive military action, but Gallieni's instructions from Lebon had specifically enjoined against this, especially the use of French troops. At any rate, this was not his method of operation and he intended to use the oil spot with its economy of men and money. The central plateau, including Imerina and Betsileo, was the most important part of the island, along with the route from Tananarive to the port of Tamatave. With order restored in this central area, pacification would then spread out from this oil spot, which included efforts to gain support of the non-Merina peoples.

In addition to the centralization of all authority in his own hands and the organization of military *cercles* a general staff of seven bureaus was set up by Gallieni to control all activities—civil and military—on the island. As pacification progressed, new military *cercles* were added and old *cercles* were grouped together into military territories. The native peoples were handled under the policy of races by which the Merina hegemony was suppressed and the former subject peoples were convened to choose their own leaders. When important rebel leaders surrendered, Gallieni made a great show of clemency in order to persuade them to use their influence with those still in rebellion and even restored some to their former positions. This tactic, along with a few executions and deportations, achieved the desired results.[45] Madagascar was fortunate in having Gallieni, whose actions compare most favorably with the methods used by the French following the Malagasy rebellion of 1947, which resulted in repression, mass arrests, and a large number of victims.

By the spring of 1897 the center of the island was sufficiently pacified to allow the grouping of the *cercles* into larger territories with greatly reduced forces. Gallieni also made use of the method he had tried successfully in Tonkin—the arming of loyal partisans so that they could defend their villages against attacks of the insurgents. With the accomplishment of this first state of pacification, he made a triumphal tour of inspection around the island in May and June, much in the style of the Merina rulers, to meet with Merina vassals. Part of the purpose of the tour was to determine the military situation for the second stage of pacification in the coastal regions during the summer and fall of 1897. One of these actions was to be under the command of Lyautey, who had come to Madagascar to serve under his old commander again.

In spite of his success, Gallieni encountered considerable opposition from a Parliament that was more concerned with "jokers and charlatans" such as Boulanger than with colonial affairs and from the civil and military authorities in a "France more mandarinized than China."[46] The second stage of operations was sufficiently successful, however, to enable him to make a second tour of inspection from June to October 1898. Whereas the first tour was primarily military, the second tour was largely political in character.

Before his departure from Tananarive, Gallieni issued his "Instructions of May 22, 1898," the most complete statement of his doctrines of pacification and administration. In it he emphasized his policy of races, or association, or indirect rule. The objective of this policy was to separate the peoples into their own racial groups without forcing them into a uniform method of organization and administration and always taking into account the manners and customs of the different peoples of the island. In his speeches to the various local groups, Gallieni emphasized that they should learn the French language in order to become "devoted associates" of the French colonists, who came to bring them "wealth and civilization," but that they were free to preserve their customs, religion, and traditional dances. Before the close of 1899 the entire island seemed to be pacified and, although there was a revolt in the south in 1904, the fact that Madagascar was singularly free from internal violence until the revolt of 1947 was largely the result of the foundations laid by Gallieni.[47]

Allied with the problem of the monarchy, but not so easily solved by a coup, was the question of religion. There had been a continuing struggle among English, French, American, and Norwegian Protestants and French Catholics, the major contestants being the London Missionary Society and the French Jesuits. The religious conflict was complicated by the fact that education was in the hands of the missionaries, with more than two-thirds of the schools under foreign Protestants, mainly the London Missionary Society. Since Gallieni considered education of the utmost importance in the establishment of French control, it was necessary for him to take action, although he noted "it was not easy to maneuver between Luther and Loyola."[48] Instructions from Lebon had called for religious neutrality and, so far as religion itself was concerned, Gallieni was in complete agreement. French Protestants and French Catholics could argue over the Malagasy as much as they wished since this did not involve the question of French domination, but Gallieni was not so neutral where foreign missions were concerned. His program in Madagascar has been compared with that of Richelieu— "to humble the House of Austria, the nobles, and the Protestants." For Gallieni the House of Austria was Great Britain, the nobles were the Merina officials and the queen, and the Protestants were, above all, the missionaries of the London Missionary Society. Like Richelieu, Gallieni felt the latter comprised a "state within a state."[49]

Although some of Gallieni's actions unfavorably affected the Protestant mission schools, such as the decrees that French be the basis of instruction and that no Malagasy who did not speak and write French be employed by the government, he had no desire to destroy such schools and even encouraged French Protestants and Catholic orders other than the Jesuits to establish new missions. He did take over some of the mission schools and hospitals after adequate compensation was given, but he never touched the churches and ordered the return of some that had been confiscated.

Perhaps the most important result of this religious-educational conflict was that Gallieni felt it necessary to establish an official lay system of education, which was the foundation of the program lasting until independence in 1960 and beyond.[50] The emphasis was upon practical education in contrast to the traditional literary emphasis in other French colonies. His aim was to train farmers and artisans not *savants* or a dangerous intellectual proletariat. All three levels of the official schools were directed toward this end. The first (rural) level emphasized handicrafts and agriculture, the second level provided more advanced training for industrial and agricultural apprentices, and the third level continued this process. At this last level the three most important schools were the Ecole de médecine to train medical assistants, the Ecole professionelle to train craftsmen and teachers of crafts, and the Ecole normale Le Myre de Vilers to train interpreters and government administrators. Almost all of Madagascar's present leaders are products of these institutions established by Gallieni. His interest in education and cultural life extended beyond the schools and, in line with his policy of association, he encouraged the scholarly activities of the Comité de Madagascar, founded the

Académie malgache in 1902, and required his subordinates to learn the Malagasy language.

Madagascar, 1900–1905

By the spring of 1899, it was possible for Gallieni to return to France for an extended leave (April 1899–August 1900). The combination of force and diplomacy had secured most of the island except for some areas of the west and south. One reason for the return was to secure finances for his expensive public works—the railway from Tananarive to the east coast, roads, telegraph lines, and the naval base at Diégo-Suarez, the construction of which was carried out under Colonel Joseph Joffre of the corps of engineers.

This period during the Dreyfus affair, between the Fashoda crisis and the outbreak of the Boer war, was not opportune for Gallieni's plans and caused his stay in France to be much longer than he originally intended. It also posed the danger that he and his subordinates might be drawn into the struggle; and Gallieni gave strict orders to his assistants, including Colonel Lyautey, to concern themselves exclusively with Madagascar. Although he claimed that Dreyfus and Zola "left him cold," there were apparently some rightist leaders and groups who viewed Gallieni as a "man on horseback" and the minister of war, General de Galliffet, is reported to have jested that if he were Gallieni, he would be sleeping at the Elysée within a week.[51] However, the delay gave Gallieni and his assistants an opportunity to gain support from various colonial groups, especially the Comité de l'Afrique française. This group included diverse personalities from politics, finance, and industry, such as Joseph Chailley-Bert, secretary-general of the Union coloniale française and founder of the Institut colonial international, and Eugène Etienne, deputy from Oran, former colonial minister, and leader of the colonial group in the Chamber. While avoiding the invitations of the rightist groups, Gallieni spoke to the Union coloniale française, the Comité de Madagascar, the Société de géographie, the chambers of commerce at Marseilles, Lyon, and Rouen, and to educational institutions. He was pleased that his speech at the Sorbonne was so well received that he had to escape from students shouting "Vive Gallieni!"[52] Only after months of work, hopes, disappointments, and anger was he able to gét the loan of 60 million francs for the railway and other public works. Once this was achieved, the growing involvement of the ministry in the separation of church and state caused Gallieni to conclude that there was no longer any reason to remain in France.

The return to Madagascar for his second tour of duty (1900–1905) involved celebrations that verged on the regal—an inspection of the naval base at Diégo-Suarez, a review of the troops, and a tour of the northern part of the island before making a triumphal entry into Tananarive with the first automobiles on Madagascar. Gallieni was always interested in the latest technical and mechanical developments and often used them to impress the local peoples. Rebel chiefs who had been exiled to Réunion were allowed to return, and the ashes of Prime Minister Rainilaiarivony, husband of queens Ranavalona II and Ranavalona III, were brought back from Algeria. Although pleased by the reception, Gallieni ordered that it be the last such celebration. In an order to the commanders of territories, *cercles*, and provinces, he noted that official festivities were formerly necessary as traditional manifestations of submission to authority but that the Malagasy had now freely rallied to the French cause and such celebrations were not in accord with principles of liberalism and democracy.

The second period was largely devoted to the organization and development of the colony, in contrast to the first, which was concerned mainly with pacification—although Gallieni's program always combined pacification and organization. However, the southern third of the island was still not under French control except for scattered centers, and this task was assigned to Colonel Lyautey as supreme commander of the south. With his most trusted lieutenant in charge, Gallieni felt free to devote himself to primarily nonmilitary matters. Although the pacification of the south was completed by 1902, Lyautey warned of the possibility of future troubles, and in 1904 rebellion broke out.[53] The uprising was not especially serious and was suppressed more by the use of tact than by force, but it aroused considerable criticism of Gallieni and his methods. He was charged with levying taxes solely for income without consideration of the needs of the people, and local French officials were accused of gross maladministration. Among the critics was Victor Augagneur, Gallieni's successor as governor-general.[54] Undoubtedly, there were many reasons for the revolt, such as unwise actions by local officials and settlers that aroused native resentment. Gallieni warned against blunders and abuses that have "most regrettable consequences" and he made much of finding the right man for the job, but he was not always able to do so. Although he probably moved around supervising his men more than almost any other colonial official, he could not detect and prevent all abuses. He always professed to be unmoved by the attacks of his critics; yet he was keenly aware of criticism and defended his actions in letters to friends.[55]

With respect to economic development, one of the major problems in Madagascar—as in the other colonies where Gallieni had served—was that of labor supply. The precipitate abolition of slavery in 1896 complicated the problem of providing the labor needed for the immense task of construction of public works as well as for the development of agricultural and industrial enterprises that would compensate France for the costly military operations of conquest. Gallieni attempted to find a solution in various ways, but his efforts and those of succeeding administrators were generally unsuccessful in supplying labor in sufficient quantity for European enterprise.

In 1896 the Merina corvée system of forced labor was reintroduced for the construction of public works. A head tax was ordered that forced the natives to work in order to obtain money to pay it. Attempts to recruit workers from Asia and Africa were, on the whole, unsuccessful. Although the system of forced labor was abolished by Gallieni in 1900, it was revived by Augagneur, his successor, and lasted until 1946. In spite of the problems with labor, Madagascar experienced an economic boom during most of Gallieni's term, aided by the public works projects. But there was also the introduction of new crops, and between 1896 and 1905 imports rose from 13.9 million to 31.2 million francs, and exports increased from 3.6 million to 22.5 million francs. Gallieni was pleased to claim that French commerce had grown from nine percent to ninety-two percent of the total trade of Madagascar.[56]

The long-range plans to increase the labor supply, aside from the educational system with its emphasis upon the training of semiskilled and skilled workers, included such efforts as the encouragement of legal marriages and large families by exempting fathers from forced labor and military service, the fostering of public health, special taxes for single persons, and the institution of the Fête des enfants, an idea that Gallieni got from Indochina. All of these efforts were particularly directed toward the Merina, as Gallieni now considered them to be the only group capable of producing a skilled work force.[57] Public health services were vital not only for the future population but also for the existing population. Continuing the work of the missionaries, a school of medicine was inaugurated at Tananarive and a territorial health system was organized. Gallieni believed that the establishment of charitable and benevolent institutions by the state was both a humanitarian obligation and an economic necessity and that no other expenditures could more effectively serve the spread of French influence and colonization.

Gallieni began with high hopes that Madagascar would become a French equivalent of Canada, Australia, or New Zealand as a place for settlers, and he urged his officers to do everything possible to assist the colonists who would develop the colony with their skills and capital. He fostered the publication of a guide for immigrants and sought the support of French colonial organizations. One of the colonization schemes called for the encouragement of soldiers to settle on the land after the expiration of their terms of enlistment, but this also proved to be a disappointment. Gallieni eventually came to the same conclusion as Joseph Chailley-Bert that Madagascar was not a colony for Eurpoean settlement; but in spite of the difficulties he believed it would not be the last of the French possessions to justify the hopes of the mother country.[58]

At the time of the resignation of Premier Waldeck-Rousseau in 1902, Gallieni put himself at the disposal of the colonial office to decide whether he should be replaced by a civil governor. Personal reasons may have partly dictated this action. He was then the youngest divisional general in the army, having been raised to that rank in 1899, and he was well aware of the attitude of the metropolitan army toward colonial officers. Gallieni had gone as far as he could possibly go in the colonial service and perhaps it was well to look toward the continuation of his military career in France. Should he return, he was assured of the command of an army corps. However, his desire to oversee the completion of the first stage of the Tamatave-Tananarive railway, and possibly the political situation in France under the anticlerical, antimilitary Combes ministry, encouraged him to remain until 1905. In October 1904 Gallieni presided over the inauguration of the first section of the railway, and he was now eager to return home, feeling that it was necessary only to continue improving upon what had already been accomplished in Madagascar. He expressed the hope that his work and the efforts of his collaborators would bring to France "not only material profits but also the honor of having brought to a new people the benefits of its civilizing influence."[59] Although he sailed for France in May 1905, he continued in his official position until November, when he was replaced by Victor Augagneur, deputy of the Rhone. Gallieni was then awarded the Grand Cross of the Legion of Honor in recognition of his services to France and appointed inspector general of the colonial army.

Madagascar was Gallieni's last real colonial assignment, the remaining years of his life being spent with military duties in France. His impact upon the island was greater than that of any other individual, "and there is almost no aspect of the island's development on which [he] did not leave his mark."[60] He was the man who "really made Madagascar" and his policy of races caused the colony to be "an interesting study, not only in French colonization, but in the wider history of comparative colonial methods."[61] If anything, his policy may have been too successful. Although it produced generally desirable results, it was "too personal, too rich in experiences and personal reflections" to be followed by other governors who were less aware of the traditions of the country. An indication of the lasting quality of Gallieni's governorship is that most of the structures laid down by him lasted until political independence in 1960, and many of them were continued by the government of the Malagasy republic.

France, 1905–1916

Following his return to France, Gallieni completed the editing of his official report *Madagascar de 1896 à 1905*, to which he later added another work covering the same material for the general public, *Neuf Ans à Madagascar*. He spent the remainder of 1905 at his home, La Gabelle, near Saint-Raphaël, surrounded by souvenirs of his colonial career, and in 1906 he returned to duty as commander of the Twelfth Corps at Clermont-Ferrand and then of the Fourteenth Corps, with the additional duty of military governor of Lyon. Aware of the fact that his colonial service had left him out of touch with the "higher study of war" and large-scale operations, he asked that a recent Ecole de guerre graduate be assigned to him. The results of his studies and thoughts on military subjects are to be found in a massive, three-volume manuscript.[62] He was such an apt pupil of operations that in the maneuvers of 1912, as commander of the "Blues," he crushed the opposition "Reds," capturing the commander and his entire staff. In time of war, it would have been a stunning victory.[63]

In August 1908 Gallieni was appointed to the supreme war council, a position he held until his retirement in April 1914. It was in this capacity that he played a major role in the great crisis in the French command in 1911. Adolphe Messimy, minister of war in the cabinet of Joseph Caillaux, was an advocate of the *offensive à outrance* and immediately upon taking office began searching for a successor to the cautious, defensive General Victor Michel as vice-president of the supreme war council. Michel's defensive proposals, envisaging a German attack through Belgium that should be met with an army increased by reserves, were completely contrary to the offensive ideas later embodied in Plan XVII and were rejected by the council. Although Gallieni accepted Michel's ideas on the German attack and on artillery, he had little faith in vast numbers of reservists because of his belief in the value of training and he did not consider the vice-president the "right man in the right place."[64]

The usual story concerning the appointment of General Joseph Joffre as commander of the French army is the one given by Messimy, who claimed he offered the position to Gallieni, the candidate of Premier Caillaux and an undoubted republican; but Gallieni refused because he had participated in the removal of Michel, was too old, and was a colonial. When asked for suggestions, Gallieni is said to have recommended General Paul Pau or Joffre; but Pau was a reactionary who demanded the right to name generals, whereas Joffre was a reputed republican and former Freemason. The latter was also attractive to Messimy as an advocate of the offensive.[65] However, in view of Gallieni's presumed reasons for refusal, his suggestions appear odd. Pau was a year older and thus had even less time before reitrement; Joffre was a colonial with far less experience in military campaigns or administration and had never commanded an army.[66] The appointment of Joffre was regarded as a victory for Colonel de Grandmaison, the "Young Turks," and the doctrine of the offensive, and Liddell Hart described Gallieni's recommendation of his former subordinate as "the one disservice he rendered to France and the worst to himself."[67]

By 1913 Gallieni saw war coming to an unprepared France, and by 1914 he was even more concerned. He urged the strengthening of defenses and troops in the north and replacement of the red trousers of French troops, but he was attacked as a general with the Grand Cross and the Military Medal, with nothing more to wish for, reaching the age of retirement, who now wanted to abandon Plan XVII and even change the uniforms.[68] Retirement was something Gallieni viewed with mixed emotions. He was under a government he considered heedless of dangers, yet he was displeased with the rapidity with which he was placed on reserve on his sixty-fifth birthday. After some delay, he was retained as president of the council for the defense of the colonies, but the first signs of the illness that was to cause his death and the illness of his wife called for rest at La Gabelle. It was a very short retirement as Marthe Savelli-Gallieni died from a cerebral hemorrhage on July 17, the day he received news of his recall to duty by the minister of war.

Upon his arrival in Paris on August 2, Gallieni was informed by Joffre and Messimy that he had been named as assistant and eventual successor to the commander in chief. But Joffre had no desire to have at headquarters his potential replacement, senior officer, and former commander or even to keep him informed of operations.[69] As a result, Gallieni was left at the war ministry as a "fifth wheel," daily growing more alarmed at the failures of Plan XVII and the battle of the frontiers. These failures forced Premier René Viviani to reshuffle his cabinet and to replace Messimy with Alexandre Millerand on August 26. Messimy's last act as minister of war was to dismiss General Michel again, this time as military governor of Paris, in favor of General Gallieni. The latter immediately set to work on the neglected defenses of the city. Unlike Joffre, he believed it essential to hold Paris, and when the government departed leaving him with all civil and military powers, his famous proclamation of September 3 made it clear that he intended to defend the city to the end.[70]

Fortunately, Gallieni did not limit himself to the defense of Paris and "by keeping his eyes on the wider horizon . . . by exceeding his duty, he perceived and seized the chance to save not merely Paris but France."[71] When he became aware of the shift of von Kluck's First Army, he urged an attack on the German flank, but he was faced with the formidable task of getting Joffre and the British under Sir John French to act. His insistence on an attack north of the Marne and his actions on September 4 in getting Joffre's agreement caused him to remark that the battle of the Marne was won by *coups de telephone*. Seeing his moment slipping away, he called Joffre, insisted on speaking to him personally, and finally got the commander in chief's approval of a strike north of the Marne on September 6.

Since Joffre had taken control of the Army of Paris, Gallieni's major role once the battle began was to supply troops and equipment, especially to the Sixth Army, under General Michel Maunoury. The most famous of these actions was his use of hundreds of taxis to speed troops to the front—one more example of Gallieni's willingness to employ modern technology and a forerunner of the motorized armies of the future.

Perhaps no battle has caused more controversy or given rise to more legends than that of the Marne. The controversy over the roles played by Joffre and Gallieni was mainly carried on by the partisans of each, but the commander in chief certainly helped to bring it on by his immediate efforts to belittle his rival. The basic argument of the supporters of Joffre is that he gave the final order and bore the ultimate responsibility, but "General Gallieni had sought to suggest the opportune moment" and had been "the inspirer of the hour."[72] Gallieni believed that he could have had a decisive instead of a limited victory had he been given the troops he requested, and he resented the fact that he was the only major participant not awarded the Croix de guerre. Nevertheless, he believed that history would justify his position.[73]

The year following the battle of the Marne was a difficult one for Gallieni. Although he remained as military governor, he was once more something of a "fifth wheel," especially after the return of the government to Paris. There were repeated promises of an active command, but they were always opposed by Joffre, who even wanted to have General Ferdinand Foch designated his successor. Gallieni eventually came to the conclusion that the commander in chief was a "clever peasant."[74] During this period Gallieni grew more concerned and critical of the military failures and stalemate in the West. By late 1914 or early 1915 he, along with Briand and Franchet d'Esperey in France and Lloyd George, Kitchener, and Churchill in England, was proposing a second front in the Balkans. Joffre, of course, was opposed, claiming he needed every man and would soon achieve victory in the West and that the idea was the result of Gallieni's personal ambition to have a command.[75] Failure of the September 1915 offensive led to the fall of the Viviani cabinet in October and its replacement by one under Aristide Briand, which included Gallieni as minister of war.

The new minister might have been tempted to turn the tables, but he loyally defended Joffre in the Chamber of Deputies and agreed to his elevation to the position of commander in chief of the French armies without any reciprocal action on Joffre's part. Gallieni's sense of duty received its greatest test when, in answer to his inquiry concerning reported deficiencies at Verdun, Joffre replied with such "offended grandeur" that Liddell Hart said it "might well be framed and hung in all the bureaus of officialdom the world over—to serve as 'the mummy at the feast,'" and Winston Churchill described it as "a letter which holds its place in the records of ruffled officialdom." Gallieni was thoroughly exasperated, but he was prevailed upon by the council of ministers to send a reply of capitulation. Joffre had "been touchy" and Gallieni had been "sat on."[76]

His term as minister of war from October 1915 until March 1916 was not one of Gallieni's most successful assignments. He had accepted the post with misgivings and they proved to be correct. The promises made to him were not kept and he was unable to carry through his reforms of the ministry and the high command. In a very real sense, he had "missed his hour."[77] Although some claimed that he had instituted four major reforms during his term—internal reorganization of the ministry, institution of an inter-Allied council, regulation and renovation of the high command, and preparation of the offensive from Salonika—only the first of these was in any sense accomplished during his lifetime although he can be credited with laying the groundwork for the other three. The explosion of a German shell in the episcopal palace of Verdun on February 21 signaled not only the beginning of the battle of Verdun but also the showdown among Gallieni, the Briand cabinet, and Joffre. The minister had concluded the task was too difficult in view of the timidity of the government and his health and age and that he must accept the advice of his doctors.[78] However, before his departure, he presented a written report on the high command. He was sure his ideas would not be accepted, but he believed it to be his duty to express them and then to offer his resignation.

On March 7 Gallieni read his "Note on the Modification of the High Command" to the cabinet. This penetrating analysis of the role of the high command and its relationship with the government concluded with the recommendations that the high command be limited to military operations, that administrative control be restored to the minister of war, and that chiefs who "adhere to anachronistic ideas and outmoded procedures" be eliminated.[79] The note created an uproar and he was asked to reconsider his resignation, but Gallieni refused, except to delay his formal resignation until a successor could be named. In spite of his bitterness toward politicians, he refused to make the high command the reason for his departure since that would have caused the fall of the cabinet. On March 10 he left for Versailles, where, after a few weeks of rest, he submitted to two prostate operations. Postoperative hemorrhaging caused his death on May 17, 1916.

Gallieni's body lay in state at the Invalides and he was given a state funeral. President Poincaré, Premier Briand, and other dignitaries—but none of the top army command—were present. General Pierre Roques, the new minister of war, made effective use of Gallieni's favorite phrase, *jusqu' au bout*, in his oration.[80] Cardinal Amette, archbishop of Paris, presided over the religious ceremony and it was, perhaps, rather ironic that a man with Gallieni's attitude of religious neutrality should receive the full treatment of the Roman church. Not until 1921 was he awarded the posthumous dignity of the rank of marshal of France.

Conclusion

Joseph Simon Gallieni was a professional soldier to such a degree that he made it difficult to separate the man from the uniform in which he had spent his life from the age of eleven. A "cold meridional," all his actions were determined by his profound, instinctive belief in "la Patrie et la République."[81] In an age of anticolonialism and anti-imperialism, Gallieni's accomplishments in Africa and Asia might be questioned, but he was a product of his time, a nineteenth-century rationalist, a reader of John Stuart Mill, Charles Darwin, and Herbert Spencer. His belief in evolution inspired his methods of association, peaceful penetration, and the oil spot. Although always deeply concerned with the progress and improvement of indigenous peoples, Gallieni saw France was his first duty. He shared the nineteenth-century European belief in white superiority and the struggle for the "survival of the fittest." Though he undoubtedly held that the French were the "fittest," Gallieni was not blind to the shortcomings of France, especially its politics and Byzantine bureaucracy. Nor was his patriotism chauvinistic since he preferred peaceful solutions wherever possible. It was his duty to carry French civilization to the "lesser breeds of men"—not to make Frenchmen of them but to introduce the advantages of modern progress.

Whereas the greatest part of Gallieni's career and his greatest achievements were in the colonial sphere, he became best known for his actions leading to the battle of the Marne, which gained him the title of "Savior of Paris." This has also been the area of greatest controversy. Decline in health most likely prevented this "most gifted soldier in the French Army" from "enforcing the advice that his genius counselled," according to David Lloyd George. Winston Churchill characterized Gallieni as a man from whom France and the Allies had "profited by his genius, sagacity and virtue, and might have profited far more." And on the eve of victory Georges Clemenceau is quoted as saying, "Without Gallieni, victory would have been impossible."[82]

Notes

1. Jean Charbonneau, *La Jeunesse passionnée de Gallieni* (Bourg-en-Bresse, 1952), pp. 15–17.
2. In 1911 General Joffre was the only other "republican" on the supreme war council; by 1913 General Sordets was included in this category—this in contrast to eight members labeled "reactionaries" in 1911 and nine in 1913. André Morizet, *Le Plan 17: Etude sur l'incapacité de l'Etat-major avant et pendant la guerre* (Paris, 1919), pp. 63–65.
3. Joseph Gallieni to Gaëtan Gallieni, quoted in Jean d'Esmenard [Jean d'Esme], *Gallieni: Destin hors série* (Paris, 1965), pp. 31–32.
4. Gallieni to his parents, quoted in Pierre Lyautey, *Gallieni*, 4th ed. (Paris, 1959), pp. 23–25.
5. Charbonneau, *La Jeunesse*, pp. 35–45; Lyautey, *Gallieni*, p. 27; Pierre B. Gheusi, *Gallieni, 1849–1916* (Paris, 1922), p. 12.
6. Charbonneau, *La Jeunesse*, pp. 48–50.
7. John D. Hargreaves, *Prelude to the Partition of West Africa* (London, 1963), p. 257; A. S. Kanya-Forstner, *The Conquest of the Western Sudan: A Study in French Military Imperialism* (London, 1969), pp. 72–75.
8. Admiral Jauréguiberry had been governor of Senegal, 1861–1863, between the two terms of Louis Faidherbe.
9. See Kanya-Forstner, *Conquest*, pp. 72–83, for a discussion of the mission to Ségou, 1880–1881. Both Kanya-Forstner and Hargreaves, *Prelude*, pp. 257–265, accuse Gallieni of duplicity and indecision.
10. Joseph Simon Gallieni, *Voyage au Soudan français (Haut-Niger et pays de Ségou), 1879–1881* (Paris, 1885), pp. 455–472. One story told was that Ahmadou had ordered the execution of all foreigners soon after stopping Gallieni and his group at Nango. They were presumably saved by the mother of the sultan, who pleaded for their lives as they were guests of Allah.
11. John D. Hargreaves, *West Africa Partitioned*, vol. 1: *The Loaded Pause, 1885–1889* (Madison, 1974).
12. Kanya-Forstner, *Conquest*, pp. 143–144.
13. Joseph Simon Gallieni, *Deux Campagnes au Soudan français, 1886–1888* (Paris, 1891), pp. 14–15, 36–37; Auguste L. C. Gatelet, *Histoire de la conquête du Soudan français, 1878–1899* (Paris, 1901), pp. 97–98.

14. The details of this campaign are to be found in Gallieni, *Deux Campagnes*, pp. 4–120.

15. Ibid., pp. 110–122; idem, *Gallieni pacificateur: Ecrits coloniaux de Gallieni*, ed. Hubert Deschamps and Paul Chauvet (Paris, 1949), p. 79, n. l; P. Lyautey, *Gallieni*, pp. 64–67.

16. Yves Person, *Samori*, 2:699–702, quoted in Hargreaves, *West Africa*, 1:71–72; Gallieni, *Deux Campagnes*, pp. 146–148.

17. Marie Etienne Péroz, "Mission du capitaine Péroz dans le Ouassoulou," in Gallieni, *Deux Campagnes*, pp. 223–291.

18. Ibid., pp. 295–297; Joseph Emile Froelicher, *Trois Colonisateurs: Bugeaud, Faidherbe, Gallieni* (Paris, 1902), pp. 223–228; Gatelet, *Histoire*, pp. 106–107; D. Bouche, "Les Villages de liberté en A.O.F.," *Bulletin de l'I.F.A.N.* 1, B, no. 9 (1949):526–540, quoted in Kanya-Forstner, *Conquest*, pp. 272–273.

19. Gallieni, *Deux Campagnes*, pp. 323–339, 349–371; Gatelet, *Histoire*, pp. 107–114; Charles André Julien, "Gallieni," in *Les Constructeurs de la France d'outre-mer*, ed. Robert Delavignette and Charles André Julien (Paris, 1946), pp. 392–394.

20. Gallieni, *Deux Campagnes*, pp. 192–221, 422–603; Hargreaves, *West Africa*, 1:78–85; Joseph Simon Gallieni, "Voyage de la canonnière *Niger* à Koriumé, port de Tombouctou," *Compte rendu des séances de la Société de géographie* [Paris] *et de la Commission centrale* (1881), pp. 68–78.

21. Archinard was commandant of the Upper River, 1888–1891, and lieutenant governor of the Sudan, 1892–1893.

22. Gallieni, *Deux Campagnes*, pp. 626–631; Froelicher, *Trois Colonisateurs*, pp. 244–249; Raymond F. Betts, *Assimilation and Association in French Colonial Theory, 1890–1914* (New York, 1961), pp. 112–113.

23. Jean Charbonneau, *Gallieni à Madagascar, d'après la documentation rassemblée par Mme Gaëtan Gallieni* (Paris, 1950), p. 19.

24. Gheusi, *Gallieni*, pp. 33–34; Maurice Barrès, *Scènes et doctrines du nationalisme* (Paris, 1902), pp. 377–378, 383.

25. Joseph Simon Gallieni, *Gallieni au Tonkin, 1892–1896*, 2d ed. rev. (Paris, 1948), p. 1.

26. Jean Gottmann, "Bugeaud, Gallieni, Lyautey: The Development of French Colonial Warfare," in *Makers of Modern Strategy: Military Thought from Machiavelli to Hitler*, ed. Edward Mead Earle (Princeton, 1952), p. 39.

27. Gallieni, "Principes de pacification et d'organisation," *Gallieni au Tonkin*, p. 215.

28. Louis Hubert Gonsalve Lyautey, *Intimate Letters from Tonquin*, trans. Aubrey Le Blond (London, 1932), pp. 89, 98–100, 106, 113–115. For the influence of this antibureacratic attitude on other colonial administrators see William B. Cohen, *Rulers of Empire: The French Colonial Service in Africa* (Stanford, 1971), pp. 64–65.

29. Lyautey, *Intimate Letters*, pp. 118–119.

30. Ibid., p. 138.

31. Ibid., pp. 173–174.

32. Louis Hubert Gonsalve Lyautey, "Du rôle colonial de l'armée," *Revue des deux mondes* 157 (January 15, 1900):310–311; Gottmann, "Bugeaud, Gallieni, Lyautey," pp. 241–242.

33. Gallieni, *Gallieni au Tonkin*, pp. 9–20; Emmanuel Pierre Gabriel Chabrol, *Opérations militaires au Tonkin*, 4th ed. (Paris, 1897), pp. 229–233.

34. Lyautey, "Du rôle colonial," pp. 309–311; Louis de Grandmaison, *L'Expansion française au Tonkin: En territoire militaire* (Paris, 1898), p. 101.

35. Gallieni to Louis Hubert Lyautey, Long Son, 1895, quoted in P. Lyautey, *Gallieni*, pp. 133–136.

36. Gallieni, *Gallieni au Tonkin*, pp. 215–216.

37. Joseph Simon Gallieni, *Neuf Ans à Madagascar* (Paris, 1908), pp. 1–2; F. Charles-Roux and Guillaume Grandidier, eds., "Avant-propos," in Joseph Simon Gallieni, *Lettres de Madagascar, 1896–1906* (Paris, 1928), pp. 5–8.

38. Betts, *Assimilation and Association*, pp. 106–109.

39. *L'Afrique française: Bulletin mensuel du Comité de l'Afrique et du Comité du Maroc* 6 (1896):245;

Louis Brunet, *L'Oeuvre de la France à Madagascar: La Conquête—l'organisation—le général Gallieni* (Paris, 1903), pp. 227–232.

40. Gallieni, *Lettres de Madagascar*, pp. 11–12; idem, *Neuf Ans*, pp. 3–4.

41. Gallieni, *Neuf Ans*, pp. 31–33; André Lebon, *La Pacification de Madagascar, 1896–1898, avec des lettres inédités adressées par Hipp. Laroche, Paul Bourde, et Gallieni au ministre des colonies* (Paris, 1928), pp. 137–150.

42. Joseph Simon Gallieni, *Rapport d'ensemble sur la pacification, l'organisation, et la colonisation de Madagascar (octobre 1896 à mars 1899)* (Paris, 1900), pp. 5–7.

43. Gallieni, *Neuf Ans*, pp. 36–37; idem, *La Pacification de Madagascar (opérations d'octobre 1896 à mars 1899)*, ed. P. Hellot (Paris, 1900), pp. 30–35.

44. Gallieni, "Instructions pour monsieur le sous-lieutenant Durand," quoted in Alfred Durand, *Les Derniers Jours de la cour hova; l'exil de la reine Ranavalo* (Paris, 1933), pp. 109–118; Gallieni, *Gallieni pacificateur*, pp. 204–205; André Lebon, "La Pacification de Madagascar," *Revue des deux mondes* 159 (15 June 1900):812. Queen Ranavalona III was later transferred to Algiers, where she lived until her death in 1917. Her remains were brought back to the royal tomb in Tananarive in 1938.

45. Gallieni, *Neuf Ans*, pp. 29–31; idem, *Madagascar de 1896 à 1905: Rapport du général Gallieni, gouverneur général, au ministre des colonies (30 avril 1905)*(Tananarive, 1905), pp. 24–27; idem, *Pacification de Madagascar*, p. 29; idem, *Gallieni pacifcateur*, pp. 213–214; Louis Hubert Gonsalve Lyautey, *Lettres de Tonkin et de Madagascar, 1894–1899* (Paris, 1920), 2:190–192, 200–201. For a brief discussion of the methods of pacification see an anonymous work (the author is identified as le capitaine P.) entitled "L'Oeuvre du général Gallieni à Madagascar: Principes de pacification et de colonisation," *Revue de géographie* 50 (May 1902):424–440.

46. Lyautey, *Lettres de Tonkin*, 2:175, 209.

47. Virginia Thompson and Richard Adloff, *The Malagasy Republic: Madagascar Today* (Stanford, 1965), p. 16.

48. Gallieni, *Gallieni pacificateur*, p. 203, n. 2.

49. Ibid., pp. 179–182, 200–202; Charbonneau, *Gallieni à Madagascar*, pp. 66–68. For the London Missionary Society side see Thomas T. Matthews, *Thirty Years in Madagascar*, 2d ed. (London, 1904), and James Sibree, *Fifty Years in Madagascar* (London, 1924). For the Jesuit side see J. B. Piolet, *Douze Leçons à la Sorbonne sur Madagascar* (Paris, 1898).

50. Nigel Heseltine, *Madagascar* (New York, 1971), p. 84.

51. Lyautey, *Lettres de Tonkin*, 2:270–71; P. Lyautey, *Gallieni*, pp. 178–179; Charbonneau, *Gallieni à Madagascar*, pp. 138–139; Gheusi, *Gallieni*, pp. 68–70.

52. P. Lyautey, *Gallieni*, p. 179; Hubert Deschamps, "Introduction," in Gallieni, *Gallieni pacificateur*, p. 16; Charbonneau, *Gallieni à Madagascar*, p. 144.

53. Louis Hubert Gonsalve Lyautey, *Lettres du sud de Madagascar, 1900–1902* (Paris, 1935), pp. 16–21, 246–251; idem, *Dans le sud de Madagascar: Pénétration militaire, situation politique et économique, 1900–1902* (Paris, 1903), pp. 11–15; idem, *Les plus belles lettres de Lyautey*, ed. Pierre Lyautey (Paris, 1962), pp. 57–60.

54. Victor Augagneur, *Erreurs et brutalités coloniales* (Paris, 1927), pp. 131–140.

55. Lyautey, *Lettres du sud de Madagascar*, p. 15; Gallieni, *Lettres de Madagascar*, pp. 40–52, 125–140, 149–156.

56. Joseph Simon Gallieni, "Allocution," *Bulletin de la Société de géographie et d'études coloniales de Marseille* 39 (April–June 1905):139.

57. Gallieni, *Gallieni pacificateur*, pp. 247–255; idem, "Mesures à prendre pour favoriser l'accroissement de la population en Emyrne," *Revue scientifique* 24 (4 March 1899):261–269. The 1905 census estimated the population of Madagascar at 2,664,000.

58. Gallieni, *Madagascar de 1896 à 1905*, pp. 564, 739–740; F. Martin-Ginouvier, "Mise en valeur de notre empire colonial: Par le soldat laboureur marié faisant souche," *Questions coloniales* (Paris, 1898), vol. 2, no. 8; Gallieni, *Lettres de Madagascar*, pp. 86–87, 121.

59. Gallieni, *Lettres de Madagascar*, pp. 162–163, 169–193; idem, *Madagascar de 1896 à 1905*, pp. 739–740.

60. Thompson and Adloff, *Malagasy Republic*, p. 15.

61. Stephen Henry Roberts, *The History of French Colonial Policy, 1870–1925* (Hamden, 1963), pp. 390, 418.

62. Basil Henry Lidell Hart, *Reputations Ten Years After* (Boston, 1928), p. 76; Joseph Simon Gallieni, "Notes militaires," 3 vols., unpublished manuscript in the Gallieni family archives, quoted in Lyautey, *Gallieni*, pp. 206–208.

63. Henri Charbonnel, *De Madagascar à Verdun: Vingt ans à l'ombre de Gallieni* (Paris, 1962),p. 244; Gheusi, *Gallieni*, pp. 87–88. Joffre passed it off by stating that "protection was badly carried out, imprudence in maneuver led to surprises." See *The Personal Memoirs of Joffre*, trans T. Bentley Mott (New York, 1932), 1:33.

64. France, Ministère de la guerre, Etat-major de l'armée, Service historique, *Les Armées françaises dans la grande guerre* (Paris, 1922), 1, annexes 3:7–11; Joseph Simon Gallieni, *Mémoires du général Gallieni: Défense de Paris, 25 août–11 septembre 1914* (Paris, 1920), pp. 7–9; Emile Mayer, *Trois Maréchaux: Joffre, Gallieni, Foch* (Paris, 1928), pp. 69–70.

65. Adolphe Messimy, *Mes Souvenirs* (Paris, 1937), pp. 74–80; Charbonnel, *Madagascar à Verdun*, p. 243, states that General Edouard de Castelnau was Gallieni's first choice.

66. Alexandre Percin, *1914: Les erreurs du haut commandement* (Paris, 1919), p. 54; Morizet, *Le Plan 17*, pp. 55–57; Messimy, *Mes Souvenirs*, p. 78.

67. Liddell Hart, *Reputations*, p. 78.

68. Joseph Simon Gallieni, *Les carnets de Gallieni*, ed. Gaëtan Gallieni and Pierre B. Gheusi (Paris, 1932), pp. 17–19; Charbonnel, *Madagascar à Verdun*, pp. 246–247. On August 5, 1914, Gallieni wrote to General Weick, "Note that the Germans are making the maneuver that I studied last March," quoted in Marius-Ary Leblond, *Gallieni parle* (Paris, 1920), 1:25. Generals Gallieni, Lanrezac, and Ruffey criticized the conceptions of Joffre and Plan XVII but to no avail. Paul Pilant, "Août 1914: L'Armée française en face de l'armée allemande," *Les Archives de la grande guerre de l'histoire contemporaine* (Paris, 1926), 17:181.

69. Gallieni, *Carnets*, pp. 31–32; idem, *Mémoires*, pp. 11–12; Messimy, *Mes souvenirs*, p. 207; Joffre, *Personal Memoirs*, 1:134.

70. Gallieni, *Mémoires*, p. 65.

71. Liddell Hart, *Reputations*, p. 81.

72. Emile E. Herbillon, *Souvenirs d'un officier de liaison pendant la guerre mondiale* (Paris, 1930), 1:82. Two British military historians illustrate the extremes. Liddell Hart, *Reputations*, gives the credit to Gallieni, whereas Edward L. Spears, *Liaison, 1914: A Narrative of the Great Retreat* (Garden City, 1931), gives all the credit to Joffre.

73. Lallier du Coudray, quoted in Jean de Pierrefeu, *Nouveaux mensonges de Plutarque* (Paris, 1931), p. 32; Gallieni, *Carnets*, pp. 198–199, 201–202; Leblond, *Gallieni parle*, 1:58; Gallieni, *Mémoires*, p. 197.

74. Raymond Poincaré, *The Memoirs of Raymond Poincaré*, trans. Sir George Arthur (New York, 1926), 3:181–183, 197–198; Gallieni, *Carnets*, p. 188.

75. Leblond, *Gallieni parle*, 1:78–79, 2:57–58; Joseph Paul-Boncour, *Entre deux guerres: Souvenirs sur la IIIe République* (Paris, 1945), 1:253–254; Georges Suarez, *Briand: Sa Vie—son oeuvre* (Paris, 1939), 3:87–91; Gallieni, *Carnets*, pp. 148–149. The idea of a second front has been attributed to various individuals, but Lloyd George gave the credit to Gallieni. David Lloyd George, *War Memoirs of David Lloyd George* (Boston, 1933), 1:333–334.

76. Liddell Hart, *Reputations*, p. 35; Winston S. Churchill, *The World Crisis* (New York, 1923), 3:89–91; Gallieni, *Carnets*, pp. 235–239. See Jere C. King, *Generals and Politicians: Conflict between France's High Command, Parliament, and Government, 1914–1918* (Berkeley, 1951), pp. 89–95.

77. Charles Bugnet, *Rue St. Dominique et C.Q.G. ou les trois dictatures de la guerre* (Paris, 1937), p. 131.

78. Gallieni, *Carnets*, pp. 267–270; Edouard Charles Laval, *La maladie et la mort du général Gallieni* (Paris, 1920), pp. 33–34.

79. Gallieni, *Carnets*, pp. 277–278; Gabriel Terrail [Gabriel Mermeix], *Sarrail et les armées d'Orient* (Paris, 1920), pp. 231–246; King, *Generals and politicians*, pp. 103–106.

80. Henry Bordeaux, *Histoire d'une vie* (Paris, 1951–1963), 5:128–129.

81. Deschamps, "Introduction," pp. 20–21.

82. Lloyd George, *War Memoirs*, 2:6, 13; Churchill, *World Crisis*, 3:99; Gallieni, *Carnets*, p. 306, note.

Louis Gustave Binger (1856–1936)

Henri Brunschwig

THERE was no lucky star over Louis Gustave Binger when he was born at Strasbourg on October 14, 1856. His father's profession is unknown, and he died shortly afterward. His widowed mother, Salomé Hummel, settled in the little village of Niederbronn, where Louis Gustave was placed with a teacher who instructed the youngster along with his own son and two other students. Binger managed to complete the third class of the secondary school curriculum without attending a lycée, and when he was fifteen his mother apprenticed him to an ironmonger. The year was 1871, in which France was compelled to sue for peace and cede Alsace to the newly formed German Reich. Binger was still too young to choose his citizenship, but after a short stay at Pont-à-Mousson he decided in 1872 to remain a Frenchman. The following year he moved to France and took a job with an ironmonger at Sedan while waiting to join the French army.[1]

The Soldier

On his eighteenth birthday Binger signed on for five years with the Twentieth Battalion of the *chasseurs à pied* at Mézières. He made rapid progress; within two years, on July 28, 1876, he was promoted to sergeant major and in 1878 was sent to the Ecole des sous-officiers at Avord. He graduated ninth on the list of 167 noncommissioned officers and was commissioned to the *infanterie de marine* regiment at Toulon. His personnel report at Toulon, dated 1881, states: "conduct, good; general education, average; family background, obscure; military service,

109

satisfactory." Binger volunteered for service in a penal battalion at Senegal, a position little sought after in the army, and left for Dakar on January 19, 1882.[2]

Binger was a nobody—an impoverished subaltern who had never known the comfort of an affectionate family, friendship, religious faith, or a woman's love. His personnel file indicates that he was a Protestant; but neither biographical studies nor his own published works give the slightest evidence of religious belief. Some of his biographers suggest, without giving evidence, that he was a Jew. Constantly haunted by poverty—an orphan, an apprentice, a poorly educated, non-commissioned officer who tried his best without being recognized by his superiors—Binger was stimulated by the ideal shared at the time by Frenchmen of all social conditions: a deep love for his defeated country. Much later, when he had reached the age of seventy-five and was invited to sit at Lyautey's right hand at the inaugural banquet for the colonial exhibition at Vincennes (1931), Binger responded to a journalist's question, "I was an Alsatian. France welcomed me, and to prove my gratitude I tried to win for her a worthwhile slice of Africa."[3]

An Alsatian patriot, commissioned at the age of twenty-five and dreaming only of martial glory, might normally be expected slowly to rise by seniority to the rank of major, at best lieutenant colonel, before retiring. Or there was the Ecole de guerre and a brilliant career on the general staff. But to get there he would have to overcome two major obstacles: a second-rate education and a modest social background.

The mainspring of Binger's personality was his will to survive, his resolve to make his way into the elite—to direct his energy, his tenacity, his patience against the injustices of fate. In order to reach the top, he braved a tough apprenticeship and the harsh reality of military discipline to serve a greater good—patriotism. Binger, like Brazza, had opted for France. But the Corsican Brazza was wealthy, well educated, well connected, and noble-born; Binger had none of these advantages.

The Explorer

On his arrival in Senegal, Binger was ready to shoulder any risk and accept the most dangerous assignments. He volunteered for a post at the yellow fever ridden camp des Madeleines near Dakar. Again he volunteered for an expedition to Casamance (February–April 1882), and then for a topographical mission in Upper Senegal. On May 25, 1883, he advanced by seniority to the rank of full lieutenant. He returned to Toulon in May 1884 but departed in October with an expedition under Captain P.L. Monteil to map the area between the Senegal and Niger rivers and to study the route for a proposed railway from Kayes to Bamako. On his return in August 1885, Binger obtained a temporary appointment to the general staff. Together with Monteil he compiled the standard map of French settlements in the Senegal (published by Challamel in 1886).

During his long stay in Africa, Binger had taken a great interest in the indigenous people, especially the Bambara, and learned their language. He wrote a monograph on the subject and sent it to Faidherbe, now grand chancellor of the Legion of Honor, who published it under the title *Essai sur la langue Bambara*.[4] Faidherbe, working at the time on his book *Les Langues sénégalaises*, appointed the young lieutenant as his aide-de-camp (January 1886) and sent him on a "linguistic mission" to study Woloff (July–August 1886). Binger did not become a captain until 1888, but he had gained an academic reputation and the violet ribbon of the Palmes academiques conferred upon him by the ministry of public instruction.

The way now seemed open to a new profession. Binger had learned to approach the indigenous Africans not as a commandant, but as an ethnographer. Moreover, he had witnessed the rise of a new profession both in France and in Europe as a whole—the métier of an explorer. In 1886 the partition of Africa had begun. The scramble in turn introduced new legal concepts into international law. The ideas of "spheres of action" and "zones of influence" had long been rejected and were still unacceptable to the diplomats at the Berlin conference; but the 1886 Anglo-German and Anglo-French agreements of October 29 and November 1 regarding East Africa introduced them into international public law, and they were accepted in the Anglo-German and Anglo-French agreements of July 1 and August 5, 1890. The boundaries traced upon the map of Africa in turn presupposed exploratory work and treaties of commerce, friendship, or protectorate status signed by African rulers. The new breed of "explorers"—Paul Soleillet used the title on his visiting card—concluded such agreements as a matter of course, with or without the consent of their governments. The Quai d'Orsay was left free to ratify these accords.

There were many new explorers. Olivier Pastré de Sanderval, who had already advocated "peaceful conquest" in his book *De l'Atlantique au fleuve Niger par le Fouta-Djalon* (1882), strongly praised the new vocation in his study *Soudan français: Kahel* (1893). During the period 1880–1890 Bayol, Noirot, Monteil, and others all were seeking fame. They looked to the explorer's crown rather than martial glory, drawing their inspiration from Brazza's triumphal career, which had begun in 1880. The aspiring explorer usually left on his first journey unknown and almost alone. He faced unexpected dangers and risked his life daily. Either he foundered or he brought back to France a bundle of treaties and new scientific findings of value to humanity as a whole. Within a short time he was famous—the Legion of Honor, gold medals from geographical societies, receptions in the great hall of the Sorbonne, his name inscribed in gilt on leather-bound tomes—prizes given by lycées anxious to honor the energy and patriotism of the author, an expert and prophet journeying on the road that would benefit his country, science, and humane civilization. Brazza, now commissioner for French West Africa, had succeeded. Binger's ambition stirred.

Binger had studied the route of the projected railroad from Kayes to Bamako. Once this line was completed, there was the question of linking Sudan to the coast. From the Lambert mission sent out by Faidherbe in 1860 to the more recent journeys of Olivier Pastré de Sanderval and Bayol (1880–1881), the French had sought a connection by way of Fouta Djallon between the Rivières-du-Sud and the upper Niger. Binger's plan was more daring; he wanted to leave Bamako for Sikasso, Tingrela, and Kong, where he would explore the Mossi country before going on to Grand Bassam. Faidherbe backed the scheme. Arthur Verdier, the largest and most restless of the European merchants and settlers on Côte d'Or, was alerted to the project. Between 1878 and 1885 Verdier had served as French *résident*, and he still claimed this function after a brief tenure by Charles Bour as *commandant particulier*.[5] Verdier was living at La Rochelle and had delegated his power to agents. He met Binger in the office of Jean de La Porte, a French cabinet minister, and tried to modify the scheme so that the Côte d'Or would serve as point of departure. But the secret leaked out. Verdier promised his cooperation; his agent, Marcel Treich-Laplène, would start from the Côte and join Binger at Kong. Both would conclude treaties of friendship and protection along the way. Verdier offered "generous financial assistance" amounting to half the 20,000 francs to be allotted to Treich.[6]

Binger was taking an enormous risk. He was not sure he would return. In February 1888 there was even a rumor of his death. Before departing, however, he settled to the last detail the financial conditions of his assignment. He obtained 35,000 francs, half from the ministry of foreign affairs, and 17,500 francs from the "missions" account of the colonial budget, the latter to be spent before his departure on "barter goods and equipment." He was authorized to draw the funds from the ministry as a "personal subsidy" of 560 francs a month; his stay in Africa would last twenty-six months; and on his return he found 14,560 francs waiting for him. An order of February 15, 1887, authorized Binger to pursue during his entire journey the official functions of ordnance officer of the grand chancellor of the Legion of Honor. His military pay of 556 francs a month would continue to come from naval funds, bringing him an additional 14,456 francs.[7] If he ever saw France again, he would be rich.

He left Médine at the end of April 1887, the only European in a team of twenty-seven men. After July 8, having sold or distributed his barter goods, he was left with ten donkey drivers, a cook, a groom, and a personal servant; only the last two were armed with rifles.[8] I shall not summarize Binger's detailed reports concerning his ventures or assess his contribution to geography and other sciences. Suffice it to say that his expedition disproved the notion that the Sudanese heartland was isolated from easy access to the West African coast by a chain of high mountains paralleling the litoral, the mythical mountains of Kong—an important discovery from a strategic standpoint.

Binger's work made him one of the champions of modern colonization. As he saw it, France had to intervene in the loop of the Niger for the sake of establishing peace, that colonial peace which was indispensable for a colonial development (*mise en valeur*). Slave raiding prevented "the normal development of the population" and therefore had to be stopped. From the Gold Coast roads must be built and railroads constructed to open up the area's great supply of gold, wood, rubber, palm oil, pineapples, tobacco, indigo, and cotton and to export Mossi textiles and coffee from Liberia and from local plantations.

According to Binger, the *mise en valeur* could be brought about only under the auspices of a state that would abstain from meddling with minute administrative details of the incipient colonies.

> We believe that direct state intervention will always be bad. Before Frenchmen come to settle, the infant colony will be overloaded with administrative, judicial, prison, and military services, etc.; private initiative will no longer be able to set up a single trading post or wharf, build a road, or fell timber without meddling from government officials.
>
> The colony will be shackled; its development will be strangled by administrative regulations. Merchants will refuse to establish themselves in our colonies and will prefer to settle abroad under British or German protection.

This is not to say that there is no place for state intervention. But its proper object is to favor, by all possible means, the settlement of French citizens in the French colonies.

Why not entrust the development of the Côte d'Or to private companies or to individual concessionnaires, subject to specific guarantees?

The state will have everything to gain without a heavy drain on its budget; it will have a prosperous colony whose tax revenues will greatly exceed its expenditures.

There is no need to rely solely on large companies; the state can also accommodate new enterprises. In return for specific privileges, the state can require various forms of compensation; for example, the setting up of supply depots for food and coal, the construction of wharfs to facilitate the landing of men and supplies, the building of schools, the organization of postal services, assistance to our brave missionaries.

Above all, the state must not demand too much. Pioneer enterprise in these regions is often painful; the beginnings are apt to be followed by years of laborious gropings, fruitless experiments. . . .

The Côte d'Or is admirably suited to the concessions system; we have nine rivers, each of whose valleys, together with its corresponding coastline, could become a concession. . . .

Gradually each company would expand its territory inland, would create new trading posts with schools—civilization would thus advance like a wedge into the center of the Niger bend.

Missionary activity would parallel the work of trading companies. On the basis of common interests, it would be easy to reach a peaceful understanding with the indigenous people of the interior.[9]

The native policy put forward by Binger reflects notions current at the time. In his work *Esclavage, islamisme, et christianisme* (1891) and later in *Le Péril de l'islàm* (1906), Binger, relying on Faidherbe's authority, rebuked those who believed that black Islam was hostile to Christianity; he stressed the humane nature of slavery as practiced in African societies and preached tolerance. There was nothing original in these views. They had all been put forward by Verdier in his *35 Années de lutte aux colonies* (1896). Most contemporary explorers shared them. In his travel notebook, *Soudan français: Kahel*, Olivier Pastré de Sanderval had written:

It is said that the colonist should follow the customs official, the tax collector, and the subprefect, and in fact these worthies always precede the colonist, whenever they arrive in time. They lead, but no one follows; hence our colonies develop but slowly. A colony, more than any other community, certainly requires an organized authority that will protect infant enterprise against adventurers and even against itself. But there is no need for this authority to belong directly to the state; it should certainly not be accompanied from the start by the restrictions of a rigorous administration.[10]

And it was well known that the undersecretary of state for the colonies, Etienne, a most influential politician, favored the great companies—though in the absence of an enabling law he did not dare to establish them by decree.

In July 1888 Binger obtained his captaincy; he was made a chevalier of the Legion of Honor in March 1889. He had become a great Frenchman, renowned, sought after, admired. The four years between his return to France in May 1889 and his appointment as governor of the Ivory Coast in March 1893 are essential to understanding his personality. He was undoubtedly a great explorer. But to him was Africa a passion, a need, an ideal, as it was to Brazza? Was he impatient to return, now that he had found his vocation and the requisite authority for its exercise?

In September 1889 he resumed his functions as aide-de-camp to Faidherbe, who died two months later, and then to his successor, General Février. In 1890 Binger consolidated his personal fortune; his avarice again is surprising. At the end of his expedition he had convoyed five Africans from Grand Bassam to Gorée without spending the full sum provided for their needs. He asked what he could do to avoid returning the remainder of the money. Haussman, Etienne's cabinet head, replied on February 24.

Monsieur Deloncle has referred to me the letter in which you ask to be excused from repaying the 256.25 francs remaining from the 1,000 francs remitted to you by the treasurer at Grand Bassam. I regret to inform you that this is impossible. The money entrusted to you was a subsidy paid for the purpose of completing your mission. . . . The 1,000 francs were destined for a specific purpose, to meet the expense of your journey and that of the five Africans who accompanied you. We cannot pay you more than you have actually spent for this purpose [to do so would require a decree on the part of the president of the republic]. . . . Don't you agree, since we have justification on our side, that this would set in motion a very large undertaking for such a petty sum?[11]

Binger subsequently had recourse to expedients of a similar kind. In 1894 he was called to Paris from Vichy, where he was taking the baths, and asked to study administrative questions regarding the Ivory Coast. He put in a claim for a special reimbursement for the period from August 30 to October 20. The auditors found the length of his stay excessive, and Delcassé agreed to pay him 600 francs for a month. Binger, who was about to leave Marseilles for Africa, refused to sail unless he were immediately paid the money owed him. The head of the colonial service wired the ministry, who replied on October 24: "Pay." In the following year Binger was censured for having met the cost of his wife's passage from Marseilles to Grand Bassam from official funds, on the ground "that she had exceeded her free travel allowance."

He was paid well for the many expeditions that he led. On December 30, 1898, he was called to Senegal to delineate with the governor-general the boundaries between Senegal, Guinea, and Dahomey. In addition to travel expenses by land and sea, he received for this assignment a special allowance of 3,000 francs charged to the colonial budget—this for a tour of about a month. In January 1900 he was appointed French delegate to a London conference meeting in April to safeguard wild birds and fish; he insisted upon and was granted an allowance of 1,500 francs. He obtained 352.53 francs in 1902 for going to Bordeaux to receive the ashes of Governor Ballay, who had died at Saint-Louis.[12]

By now Binger had become a wealthy man. On July 12, 1890, he had married Noémie Lepret, whose father owned a "large and prosperous iron foundry." She brought him a dowry valued at 40,129 francs, with "the hope of inheriting later something between 800,000 and 900,000 francs."[13]

Verdier, after declining to glorify the career of an officer "who might one day rise to the highest ranks," offered Binger the presidency of a major concessionary company controlling more than 20 million hectares. He was acting on behalf of "a reputable and wealthy financial group" and commented that "Binger accepted the offer without objection, much to my surprise." Etienne, however, was unwilling to approve a charter as long as the legislature had not authorized the minister to sanction chartered companies. The matter rested there. After a few days, however, Binger called on Verdier to suggest that the two of them, and perhaps other capitalists, might "set up an exploratory company rather than a development corporation."[14] Verdier's evidence is perhaps suspect. But, as will be seen, Binger later sought to retire on pension in order to go into business; in 1907 he succeeded in becoming chairman of the Compagnie de l'Ouest africain français.[15]

It is certain that in 1891 Binger was wavering between several possible choices. He studied for the entrance examination of the Ecole de guerre, took it in September, but failed. Disappointed, he gladly accepted an offer to preside over the French boundary commission for the Côte d'Or. On October 24 he sailed for Africa and soon quarreled with Captain Lang, the head of the British mission. Negotiations were broken off in April 1892. Binger then traveled through the northern territories of the Ivory Coast, concluded a number of protectorate treaties, and returned to Paris in September.[16] In the meantime, General Février had placed him once more at the disposition of the navy and in December 1891 had recommended that he be promoted to battalion commander. But Binger failed to secure advancement because he lacked seniority.[17]

On his return to Paris, Binger was busy with his report on the work of the boundary commission. His future seemed uncertain. There were no prospects for him either in the army or in the world of chartered companies. He had prestige, however—the publication of the two-volume *Du Niger au golfe de Guinée* further added to his reputation—and had acquired wealth and connections. But he was at an impasse until Delcassé, the minister for the colonies, decided to reorganize the administration of French West Africa. A decree dated March 10, 1893, set up three separate colonies: Ivory Coast, Dahomey, and Guinea. Binger was offered the governorship of the Ivory Coast; on March 20 he was appointed governor third class and a week later he resigned his commission in the army.[18]

The Governor

On July 20, 1893, Binger left Bordeaux for the Ivory Coast to take up residence in the government house just completed at Grand Bassam, the capital. His new domain did not amount to much. The skeleton administration consisted of the *résident* (replaced by the governor), an administrator, a secretary, a treasurer, a physician, a teacher, some occasional interpreters, 200 African soldiers, and 10 policemen headed by a European commissioner.[19] Inland penetration had only just begun, but the customs posts set up from 1890 to 1893 at Grand Bassam, Assinie, Half Jack, and Lahou provided sufficient revenue to balance the budget.[20]

This tiny administrative establishment faced an enormously complex task. The modern republic of Ivory Coast, successor to Binger's colony, covers an area larger than Western Germany and the Benelux countries. Only a very small portion of this region was under French control when Binger arrived. Inland penetration was difficult. The country was ridden with sicknesses whose causes were still unknown—malaria, blackwater fever, and other tropical diseases.

From the geographical and ethnographical standpoint, the colony was immensely diverse. The Atlantic littoral was flanked by a coastal plain that stretched forty miles or so inland; in the interior the terrain rose gradually to the rain forests. Dense woods, with their lush tropical vegetation, ran from 50 to 200 miles north, broken only by river valleys and clearings; this forest belt contained all manner of valuable timber—mahogany, African teak, and other woods. Staple crops included oil palm, bananas, cassava, and yams. Precipitation decreased in the far interior until a traveler found himself in dense savanna country changing to dry bush toward the distant north.

Ethnically, the country was divided into some sixty different tribal groups. The western part of the forest belt contained Bandama people linked to the Kru of Liberia; they were subdivided into small patrilineal groups scattered through the forests. The eastern forest–savanna region was equally mixed: matrilineal communities famed for craftsmanship and agricultural skills were organized into small states including, among others, the Agni and the Baoulé. The most numerous savanna group was the Mande (Mandigo): Malinke farming communities lived by cultivating millet and keeping cattle; in the so-called Dioula (Dyula), a social more than an ethnic category, the natives made their living mainly from trade, traveling over great distances in search of profit. The Mande people had developed considerable skills as blacksmiths, potters, and artists working in wood and leather; many of them had been influenced by the islamic region, upon which they imposed their own peculiar stamp. They also achieved political prominence. One of their greatest warriors and state builders was Samory (*c.* 1830–1900), a leader who used Islam as an instrument of conquest. Samory appealed to the more mobile groups within Sudanic society—traders, wandering scholars and poets, men who had visited European settlements, as against the more traditional chiefs. He was an outstanding soldier and one of the most formidable local rulers encountered by the French. The northeastern region of the country contained a variety of Voltaic peoples, including the Senufo and other groups who lived widely scattered in small communities.

From the French administrator's standpoint, the country's ethnic diversity posed both advantages and disadvantages. There was no sense of cohesion. There was no concerted resistance to French penetration. Thus, there was no single powerful state that the French might have used as an intermediary to dominate the country. The colonial establishment headed by Binger had neither railroads nor modern ports. Workshops, repair facilities, hospitals, schools—the entire infrastructure of modern civilization had to be built from scratch.

Only a handful of Europeans—a few settlers, merchants and planters—had come to live in the country; the most active of these was Arthur Verdier, the merchant *résident* at La Rochelle who had supported Binger's expedition in 1887. Verdier was always eager to secure monopolies and privileges for the purpose of ousting his competitors. Of these, the most enterprising was an Englishman named Swanzy, who, like Verdier, owned a number of trading posts in the country, a flotilla of river steamers, and some coffee plantations. Some whites were also interested in timber; in 1890 Etienne had ratified agreements concluded by eight Europeans with indigenous chiefs on the subject of cutting mahogany.[21] Other entrepreneurs hoped to set up large-scale companies and never tired of submitting unacceptable requests to the ministry. One Monsieur de Beauchamps demanded in 1890 "the right to exploit for a period of fifty years the natural wealth of the territories placed under French protection between the left bank of the Niger and the French settlements on the Côte d'Or . . . with freedom to operate in the as yet unexplored regions beyond this perimeter."[22] Another, J. Montet, asked for "a commercial monopoly" within "the entire region from the French posts at the Côte d'Or, from the Tanoe river to the Liberian frontier"; if his request were not granted, he threatened "to settle abroad, with all the capital and goodwill that we still enjoy." Other companies quarreled over prospecting rights, firms such as the Société française de la Côte-d'Ivoire, supported by the Comte de Fels, the Compagnie Fraissinet, and Société Despagnat; in 1897 the two groups merged under the name Société civile française d'études et d'exploration des gisements aurifères de nos possessions d'Afrique occidentale.[23]

Verdier continued to step up his demands. On September 20, 1893, he succeeded in obtaining from Delcassé for his Compagnie de Kong a monopoly over the timber rights between Tanoe and Bandama for a period of thirty years, including customs privileges respecting imports for trading posts to be set up at Kong and Bettié. Binger supported the protests of Verdier's competitors. On September 4, 1895, the company had to be liquidated as it was unable to raise its required capital of 2 million francs.[24]

The new governor did not stay long in his fief. He arrived at the beginning of August 1893 and departed nine months later with his wife and their small daughter to take a three months' furlough. Physicians at the military hospital at Vichy examined him on July 27, 1894, and granted him "an additional sick leave of three months" on the ground that he had malaria, aggravated by congestion of the liver and the spleen, anemia, and dyspepsia. These ailments had been contracted on Binger's various campaigns in Senegal, in the Sudan, and the Ivory Coast; they required a lengthy and expensive treatment. The diagnosis did not prevent Binger from spending nearly three months in Paris (August 30 to October 20). He returned to the Ivory Coast in November 1894 to stay until September 1895. Again in Paris, he asked for convalescent leave, granted by a delgate of the Conseil supérieur de santé des colonies on the grounds of "congestion of the liver and endemic diarrhea" without specifying a time limit. At the end of the year he asked to be retired early for health reasons. The professors of Val-de-Grâce who examined him on October 29 diagnosed

> intestinal dyspepsia with frequent attacks of diarrhea. Diminution of the liver and slight enlargement of the spleen. General condition good but requires a period of regular and specific diet. According to information furnished by the patient and that available in his medical file, the patient's condition began several years ago. The patient took mineral water treatment at Vichy from 1894 to 1896. We therefore conclude that his condition does not appear to be incurable.

The physicians recommended that Binger stay in France for at least a year.

Binger, now forty years old, on November 30, 1895, had been promoted to the rank of governeur de 2e classe. From March 1893 to June 1897 he had spent no more than nineteen out of fifty months in Africa.[25] His unwillingness to live on the Ivory Coast did not prevent him from effectively governing the colony but seems to indicate that he was no longer passionately dedicated to the vocation of explorer or frontiersman.

Like all new governors of French West Africa, Binger was concerned principally with running affairs in his own fashion. He preferred to deal with a problem, or a regulation, or a tax, in a manner that would differ from the pattern adopted by his neighbors. The Garde indigène of Ivory Coast was reorganized by an *arrêté* dated October 29, 1894; the force had its own hierarchy, its own salary scale, and its own uniform. The "interpreters' corps" set up in July 1898 had a pay scale much lower than those of neighboring territories. Concessionary regulations differed widely from those in the remainder of French West Africa. On his return to Paris, Binger protested against the establishment of a government-general for the whole of French West Africa (by decree of June 16, 1895)—the first attempt at political integration of the entire region. In the following year another decree (September 25, 1896) separated the Ivory Coast; its governor thenceforth corresponded directly with the ministry, required only to forward copies of his reports to the governor-general.

The first problem calling for the attention of Binger and that of his colleagues concerned land and mining concessions. In 1894, for example, Lieutenant governor Cerisier of Guinea republished his regulation of January 18, 1890, which "while awaiting instructions requested from the department," provided for "temporary permits" of a year in the Tumbo (Conakry) peninsula. He specified in article 10 that "the regulation is solely temporary and will be supplemented by permanent regulations . . . now being studied."[26] At Dahomey, Jean Bayol, lieutenant governor of the Rivières-du-Sud, similarly countersigned a regulation issued on February 18, 1890, by Victor Ballot, *résident* of Porto-Novo, stating that the local government would receive applications for provisional concessions; the relevant documents "will then be transmitted to the proper undersecretary of state for the colonies to determine their acceptance or rejection."[27]

Binger did not bother with such formalities. He drew up his own regulation during the four months he spent in Paris before returning to the Ivory Coast and submitted the draft to Delcassé. The latter replied on June 21, 1894, that on the whole he had no objection but added that "I cannot as yet sanction your scheme in its present form and I cannot permit you to put into effect a measure that does not fall within your functions. Once experience has proven the value of the proposed regulation, I reserve the right of approving the final version that you will then submit to me."[28]

Binger took immediate action on surveying the settlements. Without waiting for approval by the minister, he encouraged development of all commercial, mineral, forestry, and agricultural resources within his colony. Article 7 of the Arrêté concernant les diverses concessions à la Côte d'Ivoire, published a few days after his arrival in the colony, announced: "The governor will have final decision regarding the guidelines according to which concessions will be granted or rejected, as well as on the extent of their territories."

Permanent land concessions for trading posts and other structures were immediately granted free of charge. Renewable forest concessions for the purpose of felling mahogany were accorded for a year, their size ranging from 10,000 to 100,000 hectares, at a cost of ten centimes a hectare. Cleared lands were granted for agricultural development at half a franc a hectare, and the cost was even lower for livestock farms. Mineral research permits on parcels of 10,000 to 100,000 hectares cost 10 centimes per hectare. If the venture succeeded, developers could apply for annual concessions of 5,000 to 10,000 hectares at three francs per hectare.[29]

Binger's legislation was on the statute book well before ministerial commissions had examined the matter in Paris; the commission on mines did not complete its work until 1899, and that on land in 1904. His regulations reflected the philosophy of a professed champion of "modern colonization." Binger and his friends, however, miscalculated; few capitalists came forward to take advantage of the proffered opportunities.[30] Reasonably exact statistics are available only from the date concessions were officially registered in the *Journal officiel de la Côte-d'Ivoire*, started in January 1895. In 1896 and 1897 fifty-six small-scale concessions were granted (private dwellings, shops, trading posts, a mechanical sawmill, and two kilns); twenty-six of these went to Africans, one to a Catholic mission, and seven to agricultural enterprises ranging in size from 20 to 1,000 hectares. The concessionnaires were mostly firms already operating in the Ivory Coast at the time. Newcomers were concerned mainly with mineral prospecting. Eleven annual permits, most of them 10,000 hectares in size, were delivered or renewed. Forestry concessions, other than the eight granted to indigenous chiefs and ratified by Etienne in 1890, were not in demand until 1906.[31]

While Binger was away, decisions were made by Pascal and Couturier, his secretaries-general (1894 and 1895), and by Eugène Bertin and Louis Mouttet, acting governors (1896 and 1897). Binger was interested primarily in commercial development and in occupation of the coastline up to Cavally; thus, he extended the existing chain of customs posts, providing the colony with needed financial resources. Inland penetration was a matter for military expeditions organized by the ministry. Captain Marchand intervened in the Baoulé country by way of Bandama, and clashed with Samory. Contrary to his principle of peaceful penetration, Binger yielded to the requests of Delcassé, who dispatched a column under Colonel Monteil into the Kong region. This action reflected badly on Binger's authority within the colony, and commerce suffered. Monteil's reverse did not displease the governor. Yves Person, who studied the military details of these operations,[32] concluded that they contributed to Binger's lack of enthusiasm for returning to the Ivory Coast after September 1895.

During this period of his life the famous explorer was decidedly more interested in economic development than in the exploration of unknown country. The onetime "bush basher" who had learned the Bambara tongue in the Sudan had lost his zeal; Binger had grown wary of the bush—he was to live to be an octogenarian, yet he constantly worried about his health. But competition between major capitalists like Fraissinet and the Comte de Fels, both sponsored by the Prince d'Ahremberg, led him to dream of future financial prospects. He might retire at the age of forty, work for a private consortium, where his prestige, his African experience, and his associates could help him to stake out yet a third career. After the patriotic soldier and explorer, why not the promoter of a new El Dorado?

The Diplomat

In 1896 Binger had a stroke of good fortune. Guyesse, minister for the colonies and not one of his friends, fell from office and was replaced by André Lebon (April 1896–June 1898). Binger asked to be retired on pension, but his request was not granted.

> Because of your state of health, you have asked to apply for retirement on pension.
>
> I have the honor to inform you that the army medical officers at the Place de Paris, in accordance with orders dated 2 July 1831 and 26 January 1832, respectively, have examined you several times; they consider that the disabilities from which you suffer are not incurable.
>
> It is therefore not possible to grant you retirement on pension under present circumstances.

But it was possible to stay in Paris, and Binger did not want to go back to the Ivory Coast. The *Direction des Affaires politiques au Ministère des Colonies*, set up on March 20, 1894, had been separated in July from the *cabinet du ministre* and placed under Ernest Roume. Lebon divided the department into two sections, *Affaires d'Afrique* and *Affaires d'Asie Amérique et Océanie* (May 23, 1896). On June 18 he signed the decree naming Binger to African affairs and wrote him, in a personal letter dated September 17,

> I have the pleasure to inform you that, by an *arrêté* dated 11 September, I have set your salary at 14,000 francs a year. Your remuneration will be paid from the account established under section 1 of the colonial budget; it will become effective from 27 August 1897, the date on which the *Journal officiel de la République* will publish the *décret* appointing you *Directeur des Affaires d'Afrique au Ministère des Colonies.*

The pay of a governor second class in Europe amounted to 12,500 francs. The two colonial ministers who succeeded Guyesse, Antoine Guillain and Albert Decrais, successively raised Binger's salary to 15,000 francs (October 1899) and to 16,000 francs (December 1899).[33]

Binger thus was promoted to a central position from which he kept in touch with everything relating to Africa, including matters that concerned other departments or technical services. He was hardly required to intervene in running the colonies. The centralization of French West Africa proceeded under the auspices of Ernest Roume; land and mining concessions were regulated in 1896, 1899, and 1904 by commissions attached to the *Directions des Affaires économiques* and the *Services des Travaux Publiques*. He was not directly concerned with military operations such as the expedition against Rabah (1900) or with investigations like the inquiry handled by Brazza in the Congo in 1905. Binger's role was that of a staunch lieutenant. He was a "brilliant second," supplying the minister with information rather than advice on final decisions, writing few dispatches and official letters, but aware of everything and in touch with all who counted within his field.

The director's job was essentially diplomatic. During the decade in which Binger held office, France was run by ten ministerial cabinets under seven different colonial ministers. Senior civil servants like himself provided the administration with an element of continuity that it otherwise would have lacked. His job was exacting. He left Paris eight times on official trips, three of them of negligible importance: a conference in London on the protection of wild animals in Africa (1900), a second to Bordeaux to receive Ballay's ashes (1902), a third to negotiate financial compensation due British merchants in the Congo (1906). And there was fieldwork to protect French interests during the last stages of the partition of Africa. France had no greater expert on West Africa than Binger, and his government justly appreciated the mixture of subtlety and tenacity that he displayed during the course of these negotiations.

In 1897 he was appointed French delegate to the Franco-German boundary commission to define the limits of Dahomey, Sudan, and Togo; a convention was concluded on July 23, 1897. He then took part in the Franco-British boundary commission appointed to determine the eastern and western borders of Niger; a convention was signed on June 14, 1898. Later he left for a secret mission to Senegal during the political tension engendered by the Fashoda affair. In 1905 and 1906 Binger was sent to London to establish the frontier of Niger at Lake Chad and conclude an agreement on May 29, 1906. He finally took part in the Franco-Liberian boundary commission whose work resulted in the treaty of September 18, 1907.

Whether Binger was a diplomat would be a good subject for a historian interested in perusing the files concerning the partition of Africa, from the failure of negotiations with Lang in 1892 to the successes attained between 1897 and 1907. A scholar would have to study Binger's methods and assess the degree of initiative allowed by the government to the man on the spot in order to carry out its instructions. That margin of action was narrow. Final decision rested with the ministry of foreign affairs. Their delegates in the field resolved the relevant geographical, economic, and ethnographic problems. However well Binger accomplished his task, it seems that it did not inspire in him a more passionate interest than most of his preceding work.

What was it, then, that motivated this great Frenchman, now in his fifties, a man covered with glory that none dared to dispute? A curious document, a handwritten note, survives in the Binger file in the *Direction du Personnel et de la Comptabilité du Ministère des Colonies*; the note, anonymous and undated, makes mistakes as to details of Binger's career, yet it may provide the answer:

> Monsieur Binger, colonial governor second class on special assignment, has asked the minister to be placed on retirement pension in order to enter private industry.
>
> Monsieur Binger's long and brilliant career makes it incumbent on the government to provide him with a reward upon leaving the administration that will suitably acknowledge his excellent work.
>
> Monsieur Binger, born in Strasbourg on 14 October 1856, entered the army as a private soldier in 1874. In 1876 he was promoted to sergeant. Sublieutenant in 1880, lieutenant in 1882, captain in 1888 and as such appointed ordnance officer to the grand chancellor of the Legion of Honor, chevalier of the Legion of Honor. . . .

After numerous expeditions and military campaigns in Senegal and the Sudan from 1882 to 1889, he accomplished his remarkable mission to the Ivory Coast (1891–1892), which resulted in giving France a new and wealthy colony. Monsieur Binger accomplished this mission with the most scanty means and without firing a single shot.

The government then recognized Monsieur Binger's services by naming him to be an officer of the Legion of Honor (1892) and governor of the colony that he had set up (1893).

In service in the French Ivory Coast (1896) (he resigned from the army in 1893), on 18 June 1897 he was appointed *Directeur d'Afrique* at the ministry of colonies. A decree dated 17 June 1897 promoted him to the rank of *commander* of the Legion of Honor.

Monsieur Binger continued his brilliant public service at the ministry of colonies, bringing to that department and to its successive ministers the benefit of his vast experience, his common sense, and his faultless knowledge of African affairs.

At a time when Monsieur Binger leaves the public service in order to take up the pension to which he is entitled, the ministry of colonies considers that the government should award to this high official the cross of grand officer of the Legion of Honor.

Binger thus achieved what he had failed to secure in 1896. On October 10, 1897, he was awarded "the pension to which he [was] entitled." A few months later he was promoted to the rank of commander of the Legion of Honor. He was now able to enter private industry.

The Businessman

Binger was only fifty-one years old; he died at the age of eighty in 1936. How did he occupy his time during the remaining thirty years of his life? Despite a good deal of research, his family papers have not been found. Some documentary evidence discovered by chance during an investigation of African mining concessions and a few notes from the dossier at the *Service du Personnel et de la Comptabilité* lead to an assumption.

The regulations of 1899 regarding mineral prospecting and development encouraged speculation in gold mines. The number of applications for exploration permits rose rapidly from 1902 and 1903; those for prospecting substantially increased from 1907 and 1908. Hardly had the applicants obtained their permits than they formed companies and sold shares to the public. Speculation was rampant. The ministry, alarmed, lacked information and called for additional data. Governor-general Roume felt that the facts concerning these various societies in the official gazettes of the different colonies were inadequate; he insisted that material concerning these companies must be published in the *Journal officiel de la République française* as of February 15, 1904. The firms were obliged to provide full details relating to the "number of concessionnaires in possession of valid prospecting, research, and working licenses, the number of enterprises that had actually started development, and, finally, the amount of gold exported." From then on, lists of applicants were periodically sent to the ministry, which conducted inquiries in France before granting permits.

One of these lists, signed on September 4, 1908 by the acting governor-General Liotard, contains the name "L. Binger." On November 12 the director of public works stated that "it appears pointless for me to request information regarding Monsieur Binger, honorary governor of the colonies, whose name and reputation are sufficiently well known." Governor-general Ponty replied on December 11 that he had been unaware that Binger, the applicant, and Binger, the ex-governor-general, were one and the same person.

Binger, in fact, had financial interests in West Africa. The *Relevé des sociétés créées en vue de l'exploitation des mines d'or de l'A.O.F. en juin 1908* lists the Compagnie de l'Ouest africain français with a capital of 3 million francs; the company had issued 30,000 hundred-franc shares as well as 40,000 founders' shares, registered at the Paris Bourse on December 21, 1907. The founders were granted special privileges in their capacity as grantees of government permits. The board of directors consisted of Binger, honorary governor-general of the colonies, L. Voirin, engineer and chairman of the Banque coloniale française, J. B. Richard, engineer, E. Henry and G. Ardiller, both landowners, and G. Roux, mining and consulting engineer.

A "note on the inspection work carried out by the public works department of French West Africa with respect to the Compagnie de l'Ouest africain français (Côte d'Ivoire)" outlines the history of the firm. It had taken over the Akrizi mine —inefficiently worked by J. B. Richard—and also held five other permits; the note stated that further development work was in progress. During the first quarter of 1908 the company had managed to extract 2 kilos, 355 grams, of gold. Engineer Jordan, however, had doubts regarding the operation's profitability. Between January and June the company's shares rose from 325 to 532 francs for each 100-franc certificate issued in December; the founders' shares rose from 132 to 271 francs at a time when shares issued by most other companies were declining in value.[34]

Did Binger's name contribute to this temporary success? Perhaps his continuing fear of poverty derived from financial misfortunes rather than from his habitual parsimony. Between the two world wars salaries and pensions in the French army and administration did not keep pace with the rising cost of living; like many of his colleagues, Binger therefore may have experienced unforeseen difficulties. In 1932 the Val-de-Grâce hospital at Bordeaux requested that the ministry of colonies reimburse hospital authorities for a bill for five days in hospital, at thirty-one francs a day, incurred by the governor-general. The ministry replied that Binger, in his capacity as a retired governor second class of the colonies on special assignment, "should pay his own expenses" and supplied his address. On July 17, 1931, Paul Reynaud, the minister, informed Binger that he had been granted a special annual allowance of 14,500 francs payable from the Ivory Coast budget. "I am happy to inform you," the minister added, "that the colony thereby acknowledges the eminent services that you have rendered to it." Binger complained on April 20, 1936, that he had not as yet received anything. He was paid on April 23.

The ministry did not reply to his request that in the event of his death his widow should continue to receive his allowance. By that time Binger was living in l'Isle-Adam. On September 7, 1936, he was admitted for sciatica and a disease of the liver to the Val-de-Grâce hospital as a fee-paying patient.[35] He died on November 11, 1936.

Conclusion

In undertaking this study, I thought to find in Binger the man who—in the course of his career—successively embodied the various types of colonial administrators at work in French black Africa between 1871 and 1914. He was an army officer like Brière de L'Isle or de Trentinian, seeking to assure military expansion and a restoration of prestige for *la Patrie* humiliated by the defeat of 1871; he was an explorer passionately committed like Brazza to geographical discovery and to the peaceful spread of a humane civilization superior to any founded upon war, slavery, and ignorance; he was an organizer like Roume or Ponty, resolved to set up in anarchic Africa great bureaucratic structures that would link complementary regions into larger entities.

These concepts were certainly not alien to a man who served as soldier, explorer, governor, and *Directeur des Affaires de l'Afrique*. But Binger does not seem to have been deeply committed to any of his successive assignments. The soldier did not like war. The explorer, eager to profit from the risks that he took, did not try to continue his work of discovery in a continent as yet largely unknown. The governor, though determined to assert his authority, preferred to run his colony from Paris. The *Directeur des Affaires d'Afrique* maintained those rights that his government had won during the course of negotiations in which Binger himself had not taken part; but in his capacity as a senior public servant he failed to link his name to any particular aspect of imperialist policy. These various personae who had worked in Africa had but one ideal in common—a visceral nationalism common to most Frenchmen at the time.

To understand the secret man on guard behind the roles he so perfectly played, we have to leave the stage and consider the psychology of the actor. We then expose a deprived adolescent threatened by numerous economic and social handicaps; a brave and tenacious fighter who did not shy away from any effort. Binger rose in life; he passed from one role to another; he acquired a new post and went on to the next. At a time when money rather than birth or knowledge meant power, he dreamt of becoming one of the great capitalists of his time. Within the French administration, Binger was an exceptional character. In retrospect, he ranks as one of those self-made men ever more dominated by the lust for power, like Rastignac, a figure who might have stepped out from the pages of Balzac.

Notes on Sources

Career. Biographical information on Binger is scattered. There are two personal dossiers: the military dossier bears the number 1235 (always cited); that concerning his career as a colonial official is identified as "ANSOM Personnel Binger."

The Missions des ANSOM series contains a large box of administrative correspondence, here identified as "ANSOM Missions 12."

Binger Publications.   Published works by Binger, apart from a few brief prefaces and short articles are listed herein.

"Considérations sur la priorité des découvertes maritimes sur la côte occidentale d'Afrique aux quatorzième et quinzième siècles." *Bulletin du Comité de l'Afrique française*. Paris, n.d.

Essai sur la langue bambara parlée dans le Kaarta et dans le Bélédougou, suivi d'un vocabulaire. Paris, 1886.

"Transactions, objets de commerce, monnaies des contrées d'entre le Niger et la Côte d'Or." Paper presented at the conference of the Société de géographie commerciale de Paris, 26 January 1890. *Notes d'information et statistiques* 179 (December 1970), Banque centrale des états de l'Afrique de l'Ouest.

Esclavage, islamisme, et christianisme. Paris, 1891.

Du Niger au golfe de Guinée par le pays de Kong et le Mossi, 1887–1889. 2 vols. Paris, 1892.

"La Côte-d'Ivoire (son passé, son présent, son avenir). Conférence." *Bulletin de la Société de géographie de Marseille* 19 (1895):380–399.

Le Péril de l'islàm. Paris, 1906.

Notes

Abbreviations used:
AN   Archives nationales
ANSOM   Archives nationales, Section outre-mer

1. Michel Elbaz, "Quelques Notes sur l'origine de l'exploration de Louis Gustave Binger" (handwritten manuscript, Université de Paris, Centre d'études africaines).

2. AN, Ministère des armées, Troupes de la marine, personnel dossier 1235.

3. L. G. Binger, *Une vie d'explorateur, carnets de route* (Paris, 1938), preface.

4. L. G. Binger, *Essai sur la langue bambara parlée dans le Kaarta et dans le Bélédougou, suivi d'un vocabulaire* (Paris, 1886).

5. Paul Atger, *La France en Côte-d'Ivoire de 1843 à 1893: Cinquante ans d'hésitations politiques et commerciales* (Dakar, 1962), pp. 109 ff.

6. ANSOM Missions 12, 31 July 1888; Arthur Verdier, *35 Années de lutte aux colonies: Côte occidentale d'Afrique* (Paris, 1896), pp. 173–178.

7. ANSOM Missions 12, 5–15 February 1887, 26 April–7 June 1890, "Le Sous-secrétaire d'état au président de la Cour des comptes."

8. L. G. Binger, *Du Niger au golfe de Guinée par le pays de Kong et le Mossi, 1887–1889*, 2 vols. (Paris, 1892), 1:29.

9. Ibid., 2:347.

10. Aimé Olivier Pastré de Sanderval, *Soudan français: Kahel* (Paris, 1893), pp. 417–418.

11. ANSOM Missions 12, 11 and 24 February 1890.

12. Ibid., Ministère des colonies, Direction du personnel et de la comptabilité, minister's report, 27 December 1898, on the congress of London; memorandum from J. Decrais, 25 April 1900; memorandum from Binger, May 1900.

13. AN dossier 1,235.

14. Verdier, *35 années de lutte*, pp. 246, 249.

15. Binger, *Une Vie d'explorateur*, p. 185.

16. Yves Peson, *Samori: Une Révolution Dyula* (Dakar, 1975); 3:1644–1646.

17. AN dossier 1,235.

18. ANSOM Personnel Binger.

19. Atger, *La France en Côte-d'Ivoire*, pp. 133–134; ANSOM, Côte-d'Ivoire, 11a; *Journal officiel de la Côte d'Ivoire* 1 (January 1895).

20. Atger, *La France en Côte d'Ivoire*, pp. 138–150.

21. Ibid., pp. 162–163.

22. ANSOM, Soudan, 15, 4.

23. ANSOM, Côte d'Ivoire, 15, 5, 8.

24. Verdier, *35 Années de lutte*, pp. 344–347, 353.

25. ANSOM Personnel Binger, passim.

26. ANSOM, Guinée, 15, 1; *Bulletin officiel administratif de la Guinée française, 1894*, p.80.

27. *Journal officiel des établissements et protectorats français du golfe du Bénin*, 1 March 1890.

28. ANSOM, Côte d'Ivoire, 15, 1b.

29. Ibid., 15, 7.

30. Ibid., 15, 8.

31. *Journal officiel de la Côte d'Ivoire* for 1895–1898.

32. Person, *Samori*, 3:1646–1684.

33. ANSOM Personnel Binger, 14 November 1896. Cf. ibid., the request of Binger to Lebon of 11 September 1896, his nomination to the Direction d'Afrique, the list of his missions, and his retirement in 1907.

34. ANSOM Travaux publiques, 149, dossiers 12, 14, 19, 21.

35. ANSOM Personnel Binger.

William Ponty and Republican Paternalism in French West Africa (1866–1915)

G. Wesley Johnson

L'Afrique fut sa grande passion, elle fut sa raison de vivre, il lui a tout donné, il lui a consacreé toutes les années de sa vie d'homme.

Governor Raphaël Antonetti, *Journal officiel de l'Afrique occidentale français*, 19 June 1915, p. 424.

WILLIAM Ponty was the illustrious governor of France's largest overseas colonial possession, French West Africa, from 1908 to 1915. Ponty was popular in his own day but has been neglected by historians in favor of early conquerors such as Gallieni and Archinard or later governors such as Van Vollenhoven. I propose to look at the career of Ponty and his achievements and innovations in colonial policy and administration and to suggest that Ponty was probably the strongest and most influential governor-general who ruled French West Africa during its brief life from 1895 to 1960. This claim is based upon his activity in the following areas: ending both the traffic in slaves and domestic slavery; creating the native provident societies; defining for the first time a coherent French native policy (*politique de races*); clarifying an Islamic policy; bringing pensions and benefits to African functionaries; favoring land for African

127

use through a homestead land policy; and setting in motion the celebrated *armée noire*, the African troops who participated in World War I. In addition, Ponty created and defined the office he held as a standard for future governors.

Part of Ponty's success rested on the fact that he was a link between the military conquest and the establishment of civilian rule. He became a true proconsul of empire, a governor who could rule most of the time with little interference from the ministry of colonies. That such a strong-willed man of action was mourned by his African subjects when he died and that he inspired admiration and respect from foe and friend alike becomes less remarkable upon examination of Ponty's basic philosophy of colonialism. For Ponty was the high apostle of what I shall call republican paternalism, a blending of egalitarian concepts based upon the "rights of man" with a code of noblesse oblige. This was a reflection of nineteenth-century bourgeois France, often expressed as the *mission civilisatrice*. Ponty held humane and optimistic views for his day, believing in human progress in an era of scientific racism and giving his African subjects a basic respect that sets him apart from most early governors. At times Ponty seemed to anticipate the liberal era of the 1950s and decolonization, and at the end of his career there are hints of disillusion with the imperial task. But the daily record shows him an unabashed imperialist, proud of his vocation, strictly professional to the end (probably more so than the widely heralded Van Vollenhoven); it is this dualism—proconsul-conqueror, on the one hand, humane paternalist, on the other—that makes Ponty a fascinating study and also sheds new light on how French colonialism worked in the field. In Ponty we have a man who believed the republican ideal and dedicated his life to carrying it out.

Like Léon Faidherbe, Ponty had a keen insight into the mentality and *âme* of his African subjects—a sensitivity and compassion rare in hard-bitten colonial circles. He liked the sobriquet *vieil Africain* that he bore in later years. It was a recognition of twenty-five years of almost uninterrupted service in West Africa as a most distinguished expatriate of his time, a man of two continents. Unlike Faidherbe and Gallieni, Ponty did not write books. He was a literate man whose speeches show us his fire and compassion; but to recapture the career of Ponty the historian must use official documents and archival records. No known family or personal documents survive. Much can be learned from comments of others (both French and African), from Ponty's terse marginal notes in the archives and his reports to Paris, and especially from newspapers written by African elites. Ponty was also the subject of a thinly veiled biographical novel by Robert Arnaud, his former adviser on Islamic affairs, which is suggestive of his character and motivations.[1] Comparatively little is known about his family background and personal life.

One purpose of this essay is to suggest some points of departure, questions, and problems for a future biographer. Since Ponty's career was so intertwined with French West Africa, however, a full portrait will probably have to await a comprehensive administrative history of that colony. Moreover, I have sought to examine Ponty on his own ground—that of an imperialist of his time—rather than looking at him from the nationalist perspective of today. One has the impression that Ponty—like Faidherbe, Delafosse, and Delavignette—may weather the test of time and be remembered in African nations as a humane ruler of empire.

Early Career

Little is known about the early years of Ponty beyond the fact that he was born Amédée William Merlaud-Ponty into a middle-class family on February 4, 1866 in Rochefort-sur-Mer, in southwestern France. By the time he received his law degree at the age of twenty-two, he had opted for using his middle name and the second part of his hyphenated name—hence William Ponty. Ponty obtained an internship (*commis expéditionnaire stagiaire*) at the central administrative offices of the colonial section of the marine ministry in 1888. The earliest note on Ponty in his personnel file mentions that his first year's performance was satisfactory but cautions "he is perhaps a bit too self-satisfied." Whereas this trait appeared as a potential flaw to his examiner, it indicates a quality—great confidence in himself—that became the hallmark of Ponty as an administrator and the keystone of his success and effectiveness as governor-general for seven years. The young intern settled in slowly to his life's work: in 1889 he was criticized for having "too many absences, primarily to visit his family at home."[2]

The next year, Ponty—who did not attend the new Ecole coloniale—was abruptly torn away from family and internship and assigned as an aide to Colonel Louis Archinard in the Sudan campaigns in what was to become French West Africa. Archinard needed a secretary in the field and young Ponty needed field experience and a protector to advance his colonial career.

Arriving in Sudan (then called the Haut-Fleuve region) at the headwaters of the Senegal and Niger rivers, Ponty was quickly exposed to a series of campaigns for the conquest and "pacification" of Africans in a populous and ethnically diverse area. As one of the first professional colonial administrators, he was part of the last days of the military operation in West Africa, and throughout his career there is ample evidence of Ponty's affinity for the military.[3] This new part of France's West African dominions had become a separate political entity in embryo in 1880, with a commander who in theory was subordinate to the governor of Senegal but who in fact commanded with autonomy. A governmental shell, therefore, had existed in this area for a decade before Ponty's arrival, but African resistance from such tenacious leaders as Samory Touré had kept the nascent colony in a continual state of alert. Colonel Archinard had succeeded to the title of superior commandant after his first tour, 1880–1890, when he had taken over from General Gallieni; it was in preparation for his second tour, 1890–1893, that Archinard recruited young Ponty to serve with him in the Sudan. It was Archinard who finally conquered the once potent Tukulor empire of Ahmadou, the son of El-Hadj Omar Tall. Maurice Delafosse later credited Archinard as being the true creator of the French Sudan.[4]

Archinard was seconded in his projects of conquest and pacification by Eugène Etienne, then serving as undersecretary of state for the colonies; moreover, in 1890 the French public was more favorable to further expansion than it had been in the 1880s. Archinard therefore decided to attack Ségou and strike a blow at the hegemony of Ahmadou; he was also charged with the continuing campaigns against Samory. Ponty received a baptism by fire, serving in seventeen battles against Samory's forces alone; he was wounded at the battle of Ouassako and received his first advancement into the Legion of Honor in 1893.[5] During more than three years Ponty participated in a myriad of battles in Upper Guinea against Samory's forces. He was involved in the assault against Kouroussa and later wrote of his job at the side of Archinard: "In November of 1892, Archinard dictated while I wrote the instructions for Captain Briquelot to move immediately toward Benty, to stop the march of our English rivals, and to create a commercial route." Ponty helped formulate Archinard's strategy of building a railroad from the interior to Conakry and hence the creation of French Guinea as a viable colony. Twenty years later at the dedication of this railroad, when Ponty was governor-general, Governor Camille Guy lauded him on having "the good fortune, which is unique and personal to you, to have brought this project to completion."[6] Not only was Ponty lucky, but he seemed repeatedly to be in the right place at the right time. His coolness under fire won him the admiration of Archinard, who found it easy to recommend Ponty for promotions. He also won the confidence of Archinard's temporary replacement, Lieutenant colonel Humbert, who wrote: "Model secretary, very devoted, full of zeal, conscientious worker, indefatigable. Great deal of moral valor. Has never been sick. . . . Is tactful, and as a result, is well liked by all of the officers of the column. In battle he is cool under fire."[7]

Ponty's experiences in the final days of the conquest gave him a perspective that most colonial officers who followed him lacked. In fact, Ponty uniquely bridged the military and colonial worlds. After he became governor-general in 1908, Ponty lamented that so many of his early comrades at arms were no more or were no longer in Africa; most other colonial officials who moved up the ranks in the late 1890s had not participated in the conquest. Ponty knew Gallieni, Archinard, de Trentinian, Ballay, Bonnier, and other famous figures of the conquest because he was there. No other colonial official of such high rank knew equally well the two worlds of conquest and colonization.

In 1894, as a hardened military veteran of western Sudanic campaigns, Ponty was rewarded for his field performance by being appointed chief of the secretariat of the colony of Senegal. This brought him away from more intensive military experience to the world of the bureaucracy in Saint-Louis, which was then the capital of France's black African colonies. Ponty was on duty when the new post of governor-general was created in 1895 as the French colonial establishment tried to bring order and system to these vast new possessions beyond the traditional borders of Senegal. He had been recommended by Archinard, who saw important things in the future for his protégé: "I think that, with perseverance, someday [Ponty] will gain an important post. I have full confidence in his future. . . . [H]e knows that you must work to gain something honorable in life. . . . [He] is resolute and intelligent." Archinard, however, had to explain his glowing recommendation since the earlier notes on Ponty had painted him as a somewhat capricious young man given to frivolity. But now Ponty was firmly launched on his move up the administrative ladder, and the next year—in 1896—he accepted a transfer to the colony of Madagascar as an administrator first class.

In the Indian Ocean colony Ponty served under General Gallieni, who had first carved out his reputation in the French Sudan. Gallieni took an interest in him and reported to Paris that he showed outstanding leadership in his management of Mananjary province, where there had been a marked increase of colonial activity.[8] But Sudanic Africa was in Ponty's heart and the next year he requested a transfer back to French West Africa and was reassigned to Djenné in the Sudan as the *cercle* commandant. (This experience at the *cercle* level is what distinguished Ponty from the two other governors-general to whom he is often compared—Roume and Van Vollenhoven—neither of whom ever served in the field in this capacity. In his book on colonial life, *Les Vrais Chefs de l'empire*, Robert Delavignette placed the *cercle* commandant at the center of colonial governance.)[9]

Ponty's career illustrates the movement upward of a man who had helped carve out the colonial domain and then participated in the organization at the *cercle* level. At Djenné, Ponty collaborated with the new chief of the Sudan, General de Trentinian, vanquisher of the Mossi, who governed the new colony from 1895 to 1899. De Trentinian, a rough and ready disciple of Archinard, divided the colony (called Upper Senegal–Niger during part of this period) into *cercles* and defined the tasks of governing as colonial officials to his commandants. Even though he was a military officer who attained the rank of general during the latter part of his tour, de Trentinian called in a mission of technical experts and first investigated the feasibility of growing cotton scientifically.

When the general was called back to France, Ponty was named to replace him as governor—although without the title: he was called delegate of the governor-general until 1904, when he was promoted to governorship. The Sudan was split, several areas were organized into military districts—Timbuktu, Bobo-Dioulasso and Zinder, but Ponty retained control of the western Sudan. Even so, the question was raised why so young a man should be given such great responsibility (he was thirty-three when de Trentinian was recalled). Governor-general Ballay wrote:

> Although still young, M. Ponty is endowed with a mature attitude, which is unique; he is well behaved and possesses to the highest degree the qualities of respect and discipline. Besides, he has the considerable advantage for this period of transition in the Sudan of having been trained by the military and therefore acceptable to them with greater ease than anyone else.[10]

Starting early with the military, yet being a colonial officer, now paid rich dividends to Ponty, who assumed gubernatorial functions after only nine years in the field. In this command position he presided over the largest and most complex of the French West African colonies (from 1899 until 1908). He had the training and time to complete the work of his shorter termed predecessors. In 1905, while in Paris, Ponty wrote a descriptive analysis of his work in the Sudan for the minister of colonies. This gives us a sampling of the mind of the conquistador turned colonialist: Ponty starts by saying that the "perfect tranquility" of the colony during the past several years has allowed him to devote himself to the "moral conquest of the natives." In other words, Ponty, having gained physical possession of the Africans, is now striving for their souls. "Essentially, we are resolved with all our strength to make the natives respect [*faire aimer*] France by justifying with our actions those promises that we made the morning after the conquest."

Ponty continues by pointing out that many Africans considered the French to be liberators from the old African tyrants. He admits in outlying areas there is still mistrust of the whites, but the fact that each year it becomes easier to collect taxes bears out his argument, even after giving chiefs one percent fees for collecting. He feels that taxation has helped the African learn how to handle money and plan ahead and has helped create a cash crop economy that ultimately benefits the native sector: "Sudan is not, and cannot be, a settler colony. . . . [O]ur duty is to train the natives [in modern agriculture]."[11] Ponty reserves the role of "intermediary" for resident Europeans, who will link up Africa with France. He cites the linking of the Senegal and Niger rivers by railroad as a contribution to the economic development of the colony that will benefit both groups. And looking at the new crops of rice being developed, he is hopeful that eventually Africa will not have to be dependent on imports of Asiatic rice.

Ponty closes his analysis with remarks establishing his loyalty and faith in republicanism at a time when separation of church and state had just been accomplished by the anticlerical republicans in France. He gives orders to cut off subsidies and salaries for the Catholic teaching orders in his colony; he faults them with proselytizing rather than teaching: "The blacks, whether animists or Muslims, want to keep their customs and religion. It is difficult for them to believe we are tolerant, that we believe in liberty of conscience, as long as we seem to favor the proselytization of the missionaries."[12] In William Ponty we find the staunch defender of anticlerical principles, and it is no surprise that he became a prominent member—along with other aspiring young colonial officers—of the Masons.[13] For many colonial leaders needed a credo, and republicanism furnished an ethos that carried men into battle against foreign potentates. Ponty concludes that more lay (rather than religious) teachers are needed so they could "inculcate in the Africans the great principles that make the strength and honor of republican France." Only toward the end of his career are there hints of Ponty's faith wavering.

Ponty governed Sudan longer than any of his illustrious predecessors and brought about the transition from military to full colonial rule. It was, in fact, this consistency and familiarity with one area for fifteen years that established Ponty's reputation as an administrator and as someone who—in the mold of Faidherbe—knew the manners, mores, and language of the people. He was therefore in an unusual and advantageous position vis-à-vis his contemporaries, who suffered from *rouage*—the French policy of frequent transfers, designed to prevent corruption but often preventing a knowledge of the governed.[14] By contrast, British governors usually served six years in a colony, which allowed the kind of familiarity Ponty developed. Why Ponty was so favored is difficult to pin down, but his personnel records suggest that he became an "indispensable collaborator" because of his experience. Moreover, he seems to have enjoyed the confidence of two important governors-general: Ballay, at the turn of the century, and Ernest Roume, architect and chief organizer of the federation of French West Africa.

Ballay noted that Ponty "has always been a valuable collaborator. . . . [H]e has performed difficult tasks with distinction and discretion." Roume was even stronger in his praise:

Manages an excellent budget [1902]; . . . I think he is destined to occupy one of the highest colonial positions [1903]; . . . [he] should be advanced as rapidly as possible [1906]; . . . M. Ponty is a true man of action and has not hesitated to go from Kayes to Niamey, all along the border, to get to the heart of the problem of these attacks [1907].

Roume concluded his report by saying that "every day" Ponty distinguished himself and merited the promotions and honors requested.[15] Clearly, Ponty won the respect of his two commanders and found himself close by when the call came for him to become the new governor-general in 1908. His accomplishments as governor in the Sudan gained him his professional reputation and carried him to the top.

Governor of the French Sudan

The hallmark of William Ponty (like Faidherbe in Senegal) was an intimate knowledge of his colony, which won him the respect of many Africans. He displayed early in his career a willingness to move into the field to solve problems—a willingness that he kept intact in the governor-general's palace. Later governors became wedded to their desks, and Ponty himself toward the end of his career lamented his diminishing opportunities for field tours. His intimacy with his charges is revealed by Governor Raphaël Antonetti, a close associate, when he told the story of Ponty, who, on a visit to Liberia, was asked to pass the troops in review and found a Bambara soldier from the Sudan with a tattered remnant of a French medal on his tunic. The African and Ponty had served under fire together years before; to the astonishment of the official party, Ponty had a reunion with the man on the spot, laughing and joking. Then, in a grand gesture, he stripped the colonial service medal from the chest of his accompanying senior officer and pinned it on the chest of the Bambara infantryman. "Here my brave man, you can say it was Ponty who gave you your medal." And he shook the African's hand and pressed twenty francs into it: "That's for celebrating."[16]

As chief of the Sudan colony, Ponty early had to face the question of slavery. Some French commanders, such as General de Trentinian, had recognized the claims of masters toward slaves and their families and tended to let the social system remain unchanged. Ponty, the idealistic republican, wanted to attack the slave trade caravans, free the slaves, and resettle them in *villages de liberté* ("liberty villages"). For each governor of a colony had flexibility in handling the slavery question until 1905, when the decree of December 12 finally outlawed slavery. Only the Sudan had a coherent policy in French West Africa, and this was largely the work of Ponty; faced with greater numbers of refugees and displaced captives than other governors, he felt obliged to work out a humanitarian policy.[17] Ponty moved soon after taking over command to remove the ambiguities and double standards that had characterized French policy in the 1890s, and on October 10, 1900, issued a decree for Sudan. It ordered the arrest of any persons trafficking in slaves, promulgated slave liberation, and ordained the establishment of so-called liberty villages so former slaves could be reintegrated into a new society. From a French point of view, the villages were noble experiments, akin to the underground railway in antebellum United States, where slaves could be brought to freedom. There were several problems, however: first, many Africans, such as the Fulani, were alarmed by the departure of their serfs; French commanders let them reassert domination rather than risk further unrest and insubordination.

Second, in actual practice the villages became recruiting centers for French forced labor projects so that some Africans exchanged African for French masters.[18]

Paul Marty, Islamic specialist and government interpreter, and Pierre Mille, independent journalist, both agreed in different contemporary articles that Ponty, as governor of the Sudan, was responsible for the demise of slavery.[19] It is fair to say that this was his most important accomplishment before being named governor-general in 1908. But to bring abolition about, Ponty had to win over a number of his administrators who were not so imbued with republican idealism and "rights of man" rhetoric. Marty noted, "By a radical measure, which upset a number of his associates, but whose final success was justified once again by his far-sightedness in political matters, he officially put an end to the state of domestic captivity."[20] The slave trade itself had been vigorously attacked by the majority of French field commanders as the conquest moved forward; by 1897 the trade was considered near an end when civil authorities took over the Sudan area. But domestic slavery (*servitude domestique*) still existed; in fact, the number of captives (a more accurate term in this context than slave) actually grew as French dominion spread. And trading in private continued. Ponty, therefore, moved to resettle countless refugees who wanted to return to the land of their origin. The resettlement extended to Ségou, Kita, Bafoulabé, Kayes, Bougouni, Sikasso, Koutiala, and other centers. A captive who sought freedom paid (if he could) his annual tax, then registered with the *cercle* commandant, who gave him a pass for his destination.

More complicated was the liberty village, which grouped together refugees with no place to go on lands supposedly uninhabited. Abuses in the administration of the villages, some of which were backed by antislavery societies, finally led to their demise and ultimate phaseout. Although Ponty supported the villages, he was sympathetic to cases in which captives were virtually adopted into the master's family and emancipation would be traumatic—hence the possibility of some captive families' staying on their master's lands, with the *diangal*, a vassal's tax, transformed into simple rent. Thus, Ponty earned the reputation among his colleagues as the "emancipator" of the Sudan and did more than any other colonial governor in French West Africa to prepare the way for the abolition decree of 1900. It is perplexing, however, why Ponty has not received proper credit. Senator J. Lemaire, writing in Maurice Viollette's collection on French West Africa in 1913, wondered why Ponty had not received a medal for his antislavery achievements.[21]

Governor-general of West Africa

Ernest Roume, French intellectual and master bureaucrat, became ill in October 1907 and returned to France. His tour as head of the group of colonies known as French West Africa was now at an end; his protégé and friend William Ponty was appointed to succeed him as governor-general. In many ways, Roume, the office man, had been preparing for his succession by Ponty, the field man. Although French West Africa was created in 1895, the idea of a federation of colonies with a unified budget and supreme commander really came about under Roume, a scientific-minded bureaucrat on the Indochina desk at the ministry of colonies who had been dispatched to Africa in 1902.[22] Roume floated the first loan in France for French West Africa's economic development and thereby procured a line of credit for the new colony; he stimulated interest in railway building; he created a rational structure for administering a far-flung empire with efficiency; and he constructed a marvelous palace on Cape Verde overlooking the green Atlantic, a baroque structure to awe the Africans with its magnificence. Ponty was the heir of these policies and fittingly the first occupant of the palace. As such, it was Ponty who gave form and life to the concept of the governor-generalship and brilliantly expanded the office thanks to the powers, concepts, and agencies that Roume had created.[23]

Moreover, the capital had been transferred from Saint-Louis to Dakar to make clear that henceforth Senegal was but one of many colonies under the government-general. A decree of 1902 spelled this out. As Newbury put it, the aim of the decree was to extend the responsibilities of the government-general to financial and political control of all the French West African colonies. The main idea was that the Dakar budget would be responsible for education, justice, customs, and public works throughout the federation; in return, each colony would contribute its revenue derived from imports and other indirect sources to support the general budget. Roume determined a number of ground rules for operating the government-general: he alone would correspond with Paris or foreign territories; he alone would publish official decrees affecting all the colonies; and all administrative organizational decisions required his approval. But in the area of native policy, which varied from Mauritania's nomads to Ivory Coast's lagoon people, the governor-general would leave autonomy to each colony's lieutenant governor. Thus, Ponty inherited a viable administrative and economic federation of colonies unique in African colonial history. (It became the model for the creation of French Equatorial Africa in 1910.)

Ponty was on tour when he heard the news of his elevation to supreme commander; Martial Merlin, secretary-general to Roume, took over the reins of government until Ponty could arrive from a long and triumphal trip to Dakar via Kayes and Saint-Louis. Immediately a popular choice, Ponty was feted by French and Africans alike along the journey to the coast: in Saint-Louis he was honored for his service there more than a decade earlier, and a young man who held the post he had formerly filled, that of secretary, gave the principal toast—Joost Van Vollenhoven, later to become governor-general himself. Ponty thanked him and responded that he hoped under his rule Dakar would become the most magnificent port on the Atlantic Ocean. An indication that Ponty would be available to his public was a notice in the *Journal officiel*: "The Governor-General will receive every morning (except Wednesdays and Saturdays) from 9:30 to 11:00."[24]

Ponty started his administration in Dakar with much prestige: he was hailed as the true organizer of the Sudan colony, much as Faidherbe was memorialized as the father of Senegal. He was called "the right man in the right place" [English in the original] for his job, and it was clear that he was the first choice of Roume and the ministry of colonies. The inspector general toasted his welcome to the governing council, adding:

> The task you assume is difficult. . . . [T]he resources of Africa are scarcely developed . . . that's a job reserved for you. That work will be yours because you have the

tenacity, energy, and spirit that are indispensable, and, above all, you have had the firmness to attract to you and hold the devotion, attachment, I would even say affection [of the people] in the new territories, where everything needs to be created.[25]

Much, therefore, was expected of Ponty as chief, and Ponty, in fact, gave much. He was already a veteran of eighteen years in the field—all in Africa, save for the interlude in Madagascar—and a man devoted totally to his career; he had never married. He faced a number of problems inherited from Roume, but Ponty was fortunate to preside over French West Africa at an optimistic time when the emphasis was on development. It was an era of great hope for the colonial party as the pages of *La Quinzaine colonial* and *L'Afrique française* testify. In fact, Charles Humbert, in his survey of French colonies in 1913, called French West Africa the model colony and boasted that future historians would cite it as the preeminent example of the French colonial method.[26] Originally, many Frenchmen thought it would be impossible to develop the wide-ranging lands of West Africa —from sahel to forest—but the steady progress of Roume and Ponty changed this pessimism and created a bullish climate. Ponty's plans for expansion were altered only by the onset of war in 1914; he died in 1915 and did not live to see the disruption the war brought to his colony and the marginality of the postwar colonial world.

French West Africa during the time of Ponty was at its zenith in terms of colonial self-confidence, and this posture was, in part, the creation of the self-assured veteran himself.[27] Ponty's annual speeches before his *Conseil du Gouvernement* at times read like chamber of commerce reports; at one session, Ponty admitted that he was overweening in his pride after looking at progress reports but reminded his colleagues that French West Africa was like his family: he had devoted all his adult years to it. In fact, he presided over his government establishment like a patriarch, taking equal interest in French administrators and African chiefs, his two main groups of staff. In 1912 he was responsible for 2,403 French functionaries, of whom 341 were professional colonial administrators, who governed about 12 million Africans in five—later to become eight—colonies. He was all-powerful in a colonial world and only he had the right to correspond with Paris: all reports, requests, or complaints had to be sent to his office in Dakar, and he alone determined what would be sent to the ministry of colonies. This is why Robert Cornevin called Ponty one of the great proconsuls of empire: he held quasi-absolute power in a day when frequent political changes brought uninformed ministerial novices to power.[28]

Economic and Administrative Achievements

Ponty was in power from 1908 to 1915. He benefited from Ernest Roume's success in raising funds for an ambitious public works program in French West Africa. The heart of this program was construction of railway lines linking coastal colonies with interior markets, such as the Dakar to Bamako line, Conakry to Fouta Djallon, and Bingerville to Upper Volta. Ponty was enjoined by *La Quinzaine coloniale* "to spend wisely these millions" and, in fact, pushing the railways further became an obsession with the governor-general, matched only by his interest in the *armée noire*. In dedicating part of the Guinean line, the antislavery champion promised "that the railway will make that barbarous necessity, human porterage, disappear." Ponty, as an executor of the comprehensive plan worked out while Gaston Doumergue was minister of colonies in 1898, watched the progress of his railways; he also presided over the development of port facilities, the second great priority in the economic development scheme of French West Africa. This primarily meant building a modern port at Dakar, which now replaced the Cape Verde Island ports as the principal refueling and replenishing station for European ships on the Atlantic. Ponty could watch from his baroque palace as the work crews created an imperial city further to impress the Africans and to underline France's claim to colonial grandeur.[29]

Ponty favored agricultural development and commissioned the first serious studies on irrigation possibilities of the lower Senegal river and the Niger river at Ségou. He called for increased beef production and opened the first refrigerated packing plant in Senegal in 1914. He started experiments in raising sisal hemp and in improving breeds of sheep for market and hoped that his old colony of Sudan would someday meet a large part of France's demand for cereals and cotton. Ponty felt confident that once the infrastructure of railways and ports was completed, West Africa would take off economically. Practical and prudent, Ponty remarked that "we are only at the beginning of the rational development of French West Africa." But his enthusiasm was barely masked, and colonial publicists such as Humbert and Viollette spread the word of his success to the French public. Ponty was also pleased with the migration of Africans toward rail centers, as occurred in Senegal, where whole villages moved from the Ferlo desert to southerly peanut growing areas in Baol and Sine-Saloum.[30] It meant that the era of resistance to the spread of rails was over—as in the resistance of Lat-Dior Diop in Cayor—and that African peasants now wanted to participate in a cash crop economy.

Ponty made no secret about his desire to work closely with the large French business houses that now began to dominate the African market, to the prejudice of the old mulatto houses of Gorée and Saint-Louis and smaller independent French traders: "I favor close cooperation between the administration and commerce," he declared on several occasions, and his friends were drawn from the ranks of old line firms such as Maurel Frères, Vezia, Peyrissac, and Maurel and Prom. He was feted and entertained in Paris by members of the Union coloniale. Yet Ponty did reserve some areas for government domination: he thought private enterprise should be limited to operating feeder lines, with the government in charge of French West Africa's main lines. Ponty worried about the great number of imports from other powers, especially the fact that his colony was dependent on foreigners for energy supplies. In a day when a minimum of economic planning was done, it was presumed that private enterprise would be given free reign to develop internal markets in French West Africa; however, Ponty also had sympathy for small French traders and when he died he was memorialized as the first governor-general who had helped the *petits-colons* in their quest to benefit from the African bonanza.[31]

In two areas of economic activity, however, Ponty came out clearly on the side of the African. One of his greatest accomplishments was the establishment of the sociétés indigènes de prévoyance ("native provident societies"). Tried as experiments in Guinea and Senegal in 1908–1909, these combination seed storage and cooperatives were recognized by Ponty in a decree of June 29, 1910. He was concerned about the plight of thousands of Africans during the "hungry season"— often a period of several months before the harvest during which Africans did not have enough to eat—and about cases in which too little seed was put aside to insure sufficient planting. Ponty set up his program to provide insurance against natural disasters, to purchase adequate tools, to help Africans get credit for better terms, to provide aid in time of illness or accident, and to develop a spirit of African solidarity. The cooperatives spread all around West Africa and proved of great value especially in the 1930s—despite local corruption of administrators and African chiefs alike—in many areas serving as the model for modern cooperatives in independent Africa. Ponty was genuinely concerned about the problem of credit for many African farmers, how they easily got in debt; the governor-general personally attacked and defeated a scheme backed by important financial interests to institute a thirty percent interest rate in French West Africa: "It is not possible for the administration to authorize the collection of such onerous interest . . . without seriously compromising its responsibilities toward the natives."[32]

Ponty's concern for the welfare of his subjects is further illustrated by his staunch resistance to increasing the head tax, which many colonialists were calling for:

> It is true that the personal tax is very moderate, varying from .25 to 5.00 francs per head in different regions; at any rate, in my view, the present rate constitutes the maximum that we can legitimately require. It would be impolitic to increase it; it's only by improving our censuses that we can increase the yield.

Despite his enthusiasm for railway building, he argued against the idea that railways were designed to show a profit; rather, they were the means of subsidizing the development of agriculture. "By adjusting tariffs," Ponty declared, "we can best stimulate the development of agriculture."[33] He projected the goal of eventually substituting rice from the Niger valley for that from India, currently eaten by Europeans, and having cheap rail services to transport products to the ports was essential.

Ponty did have his share of economic problems. He geared up French West Africa for a share of the lucrative rubber market just as the world market became depressed, thanks to overproduction in Malaysia. He was aware that imports were constantly increasing in French West Africa, that the colony was dependent on foreign oil, rice, and cotton, within the framework of modified free trade (only after World War I did the French put the colony on a stricter schedule of protection). And increasingly he was criticized for allowing Syrians and Lebanese to continue immigration begun just before the turn of the century: criticism came from smaller French businessmen, whom these thrifty traders first jeopardized, and later by African merchants, who also felt threatened.

In the area of administrative achievements, it is fair to observe that French West Africa never in its sixty-five-year existence had a better prepared governor-general than William Ponty. Ponty had the further advantage of being in power at a formative time when he could, in fact, serve as a lawmaker, although theoretically he was only to promulgate decrees from France. In actual practice, Ponty deserved his gubernatorial title with the Africans as *Borom* of Dakar, and he conveyed this image of "master" of West Africa with aplomb and style. Villard characterized this as a mixture of "good humor, spirit, and skillfulness." Ponty was not offended—as were later governors-general—by genteel satirists in local newspapers who called him "Seigneur Guillaume I de l'A.O.F." or "Guglielmo Ponty Africano." In fact, there is good reason to assume that Mody M'Baye, early Senegalese intellectual gadfly and *écrivain publique*, had Ponty in mind when he wrote his famous essay on the two types of colonial Frenchmen and how Africans should learn to identify and cope with them: the one who comes to Africa to exploit the natives, whom the African should mistrust; and the other, the *bon français*, who comes to Africa to help the natives and who thinks:

> I take the opportunity of showing my love for and my gratitude to my country. In joining its service, I took an oath . . . that I would be like a father to the people in my charge. My most important task would be to educate them, and to make them into free men, capable of running their own affairs.

M'Baye argued that this kind of Frenchman could be trusted. Ponty was respected by fledgling elites and traditional chiefs alike as the model of desirable republican values.[34]

Devotion to duty was ingrained in Ponty and he expected the same standard of total commitment from his subordinates. He married only late in his career and argued that administrators who brought their families to Africa lost approximately fifty percent of their efficiency: "The comfort of the hearth [is] detrimental to good colonial administration."[35] This also reflected the fact that times were changing in two ways: first, fewer administrators lived with African women, which had been a time-honored way of initiation into the *coutumes du pays* (more European women now arrived with their husbands—Ponty's marriage followed this trend); second, as a result—and thanks to improved roads and to autos— fewer administrators took frequent tours into the bush. General Gallieni set a brisk pace in Madagascar by constantly moving about like a medieval prince, and so did Ponty. It was personal contact that counted, and Ponty later took pride in the "old school of administrators" as being composed of those who knew "little about official regulations." The *Journal officiel* of French West Africa is filled with descriptions of Ponty's official tours during his tenure, which give credence to his reputation of being warmly respected and welcomed by African chiefs; in March 1911, for example, he visited the Fama of Sansanding, an old friend, "pour lequel M. Ponty a conservé une amitié pleine d'estime."[36]

Ponty's greatest fame as an administrator was gained for his *politique des races* (discussed subsequently), which was a reflection of his interest in trying to mold and develop African leadership for French goals. Aware of the discrepancies between salaries and benefits of French and African bureaucrats and auxiliaries, he was the first high official to propose that African employees qualify for a pension after loyal service to France. Ponty described this as "cette politique qui tend à associer de plus les indigènes à notre oeuvre," and he fought for African bureaucrats to share in liberal colonial pensions. This was the *caisses de retraites* for local agents, which affected Africans who were in the administrative service. Ponty seems not to have been a party to the policy that eliminated many Africans from government service after the turn of the century. To the contrary, in 1911 he announced that "I intend to make greater use of native elements in the creation of various lesser cadres."[37]

Ponty was also vigorous in his pursuit of educational reforms; today he is probably best known for the William Ponty School, originally a normal school, which was named for him after his death and which in its heyday (1920s to 1950s) was the most important postprimary school in French black Africa. He followed the anticlerical lead of Roume in maintaining a hard line on Catholic religious congregations and favoring the development of secular schools. In Ponty's view, the essential subject was French so that the interpreter, whom he thought wielded too much power, could be eliminated: "The primordial condition for the success and duration of our domination resides in the natives' acquiring our language as rapidly as possible." He urged African chiefs to take advantage of the free French schools and to enroll their sons. He was cool to Catholic and Islamic educational institutions alike, if under French sponsorship, because animist Africans might be offended. His circular of May 8, 1911, forbade future use of Arabic in local court cases and in all administrative correspondence, thus compelling local Islamic elites to master French or hire translators and to send their sons to French classes. Ponty, however was not totally anti-Islamic and took pride in 1908 in the conversion of the "Ecole des fils de chefs et des interprètes " in Saint-Louis, founded by Faidherbe, into a *medersa* for teaching Koranic subjects—but under French control. And in the area of publications under Ponty's direction, the first colonial journal for education was inaugurated in 1913, *Bulletin mensuel de l'enseignement.*[38]

Ponty was not infallible in administrative affairs. One excellent example of his lack of judgment was Dahomey, probably farthest from Dakar in terms of colonial interest. During these years Dahomey was a brutally run colony, with Africans subject to indignities and possibly the worst French administration in West Africa. Ponty refused to face these realities and once announced to Paris that "Dahomey is a happy colony, a country almost devoid of history." He shared the bias and interest of Faidherbe for the upper Guinea coast and the Sudan; Dahomey was simply out of his ken.

In the related administrative area of medicine and sanitation, Ponty established a strong reputation in France as a farsighted leader. For example, he developed hundreds of dispensaries for medical treatment in the bush; he obtained funds for and stimulated campaigns against smallpox, yellow fever, sleeping sickness, and especially bubonic plague, which had struck Dakar. Ponty was denounced by African elites and chiefs alike for ordering the burning of towns and villages where unsanitary conditions were determined by health officials to be fostering the spread of plague; it even became a political issue in the hotly contested election of Blaise Diagne to the chamber of deputies as Senegal's representative in 1914. But Ponty held firm, convinced that modern public health services were badly needed by African urban society. New bacteriological stations at Bamako and Bingerville were founded under his direction; the famous African hospital at Dakar was finished and put into operation; new doctors and auxiliaries were recruited; and Humbert in 1913 observed that "the governor-general neglects nothing." Ponty was also lionized for his fight against alcoholism, which at first glance seems strange for the representative of a colonial power eager to export its wines and cognacs. His opposition to African consumption of hard liquor and spirits was actually aimed more at imports from Britain; he was pleased when French wine imports increased in French West Africa and observed that the Africans "are now learning to appreciate our civilization."[39]

Achievements in Native and Military Policy

William Ponty is probably best known in the literature on French colonialism for his native policy referred to as *politique des races* (policy of races"), which established him as the leading practitioner of the new policy of association. His philosophy on governing traditional African societies evolved during his years in the Sudan and came to fruition in his famous 1909 circular after completing an inspection trip across French West Africa.[40] During his governor-generalship Ponty refined this statement and tried to establish a coherent policy in relation to African chiefs and traditional societies, Islamic leaders and communities, and emerging urban elites—especially in coastal Senegal—and in the area of *justice indigène* ("native court system"). In so doing, he laid the foundation for French colonial policy in the twentieth century, which was later expanded upon and reinterpreted by governors-general Clozel, Van Vollenhoven, Merlin, Carde, and Brevié.

Having participated in the conquest of the Sudan, having fought or been allied with many of the most important African chieftains of the day, Ponty considered himself knowledgeable on native policy and conveyed in his speeches this sense of having mastered African manners, mores, and mentality. Before considering his formal doctrine of *la politique des races*, however, it is necessary to look at Ponty's fundamental assumptions about Africa, Africans, and their society. This is what can be termed republican paternalism—that is, an unswerving commitment to and loyalty toward the French Third Republic and its bourgeois, anticlerical, and materialistic ideals. Ponty was a recruit to colonial life in the "heroic age" of conquest: training in Paris just as the ministry of colonies was organized as a separate department of government; participating in the Sudan wars; called upon to lead the transition from military to civilian rule. He learned his colonial philosophy firsthand in black Africa, and this took—in addition to his dyed-in-the-wool republicanism—a paternalistic bent. That is, Ponty was in sympathy to and identified with his African charges in an emotional, personal way that differed from the attitude of colonial commanders more inflexible and less sympathetic to African problems (one thinks of his contemporaries Raphaël Antonetti, later to become infamous as builder of the Congo-Ocean railroad; Martial Merlin, who systematically persecuted urban elite Africans; and Gabriel Angoulvant, the strong-armed "pacifier" of the Ivory Coast). Ponty was not "soft" although he was sensitive and sympathetic.

It was this sensitivity that caused more than one observer to remark that Ponty was *trop bon* or *très humain*. It was at the root of his apparent popularity with peasant, chief, and urban elite alike, something few other governors could manage. Ponty interpreted French colonialism in this way when the question of land use was raised: "Our colony was not established to facilitate the emigration of white workers. The blacks, who are now our partners, make perfect settlers."[41] This, then, was a form of partnership—the blacks as collaborators with the

French; Africans were colonists to work with the French for development. The incongruity of Africans as colonists in their own land never occurred to Ponty; his views—expressed, after all, in 1908—were liberal for the day, putting the African at the center of the colonial stage. But he stopped short of believing that Africans were full partners, and it is this emphasis that turns his sympathy, understanding, and real love for them into paternalism. Clozel, asked to comment on Ponty's policies, replied, "We follow the policy of association, which permits us to bring the natives even closer to us." Ponty thought it was France's mission to win the Africans' goodwill, to bring them to respect (*faire aimer*) France and what it stood for: universal republican principles.

A good example of this was his championing of land use for Africans. "We have renounced," he told the governors assembled in the governing council, "vast agricultural concessions that have never given expected results. It's the African cultivator who more than anyone else is at the heart of agricultural production." Ponty then issued a warning to potential plantation owners: "European enterprises should not be allowed to be established to the detriment of African land-holdings, which it is our duty to encourage, support, and guarantee."[42] Ponty emerges here as the great protector of African society—which he was, certainly, in his own mind—but the ultimate benefit is always to France. His insistence on the power and the glory going to the metropole identifies Ponty, despite his liberalism and real empathy, as a colonial paternalist.

This attitude is further revealed in a word often employed by Ponty to describe his method in native policy: *apprivoisement*. Some commentators have translated *apprivoisement* into English as "taming"; that is, Ponty wanted to tame the Africans. This construal misses the intention of his thought; a better translation would be "to become accustomed." He wanted the Africans to become acclimated to French rule, to like the French, to work with them as junior partners, and—as we shall see—in exceptional cases (such as that of the urban elites) to become black Frenchmen, that is, to become assimilated. But Ponty was not an assimilationist: his long tenure had convinced him of the worth of African society and he did not wish to destroy its fabric; his practicality told him that association was the only workable policy for the millions of new subjects France added to its colonial empire during the conquest. Such was the nature of Ponty's republican paternalism. Let us now examine his own doctrines.

The policy of races, a phrase Ponty had used often during his governorship of the Sudan, was the subject of the circular of September 22, 1909. This circular may be taken as the foundation of native policy in West Africa in the twentieth century. Ponty begins not with a hard line or firm orders to his subordinates; rather his first words reveal the tenor of the circular: "It is undeniable today that in order to produce positive and lasting results, our administration should become flexible toward the diverse modalities of native policy." He then sets out the basis for this policy: "Now it seems possible today to formulate this policy into a body of principles derived from a greater understanding that we now have of the psychology of our subjects, from our constant concern not to offend them in their customs, in their beliefs, and even in their superstitions." But the heart of his policy was that African traditional societies should be governed by leaders drawn from their own people—a kind of local nationalism. Ponty accepted the idea that African chiefs were desirable and were to be part of the French colonial establishment, but he insisted that they be drawn from their own people. He opposed "carpetbaggers" from other ethnic groups or from other regions and especially the imposition of Islamic chiefs over non-Islamic peoples. Ponty was striking particularly hard at leaders of areas ruled by their erstwhile conquerors; the problem of local imperialism he expressed as the "commandements indigènes purement territoriaux calqués sur les anciennes principautés locales."[43]

How did this approach harmonize with French colonial doctrines of centralized, direct rule, so often contrasted to the doctrines of Frederick Lugard in British areas, often known as indirect rule? For Ponty, "purifying" native African rulers meant that France would in effect have greater control over its subjects; that by ousting traditional kings, warlords, and mercenaries who flunked the ethnic test, France put itself in a position to appoint African chiefs who would be partners with France, who could be led to *aimer la France*. The policy of races, then, assumed the widespread appointment in French West Africa of chiefs at the regional and canton levels since it was recognized there would never be enough Frenchmen to provide total direct rule. Paul Marty, an Islamic affairs officer who admired Ponty, summed this up: "He has freed all ethnic groups; he has proclaimed the equal human value of all peoples and their right of existence; he has brought back to life peoples who were dying under social and religious oppression."

Ponty further argued that his goal was to establish closer contact between the ruler and the ruled, and by having handpicked chiefs who would serve as French auxiliaries he would be able to transmit his republican values. "We should continue," he said, "to surround them [as we have done] with external signs of honor and esteem; to fulfill the obligations that we have contracted toward them; and to utilize their services by making them auxiliaries in our administration." He wished to bypass the interpreter as well as the alien chief; he wanted a chief who spoke the language of the people administered— but also the language of the conquerors, French, to encourage closer contact. Ponty also urged more frequent tours by his French administrators. During his first week in Dakar as governor-general he established an "open door policy" whereby Africans could carry on palavers.

> We must act wisely in the generous tradition of our people. We must draw the people near to us so that they come into direct contact with the administration. Our native policy will become wholly effective only when it becomes sufficiently flexible so as to influence the masses, to shape them in some measure, enabling them to evolve according to the needs of their *milieu*, and without doing them injury.[44]

Ponty also urged his administrators to study local customs in order to better understand their subjects.

Was Ponty anti-Islamic? In 1911 he retorted critics' remarks that he was against Muslim populations: "It is not part of my policy to interfere with the legitimate exercise of the Muslim religion. . . . [I]t is against what I've called Muslim clericalism, the *marabout*, who distorts the doctrine." Ponty argued that he wanted protection for the two-thirds of the population who were animist in persuasion. Paul Marty, who helped (with Robert Arnaud) to develop the governor-general's Islamic policy, felt that Ponty was not hostile to Islam despite the fact that he forbade Arabic in official correspondence; "the greatest liberalism" guided the governor-general, who maintained with the great Mauritanian and black sheiks "the most friendly of personal relations."[45] And it was Ponty who finally ended more than a decade of French persecution of Amadou Bamba, founder and spiritual leader of the Mourides sect, prominent especially in Senegal; Bamba had been exiled but finally returned under house arrest. Ponty flattered Bamba, sought his advice, and eventually enlisted his aid in recruiting Senegalese for the *armée noire*. Later, when Ponty died, Bamba composed an ode to his greatness, calling him "sultan" and "master" of the country. Whether this was cooption is difficult to say, but it was an indication of a successful Islamic policy.

Early in his administration Ponty and other French officials became concerned about possible links between the Muslims in French West Africa and those under the jurisdiction of the Ottoman sultan in Turkey. He sent Arnaud and later Marty to study different *tariqas* and *marabouts* to determine whether France's African subjects would be loyal and whether there was danger of subversion and propaganda from Turkey. In a world rapidly moving toward conflict, foreshadowed by diplomatic alignments, French colonial officials feared hostility in their own domains. Arnaud, in his *L'Islam et politique musulmane française*, emphasized that the "West African Muslim has not in any way been influenced by political developments in the Ottoman Empire. . . . [T]he black Muslim ignores the revolutionary dogmas of these modern times."[46] Moreover, when war came in 1914, Ponty was flooded with a number of affirmations of loyalty from diverse Islamic holy men across French West Africa, many of whom knew Ponty personally. Marty reported that Ponty had not requested this show of support, had issued no statement or proclamation; it was a genuine outpouring of respect.

Under Ponty's orders, a research office on Islamic groups and leaders in West Africa was established so that pro-French *marabouts* could be rewarded and hostile ones closely watched. Ponty was also mindful that Islam was making great progress under the French banner, possibly greater than before the conquest; this is why he wanted protection for animist groups and why he wanted to destroy many of the older chieftainships, a majority of which were Islamic and had been imposed: "We must destroy all hegemony of one race over another, combat the influence of local aristocracies, and suppress the great chieftainships, which are almost always a barrier between us and the people and which work to the profit of Muslim clericalism."[47] Ponty, the good republican, remained on the attack against both clericalism and aristocracy. His commissioned intelligence in Islamic affairs made him respect the specialist and caused him to set his subordinates studying African societies so they could be better administrators. However, the war came before Ponty's schemes could bear fruit in other than Islamic affairs; consequently, later critics such as Maurice Delafosse and Joost Van Vollenhoven thought Ponty had been anti-intellectual and disdainful of native policy research; the record does not support this claim. To the contrary, Ponty gave the impetus to this movement and inspired Clozel, who, after Ponty's death, laid the groundwork for what was to become the famous Institut français de l'Afrique noire (IFAN).

Ponty's "policy of races" placed special emphasis on the reform of the native court system. Here Ponty was clearly ahead of his times since he valued Africans as persons and wanted a better system for protecting them against administrative whim or abuse. The decree of November 10, 1903, had set up French West

Africa's basic judicial system, but Ponty and other veterans of African bush life believed the system was badly conceived and in need of overhaul. The reorganization, comprising seven chapters and fifty-five articles, was personally supervised by Ponty and announced in the decree of August 16, 1912; he considered it one of his greatest triumphs. Ponty's instructions give a brief idea of his intentions: "Our judicial organization guarantees to the natives the maintenance of their customs. Tribunals . . . will be composed of judges who follow the same customs as the parties coming before them. . . . The claimant will have the certainty of being judged according to his traditions." Special tribunals would be created for Africans living in the midst of a dominant ethnic group in order to protect minority rights. Ponty wanted to follow the general rule that local customs should determine punishments—except in well-defined areas such as murder, where French law would prevail—and should not allow punishments involving mutilation, torture, or ritual murder. He believed that Africans would be thankful for the reforms, that such an "equitable" system would draw them to French rule, and that it would help develop them intellectually, morally, and materially. His judicial reform was consistent with the policy of races, emphasizing ethnic and local differences. He said if a book were written about colonial accomplishments he would not hesitate to offer his justice reforms "as the prologue."[48]

The year after these reforms Ponty went further by announcing his intention to modify the *indigénat*, France's system of administrators who had disciplinary powers that were not dependent on court hearings. Created during the conquest in 1887, this system seemed to Ponty to be out of step with his reforms, especially since he believed the Africans had shown "goodwill" in early recruitment operations. French officials could imprison an African for two weeks without trial after a summary judgment. Ponty may have been influenced also by the celebrated Mody M'Baye case. As mentioned before, M'Baye was an African scribe and a permanent gadfly in Senegalese political matters. In 1913, after publishing critical articles, M'Baye was thrown into prison on a summary judgment by Paul Brocard, administrator of Sine-Saloum in Senegal. M'Baye appealed directly to Ponty, arguing that since he was born in Saint-Louis he was actually a French citizen and hence not subject to the *indigénat*. Ponty's subordinates had weathered M'Baye's attacks for years and were delighted Brocard had finally put him in jail. But Ponty, aware that M'Baye was well connected in France to the civil rights organization League for the Rights of Man, ordered M'Baye freed. The lieutenant governor for Senegal, Henri Cor, was astounded. Ponty explained that he believed the administrator had handed out a sentence far too stiff for merely authoring an article; that public opinion in France was now hostile to applying the *indigénat*; and that it was perfectly normal for the African to appeal to a higher authority. (Ponty often was criticized behind his back by colleagues for intervening in affairs of this type, especially in Senegal, where political consciousness was growing among urban Africans.)[49]

Ponty also made a major contribution to relations with emerging African elites. In retrospect, it is apparent that Ponty favored—indeed, fostered—advancement of Africans known as elites, or *évolués*. This is remarkable because the veteran of the bush, such as Maurice Delafosse, usually was antagonistic to the city African. Yet Ponty in his paternalism seems at times to have embraced Senegalese creoles (mulattoes) and *originaires* (inhabitants of the "Four Communes" comprising Saint Louis, Gorée, Dakar, and Rufisque. Their inhabitants were French citizens and enjoyed representative institutions.) His ambivalence is illustrated by two examples: it was Ponty who first proposed reforming Senegal's *conseil général*, the preserve of elite mulattò politicians, in order to cut its power and aid traditional chiefs; yet he early favored the idea that urban African elites from the Four Communes should have the right to vote in local elections regardless of where they lived. This ambivalence caused consternation among both elites and traditional Africans and is best explained by the fact that Ponty was above all a paternalist; if he could help or promote Africans in their milieu he would do so, provided they were loyal to France. Recall that it was Mody M'Baye, despite his published attacks on the administration, who earlier had proclaimed his loyalty to the good Frenchman, the one who stood for the principles of the French revolution. In 1909 Ponty had also tried unsuccessfully to get the ministry of colonies to authorize a number of rural Africans to vote in the Senegalese local elections. How did this interest in African elites, who were supposed to be products of assimilation, square with the doctrine of association, for which Ponty was now a leading spokesman?

Like many Frenchmen of his day, Ponty accepted the idea of evolution and applied it to non-European peoples. In his mind, some Africans were more ready for advancement to French civilization than others; he would help each group, whether elite, Islamic, or animist, toward closer association with France. There is no question that Ponty was well liked by many tradtional chiefs; his tours often spawned rivalries between local leaders who vied to entertain the governor-general. He won over such Islamic leaders as Amadou Bamba and counted the support of the powerful Sheik Sidia of Mauritania.[50] But at the same time Ponty cultivated mulatto deputy François Carpot of Senegal, representative of the old creole Catholic elite of Saint-Louis and Gorée, which had wielded much economic and political power in the nineteenth century. Idowu, in his excellent study of the *conseil général* of Senegal, concluded that Roume and Governor Camille Guy of Senegal had favored taking away political rights of the Senegalese, but that William Ponty objected, arguing that "the Senegalese deserved keeping their rights because of their long and loyal devotion to France."[51] Roume and Guy wanted to abolish the *conseil général*; but Ponty, the good republican, worked to reform it so that rural as well as urban areas would be represented. In Ponty's mind the ultimate goal was eventual assimilation since bringing Africans into the council was another step in developing their loyalty to France.

Beside M'Baye and the council, the most important urban elite problem for Ponty was the election of Blaise Diagne as Senegalese deputy in 1914. Diagne was the first full-blooded black African elected to the French Parliament, and his election caught officialdom by surprise. Even Ponty had predicted that mulatto party leader Carpot would be reelected. After the first election, when Diagne led the field, Ponty was embarrassed by not being prepared for the victory of the majority black voters; the ministry of colonies thundered telegrams at him demanding explanations. Ponty still thought the French backed candidate, Heimburger, would win. When Diagne took the runoff election, Ponty had to send a special report to Paris. Pressures on Ponty were great. First, the French business candidate was defeated; second, mulatto leader Carpot went down to defeat; both of these groups contested the idea that a simple African could win the coveted election to sit in Paris and brought pressure to invalidate the election. Moreover, many of Ponty's colonial administrators were alarmed by the prospect of a member of the African elite in high office. Ponty himself observed that "between the primary and runoff, Diagne was without scruple in threatening us with African strikes."[52] (Diagne had actually argued that unless French businessmen extended credit to African customers, he would call for strikes.)

In the face of enormous pressure to stop Diagne, Ponty received a report from Raphaël Antonetti, acting governor of Senegal, that suggested that Ponty should buy off Diagne, possibly with a high administrative post in France, or that it could be arranged simply to "get rid of him." Ponty left out these suggestions in filing his report to Paris although he must have been sorely tempted. After the election, bubonic plague broke out in Dakar; Ponty's orders were to burn part of the city and Diagne incited the Africans to rioting and resistance. Moreover, Ponty complained that Diagne was picking on him (the latter had sent telegrams of protest to high officials in Paris). Ponty's report on the election hinted that Diagne himself was ineligible to vote and hence could not be a candidate, but Ponty stopped short of suggesting that he not take his seat.

Available evidence suggests that Ponty's republican principles dictated his attitude: that Diagne had won a free election and that he was entitled to his political reward—despite the dire consequences predicted. And there is one unknown quantity: the fact that both Diagne and Ponty were members of the Grand Orient, France's most prestigious Masonic lodge.[53] Did Ponty leave the way open for his fraternal brother? There seems to be no question that Ponty could have stopped Diagne, at least in the early stages, but the fact that he did not strongly reinforces the view that his republican paternalism was applied equally to African elites.

Ponty did not articulate a policy vis-à-vis elites in official circulars. However, his attitudes and actions suggest an implicit policy of tolerance and encouragement. By freeing Mody M'Baye (who could have been left in jail under terms of the *indigénat*), by working for a broader representation in the *counseil général* (when he could have aligned with Roume and Guy to abolish it), and by not quashing Diagne, Ponty showed his basic liberal tendencies. In return, when he died *La Démocratie*, chief journal for the elites, praised Ponty and lamented his passing. It is probably not an exaggeration to say that political movement in Senegal of Diagne, Galandou Diouf, Lamine Guèye, Tiécouta Diop, and the Jeunes Sénégalais could not have survived but for the implicit recognition of Ponty. For this reason Ponty may be characterized as the most liberal governor toward Africans until de Coppet in 1936, and among certain political militants of the prewar period Ponty's name has the same ring as that of Faidherbe. Both have weathered the nationalist writing of history; whereas Merlin, Antonetti, Angoulvant, Van Vollenhoven, and others have often suffered stinging critiques.[54]

In summary, Ponty's native policy was an attempt to give French West Africa a modus operandi consistent with France's republican ideals and stated colonial needs, on the one hand, and humane and sensitive to the needs of French subjects, on the other. In the Ponty differed from earlier administrators, who were interested in consolidating the military conquest; this policy was a departure from the approach of non-Africanist Ernest Roume, who was interested principally in administrative and budgetary organization and who created a workable structure for Ponty. But none of these persons tried to bring together elements of an African policy as did Ponty. To be sure, Ponty was building on Algeria, Faidherbe, and other models and legacies. Another difference is that Ponty was a popular governor, better known among the people than any other governor-general of his time; there was a sense of relief when he replaced "the cold and aloof Roume." Ponty was not a theoretician but a pragmatist who wanted his *méthode*—in the full French sense of the word—employed by his subordinates for the greater glory of France. His devotion, patriotism, emotional attachment to Africa and Africans, and his reason for an enlightened native policy are summed up in a speech he gave before his council of government in 1912: "Excuse me for giving such a long report . . . please remember that a great part of my life, and all of my career, have been spent in this country, and that I love French West Africa in the same way one can love his homeland, and I have the same hopes and ambitions for its greatness."[55]

Closely related to native policy was Ponty's military policy, understanding of which is essential to understanding of his administration. We have seen that Ponty spent his early years with military men conquering the Sudan and that when he was elevated to the governor-generalship one reason advanced was his strong rapport with the military. His activities in the military sphere can be divided into three phases: pacification, border settlements, and the *armée noire*.

"Pacification" is a word that was never wholly accurate; today's historian has difficulty using it. Yet it appears in the literature, and Ponty believed one of his great accomplishments had been to finish the pacification of French West Africa. To him, this meant a small-scale effort on the model of France's final campaign against African resistance leader Samory Touré. The stakes were high, for Ponty believed that feudalism (and invariably resistance leaders were viewed as tyrants) is the enemy of republicanism and hence that France possessed the right to destroy leaders and institutions of the ancien régime. Ponty and his colleagues deduced that any African resistance to French rule must be an aberration impeding progress and should be rooted out. Thus, both as governor of the Sudan and as governor-general, Ponty sanctioned and rewarded pacification campaigns.

Perhaps the most hotly contested movements were in the Ivory Coast, where Gabriel Angoulvant was lieutenant governor. Ponty openly criticized policy and methods in the Ivory Coast, and little love was lost between these two commanders. Ponty felt more at home in the more northerly areas, and he gloried in military campaigns in Mauritania, Tibesti, Upper Guinea, and Upper Casamance in Senegal.[56]

He felt that once the foe was vanquished, he should immediately be invited to join the victor: "From our enemies of yesterday, we will make our auxiliaries of today." He lauded Colonel Laperrine, who recaptured Gao with *méharistes* nomads, "which shows what can be accomplished with police forces composed of elements recruited from desert populations." Ponty was critical of the southern colonies such as Dahomey and Ivory Coast because they had not always followed his policy of races, which he believed was the key to pacification. But by the time of his death in 1915 he had not eliminated the need for pacification: African resistance had continued in numerous areas and would increase in violence during World War I.[57] In the context of his tenure as chief of several colonies, however, Ponty believed—and with good reason in that day—that his policies had resulted in the pacification of many areas, and he bragged to Paris about his success.

Another military task eventually handed over to the diplomats was that of defining borders between colonies in West Africa. Ponty pushed hard for commissions to work out quarrels over boundaries, rights of passage, commercial tariffs, and other matters with Liberia, Portugal, Britain, and Germany. During his years in office most of these questions were eventually resolved, and Ponty even embarked upon a goodwill tour to Liberia. The *Journal officiel* of French West Africa listed the delimitation of the federation's borders as one of Ponty's outstanding accomplishments.[58]

His military policy hinged on the creation of the *armée noire*, a logical extension of the *tirailleurs sénégalais* of Faidherbe and the African troops first used by Archinard in the Sudan conquest. Ponty had marched with Archinard and seen the valorous African infantrymen in battle; he learned to respect African military capabilities and, in turn, earned the respect of African soldiers. Archinard had been the first to use these troops mainly by themselves, often without French support troops or cadres, and his results were encouraging. They also seemed impressive to two young men, Charles Mangin and William Ponty, who two decades later jointly would become the principal architects of France's black African army. Mangin published a book in 1910, *La Force noire*, which has been credited (or blamed) for setting in motion black Africa's contribution to France's World War I army.[59] A careful reading of the record suggests that such groups as the Comitè de l'Afrique française favored having black troops as auxiliaries, available to substitute for regular troops, which might be recalled from North Africa for metropolitan duty. France faced the problem of demographic stagnation and theorists of the day wondered openly how in a showdown France's forces could combat the numerically superior Germans? African troops had been used for short-term reinforcements in Morocco, but the alarm was sounded from Algeria, where local residents argued strongly against the deployment of black troops there. In this context, therefore, the groups supporting the idea that black Africa might be tapped for manpower decided upon a mission to study the question, and Mangin was picked to head it.

Most accounts omit the fact that Ponty *requested* the mission in the first place and that it is unlikely it could have succeeded without his close cooperation. He early recognized the value for France of using African soldiers, and in Paris he became a part of the inner circle that planned the orchestration of the campaign to use black troops. Marc Michel has called this group "les Soudanais" because many had served with Archinard in the Sudan. The first public notice that Mangin and Ponty were working in concert was in *L'Afrique française* for May 1910, where it was announced that

> Monsieur Ponty, governor-general of West Africa, requested that a special mission be sent to Africa to study the organization of the recruitment of black troops; the minister of colonies has entrusted the mission to Lieutenant colonel Mangin and to Captain Cornet of the colonial infantry and administrators Le Herisse and Guignard.

Such early dispatches and commentaries make it clear that the mission had originated with Ponty, but in later years his name disappeared from accounts, especially since he died during the war and was survived by Mangin, who wrote several books on the subject.[60]

Some influential colonial figures were against the idea. Governor Peuvergne of Senegal, for example, during the next month gave his endorsement but warned that "it was never the intention of the public powers to send a black army outside of French West Africa." Then, in his report to the council of government in June 1910, Ponty clarified speculations on Mangin's mission: they hoped to recruit 5,000 men yearly, to compose a reserve force of 20,000 "stationed in our coastal cities but available to the government to be employed wherever needed." He also announced the departure of another battalion of *tirailleurs* for Algeria to add to the two sent in 1908 to Morocco. And by November 1910 *L'Afrique française* reported that Mangin had completed his travels and had found that "the conclusions of the mission confirm the possibilities of creating a reservoir for the project that M. Ponty, governor-general, has established."[61]

Ponty and Mangin had worked closely on the first general enlistment of July 1907 to July 1908, during which 7,868 blacks were recruited for new battalions in the French Congo, the home guard in the French West Africa, and the two battalions mentioned for Morocco. This success had encouraged both men to ask for more troops. In 1910, the French authorities set up a study mission, which Ponty had believed would convince Parliament to grant their request. Ponty had not favored conscription (as did Mangin) but realized volunteers would be insufficient; so he came out for the doctrine of recruitment *à l'amiable*, which meant putting the burden on individual African chiefs to come up with quotas of recruits. His successor, Clozel, later wrote that he did not share Ponty's enthusiasm for this idea and doubted that Africans would respond; nevertheless, they were forced to cooperate, and Ponty seemed justified in his assumption of the wisdom of taking Africans into partnership in the military arena—an extension of his pacification policy of "enemies yesterday, auxiliaries today."[62]

Mangin's team visited almost all *cercles* in French West Africa, held more than 100 palavers with major chiefs, and wrote 63 detailed subreports with impressive documentation. Michel suggests that with approval from "collaborating chiefs" and urban Africans of Senegal and Dahomey—who aspired to assimilation via military service—and with Ponty's support, Mangin was able to convince his superiors that such recruiting should take place. With Archinard's patronage, Paris issued the decree of February 7, 1912, which authorized limited recruitment of Africans for four years.

The new proposal was called the Plan Ponty and had as a goal the recruitment of 5,000 Africans per year for the next four years—precisely what Mangin had wanted. Ponty's political pragmatism helped carry the day for Mangin; as Davis commented, "[Ponty's] recognized competence in colonial affairs, and the fact that he was not a military man, made the *Plan Ponty* of perhaps greater significance for the time being than Mangin's ideas." Ponty wanted the chiefs to have sole responsibility for finding the young men for military service, but few chiefs would take the responsibility—the onus—of recruiting from their own people. Within a few months Africans were fleeing to neighboring colonies such as Gambia to avoid the draft, and news reached Paris that some administrators threw aside voluntary enlistments and simply moved toward conscription. *Le Temps* observed that the situation would be put in order when Ponty returned to Africa from Paris, that recruiting had been mainly in Senegal, and that it needed to be extended to other colonies.[63]

From 1912 through 1914, 16,000 men were recruited in French West Africa, mostly in Senegal, Sudan, and Guinea. But protests continued, administrators did not share Ponty's enthusiasm, and—with complaints coming from French business houses—recruitment went back to a voluntary basis just before the outbreak of the war. As Michel points out in his seminal article, Mangin had *not*, in effect, been able to create his reservoir of black troops for France. Yet the precedent was established, and once the war started Ponty quickly recruited more men. Moreover, as Michel emphasizes, the idea—and morality—of drafting colonial subjects was now established firmly in French public opinion. When war broke out in August 1914 Ponty justified his years of support of the African troops and made recruitment the number one item on his agenda until his death the next year. The black troops to serve in France left Morocco on August 10, 1914, in time to participate in the battle of the Marne, where they suffered heavy losses. Other battalions from Morocco arrived in October, and during the rest of the war there was a constant stream of men from French West Africa for the armies of France. The troops of Mangin and Ponty were useful if deployed properly (not in the winter months) and earned a reputation for bravery under fire. When Georges Clemenceau became prime minister in 1917, he wanted more Africans for a badly depleted French army. Joost Van Vollenhoven, the new governor-general of French West Africa, balked at recruiting more Africans (he feared widespread rebellion), but Clemenceau bypassed him and sent Senegalese deputy Blaise Diagne to conduct the 1918 recruting campaign. In total, 161,000 men were recruited during the war in addition to those recruited beforehand—a considerable effort by an African society that scarcely understood or had a stake in European wars.[64]

For Ponty, it was the crowning glory of his long colonial service: "It will be the proudest and most honorable moment of my career to have served at their head," he told his lieutenant governors. In 1913 the Senegalese regiment won the Legion of Honor and Ponty boasted: "This sudden recognition by the government of our black soldiers . . . goes straight to the heart of the *vieil Africain* that I am; of the African who for more than twenty years has had the honor of marching at the side of these audacious troops."

Ponty's devotion to his *tirailleurs* eventually cost him his life since in early 1914 he began to suffer seriously from uremic poisoning and was advised by his doctors to sail for France and medical treatment. But he preferred to stay at his post, arguing that the war now made recruitment essential for France's welfare and that to leave would be the equivalent of deserting one's post in the midst of battle. Despite repeated warnings from doctors, friends, and his wife, Ponty clung tenaciously to his office, perhaps afraid his power might be seized by younger, ambitious men. Finally, on June 13, 1915, Ponty died in his baroque palace overlooking the Atlantic at Dakar, and countless Africans of the federation from Senegal to Niger went into mourning for the old Sudanese chief. Above all, there was sadness in the regiments of the 60,000 men he had recruited to fashion France's *force noire*. It was, as the *Journal officiel* observed, his "connaissance de l'âme et des milieux indigènes" that had made the *armée noire* possible.[65]

Personal Life and Conclusion

William Ponty's personal life is mostly an unknown quantity because of the paucity of original personal materials. Glimpses of his personality can be picked up in published reports of official gatherings, such as the sincere praise given by Inspec-

tor General Guyho, who welcomed Ponty to Dakar in 1908: "You have the knack
. . . of always remaining yourself, full of good humor and affable, whether in difficult or happy days." His comrade in arms Camille Guy, with whom Ponty often
disagreed, described him: "a very penetrating intelligence . . . nothing discour-
ages him. . . . [He] possesses a will that no one can thwart . . . and shows smiling
good humor in the face of fatigue and danger." Fournier, Ponty's finance director,
observed that Ponty was said to have a lucky star but that actually Ponty rarely
left anything to chance, always being prepared on smallest details when making a
decision: "his instructions . . . will be models of clarity and sagacity for generations to come." He believed that Ponty's moderation in native policy was responsible for creating the climate of African loyalty, that his generosity disarmed his
enemies. General Pineau, head of the French West African troops, called Ponty
"the kind of delightful comrade full of good humor . . . whom you hated to leave
and whom you wanted to keep track of." Pineau confirmed the fact that Ponty
was popular with troops in the army and that the organization of the black army
succeeded thanks "to Governor Ponty and to him alone" because of his knack of
cutting through red tape and inspiring African chiefs to cooperate. "We salute
him for the last time. . . . [H]e succeeded in being our chief, but even more so our
friend." Antonetti said that Ponty's name was the best known in black Africa—
especially in the Sudan, where Africans often named children, favorite horses,
and even villages after him.[66]

There is one source rich in personal materials but it should be used with cau-
tion. This is Robert Arnaud's biographical novel of Ponty's career, *Le Chef de
porte-plume*, published in 1922, seven years after Ponty's death. Arnaud, writing
under the pen name of Robert Randau, describes Ponty (called Ledolmer) in his
governor's palace in Dakar, aging and meditating upon his past glories and mistakes. The action is seen through the eyes of a young aide, Tobie—presumably Arnaud himself, who was Ponty's staff officer for Islamic affairs. The portrait of
Ponty that emerges is often critical, at times pathetic, at times humorous, and it
helps shed light on the inner man.

Ledolmer (Ponty) is famous for his knowledge of "the native mind" and for his
interest in feminine companionship. Melancholy because he lacks a permanent relationship, Ledolmer finally surprises his mistresses and colleagues by going to
France and bringing back a bride who was in show business. This corresponds
with Ponty's marriage in 1910 and with his difficulties in adjusting to marriage
and to having his wife run the governor's palace. Arnaud tells us that Madame
Ledolmer sacks the old Bambara soldiers, who were Ponty's trusted servants; to
her the palace was a military barracks to be changed. Arnaud tells of the palace
intrigues around Ledolmer with only thinly disguised characters; one subordinate
is in reality Gabriel Angoulvant, whose ambition was to replace Ponty. We find
Ponty tolerating the elite African politician Sissoko (read Diagne), who has defeated Ledolmer's candidate at the polls. Tobie's wife, Camille, describes his aging glory:

> Poor Ledolmer was once a man in the mainstream of his time. Now he is old, and
> gaga, and full of himself. All he can do is to play father confessor to civil servants.
> When in his cups, he reminds me of the old type of piratical Corsican uncle from
> the Indian Ocean, Uncle Barbassou looking for a woman.

Arnaud describes Ponty's palace, considered so magnificent by the Africans, as a place filled with "paintings purely second-rate, sent out by the undersecretary for beaux-arts . . . and a mantlepiece in the Louis Philippe style, but false." From this gilded prison, Ledolmer commands his vast empire, lost without his old colleagues who have retired or died before him; he relives his battles against native tyrants, against slavers, savors his feminine conquests in Paris while on leave. "I'm no more virtuous than the next person," he laments. "I'm not really concerned about such things, and I willingly excuse weaknesses except in the matter of duty." He fondly recalls his old friends, the *broussards*, from the conquest: "We entered into the furnace together and because we were always in action, wound up without family, home, or posterity." Ledolmer thunders to his assistant, "Never employ the term 'subjects' in administrative texts when speaking of the natives." And on native policy he waxes eloquent, expatiating "with passion on his plans for social reform among the 'least advanced' black peoples of tropical Africa, but with extreme prudence, for he does not want to infringe upon even the smallest traditional right." To his superintendent of education, Ledolmer frets about the dangers of assimilation: "Be careful! The students will become so Frenchified that they may pretend to be the only true Frenchmen!"[67]

To the ladies, Ledomer confides, "You see, Madame, I was born a good French bourgeois, but I have lived a life worthy of a hero of Fenimore Cooper." Ledolmer passes in review the African troops leaving for Morocco, wishing them godspeed first in French, second in Bambara, and third in Tukulor (Poular). Their response to his sentiments is "noisy as sirens." But one of his staff members complains: "He is the incarnation, in my view, of the colonial bohemian type. . . . [H]e likes only those who resemble him. He lives for the pleasure of his passions and claims that he has the constitution of a superman; in such a situation, it's easy to become blind to his merits!" Ledolmer prides himself on his achievements as governor of a vast empire; he delights in telling his intimates, usually mistresses or admiring women, of his recipe for success; the self-confident charm shows through, the egotistical drive to succeed:

> From a multitude of African cantons juxtaposed under my authority by the conquest, I have constituted an empire, a black France. I have the double honor of having surrounded myself with colleagues chosen from the elite and of having never had to share my power with anybody: I am a solitary figure. . . . It's true, I have become, without realizing it, an African monarch.

Toward the end of the novel, when Ledolmer has finally married and become weak from keeping up with his young wife's frenetic schedule, which includes endless receptions, bridge parties, and suppers that the old campaigner is ill-suited for, he philosophizes about his career. It is here that Arnaud provides us with his deepest insight into the twilight years of Ponty's rule, and we see doubts about the French presence in Africa voiced by the *vieil Africain*:

> Now then, my friends, there are times when I ask myself, why in the world did we come here? At the risk of our lives, we have made a lot of heroic gestures, but to what end? Our people will never adapt themselves to these tropical countries, where we will simply atrophy by interbreedings. Was it to build a fortune for several dozen merchants, more or less honest? Was it to teach the blacks, in hollow

phrases, the paradoxes of Rousseau on human goodness and the social contract? These people here, they were used to simple ideas, to uncomplicated dogmas; we profoundly trouble their psychological makeup, even despite ourselves. And why? Will they some day constitute themselves into South American type republics, on the model of Liberia? We will have spilled our blood, wasted our money and energy to bring about the triumph of racial hatred. Do you think I could be very enthusiastic about having knocked myself out to help bring about such results? And don't think that I'm exaggerating! The half-civilized inhabitants of the cities have their minds stuffed with the principles of 1789; they conclude only one thing: it's necessary to get rid of the Europeans.[68]

Notes

Abbreviations used:

ARS   Archives de la République du Sénégal (Dakar)

ANSOM   Archives nationales, section outre-mer (Paris)

JOAOF   *Journal officiel de l'Afrique occidentale française* (Dakar)

1. Robert Arnaud [Robert Randau], *Le Chef de porte-plume* (Paris, 1922).

2. The French ministry of colonies was created later (1894) than the British. See William Cohen, *Rulers of Empire* (Stanford, 1971), pp. 19–21; also William Ponty, personnel dossier, ANSOM, EE (II) 1137 (6).

3. This helps explain his willingness to build an African army when most colonial officers, who by training and temperament were separate from the military, opposed such solutions; see memorandum by Maurice Delafosse for Joost Van Vollenhoven opposing recruiting during 1917, ARS, 2-G-17-4.

4. Maurice Delafosse, "L'Afrique occidentale française," in Gabriel Hanotaux and Alfred Martineau, *Histoire des colonies françaises* (Paris, 1931)4:184.

5. M. Fournier, speech, *JOAOF*, 19 June 1915 (p. 421).

6. William Ponty, speech, ibid., 4 February 1911 (p. 86); Camille Guy, speech, ibid.

7. Lieutenant colonel Humbert, note, 4 May 1892, Ponty personnel dossier, ANSOM.

8. Colonel Louis Archinard, note, 1892, Ponty personnel dossier, ANSOM; General Joseph S. Gallieni, notes, 1896–1897, ANSOM.

9. Robert Delavignette, *Les Vrais Chefs de l'empire* (Paris, 1939), available in translation as *Freedom and authority in French West Africa* (London, 1968).

10. Governor Ballay, note, 1899, Ponty personnel dossier, ANSOM.

11. Ponty, "Note sur la colonie du Haut-Sénégal–Niger," ANSOM, Soudan I, c. 11-bis.

12. Ibid.

13. In this case, Le Grand Orient, whose members filled many important posts in the upper echelons of French colonial administration; private communication from Robert Delavignette, Paris, 14 November 1964.

14. Donal Cruise O'Brien, *Saints and Politicians* (Cambridge, 1975), p. 94; Cohen, *Rulers of Empire*, pp. 123–126.

15. Governor Ballay, note, 1901, Ponty personnel dossier; Governor Roume, notes, 1902–1907, ANSOM.

16. Governor Raphaël Antonetti, speech, *JOAOF*, 19 June 1915 (p. 425). The psychology of the moment is heightened by Antonetti's postscript: "Il faut avoir assisté à une telle scène pour se rendre compte de l'émotion qu'elle dégage. Ce grand chef des blancs qui avait reconnu un tirailleur et lui avait serré la main."

17. Denise Bouche, *Les Villages de liberté en Afrique noire française* (Paris, 1968), pp. 93, 101–102.

18. Paul Marty, "La Politique indigène du gouverneur général Ponty," *Revue du monde musulman* 31 (1915):12–13.

19. Pierre Mille, "La Fin du régime de l'esclavage," *L'Action nationale* (July 1912): 500–508; Marty, "La Politique indigène," pp. 1–28.

20. Marty, "La Politique indigène," p. 12.

21. Ponty also made available seed for African farmers in many of the villages, ARS, 21-G-127-108; see also Marty, "La Politique indigène," p. 12.

22. Roume had never visited Africa before; he was a *maître des requêtes* in 1892 and director of Asian affairs in 1895 at the colonial ministry. *Le Soir* (Paris), 11 November 1904, irreverently observed: "Il fallait un Africain d'expérience. . . . [O]n a choisi un Indo-Chinois de Paris."

23. Delafosse, *L'Afrique occidentale française*, pp. 348–349; see also Colin Newbury, "The Formation of the Government General in French West Africa," *Journal of African History* 1 (1960): 111–128.

24. Descriptions and quotations cited in *JOAOF*, 14 March 1908 (pp. 129–130).

25. Ibid. (p. 132); see speech by *inspecteur général*.

26. Charles Humbert, *L'Oeuvre français aux colonies* (Paris, 1913), pp. 9–11.

27. André Villard, *Histoire du Sénégal* (Dakar, 1943), p. 182. Villard observed that "Ponty, vieux soudanais . . . mena l'A.O.F. avec bonne humeur, esprit, et habileté."

28. Ponty, speech, *JOAOF*, 23 November 1912 (pp. 740 Off.); *L'Afrique française*, June 1912, p. 232; Robert Cornevin, "L'Un des plus grands proconsuls français: William Merlaud-Ponty," *France eurafrique* 197 (1968): 33–37.

29. Respectively, during their governorships, Roume raised loans of 100 million and 65 million francs; Ponty, 14 million and 167 million francs. *La Quinzaine coloniale* (Paris), 25 February 1908; Ponty, speeches, *JOAOF*, 4 February (p. 87), 24 June 1911 (p. 365).

30. Ponty, speeches, *JOAOF*, 26 June 1909 (p. 286), 24 June 1911 (p. 367), 23 November 1912 (pp. 738–739); see also Maurice Viollette et al., *L'Afrique occidentale francaise* (Paris, 1913), p. 12.

31. Marty, "La Politique indigène," p. 3; Ponty, speeches, *JOAOF*, 25 June 1910 (p. 406), 24 June 1911 (p. 364); also M. Masson, mayor of Dakar, speech, *JOAOF*, 19 June 1915 (p. 427). *La Démocratie* (Dakar) also carried aludatory articles on Ponty for several weeks after his death; this was during the editorship of Jean Daramy d'Oxoby, a vociferous spokesman for *petit-colon* interests.

32. *L'Afrique française*, July 1910, p. 232; Viollette et al., *L'Afrique occidentale*, pp. 33, 43; Raymond Leslie Buell, *The Native Problem in Africa* (London, 1965), 2:44–45.

33. Ponty, speeches, *JOAOF*, 25 June 1910 (p. 409), 24 June 1911 (p. 364), 15 November 1913 (p. 1010).

34. Later governors-general, such as Martial Merlin, were instrumental in clamping censorship on French West Africa. The sobriquets for Ponty were used frequently in the columns of the pro-African elite newspaper *La Démocratie*; see issue of 25 December 1913.

35. Cohen, *Rulers of Empire*, p. 122. Ponty married in 1910, after twenty years in the field.

36. Ibid., pp. 62–63; "Voyage de M. le gouverneur général," *JOAOF*, 25 March 1911 (p. 187).

37. "Informations," *JOAOF*, 8 June 1911 (p. 392); Ponty, speech, ibid., 24 June 1911 (p. 371).

38. On the William Ponty School, which as a normal school antedates Ponty's career as governor-general, see Peggy Sabatier (Ph.D. dissertation, University of Chicago, in preparation); Ponty, speeches, *JOAOF*, 25 June 1910 (p. 405), 4 February (p. 88), 24 June 1911 (p. 370), 15 November 1913 (p. 1005).

39. Marty, "La Politique indigène," p. 3; G. Wesley Johnson, "The Ascendancy of Blaise Diagne and the Beginning of African Politics in Senegal," *Africa* 36 (1966):247–248; Humbert, *L'Oeuvre français*, pp. 33–34.

40. For Ponty's original text see *JOAOF*, circular of 22 September 1909 (p. 447).

41. "Voyage de M. Milliès-Lacroix," ibid., 19 April 1908 (p. 192).

42. Ponty, speech, ibid., 23 November 1912 (p. 736).

43. See text and commentary of circular of 22 September 1909 in Jean-Baptiste Forgeron, *Le Protectorat en Afrique occidentale française* (Paris, 1920), pp. 75–79.

44. Marty, "La Politique indigène," pp. 5, 7, 8.

45. Ibid., p. 9; Ponty, speech, *JOAOF*, 24 June 1911 (pp. 369–370).

46. Robert Arnaud, *L'Islām et politique musulmane française* (Paris, 1912), pp. 3–4.

156 William Ponty and Republican Paternalism in French West Africa

47. Ponty, speech, *JOAOF*, 25 June 1910 (p. 405).

48. Ibid., 24 June 1911 (p. 270), 23 November 1912 (p. 728); Marty, "La Politique indigène," p. 17.

49. Complete documentation on the M'Baye-Brocard affair is contained in ARS, 13-G-17. It should be noted that Ponty was hypersensitive to metropolitan opinion and feared that if the *indigénat* were repealed it would complicate administrative tasks in West Africa. He favored modifying this system rather than abolishing it.

50. Ponty, speech, *JOAOF*, 26 June 1909 (p. 286); note, ANSOM, Sénégal VII-bis.

51. H. O. Idowu, "The Council General of Senegal" (Ph.D. dissertation, University of Ibadan, 1966), p. 408.

52. See reports and minutes, governor-general to minister, 1 May 1914, ANSOM, Sénégal VII-81; acting governor of Senegal to governor-general, 10 June 1914, ARS, 20-G-21.

53. Governor-general to minister, 24 June 1914, ARS, 20-G-21; governor-general to minister, 15 June 1914, ARS, 17-G-234-108. Diagne became a Freemason in Madagascar in emulation of most important colonial administrative officials.

54. Merlin was criticized for setting up censorship laws in French West Africa, among other policies; Van Vollenhoven was been suspected of being a racist by some African observers; Angoulvant became infamous for his brutalities in the "pacification" campaigns in Ivory Coast; and Antonetti has been vilified, with good reason, for his inhumane treatment of Africans in the building of the Congo-Ocean railroad.

55. Ponty, speech, *JOAOF*, 23 November 1912 (p. 427).

56. Marty, "La Politique indigène," p. 2; Ponty, speech, *JOAOF*, 24 June 1911 (p. 369); "Mort de M. le gouverneur général Ponty," ibid., 19 June 1915 (p. 419).

57. Ponty, speeches, ibid., 26 June 1909 (pp. 286–289), 23 November 1912 (p. 728). These resistance movements have not been fully studied, but dozens of reports are on file in the Senegalese national archives that testify to them.

58. "Mort de Ponty," p. 420.

59. The standard work on the *armée noire* is Shelby Cullom Davis, *Reservoirs of Men* (Chambéry, 1934), pp. 68–69.

60. Marc Michel, "Un Mythe: La 'Force noire' avant 1914," *Relations internationales* 2 (1974): 83–90; also see *L'Afrique française*, May 1910, p. 163.

61. *L'Afrique française*, June 1910, p. 193; Ponty, speech, *JOAOF*, 25 June 1910 (p. 410).

62. Davis, *Reservoirs of Men*, p. 107; Viollette et al., *L'Afrique occidentale*, pp. 64–68, 109. See also Governor-general Clozel to minister, 17 September 1915, ANSOM, A.O.F. Affaires politiques, 2801-6; Clozel felt that Ponty's enthusiasm for recruitment—especially after the onset of hostilities—was explained partially by the fact that Ponty (and others) thought the war would be short.

63. Davis, *Reservoirs of Men*, p. 112; *L'Afrique française*, September 1912, p. 376. See also *La Quinzaine coloniale* (Paris), 24 July 1912, p. 500; *Le Temps* (Paris), 18 July 1912.

64. *L'Afrique française*, September 1912, p. 376; Michel, "Un Mythe," p. 89; Davis, *Reservoirs of Men*, p. 143. On Diagne, see G. Wesley Johnson, *Emergence of Black Politics in Senegal* (Stanford, 1971). For revised troop estimates see Marc Michel, "Le Recrutement des tirailleurs en A.O.F. pendant la première guerre mondiale," *Revue française d'histoire d'outre-mer* 60, no. 221 (1973):645.

65. Ponty, speeches, *JOAOF*, 8 July 1911 (p. 392), 15 November 1913 (p. 998); "Mort de Ponty," p. 420.

66. "Arrivée officielle du gouverneur général à Dakar," ibid., 14 March 1908 (p. 132); Camille Guy, speech, ibid., 4 February 1911 (p. 86); Fournier, Pineau, Antonetti, speeches, ibid., 19 June 1915 (pp. 422, 423, 425).

67. Arnaud, *Le Chef de porte-plume*, pp. 50–139 et passim.

68. Ibid., pp. 97–241 et passim.

Governor-general Félix Eboué (1884-1944)

Brian Weinstein

FÉLIX Eboué may be the most famous governor in French imperial history, yet he is one of the least known. A single decision near the end of his life brought him into the spotlight illuminated by General Charles de Gaulle and to burial in the Panthéon next to Jean Jaurès and Victor Schoelcher, but that action also obscured the long career in Africa and the West Indies that preceded it. Eboué's blackness and colonial birth at first provided material for hagiographers and loyalists straining to find models of the successful "native" and reassurances for the continuity of empire after World War II. Later some African and Caribbean nationalists angrily rejected Eboué, calling him a traitor to the goals of liberation, and serious biographers chose to write about black revolutionaries and white innovators in colonial history. Thus accepted, rejected, or ignored on the basis of his usefulness to colonial or anticolonial ideologies, Eboué's life was never considered interesting.

In fact, his life is a striking example of how ethnic and racial elites attempt to resolve the tensions between narrow group identity and participation within a larger national system. Equally important, his career as an admininstrator for thirty-five years reflects the tensions between centralizing and decentralizing strands in the French political tapestry. Most significant, his success as a colonialist is a demonstration of the delicate interplay between interests and sentiments in the metropole and those in the colonial state, which link and separate France and Africa then and now.

Colonial Beginnings

The grant of citizenship to all inhabitants of France's Caribbean colonies, Guadeloupe and Martinique, and to the residents of French Guiana on the South American littoral after the end of slavery in 1848 opened a little further the door to a better life. For two centuries mulattoes with good contacts had been emigrating in order to enter the French middle and professional classes; more blacks could now squeeze through, but a wider gate opened after World War II, when the Caribbean possessions were more fully integrated into the French republic as overseas departments.

Limitations on this form of escape from 1848 to 1946 derived from the absence of schools in rural areas, the lack of aid, the isolation and poverty of most of the population, a complex racial belief system—particularly in Martinique and Guadeloupe—and the colonial pact that barred intercourse with neighboring islands and continental America. Even under the most favorable circumstances mulattoes and blacks needed well-placed friends, relatives, or patrons to buy the right ticket.

The solution of political independence was only briefly on the French political agenda, despite the example of Haiti's successful revolt. The "pearl of the French empire" had had resources lacking in the Lesser Antilles and Guiana (Guyane): a much larger and more defensible territory, at least five times the population of Martinique, a significant educated elite in the island, and a material wealth that far outdistanced that of other French colonies. Thus, although French forces quickly subdued the revolt of Delgrès and Ignace in Guadeloupe in 1802, Dessalines triumphed against the Europeans in Haiti the following year. And in later years the sugar cane, banana, and spice economies of the three remaining colonies became increasingly dependent on France.

In these hopeless circumstances aspiring elites saved themselves individually, rather than as members of communities, through education and careers outside the Caribbean. Men such as Frantz Fanon, psychiatrist and revolutionary writer, Gaston Monnerville, president of the French Senate, Saint-Jean Perse, white poet and diplomat, and Félix Eboué served the interests of France and other states well.

The situation in Guiana, where Félix Eboué was born on December 26, 1884, seemed the most hopeless of all despite the economic potential of the colony. A miniscule but racially varied population of 24,000 huddled in ten towns and villages strung along the coast that year, leaving Inini—a vast, unexplored, rich interior—to the few thousand American Indians and black descendants of escaped slaves who had tried to reestablish African societies. About one-third of the population lived in Cayenne, the capital, where the governor had his headquarters and where the elected council met for about a month each year. People had moved to Cayenne after the abolition of slavery and the beginning of the gold rush in 1855. The attraction of gold up the Sinnamary river, for example, robbed the developing farms, which might have provided a foundation for a more economically autonomous community, and young men and women made the town their home.

Félix Eboué's maternal and paternal families moved to Cayenne from the area of Roura, a town thirty miles away, where his African great-grandparents had worked as slaves on spice plantations. The first record of his paternal great-grandfather appears in an inventory of the Hermitage plantation. This property had been owned by a woman called Sabine, herself a slave freed about 1803. Sabine had given the land to her daughter—probably the offspring of Sabine's former white owner, Bordes—and to the European she married.

Item 94 in an inventory of 1842 is a slave called "Héboué, 46 years, invalid,"[1] but this man must have died before the emancipation of 1848 because the records contain no further reference to him. A woman, Henriette, identified as his widow, is listed in the manumission book, but the clerk spelled her surname "Eboe" and her two offspring, Alexandre-François and Marie-Gabrielle, were also called Eboe.[2] On the maternal side of the family, the manumission book lists Jean-Baptiste and his wife, Rosie Léveillé, as also born in Africa.

Judging from the approximate birthdates of Eboué's four great-grandparents—between 1796 and 1810—they may have been captured between 1815 and 1824. Despite the laws against the slave trade, it had begun again clandestinely after the Napoleonic wars in 1815. The year 1824 was particularly active because of an increase in arms sales in Africa.[3] According to the documents available, the highest percentage of slaves during this period came from the general areas of Congo, Angola, and Mozambique.[4] Family tradition placed the Eboué or Léveillé ancestors up a river from the coast. The women kept cowry shells as a remembrance of Africa. Eboué himself told Africans in two areas that he had traced his ancestors there, but this was probably a friendly gesture or a tactic to gain their confidence.

No matter where the Héboué and Léveillé came from, their famous descendant must have had a keen sense of African origins. Henriette lived until 1888, when Félix Eboué was only four years old, but her daughter lived to 1898, when he was fourteen. Henriette stayed at Roura, so the young Félix probably never met her, but Marie-Gabrielle died in Cayenne. His maternal grandmother, Palmyre Léveillé, who lived the first seventeen years of her life as a slave, died in Cayenne in 1918, when her grandson was already thirty-four. Doubtless Félix Eboué heard many firsthand stories about slavery and secondhand stories about Africa from his two grandmothers.

But if Eboué did not think of himself as an African, it is not surprising. Despite an awareness of origins in Cayenne in the late nineteenth and the early twentieth century African heritage was not something about which people were particularly proud. Black Creoles—people of African descent born in Guiana—thought Africans must be like the peoples of Inini, whom they called the "primitives," and they condemned as "savage" any exhibitions of music and drumming assumed to be African. Becoming more French was the watchword, but without important contacts in the schools, the civil service, or politics a family might have little hope to offer its children.

Fortunately for him, Félix Eboué was served some very useful names, and he learned quickly how to cultivate them. Although Yves Eboué, his father, had no legal father at his birth in 1851, family tradition named Philistrat Ursleur, a well-known Cayenne lawyer. Ursleur also reportedly fathered Maximilien Liontel and the son he did recognize as Henri Ursleur. These three half brothers knew each other well, and Liontel and Henri Ursleur achieved prominence. Liontel climbed the colonial judicial ladder, occupying the post of public prosecutor for Guiana between 1887 and 1893; then wworking in French India, Papeete, Africa, and back to Guiana as attorney general between 1901 and 1905 or 1906. The voters elected Henri Ursleur mayor of Cayenne and then deputy to the French Parliament between 1898 and 1906.

Of the three, Yves Eboué's career shown least brightly, but his reputation as a gold mine manager put him nonetheless into close contact with important businessmen such as Adolf Bailley, who agreed to be Félix Eboué's godfather. Yves Eboué was also elected to Cayenne's municipal council on the same ticket with Ursleur. Unfortunately, he died young (in 1898), a few months before Félix's fourteenth birthday. His half brothers may not have helped his family with much money, but they probably promised other kinds of assistance.

Thus, Madame Eboué, a devout Roman Catholic and well-known treasure house of local lore, supported herself and the two of her five children still at home—Félix and his eight-year-old sister, Cornélie. She took up petty trading and raised vegetables and prepared various concoctions for sale. Many years after her death Cayenne remembered this African looking black woman in a long, traditional dress and head scarf smoking her pipe as she waited for customers.

In the meanwhile, her son Félix continued his schooling at the Collège de Cayenne, considered a poor excuse for a secondary school. There he probably learned the virtues of self-control: in a multiracial society like Guiana, where European standards prevailed, schoolchildren mocked their peers who had African features. Eboué, deep brown in color (or "so black he was blue," one fair-skinned Guianese said), with a broad nose, full lips, and short, curly hair, must have heard many jokes at his expense. A naturally robust physique and a growing interest in sports made him into a formidable opponent in a fair fight, but his mother preached the need for self-control for success in life. The leitmotiv of the *dolos*, or Guianese proverbs and folktales she knew so well, was that the weak must act with economy and calculation in order to survive and prosper in a world ready to mock and crush them. Eboué learned these *dolos* well.

Watching his successful relatives, talking to civil servants and businessmen, working hard at his studies, the young man moved swiftly through school. Because it did not grant the baccalaureate, or secondary school diploma, the lucky few would finish their education in metropolitan France. Ursleur and Liontel could not have been indifferent to Yves's son, who had also been at the top of his class; thus, in 1901 Eboué left for a lycée in Bordeaux with a scholarship in hand.

Sailing to France that September, a few months before his seventeenth birthday, he must have reflected on the career options before him. A return to the stagnant homeland was out of the question unless he wanted to work in the prison administration watching over poor souls like the famous Captain Dreyfus. His mother had begged him not to go into gold prospecting, and he already knew what he would write to a relative twenty years later: "there is nothing for us in Guiana. . . . [O]ur children's futures cannot be guaranteed with the famine salaries in Cayenne."[5]

Thus, the years in Bordeaux, from the end of 1901 to the end of 1904, helped Eboué formulate career goals, articulate a personal philosophy built on the *dolos* of his mother, and find new contacts. Beginning at the Lycée Montaigne he found other West Indians such as René Maran (future winner of the Prix Goncourt for the novel *Batouala*). Eboué and Maran rejected the church of their parents and substituted a stoic faith in elites, restraint, internal withdrawal, harmony with nature, and unity of humanity. A better life depended on order and discipline, and those who could not control themselves would have to be forced into certain patterns of work. These ideas nourished Eboué for the rest of his life and sustained his confidence in the benefits of colonialism. In one of the many notebooks he kept over the years he wrote.:

> Love, Love in and of itself lets leave it to Tolstoy. We must live—to live = blows. But if we have iodine to dress the wounds, we agree on an existence that is to live and to fight. All the rest is nonsense. That is colonization—more Nietzsche than Tolstoy. We must know how to suffer. Only suffering permits organization.[6]

Becoming a colonial administrator thus was not a difficult decision. The service offered relatively high salaries, job security, and a pension; West Indians were encouraged to join the relatively unpopular administration. Both Eboué and Maran had many contacts in it, and good positions were increasingly open to graduates of the Ecole coloniale.

The Ecole coloniale, as Eboué knew it, had been founded in 1889 to train a corps of professional administrators. Unfortunately, teachers knew very little about the colonies, and Eboué must have found most courses useless. Increasingly, however, the school was the entry point into the corps of administrators from which the highest ranking officials and governors were to be drawn.

Having been accepted in the class entering in 1906, Eboué moved to Paris. Here he discovered the great intellectual life of the French capital and joined the SCUF (Sporting Club universitaire de France), where he played football along with a new friend, Yvon Delbos, future cabinet minister and candidate for the presidency of the republic. These activities and a reported affair with a young Italian woman—to say nothing of the mediocrity of the courses offered—were doubtless responsible for his poor showing at the school. In July 1908 Eboué was graduated near the bottom of his class—twenty-third out of twenty-seven students. Malgache language studies was the only area in which he had done very well.

Perhaps he knew he might be assigned to Madagascar. On November 30, 1908, a decree named him to the island, and he prepared to leave. A Martiniquan classmate begged Eboué to exchange posts, however; he had just married, and couples were discouraged from going to the French Congo, where he had been assigned. Eboué agreed to the exchange and left for Africa on Christmas Day 1908, celebrating his twenty-fourth birthday at sea.

The trip to Brazzaville, capital of the Congo, lasted from December 25 to January 21, 1909. En route Eboué glimpsed France's new empire in West Africa as the ship made stops in Senegal, Guinea, and Ivory Coast. Lagos, Britain's richer colony, must have impressed him then and over the next decades because of the higher rate of investments than in the French possessions. He also had to pass through the Belgian Congo because the French had still not built a railroad to the coast although the Belgians had built one inland to their capital by 1898. In Brazzaville, a village in 1909, the governor-general's office quickly assigned him to Ubangi-Shari, where he would spend almost twenty years.

Early Days in Ubangi-Shari, 1909–1931

Much of the Congo—which then included today's Chad, Gabon, Central African Republic, and Congo—had been explored, but very little of it was under French control. Taxes could not be collected because Africans refused to accept French authority, and administrators were too few and far between to control the huge territory (four times larger than France). Thus, the colony consisted of a few islands of administrators surrounded by a vast sea of indifference and hostility. Problems of communication and underadministration were to plague these colonies throughout Eboué's career and even to the present day.

As an *élève-administrateur* Eboué was on trial that first year, and the rule was that he work under an experienced administrator at a variety of tasks. The lieutenant governor assigned him to the Upper Shari, one of the seventeen administrative divisions. He left Bangui, the capital, by *tipoye*—a type of hammock carried by four Africans—for his posting at Bouca to the north. Another West Indian supervised his work, and he quickly understood the complications of census taking, construction, and mapmaking and began to learn an African language. Eboué's superior returned enthusiastic reports, and the ministry of colonies made him an assistant administrator third class, at the bottom rank in the corps of administrators at the beginning of 1910.

This year was also the beginning of the efforts made by Martial-Henry Merlin (governor-general of French Equatorial Africa, 1910–1917) to reorganize the administration. The name French Equatorial Africa replaced the name French Congo; more important, the first systematic administrative organization was set up. Merlin clarified his powers and those of the lieutenant governors who headed each colony. He set the frontiers of the colonial subdivisions, decentralized budgets, and sent out instructions for the weaving of a French administrative network throughout this vast area.

Despite the circulars that steadily filtered down to administrators in the field, Eboué learned early to work out his own way of interpreting them. He could do nothing, he saw, without taking into account local chiefs and French business interests, particularly in isolated places such as Bozoum, to which the governor assigned him.

The Mandjia people lived at Bouzoum, and they refused to pay their taxes. Merlin had set the tax per man and per woman at five francs, a higher figure than in the richer French West African colonies. The only way it could be paid was by the collection of rubber and ivory for sale to the private concessionary companies. Paris had told the colonies they had to be self-supporting, so that administrators' salaries came from the taxes collected on the sale of rubber and ivory and from customs duties. Little money was left for development. For example, the 1910 budget for Ubangi-Shari shows that at least sixty-three percent of expenditures went for functionaries' salaries, whereas only one percent was spent on education, less than one percent on agriculture, and slightly more than one percent for health.[7]

Under these conditions Africans failed to understand what benefits the colonial administration could offer. Recruited as porters to carry equipment toward Chad, forced to collect wild rubber for no immediate material benefit, moved to new villages near administrative posts, subjected by businessmen and some administrators to various humiliations, they naturally began to resist and flee the European and his guns.

Eboué thus participated in the last stages of what officials called "pacification," particularly in the area of Bozoum. He circulated through an endless region with armed African troops, attempted to collect taxes in some form, and somehow stopped attacks on European businessmen. The governor had instructed him to arrest the most troublesome chiefs, but the young administrator quickly showed his adaptability and cleverness.

Soon after his arrival in Ubangi he began the study of the cultures of the various people through African informants. Along with a colleague he prepared a manuscript on the Baya people that was published many years later. On the basis of his research in Bozoum he became convinced that the French must ally themselves with traditional authority in its various forms. This strategy meant convincing chiefs of the advantages they could win through cooperation: a five percent slice of the taxes collected, for example, or a gift of a few guns to be used against old enemies. Thus, instead of arresting dissident chiefs Eboué arranged palavers with them.

Eboué's willingness to negotiate went beyond temporal authority. He dealt with secret societies, particularly one he labeled *Somale*, which fascinated him for thirty years. These societies, which helped keep order, were perceived by Eboué as the type of elite organization that fit with his stoic philosophy. *Somale* was thus seen as legitimate, something he should help preserve in African society. In this troubled region he arranged a meeting with the leading spirit of the society, assumed to be a supernatural being called the *Ngakola*, after sending gifts of salt, machetes, and cloth. He traveled to the appointed meeting place during a howling storm, which his only companion, an African interpreter, saw as proof of the spirit's power. Some messages were exchanged during the encounter, and, as Eboué told the story in a speech to a group of Freemasons many years later: "His cooperation was promised, and I must admit that the contract was faithfully executed, that orders were given in the way I desired [to pay taxes, stop harassing Europeans and their agents], after which the difficulties disappeared like magic."[8] Eboué should also have added that he had recognized the spirit's interests as well.

No supernatural spirit could help an administrator's relations with the big companies, however. Because the French government had refused to spend money for development, it made immense land grants—concessions—to private companies that promised to undertake various undefined projects in French Equatorial Africa. The plan failed. Companies "without capital or spirit of enterprise" collected what they could without making any positive contribution; their "inertia paralyzed the economic life of the country" in those early years.[9] Yet they demanded that the colonial administration maintain order, which meant forcing the Africans to collect wild products for them and providing coerced labor to carry the products to acceptable ports. Even when roads opened and inland waterways were available, the businessmen often hesitated to invest in trucks and boats, preferring the cheaper human labor. Eboué and others, struggling with the problems of development, became increasingly skeptical about the role of private enterprise.

He followed these activities and maintained contact with the chiefs—particularly the select group cooperating fully with the French—by regular tours. Traveling by *tipoye*, Eboué could cover about five kilometers in an hour over the fairly flat savanna country of Ubangi-Shari. He kept little notebooks accounting for every minute spent, and they show he could not have stayed more than a few moments in most villages. Most of his time was spent haranguing chiefs who had almost exclusive access to the administrators: they must get people to pay taxes; they must supply workers and porters; they must move villages nearer the administrative post or new road.

Until the 1920s administrative problems in Ubangi seemed to be getting worse, however. At Kouango, located upstream from Bangui, for example, a rebellion had slowed tax collection and had adversely affected commerce. The governor wrote in 1914 that the French had even less control of the area than in 1912. Because of the beginning of the first world war, the soldiers in charge of Kouango had to leave for German controlled Kamerun, where the French were fighting. Thus, the governor had to choose an experienced civilian to subdue a region in which, in his words, "the villages are dispersing; the roads are abandoned; convoys are attacked."[10] The governor gave the assignment to Eboué, who had been on leave and then had been posted to Damara in 1913.

By allying himself with Sokambi, a clever Banziri chief who knew the advantages he could get from a close association with the French, Eboué succeeded in reestablishing French control and even in extending it. This effort rested on long military operations. During one of them Eboué traveled 1,143 kilometers from September 7 to November 21, 1915; another trip lasted from May 5, 1916 to July 31, 1916.[11] Without medical personnel he treated his own illnesses, including painful ear trouble; although he had some European products, he had to live off the land; and with Africans for companions he talked with them in the evening about their customs and beliefs.

Sokambi, an ally and friend, provided troops, protection for Eboué, knowledge of the area, information, and even a wife from his own extended family. In return for these services to the French, the Banziri leader won secure control over a large population, which meant money, prestige, and power. It meant he had first access to the economic and technological changes brought with the introduction of coffee and cotton a few years later. Sokambi's children received the first smatterings of colonial style European education, the French language and arithmetic, initially in a school that he himself founded and then in a French school. They thus became the first teachers and clerks, well placed to play an important role in the political evolution of the country in the years to come.

With the reestablishment of peace at Kouango the major company there, the Compagnie du Kouango français, purchased increasing quantities of products. Despite a worldwide decline in prices, this company shipped 141,000 kilos of rubber in 1915 and 191,000 kilos in 1916 compared with only 38,025 in 1914. Their exports of ivory increased from 1,060 kilos in 1915 to 1,998 in 1916.[12] On his own, Eboué shipped food from Kouango to Bangui: 9,000 kilos of manioc, 16 pigs, 11 goats, and 800 kilos of millet.[13] In 1916 these efforts were recognized by his promotion to assistant administrator first class and to full administrator third class the following year.

With the rank of full administrator Eboué could now be assigned to head a complete circumscription instead of the smaller subdivision. After a 1917 vacation in France, during which he tried to join the French army fighting in Europe,[14]

Eboué returned to direct the affairs of a much larger area under the leadership of a new, dynamic governor who reshaped the colonial state of Ubangi-Shari in the way Merlin had given new life to the organization of French Equatorial Africa.

The man was Auguste-Henri Lamblin, governor of Ubangi-Shari from 1919 to 1930. Lamblin's long tenure marked a change in colonialism, and the decade was the most important in the colony's history. He and Eboué shifted the economy from one of collection of wild products to industrial agriculture. Lamblin also supervised the construction of an extensive communication system and by these two actions showed that if a colony—even one in French Equatorial Africa, the Cinderella of the empire—had a well-staffed administration under the same, intelligent direction for more than five years, something of permanence could be built.

Lamblin assigned Eboué to Bambari from 1918 to 1921. Bambari was located in the center of the colony among the Banda people, the largest local ethnic group. Under Lamblin's direction Eboué built roads and introduced peanuts, rice, and sesame. He encouraged the development of a small sack-making industry. Significantly, also, Eboué established the largest school in the colony—at one point it had 300 students.

An enthusiastic governor proposed Eboué for an honor and a promotion, but Governor-general Victor Augagneur stood in the way. Augagneur, with the reputation of a liberal reformer, was suspicious of Eboué because of the number of people in prison in Bambari.

It is true that along with the rising rate of tax collection the number of people in Eboué's jails also increased. This is not surprising, of course, because his philosophy was that colonial officials knew best—that the African had to be forced to work for his own benefit, that he needed more discipline, and so forth. Refusal to cooperate meant punishment although there is no evidence that Eboué, like some of his colleagues, ever used any cruel or unusual methods.

On his way out of the colony to go on leave he met with Augagneur in Brazzaville in July 1921 to explain himself. Eboué pointed out that his region had the largest population in Ubangi-Shari, which was true, and that it was logical that the prisons should have a larger population than others. Doubtless he also explained his attitudes toward work. Augagneur told him he understood and praised Eboué in a general way, promising support for promotion in the near future. He probably remained suspicious of Eboué, however, and Eboué left for France and Cayenne, where two important changes in his life were imminent.

By 1921 Félix Eboué was thirty-seven years old, a bachelor with two sons—Henri, born in 1912 of a Mandjia mother, and Robert, born in 1918 of Eboué's Banziri wife. Apparently Eboué had once been engaged to marry a Guianese, but plans changed, and he seemed content with his two sons, whom he recognized legally. His sister, Cornélie, had a friend whom she encouraged Eboué to court: Eugénie Tell, twenty-nine years old, had been educated in France and was working as a schoolteacher at Saint-Laurent-du-Maroni. Her father, Herménégilde Tell, was director of the prisons, the first Guianese to hold this high post. In addition, he headed a local Masonic lodge and had many contacts in France and Africa, where his close friend Blaise Diagne had been elected to the French Parliament.

Marriage to Eugénie Tell would be convenient: new contacts would help in promotion, his two children would have a mother, and his life could achieve a new stability. However, all accounts of their twenty-two years of marriage indicate clearly that deep affection and love developed over time. And, on June 14, 1922 Eboué, giving in to the religious sentiments of his mother, wed Eugénie in the Catholic church of Saint-Laurent-du-Maroni.

One month later Eboué completed the picture of the successful Creole by joining the Cayenne lodge of Freemasons, La France équinoxiale. This action, too, would provide a wealth of new friends because freemasonry under the Third Republic was popular among political figures and civil servants. It was also powerful, forming a secret network of information and mutual help, particularly within the colonial administration. Joining this society was consistent with Eboué stoicism. The association of elites for discussions and reform of society appealed to him. The lodges had close ties with the socialist and radical parties and supported provocative political positions. For example, the federation of lodges to which the Cayenne lodge was affiliated resolved in 1922 "that natives should be educated to be on a level with the white and that natives in the colonies should be represented in parliament."[15]

Thus, with marriage contract and Freemason membership, Eboué's life changed. And he, Eugénie, and Henri—who had been staying with Eboué's mother—sailed for France. Because Eugénie soon became pregnant, Eboué requested an extension of leave in Paris, taking advantage of the time to complete his degree in law and to take some courses in anthropology. Eugénie met all his friends, with the exception of René Maran, who was still in Africa working as a colonial official.

In 1921 Maran had published *Batouala*, a novel about life in Africa from an African point of view. The book, whose introduction contained some sharp criticisms of colonialism, won the prestigious Prix Goncourt, and Eboué was filled with pride because this black man won. In addition, Eboué doubtless had contributed some details about African life—including *Somale*. He thought that the delay in his promotion might have been related to the book's publication. For this reason and because his wife began to doubt she would be happy in Africa, Eboué applied to the ministry of colonies and other agencies for a post in Paris.

In January 1923 the ministry promoted him to administrator first class, and Governor-general Augagneur asked for his speedy return to French Equatorial Africa, showing his respect for Eboué despite the full prisons at Bambari. Eboué obtained a further extension of his leave for the benefit of Eugénie, who gave birth on March 17, 1923, to their first and only daughter, Ginette. Five months later the three of them set sail for Africa, leaving Henri at school.

In Ubangi-Shari Governor Lamblin assigned Eboué to direct the Lower Mbomou region in the east. This area, inhabited by Zandé and Nzakara, had the only important monarchs left in the colony, and Eboué was fascinated by Sultan Hetman, who had cleverly supported French expansion for his own benefit. Hetman's services would be needed again because of a decline in French authority: taxes had not been collected recently, exports declined, and the people showed a general dissatisfaction with the colonial administration. A dynamic program might revive the area's economy. Because of increase demand for cotton in France, Eboué and other began to experiment with this plant.

In early 1924 cotton seeds sent from Bangui were planted. Eboué and his colleagues had distributed them to local leaders such as Hetman, who in turn distributed them to their people, as they were instructed, or to slaves. The experiment failed because of lack of experience and insufficient rainfall. The following year boded well for the colony in all ways, however. Governor Lamblin finally abolished the porter system and insisted that companies use trucks on the new roads. (Ubangi then had 3,800 kilometers of roads, the largest system in French Equatorial Africa.) Another good sign was the disappearance of the old-style large companies. Africans were now free to sell their products to the highest bidder, and they had money to spend on consumer goods.[16] The stage was set for industrial agriculture controlled by Africans, similar to the peanut industry in Senegal and the coffee industry in Ivory Coast.

The year 1925 had to be a success! To prepare himself for it Eboué read everything he could lay his hands on. René Maran, back in France, sent him books and articles, but the Belgians proved to be most helpful of all. On the south side of the Mbomou river they were getting good results with an American variety of cotton. Eboué entered into close relations with the Belgian administration and with businessmen who already had considerable economic influence in Ubangi. He obtained precious seeds from them and began his own experiments.

Introduction of cotton meant long tours and absences from Bangassou, the administrative capital. Eugénie, busy with her baby and Eboué's son Robert, who had joined them, gave birth in May 1924 to another child, Charles. With such responsibilities she could not bear her husband's absences. She also feared the drumming in the night, the thunderstorms during the rainy season, and the general loneliness of an administrator's wife. She begged Eboué to leave Africa, but he warned her his career would be broken if he did. He rushed back to Bangassou when he could, but the governor's warning about another crop failure kept him in the field.

The effort paid off. There was enought rain, and the Africans had taken proper care of the plants. Between January and March 1926 the harvest and sale took place, and for several weeks Eboué moved exuberantly from village to village supervising production. The results were spectacular: 180,000 kilos of cotton transformed the economy of Lower Mbomou in the space of one year.

To Eboué must go the credit. Lower Mbomou was the only successful region in the colony that year although others had conducted their own experiments. For the first time in the history of Ubangi-Shari, the Africans had a significant surplus of money after the payment of taxes. Businesses quickly shipped in cloth and other manufactured products to satisfy the needs of a new market.[17]

Like so many victories in life, this one was bittersweet. The personal satisfaction was there, but Governor Lamblin seemed to want to take the public bows; much worse were the complaints of the old companies that depended on the purchase of ivory and rubber from the Africans. Articles mysteriously appeared in colonial magazines and reports were written accusing Eboué of creating a famine since cotton cultivation allegedly prevented Africans from collecting or producing food. Behind the attack was the economic interest of businessmen who feared that other companies would benefit from the new crop.

A furious Eboué submitted his own article to the magazine *Le Monde colonial illustré*. At the same time, he prepared for the governor a draft decree setting forth the organization of the production and sale of cotton. Because of his growing suspicion of private business, Eboué proposed strict government control of the market, a minimum purchase price, and assurance that France would have the right of first refusal. The Belgians seemed more dynamic than their neighbors and Eboué feared their economic power in the colony, so he worked with a French businessman, Marcel Bénard, of a Paris banking family, to set up a French company for the processing and purchase of the product.

In a very brief period of time cotton had been firmly implanted in the colony's economy, and Eboué felt he could go on leave in June 1926. He had hoped to see his mother, but she died in March and he had to travel to Cayenne to settle her estate. While there, he advanced in the hierarchy of the Freemasons and received word that he had been named chevalier of the Legion of Honor.

Again in Paris, he spent long hours with Senegal's representative in parliament, Blaise Diagne. Rising black bureaucrats had similar interests and kept in close contact with each other and with the few African and West Indian politicians of importance. They pledged mutual support, seeing in their own personal success proof that black elites could obtain equality with white elites within the French nation. Diagne promised to help Eboué advance, although by the time Eboué left for Africa at the end of 1927 no decision on his promotion had been made.

The Ubangi-Shari he found on his return was undergoing another difficult period. The Baya people in the west rebelled against the French, and recruitment of workers for the new railroad—which the French finally decided to build from Brazzaville to the coast—challenged further the equanimity of administrators. Like the system of porterage, railroad recruitment paid little heed to the African workers' needs. Ill-fed, ill-clothed, and ignorant of the difficult tasks expected of them, the workers died in shocking numbers. Eboué's labor quota for the Kémo-Gribingui region, which he headed during most of 1928, accounted for less than ten percent of the total—520 out of 6,075 for the entire colony that year—but most of the workers probably never returned.[18]

Africans fled this death sentence by hiding in forest areas or by crossing the river into the Belgian Congo. Eboué, in a coded telegram to the governor, said: "Many natives have fled into the bush. I intend to have them found and request authorization to modify recruitment plan to take them for railroad rather than those who stayed to cultivate."[19] In 1929 he recruited workers from the area of Bambari, capital of Ouaka, where the governor reassigned him.

Eboué found old friends at Bambari and happily administered the region from 1929 to 1931, still as an administrator first class. Governor Lamblin and Governor-general Antonetti supported Eboué's promtion to administrator in chief, the highest rank in the corps, but the nomination was stopped at the ministry. Complaints about this matter to the Freemasons brought discreet promises of action. Eboué also wrote to West Indian politicians such as Gratien Candace, who represented Guadeloupe in the Chamber of Deputies. The ministry defended itself sharply against Candace's letter, implying racial prejudice, and Eboué received no promotion.

Work continued at Bambari. Gold had been discovered at Rohandji, near the post, and Marcel Bénard, the banker who had helped set up a cotton company in the Lower Mbomou, created the Compagnie équatoriale des mines to exploit it. Eboué purchased shares in this company while recruiting workers for it (administrators were allowed to own shares of corporations working in their areas despite what might seem to be possible conflicts of interest). He often traveled to Rohandji to observe the work there, and his wife—now more at home in Ubangi-Shari— enjoyed accompanying him. In 1930 Ginette was seven and Charles was six, old enough to free Madame Eboué a little; Henry and Robert attended school in France.

Eboué and his wife continued his researches into African culture and he sent René Maran his latest findings, but he was a little bored. He studied the upcoming parliamentary elections and asked his father-in-law's opinions about his chances in Guiana. Fortunately Eboué's career took a turn for the better; at the end of 1930 he received his long awaited promotion to administrator in chief, and one month later his friend Blaise Diagne became undersecretary of state for the colonies. The Eboué family left Bambari for France in March 1931.

That year was to be important for the nation, and it would be useful for an ambitious administrator to be in the capital. The international colonial exposition was opening to promote the colonies; Diagne held a high position; and elections were on the way. Eboué spent most of his time at the exposition, attending in particular the exhibits on French Equatorial Africa. At the opening on May 20, 1931, he met old colleagues as well as businessmen he knew. In June he traveled to Belgium apparently for a colonial conference; back in Paris he attended an international congress of anthropologists and prehistory archaeologists, at which he gave a paper on Ubangi-Shari. Part of that report also appeared in *La Revue du monde noir*, edited by West Indian intellectuals.

After a brief trip to Cayenne to settle the affairs of this father-in-law who had recently died, Eboué met with Blaise Diagne. The undersecretary of state was working to have Eboué appointed secretary-general of Martinique. In such a position his chances for a governorship would be excellent. Secretaries-general ran the day-to-day administration of a colony under the direction of the governor, and they could replace the governor temporarily. Acting as governor—if the latter went on leave, for example—gave a man the chance to prove he could do the job; thus, if the governor were to retire or be transferred, the secretary-general would be well placed to try for promotion. Such appointments were more complicated in the West Indies than in Africa because of the presence of locally elected politicians. In addition, Antillean sensitivity to fine color differences among blacks meant that fair-skinned Martiniquans might object to the appointment of a man of Eboué's darkness. Henry Lémery, Martinique's very fair-skinned and conservative senator, did in fact object, but Diagne was too well placed and the nomination went through.

The West Indies, 1932–1934

On January 26 a presidential decree named Félix Eboué secretary-general of Martinique, and he prepared to leave in two weeks. Just before his departure, however, he met with other Guianese to sign an agreement about the forthcoming legislative elections. A white journalist had held Guiana's seat in Parliament, and many Creoles thought he should be replaced. Some of them supported a more liberal white; others, like Eboué, thought a black should represent the colony. Eboué wrote friends that blacks could do the job, just as Candace represented Guadeloupe and just as Diagne represented the citizens of Senegal. It is significant that Eboué chose these two examples because both Candace and Diagne were darker-skinned than other black politicans. In the West Indies and in Africa Eboué consistently opposed special advantages for people of Euro-African ancestry. Finally, the Guianese agreed to support two Creoles instead of a white, and Eboué left for the Caribbean.

Guianese politics were probably simpler than those in Martinique, and soon after his arrival in Fort-de-France, the capital, Eboué learned the various ins and outs of the delicate and prickly relationship between the colonial administration and the elected officials. The reason for this intensity had to do with the distribution of favors such as jobs, scholarships, promotions, and the governor's influence over elections. A governor could weaken or strengthen the position of a deputy or senator by rewarding his friends and supporters and even by insuring electoral victories through failing to prevent corruption or voter intimidation. On the other hand, an elected deputy could weaken a governor's position by raising questions in Parliament to embarass a minister of colonies, or he could strengthen the position of the governor by writing letters of support.

The politicians Eboué found in Martinique were masters of intrigue, and the 1932 elections were preceded and followed by plot and counterplot. One of the two deputies, Joseph Lagrosillière, was trying to displace the governor and Senator Lémery. The governor was supported by Lémery and by the other deputy, Alcide Delmont. Each side blamed the other for various local scandals. On July 15, 1932, Governor Louis Gerbinis left for France to testify at the trial of Lagrosillière, accused of involvement in certain illegal activities, and Gratien Candace, then undersecretary of state for colonies, supported Eboué's nomination as acting governor.

From July 15 to August 23, 1932, Eboué acted as governor of a colony for the first time in his life, and he enjoyed it immensely—at first, anyway. Other good news came, for his book on Ubangi-Shari—based on materials collected over the years—began to appear in installments in the prestigious *L'Afrique française*, and his article on sports in Africa was published in *Le Monde colonial illustré*.[20] Eboué's friends moved from success to success: Maran's reputation as a writer grew, and Yvon Delbos, a fellow sportsman, was an increasingly important deputy in Parliament. Eboué loved the parties of sophisticated Fort-de-France, and he faithfully attended Masonic meetings at Les Disciples de Pythagore lodge, which welcomed him as a representative of La France équinoxiale of Cayenne. The fact that this was also Lagrosillière's lodge did not go unnoticed among the deputy's political opponents.

The following year, 1933, rumors of Gerbinis's possible retirement grew; he was already sixty-two, two years beyond the age at which he could retire, and when he went on leave in June 1933 many assumed he would never return. Gerbinis, Delmont, and others opposed again making Eboué acting governor, suspecting then that Eboué might favor Lagrosillière and his friends. On his side, however, Eboué had an impressive array: Blaise Diagne, Lagrosillière, Candace, René Maran, plus Yvon Delbos and Maurice Sarraut, who ran the influential newspaper *La Dépêche de Toulouse.* An Eboué friend, the journalist Roger Dévigne, knew Sarraut well, and doubtless the latter communicated favorable comments about Eboué to his brother Albert, who conveniently was minister of colonies. Eboué became acting governor on June 4, 1933.

Eboué's interim lasted for seven months, and he got a full taste of Carribean politics and problems. Although no labor conflicts erupted, problems in the school system shook the colony, and the mysterious death of the editor of a communist newspaper caused an uproar in left-wing and student circles. A growing group of young West Indian intellectuals, who had called for radical political change, saw in the death of the journalist the white hand of sugar interests. The affair sparked a protest meeting in Paris attended by Eboué's son Henry, who also signed a petition demanding justice in this case. Any such protest would naturally be labeled "red" in those days, so Eboué was deeply embarrassed and then infuriated by Henry's actions, which he thought might hurt his career.

Despite the problems and tensions, Eboué and his wife wanted to stay in Martinique. In November 1933, after five months as acting governor, he wrote to René Maran: "I have keenly wanted to be where I am, and [this is] where I want to be kept."[21] Many Martiniquans, too, were happy to see a black man at the head of their administration.

Surprisingly, Gerbinis returned to the colony in early January 1934, and the pushing and pulling over the next three months between supporters of Gerbinis and Eboué's friends in Paris determined the decisions of the new minister of colonies, Pierre Laval. Diagne was ill (he died in May) and could be of little help; Lagrosillière had more legal troubles; and Sarraut was out of the ministry. Laval decided to remove both Gerbinis and Eboué at the same time and by so doing avoided displeasing the different sides too much. He retired Gerbinis as part of a depression austerity program and gave Eboué a not unattractive position in West Africa.

Sudan Interim, 1934–1936

Back in France on a short leave, Eboué was having some health problems. In December he would be fifty years old, and at the time he was considerably overweight. He was already hard of hearing because of an untreated ear disease from Ubangi days and he was suffering from gout. According to the physicians he saw, the uric acid in his blood was too high. He therefore "took a cure," as they called it, in Vittel. Feeling better after a rigid diet of milk, thin soups, lean meat, and no alcohol, Eboué and the family (except Henry) left Bordeaux the last day of July 1934 on the S.S. *America* for Dakar and the trip by railroad to Sudan to become secretary-general and acting governor.

He felt at somewhat of a loss in Sudan because he could never know this huge colony—today the twenty-third largest country in the world—from the bottom up the way he had known Ubangi. Yet he stayed for two years, from August 1934 to September 1936, and acted as governor for almost half that time. The experience was a rich one and quite calm compared with the spicy Antilles.

By mid-1935 Eboué had visited all twenty-two *cercles* into which the colony was divided. He found an essentially Muslim and hierarchized population with a higher level of education than in French Equatorial Africa and began to think about the role of a growing group of educated Africans. Through his conversations with church officials, whose goodwill he scrupulously cultivated by a sympathetic ear and an open purse, he perceived the growing problems between Christian initiated social change and Muslim authority. For the first time Eboué thought French colonial policy needed to provide for a new intermediary status between subject and citizen. His notes show he wanted to call the status *noir évolué*.

For the first time in his career he had contacts with African civil servants whom he considered his equals or almost his equals, and this, too, influenced his view of colonial policy. Fily Dabo Sissoko was probably the most important one. Teacher and then canton chief, this Sudanese conducted anthropological research that interested Eboué. They had many conversations about Sissoko's work and about the role of black elites in world history. Eboué was much more race conscious than most people knew; in the dedication Sissoko wrote on an article he published and sent to Eboué, he said: "To Félix Eboué—who never despaired of the race." Eboué kept the article and all others written and sent to him by the Africans.[22] He saw these low-ranking clerks, teachers, and canton chiefs as a new African elite who should be encouraged, promoted, and cultivated to insure a continuing alliance with the modernizing colonial administration. They would, in his view, provide a link with precolonial and evolving African society and would be able to maintain order within that society alongside chiefs and others.

But Eboué had no power to undertake major reforms, and his thoughts had to be shelved for almost three years. At the end of 1935 Matteo Alfassa arrived to take up the post of governor of Sudan. Once again Eboué was a mere secretary-general, and partly to try for something higher he went on leave early in 1936, a key year in French history.

The elections of 1936 had been won by a coalition of the left, and Léon Blum, leader of the *Parti Socialiste* (SFIO), became prime minister of the Popular Front government in the midst of an economic and social crisis. Marius Moutet, also a Socialist, took charge of the ministry of colonies in June 1936, and Yvon Delbos, Eboué's friend, became minister of foreign affairs. With a Socialist government in power, a friend at the Quai d'Orsay, and an excellent record in the colonies, Eboué was in an excellent position to be promoted to a governorship.

Coincidentally, the ministry was looking for a way to solve a current uproar in Guadeloupe, Martinique's sister colony to the north. The 1936 election had brought more than the usual uproar and conflict. The governor, Louis Bouge, was already on bad terms with at least one major politican, and many thought he showed racist tendencies. The spark setting off this year's explosion was that white gendarmes fired on black demonstrators, and one important political figure went into hiding when Bouge ordered his arrest. The ministry decided to recall Bouge, and Eboué's friends calculated that if he were named acting governor and could solve the current conflict he would be well placed to claim the governorship. A group of progressive-minded men had been elevated to high positions in the Popular Front government and administration; their pro-black sentiments combined with Delbos's and Lagrosillière's weight worked, and on September 29, 1936, a decree named Eboué acting governor of Guadeloupe.

Guadeloupe, 1936–1938

Guadeloupe's 300,000 population slightly exceeded Martinique's, and the colony consisted of a series of islands instead of just one. Each island and the different regions of the two largest islands sheltered several fiefdoms of politicans whose conflicts rivaled those of the fabled Chinese warlords even though the rewards they fought for were of infinitesimal importance on the world stage. As in Martinique, the sugar mills provided most income; unlike the situation in Martinique, absentee investors controlled them.

Eboué's arrival in this colony on October 21, 1936 brought out the best in Antillean society—a warmth and cordiality and at least the appearance of solidarity.[23] In a letter to his wife, who had remained in Paris to keep an eye on his promotion at the ministry of colonies, the new acting governor wrote: "Excellent first impression. The population is showing some pride in seeing me govern their island. You should see the joyful smiles on their faces. The Martiniquans gave me a lot of [good] publicity."[24]

When the music celebrating his arrival had died down, Eboué worked quickly to lead the administration. With Jean de La Roche, a white he knew in Martinique, he prepared speeches to the population, a statement to the elected *Conseil Général*, and a plan to solve the disorders that necessitated a change of leadership in the first place. He revoked his predecessor's order to arrest a local politician and convinced the ministry to recall to France the white gendarme seen as responsible for the shootings. He traveled quickly around the two main islands making speeches and greeting people, and he settled dock and sugar workers' strikes in good order.

On October 31 Eboué proposed gradual extension of Popular Front laws, already applied in the metropole, to the colony of Guadeloupe. They included limitations on the work week, rights of collective bargaining, and other progressive measures. This began to disturb businessmen, as well as the two deputies, Maurice Satineau and Gratien Candace, who wondered how Eboué would use his soaring popularity.

Satineau, the more volatile of the two, had already openly requested Eboué to help his local political party through his agent in Pointe-à-Pitre. Never a man to engage in subtleties, Satineau wrote: "I confirm that I have complete confidence in him, and I am asking you to reserve a warm welcome to the steps he will take with you in the interest of my party and my friends."[25] Eboué responded stiffly without committing himself. He could ill afford to offend.

Then the ministry retired his predecessor, and the way seemed open. Oddly, the decision to promote Eboué to the rank of governor and then to name him to Guadeloupe seemed to be floating in the sea of bureacracy. Eugénie and some close friends reported that certain high-ranking officials opposed the advancement. Candace seemed cool to the Guadeloupe appointment despite his support over the past years; the deputy did not favor Popular Front reforms. Eboué wrote to Yvon Delbos and Henry Bérenger, Guadeloupe's senator since 1912 and chairman of the foreign affairs committee of the Senate. On November 29 the general council passed a motion praising Eboué and affirming its confidence in him.

As usual in such circumstances, Eboué became moody: the world had abandoned him and friends could not be trusted. But finally the minister decided in his favor, and on December 4, 1936 the president of the republic, Albert Lebrun, promoted Eboué to the rank of governor third class and appointed him governor of Guadeloupe. In the flood of praise and telegrams in which Eboué swam he liked one statement in particular: a Cayenne newspaper, *L'Observateur*, said that the appointment proved France wanted to show the world that there are no inferior races. This is the first time, the writer said, that a truly black man had been named governor.[26]

Thus, Governor Félix Eboué prepared for the triumphal arrival of his wife and threw himself once again into his work, which brought successful returns. Although the worldwide economic depression had damaged Guadeloupe's fragile colonial economy, sugar prices rose in 1936 so that workers could expect more money. Eboué increased the budget for the colony. Exports of refined sugar increased from 40 million kilos in 1936 to 61 million in 1937. Banana exports increased, too, so that despite devaluation of French currency, the economy improved.[27]

Encouraged by the economic progress, Eboué traveled widely; he was the first governor in twenty years to visit the small island of Désirade. He started an expansion of educational facilities and reclamation of swampland for new housing. He encouraged cooperation between Guadeloupe and Martinique.

In the midst of this Caribbean sunshine a storm appeared foreshadowing the tropical hurricane just out of sight. Strikes always took place at the beginning of the sugarcane cutting season in December and January because this was the only time cutters and hawlers could put pressure on owners. If the cane were not cut and processed, it would rot. Similarly a dockers' strike in April meant the loss of the banana crop. Thus, strikes began here and in the sugar mills.

Eboué suspected the hand of Maurice Satineau in these strikes. The deputy spent considerable time in Guadeloupe and because Eboué refused to serve his friends in the manner expected Satineau began to hate the governor. In addition, some people believed that the deputy had been recruited by some big businessmen—worried about the minimum wage laws, Eboué's recent price ceiling on retail sales goods, and his suggestion of a property tax—to undermine the governor. He began insulting Eboué in his newspaper, *La Voix du peuple*, and he wrote to Marius Moutet demanding the governor's removal. The Freemasons and other friends counterattacked with messages of support, and Moutet refused the demand.

Gratien Candace entered the fray as the senatorial elections approached. He wished to finish his parliamentary career comfortably as a senator whose nine-year term of office and limited constituency guaranteed a safe seat. (Only about 315 men voted for senator; they were the "notables" such as mayors and members of the *Conseil Général*.) But Bérenger, a friend of Yvon Delbos, had supported Eboué's nomination as governor, and Eboué thought an alliance with him would serve his career. Governors were supposed to be neutral in elections, but everyone knew they played a key role in the choice—either directly and blatantly by permitting ballot-box stuffing or indirectly by giving advice and lending their prestige to one candidate or the other. Eboué played the indirect role by advising Bérenger, taking a poll for him, and letting people associate the names Eboué and Bérenger. Candace railed against Eboué in his newspaper, *La Démocratie sociale*, but he had little influence on the government.

Satineau and Candace thus probably celebrated the fall of the government in 1938. Georges Mandel, more interested in the course of German rearmament than in the colonies, took over the colonial ministry. Unfortunately for Eboué, Mandel and Bérenger were reportedly on bad terms because of some old and complex disagreements. Thus could enemies prepare the fall of Eboué on the small stage of the Caribbean when the curtain fell on the Popular Front.

The details of the maneuvers have been lost, but Mandel resolved to recall Eboué, and Satineau and Candace knew about this decision before the governor. On July 13, 1938, Satineau sent the following telegram from Paris to his friends in Guadeloupe: "Have obtained recall Governor Eboué." The following day they printed the telegram and distributed it around the colony. A copy was brought to Eboué, who immediately telegraphed the ministry for a telegram of support to counteract what he supposed to be a canard. Mandel replied on July 15 with a terse, coded telegram: "I am asking you to come here as soon as possible; to give temporary authority to the secretary-general; and to instruct him to observe a strict neutrality during the forthcoming senatorial election campaign."

Furious about the implication he had acted improperly and that Satineau seemed to have had a special influence at the ministry, Eboué and his family quickly packed. He refused to believe he would not return after the appropriate explanations, and his friends sent telegrams and letters of support. Two Masonic lodges appealed to Grand Orient headquarters—the leading Masonic federation—and the union of civil servants appealed for help to the central trade union in Paris, the CGT. On July 26 Eboué left Guadeloupe after a large and warm send-off by the people of Pointe-à-Pitre.

In Paris Eboué waited for vindication. Mandel sent an inspector to investigate Candace and Satineau's claims; his report absolved Eboué of any wrongdoing although he wrote that the governor might have inadvertently left the impression of partiality. On October 23 Bérenger won the election overwhelmingly, and popular singers predicted Eboué's speedy return. Eboué awaited the good news, but Bérenger became silent and cold. Other friends cheered him. Behind the scenes Satineau and Candace worked against him.

Mandel called Eboué to the ministry and abruptly informed him that he would not return to Gaudeloupe but would instead go to Chad, in French Equatorial Africa. To lessen the blow Mandel raised Eboué prematurely to the rank of governor second class. He also indicated that Chad might have an important role to play in the growing tensions between France and Italy and seems to have promised Eboué a better post after some months if he would cooperate. On November 19, 1938, the decree was issued.

This appointment amounted to a demotion because the colony did not then have a governor. An administrator in chief ran its affairs since the reorganization of French Equatorial Africa in 1937, and he could do nothing without the approval of the governor-general in Brazzaville. Mandel had to create a lieutenant governorship for Eboué, but even so Eboué would no longer be able to communicate directly with Paris as he had done in Guadeloupe.

Obedient and downcast Eboué planned his return to the heart of Africa. To cheer him up Lagrosillière and others organized a party on January 21, 1939. Marius Moutet and many friends attended. Early the following morning Chad's new governor took what was proably his first airplane trip, going from Paris to Africa by way of Marseilles and then on to Algiers, Gao, and Fort-Lamy, the capital of Chad.

Chad, 1939–1940

The house waiting in that dusty, grey town reminded Eboué of some of the simple dwellings of his early days as an administrator third class. The buildings, equipment, and material belonging to the administration were deficient in every way, and conflict was sharp between the civil administration and the military. On the bright side, Eboué found some old French Equatorial Africa hands and even a cousin.

Shortly after his arrival he began his usual tours and tried to organize his administration by bringing in friends such as Jean de La Roche to occupy key vacant posts. He also made a strenuous but useless effort to increase the autonomy of the colony to facilitate decisionmaking and to increase his power.

Madame Eboué arrived in Fort-Lamy in March and found the accommodations disgusting. She had left Ginette in school in Paris, where Charles was attempting to enter military school. Robert studied for his baccalaureate examinations, and Henry got a job in Senegal. The Chad appointment must be temporary, Eboué and his wife reasoned, and—convinced it had sufficiently purged them of their alleged sins—they planned to go on leave about July 1939. Lagrosillière worked to have Eboué named governor of Martinique, governor of Cameroon, or maybe even the head of a proposed federation of the Caribbean colonies. Eboué also savored the thought of running against Satineau in the forthcoming elections in 1940.

He shelved these projects as the international scene deteriorated. When the Germans invaded Poland on September 1, 1939, thus beginning World War II, Eboué could not desert Chad. Cameroon, coveted by the Third Reich, shared a frontier with Chad, and the Italians in Libya—also one of the colony's neighbors—tried to undermine French authority. Improving communication to ease troop movements toward the border with Libya, recruiting African troops, and insuring African loyalty and cooperation depended on steady leadership.

The attitudes of African authorities took on a greater importance than ever before. Eboué cultivated the friendship and loyalty of key chiefs and sultans, including Muhammad Ourada, sultan of Ouaddai, traditional leader of almost 250,000 souls. Then he chose Henri Laurentie, who also respected African traditional authority, to direct the affairs of this region. As the war news got grimmer and as Laurentie's relations with the French military worsened, Eboué brought him to Fort-Lamy to work closely with him. But even with this help, Eboué fell into a state of depression again and requested leave; in March 1940 the governor-general, Pierre Boisson, refused.

By spring 1940 the war took a sharp turn for the worse. German forces moved swiftly into Belgium and Holland in May, and France braced for the worst. Frenchmen thought they had a strong army and sufficient defenses in the Maginot Line, but the enemy skirted neatly around the cement fortresses in early June and moved toward Paris. The Italians attacked from the southeast, and the French government moved to Bordeaux to escape the onslaught. Prime Minister Paul Reynaud resigned on June 14. Marshal Henri-Philippe Pétain, hero of World War I, took his place in the midst of chaos and flight. On June 17 the French armed forces surrendered to the Germans.

For the next week colonial governors agreed the struggle must continue. Boisson and Eboué shared this view. Both had tried to prepare French Equatorial Africa for the conflict, and they saw no reason to stop now. The proposed organization would be called the "Bloc africain," according to several colonial officials.

The signature on June 22, 1940, of an armistice between Marshal Pétain and the Germans, providing for a quasi-autonomous French government in southern France while the enemy occupied the north, including Paris, changed enthusiasm to obedience and submission. French Equatorial Africa had looked to its stronger neighbors in French West Africa and in North Africa for leadership. Everyone waited for action by Admiral Noguès, head of the colonial administration in Morocco, but he apparently feared a German invasion and declined to continue the battle. Marshal Pétain demanded obedience and promised that no German or Italian invasion of French colonies would take place. The British sinking of the French fleet at Mers-el-Kebir the first week in July gave Pierre Laval, second in command to Pétain, ammunition for his anti-British campaign.

The British, now alone in the war against Hitler, had launched a campaign in June to rally the French colonies to their side. Charles de Gaulle, a relatively unknown brigadier general, had broadcast appeals over the BBC in an effort to organize his compatriots, but he had little immediate influence. Britain needed a French involvement in the war effort because of the location of the French colonies in between the British colonies, because the French possessions might be able to provide a French leader such as de Gaulle with weapons or the money to buy them, and because they felt painfully the need "to give a broad international character [to the war effort] which will add greatly to our strength and prestige and will demonstrate to the world that we are fighting to restore freedom of oppressed peoples of Europe."[28] Eboué and Laurentie responded favorably to their messages; but in equatorial Africa the British considered Cameroon to be of far greater importance than Chad, and they had little contact with the colony's leaders.

To encourage French cooperation the British began a sea blockade of their colonies so they could neither export their products nor import food and manufactured goods. Eboué and Laurentie consulted with the British, but they were waiting for Boisson to act. Eboué requested that the British governor of Nigeria send a delegation to Fort-Lamy to discuss a continuation of the war effort and the meaning of the blockade. Cooperation would mean an end to the blockade and even the purchase of local products for which the British had "no use whatsoever,"[29] but they had no weapons to offer. With respect to Cameroon, for example, Bernard Bourdillon, governor of Nigeria, and his colleague the commander of British forces in West Africa told the foreign office that they "could not support the French in Cameroons if they were attacked by French troops from elsewhere."[30] That was exactly the reason why several Frenchmen hesitated.

Meanwhile Pétain's government reorganized itself. The marshal became head of state, Laval prime minister, and Eboué's old opponent from Martinique, Senator Henry Lémery, took over the ministry of colonies. Pierre Boisson agreed to cooperate with the new government, then located at Vichy, and they named him high commissioner over the colonies. Traveling through Fort-Lamy on his way to his new headquarters at Dakar, Boisson told Eboué on July 20, 1940, that resistance would be useless and that someday France and the colonies might reenter the war in some unspecified way. On the surface Eboué agreed, but he and Laurentie thought about ways to continue the war effort.

Further to insure loyalty, Vichy sent Admiral Platon to the colonies to explain the armistice and to warn officials that disobedience meant punishment. The threats frightened the governor of Cameroon, and the British decided they could no longer count on him. Bourdillon telegraphed London:

> Duala was at one time the bright spot in the picture. Now with the exception of Dakar itself it is almost the darkest, and that in spite of the fact that our economic help was so obviously needed and had so nearly been arranged. I cannot avoid the conclusion that the Germans are devoting special attention to the Cameroons, and that there have been contacts and propaganda of which we have no information. A demand, acquiesced by Vichy, for the return of Cameroons to Germany seems by no means impossible; at any rate German infiltration begin[ning] from Fernando Po and Muni, must be certainly expected.[31]

Eboué and Laurentie were tormented during these weeks of British and French maneuverings and hesitations. Laurentie's wife and four children were in France. Of the Eboué children, only Charles was safe. At the last minute Ginette could not leave France, and Henry and Robert had been taken prisoner by the Germans. Colonel Marchand, commander of the military in Chad, hesitated to support the British and General de Gaulle partly out of obedience to Marshal Pétain and partly because he knew his forces had no means to repulse an attack.

A report that Vichy would soon replace the acting governor-general in Brazzaville with a new man known to be loyal convinced the British and General de Gaulle that speedy action was necessary. Vichy loyalists would have to be removed, by force if necessary, and Eboué, the only governor who had never wavered in his support, would have to be strengthened. De Gaulle thus sent four military men and a civilian to French Equatorial Africa to bring the colonies into his movement, and—very important—the British were now prepared to promise military assistance.

On August 23, 1940, René Pleven and Colonel Colonna d'Ornano flew into Fort-Lamy from Lagos. In the next couple of days they discussed de Gaulle's plans with military men and civilians. When finally they promised three airplanes with pilots, trucks, and other equipment, Colonel Marchand agreed to follow them. Eboué needed no convincing, but he, too, was relieved that the commitment had been made.[32] It was decided that Colonel Marchand would announce the colony's adherence to de Gaulle in order to underscore the military aspect,[33] and on August 26, with Eboué at his side, he declared Chad would continue the battle alongside the British and under the leadership of the French general. The signal was given, and on the following day de Gaulle's representatives linked up with friendly forces in Cameroon and declared that colony would join the movement. On August 28 a group of young officers staged a coup in Brazzaville to join Chad and Cameroon. On August 29 word was received that Gabon would join the rally, but the governor of that colony then changed his mind and it was not until November that Gaullist forces defeated Vichy loyalists. Confusion reigned in Ubangi-Shari for some days, but it joined de Gaulle, too.

Vichy reacted swiftly by dismissing Eboué as governor and by threatening him and others. French West Africa and North Africa remained on the side of Pétain and Laval despite General de Gaulle's efforts. After he unsuccessfully tried to win the support of Senegal he realized that French Equatorial Africa and Cameroon would be his only basis for claiming France was still in the war, and he proceeded to visit these colonies.

On October 15 de Gaulle flew into Fort-Lamy. He and Eboué had long talks about the war effort before he flew on to Brazzaville to organize a new administration there. On November 9 he wrote Eboué that he wanted him to become governor-general. He had consulted with the British and the Belgians about naming a black man to head this important group of colonies, and they agreed with this choice despite some reservations. The British military mission wrote: "Eboué new governor of A.E.F. [French Equatorial Africa] is by all accounts a fine man but he is a Martinique [sic] native which will not help in Congo or West Africa although it may have some favorable effect on native opinion generally."[34]

Governor-general in French Equatorial Africa, 1940–1944

Eboué had never liked Brazzaville partly because of the antiblack attitude of many of the so-called *petits blancs* there and partly because he always felt freer in the field. Naturally, however, he accepted the appointment with joy. Laurentie, who would become secretary-general, flew to Brazzaville to help set up the offices, and de Gaulle named Colonal Edgar de Larminat to the newly created post of high commissioner for Free French Africa.

Eboué did not arrive in Brazzaville until December 30, 1940, and de Larminat took many measures before that date for which Africans would blame Eboué. The most significant was, perhaps, the imprisonment and execution of Balali leaders who for years had been demanding a special status and rights. Martial Sinda, a Congolese writing many years later, bitterly and erroneously accused Eboué of the severe repression of the Africans.[35] Installed in the governor-general's residence at the end of December, four days after his fifty-sixth birthday, Eboué would not grant the Balali their demands. He saw his role as keeping the population mobilized for the war effort; but he did take certain initiatives for reform that surprised the Free French Committee in London and de Larminat, none of whom could match his experience and knowledge of the problems of French Equatorial Africa.

On January 19, 1941, Eboué issued a decree that put forward broad principles of decentralization. More authority would be given to the governors and administrators in the field. Then he went on tour to make contact with his subordinates, particularly in Gabon, to find out what problems they faced. Returning to Brazzaville to meet General de Gaulle on April 18, Eboué explained that even in wartime a decentralized administration would be more effective than the centralized, Jacobin pattern typical of France since the revolution of 1789. His antagonists were the high commissioners—de Larminat and then Surgeon general Adolphe Sicé—until the abolition of the office in June 1942.

Of equal interest to Eboué and Laurentie were changes in native policy. On November 8, 1941, Eboué published his famous La Nouvelle Politique indigène, written largely by Laurentie after long consultation. The purpose of the document was to serve as an introduction to three major decrees designed to decentralize power. General de Gaulle's advisors knew little about the colonies, but because de Gaulle favored some reforms they thought the document would serve to show the world that the Free French planned major changes.

Although the Free French gave much more publicity to this document than either Eboué or Laurentie expected, these same officials ignored or fought the concrete changes subsequently proposed. These measures included the establishment of African courts and African run municipal institutions in Brazzaville and the creation of a new status between subject and citizen that Eboué had been thinking about since his days in the Sudan and called *notable évolué*. Only after energetic lobbying by Eboué and Laurentie were these proposals adopted.

Other important reforms were the expansion of the education system and the upgrading of African civil servants to a level equal to that of a few of the European functionaries. All governors had had their African protégés and favorites whom they promoted into decent jobs, but most of them were Euro-Africans, sons of French fathers and African mothers. Eboué insisted that no favoritism be shown mulattoes, partly because he had always resented this practice in the Caribbean, and he upgraded a tiny minority of four African clerks who worked in his cabinet. He met frequently with these men, encouraging them to organize themselves into cultural and discussion organizations, and he gave them money. Furthermore, he encouraged them to fight—in peaceful ways—against the segregation and overt racism of Brazzaville. These gestures seem derisory compared with changes soon to come, but in the context of the time many whites considered them subversive.

Other decisions—those concerning the war—were really outside Eboué's domain although he advised General de Gaulle on certain policies in the Caribbean, which he knew better than anyone else in the general's entourage. He passed on the orders to increase cotton production and rubber, needed since the fall of Malaysia to the Japanese. Gold mined in Equatorial Africa also helped the Free French, and the British kept their promises, including the one that obliged them to purchase coffee and bananas dumped into the ocean or burned. Gabon's wood was more useful finding its way into warplanes. And communication between West Africa and the Middle East was no longer in danger.

The personal distress Eboué and Laurentie felt did not abate until December 1942—at least for Eboué. Although Laurentie's wife had been sent to a concentration camp for helping the French resistance, Eboué's children slipped out of

France and arrived on December 20 in French Equatorial Africa. Ginette remained with her mother and father; Robert and Henry flew in March 1943 to Cairo to rejoin the army. Charles attended pilot training school in England.

At that time in 1943 General de Gaulle was fighting for his political life. British support was never complete, and once General Giraud, who outranked de Gaulle, began to set up his own movement after the Allied invasion of North Africa, his position weakened. Making matters worse, the Americans, who had opposed de Gaulle, began to support Giraud.

Eboué telegraphed his loyalty to General de Gaulle and had his African subordinates do the same. He informed the British and the Americans, who had set up a consulate in Brazzaville, that he would recognize no other leader except de Gaulle. Finally, de Gaulle and Giraud agreed to be co-presidents of the Comité français de la libération nationale, and in August 1943 the committee was officially recognized as the tide turned against the Germans.

A provisional consultative assembly meeting in Algiers in November began to plan for the future of France. The members raised the question of possible African representation and the status of African elites in postwar Frence, subjects of great interest to Eboué. Such questions might be resolved at a meeting of colonial officials scheduled for the end of January 1944 in Brazzaville. René Pleven, minister of colonies, planned a conference to bring about some reforms in the empire, but it is doubtful he wanted or expected anything profound. The choice of Brazzaville was a tribute to Eboué, about whom Colonel Leclerc, a key figure in the Free French movement, wrote, "[his] attitude in 1940 will remain a historic example for all Frenchmen."[36]

The conference lasted from January 30 to February 8. For some observers it represented the beginning of a new age in the colonies; others saw it as another missed opportunity. At the very least, it can be seen as one of a series of attempts throughout colonial history to make politicians and the public more sensitive to the needs and problems in the colonies, and it inspired some African elites to believe changes might give them higher positions.[37] Eboué was a little disappointed by the meeting, and he made little mention of it in the short time he still had to live.

The future of his own position troubled some. Eboué had been ill and now could hear only with an aid. Rumors of his replacement circulated. The British sent the colonial office a report about it, but, curiously, they destroyed the document after the war. Eboué fully planned to continue but felt he needed a vacation. Earlier he had been invited to Nigeria but could not go, and a vacation in South Africa, where his white colleagues went, was out of the question. He decided he wanted to go to Egypt and then to Jerusalem and Damascus to renew an association with antiquity that had begun with his study of the Stoics in the Lycée Montaigne. African and West Indian civil servants begged him not to leave.

On the morning of February 16 he, Madame Eboué, and Ginette left Brazzaville by car for what Eboué said would be a three-month holiday. Their driver took them first to the Belgian Congo and then to Anglo-Egyptian Sudan, where they traveled down the Nile by boat to Khartoum to meet Governor-general Huddleston. He made speeches to the British about the French colonies.

From the Sudan the family took the railroad to Cairo, where they arrived on April 4. The history of Egypt fascinated Eboué and he toured the pyramids near

Cairo. On April 15, speaking about French colonialism at the French lycée, he felt
ill. Physicians put Eboué in a hospital as a precaution, but his health quickly declined, attacked by pneumonia and then uremia. Laurentie, who had been working with René Pleven in Algiers, flew to Cairo to be with Eboué, Madame Eboué,
and Ginette. Although Eboué had never had trouble with his heart, his stoutness,
fatigue, and illness strained it too far. Seven months before his sixtieth birthday,
on May 17, 1944, Félix Eboué died.

Eboué, the Symbol

Beyond the circle of family and friends, the West Indian and growing African
elites felt Eboué's loss most keenly. The black governor-general symbolized the
France they hoped would permit them access to the highest posts within nation
and empire. Burial in the Panthéon in 1949, the monuments raised, and the streets
named here and there to honor his memory seemed to confirm a secure place for
blacks. Finally pulled along toward independence by neighboring colonies and
worldwide anti-imperial sentiments, the same elites and their younger brothers
later forgot Eboué or dissociated themselves from him.

   Yet the meaning and interest of Eboué's life transcends the colonial period and
the day-to-day politics of the successor states. He belonged to an ethnic or racial
minority, and he successfully formulated that identity in a way that permitted his
assimilation into a larger national community. Thus, his most intimate friends
(and enemies) were Antilleans and Guianese, and he kept his ties with the Caribbean by visits to Cayenne and by struggling to be named governor of Martinique
and Guadeloupe. In Africa, by supporting traditional elites and then intermediate
elites, he showed his respect for African civilization within the French empire. At
the same time he proved his loyalty to France and promoted European values and
technology through education, administrative organization, and economic
change.

   The success of this pluralism depended on decentralization of the decisionmaking process and on administrators who remained a significant period of time in
one colony. As an administrator Eboué consciously reshaped orders and took initiatives, and as a governor he encouraged subordinates to do the same while respecting parallel institutions. Success also depended on his contacts above and
below, in Africa and in France. Eboué cultivated friendships in all circles—Freemasons, clubs, political parties—and younger elites followed him when they realized the advantages to be gained.

   Playing such a game of life on two stages had its risks and costs. Eboué heard
and tolerated racist remarks and actions, but he refused to give up his French
identity in the face of such provocation. Intense desire to advance up the colonial
hierarchy meant pleasing Paris while working within the realities of the colonial
state. The development of an economy and new administration meant finding a
balance between the greed of some businessmen, who had the money, and the natural resistance of Africans, who had the labor.

   Eboué attempted to solve these tensions by objectifying them. He studied the
Stoic philosophers, who had come to terms with their own minority position in the
Roman empire; he studied and wrote about African civilization, seeking compari-

sons with what he saw in the Caribbean and Europe; and he read about and discussed colonial policy with colleagues. His heavy smoking and moodiness—even his premature death, perhaps—show he did not successfully cope with all the contradictions in his life.

But these tensions, a superior intelligence, honesty, and ambition made Eboué an innovator within an authoritarian system. It is no coincidence that he is the only black and the only colonial official to rest in the Panthéon. He is both a symbol of the contribution ethnic groups have made within the nation and a symbol of the creative role of the colonial administrator in the unfolding of European, Caribbean, and African history.

Notes

NOTE: Most of my research was conducted in Africa, France, the West Indies, and Guiana between 1967 and 1970 thanks to generous grants from the Joint Committee on African Studies of the American Council of Learned Societies and the Social Science Research Council and from Howard University. (See Brian Weinstein, *Eboué* [New York, 1974].) Another grant from Howard University permitted me to examine British documents from World War II in the Public Record Office in 1975. I am grateful for this support and for the cooperation of the Eboué family and others who helped me obtain information.

1. Paul Prévot to Brian Weinstein, 6 April 1968. Unfortunately, Mr. Prévot (a notary) found he was unable to give me further information.

2. *Nouveaus libres avec tables alphabétiques de prétiques de prénoms* (Roura, Fr. Guiana, 1848),p. 32, items 411–414, Archives nationales, section outre-mer (hereinafter cited ANSOM), Paris.

3. E. Maugat, "La Traite clandestine à Nantes au XIXᵉ siècle," *Bulletin de la Sociétfe archéologique et historique de Nantes* 93 (1954): 162–169.

4. Philip D. Curtin, *The Atlantic Slave Trade: A Census* (Madison, 1969), p. 258; data are based on British foreign office records.

5. Eboué to Félix Gratien, 10 May 1924, Félix Eboué Papers, Asnières.

6. Notebook, 1929(?), Eboué Papers.

7. République française, *Journal officiel du Congo francais* 7, no. 1 (1 January 1910): 5–6.

8. Félix Eboué, "Les sociétés d'initiation de l'Afrique noire comparées à la franc-maçonnerie moderne," Eboué Papers.

9. Catherine Coquéry-Vidrovitch, *Le Congo au temps des grandes compagnies concessionnaires, 1898–1930* (Paris, 1972), p. 15.

10. "Rapport d'ensemble pour l'année 1914," unclassified, Afrique équatoriale française, Oubangui-Chari, ANSOM, Aix-en-Provence, n.p.

11. "Rapports mensuels," Kouango, 1915, 1916, Archives de la République centrafricaine.

12. "Relevé des exportations," Contrôle des concessions, Afrique équatoriale française 8 and 12 May 1917, ANSOM.

13. "Rapports mensuels," Kouango, October 1916, Archives de la République centrafricaine.

14. The governor-general opposed letting him join.

15. Mildred J. Headings, *French Freemasonry under the Third Republic*, Johns Hopkins University Studies in Historical and Political Science, Series 66, no. 1, vol. 66 (1948):190, 93.

16. "Rapport économique pour l'année 1925," 20 April 1926, pp. 6–7, ANSOM, Aix-en-Provence.

17. Coquéry-Vidrovitch, *Le Congo*, pp. 473–479.

18. Gilles Sautter, "Notes sur la construction du chemin de fer Congo-Océan (1921–1934)," *Cahiers d'études africaines* 7, no. 26 (1967):259.

19. Telegram no. 28c, 31 August 1928, Archives de la République centrafricaine. Archives for Kémo-Gribingui were located in Bangui in the Ecole nationale d'administration in 1968.

20. He had already published a glossary of African languages, and he was working on other manuscripts.

21. Félix Eboué to René Maran, 21 November 1933, René Maran Papers, in the possession of Madame Camille René Maran, Paris.

22. Eboué Papers.

23. For a study of Antillean society see Brian Weinstein, "The French West Indies: Dualism from 1848 to the Present," in *The African Diaspora*, ed. Martin Kilson and Robert Rotberg (Cambridge, 1976), pp. 237–279.

24. Félix Eboué to Eugénie Eboué, 22 October 1936, Eboué Papers.

25. Maurice Satineau to Félix Eboué, 9 October 1936, Eboué Papers.

26. The date was 2 December 1936. The news of the nomination was known a few days before the actual decree. Other governors had African ancestry but were fair in color.

27. République française, Colonie de la Guadeloupe, *Bulletin mensuel d'information*, January 1938.

28. Telegram, 3 August 1940, FO/371/24329/6291, Public Record Office, London.

29. Cypher telegram from governor of Nigeria, 31 July 1940, FO/371/24329/6291, Public Record Office, London.

30. Telegram, 31 July 1940, FO/371/24329/6291, Public Record Office, London.

31. Telegram from governor of Nigeria, 6 August 1940, FO/371/24329/6291, Public Record Office, London.

32. Note by W. Mack, 27 August 1940, FO/371/24330/6295, Public Record Office, London.

33. According to René Pleven, the choice of Marchand had nothing to do with Eboué's color. Interview, Paris, 20 June 1969.

34. Telegram from military mission to war office, FO/371/24331/6291, Public Record Office, London.

35. Martial Sinda, *Le Messianisme congolais et ses incidences politiques: Kimbanguisme-matsouanisme-autres mouvements* (Paris, 1972), pp. 230–231.

36. On a photo dedicated to Eboué, 11 December 1942, Eboué Papers.

37. See D. Bruce Marshall, *The French Colonial Myth and Constitution-Making in the Fourth Republic* (New Haven, 1973), pp. 102–115.

Robert Delavignette: The Gentle Ruler (1897–1976)

William B. Cohen

GEORGES Balandier, the great French sociologist, characterized Robert Delavignette as "a solid and obstinate liberal."[1] The description is well deserved. Delavignette was an able man, sensitive to change overseas, who also served as the conscience of French colonialism. His African career as a governor was brief; he served in the Cameroons as high commissioner for only one year, from 1946 to 1947. Nevertheless, he played a crucial role in the evolution of the French empire, especially as a writer, thinker, and educator. In his role as writer he was unrivaled among the French colonial service. No one was as prolific. For half a century he continued in an unending stream of books and articles to make Africa known to the French public. No survey of French colonial policy can afford to exclude Robert Delavignette.

Childhood and Early Career

Delavignette was born in Sainte-Colombe-sur-Seine in 1897 in the old province of Burgundy. His family was of moderate means, Delavignette's father working as a manager at a small iron-smelting work. The picture that emerges from Delavignette's writings is that of a relatively happy youth. His life was not socially restricted; he spent much of his free time in the forge talking to the workers, absorbing their tales about life in the old days and various legends associated with the career of smiths.[2] He obtained his secondary education in Dijon, where he went to a lycée. His teachers seem to have been remarkable men, and he was especially affected by Auguste Mairey, a geographer, and Gaston Roupnel, an historian. Mairey opened to young Delavignette a window on the wider world, and overseas France was stressed in these geography lessons. In a geography textbook that Mairey had published, more space was spent on the empire than was common at that time.[3] Roupnel was part of the distinguished tradition of French social historians that culminated in men like Marc Bloch. He stressed the importance of the social foundations of French history: it was not the kings of France who had made the country but the tillers of the soil, who by generations of their effort and suffering had made human progress possible. He conveyed to his pupil a sense of empathy for the common people and an interest in their culture and life-styles. The peasant was central in Roupnel's historical scheme. The seeds planted by the teacher fell on fertile ground, for Delavignette was clearly receptive to these views. As a youngster, he had shown sympathy for the working man. And long before falling under Mairey's influence, he had devoured the descriptions of exotic lands in the pages of popular journals like *Illustration* and *Tours du monde* and in the works of Jules Verne.[4] These interests had awakened before he arrived at the lycée at Dijon and developed further while he was at school.

Delavignette graduated from the lycée in the fateful year 1914. Within months Europe was at war. In 1916 he was drafted, sent to the front, and wounded. Like so many sensitive men of his generation young Delavignette was shaken by the mixture of heroism, folly, courage, cowardice, and incompetence that so singularly characterized the Great War. What he found most despicable was the callous manner in which officers ordered men to their death merely to advance a few yards to win honors or promotion. Sixty years later anger still entered his voice as he recalled the soldiers who died merely to satisfy the *amour-propre* of some officer or other. This war experience made Delavignette suspicious of an official mind blind to the needs of real people.

In 1919, along with the rest of the French army, Delavignette was demobilized. He now had to decide on a career. It was expected that he would follow in his father's footsteps and work at the forge, but the physical and spiritual destruction that had been wrought upon Europe gave a special sense of romance to the supposed opportunities and limitless horizons of the colonial world.[5] Delavignette applied for the position of, and was appointed, colonial clerk to French West Africa. He was assigned to Dakar to the central bureaucracy of the French West African federation, working in the personnel office. The work was routine and paid very poorly. But it conferred one advantage: with some additional training he could qualify for a higher position and enter the corps of colonial administrators. In the British colonial system many of the clerical functions were occupied by Africans and further promotions into a higher administrative corps was impossible. In the French system there were few Africans in subaltern positions, and the Frenchmen who exercised these responsibilities—even with little education—could aspire to higher positions and eventually become governors. Delavignette as a veteran was required only to undergo a six-month training course at the Ecole coloniale in Paris, the school for colonial administrators. After a year in Dakar he returned to Paris and then, having had his prescribed training, in 1922 was ready to return to Africa.

Thus, except for his six months at the Ecole coloniale, Delavignette had no higher education beyond that of the lycée, but that still represented a considerable amount of formal training. The pre–World War I lycée had a heavy classical curriculum that exposed its students to a vast culture, including Latin, the literature of antiquity, and the French literary tradition. If weak on the history of other countries, the curriculum imparted a good knowledge of French history and geography—often taught together. Graduates of a lycée usually developed a high sense of reverence for learning and culture, and in the case of Delavignette this was underscored by his fondness for Mairey and Roupnel, both of whom were distinguished scholars. (In France a lycée teacher was addressed as "professeur," thus little distinction was drawn between him and a university professor.)

All his life Delavignette was to be attracted to the scholarly world; he counted among his friends many French academics, especially students of Africa—men like the ethnologists Paul Rivet and Lucien Lévy-Bruhl, the historian Charles André Julien, and after World War II the geographer Pierre Gourou and sociologist Georges Balandier. Delavignette was a teacher much of his life; his writings in the popular press in the 1930s were intended to educate Frenchmen about their colonies. Then, as head of the colonial school he was directly involved with the education of future colonial administrators, and years later when he had retired from active service he was still teaching (at the Ecole nationale de la France d'outre-mer). His interest in education was underscored by his long and active participation on the board of governors of the Alliance Française—he even served as its vice-president—an organization dedicated to spreading knowledge of the French language. Beginning in the 1950s he also served on the board of the news organization Havas, being particularly interested in seeing the press cover African affairs. His membership in scholarly organizations reveal his respect and interest in promoting the world of learning. He was an active member of the Académie des sciences d'outre-mer, an organization founded in 1921 to promote knowledge of overseas France. And at his death Delavignette was still honorary president of the Société française d'histoire d'outre-mer, the foremost French society devoted to the study of the history of overseas France.

Physically Delavignette was an imposing man; tall, with large shoulders, he carried himself well and had a solidity that tall people do not always possess (one thinks of the lankiness of the young de Gaulle). The people in his district were to remember him affectionately some fifty years later as *Tchidjan*, "Big One"; and his stepchildren nicknamed him "l'Eléphant," his students at the Ecole coloniale, "Big Bob." The size and authority of Delavignette made a lasting impression on those who came into contact with him. His habit of carefully listening to people gave him an added authority. He was patient and could wait to speak, but he was not cold. Rather, this trait of politeness added to the general impression of the man as competent and knowledgeable.

He was witty but never sarcastic and liked to tell stories. With considerable relish he would tell about the African mistress of the commandant who, when the commandant had finished his tour of duty and was ready to leave, would fall into hysterical bouts of grief. Deeply touched by this sign of affection, the administrator would generously provide for her, and as soon as he had left she would prepare the official residence, dress in her finest clothes, and ride out to meet the new commandant to insure that she would be chosen his mistress.

Some of Delavignette's stories were about himself and he did not mind having people laugh at his expense. One of his favorites was about his first experience with buying supplies for his post in Niger. He arrived from France by ship in Cotonou, Dahomey. There he bought canned goods and other supplies to last him for a year. These were carefully crated and put on the tug that was taking him to Lagos, from where he would go toward Niger. As the boat was pulling out of the wharf, a distraught employee of the trading house came running to tell him that inadvertently two years' supplies rather than one had been packed. Generously, Delavignette (as many others) offered to pay for the extra supplies; the employee gratefully pocketed the money and waved to the boat as it disappeared. Reaching Niger, Delavignette found only one year's supplies.[6] His novel *Toum* reveal a fine sense of humor; it is a satire of colonial life often showing the manner in which the white man and his ways must appear hideous to the African.

Delavignette was not a vain or self-important man. Used to commanding and to having respect, he did not feel the need to prove himself. This frame of mind led him to avoid writing about himself and his experiences. The "commandant" in his writings clearly is himself, but he did not say so. In writing about the colonial administrator in many articles and books, he drew directly on his life in the colonies without making the fact plain. A marvelous stylist able to write with great empathy and understanding about colonial affairs, he did not publish his memoirs. The last ten years before his death saw him rather halfheartedly start them, but his poor health explains why they were not finished and why even the drafts of some of the finished chapters lack focus. There was also an intellectual reason: his unwillingness to put himself squarely in the middle of events, to make himself the hero of his account. It struck him as unseemly. He was bemused by the self-importance and aggrandizement of that successful memoir writer de Gaulle, and assuming the cadence of the general's voice would say, "Général de Gaulle, il . . ." (de Gaulle wrote his memoirs in the third person, copying Julius Ceasar.)

Roi de la Brousse

The main function of members of the corps of colonial administrators was to serve as territorial administrators over the *cercle*, the basic district in French black Africa or a subdividion of it. They also occupied positions of responsibility in the government headquarters, the secretariat. To Delavignette's disappointment his first assignment was the finance bureau in Niger. Its capital, Zinder, an ancient caravan town where nomads from the desert traded with the sedentary people from further south, was still a rather picturesque city reminding the young Frenchman of the *Arabian Nights* or the world of the Old Testament. Sitting in the treasury office, Delavignette yearned for the day when he would administer his own district and perhaps emulate Commandant Henri Fleury, the administrator of Zinder, who—with red beard flowing—rode in hot pursuit of horse thieves and was appropriately nicknamed "horse thief catcher."[7]

Delavignette had to wait only a few months for his assignment. In February 1923 he was appointed administrator of the subdivision of Tessao, located west of Zinder. He had as his superior an official whom later investigation proved both corrupt and brutal. Refusing to obey his orders, Delavignette was badly rated by his commandant and reassigned after a few months, this time to Dosso. This experience was to his credit, however; the governor of Niger was impressed by Delavignette's courageous show of independence and in 1924 observed of him:

> Elite functionary of an education and culture superior to the average. Is an aide in the real sense of the word and one can count on his loyalty, his good sense, his sense of balance, and his general knowledge. . . . When this young official has acquired a little more experience and colonial initiative, he will make an excellent *cercle* commandant or bureau chief.[8]

The frequent displacement that Delavignette experienced was common in the French administration, and he was fortunate to be able to remain in the same general region. These were Islamized areas with large nomadic populations whose relationships with the sedentary peoples were always difficult; the age-old struggle between nomad and peasant went on unabated. The former tended to dominate, and the young administrator interfered when he thought their rule overly harsh and arbitrary.[9]

Although Delavignette saw French rule as beneficent, he by no means shared the low respect for the local chiefs usually exhibited by French administrators. The sultans of the upper Sudan often had sophisticated governments with a firm control over their subjects. To ignore the traditional rulers seemed to him to invite chaos and anarchy. An administrator could not afford to take such risks. Delavignette's early experience with traditional rule therefore convinced him that the French administration must prevent the worst abuses of cruelty and dishonesty in chiefs but nevertheless should respect and utilize the general institution of traditional rule.[10] Delavignette's ideas were probably an amalgam of his experience in the field and the example of the neighboring British in Nigeria. Although many French administrators were rather uninterested in the British or, for that matter, the experiences of other European nations in the colonies, Delavignette seems to have been well aware of them.

After serving in the Sahel region, Delavignette was transferred south to Upper Volta. In Ouagdougou he served as assistant to the district officer, the *cercle* commandant, the man on whom in the final analysis the efficacy of French rule depended. He administered regions varying in size and population. At the extremes were a small *cercle* like Cotonou in Dahomey, with only 85 square kilometers, and that of Timbuktu, 500,000 square kilometers (nearly as large as France, with its 540,000 square kilometers). In population, there were in 1927 ten *cercles* having fewer than 20,000 inhabitants and sixteen with more than 200,000. Most of the 115 *cercles* were somewhere in between these extremes.[11] The very large districts were subdivided, and a junior administrator served as head of the subdivision.

The commandant had enormous power: he had both executive and judicial responsibilities; he tried cases and carried out sentences. Among his duties were to preserve order and to see that the regulations of the colony and the district were observed. He was involved in political actions such as choosing chiefs—an important function since the chiefs at the canton and at the lower village level were the African intermediaries through whom French authority filtered down. He sometimes had to act as diplomat, trying to reconcile differences between antagonistic clans or ethnic groups. He had to know something about agriculture, to help encourage the planting of various kinds of crops; he built bridges and roads; he took the census; he collected taxes; at times he even gave inoculations against epidemics.

To carry out his functions the commandant found he needed a growing staff at his headquarters. Delavignette was appointed to help fill this need in the *cercle* of Ougadougou, where he served from November 1925 to January 1927. Though he did not particularly like the red tape and dreariness of desk administration, he seems to have done well and his *cercle* commandant wrote in 1926: "This is a first-class official who will always be the right man, be it in the bush or in an office."[12] After a leave Delavignette was assigned to the bush post of Banfora in Upper Volta, one of the three administrative subdivisions in the *cercle* of Bobo-Dioulasso. The *cercle* commandant in Bobo was responsible for the whole *cercle*, but direct responsibility rested with the *chef de subdivision* of Banfora: Delavignette. The region had a population of approximately 100,000. Each village had its own chief, and these in turn were responsible to an African appointed by the French, the *chef de canton*. There were nine such chiefs in the subdivision of Banfora, these supervised by the *chef de subdivision*. As such, Delavignette had all the responsibilities of *cercle* commandant with the exception that he was formally responsible to the commandant located in Bobo-Dioulasso.

Banfora had been a turbulent region that the French had had considerable trouble controlling. In 1915 it was the scene of a violent uprising that had been put down only with the greatest difficulty. Using the common device of "divide and rule," the French had brought in the Ouattara, a ruling clan from the Kong region of the Ivory Coast, to help suppress the inhabitants. As a reward for their efforts the Ouattara were made chiefs of the region. They were hated by the local inhabitants and in turn had utter contempt for the people over whom they had been given power. Forgetting that the French had put them in a position of authority, they felt they had a right to rule free of European intervention. When the French administrator of Banfora in late 1927, Livmann, fired a *chef de canton* in that district, the Ouattara precipitated violence; on January 3, 1928, Livmann was stabbed and had to be medically evacuated.[13]

It was under these difficult circumstances that Delavignette was appointed to head the Banfora subdivision. He had had previous experience with ethnic strife of various sorts, especially in Niger. By skillful diplomacy and a series of palavers with village elders he was able to arrest the would-be assassin and reestablish tranquility. Banfora was a poor region with few economic resources; the peasants lived at and sometimes below subsistence level. Delavignette saw his role as increasing their economic welfare as well as restoring tranquility in the region.

In the 1920s the colonial administration established seed cooperatives in West Africa; under government auspices millet and other foods were stored for the following year to insure that there would be sufficient seeds to plant. Delavignette actively encouraged the local peasantry to contribute to the cooperative. The world demand for peanuts was high and he saw in these legumes a cash crop that would give the people much needed money, so he toured his district preaching peanut cultivation. The peasants were naturally suspicious but overcame their reluctance. In 1927 450 tons were grown, and production increased nearly tenfold during the following two years: 8,000 tons were gathered in 1928 and 1929. Peanuts were exploited for their oil. They had to be pressed by hand, an inefficient method that yielded only half the oil of an industrial press. Delavignette helped bring an industrial press to Banfora,[14] freeing much of the population from the back-breaking work of oil extraction. Thus, the laborers could concentrate on raising food crops or on increasing peanut production.

The success of the peanut harvests of 1928 and 1929 created a sense of well-being in the population. Delavignette's espousal of cash crop production was very much a part of the concern of the interwar French administration. But unlike many of his colleagues, he made sure that his district produced more crops and he also saw to it that the newly created wealth went to the cultivators. In many districts the chiefs forcibly extracted labor from their subjects while withholding from them the fruits of their efforts. French administrators often condoned such behavior since they were interested only in high production figures for their district. But Delavignette was genuinely concerned for the peasants; by discussion rather than force, he seems to have convinced the chiefs and elders of the wisdom of letting all share in the newly created wealth. His understanding and empathy for the Africans turned him into a successful administrator. His authority was un-questioned. Delavignette's methods were seen as a model, and Governor Jules Brévié summarized his colonial career as follows:

> During his colonial assignments Delavignette has always acquired the best results at the head of the districts he has administered. Intelligent, energetic, having very good judgment and tact, and absorbed with his profession, he has acquired a profound knowledge of African affairs. A talented writer.[15]

As Brévié noted, Delavignette had become famous as an author. In 1926 he had written a semisatirical novel on French colonialism, *Toum*. Since such criticisms were not appreciated in the administration, and indeed even the publishing of general essays was frowned upon, he wrote under the pseudonym of Louis Faivre. Once his publications had received some acceptance, however, he published under his own name, and in 1931 authored the book that won him fame: *Paysans noirs*.

The title of the book is significant. Frenchmen had become accustomed to thinking of the colonial peoples as faceless "natives." Delavignette restored human dignity to them. He showed the Africans to be peasants, black peasants. He did not deny Africans their own personality, portraying them as inferior versions of French peasants. Although it was his knowledge of French peasantry that helped Delavignette understand that Africans were not uniform, they, too, had local traditions and beliefs that deserved respect. Like the French peasants, most Africans lived off the land; they were bound to it and their future depended upon how the soil was treated. The role of the French administration was to help develop that soil.

The administrator depicted in *Paysans noirs* respected the traditions of the elders and consulted them at length. By appealing to this tradition he sought support for the changes that were important if the community was to live at peace and in prosperity. Delavignette grasped what few colonial "developers" understood at the time, that ordinary people must themselves become convinced that change is to their benefit. Economic development should not be seen as a threat to a community's way of life but as the key to its survival. Delavignette thought of change as a means of saving the village life while auguring a new era. Thus, the oil press in Banfora kept the young men from migrating southward by providing jobs. The community remained intact; the villages did not lose their young men. On the other hand, the new income received by wage workers allowed them to establish their own households and become more independent of their elders than had been the custom. A new, freer social organization was evolving. Humane administration would permit traditional societies to preserve much of their structure, but it was also creating a new Africa. Within African society there were forces susceptible of development and it was these forces that, according to Delavignette, the French presence should encourage and guide.

The role of the administrator was to deal with people not in the abstract but very personally, at the village level and down to the household. The whole community's problems had become the administrator's concerns. In this sense, as Delavignette later was to write, the colonial administration was a totalitarian system.[16]

The bulk of contemporary colonial literature was self-assured with regard to the white man's mission overseas; *Sanders of the River* had no qualms about what he was doing. The mood of *Paysans noirs* was more hesitant. The characters described by Delavignette, white and black alike, were real human beings rather than heroes and villains. The white administrator at times was filled with self-doubt: had he misled his subjects, would in fact the rains come? Would the elders, so much wiser and experienced, listen to a man in his twenties whom they still considered a boy? What if all the efforts came to naught?[17] The attraction of the book was that it is a profoundly realistic colonial novel depicting in rich detail the life of Africans and of French administrators overseas. It was an immediate success and won the prize as the best colonial novel in 1931. The novel was made into a movie and in 1946 reprinted in a new edition.

Metropolitan Service

Delavignette's health had not been good while he was in Africa. He had acquired chronic malaria, some of his war wounds acted up, and he suffered from a punctured eardrum. He was to become deaf in his right ear and later in life, at receptions at his home, one could always tell who was the guest of honor—the person sitting to his left. When the Agence économique pour l'Afrique occidentale française, located in Paris, offered him a post in 1931, he welcomed a stay in France to regain his health.

The position must have further tempted him since it allowed him to remain with his new bride, Annie Mairey, the widow of his geography teacher, who had been killed in World War I. Thirteen years his senior, she was a remarkable woman; for her generation she was very well educated, having received the baccalaureate, a rare feat for women before World War I. Her father was a schoolteacher and a member of the Socialist party in the city of Saint-Etienne, one of France's industrial centers. Annie Mairey was brought up a Catholic and had at the same time developed strong socialist attachments. At the turn of the century, she married a lycée professor and socialist militant, Auguste Mairey, and had three children by him; the war left her a widow and she had to bring up her two remaining children (one died tragically in an accident) on the meager pension provided to war widows. When in 1920 the Socialist party split at the Tours conference she opted for the Communist majority and sat on the political bureau of the party, the first woman to do so. The party's increasingly rigid position and its growing subservience to Moscow—the process usually described as Bolshevization—turned Annie Mairey against it. Furthermore, it became clear to her that she could not be a Communist and a Catholic at the same time. She left the party in 1924 but continued to have many friends who belonged to or who came from left-wing political circles.

During World War II the home of the Delavignettes was a haven for resistance members; Annie's son Jean Mairey was to play a significant role in the resistance, becoming one of the seven commissioners of the republic—the superprefects appointed by de Gaulle to administer France after liberation. By her connection with academic circles from her first marriage and by her political associations, Annie Delavignette brought into their home people of intellect and sensitivity. Her husband seems to have enjoyed these visitors. But it would be hard to determine whether they or Annie had any direct influence on the shaping of Robert's career and thought. They certainly constituted an intellectual reference group different from that which most colonial officials had. It probably made it easier for Robert Delavignette to develop his strongly independent ideas on the empire, which were not in conformity with the official doctrines of the day. Although everyone who knew the couple attest to their deep devotion to each other, they were both independent-minded individuals and Annie Delavignette does not seem to have influenced her husband's thinking.

In 1931, newly married, Delavignette took the post at the *Agence économique*. The role of the agency was to attract investments to Africa and spread information about the continent. He was ideally suited for the latter role. The opening of the international colonial exhibition of 1931 was accompanied by the publication of an ambitious series of volumes on the empire. Delavignette was commissioned to author the volume on French West Africa.[18] Beautifully illustrated with wood engravings, the book is written in the style that was Delavignette's trademark. It is highly personal, revealing the experiences and feelings of the author, yet including all the official statistics usually expected of such volumes.

In a series of journal articles Delavignette wrote about the depression and its effect on Africa. The French government and people—he believed—should be concerned not only with the poverty of Europe but also with the misery of the African peasant. He argued that the African's needs were in many ways more pressing; often lacking the most simple amenities such as a water well or an iron plow, the African was particularly vulnerable to the vagaries of the weather and other uncontrollable forces. Delavignette advocated "small projects" such as the digging of a well or the installation of a water pump; they would have immediate impact on the daily lives of a village. Grandiose plans of dams, railroad networks, and ports were important, too, but they must not prevent the development of programs administering directly to human needs. In article after article he tried to educate the public about the needs of the colonies. If an empire united in purpose and goal was to be created, it had to share the experience of self-sacrifice. Delavignette scorned programs that sought to develop the colonies only the more readily to exploit them; what was needed, rather, was that people in the colonies experience a real improvement in their lot.[19]

In 1934, on the occasion of the fiftieth anniversary of the French conquest of the Sudan, Delavignette made an official journey to the Sudan and subsequently published his *Soudan-Paris-Bourgogne*. The thesis of this book is that the Sudan was as much a province of France as Delavignette's own beloved Burgundy and, like it, had a right to its own life and personality. There was a symbiosis between these two provinces—Sudan and Burgundy—and Paris. They gave human meaning to the city; they both represented the historic verities of man, his age-old relationship with the soil, and the traditions of his ancestors. Paris was pointing to the future, but in order to gain wisdom and balance it needed to draw on the life of its provinces. As in *Paysans noirs*, Delavignette was able to combine a deep appreciation of tradition with commitment to change. Men's lives could be improved by technology. The oil press in Banfora had helped enrich the peasants; the dam being built on the Niger would help irrigate new fields for the Sudanese peasant. But for his life to have meaning, the individual and the society of which he is a part has to have a culture, a central focus of beliefs. Thus, Delavignette did not advocate simply the substitution of French for African culture. Some aspects of French culture, for instance its technology, would be useful to Africans. But the culture exchange was not to go only in one direction. Frenchmen had much to learn from their compatriots overseas—their reverence for nature, their ability to live in harmony with it, and their spiritual values. By living together in a union in which each party would be allowed to preserve its own personality, the interchange of values would help enrich both cultures.[20]

As President Léopold Sédar Senghor of Senegal put it in a tribute published on the occasion of Delavignette's seventieth birthday in 1967, "What makes Robert Delavignette a pioneer . . . is that in the colonial era itself he overcame the dichotomy white-black, Europe-Africa, in order to create a symbiosis."[21] If he never quite spelled out what the future political configuration of the French empire might be, the general themes of his writings suggested a loose federation. Beginning in the 1930s, he went against common thinking on colonial questions, anticipating the evolution of the empire by more than a decade.

Delavignette also departed from contemporary orthodoxies in other ways. Western educated Africans, he argued, should play an important role in the African parts of the new federation. Such views were at variance with the attitude of French administrators, who were as a rule hostile to the *évolués*. For all their foibles, the *évolués*, Delavignette was convinced, were the symbol of successful assimilation, an example of the future Franco-African community.[22] In his personal relations in Paris in the 1930s and the following decades, Delavignette was to have close friendships with many of the outstanding African intellectuals residing in Paris.[23]

Having won a reputation for his advocacy of overseas reform, Delavignette was asked to collaborate in the ministry of colonies under the Popular Front government that had come to power in June 1936, supported by France's three largest political parties of the left—the Socialists, Radicals, and Communists. Delavignette never formally joined a political party, but it would be fair to label him a liberal Catholic; in the 1930s and the following decade he was to be an active contributor to the liberal Catholic journal *L'Esprit*, edited by Emmanuel Mounier. Although objecting to being labeled a disciple of Mounier, in many ways Delavignette paralleled the thought of the distinguished Catholic liberal in his social conscience and deep concern for the social and spiritual disruptions caused by the industrial revolution.[24] The new minister of colonies, Marius Moutet, was a Socialist with a reputation as a critic of colonial abuse. As a result of the influence of a common acquaintance, the Socialist Lucien Lévy-Bruhl, who as an ethnologist knew Delavignette and recommended him to his Socialist comrade, Moutet decided to appoint Delavignette as his *chef de cabinet*. Socialists in the colonial service were still rare in the 1930s, and appointment of a Socialist *chef de cabinet* might have alienated the service even further from Moutet, who was regarded with some suspicion since he was the first Socialist to occupy the position. The minister probably thought it useful to attach to himself a man known for his liberal inclinations who was not a member of the party.

As *chef de cabinet*, Delavignette's main responsibility was to prepare the files for ministerial decisionmaking and screen the letters and people the minister should personally see. Though formally the *chef de cabinet* was outranked by directors of various services, his position of proximity to the minister made him nevertheless important. After World War I the ministry of colonies was divided into bureaus organized along functional lines; thus, there was a bureau of political affairs, one on personnel, one on economic affairs. Each bureau was headed by a senior official with the title of director. The most powerful of these was the director of political affairs; since nearly every decision overseas had political implications he was carefully listened to.

Delavignette as *chef de cabinet* spent most of his time on the daily chores of preparing files for his minister, but he seems to have played a direct role in the establishment of a "program of small works," which he had advocated throughout the 1930s—small projects of great import to people in a village, such as digging a well or supplying tools and seeds.[25] In political decisions he seems not to have had as much impact as he would have liked; the director of political affairs, Gaston Joseph, who was also an old African hand, usually won the minister's ear. Joseph had been in the ministry for a long time; in the face of ever increasing agitation in Indochina he advocated repression. Moutet himself was ambivalent toward the overseas areas; although he desired reform, he feared the nationalist movements and was determined not to lose the empire for France.[26] In recognition of his services, Delavignette obtained the rank of governor in 1937, a distinction normally granted only to senior overseas administrators but occasionally bestowed on distinguished senior civil servants at the ministry.

Ecole Coloniale

In the same year, Delavignette received a new assignment; he was appointed director of the Ecole nationale de la France d'outre-mer (ENFOM). This training institution for colonial administrators had been founded in 1887, and for over a generation was a colorless and little regarded body that educated but a small proportion of the men serving in the colonial service. After World War I the ministry of colonies required that all men entering the corps of colonial administrators have some training at the school, and in 1926 it acquired a new director, Georges Hardy, who freed the future administrators from much of the traditional legal curriculum and stressed courses that would more closely reflect the realities of overseas life, such as languages and ethnology.

Two directors served for short and undistinguished terms after Hardy. Delavignette, however, built on Hardy's accomplishments, placing further emphasis on a curriculum reflecting the overseas evolution. He hired distinguished ethnologists such, as Marcel Griaule and Jacques Soustelle. African language teachers were also brought to the school: Diori Hamani, who taught Hausa, and later Léopold Sédar Senghor to teach Mandingo languages—both of them gifted men who in 1960 became presidents of their newly independent countries.

The school created a young group of administrators more in touch with colonial realities than their predecessors. But Delavignette himself helps explain the excitement and sense of commitment that animated the young graduates of ENFOM. He had close contacts with his students, frequently having them to his home and introducing them to his African friends. Several former students named their sons after him, and long after they had left ENFOM they continued to correspond with their former teacher. These contacts undoubtedly helped Delavignette to be so well informed on the evolution of the empire even after he had ceased to go overseas. Dozens of his correspondents throughout the empire—former students—continually apprised him of what was going on at their levels of the administration, information rarely reflected in the public media and even less in official reports to the ministry of overseas France.

Delavignette's basic concepts as teacher and administrator are summarized in his book *Les vrais chefs de l'empire* published in 1939. This book, clumsily butchered by French wartime censorship, was reprinted in its entirety in 1946 as *Service africain*; four years later it was translated into English as *Freedom and Authority in French West Africa*. Much like *Paysans noirs*, it is the account of the life of the *cercle* commandants, who, according to Delavignette, were the real chiefs of the empire. In addition, the book was a programmatic statement of the duties and responsibilities of the administrator. He is to command and exercise his authority the better to serve the people under his rule. He must respect the culture of the Africans but also bring to them the technology and gift for organization of the Western world. He must realize that the colonies are changing, moving away from their traditions and developing a new culture. The Africans who had obtained schooling in Western institutions and culture would be the new leaders of Africa; these earnest young men wanted to play a role in the new Africa that was developing. Though it was common for many European administrators to scorn educated Africans, Delavignette welcomed them as representatives of the new Africa. In Banfora in the late 1920s Delavignette had been friends with the young Voltaic schoolteacher of the town, Ouezzin Coulibally, who later became political leader of the territory. He counted Léopold Senghor among his friends, and in the book *Service africain* acclaimed him as the representative of the newly emerging African man; in 1945 each dedicated articles to the other.[27]

Service africain is a guide and program for future administrators; to those already in the field it voiced their professional credo, spelling out the mission of the colonial administrator.[28] In his writings and teachings at ENFOM Delavignette stressed French responsibility to the Africans and the need to understand their evolution by being in tune with the times. With this, it has been argued, Delavignette prepared a generation of administrators to cope with decolonization.[29] His directorship at ENFOM ended in 1946 with his appointment as high commissioner to the Cameroons.

High Commissioner

The Cameroons, which had been a German colony in 1914, was seized by England and France during World War I, the latter occupying the larger eastern part and the rest being occupied by Great Britain. After the war all former German colonies were declared mandates under the supervision of the League of Nations, and France was confirmed as virtual ruler of Cameroons by being given mandate power over the area it had occupied during the war. France had to account to the League for its rule, but otherwise its administration was generally unimpeded.

Important changes occurred during World War II, however, that weakened French control. The Free French under General de Gaulle had seized the Cameroons, and it played an important role in the fight against both Vichy and the Germans. The control of the Free French over the Cameroons and French Equatorial Africa was for a while the only territorial claim to legitimacy that they possessed. The participation of Africans in the Free French war effort both as soldiers and as laborers providing needed wartime staples put the French in their debt. To broaden their authority during the war, the Free French allowed a greater participation in political affairs, which whetted the appetite of educated Africans for further responsibilities. In both the British and the French empire the end of the war unleashed among the educated colonial elite a sense of a new era dawning. Many wanted independence; others insisted on at least enjoying equal rights with Europeans resident in the colonies. Neither the colonial administration nor the settlers living overseas, however, were cognizant of the profound changes in attitude that had occurred as a result of the second world war.

Frustrations of various sorts, including economic ones, beset a number of overseas territories, and the Cameroons was no exception.[30] In the autumn of 1945 a series of violent labor demonstrations had broken out that deteriorated into full-scale rioting; the governor was physically assaulted and French air force officers bombed and strafed Africans. Nine persons were killed and twenty wounded. Political ferment seemed to reach an all-time high; the prewar youth movement, the Jeunesse camerounaise française, now transformed itself into a political party, the Union camerounaise française.[31]

Internationally French control over the territory also seemed threatened. The draft of the French constitution of 1945 provided for full integration of French overseas territories with the metropole. But the United Nations Charter elaborated in San Francisco in April 1945 forbade such integration and gave the trusteeship council considerable control over the former mandates. Would France be allowed to administer the Cameroons; furthermore, could it be retained as part of the French empire? In considering these problems French colonial ministers vacillated between foolhardy boldness and timidity. Jacques Soustelle, minister at the end of 1945, thought the Cameroonian problem could be solved by dismantling the Cameroons, by having the territory divided up between the neighboring

French colonies of Chad and Gabon. His successor in early 1945, Moutet, was afraid that the United Nations would not even name France as trustee of the Cameroons; he thought that at best France might be able to retain the territory by joining the British in a condominium rule over the ancient Germany colony of Kamerun (which, in addition to French Cameroons, was comprised of the British Cameroons administratively joined to Nigeria). It was only in December 1946, when the United Nations General Assembly approved the French trusteeship over the Cameroons, that the French were able to breathe a sigh of relief; they would be allowed to keep the territory and administer it very much like the other French territories; the legal fiction of its separateness could be maintained by declaring it an associated overseas territory.[32]

By December 1946 the danger of losing the Cameroons had apparently passed, but at the end of 1945 it had seemed like a real possibility. To win for France a sympathetic hearing in the United Nations, it was important that violence of the kind that had broken out in the autumn of 1945 not recur, and the minister of overseas France turned to Delavignette to serve as high commissioner. Moutet, who had worked closely with Delavignette during the Popular Front government, trusted him. To the people of the Cameroons and to the United Nations this appointment would be an indication of the willingness of France to introduce reform.

Delavignette was a Catholic, and that was probably also useful. The missions were a strong force in the Cameroons; in 1946 there were 500,000 Catholics and 200,000 Protestants. As a result of the League of Nations mandate, mission activity had been tolerated to a far greater extent than in other colonies (especially the activities of foreign missionaries). The missions had come to play an especially important role in education, and Moutet seems to have desired greater state control over them; if Delavignette were to carry out such functions he could not readily be accused of being anticlerical. Also, Catholicism was politically important; there was a strong Catholic union movement and the French Catholic political party, the Mouvement républicain populaire (MRP), had reason to believe that the Cameroons would be its political bailiwick (both deputies elected to the Constituent Assembly in October 1945 belonged to the MRP). A minimum of political tensions would occur if the high commissioner were of the same political persuasion. All these considerations seem to have played a role in the appointment of Delavignette. It was his first overseas assignment in fourteen years.

When he came to the Cameroons, he faced serious problems. The colonial administration was set in its ways and failed to understand the political and economic evolution that had been accelerated by the war. Shortly after arriving he told his subordinates in a strongly worded circular:

> If you resent your loss of personal or public authority because there is a representative assembly, because your subordinates are unionized, because the *indigénat* code is suppressed, because you no longer possess judicial powers, because the Cameroons of 1946 no longer is that of 1920, you are really demanding the impossible. Catch up with the times.[33]

The settlers were another group resistant to change. The Cameroons had a well-organized European population; in 1946 there were 2,500 Europeans, of whom 1,700 were French. These settlers were wary of African participation in politics. Under the proposed constitution of the Fourth Republic, each overseas territory was to have a territorial assembly and send deputies to Paris. They were elected by two electoral colleges, the first consisting of Europeans and a few *assimilés*, the second of the mass of Africans. The first college in April 1946 elected seventeen European members of the territorial assembly and the Africans elected seventeen of their own. Even though the first electoral college had a disproportionate number of European representatives, seventeen for a few thousand voters, whereas the seventeen Africans represented 12,000 Africans—the group enfranchised out of the 3 million inhabitants—the settlers feared that they would not be preponderant. They demanded that their representatives form a separate assembly apart from the Africans, a kind of upper house that would have veto power over the African assembly. Delavignette refused to bow to settler pressure, insisting that the two assemblies meet jointly. He thus prevented exacerbation of a tense political situation, for the Africans would undoubtedly have vigorously protested administrative collusion with the settlers. The Cameroons was the first overseas territory to have a territorial assembly established, and it may well be true—as Delavignette claimed in his memoirs—that his insistence on a single chamber helped set the model for other territories.[34]

The year 1946 was a difficult one for the French in black Africa; it witnessed a transition from the old, prewar, authoritarian regime to a more liberal one. In addition to the establishment of African political participation (even if limited), other reforms were carried out: forced labor was abolished as was the *indigénat* system, which had given French administrators special disciplinary powers; the rights to free speech and unionization were affirmed. This freer atmosphere led to exaggerated fears by Europeans that their authority was breaking down and that the Africans no longer compelled by forced labor and other forms of constraint would cease working. In a speech to the territorial assembly Delavignette insisted, however, that "the old paternalist organization . . . must cede to a new organization founded on the principle of collaboration" between Africans and Europeans.[35] This collaboration was difficult, for as Delavignette wrote a friend, "There are Europeans here who are behind the times by twenty years and *évolués* [European-educated Africans] who are ahead by fifty."[36] It was important to do everything possible to bring these antagonistic groups together; little in that way had been done before. Delavignette was the first high commissioner of the Cameroons to give a reception to which both white and blacks were invited.

The economic task of developing the Cameroons, Delavignette believed, would do a lot to ease the tense political situation. Also, the stark conditions of the Cameroonian population needed to be remedied; in the urban centers most lived in slums, and those on the land barely eked out a living. Before leaving Paris, Delavignette went to see the minister of finance, André Philip, to ask for funds. The French treasury was empty and the minister received him amiably, saying: "All I can do for you, if you smoke a pipe, is to share with you my tobacco pouch."[37] A month after arriving in the Cameroons, however, Delavignette received news of an ambitious overseas development program, FIDES (Fonds d'investissement pour le développement économique et social des territoires d'outre-mer).He helped set the first plan of FIDES for the Cameroons; it was to concentrate on the infrastructure of the territory, 85.3 percent of the expenditures going to that segment of the economy during the first plan, which lasted until 1954.[38] Roads, bridges, railroads, telecommunication facilities, ports, and hydroelectric plants were built.

Delavignette's success in reducing political conflicts in Cameroons, the smooth manner in which social and political reforms had been introduced, and the economic improvements that he brought to the territory led the United Nations Trusteeship Council in 1947 to congratulate France for its accomplishments.[39] Years later, when the Cameroons attained independence, its political leaders seemed to recognize his contributions by inviting him to attend independence day celebrations. Delavignette's record was so outstanding that he was promoted to governor-general—a rank usually given only to the head of a federation who has several governors serving under him, but also an honorary distinction.

Delavignette and Decolonization

When Delavignette had completed a year's service in the Cameroons, Moutet recalled him to Paris to serve as director of political affairs at the ministry of overseas France (the new name for the ministry of colonies). He was now the highest permanent official in the ministry and occupied a key office during a critical period of French colonial rule. During the late 1940s few Frenchmen, not even the Communists, anticipated that the French empire would not survive another two decades. But already there was widespread unrest. On the very day when Delavignette took over his new office, March 29, 1947, a bloody revolt broke out in Madagascar. He sanctioned the attempt to reestablish order, which led to terrible excesses. His reaction to Malagasy nationalism may have been different from what it would be toward other national movements in the French empire because he was intellectually unprepared for the outbreak. Elsewhere, in Indochina and North Africa for instance, important nationalist movements had developed before World War II; it was not difficult, therefore, to grasp the nature of anti-French agitation. In Madagascar, where there had been no such movements since the turn of the century, such activity could be more easily dismissed as a mindless outbreak of violence. It is also possible that Delavignette, faced by revolt on the very day that he took office, instinctively ordered the restoration of order; to preserve order was the minimal expectation of any colonial official.

Delavignette, however, showed considerable understanding with regard to Indochina possibly because the evolution of a strong nationalist consciousness there had already been well known in the 1930s. Unlike Madagascar, Indochina had been severed from France during World War II, when the Japanese occupied the country. Upon defeat, Japan evacuated Indochina during the interim before the French had a chance to return; the nationalist movement headed by Ho Chi Minh was established and claimed control over Vietnam. The French were at first ambiguous in their relationship to Ho, but very soon fighting broke out. Filled with illusions, French officials prosecuted the long colonial war hoping to find some alternative to a Ho Chi Minh victory.

Delavignette was one of the few officials who understood the extent to which the changes of the interwar era, the second world war, and then finally the Indochina war itself had transformed the colonial relationship. In a series of courageous memoranda he explained to his superiors that the Vietnamese wanted genuine independence. The relationship between Frenchmen and Vietnamese had become not unlike that of Germans and Frenchmen in World War II. Attitudes had changed, and the Vietnamese now saw the French as foreign occupiers. Delavignette did not advocate outright abandonment of Indochina, but he pointed out the difficulty inherent in French insistence on remaining in their Asian colony.[40]

The war in Indochina led to the transfer of French policymaking from the ministry of overseas France to the generals in Saigon or the ministry of war in Paris. Thus, the role of the overseas ministry diminished in Asia, and Delavignette's ideas had little influence. In any case, in 1951 he left the ministry to return to ENFOM as a teacher. His role as a policymaker had ended.

Conclusion

Although no longer with the ministry of overseas France, Delavignette was still very much concerned with overseas developments. He had never served in North Africa, but in the early 1950s, he viewed French policy toward that region with increasing alarm. In Tunisia and Morocco nationalist opinion had made itself increasingly heard, and the only French response had been repression. A group of French Catholic intellectuals, led by François Mauriac, formed the Comité France-Maghreb, which advocated negotiation with the nationalists and the granting of some form of independence. Delavignette was a prominent member of this committee.

Many liberal Frenchmen could envision the independence of Tunisia and Morocco; after all, they were legally protectorates. But Algeria was different: it was technically an integral part of France and was considered fully assimilated to the metropole. In fact, however, the Muslim population did not enjoy the same political rights granted to the European settlers in Algeria or to the citizens of the metropole, and most Algerian Muslims were considerably worse off economically than their Christian compatriots. Muslim grievances could easily be channeled into nationalist agitation, especially since a similar mood had developed in neighboring Morocco and Tunisia. On the night of November 1, 1954, a small group of Algerian nationalists began the uprising that was to become the Algerian war.

Many institutions were to deal with the Algerian uprising. In the summer of 1955 the economic and social council, a high-level government advisory body, took up the Algerian question. Delavignette was a member of the council and authored its lengthy report spelling out the need for a massive French commitment to achieve the social and economic progress of Algeria. Implicit in the report was the notion that such a pledge might curtail the spread of Algerian nationalism.[41] Thus, while making clear the social matrix from which the rebellion sprung, he, too, underestimated the nationalist convictions underlying the revolt and hoped that if France carried out a genuinely egalitarian policy in Algeria, with all the sacrifices such a policy implied, the territory could be saved for France.

In an attempt to control the uprising the French army instituted a police state in Algeria. The wholesale denial of human rights and the use of torture became so well publicized that in 1957, under considerable public pressure, the government appointed a commission for the protection of individual rights and liberties to investigate the accusations made against the army and administration in Algeria. Delavignette was appointed a member of the commission, which he regarded as France's conscience in Algeria. He was committed to the notion that the total truth would be most salutary to France's colonial mission. Anything else would poison the political system both overseas and at home. However, he soon realized that the commission report would fail to clarify the extent to which the authorities in both Paris and Algeria had prior knowledge of the use of torture and other illegal activities and were unwilling to right the abuses that had been committed. He resigned in protest, having filed a severe report indicating the systematic disregard for human rights that had developed in Algeria. He also publicly spoke out on the question.[42]

In regard to black Africa, Delavignette was sympathetic toward the reforms instituted in 1956–1957, which led to internal autonomy in the overseas territories and which, from 1958 to 1960, led to independence.[43] Although many administrators had difficulty adjusting to these changes, Delavignette welcomed them because they would inaugurate a new era of full legal equality between France and its former overseas dependencies.[44] He was eager to contribute, no matter how modestly, to the success of the newly independent states. In 1959 ENFOM had been converted to a training school for African administrators, and Delavignette returned to teach—as he had in times past—the men who were to rule Africa.[45]

With the end of the empire he attempted to put the whole imperial experience in perspective and wrote books and articles trying to sum up what French rule had meant for both Africa and the metropole. He also continued an old theme: the duty and responsibility of Frenchmen to their fellow human beings in Africa. Decolonization had not diminished the moral obligation of a richer and more technically advanced society to help those less well endowed materially. Nor was there any less reason to learn from African culture those ethical values and esthetic perceptions that could enrich French civilization.[46]

Insisting on the fact that the French had contributed to the history and development of modern Africa, Delavignette had also been instrumental in advancing French knowledge of Africa. His writings conveyed to Frenchmen a better understanding of the traditional aspects of Africa, the world of the black peasant, and of the new and evolving continent with its modern cities, universities, dams, and ambitions for the future. Delavignette had seen in the French empire an institution that affirmed the unity of men by creating a symbiosis between various cultures. After the collapse of empires built upon force, he saw the opportunity of building new relationship on universal human values.

At the same time, he attempted to preserve the bonds that he first established with Africa over half a century ago. In 1974 he was still corresponding with the chief of Banfora who had been village elder when Delavignette had been the administrator there.[47] He kept very much abreast of current affairs in Africa, interrogating recent visitors to the continent on economic and political developments. When drought hit the Sahel in the late 1960s and early 1970s Delavignette was active in soliciting funds for aid to the region.[48]

On February 4, 1976, aged seventy-nine, Robert Delavignette died after a long illness. He was one of the most distinguished members of that generation of administrators whom Maurice Delafosse called *broussard*, the bush administrator, the man who was as much an African as a European.[49] By his life and writings Delavignette had tried to exemplify this ability to span two cultures. It is not surprising that President Senghor said that he thought of Delavignette "with piety."[50]

Notes

1. Georges Balandier, "Robert Delavignette, un libéral obstiné," *Le Monde*, 10 February 1976.

2. His childhood is evoked in *Birama* (Paris, 1955) and in an unpublished fragment of his memoirs entitled "La classe et la cour."

3. Gaston Roupnel, *Histoire de la campagne française* (Paris, 1932); Auguste Mairey, *Géographie générale* (Paris, 1911); idem, special texts on the colonies, *La France et ses colonies* (Paris, 1902).

4. "La Classe et la cour," p. 23.

5. Robert Delavignette, *Freedom and Authority in French West Africa* (London, 1950), pp. 9–11.

6. Retold in his unpublished memoirs, "L'offrande de l'étranger: Mémoires d'une Afrique française," pp. 71–72.

7. *Delavignette, Freedom and Authority*, pp. 9–11.

8. Personnel file, 1C 1143, Archives de l'Afrique occidentale française, Dakar (hereinafter cited AAOF).

9. On the Barmou, where Delavignette served in 1923, "Rapport politique, 1er trimestre Niger, 1923," Niger 2G 23-24, and personnel files, 1C 763, 1C 1143, and 1C 685, AAOF.

10. Robert Delavignette, "Les chefs noirs," *Le Temps*, 4 June 1931; ibid., 10 September 1931; idem, "La politique et l'administration indigènes en A.O.F.," *Afrique française* (hereinafter cited AF)43 (January 1933):7–11; idem, *Freedom and Authority*, pp. 71–84.

11. "Documentation d'ordre administratif, politique, social, et économique de l'AOF," 1927, 17G 161, AAOF; Georges Spitz, *L'Ouest africain français* (Paris, 1947), p. 90.

12. File 1C 1143, AAOF.

13. "Haute-Volta, résumé du rapport politique annuel, 1928," Haute-Volta, 2G28/15, AAOF.

14. "Rapport agricole annuel, 1928, Haute-Volta," 2G28/38, pp. 181–190, AAOF.

15. May 1932 note in file 1C 1069, AAOF.

16. Delavignette, *Freedom and Authority*, p. 22.

17. Robert Delavignette, *Paysans noirs* (Paris, 1931), p. 71.

18. *Afrique occidentale française* (Paris, 1931).

19. Robert Delavignette, "Le dispensaire au grenier," *Le Temps*, 15 January 1932; idem, "L'esprit africain," ibid., 8 August 1933; idem, "Mise en valeur africaine," ibid., 19 September 1933; idem, "Le dynamisme de l'AOF," *Afrique française* 42 (1932):578–579; idem, "L'esprit africain, l'Afrique occidentale française, et la conférence de Londres," AF 43 (1933):336–337; idem, "Le bourgeois français au XIXe siècle et les colonies noires," AF 45 (1935):279–282; idem, "Action colonisatrice et paysannat indigène," ibid.:526–530; idem, "Les idées et les actes en A.O.F., I," *Journalde débats* (hereinafter cited JDD) (9 December 1934); idem, "Les idées et les actes en A.O.F., IV," JDD (22 December 1934).

20. Robert Delavignette, *Soudan-Paris-Bourgogne* (Paris, 1935).

21. Léopold Sédar Senghor, "Un gouverneur humaniste," *Revue Française d'histoire d'outre-mer* 54 (1967):26.

22. Robert Delavignette, "Lettre pour ceux qui ne savent pas lire," *Le Temps*, 10 March 1932; idem, "La médecine en A.O.F.:—L'école de médecine de Dakar," *La Revue mondiale* (15 March 1934):15–19; idem, "Le Dahomey à travers ses journaux," *AF* 45 (1935):232–235; idem, "La vie quotidienne et les feuilles locales," *JDD* (13 August 1933); idem, "Le théâtre de Gorée et la culture franco-africaine," *AF* 47 (1937):471–472.

23. Paul Hazoumé, the Dahomean writer, has depicted the role Delavignette's home played in the easy interchange of ideas between Frenchmen and Africans, "Souvenirs d'un Africain sur Monsieur Robert Delavignette," *Revue Française d'histoire d'outre-mer* 54 (1967):31–38.

24. Delavignette contributed a short essay in a memorial publication, *1950–1975: Vingt-cinq Ans après la mort de Mounier—Témoignages*, a special issue of *Bulletin des amis de E. Mounier* 44–45 (October 1975):22–23.

25. Robert Delavignette, "La politique de Marius Moutet au Ministère des colonies," *Actes du colloque Léon Blum, chef de gouvernement, 1936–1937* (Paris, 1967), pp. 391–394.

26. William B. Cohen, "The Colonial Policy of the Popular Front," *French Historical Studies* 7, no. 3 (Spring 1972):285–286.

27. Delavignette, *Freedom and Authority*; idem, "L'union française à l'échelle du monde, à la mesure de l'homme," *L'Esprit* 13 (July 1945):214–236; Léopold Sédar Senghor, "Vues sur l'Afrique noire, ou assimiler, non être assimilés," in Robert Lemaignen et al., *La communauté impériale française* (Paris, 1945), pp. 57–98.

28. Jean-Claude Froelich, "Delavignette et le service africain," *Revue française d'histoire d'outre-mer* 54 (1967):44–51.

29. Pierre Kalck, "Robert Delavignette et la décolonisation," ibid.:52–64; Charles André Julien, "Le jubilé du gouverneur-général Robert Delavignette," *Le Monde*, 20 February 1969; interview with Pierre Alexandre, 13 October 1965.

30. On the demographic impact and changes in Duala, for instance, see Victor T. Levine, *The Cameroons: From Mandate to Independence* (Berkeley, 1964), pp. 53–57; David E. Gardinier, "Political Behavior in the Community of Duala, Cameroon: Reaction of the Duala People to Loss of Hegemony, 1944–1955," *Ohio University: Papers in International Studies*, no. 3 (Athens, 1966).

31. Levine, *Cameroons*, p. 145.

32. The best survey of the Cameroon mandate problem after World War II is David E. Gardinier, *Cameroon–United Nations Challenge to French Policy* (London, 1963), pp. 1–52; the condominium plan was anticipated to such an extent that Delavignette appointed as an aide an administrator from the New Hebrides who had had experience with the condominium relationship there. Interview with Delavignette, summer 1975.

33. Circular, May 1946, reprinted in Ministère des colonies, *Bulletin d'information* (17 June 1946).

34. Delavignette, chapter 2, entitled "Une vie politique nouvelle," in an early draft of unpublished memoirs.

35. Speech of 30 April 1946, *Journal officiel du Cameroun français* (15 May 1946):618.

36. Delavignette to Lacharrière, Duala, 23 November 1946, Delavignette Archives.

37. Delavignette, "L'offrande de l'étranger," p. 307.

38. Gardinier, *Cameroon*, pp. 29–30.

39. *Notes et études documentaires* (19 August 1949):24.

40. "Note pour monsieur le ministre Paul Coste-Floret, 17 July 1948"; memorandum, 22 February 1949; "Note pour monsieur le ministre, 24 March 1949"; "Indochine, 29 October 1949"; "Note sur la situation au Viet-nam, 30 April 1950." All in the Delavignette Archives.

41. "Rapport sur la situation économique et sociale de l'Algérie," Conseil économique, *Journal officiel* (5 July 1955):325–357.

42. The text of the report and some of his public positions on the Algerian war after resignation from the committee are reprinted in Pierre Vidal-Naquet, *La raison d'état* (Paris, 1962), pp. 168–184. The damage the war had done to France was a theme he returned to often; Robert Delavignette, *L'Afrique noire française et son destin* (Paris, 1962) p. 176; idem, "Le pus dans la plaie," *La Croix*, 30 March 1972.

43. Immediately after the war he had pointed to that kind of development already in Robert Delavignette, "Le procès de la colonisation française," *Renaissance*, no. 15 (25 October 1945):14–21; idem, "L'union française et le problème constitutionnel," *Politique* 1, n.s. (15 November 1945):413–427; typical of his later position in favor of an increasing autonomy for the overseas territories within the framework of the French union, idem, "La croissance économique des territoires d'outre-mer," *Semaines sociales de France, Dijon 1952* (Paris, 1952), pp. 213–229, and his attitude toward independence in idem, "Les transformations politiques et sociales impliquées par le développement," *Semaines sociales de France, Angers 1959* (Paris, 1959), pp. 297–311.

44. See Delavignette's *L'Afrique noire française* and *Du bon usage de la décolonisation* (Paris, 1968).

45. He paid tribute to his new students in idem, "Randonnée africaine en terre de Gaule," *Nouvelle Revue française* (1963):792–811.

46. Idem, "Tiers monde sans tiers état," *Revue de Paris* 72 (1965):82–91; idem, *Du bon usage*.

47. Hema Fedma to Delavignette, Banfora, 29 July 1974, Delavignette Archives.

48. Robert Delavignette, "Famine africaine: Signe pour notre temps," *La Croix* 17–18 June 1973.

49. Maurice Delafosse, *Broussard, ou les états d'âme d'un colonial* (Paris, 1922).

50. Senghor, "Un gouverneur humaniste," p. 25.

Great Britain

On Governorship and Governors in British Africa

Anthony H. M. Kirk-Greene

AMONG the tributes to his governorship of Tanganyika (1925–1931), one that pleased Sir Donald Cameron the most was the unexpected, rather reluctant comment from an American tourist as the governor boarded the *Union Castle* headed for Cape Town on his way back to England.

> Some of us were ashore at Dar es Salaam when your people there said goodbye to you. If that is the spirit in which a Colonial Governor is regarded on his departure from a British dependency after several years service, well, Governor, we must say that there can't be much wrong with the British Empire.[1]

Tributes of this kind were rare, for there was much to divide the British from the American gubernatorial tradition. No colonial service governor in an African colony in the twentieth century ever ran for or was elected to his office. Save under the postwar Attlee administration, few British governors were appointed on an overtly political ticket. Ex-governors rarely concerned themselves with party politics. A few went to the House of Lords in a somewhat honorary capacity. Sir Harry H. Johnston did stand as a Liberal candidate in the Rochester by-election of 1903; he failed even to reduce the small Conservative majority of 500. Nor was Sir Herbert Young any more successful as a Liberal candidate in 1945. The British governor belonged to a species not overly respected by Americans. He also enjoyed certain honorific distinctions alien to the American tradition.

It was almost unknown for a colonial service governor to be appointed under the age of forty: Sir Geoffrey Archer, a brilliant man, was promoted to commissioner of British Somaliland at thirty-two and Sir John Pope Hennessy, "the stormy petrel of the Colonial Office," was only thirty-three when he was given the first of his six colonial governorships. Just outside the limit, Sir Bede Clifford was forty-one when he went to the Bahamas and Sir Kenneth Blackburne forty-three when named governor of the Leeward Islands (which earned him a special editorial in the *London Times*).[2] Sir Hugh Foot was forty-four when he was appointed to Jamaica, Sir Frederick Crawford forty-five when he went to the Seychelles, and Sir Robert Coryndon forty-seven when he was made governor of Uganda, although he had already held almost comparable posts for nearly twenty years. Even outstanding colonial service officers like Sir Hugh Clifford, Sir Donald Cameron, Sir Alan Burns, Sir Arthur Richards, and Sir Philip Mitchell were in their late forties or early fifties on their first appointment. With several governorships apiece, they were considered to be exceptionally brilliant in earning such early recognition.

Sympathy cannot, of course, be equated with support, so that the party in power at Westminster might on occasion need an assurance—as, for instance, was required of Foot in Cyprus—that the governor would not resign over the issue of a delicate Cabinet-agreed policy. There was, too, the periodic ad hoc appointment to a colonial governorship of a former politician from outside the colonial service, such as Lieutenant colonel Sir Edward Grigg, who was Member of Parliament for Oldham until he went to Kenya as governor in 1925. As secretary of state for the colonies, Arthur Creech Jones made several such appointments between 1946 and 1948. In general, however, as Table 1 shows, the correlation between change in the British government and change in the British governors was nil.

In short, the typical British colonial governor was everything an American state governor was not: career civil servant, apolitical, aged between forty-seven and fifty-two, and therein reaching the climax of rather than achieving just another step in his public and private life. Sir Hugh Foot, lecturing in the United States in the 1960s to explain Britain's stance on her remnant colonial issues, used to tell his American audiences to take a good look at the battered figure they saw before them. It belonged to a species becoming increasingly rare and heading toward extinction.

But if the British colonial governor in the twentieth century was none of these familiar figures, who was he? A historian of the colonial office has summed him up.

> Few people, when they read in the daily press that His Majesty has been pleased to appoint Sir X to be Governor of, say, Kenya, realise the interest underlying that brief statement, or have any conception of the nature of a Governor's task and what pitfalls there are for the unwary, the unskilled, the irritable and the unfortunate.[3]

In this chapter, which is designed to serve as a curtain raiser to the case studies that follow of British colonial governors in action, I shall consider the office of governor, drawing my data principally from the African territories of the colonial empire. His official functions comprised the essence and the reality of being a colonial governor. By way of conclusion, I shall present summary data about the

Table 1. British Political Parties and Key Colonial Officials, 1912–1939

Year	British party in power	Prime minister	Secretary of state for colonies	Permanent secretary colonial office	Governor of Nigeria	Governor of Tanganyika	Governor of Kenya	Governor of Uganda
1912	Liberal	H. H. Asquith	Lord Harcourt	J. Anderson	Lord Lugard	German rule	Henry Belfield	Frederick Jackson
13								
14						Military government		
15								
16	National coalition		A. Bonar Law					
17		David Lloyd George	Walter Long	George Fiddes		Horace Byatt		
18								Robert Coryndon
19	Lloyd George Liberals and Conservative		Lord Milner		Hugh Clifford		Edward Northey	
1920								
21			Winston Churchill	James Masterson-Smith				
22	Conservative	A. Bonar Law / S. Baldwin	Duke of Devonshire				Robert Coryndon	Geoffrey Archer
23	Labour	R. Macdonald	J. H. Thomas					
24								
25	Conservative	Stanley Baldwin	Leopold Amery	Samuel Wilson	Graeme Thomson	Donald Cameron	Edward Grigg	William Gowers
26								
27								
28								
29								
1930	Labour	Ramsay Macdonald	Lord Passfield					
31					Donald Cameron		Joseph Byrne	
32	National Coalition		J. H. Thomas			Stewart Symes		Bernard Bourdillon
33			Phillip Cunliffe-Lister					
34				John Maffey				
35			M. Macdonald		Bernard Bourdillon	Harold Macmichael		
36	Conservative	Stanley Baldwin	J. H. Thomas				Robert Brooke-Popham	Charles Dundas
37			W. Ormsby-Gore					
38		Neville Chamberlain		C. Parkinson				
1939			M. Macdonald	G. Gater		Mark Young		

SOURCE: Adapted from Harry A. Gailey, *Sir Donald Cameron: Colonial Governor* (Stanford, 1974), p. 135, by Robert Baldock.

family backgrounds, educational qualifications, and career records of the British governors of African colonies over the past 100 years.

To repeat, who was—or seems to to have been—the British colonial governor? For, in the final analysis, that doyenne of British authorities on African administration, Dame Margery Perham, correctly noted in her diary after her introduction to the rigid colonial service hierarchy from governor to cadet: "There is no type British Colonial servant, only a bewildering variety."[4] The social origins of governors will be discussed in a subsequent section. These officials differed widely among themselves though they shared certain features.[5] They had mostly been to public schools; many of them to a university as well. They had been brought up on certain ethical norms expressed—as often as not—in terms like "playing the game," "gentleman's agreement," "bad form," and "team spirit." They derived mainly from the professional and middle classes. They regarded themselves as all-rounders rather than specialists and, administratively, as jacks-of-all-trades. Underneath their surface uniformity they were a diverse lot.

So varied was the makeup of the colonial administrative service—that branch of the colonial service from which at least half the governors appointed between the two world wars and over three-quarters of those appointed between 1945 and 1960 were drawn—and so dominant were the two traits earnestly sought in the would-be colonial administrator, from his initial interview at the colonial office as a fledgling graduate down to consideration of his final promotion, those of "character" and "personality," that the student of the system may be forgiven if he ends by recognizing who the British colonial governor was even if he is not fully certain who the governors were as a body. It might be said that there was always a type of British colonial governor without there ever having been a typical British colonial governor. To quote the judgment of one of its numbers, "The Colonial Administrative Service was, like a packet of liquorice, all the better for being made up of all sorts."[6]

The Office of Colonial Governor

Number and Title of Governorships.   For the greater part of the period under review (about 1874–1964) there were just under forty colonial governorships, with another dozen or so posts of independent administrative command. In 1903 the number of territorial administrations for which the secretary of state for the colonies was responsible was thirty-two. India, the Sudan, and the "white dominions" (Canada, Australia, and South Africa) comprised the portfolio of other cabinet ministers. At the end of World War II the total number of territories had risen to thirty-eight. Today there are fewer than twenty dependent territories, mostly islands in the Pacific and the West Indies, with one or two others scattered in the Atlantic and Indian oceans. As one secretary of state for the colonies is alleged to have remarked when confronted by the geographical spread of his portfolio, he had no idea where the Virgin Islands were but had to assume they were well removed from the Isle of Man. The colonial office has been closed as a separate entity for over a decade.

A third of some three dozen colonial governorships existing at the height of the empire were in tropical Africa. Four were in West Africa (Nigeria, Gold Coast, Sierra Leone, Gambia); five were in East Africa (Uganda, Kenya, Tanganyika, British Somaliland, Zanzibar); and two were in Central Africa (Northern Rhodesia, Nyasaland). The three territories in Southern Africa (Bechuanaland, Basutoland, Swaziland) were rated one step below full governorships, their senior administrative officers being comparable in status to the lieutenant governorships of the groups of provinces in Nigeria or the chief commissionerships in the Gold Coast.

Although governor and commander in chief was the most usual rank in the African colonies, there were from time to time governors-general. Lugard was accorded this title personally on the amalgamation of Northern and Southern Nigeria in 1914. Here the office was not revived until 1954, when it was held briefly by Sir John Macpherson, and finally, from 1955 until independence in 1960, by Sir James Robertson. The title, which had an honorable history in the Sudan,[7] enjoyed a momentary flicker of life during the abortive Central African Federation of 1953–1963, being held by two successive politicians—Lord Llewellyn up to 1957 and then the Earl of Dalhousie. Had the British government's plans for closer union in East Africa in the 1920s materialized, the title would likely have been conferred on Sir Edward Grigg (later Lord Altrincham), governor of Kenya. Certainly this was what they thought in suspicious Nairobi when a king-sized vice-regal palace, designed by no less an architect than Sir Herbert Baker, was erected there and another large residence was constructed at Mombasa. In most of tropical Africa the title of governor-general burst into final flame at the time of independence, the last colonial governors often momentarily becoming the first independent governors-general (Paul in Sierra Leone, Coutts in Uganda, Jones in Nyasaland).

Other current titles of gubernatorial equivalence in the modern colonial service have included captain-general (Jamaica), high commissioner (Western Pacific), British resident (Zanzibar), resident commissioner (Basutoland), chief commissioner (Ashanti), commissioner (Uganda), lieutenant governor (Northern Nigeria), resident administrator (Grenada), agent (Aden), administrator (Antigua), British consul (Tonga), and vice-admiral (Sierra Leone). The British empire may have been acquired in a fit of proverbial absentmindedness and even handed back in a mood of hasty embarrassment, but the elaboration of its gubernatorial nomenclature reflects a continuing colonial presence and several centuries of painstaking thought by colonial office clerks.

Governors were entitled within their colony to the honorific "Your excellency" when addressed and "His Excellency" when mentioned. A governor-general's wife (but not a governor's) was also granted the courtesy title of "Her Excellency"; both rated a bow or curtsy. Other top administrators such as a lieutenant governor or a chief commissioner were recognized as "His Honour"; there was no consequent title for his spouse.

At first governors were appointed for a six-year term of office. This later was reduced to five years. It was possible but not usual to have one's term extended by two years. Sir Hilary Blood's extension of the governorship of Mauritius in 1952 became the subject of a petition to the secretary of state for the colonies and of a legislative council sessional paper. Not too disgruntled, the secretary of state compromised by recommending to the queen an eighteen-month extension.[8] Sir James Robertson agreed to the Nigerian ministers' request that he see them through to independence, two years beyond his original commission. Sir Gordon Guggisberg served nearly eight years as governor of the Gold Coast (1919–1927). Governors like Sir Philip Mitchell in Kenya (1944–1952) and Sir Edward Twining in Tanganyika (1949–1958) had their tenure of office extended twice, though there is room for doubt as to whether either second extension was in anyone's best interests.[9] Sir Evelyn Baring declined to have his tour of office in Kenya (1952–1959) prolonged, recalling his predecessor's latter-day lackadaisicalness and hence arguing that "the moment you feel it is a nuisance to get out and around the country, it is time to go."[10] In Nigeria, on the other hand, Lugard wanted to go on and on. This request was firmly refused by the colonial office. But the last laugh was Lugard's: he drew a governor-general's pension for a near record twenty-six years—on top of nineteen years in Government House.

Really outstanding governors, of course, might hold two or more successive governorships. If a man were successful in the testing ground of chief secretary in a major colony (Sir Hugh Foot and Sir Arthur Benson were both tried out in this key office in Lagos, as were Sir Richard Turnbull and Sir Walter Coutts in Nairobi) or of a minor governorship (Sir Edward Twining and Sir Charles Arden-Clarke initially served as governor of North Borneo and of Sarawak, respectively), the way was open for him to aspire to the plums of the service like Nigeria or Kenya, Ceylon or Malaya, Tanganyika or Hong Kong. "It is quite a good job, of a rather large frog in a small pond variety," wrote Twining to his mother when he was appointed administrator of Saint Lucia in 1944.[11] He added that the colonial office had pointedly made "four references to its being a stepping stone to higher things."

Despite the fact that Grantham took a one-third cut in salary and would have to pay his own passage as well as that of his wife from Hong Kong and at the other end have no government quarters provided for him, he accepted the post of colonial secretary of Bermuda—but only after he had researched the careers of his predecessors and found that all of them had been promoted within three years. Similarly, although it was with regret that he said goodbye to Nigeria in 1944 on his appointment to the governorship of the Western Pacific, he commented, "Nearly everyone has their ambition to get to the top of his particular tree and my tree was the Colonial Service with a Governorship at the top."[12] The brightest stars of the colonial service firmament like Sir Hugh Clifford and Sir Arthur Richards held up to five governorships in all, giving them twenty years in colonial governorships—half the average colonial administrator's total career.

Ranking and Emoluments of Governors.   Although there were some forty colonial governorships, all carrying the style of "His Excellency" and entitling the person to the common address of "Government House" and the same salute of seventeen guns, they were by no means equal in importance as defined by status and salary. As with ambassadorships, Whitehall ranked its colonial governors in four grades. In 1946 there were ten first-class governorships, representing the pinnacle of the colonial service. Nigeria, Gold Coast, Kenya, and Tanganyika in Africa joined

Ceylon, Palestine, Straits Settlements (Malaya), Hong Kong, Jamaica, and Trinidad and Tobago. There was at that time general agreement in the colonial office that Ceylon was "the premier colony,"[13] the choicest post among colonial governorships. Thus, Sir Hugh Clifford was considered to have accepted a lesser post when, after disagreement with the colonial office, he left Ceylon in 1927 to become governor of the Straits Settlements (Malaya).[14] Colonies like the Somaliland protectorate and Nyasaland were originally designated class four governorships, though Nyasaland was advanced to class three in 1932 and to class two in 1955.[15] Kenya, Sierra Leone, Northern and Southern Nigeria, and Northern Rhodesia were all second-class governorships, but Kenya moved to class one in 1932 and the three Nigerian regions achieved first-class status in 1954.

After the independence of Ceylon and the partition of Palestine in 1948, it was always a matter of friendly rivalry in the service whether Malaya, Nigeria, or Kenya was the greatest gubernatorial plum. To a large extent the three territories played cox and box in the level of salaries, as Table 2 shows.

Table 2.　Salaries Attached to British Colonial Governorships[1]

Colony	Size (square miles)	Population	Total Administrative Staff	1945[2] (£)	1950 (£)	1955 (£)	1960 (£)
Somaliland	68,000	600,000	25	(mil.)	2,900	3,000	4,800
Gambia	3,964	278,000	25	3,250	3,250	4,000	4,900
Gold Coast	91,690	4.2m	172	6,000	6,000	7,500	—
Kenya	225,000	5.9m	350	7,500[3]	8,500	8,500	10,500
Nigeria	372,674	31.1m	521	7,750	8,250	10,150[4]	10,150
Northern Rhodesia	284,745	2.1m	160	4,000	5,500	6,500	8,000
Nyasaland	45,747	2.4m	52	3,000	4,000	5,000	6,700
Sierra Leone	27,925	2.1m	60	4,000	4,000	5,000	6,250
Tanganyika	362,688	7.6m	194	6,000	6,500	6,500	8,000
Uganda	93,981	4.9m	130	5,000	5,500	5,500	7,500
Zanzibar	640	275,000	10	3,000	3,650	4,750	5,100
Ceylon	25,332	8.1m	—	8,000	—	—	—
Palestine	10,429	782,000	—	8,000	—	—	—
Malaya	50,690	4.9m	—	7,500	7,500	9,500	—
Hong Kong	391	2.5m	—	7,000	7,300	8,500	10,000[5]
Jamaica	4,411	1.5m	—	5,500	6,000	6,300	6,300
Bahamas	4,404	86,600	—	5,000	5,000	6,300[6]	8,700

SOURCE: Data from *The Colonial Office List* (London, H. M. Stationery Office, annual) and Sir Charles Jeffries, *Whitehall and the Colonial Service* (London, 1972).

[1]Inclusive of duty allowance. Statistics are as in the mid-1950s.

[2]With the exception of Tanganyika (increase of £680) and Uganda (£1,000), the salaries paid to colonial governors in Africa were exactly the same in 1945 as they had been in 1925.

[3]Plus £1,000 as high commissioner of the three East African territories.

[4]Regional governors were paid £6,600.

[5]In 1960 the salary of the governor of Cyprus was £10,000 and that of the high commissioner for the three high commission territories of South Africa £12,000.

[6]Plus £4,200 for the upkeep of Government House.

Two ways of emphasizing the superiority of the governor's salary would be to consider the salary of the next senior colonial civil servant, the chief or colonial secretary,[16] and that of comparable overseas officials in other British imperial services or in the home civil service in the United Kingdom. For instance, in the 1920s the chief secretary of Nigeria and of Kenya respectively received, allowances aside, £2,400 and £1,800 against the governor's salary of £6,500. In Nigeria the chief secretary was paid half the salary of His Excellency. If anything, the gap widened in favor of the governor over the ensuing years so that by 1950, for instance, the ratio on the Gold Coast was five to two.

Turning momentarily to the second index, we find that at least up to the mid-1950s the colonial service was relatively well paid at the top. During the 1930s the governorships of Ceylon, Malaya, and Nigeria carried salaries of some £7,000, free of tax and with rent-free accommodation and numerous domestic perquisites. Above them among the imperial services were only the viceroy of India (£19,000), the governor-generalships of Canada, Australia, and South Africa (£10,000), and the governorships of the senior Indian provinces and presidencies (averaging £8,000 apiece). In Britain in 1947 the secretary of state for the colonies was paid only £5,000, subject to all taxes, at a time when Sir Alan Burns was appointed governor of the Gold Coast at £6,000, tax-free and virtually all his expenses paid. At the same period the permanent undersecretary at the colonial office was earning only £3,500. Even the prime minister's salary was only £10,000.

The assurance of a pension was a comfort to a colonial governor. Up to the middle of the nineteenth century there had been no such provision. Lacking private means, many governors had sought to set aside all they could during their tenure of office. More often than not the results in the quality of their administration can be left to the imagination.[17] The Governors Pension Act of 1865 changed all that, though as late as 1907 the secretary of state, Lord Elgin, found it necessary to issue a dispatch to all colonial governors reminding them that he saw no reason for them to solicit company directorships on their retirement and would not look kindly on such arrangements.[18] In principle, the pension was calculated on the governor's emoluments during the last three years of office. Hence the colonial service myth that officers who had spent their careers in East or West Africa hoped for a final governorship in the Far East, where salary scales were reputedly higher.

To qualify for a governor's pension it was necessary to have at least ten years in the colonial service. Otherwise the pension drawn was based on the officer's salary and service before his appointment as governor. This rule caused keen embarrassment on more than one occasion. Sir Robert Coryndon had served with the British South African Company for ten years and as resident commissioner for another ten before being appointed governor of Uganda (1917) and then of Kenya (1922). On his death in 1925 while still governor of Kenya, Coryndon was two years away from the statutory minimum service. The Kenya legislative council generously voted his widow a pension of £500 per annum as an ex gratia award, and the Rhodes Trust equally nobly came to the rescue by providing for the education of his three children. Sir Gordon Guggisberg, too, had served only eight years. His history, however, was unusual: Guggisberg's first colonial service post was that of governor; as director of surveys in the Gold Coast he had been a military officer. Alarmed that as a retired governor his pension would be a mere £520 per annum earned from his army career, he desperately sought another governorship and in 1928 was offered what his biographer describes as "the macabre assignment" of the governorship of British Guiana.[19] He died with his colonial service still a few months short: "£700 a year—the sum at stake—dangled tantalisingly a few months away. He never got it." All Guggisberg left in his will when he died in 1930 was roughly £1,934 (less than $5,000).[20]

A British colonial governor enjoyed substantial remuneration besides his basic salary. In most crown colonies his salary was not subject to income tax. Usually no duty was payable on anything ordered for Government House. This exemption included all liquor supplies, a highly attractive perquisite in Africa, where, as one wit put it,

> The nuisance of the tropics is
> The sheer necessity of fizz.

The governor was paid his outward passage by the British government and his homeward passage on retirement by his colonial government. The rate was fixed by the colonial office—an improvement from an earlier time when a West African governor who, on asking which party would pay his fare home on the expiry of his term of office, was told that the question had never arisen. For instance, in the 1950s the governor of Nigeria was paid £980 in passage money to be used on however many (or few) fares he liked; the governor of Gambia, £660. Here it was a question of distance and not status. In the same period, the governor of the Seychelles collected £1,300 and the governor of Fiji £1,670 in passage money. Travel by air had several advantages over a sea voyage for a new governor. Not only was there no time for expensive, official entertaining on board ship but also the governor would begin drawing his full salary earlier (from his date of embarkation for his colony he was paid half salary until taking the oath of office in the colony itself).

Another prominent item was the governor's duty or entertainment allowance. Legion, libelous, and often legendary are the service stories of what His Excellency did (or did not) with his entertainment allowance. As high as this could be—in the Gold Coast and Uganda in 1925 it was as much as an extra thirty percent on the basic salary—there were few governors who did not have to dip into their own pockets to provide the scale of entertaining that was inseparable from their office. "Members of the Colonial Civil Service generally die poor," one of its most distinguished representatives once declared, "which is proof of their honesty if not of their providence."[21] The governor, in the words of one highly class-conscious and determinedly socialist critic, was "the leader of the social life" in his colony,[22] with social responsibilities toward nonofficials as well as service ones toward his officials. He was also the target for visitors of all sorts of social size, so that many a governor—and even more so, many a governor's wife—found Government House a bewildering cross between Grand Central Station, Kennedy Airport, and the Waldorf-Astoria. It was a moot point whether air transport made things better or worse for colonial governors. Prominent guests might come more frequently, but at least they could go more quickly; yet, as the harassed staff of more than one Government House knew to their cost, a grounded aircraft or canceled flight out of the colonial capital could spell ruin to the tight roster of guests accommodated at Government House and the split-second timing of the washing of the sheets.

An idea of the social obligations of the governor can be had from this entry in Sir Edward Twining's journal for June 1950, when he was governor of Tanganyika:

> We are thankful that the last fortnight is over. Everything went very well but we hardly had a moment to ourselves. We had 17 people in the house off and on, a State dinner party for 40, a frightful Garden Party for 500 at which I wore a top hat, another given by the Aga Khan's community for 1,500; the King's Birthday parade, a grand presentation of Orders, decorations and medals, a Tattoo and a fireworks display; 3 receptions, 2 meetings of Legislative Council and 1 of Executive Council besides our ordinary work. On 3rd we go to Bagamoyo. On 6th I fly to Mombasa to open the E. African Navy as Chairman of the High Commission. . . . Then on 12th July I fly to Johannesburg to see Mining Magnates and others. On 17th I go to Salisbury for 2 nights and then to Zomba for 3. . . . On 1st August some of us set out on safari to Mahenge . . . the opening of the new railway to the Mpanda mine; to Kigoma for the consecration of an R. C. Cathedral. Then back here for a visit of 16 from the Imperial Defence College; then the week's visit of the flagship H.M.S. *Mauritius*. On 5th Sept. to Tanga, on the 9th to Lushoto for the consecration of the new Anglican Church, then to Arusha, Masailand and the Serengeti Plains. . . . Then we go down to Mbeya and drive thence to Nairobi for a meeting of the E. African High Commission.[23]

This extract would seem to confirm the observation of another governor made fifty years earlier that "it will be garnered from my narrative that if they do their duty, the luxurious life they are supposed to lead is at least not an idle or easy one."[24]

On tour, too, the governor would make a point of bringing with him food and drink from Government House, both for official entertaining and so as not to inconvenience his officials up-country. Laura Boyle, wife of a district commissioner on the Gold Coast, noted in her diary as she sat outside a bush rest house somewhere in Ashanti:

> I was suddenly informed that David [her husband] would be returning with H[is] E[xcellency] and his party for luncheon—eight in all—and that I was to prepare the table, seats, and trimmings while Slater's [the acting governor] own servants were bringing food and drinks and everything else that would be required. Slater always conformed with the accepted rule of the Service that senior officers when on tour always entertained their subordinates and not the other way round.[25]

Inevitably and acceptably, much of the governor's official entertaining was a one-way business. For reasons of protocol the governor rarely dined out with any official in the capital other than the chief justice and the colonial secretary. The governor must, to follow the dictum of one of their number, be discriminating but not exclusive in the social entertaining that he offered and accepted. Many governors made it a rule not to accept private invitations of hospitality. "We seldom lunched or dined out at private houses," noted Grantham.[26] But in a capital like Hong Kong—cosmopolitan, more foreign office than colonial service—the governor allowed himself to dine with service chiefs, consuls, and members of council.

Another made it a rule not to attend cocktail parties other than those given by public bodies and the services. Even for this there was a rigid routine. After about fifteen minutes the aide-de-camp would discreetly sidle up to the governor to remind him, in the hearing of his host, that he had another appointment to keep. Their Excellencies might then take their leave and the party would assume a more relaxed tone.

Sir Geoffrey Archer, governor of Uganda (1922–1925), noted in his diary how pleased and surprised he was to have his Government House hospitality repaid by one of his unofficial visitors, Sir Thomas Pilkington, Baronet, who asked Archer to stay with him in Yorkshire to shoot over his grouse moors.[27]

Government House and Its Staff. In addition to the emoluments—adequate rather than generous—earned by a British colonial governor, an official residence was provided, very comfortably furnished and rent-free, along with an extensive household of private staff and servants. Generally this imposing residence was known as Government House, but in Jamaica and Malaya it was King's House and in Saint Helena, Plantation House. In Accra the governor lived in Christiansborg Castle. "To a colonial governor," noted a peppery judge at the turn of the century, "two things are of supreme importance. One is Government House and the other the Government yacht."[28] Often there was a government lodge up-country as well, to allow the governor to get away from it all in the often humid capital and unwind in a cooler and quieter atmosphere. The governor's lodge in such hill stations as Jos in Nigeria or Lushoto in Tanganyika—a favorite retreat of Sir Edward Twining—or Le Réduit in Mauritius, romantically described as a cross between a shooting lodge and a private house built in the Dutch colonial style, were havens of peace.

The result was without doubt impressive. Government House at Zungeru, capital in 1906 of the protectorate of Northern Nigeria, could scarcely have passed muster as a third-rate hotel in London or Los Angeles but to Constance Larymore, wife of a district officer coming in from a remote outstation, here was a "veritable oasis in the desert, luxuriously furnished with costly English furniture, soft carpets, bright chintzes and silk curtains, and fitted with electric light."[29] Lugard, later arguing for moving his headquarters from Zungeru to Kaduna, condemned the same building as intolerable,[30] a level of abuse reminiscent of Sir Richard Burton's abrasive description of the equivalent building in Lagos as "a corrugated iron coffin or plank lined morgue, containing a dead consul once a year."[31] Margery Perham entertained no qualms about the attractions of Government House to a dust-stained traveler as she "slipped happily into Government House luxury—a suite of rooms, a glorious bath, two white and scarlet clad Africans, and an English maid."[32] A perennial problem at Government House was not so much those who were invited to stay but those who thought they ought to have been.

Comfort in Africa was perhaps a relative term. The secretary of state for the colonies could, even in the age of air conditioning and first-class jet travel, admit to being impressed by the standards of Government House. Arriving at that residence in Hong Kong, then under the chatelaineship of Lady Grantham (a citizen of San Francisco), Oliver Lyttelton relished the fact that "everything was perfectly mounted—the scarlet liveries of the Chinese servants, curtains, carpets, furni-

220

ture, flowers and food all showed what discernment and discrimination can do."[33] Flying on to Nairobi, he found "life at Government House congenial under the calm and humorous rule of Molly Baring. She had made the gaunt impersonal uniform house liveable and had done up some of the rooms to her own standards of taste and comfort."[34]

Table 3. Example of Government House Expenditures for a Major African Colony, *c.* 1959[1]

Staff (£30,000)[2]	Governor
	Private secretary (seconded from administrative service)
	Aide-de-camp (seconded from army)
	Personal secretary
	Confidential clerk
	Housekeeper
	Government House supervisor
	Typists (two)
	Chauffeur
	Orderly
	Messengers (four)
	Head chef
	Head steward
	Head gardener
	Head houseboy
	Senior cooks/stewards (three)
	Cooks (four)
	Washermen (four)
	Caretakers (two)
Other charges (£12,000)	Local transport and traveling
	Office and general
	Upkeep of Government House
	Upkeep of Government House grounds
	Upkeep of Government House public rooms
	Utility charges

[1]Only expenses chargeable to public funds are recorded herein.
[2]This Government House establishment excludes the staff of the governor's office, totaling thirty-three persons, at a cost of £70,000. Of this sum, over half was allocated to air transport for the governor and his staff on tour in the colony.

Most of the Government House servants were permanent, seeing a succession of governors come and go. Counting the housekeeper, majordomo, stewards, chefs, chauffeurs, houseboys, gardeners, and laundry workers, Government House staffs could easily number thirty to forty. Alexander Grantham made history and nearly created a strike as acting governor of Nigeria when he sacked two Government House servants who had been there since time immemorial. But Grantham may not have had the knack of dealing with such extraordinary snobs as Government House staff. While he was acting as governor of Jamaica, the butler and footman—both soldier-servants—suddenly gave him notice just minutes before the guests arrived for a large, official luncheon party. Later, taking up his appointment as governor of Hong Kong, he noted that constant supervision was necessary over the staff of Government House and that all three cooks had to be "kept up to the mark. . . . In the same way," he went on, "the table boys, if not watched, might appear in grubby uniforms, or during lunch or dinner stand round day-dreaming, failing to notice that the water or wine glasses needed replenishing."[35] He adds that his wife had periodic post-mortems with the No. 1 Boy, telling him what had been done correctly or incorrectly: "It needed eternal vigilance to maintain a high standard," he concluded.

Many governors, however, found that one of the chief attractions of the job was the way Government House functioned as a smooth, magnificent machine for entertainment. Old Africa hands like Sir Philip Mitchell and Sir Edward Twining gave jobs in Government House to retainers who had served them many years earlier in World War I. Mitchell appointed his color sergeant Alfani as hall porter in Government House, Entebbe, twenty years later. In the 1950s Twining brought with him to Government House at Dar es Salaam the Comorian manservant Ali, who had been his personal servant when he was a subaltern in the King's African Rifles in the 1920's. Grantham, returning to his first colony as governor, found jobs for a houseboy, cook, and chair bearer but could only make his rather useless, onetime Cantonese teacher his personal pensioner to the end of his days.

There was another category of personal staff, namely, the governor's private secretary and his aide-de-camp. Some colonial governors appointed their private secretaries from among friends and relatives outside the service. Archer started his African life as a sort of supernumerary private secretary to his uncle, Sir Frederick Jackson, then acting commissioner for Uganda. Sir Frederick Lugard's brother Edward and Sir Harry Johnston's brother Alex were both private secretaries to their siblings for many years. Rupert Gunnis, savant and collector of fine art, was employed personally as private secretary by both Archer in Uganda and Storrs in Cyprus. By the 1930s, however, it had become more usual for the governor to select from his administrative service a young district officer of from five to seven years' seniority and appoint him private secretary for a couple of years.

Generally, such men had already made a certain name for themselves as likely high-flyers, and with experience as private secretary behind them, many went on to be governors themselves. Sir Alan Burns, who held several governorships, counted himself as exceedingly fortunate in having acted as private secretary successively to Lugard, Clifford, and Cameron in Lagos. Sir Stewart Symes, governor of Tanganyika (1931–1934), had been picked out as both aide-de-camp (1906) and private secretary (1913–1916) to the governor-general of the Sudan. Hugh Patterson, whose father had been chief commissioner of the northern provinces of Nigeria, quickly was named private secretary to one of his father's successors. So, too, was Imbert Bourdillon, the young assistant district officer, son of a former governor of Nigeria. Both brought additional skills to the office. A.C. Hollis was private secretary to Sir Charles Eliot but could not stand his successor, Sir Donald Stewart, and soon moved out of Government House.[36] Often the reward for having served as private secretary to the governor was to be allowed to choose the division over which one became district officer. In Nigeria there was a regular flow of former private secretaries to remote areas like Mubi and Tangale Waja, "back of beyond" outstations long favored by the stereotype squirearchy of British district officers.

Life as private secretary was no featherbed. Like the governor, one was scarcely ever off duty. In the middle of a dinner party for the queen, one private secretary had to perform a complicated ballet step among the Spode and silver on the dining room table in order to release the ceiling fan that had become jammed and so allow Her Majesty to breathe more freely in the airless atmosphere of Lagos. Then there is the story, not necessarily apocryphal, of another distinguished dinner party at Government House from which the governor was called away by his private secretary in the middle of the entrée and claret because a top-secret cable had just come in from Whitehall. The secretary had properly decoded no more than "To be read only by Governor." A few minutes later the governor returned, interrupted his secretary as he was making up for lost time on the soup and sherry, and sent him off to decipher the rest of the cable. It continued: "or by Priv. Sec." As another governor was to say, speaking from experience as both private secretary and aide-de-camp, such a post called for "protean, maid of all work duties."[37]

The social side of Government House life fell largely on the governor's aide-de-camp. Sometimes he was a junior administrative officer, again picked out by the governor for his savoir faire. In later years he was a military or police officer who would be of help to the governor at the latter's frequent ceremonial appearances. Guggisberg, depicted by his biographer as every inch a governor, superb and regal, "almost too good to be true," modestly appointed as his private secretary a brigadier general and as aide-de-camp a rear admiral.[38] In the period of decolonization such a posting often came the way of the first African police or army officers, an example splendidly set by Sir James Robertson's and Sir Richard Turnbull's choices of aides-de-camp in Nigeria and Tanganyika. For an occasion such as a royal visit to the colony, the governor might appoint as equerry an additional aide-de-camp from among his younger district officers. Now and again the novelist's dream came true and the aide married the governor's daughter.

It was a sensitive job, one in which—in the opinion of such an infallible picker of winners as Sir Ralph Furse, ruling deity of the colonial officer selection board—wisdom and tact could do much for a governor's reputation. The beau ideal aide-de-camp would need to be able to turn his hand to all things at all times of the day —and night. In Kenya the governor's aide was to be seen unloading coal from a ship in Mombasa harbor during a dock strike. At Dar es Salaam one aide found himself giving a discreet helping hand to the new governor, whose knee "inclined to creak like an old motor lorry,"[39] as the latter limped down the gangplank with his sword dangling dangerously between his legs. In the same capital another aide received a massive dressing down from the postmaster general when by mischance an unexpected guest at Government House took the latter's nobly lent dinner jacket off to South Africa on the next mailboat.[40] In Lagos Sir Hugh Clifford called in one of his few fellow Catholics to act as aide-de-camp for church on Sunday. After the first unfortunate service, when the priest failed to recognize the king's representative and escort him to his reserved pew, this weekly expedition involved the additional chore of wearing full-dress uniform. Commenting on the role of the aide-de-camp at Government House in Northern Rhodesia, one guest, caught in the crossfire between Lady Maxwell and His Excellency ("who was—had to be— all that she was not"),[41] came to the conclusion that there was nothing left for him to do but to imitate total nonexistence. With long practice, she observed, the aide could even fall asleep with necessary inconspicuousness during those after-dinner chats between the governor and his guests.

An itinerant secretary of state for the colonies has left this vignette of the archetype aide, drawn from the graceful figure who met him on behalf of the governor at a certain colonial airport: "benignant and immaculate, his newly pressed tussore silk suit crowned by an orchid, his curling moustaches trimmed to perfection, his brown and white shoes a masterpiece."[42]

As for a bad aide-de-camp, he was best returned to his normal duties as expeditiously as possible and quickly forgotten by all concerned in the traumatic appointment. Now and again one came across a woeful police officer or administrative cadet plodding through the swamps of some malarial "punishment station," with the luster of Government House balls and banquets now but a memory of the past and unbelievable glory in his fevered, fitful conversation.

History of the Office of Governor. The office of British colonial governor reaches back for several centuries; the first such official was appointed to Bermuda in 1612. Our own story, however, centers on the modern years between the scramble and decolonization. Emphasis is on developments during the present century, an era of momentous changes.

At first, colonial office governance solidified. For instance, in 1900 Nigeria became a crown colony; three years later Uganda was transferred from the foreign office to the colonial office, to be shortly followed by the East Africa protectorate. Little more than half a century later decolonization began to get under way. In 1957 Ghana became independent, and during the late 1960s the last of Britain's African territories—Gambia and the three former high commission territories of Bechuanaland, Basutoland, and Swaziland—became independent and history bade farewell to the British colonial governor in Africa.

The nomenclature of the British colonies varied. In 1923 Southern Rhodesia was granted internal autonomy and assumed the hybrid title of "self-governing colony." British Somaliland between 1941 and 1948 was under military administration. The remaining African possessions were technically known as crown colonies and/or protectorates. Most of those in the Caribbean were officially described as possessing first "representative institutions" and finally "responsible government"—defined in Africa as "full internal self-government." The difference might be said to be one of history expressed in the constitution. In essence, under the traditional "responsible government" arrangement on the West Indian model, the crown reserved only the power of disallowing legislation; the secretary of state had no control over the filling of any public office other than the governorship; and in all matters affecting the internal affairs of the colony, the governor was obliged to act on the advice of his ministers, who were responsible to the legislature.

The governor of a crown colony could not be said to come under the direct jurisdiction of the British Parliament. Parliamentary questions might arise over the administration of a colony, but these were directed at—and answered by—the secretary of state. It was he, the elected minister, who defended a governor's actions, who praised his handling of affairs. Unlike the French colonial administrators, the British needed only the agreement of the colonial office for the colony's estimates and never the approval of Parliament. The House of Commons likewise had no control over the appointment or dismissal of any African colonial governor. His authority derived directly from the crown, and it was to the crown, not Parliament, that he was responsible. On this point the regulations issued by the colonial office were brief, unambiguous, and sustaining in moments of perplexity: "The Governor is the single and supreme authority responsible to, and representative of, Her Majesty."[43]

The triple classification used by the colonial office itself is perhaps the most succint definition of distinctions that do not always seem to the outsider to be differences in the terminology of colonial government:

> First, *crown colonies*, in which the crown has the entire control of legislation, while the administration is carried on by public officers under the control of the home government. Second, *colonies possessing representative institutions but not responsible government*, in which the crown has no more than a veto on legislation, but the home government retains the control of public officers. Third, *colonies possessing representative institutions and responsible government*, in which the crown has only a veto on legislation, and the home government has no control over any public officers except the governor.[44]

In crown colonies or non-self-governing ones, the administration consisted of the direct personal rule of the governor: all power and all responsibility were centered on the governor and he personally dominated the whole administration. To quote the opinion of one of the shrewdest colonial office mandarins, the governor "combined the functions of King, Prime Minister, Speaker and Head of the Civil Service."[45] As the sovereign's representative he earned and expected nothing less than the recognition customarily paid to royalty.

All the African territories were either crown colonies or protectorates—or both, such as the "Colony and Protectorate" of Kenya or of Nigeria, to give them their full titles. The difference was a historical one dependent on the mode of acquisition and did not really affect the governor's administration of the territory.[46] A plausible exception to this taxonomy may be made for Tanganyika, which as a "B" mandate was technically known as "Tanganyika Territory." Whereas the mandated territories of the Cameroons and of Togo were administered as an integral part of Nigeria and the Gold Coast, respectively, Tanganyika was large enough to warrant a separate administration. In the 1920s Sir Donald Cameron was able to invoke its special status under the League of Nations mandate to disrupt plans of the British government to draw Tanganyika into some sort of merger with settler dominated Kenya. Pleading the concept of "sacred trust" and the principle of paramountcy of African interest, he resisted all approaches for an East African federation.

The Governor's Functions. The duties of a British colonial governor were laid down at a general level as a group of rules and regulations and, informally, through his day-to-day relationships with the colonial office. The appointment of a governor was made by the sovereign on the recommendation of the secretary of state for the colonies. The appointee was always asked whether he would be willing to accept the governorship under consideration.[47] The prime minister was consulted—closely in the case of the more sensitive governorships; otherwise, according to the testimony of some secretaries of state, the convention was usually a formality. On leaving Britain to take up his appointment, the governor was received at Buckingham Palace to "kiss hands"—"which is something of a disappointment," commented one governor, "because you don't." Another noted in his diary, "You no longer literally kiss the King's hand; in fact His Majesty, the general presentation made, was delightfully informal."[48] Unusually, Sir Alan Burns on the same day kissed hands along with no fewer than two other new governors, both former colleagues of his from the Nigerian secretariat. Governors-general of the quasi-dominion type that characterized the ultimate crown appointment to most African territories at independence enjoyed the additional privilege of a private luncheon with the queen.

The tangible tokens of a British colonial governor's appointment comprised three documents, the style of which dates back to the appointment of royal and proprietary British governors for the plantations and colonies of the West Indies and America. Two of these were royal documents—a commission in the form of letters patent, passed under the great seal, and royal instructions in the form of letters close, passed under the royal sign manual and signet. The former traditionally opened with the royal command of "We do hereby empower and command the said Governor XYZ to do all things that belong to his said office in accordance with these Our Letters Patent."[49] The latter would include such matters as the constitution of the governor's executive council and rules for the making of legislation. Typically, royal instructions laid down that the governor

> is to the utmost of his power to promote religion and education among the native inhabitants. He is especially to take care and protect them in their persons and in the free enjoyment of their possessions, and by all lawful means to prevent and restrain all violence and injustice which may in any manner be practised or attempted against them.[50]

Together, these letters of appointment have been described as a "sort of organic law of the colony."[51] The governor's constitutional responsibilities were specified in a third document, an order in council, by which the legislature—or where there was no legislature the ordinance making authority—was constituted.

Finally, there are the *Colonial Regulations*, first published in 1837 as "Rules and Regulations for the Information and Guidance of the Principal Officers in His Majesty's Colonial Possessions." Major revisions were undertaken in 1908 and again in the 1950's; by this time the list had increased to over 400 regulations. Today they are issued in two parts—"Public Officers" and "Public Business"—the latter applying principally to the conduct of the governor. Technically, *Colonial Regulations* may be looked at as the directions given by the secretary of state on behalf of the crown for the guidance of governors. As such, their legal force might be held to be doubtful, but instances of their having been questioned by a colonial governor are understandably rare. From time to time it was necessary for the colonial office to issue special instructions to a new governor, as when Sir Gerald Templer was assigned to Malaya, Sir Hugh Foot to Cyprus, and Sir Charles Johnston to Aden—all at moments of international crisis, potential or realized.

Sir Charles Bruce, drawing on the experience of his several colonial governorships including seven years as governor of Mauritius (1897–1904), advocated briefer counsel. He believed that there could be no better rule of conduct for the colonial governor than to abide by the Jesuit dictum "It is surprising how much good a man may do in the world if he allows others to take credit for it."[52]

On arrival in his colony, the first thing the new governor had to do was to take the oath of office. Without this formality his tenure was not legitimate nor were his acts legal. Among the obligations undertaken by the governor was the promise that he would "do right by all manner of men according to the laws and usages of the Colony, without fear or favour, affection or ill-will."[53] The oath was administered at a small ceremony by the chief justice, with senior officials present in full colonial service uniform. On one occasion, in a small territory, it is reputed that the ceremony, which began with the reading aloud of the royal commission, was punctuated with a quick gin between each oath. Of another, the governor's own account is distinctly acid: "The swearing-in ceremony was rendered amusing by the Judge who administered the three oaths insisting on reading them aloud for me to repeat, although I had meekly attempted to express my objections to that procedure [on the ground that] I could read quite fluently."[54]

One or two points in the governor's functions and power require elaboration. In most African colonies the governor was described as having "reserve powers." This meant that he retained the power of veto over legislation, a stalling device to which he could—but rarely did—have recourse so as to guarantee law and order or to insure the continuation of good government in compelling circumstances. Technically, this power permitted the crown to disallow ordinances or to legislate by order in council in cases of emergency. Governors also held emergency powers. Sir Bryan Sharwood Smith invoked these at the time of the Kano riots in 1953, giving wide prerogatives to his provincial administrators. Sir Philip Mitchell regretted that the British government would not grant him the same powers as the home secretary had in Britain during wartime to detain dangerous people. The secretary of state would go only so far as to allow that an inquiry before a judge or magistrate might be held in camera.

Then there was the matter of the governor's authority over the movement of troops within his colony. Despite the fact that in nearly every case the governor was also Commander in Chief, he could not direct the imperial forces stationed in his territory. This was so even when, as quite frequently happened, the governor held—in his own right as a previous career officer—a military or naval rank superior to that of the officer commanding the colony's troops (e.g., in Kenya, among successive governors were Major general E. Northey [1919], Lieutenant colonel E. W. M. Grigg [1925], Brigadier general J. A. Byrne [1931], and Air chief marshal R. Brooke-Popham [1937]). Nevertheless, as the sovereign's representative the governor alone could "give the word," and he was entitled to ask for information on the strength, condition, and disposition of the troops and the military defenses at all times. Military units such as the Royal West African Frontier Force, the King's African Rifles, and the Somaliland Camel Corps were colonial and not imperial forces. Here the position of the governor was different. Raised in the territory and controlled by individual colonial governors, albeit under the general supervision of their inspector general at the colonial office, they came under the direct control of the governor acting the consultation with the local force commandant.

Finally, there was the prerogative of mercy. This has been described by one legal authority on the colonial service as "the Governor's highest endowment."[55] It was held directly from the sovereign. Consequently, it could in no way be interfered with by the secretary of state or the colonial office. Of all the functions a governor was expected to fulfill perhaps few could be so solemn and grievous a charge as this. The papers, contained in a specially colored file jacket to remove all chance of loss or oversight, would be reviewed by the governor in executive council. But the royal instructions authorized the governor, notwithstanding any advice from his executive council, to use his own judgment in deciding capital cases. The decision to exercise or refuse the prerogative of mercy was the governor's alone. One of the most publicized of these cases was the so-called *juju* murder trial in the Gold Coast in 1945–1947, which went right up to Parliament in Westminster and the privy council.[56]

Pomp and Circumstance. For one who had to combine the position of sovereign, prime minister, and head of the civil service, as well as the office of leader of the social life of the colony, the outward recognition symbols of the governor had to be supreme. Nowhere was this more important, men like Sir Stewart Symes believed, than in the context of native races and their rulers. Arguing that full ceremonial may help to invest the hard skeleton of government with a flesh and blood personality, Symes maintained that "Eastern people who habitually associate decorum with superior authority wish to be assured that their King's local representative can dress up and look the part."[57] He saw it as the price a governor must pay on ceremonial occasions for the privilege of being able at other times to waive formality, meet all and sundry, and move around freely. Even if His Excellency was not quite the king—and one recalls the observation of the Kamba chief who, having been told by his district commissioner that the visitor was the Duke of Connaught, said to the latter, "I hear you're a very important person, I suppose you must be the [district commissioner's] brother"[58]—he certainly could have fooled most observers.

Colonial Regulations laid down the punctilio of salutes for colonial administrators: seventeen for governors and fifteen for lieutenant governors or chief commissioners (twenty-one for the viceroy of India). The general orders of each colony supplemented these regulations with tables of precedence. The governor could be second only to the sovereign should she decide to visit her colony, as Queen Elizabeth II did so unsparingly and so inspiringly. As a guest of the governor of Northern Rhodesia, Margery Perham was careful to curtsy to him each morning at breakfast beside the bacon-and-egg-laden sideboard. Sir James Robertson was embarrassed by the way that the prime minister, Harold Macmillan—"a stickler for correct protocol"[59]—when staying at Government House punctiliously gave him each morning the bow reserved for royalty. It took an outside governor like ex-foreign service officer Sir Charles Johnston or an unusual insider like Sir Richard Turnbull to break the Government House staff of the hallowed tradition of serving the governor at table before everybody else.

Like royalty, the governor always had to sit behind the chauffeur so that nobody might be seen to be honored by sitting at the former's right hand. This was a lesson that many a fledgling aide-de-camp had to learn quickly as he summoned the Government House Rolls Royce to the porte cochere. One senior colonial office official was amazed at the governor's flexibility when the latter insisted that as his guest he should sit in the right-hand seat of the Government House car as they set out on tour. Later the official found that the left-hand side of the car on that particularly hot journey was the one in the shade.

Dining out, it was the governor and not his wife who was de rigueur placed next to the host and he, rather than she, who entered the dining room first. Conventionally, the loyal toast was not drunk at Government House dinner parties unless there were more than eleven persons at the table. Table 4 shows the approved seating plans for even small dinner parties and indicates the level of Government House protocol, which was strict. Governors coming from outside the service found colonial life starched and stratified. Former diplomats have expressed surprise at the markedly different style of relationship between governor and ambassador with those around him.[60] The wife of a colonial official always took her husband's seniority, and few wives were unaware of the pecking order in the local staff list. "The question of precedence is treated with immense seriousness in colonial circles," recorded Sir Hesketh Bell. "The unfortunate aide-de-camp who at a dinner party places an official—especially an official's wife—in a seat which they do not consider to be the proper one comes in for a bad time."[61]

On leave and on other ceremonial occasions, there was a guard of honor to greet the governor on his departure and his return. In parts of tropical Africa senior officials and, when they came into being, local cabinet ministers and parliamentary secretaries were required to turn up at the railway station or airport to bid farewell and welcome whenever a major tour or journey was involved. Outside Government House a regimental guard of one noncommissioned officer and five men presented arms every time the governor drove through the gates. The Union Jack flew above the building whenever the governor was in residence. At sunset the flag was often lowered with full ceremony. The national anthem was played anytime the governor appeared at a public ceremony.

With the disappearance of calling cards after World War II, signing the visitor's book by the sentry box at the gates to Government House was essential protocol for anyone, especially a colonial official, arriving in the capital. He signed it again when going on leave, adding "ppc." The book was removed at dusk and perused by the aide-de-camp for it was on the basis of this record that invitations to Government House functions were issued. When the governor went on tour he took his visitor's book with him and it would be solemnly put out in *boma* and bush for all officials to sign.

The British colonial officer's uniform was also a matter of gravity. Sir Geoffrey Archer, governor of Uganda, enjoying the relaxation of traveling up-country by car in a comfortable alpaca jacket and a trilby, found on his arrival in a district receiving its very first gubernatorial visit that the local populace was saluting the Government House chauffeur, being the only person in a distinctive uniform. But the colonial governor in full dress was a gorgeous sight. He was entitled to wear either a white uniform with white and red plumes in his colonial helmet or, in cooler climates, a dark blue uniform with a cocked hat and white plumes. Gold and silver gorgets, epaulettes, buttons, and frogging and an elaborately decorated sword completed the uniform. Outside the tropics and occasionally in Africa, the governor wore a grey top hat and formal morning dress.

The cost of this outfit was enormous. On his first appointment as governor Sir Edward Twining determined to buy a secondhand full-dress uniform. It cost him $350 in 1946; a decade later, according to his successor in Tanganyika, the figure had passed the $1,000 mark. Twining's biographer described the governor's full-dress uniform as having the capacity to make the most ordinary of men look like Admiral Nelson or Charles Laughton. Outsize in every way, Twining was so frustrated later on by the colonial office's refusal to buy him a larger aircraft that could reach the less accessible districts of Tanganyika that he ordered his press attaché to photograph him leaving the plane in full-dress uniform before the assembled chiefs, stern first. Thereafter Twining was able to fly in comfort whenever he wished. Governors in the postcolonial age relate how difficult it was to purchase a full-dress uniform even from theatrical costumers. One, living near the Thames swans at Windsor, confided in the writer that he was almost driven to secretly plucking his own brand of feathers for his governor's plumes.

Table 4. Seating Arrangements for Dinner Parties at Government House

A:	M4	L1	HE	L2	M3	
ADC						PS
	L3	M2	LHE	M1	L4	
B:	M4	L1	HE	L3	M2	
ADC						PS
	M3	L4	M1	L2	M5	

Legend: A = table arrangement when the governor's wife is present
             B = table arrangement when the governor is not married
            HE = the governor
           LHE = the governor's wife
            M1 = first (in seniority) gentleman guest, and so on from M2 to M5 +
            L1 = first (in seniority) lady guest, wives taking their husbands' seniority
            PS = private secretary to the governor
           ADC = aide-de-camp to the governor

SOURCE: Based on "Notes on Procedure, etc., for Colonial Governors," unpublished document issued personally to new governors by the colonial office (c. 1948) (by courtesy of Sir Richard Turnbull and Sir Kenneth Blackburne).

Administration of the Colony

So much for the formal side of the office of the British colonial governor. We may now turn to his functions in his daily life as governor and commander in chief. The day-to-day structure and nature of the governorship were conditioned by a network of relationships and responsibilities that though partly formalized were in the final analysis qualified by the governor's personal characteristics: his traits and quirks and moods, his interests, his strengths and limitations. His functions may be examined at a number of levels: his relationship with the colonial office, with the colony's legislature, with the colonial administration, with all sorts of resident nonofficials, and with Africans. If his relations with "the natives" seem to have a conspicuously low priority in this list, on occasion this could be at once a reflection of and on the situation. In J. M. Lee's view, "the kind of men who were recruited from Britain for service in the colonies appeared to believe that the official classes constituted the state."[62] Finally, we may consider the governor's occasional relations with other colonial governors.

Relations with the Colonial Office.   The relationship between colonial governors and the colonial office was complex. The autobiographies of governors and the memoirs written by secretaries of state and by diverse permanent officials at the colonial office indicate that in every case the balance of power depended upon the determination and character of both the secretary of state and the colonial governor. Lugard, in his biased fashion, endorsed Sir Henry Taylor's remark that "the whole history of the office is a history of conflicts with the ablest and even the most trusted governors."[63] But Taylor simplified the issue. Given the relative permanence of the colonial office staff and given the power of precedent, the governor was likely to come off second-best in any of those rare conflicts between Government House and Whitehall—unless, of course, a governor happened to be dealing with an absolute weakling in the position of secretary of state or permanent undersecretary in the colonial office. To adopt the analogy of one of the closest observers of the colonial office, the apron strings were there all right; the real question was how tightly they were pulled.[64]

Of course, the shepherds of Great Smith Street, whither the colonial office moved from its Downing Street home (to the confusion of Oliver Lyttelton, who, remembering his father's office in 1904, arrived at Downing Street the day after his own appointment as secretary of state for the colonies in 1951 only to find himself about to enter the commonwealth relations office), had their ewe lambs as well as their bêtes noires in their flock of governors. The colonial office view was that Lord Lugard was a difficult man; that Sir Edward Twining and Sir Philip Mitchell could do nothing wrong—at first. With Andrew Cohen as Arthur Creech Jones's right-hand man—though only third in the colonial office hierarchy—in 1947 governors like Sir Arthur Richards, Sir Alan Burns, and Sir Philip Mitchell probably were seen as the reactionary old guard when set beside up-and-coming radicals like Sir John Macpherson, Sir Charles Arder-Clarke, Sir Hugh Foot, and Sir Maurice Dorman.[65]

At the colonial office conference of 1927, the secretary of state could hardly mention Sir Hugh Clifford's name without referring to his "trenchant memoranda" and his "formidable indictments."[66] In Nairobi, Michael Blundell had no doubt that the British government, having at last selected Sir Evelyn Baring for the Kenyan powder keg, would back him up through thick and thin. Alan Lennox-Boyd as secretary of state felt this commitment strongly enough to offer to resign over the Hola affair when eleven Mau Mau detainees died from ill treatment in a detention camp. Yet Prime minister Harold Macmillan was ready to sacrifice Sir Robert Armitage after Nyasaland fell apart in 1959.[67] And private minutes by colonial office staff were often less complimentary on the governors than were the public comments of their political master. The head of the East Africa division set forth his opinions on why the East African governors should not be consulted on the implications of Lord Hailey's *An African Survey* in scathing terms:

> I deprecate any attempt to elicit opinion from the African Governors, either individually or collectively on the far-reaching suggestions put forward in Lord Hailey's chapter 9. Some Governors, who have the necessary time, inclination and experience, have no doubt studied Lord Hailey's remarks with sedulous attention and are already pondering his suggestions without waiting to be prompted from [the colonial office]. Others, lacking the necessary leisure or intelligence, or both, will perhaps have skipped the Chapter. But the chances are remote that their several views . . . will possess any highest common factor of significance or value.[68]

At the colonial office, Sir Ralph Furse was of the opinion that H. M. Foot, P. M. Renison, and A. T. Benson were the best governors that emerged from his brilliant recruitment policy of the 1930s,[69] though Benson failed to gain admission into the colonial administrative service the first time round, Renison—never at ease with politicians[70]—came to a sticky end, and Foot was never given a governorship in Africa. Sir Andrew Cohen would likely have followed Sir Samuel Wilson (1925–1933) and Sir John Macpherson (1956–1959) as one of the two colonial governors to become permanent secretary in the colonial office (Sir John Maffey was ex-Indian civil service (ICS) and Sudan, not colonial service) had the Conservative party not kept Labour out of office in 1956. Despite the denouement to his performance as governor of Uganda (a post he may have specially asked the secretary of state for),[71] culminating in the deportation of the *Kabaka* (King of Buganda) in a curious cloak-and-dagger operation—a crisis that would have spelt nasty nightmares and an early pension for most colonial governors—his reputation was high enough in the colonial office and his competence sufficiently demonstrated for him to return to Britain to become permanent secretary of the new department of technical aid. Ironically, as the renamed ministry of overseas development, this department was to inherit many of the responsibilities of the colonial office after the latter's decease. Sadly, Cohen, too, was dead by then.

Correspondence with the colonial office was carried out under several categories. Official dispatches, letters, telegrams, and savingrams [sic] could be marked unclassified, restricted, confidential, or secret. There was also the "secret and personal" series frequently used between Government House and the colonial office. This category of correspondence, whether by mail or telegram, was always filed separately and became a common feature of communication in the delicate days of the constitutional proposals that preceded the transfer of power. Within a territorial service its parallel was the "d.o." (demi-official) letter.

Dispatches from the governor were generally expected to be full, reasoned, and expository, supported by a wealth of confirmatory reports and documents.[72] Replies from the secretary of state were aimed at brevity and conciseness, "framed in a style which long experience has perfected, distinguished alike by reserve and lucidity, at once considerate and conclusive."[73] The Creech Jones papers show that he went further than most other secretaries of state and invited certain governors he believed sympathetic to his ideology to maintain a private and personal correspondence with him.[74] Other than the "secret and personal" letter to a colleague in the colonial office, every item of correspondence had to be addressed to the secretary of state even though he might never see it if it touched on some minor matter. Similarly, every dispatch leaving the colonial office had to issue over the secretary of state's signature. Since it was a physical impossibility for him to read everything issued in his name or sign each dispatch up to fifty times (in 1953 the colonial office sent out nearly 90,000 communications to its colonial governors), the rubber stamp was introduced in the 1920s. On the very first day of the 1927 colonial office conference this innovation led to a remarkable amount of recrimination by a number of the older governors.

Links between Whitehall or Westminster and the colonial governors became much firmer once air travel had established itself and, whatever governors might think of the impact, stronger still in the decade of decolonization, when a secretary of state could at any moment fly out to Lagos or Lusaka or the governor be flown home for a crucial conference. No longer could Winston Churchill say, as he had promised at a colonial service dinner gathering forty years before, that "it would not be possible to govern the British Empire from Downing Street, and we do not try."[75] The royal visits to Kenya in 1952 and to Nigeria in 1956 enjoyed a certain precedent in the Prince of Wales's African tour of 1925 and the King Emperor's Durbar visit to India in 1911. But Harold Macmillan's whirlwind of change tour of Africa in 1960 was quite without precedent. Colonial secretaries, too, like Oliver Lyttelton, Iain Macleod, and the inspiring Alan Lennox-Boyd had improved even on the travel record of their predecessors James Griffiths and Arthur Creech Jones, and very welcome they mostly were at Government House. Colonial office officials in the 1950s likewise were seasoned travelers. This was a far cry from the time when Sir Augustus Hemming, head of the West Africa department in the colonial office, asked permission to accept an invitation from the governor of the Gold Coast to come and see for himself what the colonial service was all about and met with the pained reply from his superior, "But what on earth do you want to go and do a thing like that for?"[76]

Once or twice the governor had to remind visiting United Kingdom ministers which of the two of them constitutionally took precedence in the colony. On one occasion even a prime minister had not fully appreciated the position. As he was leaving Government House in the company of the governor, the morning after his arrival in the colony, he noticed the guard drawn up ready to salute. The sergeant of the guard barked out the order, "Royal salute—present arms!" Turning to the governor, the prime minister asked, "Why *Royal* salute?" The governor had to explain that it was the custom for the guard to give that salute the first time the governor left Government House each day. "Oh," remarked the disappointed minister, "so the salute was for you, was it?"[77] Lesser ministers of state could on occasion be more of a nuisance than their superiors. One governor had to protect his aide-de-camp from an angered junior minister who, when for speed of departure the minister was placed in the second car of the cavalcade at the airport, asked whether the governor's aide were unaware that a minister was more important than a governor. There was the incident, too, of a parliamentary secretary visiting Government House who took it upon himself to order one of the official cars to take him to the brighter lights of the city and then on to the cinema. Since he had failed to check any of his arrangements with the aide he missed the cinema performance and on his chagrined return to Government House found that he had missed dinner as well.[78]

"Beachcombing" was another device for bringing the quite separately recruited, paid, and promoted staffs of the colonial office and the colonial service closer together. This was an arrangement whereby a few colonial service officers were seconded from their colonies to work in the colonial office for two years.[79] Such an assignment could be an entry on the credit side of an ambitious colonial service officer, if only because of those in Whitehall whom he got to know. Not all officers jumped at the opportunity. Like the newspaper editor who offered the winners of a crossword competition a first prize of one week in Edinburgh and a second prize of two weeks in Glasgow, Alexander Grantham—anxious for a spell back in the United Kingdom after long service abroad—preferred a one-year course at the Imperial Defence College to a two-year secondment to the colonial office. When the colonial services were unified in the 1930s there had been talk of merging the colonial office and colonial service into one overseas service. This came to nought, but as a result arrangements were made for beachcombing in reverse, so that a few colonial office officials were seconded to colonial administrations for a short spell. A notable instance was J. M. Martin's secondment to Malaya in 1931; later he became deputy undersecretary of the colonial office. At one time it was even accepted that it would be valuable all-round to second a serving governor to the colonial office for two years. Three of these experimental postings actually took place. In 1938 Sir Henry Moore, governor of Sierra Leone, took up residence in the colonial office until his promotion to Kenya in 1940; he was followed by Sir Alan Burns from British Honduras and finally, in 1941, by Sir William Battershill, who eventually went as governor to Tanganyika. But there were grave personal disadvantages of salary and status to home service, and the scheme was abandoned in 1945. (The appointment of Sir John Macpherson as permanent undersecretary was not quite in the same mold.)

Relations with the Legislature.   In contrast to colonies with responsible representative institutions or responsible government, where the governor was very much the governor in council constrained by the will of his legislature, the governor of a crown colony, though obligated to have a council, was in no way obliged to heed the advice he was bound to seek from it. At first the governor's council in the African territories was the executive council, consisting of a handful of senior officials. Soon a legislative council was added. Initially made up of members nominated by the governor, this body subsequently added an elective African element—in 1922 in Nigeria and three years later in Gold Coast, but not for another quarter of a century in Kenya.[80] A simultaneous development was the appointment of nonofficials to the governor's executive council, predominantly European merchants and missionaries until the 1940s, when the first African members were appointed. Not until after World War II, following such reforms as the Burns constitution in the Gold Coast and the Richards one in Nigeria, were the legislative councils developed to become fully representative. Throughout this period the governor presided over both the executive and the legislative council and his senior officials acted as a sort of "front bench."

The final steps of constitutional development saw the elective principle extended to full suffrage; the provision of a speaker to preside over the legislative council, now restyled the house of assembly; the introduction of elected ministers to replace officials in both councils; and, as a last stage, the governor's handing over the presidency of the executive council to an elected prime minister and that body reconstituted as a council of ministers. With the reformulation of the house of assembly as parliament and the council of ministers as a cabinet, the constitutional transfer of power was complete.

Although few governors ever balked at presiding over the executive council, many of them protested against their role as president of the legislative council. Indeed, a whole session of one of the colonial office conferences, attended by over a score of governors and chief secretaries, was devoted to a discussion of this item of genuine concern.[81] Governors had no parliamentary training for this important function. Furthermore, as Burns observed, sitting as president of the legislative council the governor could not help now and again joining in the hurly-burly of debate. At once he laid himself open to attack, something that was clearly harmful to the prestige of the king's representative. Another colonial governor pointed out that there was an innate and insoluble contradiction in the governor's being above politics like the monarch he represented and being as impartial in his judgments as speaker in the House of Commons and yet, as head of the government, being in his role as prime minister positively biased toward upholding governmental measures. Few governors presiding over their legislative council found it easy to keep compartmentalized the three functions of the aloofness of the king's representative, the impartiality of the speaker, and the partiality of the prime minister.[82] The remedy did not come about for another twenty years or so, when Sir Philip Mitchell decided in 1948 to appoint a speaker for the Kenyan legislature. In the final stages of the transfer of power the governor exercised the role of more of a constitutional monarch, opening the annual legislative session with a full ceremonial guard of honor and a speech from the throne written for him by his prime minister and then leaving the chamber to its own devices.

Relations with the Colonial Administration.   Despite Lugard's struggle with the colonial office to create the post of deputy governor while he was away on a working leave for six months each year in Britain, the standard procedure was for the senior official in the colony to act as governor. In these cases, as during the interregnum between one governor's departure and his successor's arrival in the colony, the officer was properly known as the officer administering the government. Only in one or two penultimate constitutions was the office of deputy governor created. It was a temporary measure quickly lapsing when it was found that, in limbo between the governor and the prime minister, the incumbent had virtually nothing to do. "I am so glad you sent me an offprint of your article," wrote one deputy governor to this writer, "as I have all the time in the world to read it in the office just as soon as I have finished *The Times* crossword." A similar complaint was sometimes heard among the last proconsuls. "You *are* lucky at being rung up at lunchtime. Nobody rings me up now at all," a terminal African governor, now translated to an honorary governor-generalship, remarked nostalgically to a latter-day colleague.[83]

In nearly every case the administering officer was the chief secretary (in some territories he was called the colonial secretary). The chief secretary's position in a colony could be likened to that of an adjutant to a colonel or, depending on the size of the territory, of a chief staff officer to a general. Very often a spell as chief or colonial secretary was indispensable to an officer in whom the colonial office described a potential governor. As the senior official in the colony next to the governor (the chief justice might enjoy a higher salary but he was apart from the colonial service hierarchy in the colony), every item of policy and many—too many—routine matters ended up on his desk. All dispatches from the colonial office or directives from the governor were channeled through the chief secretary for implementation. His was the last signature on all minute papers passed to the governor for decision; from there they might return duly covered in red ink (a privilege exclusive to governors),[84] bearing such cryptic and occasionally indecipherable minutes as "Accordingly," "As advised," or "I disagree. Pl. spk."

Within their own provinces the lieutenant governors of Nigeria took precedence over the chief secretary, but it was the latter who became the senior official in Lagos once Cameron had reduced the Lugardian hierarchy. As senior officer in the colony's administrative secretariat, the chief secretary naturally channeled all information from and instructions to the provincial and district commissioners. On tour or in the capital, the governor would no more think of issuing a directive to one of his field administrators than a colonel would of giving orders to a sergeant rather than to his company or platoon commanders. But the chief secretary's authority went further than this. Heads of the colonial service's technical and professional departments, missionaries and merchants, settlers and planters, supplicants and sinners—all had to go through the chief secretary if they wished to approach the governor or—galling enough for departmental officers—merely keep him informed of a matter within their competence.

Such a vast bureaucratic pyramid underneath a solitary figure at the top led many governors to reflect on whether the system was the best one. Lugard, authoritarian and quite incapable of devolving the power of decisionmaking, tried to run the Lagos secretariat himself. His successor, Sir Hugh Clifford, took one look at the morass, wrote it off as "the memory of one man," and appointed Donald Cameron to the new post of chief secretary.[85] Within a few years he had built up one of the two finest secretariats any African colony has known. At one time no fewer than six of its officers were to hold governorships simultaneously.[86] The other model secretariat was set up in Dar es Salaam—by none other than Sir Donald Cameron when he went to Tanganyika in 1925. There, too, many of the top officials were to go on to colonial governorships.[87]

Colonial government became more and more complex as it turned into ministerial government. Hence, the postwar African colonies ended up with twelve to twenty ministers and permanent secretaries running a central bureaucracy that before World War I had been handled by the governor and his triumvirate of chief secretary, financial secretary, and attorney general. It was then that echoes of the old Lugard versus Clifford and Cameron and Burns debate were heard again. Would it not be more efficient to have two services, a secretariat one producing highly trained staff officers and a field one consisting of experienced district administrators? With the exception of the finance side, where officers did inevitably tend to specialize, the colonial service in Africa remained adamant in its rejection of dual services and preferred a system of continuing interchange between provincial and secretariat postings. The majority of governors continued to be appointed from among the experienced district officers.[88] The chief secretary's office was abolished as new constitutions created ministries. Some of his responsibilities and much of his status were transferred to the new post of secretary to the prime minister. With it often went the novel designation of head of the civil service.

The governor's relations with his professional officers sometimes ran into troubled waters. Probably they were colored by the seemingly continual "civil war" between the administrative and departmental officers that plagued many colonies.[89] Clifford never entertained any doubts about the correct relationship. He circulated to all officers in the colony a minute in which he affirmed that the resident in his province and the district officer in his division were the senior officials, regardless of how much younger or junior he might be to technical and professional officers serving in the same area, and as such was the governor's—and hence the sovereign's—representative.[90] Once again a conference of governors held at the colonial office spent a whole session on the subject of relations between the administrative officer and his technical colleagues.[91] Quiescent for the next twenty-five years, this issue came to the fore again when the departments were merged into ministries and the poor professional officer found himself not only deprived of his erstwhile director but actually subservient to the administrative officer, now restyled as permanent secretary or undersecretary. Creech Jones's appointment of a professional officer to the governorship of Seychelles in 1947 was seen by some as an attempt to discomfit the administrative service.

One more index of a governor's relations with his colonial administration might be how soon—and afterward, how often—an assistant district officer met his governor. At one end of the scale it was seven years before Charles Dundas, in early Kenya, ever set eyes on the governor. Arthur Ramage, an administrative cadet in the 1920s, saw the lieutenant governor of Southern Nigeria only twice in eight years.[92] At the other end, Sir John Macpherson insisted that all cadets should have a two-day conducted tour of the Lagos secretariat and meet the governor informally at a cocktail party before taking the boat train to the interior. One administrator still remembers that nervous moment on his second day in the colony:

> [His Excellency], as we had already learned to call the Governor, although a sick man, had us up one by one for a chat. He asked me how long a career I thought lay before me. "A certain five years, a probable ten, and a lucky fifteen," I replied. "My boy," he said, patting me on the knee, "you have thirty years or more ahead of you, my own son is coming into the service next year."[93]

Nigeria became independent nine years later.

More typical, perhaps, was the experience of the cadet who first met His Honor on a tour of the provinces after two years; the administering officer, up-country to install an emir, after four; the governor himself after five, when the latter was making his inaugural tour of the country. Not that the young administrator was always desirous of seeing the governor. When the governor was on tour there would be the donning of the uncomfortable, overstarched colonial service uniform, perhaps the mounting of an unaccustomed steed to escort the governor, and the general whitewash and smartening up involved in any such tour inspection. In the capital, where senior officers were a dime a dozen, the reception at Government House was either above the young administrative officer's social level or too awe-inspiring an affair. Perhaps the district officer in a remote northern Cameroons province got it right when he replied to the governor, who was grandly apologizing because unexpectedly heavy rains had prevented his reaching the district and was asking the officer to convey his apologies to the assuredly disappointed chiefs and their people, "Actually, Your Excellency, the people much preferred the planting rain."[94]

Relations with Nonofficials. The governor's relations with nonofficials were more prominent, if not paramount, in areas of white settlerdom or missionary endeavor. Sir Hugh Clifford might bring his gubernatorial guns to bear on Lord Leverhulme and snub that merchant prince into withdrawal,[95] but the governor was fortunate in that the noble lord was not resident in the colony. Not so the governor of Kenya, where Lord Delamere could drum up a powerful lobby in Parliament and in the influential country-house circles of British political life of the period should the governor show himself to be pro-African rather than pro-settler. "Flannelfoot" was the irreverent title given to a governor like Sir James Sadler, who hesitated before committing himself to any policy at all.[96] In Kenya the white settlers were not averse to marching on Government House (1908), to planning to kidnap the governor (1922), or to staging a noisy demonstration outside Government House and calling on the governor to resign (1952). In Tanganyika the expatriate planters gave Sir Stewart Symes a tough time during the depression, when the hateful word "retrenchment" was in the air. In Northern Rhodesia Sir Evelyn Hone was forced into a final decision to ban the nationalist United National Independence Party (UNIP) and keep its leaders from entering the western province after the outraged reaction of the copperbelt community to the brutal incineration of Mrs. Lillian Burton at Ndola in May 1960.[97]

Equally formidable could be the church militant. H. R. Palmer, lieutenant governor of Nigeria's northern provinces, was determined to protect the Moslem emirates from Christian proselytization and in consequence had coals heaped on his head by the Church Missionary Society; fortunately for him, Palmer was something of a sadhu where fire was concerned. An earlier Missionary Society worker of beloved name, Walter Miller, was a friend of Lugard's yet a fearless critic of indirect rule, which he publicly condemned as subjecting the peasantry to whips and scorpions. Sir Percy Girouard, too, incurred the displeasure of the missions by tightening the rein on their activities in Southern as well as Northern Nigeria. In tightrope Kenya—few governors would have disagreed with Sir Philip Mitchell's confidence to his diary that Kenya epitomized all East Africa's problems and was the most tricky of all the African colonial governorships[98]—Sir Edward Grigg found himself in the eye of a Church of Scotland Mission Society storm that blew up between 1929 and 1931 over the issue of female circumcision among the Kikuyu.[99] In Uganda no governor could ever afford to relax his sensitivity to the historical rift between Protestants and Catholics, which affected adherents as much as church leaders.

Relations with Africans.   While this relationship often assumes a low profile in the literature outside the level of innumerable individual personal friendships, in real, unrecorded life it was an aspect of the office that offered most governors constant current concern and plenty of retrospective pleasure. Here governors who had served their apprenticeship as district officers started off with an advantage, often predicted on their fluency in the local language. Sir Edward Twining was able to reemploy in Government House his former friends and servants. Sir Philip Mitchell invited his erstwhile clerk to come with his wife and stay in Government House for a weekend. The blanket-covered Masai *laibon* whom he also invited, from a friendship of twenty years earlier, understandably preferred the easier atmosphere of the governor's cook's quarters. In Northern Nigeria every governor save two had spent a lifetime in the country and knew many of the chiefs and native officials (and their sons, too) as friends—and just occasionally as opponents—of long standing.

But Government House was not the *boma*. Personal and private relations often had to be subordinated to official and public ones where the governor was concerned. Some governors, such as Lugard, positively disliked the cosmopolitan society of a colonial capital and never were at ease with the African professional classes. There was all the difference in the world between Sir Hugh Clifford's contemptuous remarks to the Nigerian legislative council and Sir James Robertson's warm geniality with the Nigerian executive council thirty-five years later. Others, like Sir Edward Twining and Sir Philip Mitchell, could not adjust to the times and establish those close relations with the nationalists that spoke such volumes for the quality of men like Sir Charles Arden-Clarke, Sir Maurice Dorman, and Sir Richard Turnbull in the age of decolonization. In Sir Walter Egerton's time (1904–1912) the African elite in Lagos thought back to the golden age of the popular Sir William MacGregor (1899–1904) and complained that nowadays they were markedly less welcome at Government House. Indeed, the record of private dinner parties given by the two governors suggests that they were not wrong. Egerton gave forty-nine such parties in 1906 against MacGregor's thirty-six; but the latter's guests comprised 55 Africans and 186 Europeans against the former's 32 Africans and 455 Europeans.[100] Sometimes, of course, it was just a difference of temperament among governors.

In the latter-day empire, the governor's role was less to govern and lead, more to act as mediator and moderator. Decolonization called for special qualities in a governor, prominent among them being one that had been in notoriously short supply throughout the history of Britain's imperial district administrators in India and the Far East as well as Africa: the ability to get on well with the nationalist leadership. Seldom was this gift of greater value than in the final years of African empire. The difference in relations between Sir James Robertson and Prime minister Abubakar Tafawa Balewa, on the one hand, and Sir Edward Twining and Julius Nyerere or Sir Arthur Benson and Kenneth Kaunda, on the other, has been taken by some as an indictment of the stereotype colonial service officer.[101] One has only to think of Kwame Nkrumah's depiction of Sir Charles Arden-Clarke as the latter summoned him straight from prison to Government House and invited him to become leader of government business;[102] or Sir Richard Turnbull's first words to Julius Nyerere while the latter was awaiting sentencing, "Well, Mr. Nyerere, you and I working together have got to solve some very big problems in

Tanganyika";[103] or again, Sir Evelyn Hone's brave attempt to cut the Gordian knot and invite Kaunda to come and talk with him at Government House—"the first glimmer of light."[104]

Such statesmanlike acts will surely emerge as celebrated entries on the credit side of the British governor's relations with the African intelligentsia. Or against, on the debit side, the notorious record of Sir Hugh Clifford's sarcastic apostrophizing of the national congress of British West Africa as "farcical" and "gaseous"[105] or Sir Patrick Renison's unfortunate public description of Kenyatta as "a leader into darkness and death."[106] The average administrator's relations with the nationalist intelligentsia may turn out to have been the Achilles heel of the British empire.

Whether, as the French would have it, it was the absence in Britain's history of anything like the tumbrils of 1789 that gave the British colonial administrator his affection for aristocracy, the British colonial governor nearly always seemed to enjoy his best relations with the chiefly class. Lagos probably never forgave Lugard that on his return to Nigeria as governor-general in 1912 he could not shake the capital's dust off his feet quickly enough: within twenty-four hours of disembarking and being sworn in, he was on that train headed for the northern emirates, where a man—at least a man like Lugard—could breathe unpolluted air. By extension this kind of governor was at his happiest when he was out (often for him it was a case of "back") in the bush far from the telephones, cyphers, and the generally madding crowd of vulgar Lagos and Accra or artificial Lusaka and Entebbe. Sir Philip Mitchell had a private farm as his retreat; Sir Evelyn Baring found his relaxation in an "assault course" in the Pugu hills or in gossiping with the dockers and market women as he rode round Dar es Salaam on his bicycle at dawn. Sir Edward Twining was seldom happier than when joining in some tribal dance or conducting the police band's rendering of the regimental march of the Sixth Battalion, King's African Rifles, "Funga Safari." One of Sir Andrew Cohen's final acts was a recreational journey to the remote—in time as well as place— Karamojong.[107]

Relations with Other Governors. There is little guidance in the problem of identifying the correct collective noun for the sumptuous sight of two or three governors gathered together. Some have tried "a Galaxy" of governors; some, with faunic leanings, "a Pride"—of peacocks rather than of lions. Others, of military background, have played with "a Stick of H.E.s," while others again have thought of "a Provenance of Proconsuls." Twining favored an "Excess of Excellencies."[108] Another of their number compared an assembly of governors to a zoological garden "containing prominent and formidable animals."[109] In practice, the need to cull the dictionary rarely arose. The East African governors conference was limited to three governors, on occasion five; and they often sent their chief secretaries instead. The West African governors met more rarely still—only during World War II, when their 1939 conference was unexpectedly transformed into the high-powered West African war council with no less a go-getter than Lord Swinton as resident minister. Its successor, the West African interterritorial secretariat, did not last long. On one occasion when the governors of Nigeria and Sierra Leone met with their host in Accra they found themselves ignominiously locked out of Government House. Dressed in their civvies they failed to persuade a stubborn Royal West African Frontier Force sentry that they were who they were. Fortunately all Oxbridge graduates, they and their colonial office companion knew all about the art of climbing in after the gates were closed.[110]

Three notable occasions on which there was a gathering of governors par excellence were the colonial office conferences of 1927, 1930, and 1947. The first two were thought up by Leo Amery, secretary of state, as a way of identyfying his powers over the governors and converting them to his plans for the unification of the colonial services and the colonial office. The third was seen by Arthur Creech Jones and his alter ego, Andrew Cohen, as the right moment to warn the old guard of colonial governors and encourage the young guard that the wind of change, though no larger in 1947 than a little cloud arising out of the sea like a man's hand, was already inspiring colonial office thinking about constitutional, social, and economic reforms as a prelude to decolonization prestissimo. In their turn, the governors called on the secretary of state to grant them greater devolution of authority on financial matters, a request granted by his dispatch of June 1948.[111]

Perhaps the most splendid if not the most significant occasion for a gubernatorial gathering was the annual Corona Club dinner. Founded in 1901 by Joseph Chamberlain when he was secretary of state, the club did little more than hold a dinner each June. By tradition the secretary of state addressed the dining members, some 300 or 400 officials of the colonial service on leave in Britain. Both Oliver Lyttelton and his successor, Alan Lennox-Boyd, made it an inviolable matter of honor to keep this engagement year after year. The secretary of state often would use the opportunity to make an important speech. In 1956 Lennox-Boyd, on the night before the news was released to the press, told the Corona Club of the change in title from the colonial service to "Her Majesty's Overseas Civil Service."[112] The head table on those dining evenings was indeed a sight to behold, a night to remember. Begartered and bemedaled, festooned with colorful decorations, here were the British colonial governors in all their dazzling splendor—even though, as at one such dinner, a junior district officer was heard to remind his neighbor, understandably sotto voce, that all that glistered [sic] was not gold.

There is one more venue for governor meeting governor that ought not to be overlooked even if it cannot be adequately evaluated. This is London's clubland and its comparable societies. The leather armchairs in the Athenaeum and the Royal Empire Society have eavesdropped on many a gubernatorial gossip. Among the grandest gatherings of former governors in the postcolonial age was a Royal Commonwealth Society lunchtime meeting in March 1975 at which Sir Roy Welensky came to talk about the state of South Africa.[113]

A final dimension of this intergovernor relationship is that between an outgoing and an incoming governor. Colonial service convention dictated that the two should not meet, at least within the colony.[114] An administering officer always looked after the interregnum. Partly this was for financial reasons: a colony could afford to pay only one governor at a time. Hence, the new governor could not take up his appointment until his predecessor's leave had expired. More important, the idea was that the new governor should not feel bound by his predecessor's policies or inhibited by his last will and testament delivered in situ. This respect for feelings allowed Sir Donald Cameron to turn Sir Horace Byatt's policies upside down; Sir John Macpherson to take one look at Sir Arthur Richards's constitution and terminate it in midstream; and Sir Edward Twining to make a clean sweep after Tanganyika's eighteen years in the doldrums since Cameron's departure in 1931. In the judgment of his biographer, Twining was dispatched to Tanganyika when that country wanted not so much an infusion of new spirit as an electric spark to ignite it.[115]

There was also the positive advantage of a fresh eye, maybe followed by the proverbial new broom. District commissioners varied in their enthusiasms: one had road building as his passion in life, a second agricultural extension, and a third had a bee in his bonnet about native treasury policy and native courts. So, too, might one governor's policy be the opposite of another's in the same colony. For all the lip service paid to continuity, change was the essence locally of British colonial policy. Many governors carried the colonial service convention of "ne'er the twain shall meet" to extremes. Sir James Robertson wished that Sir John Macpherson would have let him pick his brains on the complexities of the Nigerian federation.[116] On his appointment to Gambia, Sir Percy Wyn-Harris decided he would consult his predecessor, Sir Andrew Wright, by then in Cyprus.[117] In his turn, he left his views on constitutional development recorded in a long minute in the files—in startling contrast to what Sir Kenneth Blackburne discovered in the Government House safe when he took over from Lord Baldwin.[118] The colonial office was careful to keep from Bourdillon and Lugard the proposals by the former's successor, Sir Arthur Richards, for constitutional reforms in the mid-1940s until they were a fait accompli. Most governors when quizzed on this point have replied that they had absolutely no direct contact with their successors—and could have wished for it. On the other hand, the colonial office was by and large remarkably adept at briefing governors on their first appointment. Few of them have complained of inadequacy there.

The Governor's Office Reviewed

To cap the network of relationships that involved the governor of a colony, it will be appropriate to have a look at the kind of work he did. Lugard's vision of the colonial governor is too shot through with his own mistrust of the colonial office to be of more than passing value. "The apparent autocracy of the Governor," his special pleading ran, "is limited by the control of the Secretary of State, who exercises a real autocracy."[119] Hailey's disquisition, too, is dry and legalistic.[120] Far more entertaining and at least as informative are excerpts from the diaries and letters of two colonial governors who, big men in all senses of the word, lived their exhausting office to the full. A typical day in the life of "Twinks" Twining, at Government House in Dar es Salaam, went like this:

> Ali brings me tea at 5 A.M. I get up at 5.15 and write letters or work on the files. 7.15 shave, bath, dress and have breakfast. 8 A.M. to office and dictate minutes, letters, despatches and memoranda which have formed in my mind. 9 A.M. The Chief Secretary comes in for his daily hour. 10–12.15 interviews. 12.30 lunch and forty winks. 2–4.14 meetings. 4.15 tea. 5–6 walk or deck tennis. 6–8 files. 8 dinner. 9.30 bed. One gets [he concluded] into a pretty cast-iron routine which is the secret of good health.[121]

Nor are there many more revealing descriptions of the nonstop program of the governor away from Government House and up-country on tour than that given by Sir James Robertson as he described his first visit round the huge federation of Nigeria:

> Once I had settled in I made it my first aim to go around the country to obtain a rapid view of it as a whole and to meet as many people as I could. . . .
>
> [During the next fifteen days] I paid a preliminary visit to Ibadan shortly after my arrival. Early in July I set off on a two-week tour of the other Regions. I went by train from Lagos to Kaduna, the capital of the North, where I stayed with the Governor, and met the Northern ministers and leading officers of the Northern Government. . . . While in the North I also visited Zaria and Kano before flying to Sokoto to meet the Sultan. I next went to Maiduguri to meet the Shehu of Bornu, one of the most important emirs in the North. After Maiduguri we flew to Jos on the Northern plateau, the centre of the tin-mining area, and then on by train to Makurdi on the Benue. . . .
>
> I went directly from the North to the Eastern region, beginning my tour at Enugu, the capital. Next morning I went by train, and after calling at Umuahia and Aba, where I met officials and notables on the station platforms, we reached Port Harcourt in the afternoon in a storm of rain. I had to inspect a guard of honour at the station and went on through damp crowds in pouring rain to the Roxy Hall where I was greeted by parades of Boy Scouts and Girl Guides, and by the time I had inspected them I was just as soaked as they were. Then, in the Hall, there were speeches, singing and introductions to the leading citizens of Port Harcourt. We had a large dinner party that evening, and next day I was shown round the town and the port. . . . After a lunch for administrative officers I took the afternoon off and had a game of golf on the Port Harcourt course . . . But in the evening, I was on the job again with a visit to the sports club, and a dinner party at the Residency for leading personalities.
>
> Calabar was the next stop, a journey of about forty minutes by air. . . . There the usual programme: a reception at the Council Hall, a luncheon party for local notables, a visit to the Hope Waddell Institute, . . . a drinks party followed by a dinner party, and after that a visit to the club where there was a dance. Next morning I was taken into the country to see rubber estates and visited a palm oil plantation and factory, returning in time to call at the Calabar Africa Club, where there were speeches and dances, and then back to the Residency to give lunch to the Nigerian and expatriate administrative officers.[122]

Diversity and versatility were inherent in the recruitment of the colonial administrative service, right from the range of reasons given by former administrators on why they joined the colonial service[123] to the spectrum of grounds on which they were selected. There was likewise great variety in the retrospective views of colonial governors on their careers in Africa. Guggisberg, professional engineer, was proud of his vision in creating the new harbor at Takoradi and founding the new and famous Achimota College, though fifty years later he is remembered with equal affection for his devotion to a blueprint (it proved to be little more) for the africanization of the civil service. His own image of his kind of governor was, in his biographer's analysis of the springs of action, a cross between paterfamilias and captain of the soccer team:

It is as head of a family that I wish to govern this country—a family of officials, merchants and natives. My ear will always be open to any member; suggestions and helpful criticism will always be weighed; but once my decision is given I ask all those in the family who do not agree with me to sink their private opinion and to give loyal support for the sake of their side.[124]

Mitchell, humanist and amateur anthropologist, like Lugard was proud of his role in encouraging higher education: "I saw that my duty lay in promoting to the utmost the development of university education."[125] But he clung to multiracialism as the key to Kenya's economic development, at the same time believing no less sincerely that Britain's mission in Africa was to plant the seeds of Europe's unparalleled civilization:

He argued in 1954 that conditions in Africa were not yet suitable for the establishment of democracy. Such an attempt could lead only to tyranny. To allow this to happen would be an abrogation of trusteeship, would negate what had been achieved by the European presence in Africa. He considered the emotionalism and fanaticism prevalent in mass movements as a reversion from civilization towards something sub-human.[126]

Robertson one of the last governors-general in Africa, was naturally unwilling to separate his own goals from the whole imperial story. Conscious—like Hesketh Bell before him—of the prime need for economic development, he found that in both the Sudan and Nigeria the problem far from being that of excess exploitive capital was simply that of trying to find sufficient financial resources.[127] Sixty years earlier MacGregor had obtained minimal satisfaction from his governorship of Lagos, apart from the pleasure of his personal relations with the Yoruba chiefs and Lagosian elite, and looked back on his governorship with bitterness. "West Africa is the arena for ribbons and crosses and medals," he wrote privately on his disappointed departure in 1904. "A man of peace is not wanted nor liked there."[128]

It is Archer's limited level of satisfaction that classically mirrors that of many governors:

As I look back now in the mellowed years of my retirement to the days of which I write, I can confidently claim that those early years were the happiest years for the British administrator in Africa. Personally I had a meteoric career. . . . But a "career" is not the only thing. What gives me far greater pleasure is to know that I gained in an exceptional degree the goodwill, the esteem and trust, even the affection, of large sections of the native communities over whom I was called upon to rule.[129]

As for Twining, in his recipe to the secretary of state in case there should be talk of a successor in 1957 there were—as his biographer wryly notes—certain familiar figures of a self-portrait style:

The next few years are likely to be very crucial for the territory and it is therefore of great importance that its affairs should be guided by somebody with the right qualities. . . .

On the political side it is likely to prove desirable to have a slowing down of the progress rather than advancing it. This will have to be handled with great tact, diplomacy and strength. . . . But the greatest emphasis of all will be on economic development.

Therefore what is needed is a man, not with a brilliant record, but with steady common sense, willing to take a strong line when necessary, but having at the same time a real sympathy for African aspirations. He must be a good administrator and should have a bent for economic development. I have found during the last eight and a half years that the position of the Governor has changed markedly and he is expected to be less authoritarian than he was, particularly now that the ministerial system has been introduced and a great deal of the responsibility has been off-loaded on to the shoulders of the Ministers. Nevertheless his role is one of great importance and in fact the burden is much greater now than it was. It is essential that he should know the country thoroughly and should be well-acquainted with the problems of every area or even district. He must be good at management. While I do not regard it as essential for him to have had African experience, this is certainly a valuable asset as is a knowledge of Swahili.[130]

For Lugard, perhaps the greatest of all the African proconsuls, the retrospective wish was the simplest. To quote the epitaph on his tomb, "All that I did was to try and lay my bricks straight."

The Person of the British Colonial Governor

From the foregoing account of the office of the British colonial governor in Africa, his functions, and the frequent splendors of the way of life, it is possible to sympathize with King George V who, at the end of the audience he had granted to a particularly distinguished imperial governor, turned to his equerry and whispered, "Now I know what it feels like to meet Royalty."[131]

But if we understand the role—defined in the early editions of *Colonial Regulations* as a position of "considerable rank, trust and endowment"—do we yet recognize the actor? Who were the colonial governors of the British territories in Africa during the past 100 years? What were their social profiles and career patterns? To study the familial background and upbringing, the education, career, and related affiliations of this brotherhood of imperial proconsuls is ineluctably to study a slice of British social history. By one of those unaccountable vicissitudes of imperial history, it was not until after the end of the British empire and the twilight of its imperial services that a sociological interest was taken in who the governors of yesteryear were. Robert Collins's compelling rationalization of an American's profound interest in the Sudan political service is no less relevant in the context of the colonial service:

Although the imperialists have departed, many independent countries in Africa are the creations of the half century, or more, of British administration, and the Africans will continue to make use of the institutions and instruments of government and administration which the British left behind. These institutions and instruments, indeed the whole tone of many of the African nations, clearly reflect the imperial heritage and will continue to do so for many decades. Without some under-

Robert Coryndon, right, with Cecil Rhodes, center

Sir Hugh Clifford

Sir Gordon Guggisberg

Lord Lugard

Pierre Ryckmans and his wife return to Leopold-ville, 1955

Felix Eboué

Robert Delavignette (in civilian clothes)

Martin Rutten

William Ponty

Heinrich Schnee

Julius Zech

Left, Government House, Christiansborg Castle, Accra, Gold Coast. Right, Joseph Simon Gallieni.

Freetown, Sierra Leone

Accra, Gold Coast

Government House, Nairobi, Kenya

Government House, Lagos, Nigeria, in the early 1890s

Garden Party, Hill Station, 1909

Government House, Entebbe, Uganda

Palace of Regent of Zanzibar

Interior of Palace of Zanzibar

Residency, Fort Kumasi, Gold Coast, 1890s

Royal meeting at Oyo, Southern Nigeria

standing of the imperialists themselves, it is impossible to examine imperialism, to assess its impact, or to comprehend the social and political relationships, attitudes, and states of mind it creates.[132]

To the summary biographical statistics of H. L. Hall (1937), K. E. Robinson (1965), J. M. Lee (1967), Colin Cross (1968), R. V. Kubicek (1969), and J. W. Cell (1970), we can today add a full-scale familial survey of over 200 governors carried out by I. F. Nicolson and C. A. Hughes (1975).[133] Here we shall first consider the personal background of the generality of British colonial governors and then bring together, in tabular form, somewhat different data from that presented by other scholars on the origin and career of eighteen eminent African governors by way of specialist illustrations.

It was the Reform Act of 1832 that was to curtail, if not immediately to halt, the grosser abuses of governors' appointments that had distinguished the eighteenth century—a system whose notoriety was summed up by one historian's interpretation of the nomination of Sir Henry Morgan to be governor of Jamaica as being "presumably on the principle of setting a thief to catch a thief."[134] From the middle of the nineteenth century the professionalization of the governors' cadre began noticeably to increase, with a corresponding decrease in the number of appointments that were political, haphazard, curious, or downright dubious, so that the *London Times* was at last able to editorialize on its belief that "the more distinguished among our fellow subjects in the colonies may feel that the path of imperial ambition is henceforth open to them."[135] Apart from the Australian states, the lie could gradually be given as the century neared its close to the myth that Disraeli had once laid down that governors must be peers of the realm, or the sons of peers, or at least married to daughters of the nobility. Excluding the "fortress" colonies of Gibraltar, Malta, and Bermuda, the steady professionalization of governors in the second half of the nineteenth century is clearly demonstrated in Table 5.

Table 5.   Career Origins of Colonial Governors, 1851–1901

Year	Total in survey	Military[1]	Political	Professional[2]
1851	9	5	1	3
1861	33	12[3]	4	11[4]
1871	30	7	9	10
1881	30	8	5	13
1891	31	7	5[5]	14
1901	29	?	2[5]	15

SOURCE: Data from Henry L. Hall, *The Colonial Office: A history* (London, 1937), pp. 88–89.
[1]One needs to enter the caveat that many army men decided to remain in the colonial service so that if they had entered when they were relatively young the length of career before them might well justify their final classification as professionals.
[2]The earliest use of the term "the professional class" that I have found to describe career service governors is Sir Charles Bruce, *The Broad Stone of Empire*, 2 vols. (London, 1910), 1:205 ff.
[3]Including two naval officers.
[4]In addition, three lawyers who had been in the colonial service and one each from the foreign and colonial offices might be said to earn classification as professionals.
[5]All holding a governorship of an Australian state.

Cell's data on some 260 British governors and lieutenant governors of African colonies and Indian presidencies between 1830 and 1880 show that 139 were English, 34 Scottish, and 33 Irish. They were largely from what are generally recognized as families of the gentry or the upper middle class, twenty-one of them being nobility. Fifty-four had attended a university (up to the 1920s this was by no means coterminous with taking a degree), and about the same number—but not necessarily the same persons—had been through the British public school system.[136] Half of these governors had had a career in the army or navy before their appointment.[137] Another quarter had enjoyed a career in politics, the diplomatic corps, or the home civil service, and some ten percent had been called to the bar.

Robinson's summary relates to the 103 men who held office between 1919 and 1939 as governors of British colonies throughout the world other than the three so-called fortress posts traditionally filled by a serving general. The increased degree of professionalism is shown by the fact that just over half of these had started their careers in the colonial service: sixteen had joined as eastern cadets (selected for service in South-East Asia), twenty had begun in tropical Africa, six had started as clerks in the West Indies, three had been personally appointed as private secretary or aide-de-camp, one had been a doctor, and another a lawyer. Of the forty-nine whose first job was not in the colonial service, as many as twenty-eight had been army officers. Seven of the remaining twenty-one came from the home civil service; four from the Indian, Sudanese, or Egyptian civil services; and two had been private secretaries to dominion governors-general. Another seven had served in South Africa, either in the British South Africa Company or as part of the reconstruction era after the Boer war. In terms of educational record, only 54 out of the 103 were graduates (Oxford 27, Cambridge 18, Edinburgh 5, London and Dublin 2 each), the proportion being twice as high, however, among those appointed to the public service or the armed forces after 1900. No fewer than twelve of the British colonial governors appointed during the interwar years came from outside the colonial service: eight of them were professional soldiers.

Colin Cross considers only the thirty-four persons holding governorships in 1922. Their ages ranged from forty-two to sixty-five, and nineteen of them were career colonial administrators. Lee advances the Robinson data chronologically by analyzing the 110 governors appointed throughout the British colonial empire between 1940 and 1960, which he looks on as the period of decolonization. Of these, seventy-eight had had a full career in the colonial service; seventeen came from elsewhere, including the army (four), home civil (three) or other imperial services (one) and five from the legal profession. The proportion of outside appointments to a colonial governorship increased in 1940–1960, totaling 15 out of 110, compared to 12 out of 103 for the period 1919–1939. Educationally, the figures reflect a big advance. Eighty-two of the governors were university graduates (Oxford, forty; Cambridge, twenty-seven). Exactly the same number had been to public schools, but only twenty-four of them to one of the nine leading (Clarendon) schools of Eton, Harrow, Winchester, Rugby, Westminster, St. Paul's, Charterhouse, Merchant Taylors, or Shrewsbury.

In view of this wealth of social data now available to the researcher, the gubernatorial data presented in this chapter will focus on career statistics. Table 6 brings together the Robinson and Lee figures, and Table 7 offers a comparative summary of the career profiles of eighteen distinguished British colonial governors between 1891 and 1961. Grouped by service generations, these names represent probably the most outstanding governors of tropical Africa in the four distinct phases of its imperial interlude: the period up to World War I, the interwar years, the age of nationalism, and the era of decolonization with its last (or penultimate) colonial service governor. Between them these men held forty-four governorships, including every one of the senior African posts.

Table 6.   Career Profiles of Colonial Governors, 1919–1960

	Total appointed 1919–1939	Three "generations" holding governorships between 1940 and 1960[1]			Total appointed 1940–1960
		Date of birth			
		1883–1891	1892–1899 war generation	After 1900	
1. Full-time career in colonial service (or associated work) excluding war service					
(a) as eastern cadet, MCS, or Ceylon	16	7	8	5	20
(b) in tropical Africa	20	9	7	33	49
(c) in other colonies	15	4	1	1	6
(d) as aide-de-camp or private secretary	3	1	1	1	3
	54	21	17	40	78
2. Began in other careers. Appointed to colonial service below the rank of governor					
(a) formerly army	22	1	3	—	4
(b) formerly home civil (CO) service	3	—	1	—	1
(c) formerly home civil service, other departments	3	—	1	1	2
(d) formerly Egypt, Sudan, or ICS	4	—	1	—	1
(e) legal profession	—	—	2	3	5
(f) all other	5	2	2	—	4
	(37)	(3)	(10)	(4)	(17)
Appointed directly to governorship					
(a) from politics	5	1	1	—	2
(b) from army	6	—	3	—	3
(c) from home civil service	1	1	1	1	3
(d) from diplomatic service	—	—	—	1	1
(e) all other	—	1	2	3	6
	(12)	(3)	(7)	(5)	(15)
Total of 1 and 2	103	27	34	49	110
3. Education of 1 and 2					
School (a) Clarendon	N.G.	6	6	12	24
(b) other public	N.G.	10	21	27	58
(c) other	N.G.	11	7	10	28
University (a) none	48	8	18	2	28
(b) Oxford	27	9	8	23	40
(c) Cambridge	18	6	3	19	27
(d) other	10	4	6	5	15

SOURCES: J. M. Lee, *Colonial Development and Good Government* (Oxford, 1967), p. 138; Kenneth E. Robinson, *The Dilemmas of Trusteeship* (London, 1965), pp. 46–47.

[1]All figures exclude the governorships of Gibraltar, Malta, and Bermuda. The 1919–1939 figures relate to thirty colonies; the 1940–1960 to thirty-two colonies but exclude Ceylon and Palestine.

Table 7. Selected Career Landmarks of Eighteen Leading British Colonial Governors in Africa, 1891–1961

	1891–1919			1919–1939			1939–1949				1949–1961							
	Johnston	Lugard	Bell	Clifford	Guggisberg	Cameron	Burns	Richards	Mitchell	Macpherson	Arden-Clarke	Twining	Benson	Renison	Dorman	Crawford	Turnbull	Coutts
Age at first governorship	33	42	41	46	50	52	47	45	45	50	48	47	47	41	44	45	49	49
Length of previous service	6	3	23	29	0	34	29	22	23	27	26	17	22	20	21	22	27	27
Post held immediately prior to governorship[1]	Consul.	Comm. of WAFF	Admin.	Chief sec.	Brig.	Chief sec.	Dep.-chief sec.	Dep.-chief sec.	Chief sec.	Comp. Carib.	Resident comm.	Admin.	Chief sec.	Chief sec.	Chief sec.	Dep. gov.	Chief sec.	Chief sec.
Colonies served in previously	3	1	5	3	1	3	3	1	2	2	3	3	2	2	5	4	1	2
Experience outside Africa	No	No	West Indies	West Indies Malaya	No	West Indies Mauritius	West Indies	Malaya	No	Malaya Palestine West Indies	No	West Indies Mauritius	No	West Indies	Pales.	No	No	West Indies
Experience as district officer	No	No	No	Yes	No	No	No	Yes	Yes	Yes	Yes	No	Yes	No	Yes	Yes	Yes	Yes
African governorships held	Nyasaland	Northern Nigeria	Uganda No. Nig.	Gold Coast Nigeria	Gold Coast	Tangan. Nigeria	Gold Coast	Nigeria	Kenya	Nigeria	Gold Coast	Tang.	No. Rhodesia	Kenya	Sierra Leone	Seych. Uganda	Tang.	Uganda
Total governorships held	2	3	4	4	2	2	3	5	3	1	2	2	1	3	2	2	2	1
Total years as governor[2]	8	19	(6) + 19	17	10	11	17	17	17	7	(9) + 11	(2) + 12	5	10	16	10	6	2
Age at first civil honor	38	37	39	34	39	46	40	48	43	43	43	44	45	39	43	39	44	37
Age at knighthood	38	43	44	43	52	50	49	50	47	47	48	50	47	44	45	47	49	49
Final honor awarded	GCMG	Baron GCMG	GCMG	GCMG GBE	KCMG	GCMG	GCMG	GCMG	GCMG	GCMG	GCMG	Baron GCMG	GCMG	GCMG	GCMG	GCMG	GCMG	GCMG
Age on retirement from governorship	43	61	60	63	61	63	60	62	62	57	59	59	52	51	60	55	58	51
Total years in colonial service	0	19	42	46	10	45	42	39	40	38	27	29	27	30	29	32	36	27
University	London	Sandhurst	No	Sandhurst	Woolwich	No	No	Oxford	Oxford	Edinburgh	No	Sandhurst	Oxford	Cambridge	Cambridge	Oxford	Lon.	St. And.
Father's occupation	Col. sec.	Rev.	?	Military	Trader	Planter	Col. Service	?	Army	?	Rev.	Rev.	Rev.	?	?	Doctor	Acct.	Rev.

SOURCES: Data from *The Colonial Office List* (annual), *Who's Who, Who Was Who*, biographies, and autobiographies.

[1] In this table chief secretary and colonial secretary are not distinguished.

[2] Service as resident commissioner of a high commission territory or as administrator in the West Indies is shown in parentheses.

The biographical data on British colonial governors assembled by Nicolson and Hughes is the most extensive to date and the two following paragraphs draw on their survey. Covering some sixty years under twenty-nine secretaries of state for the colonies, their study examines 214 governors of the thirty colonial territories of the British empire from Aden to Nyasaland and from Fiji to Trinidad. Some 100 further comparable appointments are excluded for reasons that the authors carefully explain. Of the final cohort, 200 were career or professional appointments and only 14 were political ones—"cuckoos in the nest," to use Sir Edward Grigg's self-description as one of them.[138] Clearly, the colonial office wheel had come full circle between the 1850's and the 1950's.

No fewer than thirty-four out of the ninety-five career governors whose fathers' occupations these researchers were able to trace were the sons of Anglican clergymen: the way from vicarage to Government House was a well-trodden route.[139] Nearly ten percent of the career governors were Catholics (six) or Jews (three). Eighteen of the ninety-five had fathers in the armed forces, sixteen were sons of doctors, and thirteen sons of civil servants, mostly in overseas service. Nicolson and Hughes note that out of the 200 governors there were fewer than a dozen scions of landed gentry. The handful of Scots (seventeen), the odd Irishman, the occasional peer, and the single governor from a working class home all tend to confirm the writers' thesis that the career governors of the colonial service in the twentieth century were overwhelmingly drawn from the English middle and professional classes.

With regard to education, out of the 168 English governors, 8 went to Eton—a high proportion among the limited number of Etonians who joined the colonial service at all—and 3 to Harrow. Nearly fifteen percent of the total 200 were educated at one of the other seven Clarendon schools, of which Charterhouse (8), Winchester (7), and Rugby (6) had the highest scores. Among what may for convenience be termed the lesser public schools, forty-two of which were to provide 80 out of the 200 governors, as many as 10 came from Cheltenham, 6 from Clifton, and 5 each from Tonbridge and Marlborough. State secondary schools provided the high figure of thirty-two governors. At the level of postsecondary education, 127 of the 200 had been to a university (103 were at Oxbridge) and 36 had, in addition or instead, legal qualifications.

Any analysis of the social background and career profile of the British colonial governors makes clear their heterogeneity. Soldier, sailor; medicine, church; rich man, poor man; lawyer, politician, left in the lurch—nearly all but one of the cherrystone categories are applicable to the governor's career. Portraits of the African colonial governor in the modern English novel—like Elspeth Huxley's by-the-book Sir Frederick Begg or Edgar Wallace's pompous Sir Macalister Cairns, David Unwin's Fabian Sir Christopher Mountclair or David Karp's no less liberal Lysander Pellman, and Norman Collins's proconsular Sir Gardner Hackforth—are just as much fact as fiction, no more or less improbable characters than they are quite possible personalities. As Graham Greene once said about a personal friend of his who ended up as governor of Mauritius, "I don't think the Colonial Office can ever have realised how strange a servant they had enlisted."[140]

If their characteristics and careers were so varied, so, too, were their individual fates. In the twentieth century alone, colonial governors have been elevated in retirement to the House of Lords (Lugard, Richards, Twining—a very select band), neglected (H. H. Johnston, Guggisberg), quietly demoted (Sadler, Bell), more or less dismissed (Renison, Armitage, Girouard), or resigned in the nick of time (Eliot, Archer). They have had attempts on their lives (Harding, Trevaskis), had Government House burned down over their head (Storrs), been assassinated (Gurney, D. G. Stewart), or died in office (Sir Donald Stewart, Gent, Coryndon). They have had statues erected to them (Guggisberg), museums built to honor them (Coryndon), and their coffins stoned by hostile mobs (Denham). Many have retired in broken health (Guggisberg, Graeme Thomson, Bourdillon), and most to a humble way of life sadly removed from the style to which they had grown accustomed in Government House. Some have made a second name for themselves, particularly as authors (H. H. Johnston, Clifford, Luke, Burns, Grimble). At least one went on to take holy orders (Champion).

In their colonial careers, or course, their hobbies and their interests were legion: ornithology (Bourdillon, Jackson, Archer), big-game hunting (Coryndon), mountaineering (Wyn-Harris), Maliki law (Ruxton), languages (Burdon, H. H. Johnston), historical research (Palmer, Burns), and founding learned journals and institutes (Wilkinson, MacMichael, Young). They included internationally recognized authorities on botany (Moloney, H. H. Johnston), on crown jewels (Twining), and on sea slugs (Eliot).

The Selection of Governors

With such a range and richness of personal talent and career data available to the colonial office—although only gradually accessible over the past few years to the social historian—the reader might be excused for thinking that the selection of "the next governor" would be a simple matter of computer programming and infallible printout. The reverse was the truth. There was not exactly unerring method in the colonial office's filling of governorships during the twentieth century, nor was there overmuch madness in the results (though not every secretariat official or passed over provincial commissioner might accept such an assumption). The analytical literature on the colonial service, already scant, is silent on this point. Nowhere is the procedure for the selection of governors described in detail. The following paragraphs owe a debt of gratitude to some thirty ex-governors and senior colonial office officials who have given much time to answering my inquiries.[141] In passing I might add as a relevant fact in itself that many of the governors replied that they had no idea as to how or, with characteristic modesty, why they had been selected.

In the colonial service division of the colonial office two critical crème de la crème lists were mentioned. List A included incumbents under the age of fifty-five who could be considered eligible for promotion to a governorship when a vacancy occurred. List B performed a similar function for those thought suitable for appointment to a chief or colonial secretaryship. Persons on List A were usually already chief secretaries, though now and again a provincial commissioner of outstanding promise might be considered. It also included the names of incumbent governors who might be considered for advancement to a more important governorship: for these, an essential qualification was to have already demonstrated complete competence in an independent command. A person was unlikely to reach List B when he was still a district commissioner, though such cases are not unknown.[142] Just a few names never got off either list until time and pension removed them; administrators, like athletes and roses, could reach their peak too soon and then see their early bloom fade.

Physically, the lists took the form of a card index on which were noted all the pros and cons of a potential governor's or chief secretary's career and character. These lists were built up from the annual confidential report on his staff submitted by every colonial governor.[143] Often, of course, the governor was merely initialing the detailed report written on a district officer by the latter's resident or provincial commissioner; but on occasion for high-flying district officers and always for provincial commissioners the governor would make his own careful, confidential comments. The keeping of annual reports was one of the tasks of the private secretary. Copies of all the reports were filed in the governor's office—except that of the private secretary himself, as a midnight search revealed to at least one over-curious newcomer to the post.

When the confidential reports reached the colonial office, they were scrutinized by the "geographic" departments (e.g., East Africa, Hong Kong, and Pacific) and the "subject" departments (e.g., economic or social services). Individuals with particular promise would be passed to the personnel department with the suggestion that the names might be "noted" for either List A or List B. However, the ultimate decision as to whether to add a name was invariably taken by the permanent undersecretary (PUS) himself. Officers who had been "noted" were often invited to call at the colonial office when they were on leave, often quite informally and probably innocent of why or of the fact they they were being sized up at all. Nor was a spell of beachcombing—being seconded to the colonial office for a couple of years—expected to do one's career any harm. Visits to the colonies in the 1950s by senior colonial office officials meant that men like Andrew Cohen as head of the Africa department used to come back with a mental list of who he thought would (and knew would not) make governor. In short, there was little doubt that by the 1950s colonial office officials had a pretty thorough personal knowledge about colonial service officers who were in the promotion zone. Gone were the days when, as Sir Ralph Williams did to secure Newfoundland and others did for different appointments before 1910, one might legitimately offer oneself for the next colonial governorship to fall vacant.

Some six months before a vacancy was due in a governorship, the names on List A would be examined by a small ad hoc committee of senior colonial office officials and a short list would be drawn up. Comments on competing claims were made by the personnel department and, where necessary, an explanation of names omitted was added. Usually, though not necessarily, these minutes ended with a specific recommendation by the head of the colonial service department responsible for administrative appointments. Other minutes would be added as the file made its way upward. After reading these, the final recommendation was made by the permanent undersecretary. The colonial office machinery after 1945 was very different from that of 1909, when submissions for governorships "were discussed in secret between the Secretary of State and Permanent Under Secretary."[144]

Colonial office lore maintains that it was a rule that nobody could be promoted to governor from within the territory in which he was currently serving.[145]

However, this convention was now and again overridden or overlooked. For instance, there was Sir Bryan Sharwood Smith's appointment to Northern Nigeria in 1954. This might be argued as a case of straight promotion since he already held the post of lieutenant governor. No such argument can be made for the choice of Sir Evelyn Hone to succeed Sir Arthur Benson as governor of Northern Rhodesia in 1959 since Hone was serving as chief secretary to Benson in Lusaka at the time. As Sir Evelyn modestly described this signal distinction, "This was something of a break with precedent which made me treasure my appointment as Governor more than ever."[146] On the other hand, an officer who happened to have served with distinction in the colony whose governorship was now under consideration could be expected to have a certain advantage over his competitors.

In the case of less important governorships where neither the secretary of state nor the permanent undersecretary might have much personal knowledge of the candidates under consideration, they would lean heavily on the information and guidance offered by the colonial office's colonial service division. For example, the colonial office produced a list of no fewer than eight colonial service names for the resident commissionership of Bechuanaland in 1928 when the dominions office favored an appointment from outside the service.[147] In the case of the highest appointments, consideration at an informal level could be expected to have been given from time to time over a long period and well in advance of the vacancy occurring. "In such cases," noted A. R. Thomas, CMG, doyen of latter-day colonial office procedures,

> the field of possible candidates was necessarily limited and fairly obvious. A Governor serving in a less senior appointment might have become naturally earmarked as the obvious choice. Indeed, "career planning" might go as far as to have a later higher appointment in mind for him when appointing a person to a smaller or intermediate governorship. In this, the interest in and knowledge of the Colonial Service on the part of Senior members of the [Colonial Office] was a vital factor.[148]

This was the case with Twining when he was offered Saint Lucia in 1944. Cameron refused to let Mitchell leave Dar es Salaam to take the chief secretaryship of Nyasaland. He promised him he would not be the loser. Nor was he. After promotion to chief secretary, Tanganyika, Mitchell was quickly offered the governorship of Uganda. He himself turned down the governorship of Tanganyika—"there was no post I desired more"[149]—but in due course Kenya came his way.

Although the final recommendation was that of the permanent undersecretary, the appointment lay in the hands of the secretary of state. Often he had strong views of his own. Arthur Creech Jones's touch was visible in the unusual appointment of a director of medical services to the governorship of the Seychelles. Awkwardly, it fell to Oliver Lyttleton to tell the chief secretary and acting governor of Malaya, del Tufo, while staying with him and watching him in action, that he regretted he did not feel able to recommend him to the queen for appointment as substantive governor (he did, however, secure him a deserved knighthood). Lennox-Boyd, Iain Macleod, and Duncan Sandys all had positive views on the governors appointed, inherited, or removed during their tenures of office. The prime minister had the right to be consulted on the name finally recommended.[150] Oliver Lyttleton notes that this was something of a formality although there is evidence that both Harold Macmillan and Clement Attlee took a personal interest in gubernatorial nominations—sometimes with calamitous results. Finally, of course, there was the sovereign. Queen Victoria took a close interest in who was appointed. No case in recent history is on record of Buckingham Palace's having turned down the secretary of state's recommendation. Sir Hilton Poynton has observed, however, that up to a few years ago the colonial office would have been careful not to submit the name of anyone who would not have been admitted to the royal enclosure at Ascot.[151]

Apart from political nominations and military men in an earlier age, most of the governorships were filled from within the service. From the 1930s onward this practice was in accord with a positive recommendation from the powerful civil service reform committee under Warren Fisher, permanent secretary of the treasury.[152] In nine cases out of ten this meant the colonial administrative service, "the normal nursery" for such appointments.[153] Professional officers were rarely considered to have the right qualities; the few exceptions included the outstanding Guggisberg and the less distinguished Selwyn-Clarke. For the most part, the incoming governor came from a chief or colonial secretaryship (see Table 7), though the post of financial secretary could also be a launching pad. Very occasionally a man went straight from administrative officer to a minor governorship, e.g., Anthony Abel to Sarawak, Geoffrey Archer and Theodore Pike to Somaliland; indeed, in East Africa officers distinguished something of a royal line of succession from Kenya's northern frontier district to the governorship of Somaliland—Archer, Kittermaster, Glenday, Reece, and Pike. Colonial office staff were not allowed to feature in either List A or List B, but governorships were now and again filled from within the office—for instance, Sir Gerald Creasy to Gold Coast in 1947 and Sir Andrew Cohen to Uganda in 1952. These would seem to have been more in the nature of positive decisions by the secretary of state than the outcome of the normal colonial office practice for the selection of governors.

The choice of the last governor for the final stages of a colony's dependent status or of governor-general for the first year of its prerepublican status was also often that of a noncolonial service man. This might be a politician like Lord Listowel to the Gold Coast in 1957 and the remarkable Malcolm Macdonald to Kenya in 1963, or he might be drawn from the former Sudan political service such as, to quote two outstandingly successful cases, Sir James Robertson to Nigeria in 1955 and Sir Gawain Bell to Northern Nigeria in 1957.[154] At this sensitive period, too, the views of the local prime or chief minister also were consulted. The chief minister of Guiana made an a priori decision not to accept Sir Richard Luyt as governor because of his South African origins, but a very warm testimonial from Kenneth Kaunda, whose chief secretary Luyt had been in Northern Rhodesia, persuaded Jagan to change his mind.

Quot sententiae, tot proconsulares. Is it, then, possible to identify the qualifications for a colonial governor from so many men of so many parts? Certainly not in the way a computer programmer would require. If any qualities can be isolated, they might be said to include proven ability, wide experience, a "good name" in the service—more easily recognized in its negative than in its positive respect—and a certain but by no means a statutory seniority. Furthermore, there were very few exceptions to give the lie to the belief, as widely held in the service as in the colonial office, that a sine qua non in a potential governor was secretariat experience. Classically, this took the form of a colonial secretaryship of a West Indian colony perhaps followed by the chief secretaryship of a major African colony (see Table 7). Finally, as in so many cases of getting to the top, there was that element of luck in having the right qualifications at the right time for the right place. If the methods were open to question by those brought up in trade unionist suspicions or committed to the ideals of democratic socialism, at any rate the results of colonial office pragmatism were on the whole remarkably successful. Even if the colonial office had not by the 1950's fully subscribed to Charles Buller's view, expressed a century earlier that its "sole business should be to breed up a supply of good colonial governors and then leave them to manage their own affairs,"[155] it had nevertheless moved a long way beyond Lord Steyne's not so altruistic patronage in *Vanity Fair* and Gladstone's gloomy reflection that nobody in England who was well known would even dream of accepting a colonial governorship.[156]

Perhaps the last word on the selection of British colonial governors should go to one of the most successful of their number (though not a career colonial service man himself). Cabling the secretary of state for a governor to replace D. G. Stewart, assassinated in 1949 as he was inspecting a guard of honor in Sarawak, Malcolm Macdonald, commissioner general for Southeast Asia, asked in effect for the names of three outstanding district officers on its books. "We don't want a Governor as such," he said. "We want the best District Officer in the Colonial Empire."[157]

Honors.   Honors were for governors what automobiles supposedly are to Californians: it would be virtually unheard of not to have one; many had two and some three. Nearly every governor was knighted during his term of office. "The Colonial Service?" remarked an Oxbridge tutor when one of his pupils told him of his career plans after taking his final examinations. "Now that's where you get a C.M.G. after twenty years and a K.C.M.G. after thirty, isn't it?"[158] Burns complained that it was a pity that a governor should sometimes have to take up his appointment without the inevitable honor that quickly followed, as it belittled him on his arrival in the new colony: "I have thought it would be wiser," he argued, "if the Secretary of State were to recommend to Her Majesty that this honour [knighthood] should be awarded to the Governor of even a small colony before he assumes office."[159] Furthermore, surprise would be expressed in the colony when the sovereign's birthday or the New Year honors lists were published and still no knighthood for the governor: "This gives rise to speculation and affords the opportunity to agitators to ascribe the withholding of the honour to Colonial Office dissatisfaction with the Governor's activities."

Two orders were particularly associated with the colonial service: the Order of St. Michael and St. George and the Most Excellent Order of the British Empire. The chancery of the former order, which goes back to 1818, was located in the colonial office. Designed for service to the crown overseas, in precedence it ranked between the two Indian orders—the Star of India and the Order of the Indian Empire. Promotion within an order was a frequent feature of a distinguished career. In the former the ranks were, in ascending order, companion (CMG), knight commander (KCMG), and knight grand cross (GCMG). The most common award to British colonial governors was the KCMG, whose holders are allotted a stall in the order's chapel in St. Paul's Cathedral. It was a mark of special distinction to be advanced to GCMG. Many a longtime official who got no further than colonial secretary or senior provincial commissioner ended up with a CMG. Among members of the service, inured to occasional exhibitions of pompous pride, these decorations were known—in an inflating order of *folie de grandeur*—as Call Me God, Kindly Call Me God, and God Calls Me God. The Most Excellent Order of the British Empire, founded in 1917, consists of member (MBE), officer (OBE), commander (CBE), knight commander (KBE), and knight grand cross (GBE). Though finite, the order was much larger than that of St. Michael and St. George. In 1924 the latter was limited to 100 GCMGs—of which 30 were assignable for services rendered abroad—300 KCMGs, and 725 CMGs. Whereas it was very unusual—but not unknown—for a colonial service officer under the rank of colonial secretary or its comparable grade in the provincial administration to be awarded the CMG, outstanding senior district commissioners were sometimes the recipient of the OBE and high-flying district officers might be awarded an MBE.

There were two other styles of knighthood bestowed on governors. Among them, the knight bachelor (Kt) was generally looked on as the least prestigious of the four knighthoods that could be awarded. Whereas all these orders were awarded by the sovereign on the recommendation of the governor (other, of course, than his own honors) made through the secretary of state for the colonies, the Royal Victorial Order is in the sovereign's personal gift. Awards like GCVO, KCVO, CVO, and MVO are therefore indicative of recognition for a personal service rendered to the royal family. In the colonial context, the KCVO was often bestowed on the governor for having been the queen's host at Government House during the course of a royal visit to the colony. It was possible for a governor to be awarded more than one knighthood, especially when one of them was a KCVO.

The Governor's Wife. For all her exalted position as the first lady, not even the governor's wife might forget in public who her husband was. Sir Gordon Guggisberg hissed furiously at his wife, the actress Decima Moore, when—with the stage in her blood and the spotlight in her heart—she stepped forward before him to curtsy to the Princess Marie Louise. He had physically to pull her back before bowing himself. Other governors' wives have been known to fly the pennant on the Government House car when out shopping without His Excellency being in the car. Protocol could go to the head of some first ladies. Margery Perham found Lady Rodwell extremely frightening and rather odd, "a bundle of nerves" and "intimidating," and could compare Lady Maxwell only with "a large splendid cabbage rose just tumbling over its prime."[160] Another such lady—but the wife of the officer administering the government—insisted that the aide-de-camp draw up a table plan even when there were just six people for dinner at Government House. When K. G. Bradley was administering officer of another colony, his wife confessed she felt like a Victorian wax posy under a glass dome.[161] The quip that governors' wives were either actresses, aristocrats, or Americans would have added truth to it if one were to extend the classification to Caledonian, couthie, or slightly crazy. On occasion one met with a confusing, tutti frutti combination of all these ingredients.

But ideally—and frequently—the governor and his lady were a real, hard-working team. Lady Clifford directed a magnificent *tableau vivant* on the Gold Coast in 1918; Lady Dundas and Lady Coryndon typified many other governors' wives by their tireless charitable activities; Lady Twining was a qualified doctor. Lady Guggisberg was one of the "actress" governors' wives; Lady Grantham and Lady Bede Clifford were among the "American" governors' wives; whereas Lady Robertson was one of the warmhearted, motherly types who never forgot her supreme role as the ideal wife of the beau ideal district commissioner. Aides-de-camp and private secretaries were more often than not looked on with genuine affection by the governor and his wife as part of the family. Just now and then, as Leo Amery once observed from his long and intimate experience of colonial governors, he would have liked the secretary of state to be granted special papal powers so as to divorce Governor A from his lady and marry her to Governor B, thereby forming the best colonial team for the best colonial occasions.[162]

Conclusion

Such being the facts of the man and his office, the case studies in the following chapters can be no more than samples of the British colonial governor in action. They must be taken as illustrative rather than exhaustive. Two of the governors selected by the editors, Lugard and Clifford, rank among the half dozen most distinguished and experienced governors of sixty years of the British administrative presence in Africa. The third, Coryndon, was resident commissioner of two of the three high commission territories in turn and then went on to become governor of two out of the three East African territories, all within the space of twenty years. The fourth, Sir Andrew Cohen, for ten years a key figure in the colonial office before moving to a governorship, is better known for his role in decolonization than in actual governance.

The five essays on British proconsuls do more than constitute a contribution toward filling in the real lacunae in our knowledge of the British colonial governor. They may well, in their turn, arouse more interest from imperial historians and so generate further study of the whole story of the British colonial service. Set alongside the few—all too few—biographical studies that we now have of British colonial governors in Africa like those of Guggisberg, Johnston, and Twining and monographs such as those on Cameron and Mitchell, as well as the somewhat better served genre of autobiographical memoirs (all of which have been happily drawn on in the writing of this chapter), the total literature on the British colonial governors still does no more than reflect the mixed feelings of the organizers of many a charitable institution: grateful for the little they have, they would still welcome much, much more.

As the high noon of imperialism recedes, a younger generation of scholars and informed readers has begun to realize that in talking of British colonial governors they are dealing with a breed that is rapidly approaching extinction. In place of living cheek by jowl with a colonial service—a situation that, to judge from the paucity of critical literature on the men who served abroad, confirms the proverbial conclusion of familiarity breeding contempt or at least indifference—today the rarity of the colonial service career and the dwindling numbers of those whom Robert Heussler has neatly labeled "yesterday's rulers" are giving rise to a renewed interest in who they were, what they did, and why they did it; the balancing proverb, perhaps, of absence making the mind if not the heart grow fonder.

The Indian civil service has been fortunate in its memorialist, and Philip Wood-ruff's work has a niche all of its own in the annals of those who by profession helped to make imperial history. The Indian political service has recently had its story told by Terence Craig Coen, and the history of the Malayan civil service is presently in hand. On the French colonial service, a fine start has been made by William Cohen. But for all the sterling attempts by Heussler and Jeffries, Bertram and Furse, the history of the British colonial service remains not so much in arrears as in default.

Meanwhile, if a start is to be made, there is no better place to start than at the top. For if the British colonial governor has today virtually left the stage, his audiences have not yet forgotten his performance. There can be few better ways to take leave of the governor than by recalling the once familiar scene of pomp and circumstance that used ritually to mark a colony's farewell to the governor as he set sail for home and retirement.

I opened this chapter with Sir Donald Cameron's final departure from Dar es Salaam in 1935. I close it with Sir James Robertson leaving Lagos in 1960. The sunlit marina was crowded with thousands of spectators, waving and cheering excitedly as the governor-general, magnificent in his full-dress uniform, drove down to the lagoon and boarded the launch to transport him across the harbor. On the quayside the band was playing and an immaculate guard of honor was mounted. Final inspection; salutes and handshakes; the last goodbyes, thank yous, good wishes for the future; slowly up the gangplank. The ship pulls away almost imperceptibly from the quay, Standing to attention along the mole, the buglers play the nostalgic "Hausa Farewell." As the great liner moves gracefully into the open sea the strains of the massed bands on the quayside can just be heard, rendering the traditional tune with which for sixty years the colony had bid farewell to the departing governor, "Will ye no' come back again?"[163]

Whereupon Sir James turned to his wife and, with that characteristic twinkle in his eyes that had calmed so many moments of political passion, whispered to her, "They'd be upset if we did!"

Notes

1. Sir Donald Cameron, *My Tanganyika Service and Some Nigeria* (London, 1939), pp. 289–290.

2. *London Times*, 12 May 1950.

3. Henry L. Hall, *The Colonial Office: A History*, Royal Empire Society Imperial Studies Series, no. 13 (London, 1937), p. 87.

4. Margery Perham, *African Apprenticeship* (London, 1937), p. 232.

5. For a detailed examination of the biographical data on some 200 governors see Anthony H. M. Kirk-Greene, *A Biographical Dictionary of the British Colonial Governor in Africa* (Stanford, in press).

6. Idem, "Reflections on a Putative History of the Colonial Administrative Service," *Journal of Administration Overseas* 14 (January 1975):39–44.

7. The Sudan had a monopoly on this rank in the African context; but officials who elsewhere might have been recognized as provincial commissioners or residents were in the Sudan dignified with the title of governors of provinces.

8. Mauritius Legislative Council Sessional Paper No. 9 of 1952; secretary of state's dispatch 21106 CR, no. 59, dated 1 March 1952.

9. Sir Alexander Grantham, governor of Hong Kong 1947–1957, enjoyed three extensions. But among African governors the lore ran that the Chinese were so courteous that a governor whose appointment they did not ask to be extended must have been a disaster indeed.

10. Quoted in Sir Michael Blundell, *So Rough a Wind* (London, 1964), p. 97.

11. Quoted in Darrell Bates, *A Gust of Plumes* (London, 1972), p. 130.

12. Sir Alexander Grantham, *Via Ports* (Hong Kong, 1965), p. 67.

13. Sir Charles Jeffries, *Whitehall and the Colonial Service* (London, 1972), p. 41; see also Sir Bede Clifford, *Proconsul* (London, 1964), p. 183.

14. However, it must not be overlooked that in accepting this transfer Clifford was returning to Malaya, his first colony and the one he had loved and written about. It was a privilege denied to another great "Malayan," Sir Arthur Richards. Interview, 22 February 1969, Oxford Colonial Records Project (hereinafter cited O.C.R.P.), Rhodes House Library, Oxford University.

15. The legislation is contained in the periodic issuance of orders made under the Pensions (Governors of Dominions, etc.) Act of 1911. I am grateful to the archivist of the Foreign and Commonwealth Office for assistance in tracing the different regulations.

16. In brief, the difference in title of the senior executive officer may be said to be that in a colony he was known as colonial secretary and in a protectorate as chief secretary.

17. Not that a private income necessarily insured a peaceful administration. In the Bahamas, His Excellency the Honourable Bede Clifford followed up his legislators' agreement to turn the island into a tax-free haven and tourist attraction by himself purchasing a hotel, a beach, and a golf course, which he then proceeded to sell to his own Bahaman government. Clifford, *Proconsul*, pp. 196–197.

18. Dispatch dated 15 February 1907, quoted in Sir Charles Bruce, *The Broad Stone of Empire*, 2 vols. (London, 1910), 1:213. In addition to the Pensions (Governors of Dominions, etc.) Act of 1911 and its subsequent amending legislation (e.g., in 1929, 1935, 1936, 1948, 1949, 1959, and 1964), the debate in the House of Commons on June 29, 1956, and in the House of Lords on July 23 in connection with further amending legislation is of prime importance. See also *Colonial Governors Pensions*, (Parliamentary Command Paper) Cmd. 3059 (London, 1928); Sir Kenneth Roberts-Wray, *Commonwealth and Colonial Law* (London, 1966), pp. 314–316.

19. R. E. Wraith, *Guggisberg* (London, 1967), p. 297.

20. Ibid., pp. 329, 336. When H. H. Johnston died in 1927, a quarter of a century after his retirement, his pension was a scant £500 a year. The foreign office treated Sir Francis Wingate in almost as cavalier a manner; after seventeen years as governor-general of the Sudan, they offered him a pension of £600 annually.

21. Sir Alan Burns, *Colonial Civil Servant* (London, 1949), p. 10. Cf. Sir Charles Jeffries, *Partners for Progress: The Men and Women of the Colonial Service* (London, 1949), p. 110. Christopher Fyfe has much interesting information on a governor's emoluments in *A History of Sierra Leone* (Oxford, 1962).

22. Rita Hinden, *Downing Street and the Colonies* (London, 1942), p. 22.

23. Quoted in Bates, *A Gust of Plumes*, pp. 228–229.

24. Sir G. William des Voeux, *My Colonial Service*, 2 vols. (London, 1903), 1: ix.

25. Laura Boyle, *Diary of a Colonial Officer's Wife* (Oxford, 1968), pp. 134–135. For further advice on how a district officer's wife should and should not entertain the governor on tour see Emily Bradley, *Dearest Priscilla* (London, 1950), pp. 136–138.

26, Grantham, *Via Ports*, p. 125.

27. Sir Geoffrey Archer, *Personal and Historical Memoirs of an East African Administrator* (Edinburgh, 1963).

28. Quoted in Roy Lewis and Yvonne Foy, *The British in Africa* (London, 1971), p. 137.

29. Constance Larymore, *A Resident's Wife in Nigeria* (London, 1908), p. 65.

30. *Report by Sir F. D. Lugard on the Amalgamation of Northern and Southern Nigeria and Administration, 1912–1919*, Cmd. 468 (London, 1920), paras. 62–66.

31. Quoted in Ellen Thorp, *Ladder of Bones* (London, 1956), p. 65.

32. Perham, *African Apprenticeship*, p. 235.

33. Lord Chandos (Oliver Lyttelton), *An Unexpected View from the Summit* (London, 1962), p. 362.

34. Ibid., p. 382.

35. Grantham, *Via Ports*, p. 122.

36. G. H. Mungeam, *British Rule in Kenya, 1895–1912* (Oxford, 1966), p. 117.

37. Sir Harry Luke, *Cities and Men*, 3 vols. (London, 1953), 1:192. Dr. Ivan Lloyd Phillips recounts Sir John Macpherson's story of how, when Sir Harold Macmichael eventually returned his private secretary to district administration after many years in Government House, the secretary was referred to in the service as being released "to do some ditching and hedging." In a well-known Nigerian case, the governor was heard to complain that his main trouble on tour was getting his private secretary to the railway station on time.

38. Wraith, *Guggisberg*, pp. 244, 306. Comparable problems of potential ranking were amusingly contemplated among the bursars of Oxford and Cambridge colleges during the 1960s, when senior officers from the armed forces distinguished many a common room.

39. Quoted in Bates, *A Gust of Plumes*, p. 205.

40. Kweli, "Borrowed Plumes," *Corona* 8 (September 1956):359–360.

41. Perham, *African Apprenticeship*, p. 235.

42. Chandos, *An Unexpected View*, p. 349. For Perham, the perfect aide-de-camp was "spruce, kind, soothing, and self-effacing to the end" (*African Apprenticeship*, p. 241). The obverse portrait is seen in one of the stories submitted for Lady Clifford's essay competition in aid of the Red Cross at Accra in 1918; it was meaningfully entitled "A Happy Day at Government House, by the ADC."

43. *Colonial Regulations*, Col. No. 270–2 (1951), part 2, no. 105.

44. Paul Reinsch, *Colonial Government: An Introduction to the Study of Colonial Institutions* (New York, 1916), p. 167 (italics in original).

45. Jeffries, *Partners for Progress*, p. 108.

46. Without entering into the juridical classification of the British colonial empire, "colonies" may be said to have been dependencies that had been annexed by the crown whereas "protectorates" were territories in which the crown had acquired control of foreign relations and defense. In the first, the inhabitants were British subjects; in the second, British protected persons. For a detailed discussion see Martin Wight, *British Colonial Constitutions* (Oxford, 1952), pp. 5–14; Roberts-Wray, *Commonwealth and Colonial Law*.

47. "It was shortly afterwards that, having intimated that I did not wish to be considered for the vacant post of Governor of Trinidad, I was asked whether I would cut short my leave and go to British Guiana" (Sir Kenneth Blackburne, *Lasting Legacy* [London, 1976], p. 153). "Grateful your opinion before I consult Palace" ran the telegram from the secretary of state to another governor seeking his views on the promotion of a member of his staff. See also the correspondence in Archer, *Personal and Historical Memoirs*, p. 158.

48. John Hilary Smith, letter to the author, 2 April 1975; Sir Harry Luke, *From a South Seas Diary* (London, 1945), entry for 26 July 1938.

49. Quoted from an address given by Sir John Shuckburgh to the Oxford University Summer School on Colonial Administration, 1937. However, a more recent royal commission appoints "the said XYZ to be Our Governor of ABC during Our pleasure, with all the powers, rights, privileges and advantages to the said Office belonging or appertaining," Although the commission is issued to the governor personally, it has to be published in the *London Gazette*.

50. Quoted in Jeffries, *Partners for Progress*, p. 64; see also J. C. Beaglehole, "The Royal Instructions to Colonial Governors, 1783–1854" (Ph.D. dissertation, University of London, 1929).

51. G. V. Fiddes, *The Dominions and Colonial Offices* (London, 1926), p. 49.

52. Bruce, *The Broad Stone*, p. 225.

53. Sir Philip Mitchell, *African Afterthoughts* (London, 1954), p. 115.

54. Cameron, *My Tanganyika Service*, p. 20.

55. Sir Anton Bertram, *The Colonial Service* (Cambridge, 1930), p. 25.

56. See Burns, *Colonial Civil Servant*, pp. 219 ff.

57. Sir Stewart Symes, *Tour of Duty* (London, 1946), pp. 153–160. On the transatlantic myth that all colonial governors had to be over six feet tall see Margaret Laurence, *The Prophet's Camel Bell* (Toronto, 1963), pp. 204, 208.

58. Sir Charles Dundas, *African Crossroads* (London, 1955), p. 16.

59. Sir James Robertson, *Transition in Africa* (London, 1974), p. 236.

60. Interview with Sir Dennis Wright, Oxford, 19 November 1974; interview with Sir Charles Johnston, London, 17 November 1975.

61. Sir Hesketh H. Bell, *Glimpses of a Governor's Life* (London, 1946), p. 123.

62. J. M. Lee, *Colonial Development and Good Government* (Oxford, 1967), pp. 1–2.

63. Lord Lugard, *The Dual Mandate in British Tropical Africa* (Edinburgh, 1922), p. 158 n.

64. Sir Charles Jeffries, *Transfer of Power* (London, 1960), p. 35.

65. I am grateful to Ronald E. Robinson, Beit Professor of Commonwealth History in the University of Oxford, for this information, taken from his forthcoming biography of Sir Andrew Cohen.

66. Colonial Office (hereinafter cited C.O.) Misc. 416 (confidential), 1927, meeting of 10 May.

67. Harold Macmillan, *Riding the Storm* (London, 1971), pp. 734–736; see also Anthony Eden, *Full Circle* (London, 1960), p. 402.

68. Minute by A. Freeston, 23 February 1939; C.O. 847/13/47100. I am grateful to Dr. Curtis Nordman for this reference from "Prelude to Decolonization in Africa: The Development of British Colonial Policy, 1938–1947 (Ph.D. dissertation, Oxford University 1976).

69. Robert Heussler, letter to the author, 12 February 1975. Cf. Sir Ralph Furse, *Aucuparius* (London, 1962), p. 227.

70. Blundell, *So Rough a Wind*, p. 293.

71. This is the view of David Goldsworthy, *Colonial Issues in British Politics, 1945–1961* (Oxford, 1971), p. 52. It is denied, however, by Cohen's biographer, Ronald E. Robinson (personal information).

72. "So you thought I was going to reply to the Treasury despatch by a minute, did you?" asked H. H. Johnston. "Why, I never reply to anything in less than two volumes octavo!" (quoted in Roland Oliver, *Sir Harry Johnston and the Scramble for Africa* [London, 1957], p. 197).

73. Bertram, *Colonial Service*, p. 27.

74. Lee, *Colonial Development*, p. 11. The Creech Jones papers are now in the Rhodes House Library, Oxford.

75. Address to Corona Club, London, June 1921.

76. Quoted in Bruce, *The Broad Stone*, p. 222.

77. Sir Cosmo Parkinson, *The Colonial Office from Within* (London, 1947), p. 136.

78. Grantham, *Via Ports*, p. 175.

79. Cf. Hugo Williams's poem "Beachcombers," from *Some Sweet Day* (London, 1975):
    The same train each night
    Enters the same station a little late
    And different passengers going home
    Look up from different books with a start
    Their eyes narrowing back into a world
    Hardly more shared
    As they rake the length of the platform
    For something they should find there
    The thread of their lives
    Difficult to recognise in the gloom.

80. For a fuller discussion see Martin Wight, *The Development of the Legislative Council, 1606–1945* (London, 1946); H. V. Wiseman, *The Cabinet in the Commonwealth* (London, 1958), part 2.

81. See Cmd. 2884, 1927, Appendix 7.

82. Sir Ronald Storrs, *Orientations* (New York, 1937), p. 533.

83. Sir Charles Johnston, *The View from Steamer Point* (London, 1964), p. 178.

84. Green pencil was restricted to the audit department. The premier of Northern Nigeria, searching for a distinctive medium in which to match the gubernatorial red ink, effectively institutionalized the use of green ink.

85. Cameron, *My Tanganyika Service*, p. 142. Cf. Harry A. Gailey, *Sir Donald Cameron: Colonial Governor* (Stanford, 1974), pp. 25–27.

86. Sir Donald Cameron, Sir Shenton Thomas, Sir Selwyn Grier, Sir Douglas Jardine, Sir Henry Moore, and Sir Alan Burns.

87. See Mitchell, *African Afterthoughts*, p. 125. For a glorification of the secretariat-*wallah* see the poem by C. W. Welman in Lady Clifford, *Our Days on the Gold Coast* (London, 1919), with its paeon of:

    Fill, fill my inkpot to the brim,
    Put nib into my pen,
    And I will vault into my chair
    To bandy words with men.
    The warrior's joy is famed in song,
    What of the penman's glee,
    Why through the Secretariat
    Swops phrases with H.E.!

    In a similarly light vein see Anthony H. M. Kirk-Greene, "Just a Minute," *Corona* 9 (May 1957):185–188.

88. Interestingly enough, Lugard, for all his admiration of the field service, never was a district officer. The general opinion in the service was expressed by a non-colonial service governor in these words: "Nobody can really know about the Colonial Service unless he has sweated all the way up the ladder; unless, in particular, he has been a District Commissioner or the equivalent, and has thus acquired that 'D.C. outlook' which is like the Ark of the Covenant or the corporate essence of the Service" (Johnston, *The View from Steamer Point*, p. 191). The debate is likely to be revived as the colonial administrative service is subjected to posthumous scrutiny.

89. See, for instance, G. B. Masefield, *A History of the Colonial Agricultural Service* (Oxford, 1972), pp. 144 ff.

90. See *Nigerian Gazette*, 21 November 1920.

91. See Cmd. 2883, 1927.

92. J. J. White, "The Development of Central Administration in Nigeria, 1914–1935" (Ph.D. dissertation, Ibadan University, 1970).

93. John Smith, *Colonial Cadet in Nigeria* (Durham, 1968), pp. 6–7.

94. This paragraph is based on personal experiences. A rich example of how the young administrator looked—both askance and in admiration—at a succession of governors is to be found in Robin Short, *African Sunset* (London, 1973). Compare another district officer's description of a governor of Nigeria under whom he served as "not a Governor who gave you the impression he was pleased to see you. Men trod warily when Old Sinister was around" (Ian Brook, *The One-eyed Man Is King* [London, 1966], p. 150).

95. See Sir Frederick Pedler, *The Lion and the Unicorn* (London, 1974), pp. 187–189.

96. Cf. John Lonsdale's cryptic portrait of one of his successors—"In Grigg, the settlers had not so much a governor as a trumpeter"—in a paper presented to the conference on "The Political Economy of Kenya," Trinity College, Cambridge, June 1975, quoted here with the author's permission.

97. David C. Mulford, *Zambia: The Politics of Independence, 1957–1964* (London, 1967), p. 153.

98. Mitchell, *African Afterthoughts*, p. 213.

99. Carl G. Rosberg and John Nottingham, *The Myth of Mau Mau* (Stanford, 1966), chap. 4.

100. For these statistics, taken from "The Dinner Book, Government House, Lagos" (NNA, Ibadan, CSO 2/17, 1899–1907), I wish to express my gratitude to Dr. Kristin Mann, who drew my attention to this source. For an illuminating account of dinner parties at Government House in Lagos a

generation earlier see John Whitford, *Trading Life in Western and Central Africa*, 2d ed. (London, 1967), pp. 95–96.

101. Kenneth Kaunda, *Zambia Shall Be Free* (London, 1962), Awolowo, *Awo* (Cambridge, 1960), Kwame Nkrumah, *Ghana* (Edinburgh, 1957), and Sir Ahmado Bello, *My Life* (Cambridge, 1962), are specimens of that important but so far rare genre, the African politician's autobiography, which we need to complete the portrait of any latter-day colonial governor.

102. Nkrumah, *Ghana*, p. 136.

103. Judith Listowel, *The Making of Tanganyika* (London, 1965), p. 334; this wording should be compared with Nyerere's version, cited in ibid., p. 424.

104. Richard Hall, *Kaunda: Founder of Zambia* (London, 1964), p. 36.

105. Proceedings of the Nigerian Council, 29 December 1920.

106. Rosberg and Nottingham, *Myth of Mau Mau*, p. 318.

107. R. N. Posnett, "Debasien Gubernatoris," *Corona* 9 (October 1957): 390–392.

108. See, e.g., Anthony H. M. Kirk-Greene, "A Galaxy of Governors," in *West Africa* (24 November 1975), pp. 1405–1407; and *West Africa* (1 December 1975), p. 1443; Bates, *A Gust of Plumes*, pp. 198–199; and I. F. Nicolson and Colin A. Hughes, "A Provenance of Proconsuls: British Colonial Governors," in *Journal of Imperial and Commonwealth History*, vol. 55, no. 1, October 1975, pp. 77–106.

109. Cmd. 3628, 1930, p. 13. This remark of Sir Edward Stubbs (Jamaica) was capped by Sir William Gowers' (Uganda) observing: "It also contains shy, retiring and insignificant animals."

110. Sir Charles Jeffries, "Excellencies excluded," *Corona* 9 (July 1957):277–278.

111. Lee, *Colonial Development*, p. 55. It has been suggested that Macmillan called a special meeting of African governors and senior colonial office officials to secure their backing before embarking on his famous "wind of change" tour of Africa in 1960, but this has been denied by Sir Richard Turnbull (interview, Henley-on-Thames, 29 August 1975). A conference of East African governors did, however, take place at Chequers in 1959. With pardonable exaggeration, Colin Cross has defined the niggling supervision over finance: "A Governor with powers of life and death might have to get permission from London to buy a bicycle for a court messenger" (*The Fall of the British Empire* [London, 1968], p. 143).

112. See Cmd. 9768, 1956 on Her Majesty's Oversea Civil Service. See also Jeffries, *The Colonial Service*, 1969.

113. See *London Times*, 7 March 1975, p. 14.

114. Cf. Dundas, *African Crossroads*, p. 197.

115. Bates, *A Gust of Plumes*, p. 222.

116. Interview with Sir James Robertson, Cholsey, 17 November 1967.

117. Letter to the author, 10 March 1975.

118. Blackburne, *Lasting Legacy*, pp. 130–131. Later he was to comment: "Despite popular belief in the colonies that Governors were just 'lackeys of the Colonial Office,' I had been given no instructions and very little advice" (ibid., p. 140).

119. Lugard, *Dual Mandate*, p. 124.

120. Lord Hailey, *An African Survey* (London, 1938), p. 160.

121. Bates, *A Gust of Plumes*, p. 230; see also Jeffries, *Partners for Progress*, pp. 110–111,

122. Robertson, *Transition in Africa*, pp. 183–186; for the reverse side of gubernatorial tours see the splendid anecdotes in such district commissioner memoirs as Charles Chenevix Trench, *The Desert's Dusty Face* (Edinburgh, 1964), and Harry Franklin, *Flagwagger* (London, 1974).

123. This conclusion is based on interviews conducted with former colonial service officers when I was research officer of the Oxford Colonial Records Project (1962–1972), directed by J. J. Tawney. See J. J. Tawney, "The Oxford Colonial Records Project," *African Affairs* 67 (October 1968):345–350. O.C.R.P. transcripts are in the Rhodes House Library, Oxford, but not all the interviews are yet open to readers. For a checklist see Louis B. Frewer, *Manuscript Collections of Africana in Rhodes House Library, Oxford* (1968), and *Supplement* (1971).

124. Quoted in Wraith, *Guggisberg*, p. 245.

125. Mitchell, *African Afterthoughts*, p. 180.

126. Fay Carter, in Kenneth King and Ahmed Salim, eds., *Kenya Historical Biographies* (Nairobi, 1971), p. 38.

127. Robertson, *Transition in Africa*, p. 251.

128. R. B. Joyce, *Sir William MacGregor* (Melbourne, 1971), p. 299.

129. Archer, *Personal and Historical Memoirs*, p. 257.

130. Bates, *A Gust of Plumes*, p. 271.

131. Quoted in W. R. Crocker, *Nigeria: A Critique of British Colonial Administration* (London, 1936), p. 266.

132. Robert Collins, "The Sudan Political Service," *African Affairs* 71 (July 1972):293–303.

133. Hall, *Colonial Office*; Kenneth E. Robinson, *The Dilemmas of Trusteeship* (London, 1965); Cross, *Fall of the British Empire;* Lee, *Colonial Development;* John W. Cell, *British Colonial Administration in the Mid-Nineteenth Century* (New Haven, 1970); I. F. Nicolson and Colin A. Hughes, "A Provenance of Proconsuls: British Colonial Governors, 1900–1914," *Journal of Imperial and Commonwealth History* 4 vol. IV, no 1 (October 1975):77–106.

134. Hall, *Colonial Office*, p. 87.

135. Quoted in ibid., p. 88. A similar rise in standards can be seen in the recruitment of colonial office clerks from *c.* 1870; see Brian Blakeley, *The Colonial Office, 1868–1892* (Durham, 1972), pp. ix, 13 n.

136. An important study on the influence of the British public schools on recruitment for the colonial service is Robert Heussler, *Yesterday's Rulers* (New York, 1963).

137. One is reminded of Joseph Howe's strictures on colonial governors appointed from the armed forces, "rulers snatched from the tented field or quarter-deck," and his insistence that they henceforth be "men to whom the British Constitution does not appear a prurient excrescence . . . and possessing great command of temper" (J. A. Chisholm, ed., *Speeches and Public Letters of Joseph Howe*, 3 vols. [Halifax, 1909], 1:619).

138. Lord Altrincham, *Kenya's Opportunity* (London, 1960), p. 56.

139. Collins, "Sudan Political Service," p. 301, calculates that one-third of the 400 men who joined the Sudan political service were the sons of clergymen. Cf. Anthony H. M. Kirk-Greene, "More Memoirs as a Source for a Service History," *Journal of Administration Overseas* 15 (October 1976):235–240.

140. Graham Greene, "The Lines on the Palm," *London Daily Telegraph Magazine*, no. 101 (19 November 1974), pp. 53–56.

141. Out of these, three former colonial office officials merit a special mention of thanks: Sir John Martin, Ambler Thomas, and W. A. C. Mathieson. Among the many former governors who have given generously of their time in interview and letter in collection with this essay, a particular debt of gratitude is due Sir Richard Turnbull for having read the whole chapter in draft and saved its author from several pitfalls.

142. Cf. letter to the author from Sir Miles Clifford, 24 January 1975. In being appointed to take over the administration of Somaliland in 1913, Archer, still a district commissioner himself, was promoted over the heads of six provincial commissioners and thirty-two other district commissioners on the same grade as he.

143. This was the document so castigated by Crocker; see idem, *Nigeria*, pp. 244 ff. There is an informed discussion of what happened to these reports in the colonial office and of the famous card index in Blackburne, *Lasting Legacy*, pp. 45–47.

144. Parkinson, *The Colonial Office*, p. 44.

145. Cf. Hailey, *African Survey*, p. 225: "Governors and Colonial Secretaries are not normally appointed to the territory in which they have done most of their service."

146. Letter to the author, 17 February 1975.

147. For this information I am grateful to the late Dr. Anthony Sillery.

149. Letter to the author, 7 June 1975.

149. Mitchell, *African Afterthoughts*, p. 189.

150. Interview, Lord Boyd, Oxford, 12 December 1974. Cf. R. B. Pugh, "The Colonial Office, 1801–1925," in *The Cambridge History of the British Empire*, 8 vols. (Cambridge, 1959), 3:728, where he observes how the appointment of a colonial governor was such "an act of high policy" that the prime minister, if not the whole cabinet, had to be consulted.

151. Letter to the author, 23 January 1975; see also Queen Mary's firm directive to Sir Edward Grigg when he was appointed governor of Kenya, in Lord Altrincham, *Kenya's Opportunity* (London, 1960), p. 74.

152. Report of a committee on the system of appointment in the colonial office and the colonial service, Cmd. 3554, 1930, p. 31. This was called "the Magna Carta of the modern Colonial Service" by Sir Charles Jeffries, *The Colonial Empire and Its Civil Service* (Cambridge, 1938), p. 55.

153. Jeffries, *Partners in Progress*, p. 107.

154. The colonial service seemed less pleased with an earlier appointment from the Sudan, that of Sir Harold MacMichael, one of the greatest Sudanese officials, to the governorship of Tanganyika in 1934. However, some have seen this as an evening of the score after the way the Sudanese service forced the resignation of one of the most rapidly promoted colonial service governors, Sir Geoffrey Archer. For a perspective on the qualified success of transferring Indian civil service officials to colonial governorships see L. S. S. O'Malley, *The Indian Civil Service, 1601–1930* (London, 1931), pp. 259 ff.

155. Quoted in Cell, *British Colonial Administration*, p. 45.

156. Quoted in Hall, *Colonial Office*, p. 91.

157. Rt. Hon. Malcolm MacDonald, letter to the author, 1 September 1975.

158. Quoted in G. F. Sayers, "What's in a Name?" *Corona* 5 (November 1953):423–424.

159. Burns, *Colonial Civil Servant*, pp. 147–148.

160. Perham, *African Apprenticeship*, pp. 248, 235.

161. K. G. Bradley, *Once a District Officer* (New York, 1966), p. 155.

162. L. S. Amery, *My Political Life*, 3 vols. (London, 1953), 2:370.

163. See Robertson, *Transition in Africa*, p. 244.

Sir Hugh Clifford (1866-1941)

Harry A. Gailey

HUGH Clifford was one of the most unusual colonial governors in British history. He was distinguished as a writer and a novelist. He derived from an ancient aristocratic lineage. He was a Catholic, one of the few Catholics to attain gubernatorial rank in the colonies. Hugh Clifford was born in London on March 5, 1866, the eldest son of Colonel, the Honorable Henry Clifford and a nephew of the seventh Baron Clifford of Chudleigh in Devon. The Cliffords were among the leading Catholic families in England, tracing their holdings to the time of Henry II. The first Baron Clifford of Chudleigh, a principal secretary of state and lord treasurer to Charles II, had given his initial "C" to the ministers of the king known as the Cabal. The punitive acts directed at Catholics in the late seventeenth and eighteenth centuries limited the services the Cliffords could render the crown. There were, nevertheless, a number of Cliffords who served the armed forces and the church in the nineteenth century. One of Hugh Clifford's uncles became bishop of Clifton, and his father, Henry Clifford, had an outstanding military career serving in South Africa, the Crimean war, and the opium wars in China. Henry Clifford won the Victoria Cross in the Crimea for gallantry at the battle of Inkerman. His skill at painting and drawing enabled him to make a number of sketches of the battlefields of the Crimean war, which were later published and brought a brief period of fame to their creator. During Hugh's boyhood, his father was on staff duty in England and was ultimately promoted to major general and was made a knight commander of the Order of St. Michael and St. George (KCMG).

Josephine, Hugh Clifford's mother, was the only daughter of Joseph Anstice, who had been a brilliant student at Oxford and later a promising young professor of classical literature at King's College. He died at the age of twenty-eight, at the very beginning of his career. In her youth, Josephine had literary aspirations and had contributed some of her work to London periodicals. Thus, not only was Hugh Clifford's early life comfortable, but his parents had exposed him to the world of literature and art to an unusual degree. The love of letters he acquired later sustained him through many lonely months in Malaya and served him well when he decided to write of his own experiences.

Hugh Clifford's childhood was spent to a large extent in the manor houses belonging to the family or to friends in Devon and Somerset. He was not educated at a public school but at Woburn Park, a private Catholic school run by a priest, Lord Petrie, who was a peer and friend of the family. Clifford's education, although scant in terms of time spent in school, appears to have been more than adequate since in 1883, at the age of seventeen, he passed the entrance examination for Sandhurst. His command of the English language as evidenced by hundreds of lengthy, well-phrased official dispatches and by his many stories and novels was far beyond that of most of his contemporaries in the colonial service. Perhaps the major factor in Clifford's success as an officer in Malaya was his knowledge of the extremely difficult Malay language, which he acquired in much less time than did most other Europeans. Those who worked closely with Clifford and later left accounts of their association always stressed his intelligence, grasp of detail, and understanding of the broad, general principles underlying certain policies. The young man who arrived in Malaya in the fall of 1883 had qualities that would have assured his success in almost any field.[1]

Southeast Asia and the West Indies

No one knows for sure why Clifford did not take advantage of his Sandhurst connections and enter the military. Perhaps he had merely bowed to his father, who might naturally have wanted his son to follow in the parental footsteps. His father, however, died in April 1883, and Hugh Clifford decided to embark upon a different career. Colonial service was an acceptable alternative. Hugh Clifford was a man of his time and his class. He shared the convictions of superiority and the cultural optimism that animated much of the middle and upper classes of nineteenth-century England. In many families such as his, there was a long tradition of service; this was bolstered by the conviction that it was a duty to bring the blessings of English civilization to warring, backward peoples throughout the world. Clifford must have felt deeply the need to serve the empire in some tangible way and probably rejected the military because he was already assured a position in the colonial service. His father's cousin, Sir Frederick Weld, had been appointed governor of the Straits Settlements in 1880 and was concerned with speeding up the processes by which the British could control the independent actions of the Malayan rulers.[2] Empowered to employ a number of cadets for his administration, he asked Hugh's mother whether any of her sons would be interested. In this manner Hugh Clifford received his appointment in the Malayan service. On his arrival in September 1883, Clifford was posted immediately to Perak, the first of the Malay states designated a protectorate. He was fortunate in this assignment since his superior in Perak was Sir Hugh Low, one of the best of the early British administrators in Malaya.

Clifford came to Malaya just when the fifty-year-old British policy against territorial acquisition was beginning to change. The same forces that impelled Britain to carve out a dependent empire in Africa and the South Pacific were at work also in Malaya. Foreign powers, especially France, Germany, and the United States, were challenging Britain for manufacturing and trading supremacy throughout the world. Markets that previously had been considered British spheres were being closed to British traders because of the territorial expansion of other powers. Reluctantly the officials at Whitehall came to agree with their agents in the field that if any portion of a given area were to remain under British economic domination, the entire territory would have to come under British protection.

The French were particularly active in Southeast Asia in the latter nineteenth century. In 1884 they had secured protectorates over Cochin China, Tonkin, and Annam. Less than a decade later, with the declaration of a protectorate over Laos, France had secured all of the territories later known as French Indochina. Their agents were also active in Siam. Some British officials and entrepreneurs viewed these French activities throughout Southeast Asia with growing alarm. Eventually their concern forced a reluctant redefinition of British policy in Malaya.[3]

Economic reasons for expansion in Malaya were not as important as elsewhere since the bulk of exports from the states was already under British control and only tin mining was an important source of revenue for the states. Possession of these mines was not sufficient reason to propel Britain into direct intervention in the politics of the independent kingdoms. But the British had to contend, above all, with a unquiet frontier between the Straits Settlements and the states. Once they had decided to "pacify and civilize" Perak, they found they could not stop there but had to continue until the entire peninsula had been brought under control.

Initially British influence was exercised through residents. The first residents were gazetted to Perak and Selangor in November 1874. Their task was all but impossible. They were to make certain that the rajas ruled justly, did not overtax the people, or maltreat their subjects. They were not to precipitate conflict with the Malay rulers but were to make certain that the rajas and chiefs consulted them on major policies. Each resident had a small force of Sikhs and Pathans sufficient to overawe minor rulers but not to prevent the more important leaders from continuing their rule as before. Andrew Clark's successor, Sir William Jervois, insisted that the residents assume more direct control of central administration. Such a forward policy brought open conflict between the residents and the native rulers. The worst crisis developed in Perak. Resident James Birch was openly contemptuous of all things Malay, and enthusiastically favoring Jervois's policy he "dashed into Perak like a Victorian rationalist schoolmaster, confident that decision and firmness would soon remedy abuses."[4] He alienated all factions and was not even supported by Raja Abdullah, the creature of British administration. Birch's attempts at implementing Jervois's reforms of the resident system resulted in his murder. The British then mounted a major offensive against Perak. Those responsible for Birch's death were tried, sentenced, and executed.[5]

The colonial office, reacting to the Perak incidents, repudiated Jervois's policies and emphasized that the residents were sent to the Malay states to give advice, not to rule. Nevertheless, the campaign against Perak was the turning point in British intervention in the independent states. Whether the colonial office wished it or not, the British slowly became dominant and ruled the land through residents. The colonial office expected them to perform a variety of tasks without overcommitting Britain to expensive campaigns or support of a native regime. In the 1880s, the residential system became a compromise between the complete control of the government, as recommended by Jervois, and the mere giving of advice, as envisioned by the colonial office. Sir Frederick Weld understood the ambivalence of the residents' position better than the central government; he accordingly gave his full support to the residents in their attempts to reform the Malay states even though these actions deeply undercut traditional rule.[6] The residents, largely isolated from all but the most perfunctory interference from the central authorities by the country's hills and forests, came to be the real rulers of the states of western Malaya.[7]

One of the best of the Malayan residents was Clifford's superior, Sir Hugh Low, who became the resident in Perak in September 1877. He had spent over thirty years as an administrator in Sarawak and North Borneo, was a Malay scholar, a naturalist, an explorer, and he understood what was needed to establish good government in a Malay state. During his residence, Low led the state out of debt, created a budget surplus, and firmly established a British styled administrative and courts system. He associated the powerful lesser chiefs with the central administration, reformed the tax system, abolished the institution of debt slavery, and helped promote the cultivation of rubber in Perak.[8] Hugh Clifford thus served his apprenticeship with the most experienced resident in Malaya, a man who was concerned with changing Malay society for the better without trampling on its culture.

As Low's assistant, Clifford began to apply his considerable intelligence to the task of understanding Malay customs and laid the groundwork for his later linguistic accomplishment in the various Malay dialects. In January 1887, at an age when many of his contemporaries were still at a university, Clifford was entrusted with a most important mission to Pekan, the seat of government of Pahang. In the 1880s, the arrival of more Europeans in search of supposed riches in gold and tin had led Pahang's ruler, the Bendahara Ahmad, to grant huge mining concessions. Sir Frederick Weld was determined to exercise some type of control over Pahang and young Clifford was chosen as agent to secure a minimum of supervision over the state.

In Pekan Clifford was almost completely isolated from the outside world and thus he alone was responsible for representing the British position in the protracted negotiations. Two weeks before Weld retired as governor, his protégé finally managed to convince the raja of the good intentions of the British. Perhaps the Bendahara misread British power since the sole agent was a very young man who seemed to pose little threat to the raja's despotic rule. By an agreement signed on October 8, 1887, the ruler of Pahang agreed to allow a permanent British government agent with consular powers to reside at Pekan.[9] Clifford was confirmed in this position. He remained the only British official there until November 1888 and took a major part in the negotiations that subsequently compelled the raja to make further major political concessions to the British.[10]

Hugh Clifford was too young and perhaps too well known to the Raja to be appointed resident. Instead, he stayed on as the assistant to the new resident, John P. Rodger. Clifford, however, lost little by being passed over for an older officer. He soon went home on sick leave and did not return to Malaya until early 1891. By then the full realization of what the British system of residency meant had come to the great and petty rulers of Pahang. British agents interfered at all levels with decision making and were intent upon forcing the chiefs to accept British concepts of right and wrong, as well as administrative and legal systems alien to Pahang. The resultant friction caused what Clifford later called a "heart-breaking little war."[11] The rebels were gradually forced to abandon Pahang, retreating into the Trengganu and Kelantan. From there the rebel chiefs continued to raid into Pahang and thus created a further unstable frontier.[12] In 1894 the British invaded these areas, and Clifford again played a crucial role.

Clifford left two first-rate accounts of these events. One is his official report of the military action against the rebels; the other is part one of *Bush-Whacking and other Tales from Malaya*. Many of Clifford's early stories are fictionalized accounts of events or people he had observed. However, the first two segments of this book are straightforward records of Clifford's experiences in Pahang from 1891 to 1895. He is the political officer in each of the long, primarily factual accounts of the campaigns. In both actions Clifford distinguished himself. His knowledge of the Malay language, the geography, the customs of the people, and the habits of many of the rebellious rulers proved invaluable to the military and police officers, many of whom were in Malaya for the first time. His friend, fellow author, and first resident-general of Malaya, Sir Frank Swettenham, gave Clifford almost the entire credit for the success of the final move in the pacification of Pahang.[13] After 1894, Clifford found himself in charge of the day-to-day administration, a role in which he displayed considerable ability.

The year 1896 stood out as a landmark in Hugh Clifford's life. At the age of thirty he married. This marriage to Minna à Becket was apparently very happy; it ended after ten years with his wife's death in a tragic accident in Trinidad. The Cliffords had three children, two daughters, Mary and Monica, and a son, Hugh, who was killed on the western front in 1916. Clifford's feelings for his wife and the anguish of the typically long separations can be glimpsed in the romantic short story "Rachel," which he wrote in 1903.

In 1896, moreover, the colonial office finally decided to standardize the government of the Malay states. This move toward a closer union had been opposed by the high commissioner, Sir Charles Mitchell, on the ground that the interests of the Malay states and the colony were divergent and in some cases antagonistic. Eventually he was forced by the colonial office to put into effect a loosely constructed federal scheme.[14]

Clifford's task in Pahang was more difficult than that facing the other residents. Pahang was deficient in population, valuable exports, and transportation facilities. Even after the completion of the trunk road from Selangor to Pahang, the only mode of travel was bicycle or bullock cart. The journey from Singapore to Kuala Lipis, the administrative capital of Pahang, took a fortnight. Until the introduction of the automobile, Pahang was effectively cut off from the rest of Malaya. Nevertheless, Clifford, aided in part by the psychological effect of a *durbar* (a grand public levee) called in 1897, achieved internal reforms almost as significant as those of Hugh Low earlier in Perak. British concepts of administration and justice were readily accepted by the same chiefs who a few years before had been aggressively hostile. Malays of all levels learned to place their confidence in the government and cooperated in all matters that required their assistance.[15] The success in building a functioning bureaucracy in such a remote area must be attributed to a large degree to Clifford's administrative skills and his knowledge of and respect for Malay institutions.

In 1896 Clifford resolved also to write seriously of his experiences. No doubt he was influenced in this by the relative success of Sweetenham's *Malay Sketches*. Clifford's first attempts were so successful that he devoted more and more of his free time to prose. In the following two decades, he produced dozens of articles, many short story collections, some good novels, as well as a few nonfiction accounts and book reviews. His total literary output would occasion envy among many to whom writing is not an avocation but a career. Almost all of these stories have the Malay states as their locale and betray Clifford's love of the area and his profound respect for the people. Some of his short stories rank with the finest written in the early twentieth century. Such collections as *Bush-Whacking* and *The Further Side of Silence* gave Clifford an international literary reputation and brought him new friendships. He became a very close friend of Joseph Conrad and was known to most serious writers of the first two decades of this century. Writing became for Clifford not merely a pastime but a serious secondary vocation in which he became as successful as in his primary career.

In January 1900, presumably as a reward for his outstanding services, Clifford was offered the governorship of North Borneo. This office was considerably more circumscribed than that of a chief executive in charge of a normal colony. North Borneo fell within the jurisdiction of the high commissioner at Singapore, but practical rule of the territory was vested in the North Borneo Company. The company's policy after 1894 had been determined very largely by an ex-Borneo trader, William Cowie, who convinced the shareholders that larger dividends would result if the scope of the company's activities were increased. Clifford's predecessor was Leicester Beaufort, a lawyer with no administrative experience and unacquainted with Asia. For a time Beaufort appeared to be a perfect choice since he did not question the decisions made in London. He began two grandiose projects, a trunk road and telegraph line across the country and a railway to link Brunei bay and Cowie harbor. The subsequent infringement on native treaty rights and the increase in taxes combined to create a rebellion.

Clifford's new task was a hard one. He arrived just in time to keep the police commandant from shooting the captured survivors of the pacification campaign. Clifford supervised the collection of arms and destruction of fortifications. He appointed to high positions men he believed knowledgeable and tactful. He tried to placate the interior people by keeping coastal populations from moving into their areas. Before Clifford left North Borneo in 1901, most of the disaffected areas had been pacified and company administration had become more responsive to the needs of the people.

Clifford, however, came under attack from his superior in Singapore, Swettenham, who believed the company's actions were not lawful. More important were Clifford's differences with the London board and William Cowie. Clifford had discovered that he had no control over the railway superintendent or the builders. His criticism of railway policy, standards of construction, and treatment of laborers was not well received by the board. He was informed that he had not been posted to North Borneo to criticize but to carry out policy and write favorable reports that would be published to help the company raise money in England. After several rebukes for his actions, Clifford found his position untenable. As one historian observed, "By nature direct, forthright and impetuous, a giant of a man, he would stoop for no one. He would have none of this deceit, nor any more of this studipity. He resigned."[16] Clifford's adamance obviously did not damage his reputation. He was welcomed back to Malaya and was reappointed resident in Pahang.

In the summer of 1901, Clifford was directed by the Malay office to attend Sultan Sir Idris bin Iskander, the senior colonial guest at the coronation of King Edward VII. As with so many of his experiences at this time, Clifford used the opportunity to write a factual article that was later published. The work, entitled "Piloting Princes," is only partially descriptive since Clifford expanded the story to speculate on the nature of rule, imperialism, and particularly the impact of Western ideas upon the Malay mind.[17]

At the conclusion of the coronation ceremonies, his guests departed for Malaya, but Clifford remained in England. He was desperately ill as a result of an unsuccessful attempt on his life by poisoning. For a time his doctors despaired for his life, but he was given a clean bill of health in early 1903. His old friend Swettenham wanted him to return to Pahang, but Clifford accepted a decrease in salary to take up the appointment of colonial secretary of Trinidad and Tobago, a recognized posting for men on the way up. He did not welcome the new post but had been informed that his career could be damaged by a refusal of the colonial office's offer. Clifford thus left a land to which he had a deep emotional attachment for an administrative position half a world away. He would not return to Malaya again for almost a quater of a century. In late 1903, Clifford began a ten-year period typical of senior civil servants who had been chosen for possible selection as governors of the empire. The similarity of British forms of administration was such that it was not necessary to be completely familiar with the people, language, or customs of a territory. Clifford was sent to oversee and develop, if necessary, the central secretariat of the colony and to act as the major administrative advisor to the governor. He was acting governor of Trinidad from March to August 1904 and from April to October 1906. But this was not his administration and he could make only an indirect impact through his influence with the governor and by improving the efficiency of the secretariat. In 1907 Clifford was given a further promotion when he was appointed colonial secretary of Ceylon, a position he retained until his appointment as governor of the Gold Coast. In 1909 he received a KCMG, a decoration that indicated his professional success.[18]

The historian has only a few glimpses of Sir Hugh Clifford during this period. Some of his more interesting and important books were written them. He published *A Free-Lance of Today* in 1903; *Further India* and *Sally: A Study* in 1904;

Heroes of Exile in 1906; *Saleh: A Sequel* in 1908; and *The Downfall of the Gods* in 1911. His correspondence with Joseph Conrad indicates a deepening relationship with this master of the adventure story. In 1910 Clifford had talked admiringly of Conrad to Gordon Bennett of the *New York Herald* while the latter was visiting Ceylon. He loaned Bennett some of Conrad's works to read on his yacht during the voyage from Colombo to Bombay. Bennett at once cabled his New York office to "buy Conrad," resulting in a contract and eventually the publication of Conrad's novel *Chance*.[19] Clifford's first wife was the victim of a carriage accident in Trinidad, and in January 1907, at the age of thirty-nine, he was left a widower with three children. Three years later Clifford remarried. The new Lady Clifford was the widow of Henry de La Pasture, a bright, adventuresome woman who was herself a writer of considerable merit. For her service to the war effort and for her writing she was awarded a CBE in 1918. Clifford's stepdaughter also became a very successful novelist, writing under the name of E. M. Delafield.

At this juncture one should note briefly some of Sir Hugh's specific personal attributes. Well over six feet tall, heavyset, with broad shoulders and deep chest, he towered over most of his staff. Despite malarial attacks, periodic bouts with a number of other tropical diseases, and a serious poisoning, he had remained in the field in Pahang, Trengganu, and North Borneo for longer periods than his European associates. Clifford loved sports and was quite proficient at tennis, cycling, and swimming, activities he continued until his retirement in 1929. His great physical strength enabled him to undertake a killing workload as a senior administrative official and also as a practicing author. After succeeding Lugard as governor of Nigeria, he regularly worked over seventy hours a week on official business. This was considerably more time than he had devoted to administration in the Gold Coast. He complained to the colonial office of the long hours not because it taxed his vigor but because the system was inefficient.

Those who knew Clifford generally remarked of his intellectual prowess. Master of a number of languages, a voracious reader, and a prolific writer, he was noted for his ability to brush aside extraneous details and go to the very heart of a problem. He knew very well what type of administration he wanted and the methods to use to achieve his ends. Clifford did not suffer fools or charlatans gladly and had no fear of expressing his viewpoint either to his subordinates or to his superiors. His temper, according to some of his associates, could be volatile, leading him at times to actions he later regretted. However, when at fault, particularly after reprimanding a junior, he would attempt to amend his hasty judgment and in many cases went to great lengths to apologize for his mistake. Clifford nurtured extreme dislike of certain of his contemporaries such as Sir Gordon Guggisberg and was not above trying to embarass them.[20]

Malaya and Clifford's close direct contact with the people and their rulers during his "thirteen years of intensely interesting and in the main enjoyable exile and isolation" are fundamental to understanding his attitudes. There is no indication that he ever altered his basic concepts concerning the value of British rule and the worth of individual native societies. Moreover, Clifford's attempt to translate his ideals into practice were remarkably free from sham theorizing. Unlike many other twentieth-century administrators, he did not base his actions on ideology but upon the practical realities of the time and circumstance. However, Clifford's most fundamental difference with many of his fellow administrators in the colonial service was a matter not so much of practical approach as of genuine respect for alien cultures and the conviction that nonwhite societies should be governed by rules that had meaning for their peoples. Empathy with the indigenous people placed Clifford with the minority of the policymakers of the new empire. He knew and understood the value of the laws and customs of a given people and how, wherever possible, those should be gently modified in the direction of accommodation with Western forms. British officials in the protected states in Malaya, like their counterparts at the same time in much of Africa, were in no position to mandate a revolution. They had no choice but to accept the major portion of the indigenous culture and even to rule through its framework with only minor alterations.

Clifford's ambivalence toward the shattering of older cultures in Asia and Africa can be seen clearly in much of his writing. Of those rebels who had opposed him in the 1890s, he wrote,

> They are the last of their breed—the last of the men who dared to pit their puny strength against the might of the British Raj. They are men who have loved, and enjoyed life greatly in the days before the coming of the white folk, who have fought manfully for years for those pleasures and privileges which mean the misery of the peasants born beneath their heels, and now comes a merciful ending to the struggle so wearily prolonged.
>
> Here let us leave them, the dreamers of dreams, the lost heroes of a day too late. "Here is tears for their love; joy for their fortune; honour for their valour; and death for their ambition!"[21]

This romantic comprehension was modified by the reality of native rule and the necessity for British control. After he had left Malaya he wrote,

> Looking back upon those days, I reckon them as the happiest and most interesting of my life; but the end of them found me a firm believer in the necessity for the intervention of Great Britain in Malaya which in my own time, I had seen transform conditions bordering upon anarchy into those appropriate to a peaceful, prosperous and contented countryside.[22]

Clifford never wavered from his conviction that British rule meant the end of internecine war, arbitrary rule, and tyranny and the beginning of good government and peace and happiness for the people of a dependency. But Clifford's intelligence was such that he understood the complexities of the clash of civilizations, first in Malaya and then later in Africa. He understood that what was being done to subject peoples was not simple and the results were not always what had been planned—or even good. In his introduction to Claridge's *History of the Gold Coast* he was very frank and critical of British relations with the people of the Gold Coast. He noted that "it may be that modern civilisation is the lion and that barbarism is the lamb; but the two cannot now days lie down side by side." Evincing sadness at the passing of the Ashanti empire, he wrote that few people would question that the Ashanti people of 1915 who devoted the bulk of their energies to peaceful agriculture were far happier than their "bloodstained ancestors, who spent a goodly portion of their time in ravaging their neighbour's homesteads, taking other people's lives, and enslaving their womenkind and their children."[23]

That he was active in this great transformation was for Clifford a matter for justified pride rather than a mere excuse for imperialism.

Gold Coast

After almost thirty years of distinguished service, Sir Hugh Clifford was finally rewarded with an appointment as governor of a British territory. He was selected to replace his old Malayan acquaintance and friend, Sir John Rodger, as governor of the Gold Coast. He arrived in Accra late in 1912 to assume the responsibility of his first administration.

The Gold Coast presented a curious amalgam of peoples and cultures.[24] The coastal groups who lived in the colony area—the Fante, Ga, and Ewe—had differing languages, histories, and cultures. There existed deep divisions even among a single national group. All coastal people had been accustomed to accommodating themselves to the Europeans; they traded with foreigners; many had become Christian and some were highly educated. These few had provided the westernized leadership for the urban population. They had, with official encouragement, framed the composite, liberal Mankessim constitution in 1871, only to see this repudiated by British authorities reacting to Ashanti disturbances. These Western oriented elite groups provided the doctors, lawyers, teachers, and civil servants for the Gold Coast. By Clifford's time they were highly dissatisfied with the roles assigned them by the British government. They wanted to be consulted more in the governance of the Gold Coast and demanded the removal of all color barriers in the civil service.

In the interior the Ashanti, the proud nation that had opposed European domination for over two centuries, were disorganized. A scant ten years before Clifford's appointment some of the Ashanti chiefs led their followers in revolt against the British. The governor had been besieged and the British had to send a major relief expedition to extricate him. This uprising, however, was the final armed action against British control, and the Ashanti territories afterward were considered a part of the protectorate and were governed from Accra. The *Asantahene* (king), Prempeh, was exiled and the chiefs of Ashanti continued to be suspicious of Europeans and even more of educated Fante. North of the Ashanti were the northern territories, scantly populated by a diverse group of Akan and Mossi speakers. The British governor controlled this area through the agency of a chief commissioner. Extremely poor, the northern territories would continue to receive little in terms of development money throughout the earlier part of the twentieth century.

Government of the northern territories, Ashanti, and much of the colony was exercised through local chiefs. This system of government in Africa was later glamorized under the term "indirect rule." It was, however, basically a pragmatic solution to the problem of governing large numbers of people without the expenditure of great sums of money. The dilemma faced by Clifford and all the other British governors of Africa was how to continue this economical system while still accommodating the demands of influential, Western educated nationalists. Clifford's work in the Gold Coast and later in Nigeria should be evaluated with this dichotomy in mind. There was no way that a governor could satisfy completely the conflicting demands of the traditionalists and the educated. After 1906, moreover, the romantic period of empire building was past; territorial conquests were completed, and the colonial office was resuming control over the man on the spot.

Despite the difficulties he faced at the outset, Clifford achieved much in the Gold Coast. He bequeathed to his successor, Sir Gordon Guggisberg, the foundations for the reforms that would bring Guggisberg rightful acclaim.[25] Not the least of Clifford's accomplishments was the £1.6 million in revenue surplus he left behind when he departed the Gold Coast in 1919. Clifford held down expenditures at a time when the cocoa industry was entering into a boom period and profits were high. Clifford early recognized that in order to facilitate the continued expansion of cocoa exports, the government had to improve communications. In 1912 there were only a few miles of railroad in the colony, and the roads were inadequate. In that year Clifford proposed to the secretary of state a long-term plan of railway and road construction. In his correspondence throughout his term, Clifford returned to this theme over and over again as the key to the future of the Gold Coast.[26] Lack of skilled engineers and construction men caused by wartime conditions prevented Clifford from doing as much as he wished. His administration completed only 26 miles of railway but built 165 miles of first-class road and added 650 miles of secondary roads, capable of supporting light trucks. Clifford also recognized the inadequacy of the harbor at Sekondi. In February 1918, he appointed a commission to study this problem and make recommendations. The commission's report, issued in May 1919, suggested the construction of a deep water harbor at Takoradi. Clifford's ability to bring change to the Gold Coast was restricted in many ways by the first world war, but he did begin to plan to meet the needs of the economy of the Gold Coast.[27]

Limited improvement was made in two other areas during Clifford's tenure. One of these was the field of education and the other concerned African appointments to the civil service. Education facilities in the Gold Coast were provided largely by missionary organizations. Soon after his arrival, Clifford had to mediate differences between some government officials and the missionaries. He warned his chief commissioner in the north to stop harassing and instead render every assistance to the religious agencies in their educational endeavors. Clifford was certain that they, in the short term, could be more effective than the government in extending primary education. He believed that this was essential for the development of the Gold Coast.[28] Primary schools could provide the necessary foundation training for artisans and agriculturists, who were in increasing demand by the Gold Coast economy. Clifford was not as convinced of the necessity for government subsidies for secondary education. Secondary schools turned out "black Englishmen," who had proven to be thorns in the side of the administration. Clifford, like so many of his contemporaries, deeply mistrusted most Western educated Africans. Despite this personal conviction, Clifford commissioned the board of education in 1915 to study secondary education in the Gold Coast and make recommendations for its improvement. The director of education and the Europeans on the board shared Clifford's misgivings, but the two African members attacked the board and the director of education for what they considered archaic ideas. Finally in 1918, Clifford appointed a special committee on education in which there was significant African representation. Its report, issued in October 1919, gave Guggisberg an immediate, contemporary Gold Coast view of education.[29]

The Aborigines' Rights Protection Society, the chief political agency of the coastal educated, had long asked that "competent and worthy natives" be appointed to administrative positions. Colony nationalists such as T. Hutton-Mills later reported their surprise when Clifford in 1913 agreed with them. Convinced by his experiences in the east, particularly in Ceylon, that "natives" had to be integrated into government service at all levels, he began in 1914 to make such appointments. For example, E. C. Quist, a Ga, became the first African crown counsel in 1914. Perhaps the most significant change instituted by Clifford was in opening positions for Africans in the medical department. To do this he had to take issue not only with the concerted opinion of most of the European medical staff on this matter but also with colonial office policy, which had been enunciated in 1912. By openly challenging the secretary of state on the question of African staffing, he was able to create six positions for African doctors in the medical service by the end of 1914.[30]

The rank and file of African civil servants in 1913, prevented from working their way up to senior posts, also received lower salaries than Europeans in comparable positions. The remuneration of beginning clerks was only £36 a year. Although salary discrepancies in the Gold Coast were still not solved even when Nkrumah became head of an independent Ghana, Clifford did make some headway in his attempt to upgrade African salaries. A committee appointed soon after his arrival made its report in 1914, and the governor followed most of its advice in completely reorganizing African salary scales, which cost the government an additional £6,000 per annum. Clifford later also lent his support to the petitions of the civil service clerks who in 1918 complained of the insufficiency of the ten percent war bonus proposed by the colonial office. Partially because of Clifford's intercession with the secretary of state, Lord Milner, this was increased in June 1919 to a bonus salary adjusted on a sliding scale of twelve to twenty percent.[31]

Normal government operations were interrupted briefly in August 1914 by the onset of World War I. Once again Clifford was involved with troops engaged in hostilities against an enemy. But Clifford was no longer a young political officer leading troops into action against a dedicated foe. He was the governor of a British territory. The enemy, the Germans in Togo, had few troops. They had, however, constructed a very powerful wireless station there which, unless neutralized, could conceivably play an important role in the sea war in the southern Atlantic. The small contingent of British troops available in the Gold Coast immediately invaded Togo and, in cooperation with a still smaller French force from Dahomey, succeeded within a few weeks in forcing the surrender of all German troops in Togo although they failed to prevent the destruction of the wireless station. By the end of September Clifford was thus able to dispatch the bulk of the Gold Coast military to Duala to aid Sir Frederick Lugard in the much more difficult campaign against the Cameroons. Clifford, working in close conjunction with the foreign office, later met French representatives a number of times to establish the temporary boundaries between the British and French spheres in Togo.[32]

The most significant change wrought by Clifford during his tenure was the reorganization of the Gold Coast legislative council. Some members of the Aborigines' Rights Protection Society had long pressed for more African representation on the council. They claimed that to have only two African members was farcical and an insult to the educated community, particularly since the appointees were expected to vote with the government. More representatives had become an even more crucial issue to the Africans after the palm oil revenue ordinance was passed against the opposition of the unofficial members of the council. The educated Africans did not expect any significant support for their postion from the new governor. Clifford, however, was not an ordinary administrator. Within a few months he had come to conclusions similar to those of the Aborigines' Rights Protection Society. He was impressed with the phenomenal development of the cocoa industry and with its social consequences. He concluded that the most severe problem facing his government was its inefficiency in explaining to Africans why certain acts affecting their interests were passed. Clifford's experiences with the elected non-Europeans on the council of Ceylon convinced him that more and better balanced African representation would go far in achieving the needed better communications with the people of the Gold Coast.

The impetus to reform the central government of the Gold Coast came not from England but from Clifford. Soon after his arrival in the Gold Coast he communicated his opinions on this subject to the colonial office. Lord Harcourt, the secretary of state, and almost all of the colonial office staff either openly opposed more African representation or took no position on the matter. In a series of detailed dispatches in 1915 Clifford laid out his proposals in such a fashion that the colonial office reluctantly gave way and allowed his reforms.[33] He proposed that the size of the council not be increased until it became unwieldy but should be restructured to admit of "direct tribal representation." He wanted no change in the method of appointments or in the method of operations of the council since he did not believe that the people of the Gold Coast were ready for direct elections. Most of them were not well enough educated. Where the taxpayers did have the franchise, they made little use of it. Direct elections would widen tribal differences instead of promoting the harmony Clifford sought. He wanted to appoint select members from the ranks of the chiefs. Such appointment of "the natural leaders" of the people could offset the growing influence of the educated African. Clifford wished to avoid unnecessary divisions in the council between officials and nonofficials. The legislative council was not a parliament where there could be the interplay of an opposition and a government position.

The colonial office accepted Clifford's proposals and in 1916 the legislative council was enlarged to twenty-one members. Of these, nine were nonofficials and six of these were Africans. Aside from tripling the African membership, the most important immediate result of the reform was the appointment of three paramount chiefs to the council. Thus, despite Clifford's continuing difficulties in reforming the government of the protectorate, he had succeeded in bringing some of the chiefs into direct participation in policymaking.

Clifford has never received the credit due him for reforming the legislative council. Perhaps the major reason for his lack of recognition was Clifford's outspoken contention that the Gold Coast was, at that time, only a collection of differing, sometimes hostile groups and therefore the territory could not aspire to being considered a single state. His statements on this issue provoked the educated coastal community, which had wanted a legislative assembly and not just an enlarged council. Clifford's reputation with some of the educated Africans was damaged also by colonial office pressure, which induced him to force through the legislative council the palm kernels export duty bill, a piece of legislation with which he vehemently disagreed. He had argued throughout 1916 that this bill, by levying a duty on palm kernels, would seriously harm a trade that already was damaged. He repeated his arguments in 1917 but could not prevail. The second reading of the bill provoked the nonofficials to vote en bloc against it. Clifford's position was misunderstood and Guggisberg inherited a bad law, which remained in effect until 1922.[34]

Clifford was not as successful as he hoped in bolstering the positions of the chiefs by enacting legislation to replace the old native jurisdiction ordinance. When he arrived in the Gold Coast, he found the chiefs under considerable pressure. This derived both from the coastal elite and from their own young men, many of whom had some education and more of whom were prosperous cocoa farmers. In Fante areas, young men were using the traditional military bodies, the *Asafo* companies, to limit the chiefs' power. They also utilized the traditional check of destoolment to express their discontent with the slowness of action and frequent corruption of the chiefs. Few of the traditional rulers, on the other hand, had any Western education. Hence, there was little that Clifford could do to implement dramatically his ideas of indirect rule. He did, however, change the tone of the administration. Soon after his arrival he reminded all district officers of their responsibility to support the chiefs and their advisors. British administrators were to consult with the chiefs on any action affecting the areas ostensibly under traditional authority. Chiefs received invitations to see the governor and explain their views to him. He was careful in informal and formal meetings with them to try to set forth the government's position on major legislation.

Clifford was dissatisfied with the old native jurisdiction ordinance. In 1916 he circulated among the chiefs the draft of the government's proposal to amend it and asked for their opinions. Closer study of the ordinance and information from Africans convinced the governor and his advisors that amendment would be useless. Instead, they prepared a new bill. This was intoduced in the legislative council in February 1919 and caused a furor among the coastal elite, who accused the government of propping up the power of ignorant chiefs against the just demands of the educated. They claimed that the new ordinance was designed to make the chiefs into tools of Europeans. All the important coastal organizations and newspapers campaigned against its adoption. Clifford had departed the Gold Coast long before the virulent debate over this issue had subsided. His successor, Guggisberg, removed the bill from consideration and in 1922 introduced a greatly modified bill.[35] This also met a hostile reception and was withdrawn. Eventually, only a stopgap revision of the original ordinance was made in 1924. Until after World War II, no governor seriously disagreed with Clifford's conclusion that the future government of the Gold Coast would have to be through the agency of rule by traditional authorities.

Despite the controversy over indirect rule, Clifford's stewardship of the Gold Coast was by no means unappreciated by the elite. At times he received almost fulsome praise from his African associates. In 1916 after Clifford had introduced his legislative council reforms, one of the most influential Africans, T. Hutton-Mills, stated that he wished that day to be remembered in the Gold Coast as "Clifford Day."[36] Perhaps as important as any concrete achievements was the spirit Clifford infused into his staff, both British and African. Another African colleague, A. Duncan-Johnstone, recalled later that Clifford gave his subordinates something that he had never felt under any other governor. This was a "renaissance spirit," which impressed his government with the idea that they were "a first-class team."[37]

Nigeria

In 1919 Clifford learned that he was to go to Nigeria to replace Lugard as governor.[38] He had to hand over the Gold Coast to Sir Gordon Guggisberg, a man he detested. There is no concrete evidence to show why he felt such animosity toward his successor. Clifford had earlier turned down Guggisberg's application to be chief commissioner of the northern territories on the ground that Guggisberg was not qualified. Ironically enough, Clifford soon found himself in open opposition to the policies of Lugard, a man he liked and respected, whereas Guggisberg, whom he considered incompetent, successfully completed many of those reforms that Clifford had begun in the Gold Coast.

Sir Frederick Lugard, the conqueror of the north, had received unprecedented powers as governor-general from the colonial office in 1912 in order to effect the amalgamation of the northern and southern protectorates. In securing this and other correlate goals he had set for himself, Lugard had been successful. The two disparate governments had been joined, and a potentially serious threat from the Germans in the Cameroons had been removed in a tedious, difficult campaign. Lugard had also had considerable success in converting the native authorities to his ideas of indirect rule and taxation. All of these things had been accomplished during wartime, when the government had been hampered by a shortage of staff and supplies. Officials in the colonial office had ambivalent feelings toward him. Few questioned the evidences of his success, but by 1917 many had grown tired of his arguments for his viewpoints and wanted an end to his unique position as governor-general. The colonial secretary, Walter Long, undoubtedly welcomed Lugard's resignation over a minor issue.[39]

Lugard's prerogatives and his massive, articulate, but verbose defense of his concepts of rule in Africa had a direct effect upon Clifford's freedom of action in Nigeria. Before Lugard's resignation, the colonial office had already decided that his successor would not have special privileges but would be treated like other colonial governors. Much discretionary power accordingly returned to the officials in London. For all his reputation, Lugard, while in office, was a minor irritant. Removed from office, he began to assume a larger than life stature in the eyes of those who administered the empire. From the official point of view, success or failure in governing African territories in the postwar years was, in many cases, measured by adherence to or deviation from Lugard's doctrines. Other governors might be slightly handicapped by Lugard's elevation to the status of demigod. Clifford, as his successor in Nigeria, was more directly affected. Major alterations in Lugard's system in Nigeria had to be fought out with the home authorities, who preferred the older methods. Of more immediate importance to Clifford in mid-1919, however, were the problems he inherited from Lugard.

The colonial office expected the western areas to be subjected to a standard system of traditional rule. It desired a viable central administrative structure that would curb the northern administrations in their tendency to develop policies at variance with the rest of Nigeria. The colonial office also called for improved relations with the educated elite. It wished to extend taxation to the eastern provinces. With regard to each of these, Lugard had, by design or inadvertence, either ignored the existence of trouble or had forced unwanted policies upon Africans. Certainly when Clifford left the Gold Coast, he little realized the scope and complexity of the difficulties that he would confront in Nigeria. Nigeria had seemed to him, as it did to all casual observers, a model British territory. He was soon disabused of any such idea.[40]

Clifford's first major problem concerned the troubled Abeokuta region. In 1893 Governor Carter had signed a treaty with the Egba people, a compact that differed considerably from the protectorate agreements with the other Yoruba rulers of the west. In return for promises of good behavior and cooperation, Britain had recognized the independence of the Egba state. During the following twenty years, the Egba constructed a state government that attempted to blend British practices with Egba traditions. Despite difficulties, their governmental system was functioning in many areas better than those of neighboring polities under British protection. Nevertheless, British economic interests in Egbaland continued to mount and the Lagos government became particularly concerned over the security of the main railway line that ran through Egba territory. By the time Lugard returned to Nigeria as governor-general, the freedom of action of the officials of the independent Egba state had been further circumscribed by other treaties with Britain.

Sir Frederick from the beginning viewed the anomaly of this independent state on the very borders of the colony with distaste. It was a threat to his vision of a united Nigeria under British control and he took the first opportunity that presented itself to subvert the Egba government. This came in the form of a minor conflict between sections of the Egba at Abeokuta, which resulted in an appeal for British assistance by the Alake. Troops were dispatched from Lagos to Abeokuta and these were so badly controlled by their officers that on August 8, 1914, they fired on demonstrators in the Ijemo quarter, killing Chief Aluo and six of his retainers. Using this affair as an excuse, Lugard then abrogated the 1893 treaty and declared Egbaland to be a part of the protectorate of Nigeria. An official investigation of the shooting at Ijemo was made in 1915, but the report was never made public.[41]

Although a part of Nigeria, Egbaland continued to be administered differently from the neighboring Yoruba areas after the Ijemo affair until 1918. Then Lugard, with the acquiescence of the colonial office, extended his scheme of indirect rule and taxation to the area. In June of that year, the most serious civil disorders ever to strike Nigeria under British governance occurred in the Abeokuta area. These were caused by a combination of factors; the most important were remembrance of the Ijemo massacre, dissatisfaction of the chiefs, hostility toward the chief Egba advisor to the resident, weakness of the Alake, and open opposition to Lugard's schemes, which ran counter to Egba tradition. Many of the towns surrounding Abeokuta sided with the protesters, the railway and telegraph lines were torn up, property was looted and destroyed, and one European was killed. Fortunately for Lugard, there were troops in Nigeria returning from the East African campaign, and he was able to deal swiftly with the uprising. In the ensuing campaign—which lasted from June 11 through July 10—the British deployed a total of 70 Europeans and 2,500 African rank and file, and an estimated 564 Africans were killed in the fighting.[42]

The uprising at Abeokuta was an embarrassment to the home government and called into question Lugard's management of the Egba problem. The colonial office could not ignore the Abeokuta disturbance as they had ignored the affair at Ijemo. Lugard reluctantly appointed a five-man committee under the direction of Dr. James Maxwell to investigate the uprising. Their report, presented to the Lagos government in the fall of 1918, was sharply critical of the actions of several British officials, particularly Resident Syer. Lugard left Nigeria before any decisions had been made concerning possible guilt of British officials, indemnification, changes in administrative procedure in Egbaland, or whether Maxwell's report should be made public. These decisions were all left to the colonial office and Clifford.

Clifford read some of the files on board the ship taking him to Nigeria. He arrived in Lagos on August 8 and in the next three weeks examined all the available material related to Egbaland and conferred with Lieutenant governor Boyle and the acting resident, C. W. Alexander, at Abeokuta. On August 29, he addressed a very long memorandum on the subject to Lord Milner. This was the first comprehensive, historical analysis of the situation ever presented to the colonial office. What Clifford had to say so disturbed the London officials that a number of them commented disparagingly and at length in minute papers. They concentrated not on Clifford's well-researched and reasoned analysis but upon his boldness in informing them of what he considered to be the worst type of bungling by almost everyone who dealt with the Egba after 1914. They considered that Clifford was premature in criticizing so harshly Lugard's administration and ascribed this not to Clifford's logic and honesty but to jealousy of Lugard.[43]

Clifford criticized not only the actions of individual officers but also the policy they had been ordered to carry out. He disagreed with Lugard's excuse that near anarchy had prevailed at Abeokuta in 1914 and that Britain therefore had to assume control. Egbaland, Clifford argued, was then as calm as many of the northern and southern parts of Nigeria where Britain still maintained armed patrols in 1919. The residents at Abeokuta, Young and Syer, had been derelict in their responsibilities; under no circumstances should Young ever be sent to Nigeria again. Sir Hugh likewise censured the timing and nature of Lugard's reforms of the Egba local government system. The administration had appointed the wrong people as district heads and had ignored the traditional Egba chiefs. The problem had been compounded by the premature introduction of taxation. Some of the most important Egba had not forgotten the Ijemo massacre and the loss of their freedom. By 1918 they had become convinced that only violence would move the British. Clifford concurred with the Maxwell report, recommended its publication, and suggested full government indemnification to all parties injured during the uprising. He approved the ad hoc measures taken by Lieutenant governor Boyle and Resident Alexander at Abeokuta and proposed to continue restructuring the local government system to support the powers of Egba traditional leaders.

The Abeokuta affair has been considered in some detail since Clifford's response to it was elicited so early in his tenure. His interchange with the colonial office, moreover, established a relationship with his superiors that he was never able to alter. In January 1920 the colonial secretary, Leopold Amery, closed the

Abeokuta discussion by denying most of Clifford's recommendations.[44] The Maxwell report was not published and Clifford's suggestion for a more equitable distribution of the Egba taxes was rejected. Even those actions that could not be avoided, such as indemnification and restructuring the native authority, were accepted reluctantly. The pattern of Clifford's relations with the colonial office was set. He would be forced to struggle with London for the approval of even the most obvious reforms. Suggestions for revisions in the protectorate government, particularly in the south, would be either ignored or denied. Important recommendations designed to arrest the development of a separate attitude and practice toward the Muslim north were debated upon and then ignored. Clifford was able to avert the premature extension of taxation to the east, before the local government system had been reformed, only by resorting to clever delaying tactics. Although absent, Lugard through his reputation in official circles still continued to exercise tremendous influence on the government of Nigeria.

Clifford very soon noted with distress the growing differences between the government of the northern emirates and the rest of Nigeria. Many district and provincial officers in the north had become overly enamored of the Hausa-Fulani and Kanuri systems and allowed the traditional rulers to govern with only minimal reference to what was being done elsewhere or to what Lagos wanted. In a series of long dispatches Clifford analyzed what he considered to be a potentially dangerous development.[45] He drew on his observations of the Nigerian system for his criticisms, as well as upon his long experience working with Muslim rulers in Malaya. His communications touching on the north were couched in general, introductory terms. Clifford's ideas received a cold and in some cases a hostile reception. Some officials simply dismissed his analysis as the work of a novice in Nigerian government. Others could see no connection between the possible actions of a Muslim emir in Africa and those observed in other Muslim rulers in another part of the empire. Still others saw Clifford's criticisms as a further manifestation of envy of Lugard.[46] Although he would mention the subject continually in later communications, Clifford realized that any major reform program in the north could not be attempted until the colonial office was willing to concede the necessity for it. Unfortunately for Nigeria, this general revision was never completed, and even in the decade before independence the government of the northern areas was substantially different from that in the rest of Nigeria.

Clifford inherited from Lugard another set of imperatives concerning local government. Lugard had been convinced that true native administration could be effective only when there were functioning native treasuries. This dogmatic concept had led to premature introduction of taxing systems to the Yoruba states. Only World War I and the opposition of the colonial office had prevented the extension of taxation to the Ibo and Ibibio peoples of the east.[47] The colonial office in the early 1920s began to pressure Clifford to tidy up the financial system of Nigeria and impose taxation on the five provinces of the east. Clifford knew very well that these areas were inhabited by people who had never experienced direct taxation. Furthermore, he was aware of the need for a general reform of native administration in the east. He believed that to collect revenue there without substantial reform of the government was to invite African opposition, perhaps a repetition of Abeokuta on a broader scale. The opinions of district officers in the east supported this conclusion. Even if African reaction were minimal, forcing another unknown and unwanted system on Africans was to violate the most basic precepts of indirect rule.

Sir Hugh could not, however, refuse to investigate the possibilities of taxation of the east. Therefore he temporized. In 1922 he sent S. M. Grier, the secretary for native affairs, on a two-month fact-finding mission to the five provinces. Grier's report, although not completely ruling out the possibility of taxation, was nevertheless highly critical of the operation of the warrant chief system in the east.[48] He advised that the local administration and courts system be thoroughly revised before any system of taxation was introduced. This revision should seek to discover the natural rulers and insofar as possible the natural boundaries of districts. If levied, any tax should be a simple capitation tax and should be collected by the chiefs. Otherwise, there would be trouble. Clifford agreed that warrant chiefs without traditional standing should be removed and noted that any such process of revision would have to be gradual.

Grier's report was so critical of the eastern system and so unpopular with the colonial office that Clifford in January 1923 sent the assistant secretary for native affairs, G. J. F. Tomlinson, to the east for further investigations. He, too, spent two months in the field. His report, although not as abrasive or as critical of Lugard's system as Grier's, underscored the need for a general revision of the administrative system. It called for an end to corruption in local government affairs and a gradual approach to taxation.[49] Any scheme of taxation ought to be preceded by a long, introductory campaign to inform the people about what was going to happen. After receiving this information, Clifford did nothing to further the colonial office's wishes until August 1924. In response to more pressure, he then instructed Colonel Moorhouse, the lieutenant governor of the southern provinces, to investigate the subject. Moorhouse's memorandum guardedly recommended the extension of taxation to the east.[50] But Sir Hugh would not initiate such a wide-sweeping reform in eastern Nigeria during the short period remaining of his term. Clifford's delaying tactics postponed the introduction of a system that he disliked. But he could not, for all his arguments, convince the colonial office. His successor, Sir Graeme Thomson, proceeded with all haste to enforce taxation. He instituted a hurried assessment of property in the five provinces and transferred to the east a complex system borrowed from the north. The result, as Sir Hugh had known, was resistance. The women's disturbances of December 1929, contained by hundreds of soldiers with dreadful loss of life to Ibo and Ibibio women, was directly caused by Thomson's implementing the colonial office's taxing policies.[51]

Whereas Clifford was prevented from instituting necessary reforms by a neutral or hostile colonial office staff, they did recognize the need for reorganization of the central administration of Nigeria. Lugard had certainly not been a good administrator. He liked to be at the center; he would not delegate authority to anyone. Instead of supporting his secretariat, he chose to ignore it in many cases, preferring to labor unnecessarily hard on the mountains of paper that accumulated on his desk. In proposing his reforms in 1920, Clifford noted that he was forced to devote an extraordinary amount of time at his desk a week just to keep up with the three separate administrative entities.[52] Even the colonial office had remarked how slow Nigeria was in turning in annual reports and budget estimates by comparison with other areas.

Clifford outlined the nature of the central administration and proposed general remedies as early as December 1919. Five months later, he was still complaining to Lord Milner about the slowness of the colonial office in approving his plans. These were not accepted until July 1920. By this date Clifford had found that his chief secretary, Donald Cameron, a man largely ignored by Lugard, matched his own brilliance and was in addition a complete master of the bureaucratic complexities of the government of Nigeria. There developed a close bond between the volatile, aristocratic Clifford and the dour, efficient Cameron. The bulk of the work of investigating the Nigerian administrative system fell to Cameron and his staff, who by November 1920 provided Clifford with detailed plans for a single secretariat. Clifford approved Cameron's suggestions with only minor modifications, the colonial office concurred, and the new system went into effect on January 1921.[53] Cameron, as chief secretary, became the second in command. Supported by Clifford, he set himself the task of creating the most efficient government instrument possible within the limits imposed by extreme financial stringency. One articulate member of that staff, Sir Alan Burns, noted the contrast between the Clifford days in Nigeria and the near anarchy of the central government during Lugard's tenure. Under Cameron, the staff of the central government became an excellent training ground for young officers. Within a few years no fewer than six of the officers schooled by Clifford and Cameron were serving as governors of dependencies.

Clifford, according to his critics, did not like the African educated elite. In a much quoted speech to the Nigerian council in December 1920, Clifford indeed gave ammunition to his censors.[54] He denounced the idea that a few British oriented Africans should govern the mass of the peoples of the hinterland without sanction of the traditional rulers. He ridiculed the concept of a united British West Africa and stated "that there is or can be in the visible future such a thing as a 'West African Nation' is as manifest an absurdity as that there is, or can be, an 'European Nation', at all events until the millennium." There was not even any such thing as a Nigerian nation. In Nigeria, as in the Gold Coast, there were too many separate peoples with fundamental racial, political, social, linguistic, and religious differences. It was without unity except that imposed by Britain.

Clifford's statements have been taken out of context by many present day nationalists. Combined with his hostility to the national congress of British West Africa and his handling of the *Eleko* affair, these pronouncements supposedly show his opposition to progress.[55] Actually, Clifford's attitudes toward self-rule by indigenous peoples had altered little since his Malayan days. He was not opposed to the development of representative institutions, but he believed these had to be firmly based on the traditions of the people. Throughout his tenure he did everything possible to upgrade traditional institutions and he hoped that in the future more chiefs with a modicum of Western education could be chosen. Provincial and district officers in the protectorate were specifically instructed to cooperate with the chiefs and their councils. Clifford and his chief secretary, Donald Cameron, viewed the early Nigerian nationalists such as Herbert Macaulay not as patriots but as potential troublemakers, without any constituency even in Lagos. Clifford's removal and deportation of Eshugbayi, the *Eleko* (traditional ruler) of Lagos, was conditioned not by Eshugbayi's actions as traditional ruler but by his involvement with Macaulay and others in local politics.

Clifford was not blindly opposed to educated Nigerians. In fact, he reinstated the legislative council as an important part of the central government machinery. In 1914 Lugard had emasculated the old legislative council and renamed its impotent successor the Nigerian council. Only six nominated Africans had seats on this unrepresentative body. Clifford, however, was committed to having a vehicle through which African opinion could be ascertained and information could be efficiently channeled down to the governed. In 1920, Sir Hugh approved the reorganization of the Lagos town council on the elective principle. His recommendations for a restructured Nigerian legislative council were approved two years later by the colonial office. This revision called for a council of forty-six members: twenty-seven officials and nineteen nonofficials. Three of the unofficial members were elected by prominent male residents of Lagos who could meet the property and literacy qualifications. Clifford saw the Lagos based elections as a first step toward the eventual extension of elections to other urban areas of Nigeria and perhaps in time to more representative self-government in the protectorate. The constitutional reform of 1922 was the most fundamental extension of responsibility to educated Nigerians before World War II. It had been done by Clifford not for ideological reasons but simply to improve the workings of the Nigerian government. As Clifford noted of the reform, he wanted the legislative council "to be real and effective or not to have it at all."[56]

Clifford's term ended in late 1924, but he delayed his departure to act as host for the visit to Nigeria of the Prince of Wales. Clifford had hoped that this visit might obtain publicity for the colonial service and help in recruiting good officers by dispelling fears concerning West Africa's unhealthy climate. But an outbreak of yellow fever and of plague that year seemed to justify the older belief. Sir Hugh knew when he left Nigeria that he was to be the governor of Ceylon—the top post in the colonial service. Before his arrival in Nigeria in 1919, the *Lagos Weekly Record* in a major editorial welcomed him as one whose "golden record in Crown Colony administration" promised well for Nigeria in the wake of Sir Frederick Lugard's "nefarious administration."[57] When Clifford left in 1925, there were no such fulsome outpourings. He could, nevertheless, look back on six years of constructive change. The Nigerian government at all levels was far stronger than the loose, almost chaotic entity he had inherited from Lugard.

The Final Years

Clifford's career after leaving Nigeria can be briefly summarized. He returned to Ceylon, where he had been so successful as colonial secretary in the years just before World War I. But now the political climate had changed. Constitutional advance had been rapid, particularly after the institution of the Montagu-Chelmsford reforms in India. In 1920 the Ceylonese legislative council had been increased in size and an unofficial majority had come into being. Additional elected territorial and communal members were added in 1923. The governor could no longer veto legislation but could only recommend such action to the secretary of state. Neither could he arbitrarily cut off debate in the council. The governor still retained his powers of certification and he alone could initiate financial legislation.

Clifford disliked these constitutional arrangements and vehemently denounced them. Some observers accused him of not wanting the constitution to
work; some attribute his implacable hostility to his growing instability. In fact,
the 1923 reforms had taken power from the governor and transferred it to the
council without giving that agency commensurate responsibility. Sir Hugh's criticisms, transmitted to the colonial office, resulted in the appointment of a commission in 1927 headed by the Earl of Donoughmore to investigate the government of
Ceylon. Its report, presented in the following year, supported many of Clifford's
criticisms and resulted eventually in the abolition of communal seats and the grant
of adult franchise.

The office of governor and high commissioner of the Straits settlements and
the Malayan federation fell vacant in 1927 and the colonial office acceded to Clifford's request for the position. After twenty-five years Clifford thus returned to an
area that in many ways, intellectually and emotionally, he had never left. Yet
Malaya, like Ceylon, also was in the process of change. Given Clifford's experience in administration and vast knowledge of the area, one might have expected
him to make a considerable impact. This, however, was not to be. Sir Hugh had
always been a man of decided opinion and quick temper. Associates had noticed,
even during the latter stages of his tenure in Nigeria, increased moods of depression and unusual behavior. These eccentricities increased while he was in Ceylon,
and eventually Clifford's instability caused his premature retirement.

By 1929, Sir Hugh Clifford's condition had worsened to such an extent that it
became necessary for him to resign as governor. According to the official explanation, Lady Clifford's health was waning and therefore it was necessary for them to
return to Britain. This was not true. Lady Clifford's health was not a problem,
but Clifford's growing instability was. His family and friends wanted Clifford to
return to England, where—with expert care and freed from the burdens of office
—with proper rest he could recuperate. Sir Hugh, however, never completely re-
covered. His retirement was not just a personal tragedy; it was also a major loss to
the government. It was likewise a loss to letters and history because he might have
contributed much to both in a happier retirement. Clifford was one of the most
brilliant men ever to serve the empire. He never again held a responsible position.
His death in 1941 brought to an end a remarkable career. In pursuit of his avocation of writing, he had achieved a stature just below the first rank of his contemporaries. As a colonial governor, he had brought his intelligence and integrity to
bear upon the problems of five major territories.

Clifford's service in Africa, though not as dramatic as was his earlier career in
Malaya, had far-reaching effects. His tenure in the Gold Coast laid the foundations upon which Guggisberg would later build. In Nigeria, his reforms of the central government were fundamental. He possessed an introspective empathy with
subject peoples that was shown in his conceptualization and practice of indirect
rule in Asia and Africa. His approach was more logical and more humane than
that of his famous contemporary Lord Lugard. Clifford played as important a
part in the formulation and development of the principles of indirect rule in West
Africa as Lugard did. His work deeply influenced many of the outstanding governors in Africa in the period between the wars. Among these was Sir Donald
Cameron, who angrily repudiated the suggestion that he was Lugard's disciple

and insisted that he had learned the positive principles of native administration from Sir Hugh Clifford.[58] He was one of the great governors of the twentieth century.

Notes

1. For further basic details of Clifford's early life see William R. Rolff, ed., *Stories by Sir Hugh Clifford* (Kuala Lumpur, 1966), pp. viii–x. Considerable help in the preparation of this chapter was obtained from Sir Hugh's grandson, Hugo Holmes, particularly those portions relating to Clifford's private life, and from I. F. Nicolson, who read the chapter.

2. For Weld's contribution to Malaya see Alice, Lady Lovat, *The Life of Sir Frederick Weld* (London, 1914).

3. For the background to European expansion in Southeast Asia and Indonesia see Sir Richard O. Winstedt, *Malaya and Its History* (London, 1951); Virginia Thompson, *Thailand: The New Siam* (New York, 1967), pp. 154–165.

4. Winstedt, *Malaya*, p. 66.

5. Chai Hon-chan, *The Development of British Malaya, 1896–1909* (New York, 1964), p. 11.

6. Lady Lovat, *Sir Frederick Weld*, p. 393.

7. Clifford noted many times how contented he was with such isolation from bureaucratic control. See, for example, Sir Hugh Clifford, *Bush-Whacking and Other Tales from Malaya* (London, 1929), pp. 120–121.

8. Chai Hon-chan and E. Sadka, "The Journal of Sir Hugh Low, Perak, 1877," *Journal Malayan Branch of the Royal Asiatic Society* (November 1954).

9. W. S. Maxwell and W. S. Gibson, eds., *Treaties and Engagements Affecting the Malay States and Borneo* (London, 1924).

10. Sir Hugh Clifford, *The Further Side of Silence* (Garden City, 1927), p. x.

11. Clifford, *Bush-Whacking*, p. 6.

12. Ibid., pp. 85 ff.; Chai, *Development of British Malaya*, pp. 28–29.

13. Sir Frank Swettenham, *British Malaya* (London, 1906), p. 271.

14. For details of the establishment of the federation see Chai, *Development of British Malaya*, pp. 36–37, 43–44; K. S. Tregonning, *A History of Modern Malaya* (Singapore, 1964), pp. 164–165.

15. Chai, *Development of British Malaya*, p. 271.

16. K. G. Tregonning, *Under Chartered Company Rule: North Borneo, 1881–1946* (Singapore, 1958), p. 59; also see John Bastin and R. W. Winks, *Malaysia: Selected Historical Readings* (London, 1966), pp. 236–246.

17. Clifford, *Bush-Whacking*, p. 193.

18. A few references to Clifford at this time can be found in Leonard Woolf, *Growing; An Autobiography of the Years 1904 to 1911* (London, 1961), pp. 137–138, 144–145, 170–171.

19. Joseph Conrad to Sir Hugh Clifford, 22 June 1911, in G. Jean-Aubry, *Joseph Conrad; Life and Letters*, 2 vols. (Garden City, 1927), 2:131–132.

20. Interview with Sir Alan Burns, London, January 8, 1975; R. E. Wraith, *Guggisberg* (London, 1967), pp. 74–75.

21. Clifford, *Bush-Whacking*, p. 132.

22. Sir Hugh Clifford, *A Prince of Malaya* (New York, 1926), foreword.

23. W. W. Claridge, *History of the Gold Coast and Ashanti*, 2 vols. (New York, 1964), 1:23.

24. A good account of Gold Coast conditions is David Kimble, *A Political History of Ghana: The Rise of Gold Coast Nationalism* (London, 1965).

25. Wraith, *Guggisberg*, pp. 73–97, devotes an entire chapter to Clifford as the originator of many of those advances attributed to Guggisberg.

26. See. for example, the dispatch from Clifford to Harcourt, 3 March 1913, Colonial Office (hereinafter cited C.O.) 96/528.

27. Wraith, *Guggisberg*, pp. 80–81.

28. Kimble, *Political History of Ghana*, pp. 81–83.

29. Gold Coast, *Sessional Paper*, no. XVII of 1918–1919.

30. Wraith, *Guggisberg*, pp. 89–90.

31. Kimble, *Political History of Ghana*, pp. 102–103.

32. Colonial Office Paper, Africa (West), no. 1065, confidential, *Memorandum on Togoland* (London, 1918).

33. Clifford's early dissatisfaction with the government is reflected in Clifford to Harcourt, 3 March 1913, C.O. 96/528. The bulk of correspondence concerning revision of the legislative council is in Gold Coast, *Sessional Paper*, no. VII of 1916–1917.

34. Great Britain, Parliamentary Papers, Cmd. 1600, *Report of a Committee on Trade and Taxation for British West Africa* (London, 1922); Kimble, *Political History of Ghana*, pp. 54–55.

35. An excellent short discussion of Clifford's attempt to change the native jurisdiction ordinance is in Kimble, *Political History of Ghana*, pp. 471–476.

36. Gold Coast, *Legislative Council Debates*, 25 September 1916.

37. Wraith, *Guggisberg*, p. 97.

38. Clifford had earlier been seriously considered as Lugard's successor as governor of Northern Nigeria in 1906. I. F. Nicolson, *The Administration of Nigeria, 1900–1960* (London, 1969), p. 109.

39. Correspondence between Walter Long and Lugard from April 1917 to December 1918 in Lugard Papers, Mss. British Empire S. 73, Rhodes House, Oxford.

40. For a reinterpretation of Lugard's administration see Nicolson, *Administration of Nigeria*, pp. 180–250.

41. For the background of British activity in Egbaland see A. K. Ajasafe, *A History of Abeokuta* (Abeokuta, 1924); Margery Perham, *Lugard: the Years of Authority, 1889–1945* (London, 1960), pp. 456, 449–450; Colonial Office Paper, Africa (West), no. 1070, confidential, *Report by Sir F. D. Lugard on the Amalgamation of Northern and Southern Nigeria, and administration, 1912–1919* (London, 1919); for the commission of inquiry report, March 1915, see C.O. 583/34.

42. The most comprehensive treatment of the Abeokuta uprising is contained in the Maxwell report in C.O. 583/72; see also "Report from Lt. Col. Feneran, O. C. West African Service Brigade, to Lugard, 9 Aug. 1918," in C.O. 583/68.

43. Minute papers attached to Acting governor Boyle's dispatch, July 1919, C.O. 583/75; Clifford to Milner, confidential, 29 August 1919, and minute papers appended to dispatch, C.O. 583/77.

44. Amery to Clifford, 8 January 1920, C.O. 583/77.

45. See, for example, Clifford to Milner, confidential, 24 June 1920, C.O. 583/89.

46. See A. J. Herbert's minute in ibid.

47. Harcourt to Lugard, 14 August 1914 and 30 April 1915, in Chief Secretary Office (hereinafter cited C.S.O.) file 9/1/18, Federal Archives, Ibadan.

48. S. M. Grier, *Report on the Eastern Provinces by the Secretary for Native Affairs* (Lagos, 1922).

49. G. J. F. Tomlinson, *Report of a Tour of the Eastern Provinces by the Assistant Secretary for Native Affairs* (Lagos, 1923).

50. Memorandum by Sir Harry Moorhouse, C.S.O. 26/2, file 17720, vol. 1.

51. For these disturbances see Harry A. Gailey, *The Road to Aba* (New York, 1970).

52. Clifford to Milner, confidential, 26 May 1920, C.O. 583/88.

53. See various long, detailed dispatches in C.O. 583/88 and C.O. 583/94.

54. Sir Hugh Clifford, *Address to Nigerian Council* (Lagos, 1920), p. 29; over 300 pages long, it covered every aspect of the Nigerian scene and Clifford's reactions to the major problems of the day.

55. For the government's position on the *Eleko* affair see Acting governor Cameron's dispatch to the Colonial Office, 10 June 1921, C.O. 583/101.

56. Michael Crowder, *A Short History of Nigeria* (New York, 1966), p. 256.

57. *Lagos Weekly Record*, 14 June 1919, reprinted in A. H. M. Kirk-Greene, ed., *Lugard and the Amalgamation of Nigeria: A Documentary Record* (London, 1968), pp. 278–281.

58. Sir Donald Cameron, *My Tanganyika Service and Some Nigeria* (London, 1939), p. 150.

Frederick Lugard: The Making of an Autocrat (1858-1943)

John E. Flint

IN their political, constitutional, and legal history the British have rightly been characterized as a people not given to dogma and inflexible insistence upon the application of political theory to administrative practice. Rather, such characteristics have been assigned to the French, over whose fertile and ebullient minds logic and rationality are said to have held sway since the revolution of 1789; whereas the British muddled from one pragmatism to another—with infinitely preferable results, the Englishman would add. These generalizations have been taken to fit, with a special appropriateness, the evolutionary (and nonrevolutionary) history of the British empire, founded, developed, matured, and ultimately transformed into the Commonwealth in what Sir John Seeley memorably termed "a fit of absence of mind."

In the development of British colonial administration in Africa, however, the period 1890–1945 exhibits quite the contrary appearance. Steadily the men and machinery of colonial administration, whether in London or in Africa, developed a credo of political theory upon which the administration of Africans was based and strove dogmatically to maintain and extend its practices and principles over peoples and territories to which its application was often singularly inappropriate. The extent to which the British had become adherents of a doctrine is shown by the precise meaning that came to be attached to the words "native administration." In the English language these words carry no more meaning than that of categorizing all the ways in which locally born people might be governed. In

British colonial jargon, however, "native administration" referred to a specific system for integrating the traditional African rulers into the colonial administration, the system often more loosely termed "indirect rule." In "discovering" the system, the British imagined they had lighted upon the secret of successfully ruling "Africans," and they made of native administration both a blueprint for action and a moral and theoretical philosophy with which to justify imperial rule in twentieth-century conditions.

To assign the emergence of such a colonial doctrine to the career of one man would obviously be simplistic: the roots of the indirect rule philosophy run deep in British imperial history. But one man, Frederick Dealtry Lugard, exercised such a profound influence over the development of native administration in British colonial Africa that it is justifiable to speak of "the Lugardian system" and to term its philosophy that of "Lugardian principles." It was Lugard who, after playing a significant role in the partition of Africa in the 1890s and in the transition of British public opinion to support of imperial expansion in Africa, himself set up the classical system of indirect rule in Northern Nigeria from 1900–1906, extended its principles into Southern Nigeria, when the country was "unified" by him after 1912, created the "blueprints" of "native administration" by the issuance of his "Political Memoranda"[1] for the instruction of administrators, and finally formed indirect rule into a justification and apologia for colonial rule in *The Dual Mandate in British Tropical Africa*.[2] No other British colonial governor in Africa had a comparable impact on the shape and nature of colonial rule.

Early Career

Lugard, born in 1858,[3] grew up in the period that has been described as "the climax of anti-imperialism"[4]—the years in which the British colonies favored by white settlers increased their autonomy through the institutions of responsible government, in which the Manchester school of free trade pursued commercial expansion while avoiding territorial empire, and in which African annexations in particular were looked upon with disfavor. But these influences had no impact on the young Lugard; his family stamped on him a familiarity with Britain's imperial role and propelled him toward an imperial career. His mother had been a Church Missionary Society worker in India and his father (the son of a soldier) served as East India Company chaplain at Madras. Both were evangelical Anglicans. And Lugard's mother could be seen as a martyr to the cause: in 1863 ill health drove her back to England, where she died in 1865, when her son was seven years old. The Reverend Frederick Lugard had secured a modest living as rector of St. Clement's, Worcester, and managed to provide his son with an indifferent education at Rossall, an Anglican public school that enjoyed little academic reputation.

At this time young Lugard's hero was Livingstone, and his ambition was to enter the Indian civil service but he failed the entrance examination. Family background now determined Lugard's choice of an alternative career; the most distinguished of the Lugards was his uncle, General Sir Edward Lugard, who from 1861 to 1871 had served as permanent undersecretary for war. With his advice Lugard took the army examinations at the end of 1877 and passed, sixth of nearly 1,000 candidates. In 1878 he entered the Royal Military College, Sandhurst, and there followed nine years of service with the East Norfolk Regiment in India. He saw fighting in the Afghan campaign of 1879, passed the higher examinations in Hindi and Urdu, shot tiger, hunted wild boar, played polo, and immersed himself in the social life of the British in India. In 1885 he saw his first active service in Africa in the Suakin campaign, but this seemed to have made little impact on him; the next year he joined the Burma campaign. Early in 1877 it might have been expected that Frederick Lugard was well set upon a modestly successful military career.

Lugard now suffered a traumatic emotional experience, which was to prove the turning point in his life. He had fallen deeply in love with a remarried divorcée in Lucknow, whose identity remains shrouded in mystery by his biographer.[5] That lady used him so badly that she almost drove him to suicide. In the middle of 1877, while still in Burma, Lugard received a telegram that she was dying after an accident in which she had overturned a coach. Rushing back to India, Lugard found the lady gone to England; he sailed for England, where he found her, hale and hearty, surrounded by a circle of "fast" friends, with her emotional needs quite satisfied elsewhere. The affair made him utterly desperate; he lost his religious faith and flung himself into a series of dangerous pursuits that may well have been designed to end his life in useful but hazardous work. For two months he fought fires as a volunteer with the new London fire brigade. Then he resolved to leave England, emulate his hero Livingstone, and seek danger and perhaps a noble death fighting the slave trade in East Africa.

He sailed for Italy on a rather wild plan to join the Italian forces preparing to attack Ethiopia but, finding that the Italians would not have him, took a deck passage on an Italian ship bound for Aden. There he picked up a British ship traveling down the East African coast and was forced to take second-class passage as white men were not permitted to travel with the Arabs and Africans as deck passengers. He thus was able to meet Colonel Euan Smith, the British consul at Zanzibar, who provided him with a letter of introduction to the British consul in Mozambique, in the hopes that he might find employment with the African Lakes Company then fighting Arab slave traders at the north end of Lake Nyasa in support of Scottish missionaries. These contacts bore fruit, and in May 1888 Lugard made his way to Lake Nyasa to lead a military attack on the Arab stockade at Karonga's settlement. But these actions were hardly triumphant; repeated attacks, culminating in March 1889, failed to dislodge the Arabs, and Lugard returned to England to turn public opinion in favor of official British intervention in Nyasaland to establish a protectorate. His ambitions were already political. He hoped to make his name known by writing about his adventures in Nyasaland and arguing for British control there, and he had high hopes that he himself might secure the appointment to carry the policy through. In this he was disappointed; Britain did eventually, in May 1891, declare a protectorate over Nyasaland, but the new territory was to be administered by Harry Johnston, much to Lugard's humiliation and bitter chagrin.

Uganda Pioneer

Lugard had made his mark in British African circles. He published four articles on Nyasaland in 1889 and had developed close relationships with Scottish humanitarians active in the antislavery movement, as well as with British officials on the

East African coast. Through these, Lugard later that year secured a vague appointment to serve the newly chartered Imperial British East Africa Company. After leading caravans and founding stations in Kenya, he was appointed in mid-1890 to lead an expedition into Uganda. By this time his ambitions had matured, and an imperious streak in his character displayed itself in his insistence that he should have complete command of the expedition, independent of the company's administrator, Sir Francis de Winton.

Lugard's experiences in Uganda, and even more his political activities in England that followed, were to place him in the forefront of British African politics. This was not because his activities in Uganda were particularly successful. As earlier in Nyasaland, Lugard overstretched the resources at his disposal and was himself largely responsible for hastening the bankruptcy of the Imperial British East Africa Company, which employed him. In the process he also became the central figure in a bitter controversy with the French government. The kingdom of Buganda on the north shore of Lake Victoria had—since the entry of British Protestant missionaries in 1877 and that of the French Catholics two years later—become a battleground for religious factions. Lugard took the decision to arm the Baganda Protestants and help them with his company troops in their attack on the Catholics. No doubt the chartered company would eventually have bankrupted itself without Lugard's help, and at some stage a struggle for power between Baganda Protestants and Catholics would have taken place. Nevertheless, the official report on Lugard's activities by Captain J. R. L. Macdonald was highly critical, condemning Lugard for religious partiality, for leaving the capital city of Kampala virtually undefended while he wandered westward to collect Sudanese soldiers, and worst of all, in Macdonald's opinion, for the fact that "by adopting a high-handed policy and by injudicious management of the crisis, he precipitated civil war in Uganda."[6]

Macdonald's report was never published. For during the time in which Macdonald was conducting his investigations Lugard was assiduously at work in Britain, developing the techniques of self-advertisement that he had used after his return from the (likewise unsuccessful) foray into Nyasaland. This time, however, the Uganda question occupied a much more central position on the British political stage. The bankruptcy of the Imperial British East Africa Company, and the claims of the French government for compensation for its missionaries in Uganda, raised two questions for the British government in acute form. What were the responsibilities of the British government for the actions of chartered companies? And given that the Imperial British East Africa Company was bankrupt, should Britain withdraw from Uganda or assume direct colonial responsibility? Uganda became the catalyst for a central decision in British policy: would the "reluctant expansion" of the 1880s, achieved through vague methods such as "spheres of influence" dominated by chartered companies (which cost the British taxpayer nothing and supposedly relieved the imperial government of direct responsibility), have to be replaced by a direct and vigorous policy of imperialist expansion? As these questions became the center of public and parliamentary debate, Lugard was able to abandon his posture of defense against the charges of the French and take his stand for the British retention of Uganda, imperialism, and expansion. This was also the way in which British political forces were moving.[7] In mid-1894, with Gladstone resigned and the Liberal imperialist Lord Rosebery prime minister and foreign secretary, the decision to retain Uganda was finally sealed. In the

public mind Lugard had emerged as the prime mover in the campaign for retention.

Royal Niger Company

Political success did not bring the rewards of office for which Lugard had hoped.
Repeated efforts to secure a high post in the new East African administration were
rebuffed. As Lugard finally understood the position, "Lord Rosebery considered
that my return would be regarded as an affront to the French government."[8]
Lugard therefore accepted an offer from Sir George Goldie[9] to work with yet
another chartered company. His task was to protect the northwestern area of the
territories of the Royal Niger Company in Borgu, where French incursions threatened to break the company's control of the navigable portion of the Niger from
Bussa to the sea. Lugard was to lead an expedition into Borgu to make prior
treaties with the kings of Borgu in which they would cede their territories to the
company.

The story of Lugard's expedition to Borgu from July 1894 until his return to
England in May 1895 has been considered in detail elsewhere.[10] Once again, however, this mission to Africa must be considered a failure, but a failure that was inevitable because of the constraints under which Lugard was made to operate.
Goldie insisted that Lugard have only a small, inexpensive force, no "occupation"
of the Borguan towns was contemplated; the French encroachments would be resisted with pieces of paper, not soldiers and officials, for the company made its
money by trading, not administering. It was therefore inevitable that Lugard's
treaty making would be challenged by the French, whose forces were in a position
to occupy the towns in which Lugard had claimed previously to have made
treaties. Accordingly, the best Lugard could do was to establish legalistic claims
for the company. Unfortunately, he failed even to do this convincingly. At the
town of Nikki, which was later to become the focus of British and French claims to
Borgu, Lugard was unable even to secure a meeting with the African king. Instead
he obtained the signatures of a local imam, or holy man, and two of the king's
councillors (one of whom was the head butcher) to a preprinted, formula treaty.
He nevertheless wrote in to the document that it had been made "between the
King of Nikki (which is the capital of Borgu)" and the Royal Niger Company; the
Arabic signature of the imam was described on the treaty as "signature of native
ruler." Lugard also inserted a name for the king in the treaty, which was later
shown to be the name of a king who had been dead for six years.[11] Shortly afterward he had to fight his way out of Borgu and abandon his original plan to strike
further westward to make more treaties that would serve as counterweights to
French claims.

Returning to England in May 1895 Lugard once again threw himself into writing and speaking, this time on West African affairs and the Royal Niger Company
and Borgu in particular. His productivity was astonishing; articles in *Blackwoods*
and the *Nineteenth Century* in June, a paper read at the Royal Geographical Society in July, two more pieces in the *National Review* in July and August, and five
more articles in various magazines before the year was out.[12] All this was interspersed with a round of speaking engagements, letters to the press, and interviews

with colonial office and foreign office officials and politicians of the day. Again the times favored him; the Borgu question was slowly growing, in the years from 1895 to 1898, into the "Niger crisis," and the British and French would not settle their differences over the frontiers of their West African colonies until August 1898. Indeed, the problem of defending the northwestern frontiers of Nigeria would eventually bring Lugard the official position he so eagerly desired. But not at once; throughout 1895, despite the patronage and persistent lobbying of Goldie, despite the lionization of London society, and despite the award of a C.B., the British government would offer him no post of consequence in either East or West Africa. Once again Lugard was forced to accept employment by a private company.

His new post was with the British West Charterland Company and his task was to lead an expedition to the area around Lake Ngami, in the Kalahari desert, to prospect for gold and diamonds. The terms were extraordinarily generous, £6,000 a year in salary, a seat on the board, a post for his younger brother as second in command, and the right to resign at once if he should be offered official employment. His real interest in the post, however, lay in the possibility that the company might gain powers of government in the area, either by royal charter or by delegation from Rhodes's chartered British South Africa Company, which had rival claims to the area. Neither of these prospects materialized, nor did the gold or diamonds, and throughout his stay in Ngami country Lugard longed for "a higher class of work, with greater results, the building of an Empire."[13] At the same time his ambition remained fixed exclusively on a post in which he would command and be under no man's orders; he had "much misgiving that I am not suited to work under *any* man!"[14] It was with bitter disappointment that in January 1897 he received a letter from Lord Salisbury indicating that there would no post for him in the British administration of East Africa.

West African Frontier Force

In the colonial office, however, Lugard's prestige was greater. The Borgu question and Anglo-French rivalry on the Niger bend were still unresolved, and Goldie's Niger Company was not an effective instrument with which to face the increasing activities of French officers commanding small parties of trained African troops and proclaiming the doctrine of "effective occupation." By July 1897 the imperialist colonial secretary, Joseph Chamberlain, had resolved to resist the French in West Africa with their own methods by the creation of a British West African colonial army. At the end of the month Chamberlain cabled Lugard in Ngamiland, offering him the command of the new force, with the title of commissioner and commandant and the local rank of lieutenant colonel.[15] In choosing Lugard, whose reputation in France was still that of an archenemy, Chamberlain threw down the gauntlet to the French.

With the command of the West African Frontier Force, as it was later to be known, Lugard, at thirty-nine years of age, assumed his first government post. It was not a role exactly to his liking or ambitions for he wished above all to be a colonial administrator, had lost all desire for soldiering, and wanted political not military command. Yet the vague title of commissioner gave some promise of a political role, and the very fact that the British taxpayer was supporting an army to defend the Niger Company's sphere made it clear that at some not distant future date Joseph Chamberlain's direct brand of imperialism would establish colonial office control and abolish the Niger Company's anachronistic powers.[16] If Lugard carefully served Chamberlain, he could expect to assume the governorship of the company's former territories in due course once the French threat had been contained.

It is revealing of Lugard's imperious character, his will to domination and fanatical desire for autonomy of decision, that in this delicate position, from the outset of his first official appointment, he showed no disposition to accept the normal and recognized constraints of his office or even to cooperate with Chamberlain's ideas and plans. At this time Lugard was much under the spell of Sir George Goldie and had accepted Goldie's views of handling the situation even before he discussed the matter with Chamberlain. Goldie had particular axes to grind; with his company about to be taken over by the colonial office he wished to achieve a favorable financial settlement while the French pressure was most intense and the British government had need of his cooperation in providing men, transport, and supplies. But Chamberlain wanted the French question settled before he would turn to the problem of taking over the company's administration. If Goldie would not cooperate, the business could be worked through the Lagos colony in the south, where the government was directly under the colonial office.

But now Chamberlain was to find Lugard obstructive to any such alternative and determined to play the game Goldie's way. At his first interview with Chamberlain on November 12, 1897, the latter expounded the policy that he expected his subordinate to follow. Chamberlain's plan was to resist the French with what was called the "chessboard" plan; where the French had occupied towns claimed as being within the British sphere Lugard was ordered to move parties of soldiers around and behind them, occupying towns and villages and running up the Union Jack, until "effective occupation" would become no more rational than treaties as a claim for jurisdiction and the matter would have to be settled by diplomacy, with the French position weakening daily. Chamberlain judged that the French would not fight, and his judgment was sound here.

To all this Lugard first stalled, saying that it would be months before he could train a force for such activity. Then, to Chamberlain's annoyance, Lugard announced that his base would have to be at Lakoja, in the company's territories (where he would need the company's cooperation), and that he could not operate from Lagos. ("My *main* reason," he wrote later in his diary, "was to be out of the jurisdiction of Lagos and its Governor.")[17] Finally, Lugard insisted that he could not agree with the chessboard policy; he boldly put forward a completely different proposal, which was both naive and impudent, in which France should be told that British troops would advance up the river and that if the French did not withdraw from Borgu there would be a "collision." As a sop to France they could be offered the Sokoto empire north of twelve degrees latitude in return for a settlement of the Nile question. This so-called solution already had been proposed by Goldie and it angered Chamberlain, who could see it for what it was—a sacrifice of future British control of Northern Nigeria in return for the safeguarding of the Niger Company's monopoly of the Niger waterway below the Bussa rapids. Not surprisingly, Chamberlain was incensed, and Lugard would have resigned had not Goldie insisted that he must not do so.

It is extraordinary that this conflict was never really resolved. Chamberlain to the last insisted on his chessboard scheme, whereas Lugard continued to oppose it. Lugard delayed and delayed his departure for the Niger and as the months dragged on became in effect a conspirator with Goldie against the colonial secretary. Goldie was still fighting for his company and hoped that it could continue as a purely administrative body, like the East India Company after 1833, with himself as a governor in England and Lugard as the administrator on the spot. The two even attempted to set the chancellor of the exchequer (who would have to find the money to buy out the Royal Niger Company) against Chamberlain on the issue, tempting him with their "cheaper" scheme of continued company rule. Meanwhile, Lugard was engaged in continual skirmishes of a lesser kind from his office in London; he would not be subject, as a soldier, to war office control and insisted on choosing all his own officers. He would have as his second in command Colonel James Willcocks, who would look after the actual operations in the field, leaving Lugard to concentrate on the paperwork and "administration" on the Niger. Lugard made it clear that if he were to be placed in any way under the authority of Lagos he would resign at once. On all these issues he had his way.

But on the main issues Chamberlain prevailed. Lugard was forced to go out to the Niger, at long last, leaving Liverpool in March 1898 with the question of compensation to the Niger Company unsettled and the chessboard strategy still in his orders. Arriving at Lagos, where he carefully avoided a "very civil" invitation to visit the governor,[18] Lugard proceeded to the Niger, where he immersed himself in the creation of mountains of paperwork, plunging himself into the minutest details of organization and working such long hours that he became ill, delegating nothing—except the actual conduct of the chessboard policy in the field. This strategy was implemented by Colonel Willcocks and his soldiers, with all the successful results that Chamberlain had expected. The French did not fight; they came to terms and in June 1898 all the outstanding questions of Anglo-French frontier rivalry were settled by the signature of a convention.[19]

Conquest in Northern Nigeria

Chamberlain was now ready to proceed with the reorganization of Northern Nigeria. There were long and tedious negotiations with Goldie over compensation to the Royal Niger Company,[20] but well before these were completed Chamberlain was forging ahead with setting up the new regime. It appears from the documents that early in 1898 Chamberlain had Goldie in mind as governor for the new region,[21] but Goldie either withdrew or was dropped. In November 1898 Chamberlain offered the post to Lugard, who accepted.[22]

Already the main lines of policy for governing Northern Nigeria had been laid down in the report of the Niger committee in August 1898.[23] Chaired by Lord Selborne, the colonial undersecretary, with Goldie and the governors of Lagos and the Niger coast protectorate as the "expert" members, the committee favored a policy of gradualness and moderation. There must be no attempt to take control of the Muslim emirates of the north by sudden military conquest, nor should there be any attempt to tax the people directly. The general tenor of the report was for continuity—military and political provocation must be avoided, authority established over the emirs one by one, and efforts concentrated on expanding trade, and therefore customs revenue, with Southern Nigeria the model for steady development. Its emphasis was therefore one of the gradual assertion of British overlordship in the region by peaceful means in which British influence would slowly be transformed into British control.

Lugard had played no part in the formulation of this policy, and when he assumed office on January 1, 1900, as high commissioner for Northern Nigeria he was determined to carry through an altogether different program. His was not the temperament to carry out policies designed by others. He had waited until middle age for this appointment; from it he intended to carve a place in history; and for him the slow process of peaceful penetration represented the road to obscurity. Moreover, Lugard's long experience with chartered and would-be chartered companies had exhausted his patience with the vaguenesses of informal penetration, spheres of influence, treaty making, and such expedients. Though he frequently expressed to his friends and in his diaries his growing dislike of soldiering and fighting, he had developed to an almost obsessive degree a somewhat simplistic military view of the nature of colonial politics and administration, in which the hierarchy of command and the flow of decision down through the structure of administration remained the key to effective administrative action. Lugard saw his position as governor almost exactly upon the analogy of a general commanding an army. He was the general, the British members of the administration were his officers to carry out his orders, whilst the colony itself was seen as a region undergoing a long-term and beneficient military occupation by English officers and gentlemen imbued with a code of military chivalry. The Niger committee's plans and policy called for an administration of tactful diplomatists with a keen eye for trade and commerce; with Lugard in charge, and with his insistence on controlling every detail of recruitment and local policy, a very different course would be set.

As Lugard assumed office there could have been no worse time for him to seek what he regarded as the key to successful administration: the military conquest of Northern Nigeria. The Anglo-Boer war in South Africa had erupted in October 1899, and British troops and money were being diverted there on an every increasing scale throughout 1900 and 1901. South Africa became the focus of British concern, and governors elsewhere in Africa were expected to lead a quiet life. Only three months after Lugard assumed office his troops had to be sent to the Gold Coast to assist in the campaign against Ashanti and did not return until December 1900. Nevertheless, Lugard was itching to establish some real control over at least some of the northern emirates. Steadily the colonial office resisted any such suggestions. In response to requests from Lugard to be unleashed[24] Chamberlain replied firmly, "We must not have another native war."[25] But Lugard was not to be bound by these restraints. He knew that the man on the spot could, as the only man "fully informed," wield enormous influence in the field and on British opinion by stressing the dangers of the situation and the need for effective and immediate action.

In addition, Lugard now developed a special tactic—the appeal to antislavery considerations. The theme of widespread slave raiding, developed in dispatches to the colonial office carefully written with a view to possible subsequent publication and stressed in the published *Annual Reports* of these early years, was one that Lugard played up for all it was worth. These accounts were often exaggerated to an absurd degree, as when Lugard in August 1900 described the effects of raids by Bida and Kontagora:

> Large slave raiding bands have been out devastating the country during the last month or two. . . . The populous country to the north of the Niger is rapidly becoming as depopulated as the country to the south became, where, owing to Nupe raids a mere fraction of the people now remain, and the traveller passed deserted and ruined villages one after another.[26]

In the months that followed Lugard repeatedly railed against local rulers, adding to the antislavery argument that of the disastrous effects that delay in dealing with them would have on the prestige of the British administration. In January 1901, almost immediately after the troops returned from the Gold Coast, expeditions were launched first against Kontagora then in February against Bida. The dispatch on these actions was not written until March 12, and it was largely taken up with painting the horrors of the country laid waste by the wicked rulers, where "many thousands have been carried off as slaves" and the country "almost depopulated."[27] Lugard used even more lurid terms in the *Annual Report* for 1900–1901, which ended by announcing (though the colonial office had sanctioned no such moves) that "there still remain the great slave raiders in the east—Yola and Bautshi—and these I propose to coerce this year."[28]

In April 1901 Lugard returned to Britain, where he was to spend the next seven months. He did not, however, leave Nigerian affairs in the hands of Acting governor Wallace but installed himself in the colonial office and proceeded to direct the affairs of the colony from there. The conquest of the Benue valley was now undertaken, with Wallace supplying the information that Yola was the scene of the worst slave raiding in the protectorate, Lugard concurring, and Chamberlain eventually sanctioning the Yola expedition.[29] Returning to the Niger in November, Lugard was soon informing Chamberlain that Bautshi "long . . . the scene of continued warfare and slave raiding" must soon be conquered[30] and that it was duly subdued early in 1902. The Bautshi expedition marched on to Bornu, where the French had deposed the sheik; the British invited him back, reinstated him, and secured his allegiance without bloodshed in the first major triumph of peaceful penetration of Lugard's regime.

The *Annual Report* for 1902 translated the need for military conquest into political-anthropoligical theory. Lugard announced: "It is unfortunately true that the African savage in his primitive state can, as a rule, understand nothing but force, and regards arguments and verbal lessons as weapons of the weak, to be listened to for the moment and set aside when convenient." The purpose of such phrasing was purely propagandist; Lugard was well aware that the regimes over which he was establishing military control could by no stretch of imagination be described as "savage" or in a "primitive state" even by the Eurocentric standards of the time. Moreover, the sentiments contradicted his actions for at each conquered place he busied himself with installing Fulani rulers, usually close relatives of the leaders he had deposed. This he did "not without some reluctance" and "as an experiment," yet he wished to "utilize, if possible, their wonderful intelligence, for they are born rulers and incomparably above the negroid tribes in ability."[31]

The conquests of 1900–1902 had resulted in the military control of the Niger and Benue riverine states; there still remained, however, the heartland of the

Fulani empire, the sultanate of Sokoto, the suzerain head of the caliphate (the emirate of Gwandu controlling the western half of the empire). This northern region was the cultural and economic center of the Hausa-Fulani society and included the major city of Kano. From the early days of the West African Frontier Force the colonial office had consistently made it clear that a collision with Sokoto and the northern emirates was to be avoided. The fact that Sokoto was the religious head of the caliphate made the British doubly circumspect, for the murder of General Charles Gordon by the Mahdists in the Sudan was still remembered as a national disaster. Experienced hands like William Wallace, who had served for many years with the Niger Company, supported the view that gradual and peaceful development of relations with Sokoto was possible. Wallace felt that a resident might be appointed in Kano "with the consent of the people in a couple of years," and at the end of 1901 he himself volunteered to undertake a mission to Sokoto as he thought it "only fair" that the sultan be approached with friendly advances.[32]

From the first Lugard seems to have been bent on settling matters with Sokoto by a military showdown. There is no evidence that he made any attempts to build a relationship with Sokoto or Gwandu by diplomatic overtures. He canceled the payment of the subsidies due to them under their treaties with the Royal Niger Company, obligations that the protectorate government assumed, with no explanation to the Fulani. The colonial office was told that this action was in retaliation for "the unfriendly attitude of these Emirs." In the *Annual Report* for 1900–1901 Sokoto and Gwandu were described as dangerous and menacing, "great centres of the slave trade," and it was suggested that their populations would welcome a British conquest.[33] In a dispatch of March 1902 Lugard made reference to "the Sokoto faction, viz. the zealous Mohammedan and Fulani clique"[34]—an extraordinary way to describe the governing class of one of the major states of Africa.

But it was from October 1902 that Lugard began to pile up the pressure to persuade the colonial office that he should be allowed to attack the sultan and the northern emirs. He now had provocation, with the murder in Zaria of Captain Maloney, the British resident. The murderer fled to Kano, where he was treated as a hero by the emir. At the same time Lugard was told to provide protection for the Anglo-French commissioners who were to delimit the frontier agreed upon in the convention of 1898. This, Lugard announced, would mean that a force would have to visit Sokoto "to put an end to the present unsatisfactory position."[35] Toward the end of November 1902 Lugard warned the colonial office that the conquest of the remaining Fulani emirates "cannot be delayed" and that the arrival of the boundary commission would precipitate the conquest.[36]

In response to these proddings Lugard received no encouragement, let alone authorization, from the colonial office to proceed with an attack on Kano or Sokoto. Indeed, the colonial office seems not to have read his dispatches with sufficient care to realize that Lugard was likely to move. Thus, when on December 5, 1902, the *London Times* printed a Reuters report that Lugard was about to attack Kano there was alarm in the colonial office and not a little indignation when it was discovered that the plans seemed to be known in Liverpool and Paris but not at the seat of the empire. Lugard was telegraphed for an explanation and in reply alleged that Kano had prepared the war:

Safety of garrison of Zaria, prestige of British Government, possibility of delimitation of frontier, depend on energetic action. Paramount chiefs of this country await
result and if action deferred they would attribute to fear of them possibility of deplorable result.

The colonial office attempted to pull in the reins: "His Majesty's Government are
anxious to avoid military actions in West Africa. We have full confidence that you
will not engage in them unless they are absolutely necessary for defensive purposes." Lugard was asked for a full report.[37]

There followed almost a month of telegraphing, during which Lord Onslow,
the undersecretary at the colonial office (Chamberlain was in South Africa) attempted to keep control of Lugard and delay the expedition until the office could
be convinced of its necessity. The exchanges throw an interesting and revealing
light on the autonomy that could be enjoyed by an authoritarian governor who
was willing to act without too much concern for the truth. The colonial office
shrank from positively forbidding the expedition because the safety of British officials had to be entrusted to the discretionary power of the man on the spot.
Lugard repeatedly insisted that "for safety and defensive measures I am compelled to take energetic action."[38] As the controversy raged on into January
Lugard demanded that he be formally ordered to stop or allowed to go on, knowing of course that he alone was in a position to judge necessity. As Onslow continued to suggest alternative courses, including an attempt at diplomacy, Lugard
became angry and aggressive and his descriptions of the situation grew ever more
lurid. He suggested that those who advocated conciliation risked the murder of all
the British in Northern Nigeria.[39] On January 16, 1903, he described Kano and
Sokoto as towns "ruled by an alien race [i.e., the Fulani, the same people whom
he was installing as rulers in the conquered emirates] who buy and sell the people
of the country in large public slave markets" and referred to his task as that of
"prevention of the daily bloodshed which has already denuded this country of
probably half its population."[40] In the end Lugard had his way, being told that
the government "regret[ted] the necessity" of the action against Kano but accepted it as "inevitable."[41] The troops marched on January 29, taking Kano on
February 13 and moving on to Sokoto in March. By early April the resistance of
the northern rulers had collapsed and the Fulani empire was in British hands.

Paper Autocracy

The northern campaigns of 1903 did not put an end to the use of military force in
Northern Nigeria; indeed, the last few months of Lugard's tenure of office in 1906
were marked by fighting on the Benue and by the bloody massacre of peasant
rebels in Satiru.[42] But after 1903 the pattern of African resistance had changed;
the Fulani became the staunch allies of Lugard's regime, whereas those whom the
Fulani had traditionally oppressed, like the pagans of the Benue valley or the
peasant rebels of Satiru, resisted the British presence. The winning of the
allegiance of the Fulani ruling class was a crucial factor lending credence to
Lugard's claim, steadily developed from 1900 to 1906 and again after 1912, that
he had brought genius to the realm of colonial administration in Africa, that he

had discovered mystical secrets of African administration, and that he had developed a model regime, which his biographer described in 1960 as "the most comprehensive, coherent and renowned system of administration in our colonial history."[43] This was the system of indirect rule, or native administration. What was Lugard's role in the creation and shaping of what was to become the characteristic dogma of British rule in twentieth-century Africa?

It may be accepted, in Dame Margery Perham's words, that "Lugard's policy of ruling 'indirectly' through the Nigerian Emirs cannot . . . *as a general principle*, be claimed as either inventive or *original*."[44] British colonial rule over tropical areas and non-European peoples had never been strongly assimilationist, only mildly so in restricted enclaves, usually coastal towns, where traders and missionaries could have a decisive cultural impact on Asians or Africans. The partition of Africa brought vast areas under the control of tiny numbers of British officials and soldiers, and common sense brought to bear on limited resources quickly persuaded all the "experts"—Goldie, Mary Kingsley, all the West African colonial governors, the British traders, and the colonial office—to pursue the idea that Africa should be ruled through its traditional chiefs, its social institutions preserved, and "progress" introduced slowly and carefully. Even slavery could not be abolished at one fell swoop lest the social fabric disintegrate in chaos.

The fundamental problem in developing a system of indirect rule thus was the emphasis that must be placed on the two apparently contradictory words. How "indirect" should the "rule" be? What power of decision should be left with the "native chief"? There was general agreement that certain elements of sovereignty must be taken away. Imperial control necessitated the removal of an African ruler's right to make war, to command an army (as distinct from a police force), and to conduct foreign relations. These ideas were enshrined in the earliest protectorate treaties of the 1880s, as were assumptions that Britain must at once suppress "barbarous customs" such as trial by ordeal, human sacrifice, cannibalism, and twin murder. But beyond these limits there was implicit in the ideas current in the 1890s the theory that African states might continue to exist as living entities, with wills of their own, making some decisions on what should be preserved from tradition and how to effect modernization and "progress" in an organic way. In Southern Nigeria before 1912 there was considerable development along these lines in some of the states of Yorubaland and in the Niger delta.

Such an approach was well suited to British traditions; at the least it represented institutionalized muddling through and at best a sophisticated attempt to mitigate and control the destructive results of contact between alien cultures.

It is consistent with what has been said here of Lugard's career and temperament to argue that he was essentially opposed to this tradition. In the sense just described Lugard was not an indirect ruler. He did not regard the imposition of British rule in Northern Nigeria (and later in his writings this attitude was extended to the whole British African empire) as an imposition of "protection," with initiative left to the African precolonial states. His military conquests were designed to destroy *all* preexisting rights to sovereignty and to establish the British claim to rule by right of conquest. At the moment of conquest the precolonial state ceased to exist. If Fulani rulers were then installed by Lugard this was at his discretion; thereby the new sovereigns in effect became his officials and they could be removed by him at will. They had to swear to obey all "the lawful commands of the High Commissioner and of the Resident."[45]

Lugard's speech to the elders of Sokoto on March 21, 1903, immediately after the occupation of the town, left them in no doubt that the new sultan and his emirs would be appointed and subordinate officials

> They . . . have by defeat lost their rule which has come into the hands of the British. . . . Every Sultan and Emir and the principal officers of state will be appointed by the High Commissioner. . . .
>
> The Government will, in future, hold the rights in land which the Fulani took by conquest from the people, and if Government require land it will take it for any purpose. The Government hold the right of taxation, and will tell the Emirs and Chiefs what taxes they may levy, and what part of them must be paid to Government. The Government will have the right to all minerals. . . .
>
> When an Emirate, or an office of state, becomes vacant, it will only be filled with the consent of the High Commissioner.[46]

In Lugard's philosophy the Sokoto empire was not to be ruled indirectly in a fashion such that an overall British control would gradually influence the old system toward reform and progress. Instead, it was to be an integral part of the colonial regime, with a definitely subordinate status. At the same time, however, the traditional authorities ought to appear to the people as still in control and operating the old system so as to assure the population that no violence was to be done to their way of life. Thus, the residents appointed to each emirate must keep themselves in the background and appear not to interfere in the emir's government. There was about this concept much of the essence of a confidence trick.

In reality, however, there was "indirect rule" in Northern Nigeria, and in the history of the country in the years to 1966 the indirect element increased at the expense of British (and after 1960, Nigerian) rule. Whatever might be Lugard's theories, and his military concept of an autocracy with himself at the head, he lacked the men and the money before 1906 to do otherwise than allow the day-to-day government of the towns and countryside to remain in the administrative control of the emirs. There was little the residents could do except tackle the glaring abuses, and often this was of small effect. Indeed, the contrast between Lugard's claims of achievement and the reality of Northern Nigeria when he left office in 1906 is staggering.

I. N. Nicholson has argued convincingly that Lugard's major achievement was propagandistic; that by his *Annual Reports*, his dispatches to the colonial office, his "Political Memoranda" (published in 1906), and his and his wife's (Flora Shaw) published writings and speeches, he created the myth of his own genius and the myth of Northern Nigeria as a model administration.[47] Yet when Lugard left Northern Nigeria in 1906, there was little to show. The protectorate was unable to live off its own revenues. It had little external trade; no roads or railways of significance; no proper secretariat or government departments; and no colonial educational system or social services of any kind. Administration had consisted of military activities and mountains of paper issuing from Lugard's own hand.

It was thus a paper autocracy, one in which Lugard exulted. "I love this turgid life of command," he wrote to his wife, "when I can feel that the sole responsibility rests on me for everything."[48] Indeed, it was his unreasonable desire for permanent control that led him to resign in 1906, when he failed to persuade the colonial office to accept his scheme for "continuous administration," which would have allowed him to spend six months of each year administering Northern Nigeria from an office in London.

From 1906 to 1912 Lugard served as governor of Hong Kong. During these years the cadre of residents he had brought to Northern Nigeria developed its administration in a way that strengthened their own and the emirs' autonomy and powers. This they were able to do under British governors whose main interests and experience were in supervising the construction of the Northern railway. One of the most important developments of this period was the growth of the system of native treasuries whereby local revenues, after payment of the share due the central government, became available for spending by the emir's government. This policy introduced an element of initiative and autonomy into each emirate and brought the system much more into line with the ideas of indirect rule current in the 1890s.[49]

At the same time these developments, and the character and social background of the residents, continued to emphasize the growing divergence between Northern and Southern Nigeria. The north retained and even developed its feudal character, with the British serving as suzerains in the feudal sense. The system was essentially alien to tropical Africa for very few precolonial states rested on feudal principles. Southern Nigeria in these years saw the penetration of British and European capitalist activities and ideas and the spread of capitalist ethics through trade and missionary activities.[50] Meanwhile, the contrasts became exceedingly awkward for the colonial office; while the revenues of the south grew and surplus could be invested in railway and harbor works, feeder roads, and other forms of economic development, the north remained poor, failing to balance its budget and in constant need of treasury grants-in-aid. Amalgamation, in which the south's revenues could be used to create a balanced budget for a unified Nigeria, was an obvious solution that could remove the awkward dependence on the treasury.

Nigerian Unification

In 1912 Lugard was brought back to unify Nigeria. There could hardly have been a worse choice for this task. It needed little imagination to visualize that the unity of Nigeria could have been a momentous turning point in the history of the country, a stage in the building of a new nation,[51] yet there was scarcely any discussion along these lines in the colonial office. The plain facts ought to have been clear. Southern Nigeria, with its cash crops, expanding mission schools, growing numbers of wage earners and clerical workers, African entrepreneurs and petty capitalists, was a success in the terms of European imperialism, whose purpose was the integration of such regions into the British and world trading system. How was the feudal north, with its conservatism, Muslim law, and emirate government to be brought into this system and its administrative poverty brought to an end? The choice of Lugard in effect turned this question upside down. With his return to Nigeria there could be no question of devising measures whereby the northern administration would be adapted to the new conditions. Instead, the south would have to bend to northern dogmas.

Lugard in 1912 was still the same man, autocratic in temperament (he successfully insisted on his scheme for continuous administration as a precondition of his appointment)[52] and dominated by ideas of tidiness and hierarchy in government. The south repelled him as it always had, and he looked at its administration "with something very close to disgust."[53] Its people, except perhaps the Yoruba (redeemed by their institutions of kingship, which he saw as capable of being "developed" toward feudalism), were of a "low and degraded type."[54] The administration in Yoruba country was "perfect chaos,"[55] whereas in the southeast "native policy is non-existent."[56] These imperfections could not be tolerated merely because the south had made "astonishing" material progress, about which there was something immoral in the amount of revenue gained by taxing alcoholic beverages. The Northern administration was a "native policy whose aim was primarily administrative"; in the south, policy was "commercial and directed primarily to the development of resources and trade." The contrast was meant to emphasize the "higher" considerations of Northern administration.

The south was blamed on almost every count: its provincial system was a failure; the regime was lethargic; it had no direct taxation; chiefs took "no effective part in the administration" (but at the same time Lugard attacked the semi-autonomous position of states such as Abeokuta); and the judicial system he implied was a farce.[57] The north, by contrast, received no hint of blame on any score (even though Lugard privately disapproved of much that had happened in the north since 1906).

The most striking characteristic of Lugard's proposals for amalgamation was that he did not really propose amalgamation. Only the railways, the marine department, and the customs service were to be unified. As the colonial office had raised the issue of amalgamation primarily to pool revenues and create a unified transport system, he could hardly have done less. Medical, postal, telegraphic, and survey departments were each to have a single head, and the West African Frontier Force would be under a single command; yet all of these entities would have separate Northern and Southern establishments as before. Lugard's motive in retaining, in effect, two colonial systems was twofold. First, he needed time to "reform" the administration of Africans in the south on Northern lines. Second, the scheme concentrated amalgamation into the one overall, unifying office, that of the governor-general. Lugard himself would fill this post. Lieutenant governors would conduct administration under supervision from Nigeria or London by the scheme of continuous administration. Lugard in essence tried to create for himself the position of a controlling buffer between the colonial office and Nigeria.

The main substance of the amalgamation report concerned the Southern administration. In effect, Lugard recommended the introduction of the Northern system. He seemed completely unaware of the qualitative differences between Fulani feudalism and Yoruba kingship (as he had always in his writings on the north used the terms "chief" and "emir" interchangeably), let alone concerned with the problems of chiefless societies in the southeast. The south must be divided into provinces like the north, district officers granted executive and judicial powers, and in time chiefs would be "found and trained" and later "entrusted to exercise control." Native courts must be established, and barristers excluded from them and the provincial courts. The supreme court's powers must be restricted to the area of the coastal towns only and to cases involving foreigners or retrials ordered by the governor-general.

The historical spread of English legal ideas, traditions, and institutions in the south, a process regarded by educated Africans with a special concern, was thus to be reversed. Lagos, the cultural center and social capital of the educated element, Lugard especially challenged. It must never become the capital of Nigeria—its "native population" was too large for that purpose so that "segregation [was] practically not feasible." It should be detached from the south, ruled separately by an administrator, and a new capital built in the north. To add insult to injury the legislative council, regarded by Africans as the nucleus and symbol of eventual democratic participation in legislation, was reduced in status to that of a town council for Lagos. There would be no legislative council for the new Nigeria, as there was in all other British colonies and protectorates, because the emirs of the north could not debate in English, the educated elements were unrepresentative, and the interests of the masses could not be subordinated to the will of an unrepresentative authority.[58] Instead, there would be established a Nigerian council, composed of nominated notables, that would meet for three days in each year and hear addresses from the governor-general.

Lugard's amalgamation proposals were adopted with hardly any fundamental discussion in the colonial office, though it may be added that they were not regarded with anything like the enthusiastic spirit in which Lugard made them. Official minutes described them as "hardly . . . a permanent solution" and as "temporary" and "tentative." Most criticism was reserved for the scheme of continuous administration, which was still disliked in the office. The reduction of Lagos was even welcomed as "a bold new departure" by one official, who commented that the Southern provincial system "will die unlamented by me."[59]

The amalgamation of 1914 appeared to be a turning point in British policy, and to the Southern Nigerian educated elements it appeared that Britain had abandoned the liberal and humanitarian ideals of the nineteenth century. It was doubly unfortunate that these decisions were taken on the eve of the first world war, which unleashed new forces of nationalism that Lugard's measures were expressly designed not to accommodate. His tenure of office was therefore marked with growing hostility and opposition from the Lagos press and the Southern elite, and his attempts to remodel the southern Yoruba kingdoms along Northern lines were to cause widespread popular resistance, especially after the introduction of direct taxation, which provoked riots and revolts. In the postwar period it was fortunate that Britain was able to find, in Sir Hugh Clifford and Sir Donald Cameron, courageous and able critics prepared to dismantle and reorganize much of Lugard's dogmatic "reforms" in the south.

Lugard the Proconsul

To the end Lugard continued to maintain his own reputation through his published writings and in particular to use *Annual Reports* as a means of self-advertisement. His final report, published in 1920, was a kind of testament to his work since 1912, running through the theoretical basis of his administrative policies in the north, extolling their wisdom and subtlety, and going on to express their universal applicability "even to the most primitive communities," where the "first step is to find a man of influence as chief," from there "to group under him as many villages and districts as possible," to establish his "native treasury," and so forth. The story of the introduction of "principles" into the south was written up almost as an idyll. When taxation was introduced among the Yoruba, the people were so convinced of its "advantages," Lugard confessed to the British public, that "there was something almost approaching enthusiasm in the way the money poured in." From this happy circumstance, "The inauguration of Native Administrations was then a comparatively easy matter." All would live happily ever after, for thus

> the disintegration of Yorubaland was arrested, and the supreme authority of the Alafin recognised by all, to the immense benefit of the country. . . . A strong Native Government is in process of being built up under its own rulers, which will be able to resist the sinister influence of more or less educated aliens which was rapidly destroying it. The Native Courts are reported to be a 'huge success.' The difficult task still remains of extending these principles to the remainder of the Southern Provinces.[60]

Lugard's career in Africa spanned almost exactly the years in which the European powers partitioned the continent and set up the rudiments of administration. His career illustrates the opportunities available to a determined, adventurous, and literate Englishman, for he lacked powerful or influential backers until Chamberlain appointed him first to the West African Frontier Force and then to the high commissionership in Northern Nigeria. Failing to secure official appointments until that time, Lugard used the opportunities presented by the chartered companies to build a career of action in Africa and skillfully capitalized on growing popular interest in African issues to put his name before the public view in his writings. During his career as a colonial official he showed from the first an imperious, autocratic temperament and a determination to command, control, and carry out his own policies, which involved him in constant conflicts with the colonial office. The success with which he maintained this position until his virtual dismissal from Nigeria in 1918 aptly, though in extreme form, illustrates the difficulties of maintaining imperial control over the man on the spot in the conditions of early administration in the African colonies. The local governor, with his skeleton staff and tiny military force, as the sole "reliable" channel of information, could present the fearful argument that if his proposal were not accepted the colony would be in imminent danger of revolt, war, bloodshed, and threat to European lives. It was a bold man indeed who was prepared to override such arguments from the comfort and security of his office in Whitehall.

Retirement

Lugard left Nigeria in 1918, bitter at the colonial office, which he felt had sacked him.[61] He would never again rule over a British colony. In retirement, however, he built a second career in which he remained active in African affairs until his death in 1945 at the age of eighty-six. With advancing age men generally are assumed to adopt increasingly conservative attitudes, but in Lugard's case it appears that, bereft of power and authority, his attitudes and activities became increasingly contemplative, analytical, and, in the African context of the times, progressive.

Immediately after leaving Nigeria Lugard began writing extensively. The first task was the revision for publication of his "Political Memoranda," his instructions to political officers in Nigeria, which set out the detailed structure of his indirect rule system. When this volume was published in 1919 Lugard was moving ahead with *The Dual Mandate in British Tropical Africa*,[62] which came out two years later. This was his major work, in which he translated the specifics of the indirect rule policy into a political philosophy of African administration. The book may be seen as an apologia for British rule in Africa, set against the background of international criticism of imperialism emanating not only from Lenin and the Russian revolution but also from Wilsonian idealism in the United States, the social democrats in Europe, and the British Labour party. In meeting these criticisms the British and the French, in distributing the conquered German colonies after the first world war, had developed the mandates system in the League of Nations, accepting, in theory at least, the doctrine that these territories were held in trust for the benefit of their inhabitants and the world at large. Lugard's essential argument was that the British colonies in Africa, and more particularly those in West Africa, which were ruled on his principles of native administration, had in effect long exhibited the principle of the dual mandate. Britain's task was to develop them economically to produce for the world, while administering them through their traditional rulers and institutions so as to protect Africans against exploitation, loss of their land, and destruction of their culture. In following this line of argument, Lugard naturally felt the need to criticize policies of direct rule and even more the alienation of land and the "detribalization" of Africans in places such as Kenya, Rhodesia, and South Africa.

The Dual Mandate was not a popular book; it was directed at the specialist. Though it went through four editions by 1929, it was expensively produced and sold only 2,242 copies.[63] Yet its impact was significant in the quarters to which it was directed. It affected colonial office and parliamentary opinion, including that of the Labour party, and became a standard work for students of Africa. It also made an impact in League of Nations circles, and this affected Lugard's subsequent life.

In 1922 the colonial secretary (the Duke of Devonshire) nominated Lugard as British representative to the League of Nations Permanent Mandates Commission, where he served for thirteen years. This post formed a base from which Lugard developed interests in, and membership of, several committees (both British and international) concerned with African affairs. In all these activities Lugard slowly moved to more and more reformist and progressive opinions, generally because he adopted British West African policies, and those of Nigeria in particular, as a yardstick to judge other territories. He was harshly critical of South African policies in the mandate of (formerly German) Southwest Africa and more and more adopted an anti–white settler stance. After 1924 he joined the International Labour Organization's committee of experts on "native labor." The year before he joined the colonial office advisory committee on education in tropical Africa and through that body developed close links with Dr. J. H. Oldham, the gray eminence of the missionary party, which was busily resisting settler demands for increased political control in Kenya. This was to throw Lugard directly into the controversies over Kenya politics in the years 1923–1931, during which he would even establish friendly contacts and occupy some common ground with Labour politicians like Sidney Webb. From his educational work and interests Lugard became active in the governing bodies of academic and research institutions such as the Imperial College of Tropical Agriculture, the School of Oriental and African Studies, and the International African Institute.[64]

None of these positions was salaried. Lugard continued his journalistic activities, publishing more than 100 articles between 1919 and 1940, but these, and his book royalties, hardly provided a secure income. After 1922 he obtained his livelihood from company directorships, each of which was linked in some way with his African interests. The first and most important of these was a directorship of the Colonial Bank, which in 1925 became Barclays Bank, the major British imperial banking institution. In 1928 Lugard was elevated to the central board of Barclays. He also accepted directorships of the Empire Cotton Growing Corporation, its subsidiary the Kassala Cotton Company (which operated in the Sudan), and the Huileries du Congo belge, the Belgian subsidiary of Unilever. His decorative value to these companies was enhanced in 1928, when he was raised to the peerage and took his seat in the House of Lords. These commercial connections seem little to have influenced Lugard's attitudes on land, labor, and educational questions; rather, they appear to have served as a financial base that allowed him to devote time and energy to his political and academic interests.

Lugard may be seen as a man with two interrelated careers. In the first—the career of action in Africa as soldier, conqueror, and governor—he emerges as a successful opportunist, imperious, disdainful of superiors, manipulative in his exploitation of situations, determined to push through his own policies. A superb self-propagandist, Lugard elevated his own pragmatic practices into a theory of native administration, which during his period as governor-general of Nigeria he imposed upon the south. Through his policies, and in his writing, he did more than any other individual to fix the concept of indirect rule firmly in British policy as a conservative philosophy, hostile to the ambitions of educated Africans and those influenced by Christian missionaries, to urban growth, to the spread of the money economy, and to the vision that new African nations were in the making. Yet after his enforced retirement, stripped of authority, while still striving to perpetuate the myths of his own creative administrative philosophy, the wider stage of memberships in League of Nations and colonial office committees had the curious effect of mellowing Lugard's views into a progressive, reformist mold. The elaboration of a defense of his policies in British West Africa inevitably implied, as the arguments were developed, hostility to alienation of African land, forced or manipulative labor arrangements, the destruction of African culture and chiefly authority, and the neglect of education—which characterized settler dominated Kenya, Rhodesia, and South Africa. From the 1920s the imperial debate over African questions had shifted ground; imperialist expansionists and little Englanders had become irrelevant, and as yet the grand question of decolonization lay over the horizon. The question had become not whether to have an empire but how should it be best governed and in whose interests. In this debate Lugard firmly stood with the paternalistic school of trusteeship, and this moved him steadily into closer sympathy with the missionary lobby, the humanitarian tradition, and even the Labour party. This was the Lugard whom Margery Perham knew so well, and loved. After his death she became the upholder of his tradition and the leader of an academic and intellectual school of Africanists who helped to orchestrate and perform the overture to decolonization.

Notes

1. The "Political Memoranda" were printed and circulated to officials in 1906 but published as *Revision of Instructions to Political Officers on Subjects Chiefly Political and Administrative* (London, 1919). A. Kirk-Greene, *The Principles of Native Administration in Nigeria: Selected Documents, 1900–1947* (London, 1965), reprints extensive portions of the "Political Memoranda."

2. F. D. Lugard, *The Dual Mandate in British Tropical Africa* (London, 1922).

3. This chapter, like all writings on Lugard, must draw heavily on the biography of Lugard by Dame Margery Perham, vol. 1: *Lugard: The Years of Adventure, 1858–1898* (London, 1956); vol. 2: *Lugard: The Years of Authority, 1895–1945* (London, 1960) (hereinafter cited Perham 1 and Perham 2). The work is monumental, with massive documentation from the Lugard papers, British official sources, and other private papers. Dame Margery writes with strong sympathy for Lugard but uses and quotes the evidence in such a comprehensive way that it is clear that she has made no attempt to conceal unfavorable information. Thus, views expressed in this chapter that are highly critical of Lugard's career and character can often be supported by evidence quoted in Miss Perham's work.

4. R. L. Schuyler, "The Climax of Anti-imperialism in England," *Political Science Quarterly* 37 (September 1922):415–439.

5. Perham 1:61–67, 253, 563.

6. Macdonald's report, 7 April 1893, p. 13, Foreign Office (hereinafter cited F.O.) 2/60.

7. See D. A. Low, "British Public Opinion and the Uganda Question: October–December 1892," *Uganda Journal* 18 (September 1954). Perham 1:422 n. lists Lugard's heavy round of speaking engagements.

8. Perham 1:477.

9. For details of Goldie's life see J. E. Flint, *Sir George Goldie and the Making of Nigeria* (London, 1960).

10. Perham 1:part 4; Flint, *Goldie*, pp. 220–225.

11. Flint, *Goldie*, pp. 224–225.

12. Perham 1:544, n. 1, gives a list of these.

13. Ibid., p. 613.

14. Ibid., pp. 613–614, from Lugard's diary 17 January 1897.

15. Text in ibid., pp. 616–617.

16. This had been clear to those in government circles and to Goldie since Chamberlain assumed office in 1895; see Flint, *Goldie*, pp. 214–215.

17. Entry for 13 March 1898, quoted in Perham 1:640.

18. "Very civil" was Lugard's own comment on the letter, yet in his diary he made the almost paranoic remark that "[the governor] wants to make it appear, I suppose, that I am his puppet, who is to dance to his tune" (ibid., p. 680).

19. For details of the convention see Flint, *Goldie*, chap. 12.

20. Ibid., pp. 307 ff.

21. Ibid.

22. Perham 2:7.

23. Report of the Niger committee, 4 August 1898, Colonial Office (hereinafter cited C.O.) 446/3.

24. Lugard to Chamberlain, 5 August 1900, p. 41, C.O. 879/58 580.

25. Minute by Chamberlain in Lugard to Chamberlain, 23 August 1900, C.O. 446/10, quoted in Perham 2:89.

26. Lugard to Chamberlain, 8 August 1900, C.O. 879/58 580.

27. Lugard to Chamberlain, 12 March 1901, C.O. 879/58 580.

28. Northern Nigeria, *Annual Report*, 1900–1901, p. 116.

29. Wallace to Chamberlain, 3 July 1901, C.O. 879/58 580.

30. Lugard to Chamberlain, 28 December 1901, C.O. 879/72 684.

31. Quoted in Perham 2:46–47.

32. D. J. M. Muffett, *Concerning Brave Captains* (London, 1964), pp. 53–55.

33. Northern Nigeria, *Annual Report*, 1900–1901, p. 114.

34. Lugard to Chamberlain, 15 March 1902, C.O. 879/72.

35. Muffett, *Brave Captains*, p. 63.

36. Lugard to colonial office, 21 November 1902, C.O. 879/79 712.

37. The telegrams, reproduced in C.O. 879/79 713, were exchanged 10 to 13 December 1902.

38. The words are those used in a telegram of 24 December 1902.

39. Lugard to Chamberlain, 15 January 1903, C.O. 879/80 718.

40. Perham 2:101.

41. Ibid., p. 103.

42. "Massacre" is not too strong a word. Two thousand peasants, armed for the most part with hoes and axes, were destroyed. A Sokoto chief described the scene tersely: "Someone gave an order, everyone fired, then a whistle blew; everyone stopped and there was no one left alive in front" (quoted in ibid., pp. 259–260).

43. Ibid., p. 138.

44. Ibid., p. 141.

45. Emir's oath of allegiance reproduced in ibid., p. 149.

46. For full text see Kirk-Greene, *Selected Documents, 1900–1947*, pp. 43–44.

47. I. N. Nicholson, *The Administration of Nigeria, 1900–1960: Men, Methods, and Myths* (Oxford, 1969). Nicholson's book is written in language extremely hostile to Lugard, and at times the author resorts to sarcasm, emotionalism, and innuendo. But the fundamental thesis summarized here is argued with trenchant insight and conviction. Nicholson argues that Lugard's influence on Nigerian history was a baleful one and, using different evidence and approaches, comes to very similar conclusions to those in J. E. Flint, "Nigeria: The Colonial Experience, 1880–1914," in L. H. Gann and Peter Duignan, eds. *Colonialism in Africa* (Cambridge, 1969), vol. 1.

48. Lugard to Lady Lugard, 2 February 1906, quoted in Perham 2:248.

49. For detailed treatment of the period 1906–1912 see Mary Bull, "Indirect Rule in Northern Nigeria, 1906–1911," in K, Robinson and F. Madden, *Essays in Imperial Government Presented to Margery Perham* (Oxford, 1963), pp. 47 ff.

50. See Flint, "Nigeria: The Colonial Experience," pp. 244 ff.

51. Such thinking in many ways dominated the discussions of the federation of the British North American colonies in 1867 and of Australia in 1900.

52. Perham 2:364–365. Lugard asked for agreement to his working six months in Nigeria and six in London. The colonial office accepted this arrangement for the first year but modified it later to eight months in Nigeria and four in London for subsequent years.

53. Dame Margery Perham's phrase; Perham 2:422.

54. This and subsequent phrases in quotation marks, not footnoted, are taken from Lugard's amalgamation report, C.O. 583/3, enclosure in Lugard to Harcourt, 9 May 1913, also printed as C.O. Confidential Print 1005.

55. Perham 2:392, quoting Lugard to Lady Lugard, 13 November 1912.

56. Lugard to Lady Lugard, 12 December 1912, quoted in ibid., p. 198.

57. Nicholson, *Administration of Nigeria*, p. 198, describes Lugard's characterization of the Southern Nigerian administration as a "gross travesty of the facts," and Nicholson's discussion of the nature

of administration in the south reveals a totally different picture, making it difficult to believe that Lugard was not engaged in deliberate distortion of evidence.

58. This was an extraordinarily misleading argument: at this time there were no elected members of the legislative council whatsoever, and its purpose was specifically to do that which Lugard opposed, viz., to give some voice to minority, unofficial interests such as British traders and educated Africans. His argument therefore condemned the whole historical evolution of representative institutions in the British empire.

59. Minutes on Lugard to Harcourt, 9 May 1913, C.O. 583/3.

60. *Report by Sir F. D. Lugard on the Amalgamation of Northern and Southern Nigeria and Administration, 1912–1919,* Parliamentary Command Paper (hereinafter cited as Cmd.) 468 (London, 1920); extracted in Kirk-Greene, *Selected Documents, 1900–1947,* pp. 46–47.

61. At the end of November 1918, during the course of a bitter controversy with the colonial office over his proposed scheme for "continuous administration," Lugard remarked in a letter that his work in Nigeria was completed. The colonial secretary immediately took this as a resignation offer and accepted it despite Lugard's protest that it was not meant as such. Perham 2:633–636.

62. Useful extracts are reproduced in Kirk-Greene, *Selected Documents, 1900–1947,* pp. 149–173.

63. Perham 2:645.

64. These details of Lugard's activities after retirement and those in the following paragraph are based on the account in part four of Margery Perham's biography, the only source that discusses this phase of Lugard's life.

Sir Robert Coryndon (1870-1925)

Peter Duignan

Robert Thorne Coryndon was one of the great representatives of British colonialism in Africa. He was born in the Cape Colony, South Africa, and served the cause of British South African imperial advance in the Rhodesias; he then joined the British colonial service and administered Swaziland and Basutoland as resident, and Uganda and Kenya as governor. He was one of those empire builders who added vast territories to the British crown in the 1890s—a friend of Rhodes, Smuts, Grey, Selous, Delamere, and others who made African history. His achievements have been somewhat neglected by historians, yet he was an outstanding administrator and a man of vision. Indeed, Coryndon was one of British Africa's more romantic figures.

To Coryndon, the British empire was a living power bringing progress and development to Africa. He loved Africa, was interested in the welfare of its people, and did much to improve the lives of those he ruled. His talents were many. He was an excellent draftsman and a sculptor. He had some literary skills; he sent occasional pieces on events in Rhodesia to the *Illustrated London News*, *The Field*, and *Pall Mall Gazette*. He did a good article on Swaziland for the *Journal of the African Society* in 1915 and one entitled "Problems of Eastern Africa" in 1922, and he wrote forewords for two books. He was a skilled hunter, fisherman, and outdoorsman. He grew from a frontier specialist into a skilled administrator and developer. He died in 1925, before his vision of an East African confederation could be tested.

Coryndon and his career were in many ways remarkable. Although he fought in the Rhodesias and in World War I in East Africa, he was not a militarist like Lugard or Meinertzhagen. Nor was he a great bureaucrat like Clifford or Cam-

313

eron, but he established the administrations of Barotseland and Swaziland and improved the governments of Uganda and Kenya. He built as much as a Guggisberg: he expanded the railway in Kenya and Uganda and started work on improving the Kenya harbor of Kilindini (Mombasa). Coryndon left his mark on every colony in which he served and participated in some of the most important events in colonial history. He belongs, then, in the Pantheon of colonial heroes, along with Lugard, Johnston, Clifford, Cameron, and Guggisberg. He is one of only two South Africans to have risen so high in the British colonial service.

Marshall Hole, Coryndon's friend, characterized him as having a robust, healthy, commonsense view of life. He had a passion for orderliness and good things—books, pictures, clothes, guns, fishing gear—and a contempt for anything ugly, paltry, or mean. Coryndon was a man possessed of a strong sense of duty to which everything else was subordinated. He was a determined—even dogged—individual with outstanding energy and force. In appearance he was handsome: five foot ten inches tall, a broad forehead and oval face, straight nose and square chin, dark hair and complexion, and blue eyes. His physical strength and courage were extraordinary. Hole and others have recounted that Coryndon could tear a deck of cards in half and then tear the halves into quarters. Or how, for a wager, he would carry a pony around the stable or bend half-crown pieces in half with two fingers. A daring horseman, he would charge wounded lions, rhinos, and hippos.

Coryndon was trusted by all who knew him—whites, blacks, and Indians—for he fought for their interests when he felt them to be right and just. Men had confidence in his judgment, in his singular sense of proportion and judiciousness, as well as in his ability to deal with the essentials of things. He had great moral courage. He was devoted to the expansion of the British empire and to the promotion of the well-being of the people within that empire. Above all, Coryndon was a builder and a man who loved the rough and rugged life of the outdoors. One friend felt that his many abilities were not fully used in Africa, suggesting that he might have fared better in more turbulent and freer times such as faced Clive and Hastings in India.[1]

Background and Training

Coryndon's father, Selby, was a solicitor. He came from Devon and settled in Queenstown, Cape Colony, where Robert was one of twin brothers born on April 2, 1870, to Selby's wife, Emily Caldecott of Grahamstown, the daughter of a member of the legislative assembly of Cape Colony. Robert's twin died in infancy. Young Robert attended St. Andrew's College, Grahamstown, and Cheltenham College (1884–1887) in England. After his father's sudden death, he returned to South Africa in 1889 to prepare to become a solicitor, planning to join his uncle's firm of Caldecott and Bell in Kimberley. No employment could have been more uncongenial to Coryndon than working in a lawyer's office for he was basically an outdoorsman who loved horses, dogs, and guns. In any case, too much was going on in Kimberley to keep him for long in the office.

Kimberley was Cecil Rhodes's town. It was in Kimberley that Rhodes regained his health; here he first dreamed of imperial expansion and later won the fortune in diamonds that let him carry out his dreams. Diamonds had been discovered in the early 1870s, and Rhodes at nineteen had taken money from the sale of his cotton crop and moved to the Kimberley fields. He soon controlled the mines and surrounded himself with followers who shared his vision of going to the "Far North."

In 1889 Coryndon had started to work but his salary of £12 a month was usually mortgaged to pay for horses he bought. Fortunately, his uncle provided him with the costs of lodging and meals at a boardinghouse kept by two English ladies. Among his friends at that time was Marshall Hole (later an official in the British South Africa Company and historian of the settlement of Rhodesia), Charles Coghlan (then a solicitor, later prime minister of Southern Rhodesia), Perry Rose Frames (a solicitor, afterward chairman of de Beers Consolidated Mines), and Archdeacon Gaul (later bishop of Mashonaland). Coryndon was popular for himself and as his father's son to old Kimberley stalwarts such as Rhodes, Jameson, Rudd, and others who were to become familiar in Rhodesian and South African history.[2]

Hole and Coryndon often had Sunday dinner with Archdeacon Gaul. For culture, the two young men met with the local musical and literary society. Kimberley had few amusements in those days other than shooting and horseback riding—no golf or tennis and little cricket. Shooting was expensive, so most young men would hire horses and canter around the outskirts of the town. Coryndon earned the reputation of being a fine horseman.

Rumors soon swept Kimberley of a new scheme of Rhodes in the far north. There was talk of undiscovered golden riches in the interior and of a chartered company to explore them. In October 1889 Coryndon and some friends were invited to participate in the project. Twelve young Kimberley men left for Bechuanaland on November 9 of that year, each provided by Rhodes with a horse, a saddle, and £10. These youths were later dubbed "Rhodes's Apostles," and most were to gain fame in the Chartered Company's territories in Northern and Southern Rhodesia. But this was in the future. None cared very much where they were going or what they were expected to do, Hole recalls, and they set off cheerfully, hoping for fame and fortune.

Coryndon was first attached to the Bechuanaland Border Police at Mafeking but in 1890 was transferred to the British South African Police, formed by the Chartered Company to accompany the pioneer column into Lobengula's territory across the Limpopo river. Rhodes had decided to occupy Mashonaland for four reasons: to place a British community in the interior of South Africa; to shut off the Boers of the Transvaal; to discover the second Rand he believed lay buried beneath the northern veld; and to advance British civilization among African tribesmen. He entrusted the venture to Frank Johnson, a twenty-four-year-old frontiersman with extensive experience in the north and a background of service in colonial mounted units. For a fee of £87,500 (later increased to £90,400) and a land grant in the area to be occupied, Johnson signed a contract to organize a pioneer corps on semimilitary lines. The corps contained a large percentage of young volunteers of good social standing, such as Coryndon. Sons of peers served next to cowpunchers. There was even a troop of brokers. A large proportion of the men hailed from the South African Cape, from Kimberley, or from Natal.

Johnson's original plan to advance with a small body of men was vetoed by the high commissioner of South Africa, who feared another bloody defeat of the kind inflicted on a British force by the Zulu at Isandhlwana in 1879. The Chartered Company unwillingly had to organize a mounted force. Coryndon and his Kimberley friends became part of this group, the nucleus of which came from the Bechuanaland Border Police, which he had joined. The expedition was made up of some 80 men known as the Pioneer Corps and 500 British South Africa Police. The Ndebele (a Zulu-descended warrior people dominant in the area) feared the British. The Ndebele warriors' best chance would have been to catch the column by surprise in broken country or at night. But Lobengula hesitated to launch his regiments against such a strong force, and it proceeded without a fight. The pioneers safely reached their destination on September 12, 1890, and established Fort Salisbury. They then dispersed to look for gold.[3]

Coryndon joined the administrative staff under A. R. Colquhoun as a clerk in the government survey department. He had beautiful handwriting, was a skilled draftsman, and had strong powers of observation. He made one of the first surveys and sketches of the Zimbabwe ruins near Fort Victoria, and he discovered and kept two of the famous soapstone birds found there. His job required that he sketch maps from information provided by others. Years later, while serving in 1914–1916 on the Southern Rhodesia native reserve commission, he would astound members of his party by describing what the land ahead would look like even though he had only drawn it from other people's descriptions twenty-four years earlier.

The first months of occupation in late 1890 were harsh owing to heavy rains and lack of supplies. Coryndon lived in the "administrative compound," a series of mud huts that only he had the skill to make attractive and livable. Throughout his life he demonstrated the knack of using whatever materials were at hand to make his environment attractive. Coryndon was by temperament a builder; he laid out capitals in Barotseland and Swaziland, and he planned the relocation of an administrative capital in Uganda. In Salisbury his house soon was the showplace of the new settlement.

Life as a clerk bored him; he wanted more venturesome tasks and took more and more to hunting, showing great skill in stalking and tracking big game. Like Selous, the greatest of Africa's hunters, Coryndon worked close to game before firing from a distance of fifty to sixty yards. He preferred, as more sporting, a single-shot "303" to magazine loads. Coryndon shot a white rhinoceros, an exploit that earned him a commission from Lord Rothschild to secure other specimens. Shooting two more white rhinos—one went to Lord Rothschild and is now in the Natural History Museum of London, the other to the Cape Town Museum—he received other commissions and became a professional big-game hunter and naturalist.

Things were not going well, meanwhile, for the pioneers and the Chartered Company. No big mines were found, and the administration was costing a great deal of money. Then Lobengula's raiding economy gave Jameson—now the administrator—the chance he wanted to end Ndebele rule. At first the chartered administration had not wanted war. It hoped slowly to erode the social system of the Ndebele by getting them to work for wages. But Lobengula could not redirect his raiding regiments, and they kept attacking parts of Mashonaland held by the company. A Ndebele raid on the Shona people around Fort Victoria gave Jameson and Rhodes the excuse they needed to attack Matabeleland. When the war started in 1893, Coryndon joined the Salisbury Horse under Major P. W. Forbes.

Lobengula mobilized about 12,000 men to face the 1,100 in the colonists' force. Ndebele regiments were experienced and disciplined; they fought with spear, shields, and knobkerries. But their foot soldiers were easily defeated by the mounted colonials supported by Maxim guns and wagons. After a few bloody battles, the Ndebele "spear kingdom" collapsed with surprising ease. Forbes's unit, however, faced tough fighting and barely escaped destruction in pursuit of the fleeing Lobengula. Coryndon saw action only briefly, for he caught pneumonia.

The settlers had conquered Matabeleland, but they lacked men and resources for its effective control. Administration remained a scratch affair, oppressive and inefficient. After the war Coryndon became a mail cart driver between Salisbury and Kimberley, a distance of over 500 miles. Rhodes was a passenger on one trip in 1896; later that year he hired Coryndon as his private secretary.[4] After the Jameson raid into the Transvaal, the Ndebele and many of the Shona people rebelled. Coryndon accompanied Rhodes to London, where Rhodes had to explain the raid to Chamberlain and the colonial office, but he did not take part in the historic meeting between Rhodes and the rebellious Ndebele chiefs, the negotiations that ended the Ndebele rising. Coryndon, although a staunch supporter of Rhodes, in fact did not like the post of private secretary. In 1897 Rhodes sent him as resident and representative of the British South Africa Company to prepare for the British takeover of the Lozi kingdom (Barotseland), a powerful African state on the upper Zambezi.

The choice was a good one. Not only did Coryndon share Rhodes's views about empire and white settlement, but he had become toughened by his life in the veld and was an experienced frontiersman. He was, as L. H. Gann has written, "able, keen, enthusiastic and self-confident, all qualities in great demand at a time when the company was still quite unable to spend even the barest minimum on its Northern possessions."[5]

Coryndon showed himself to be a resourceful and purposeful administrator. Although he had had little formal bureaucratic experience, he proved to have other skills more needed at that time—patience, tact, and a likable personality. In these first years he was primarily a diplomat and negotiator at the court of Lewanika, sent there to win more concessions for the company. He was by birth, training, and outlook a perfect exemplar of a European settler and a proponent of company rule. After 1900 he began to act more as an administrator and less as a diplomat, and his views about the benefits of settlement and Chartered Company rule changed somewhat.

Coryndon arrived at Lealui, Lewanika's capital, in October 1897 with his private secretary, Frank Worthington, and five European policemen. All were unarmed, to Lewanika's disappointment—he had hoped for a larger, more imposing body of soldiers to accompany the queen's first resident to Barotseland. Lewanika was suspicious that the young Coryndon represented only the British South Africa Company and not the British queen. After all, queen and company had ignored Barotseland from the time Lewanika had signed the treaty with Frank Lochner in 1890 until Coryndon arrived in 1897.

Lewanika, however, had had strong motives for arriving at the 1890 agreement, and these considerations still operated. He looked to British protection against the Ndebele from the south and against European settlers—Boer and British—who might intrude upon the country in the future. He looked to British aid against encroachments on the part of the Portuguese in the west. He desired British assistance regarding a number of boundary disputes with chiefs like Segkhomi in the southwest. In addition, he hoped for support against domestic upheavals and claims from possible rivals. Lewanika did not stand alone; there was a substantial party (the modernizers) among the Lozi magnates who believed that their nation's supremacy could continue only if the Lozi ruling class acquired the religious and technological knowledge made available by European missionaries and if the Lozi and the British worked in alliance. This pro-British party received strong support from local missionaries, including François Coillard, a French Protestant of anglophile conviction who did more than any other European to place Barotseland under British protection.

Six days after reaching Lealui, Coryndon addressed a great assembly at the council house. He spoke simply and clearly, stating that he was the envoy of the queen and the British South Africa Company. His mission was to assist the king of the Barotse by his advice, to see that the Lochner treaty was observed, and to facilitate relations between the Barotse and the whites who would be coming into the country. Lewanika's kingdom was now a British protectorate, but Coryndon promised not to interfere between the king and his subjects. He came in peace; his police were unarmed so as not to alarm the people. Lewanika asked for a letter setting forth all these things and Coryndon gave it to him; when the letter had been translated, the council saluted and dispersed.[6]

Having set up his headquarters in Barotseland, Coryndon had as first task to ready Lewanika for direct control by company officials and to secure more liberal concessions from the paramount chief than those contained in the Lochner treaty. As resident, Coryndon seems to have gotten on well with Lewanika, and in 1898 he secured wider powers along with mining and commercial privileges for the company. A treaty was negotiated by Sir Arthur Lawley, but it was Coryndon the diplomat who got the king to agree to sign it. Major land and mineral rights were granted to the Chartered Company; in return, the company promised to assist in educating the Barotse and to pay an annual subsidy of £850 to Lewanika. The treaty effectively put Barotseland under company control, for it allowed them to make land grants anywhere in the kingdom. The missionary François Coillard felt that the treaty was unfavorable to the Barotse and refused to sign. Coryndon, who was a keen advocate of European settlement, wanted the agreement, as did company officials. The British colonial office and the high commissioners, Milner and Selborne, were unsuccessful in their efforts to discourage white settlement beyond the Zambezi river. The colonial office disapproved of the Lawley concession; Coryndon then got Lewanika to sign two other concessions in 1900. Under Coryndon, permission to grant parcels of land were requested from the king; but after 1905, grants were made without his consent for he did not want to be bothered.

The British government was not willing to give the company a free hand; hence, northwestern Rhodesia was to be administered under the high commissioner for South Africa. The company, however, was able to choose the administrators and other officials to run the country, and in 1900 Coryndon was named administrator of northwestern Rhodesia, a position he held until 1907. Aided by Frank Worthington and Colin Harding, who organized the Barotse native police force in 1899, Coryndon established an administration and suppressed the Mambari slave trade. Administrative stations were established at Mongu, Kalomo, Kazungula, and Monze. Coryndon also negotiated the western boundary of the

Barotse kingdom with the Portuguese. The matter was arbitrated by the king of Italy, who in 1905 gave Lewanika a strip of about 200 miles running from the Congo to German Southwest Africa. Lewanika and the company did not get all that they claimed, but Lewanika probably obtained a lot more than he had ever controlled.[7] In 1906 Coryndon finally succeeded in abolishing slave holding in Barotseland—an estimated 300,000 slaves were set free.

The final act of establishing a basic administration was to impose a hut tax; this Coryndon accomplished in 1904–1906. It was not just a device to raise money to pay the costs of administration; Coryndon believed that the payment of the tax symbolized African recognition of the white man's authority. He therefore insisted that people who refused to pay have their huts burned and ordered Colin Harding to take his police and punish defaulters. Harding protested to Johannesburg against these punitive raids, and the high commissioner forced Coryndon to stop. The company did not take kindly to Harding's interference, and he resigned from the administration.[8]

White settlers and prospectors came into the territory in greater numbers after 1900. Roger Williams and George Grey demonstrated that Northern Rhodesia had copper deposits. By 1902 mining was under way at Broken Hill and later at Bwana Mkubwa, further north. The railroad reached Victoria Falls in 1904. As administrator, Coryndon played a role in what contemporaries described as "opening up" the territory.

During Coryndon's residency, the whole style of life of the Barotse leaders was transformed. When he arrived in 1897,

> they were then content with very simple clothing, little furniture, and unadorned huts, while they lived entirely on the products of their cattle and their lands; now [1905], however, very many of them wear European clothing; many own horses and saddlery, and there are a few of the more important chiefs who do not possess at least some English furniture and who do not use such things as coffee and sugar.[9]

Within ten years Coryndon set up a small African police force, pacified the territory, and organized a small civil service and district administration over a territory of almost 200,000 square miles. Northwest Rhodesia became safe for British travel, trade, and settlement. A member of the colonial service, C. H. Rodwick, who was attached to the high commissioner's office in Johannesburg, remembered Coryndon as a remote—and at times disturbing—figure, for he was no office man in those days: "His work lay in the bush and on the Zambesi—of which we clerks and secretaries knew as little as he cared about writing despatches and preparing estimates."[10] The high commissioner's office wanted fuller reports and stricter compliance with colonial office methods, which to Coryndon must have seemed fussy and unnecessary. But the people in the high commissioner's office came to regard him as one of their best administrators.

During his ten years in Barotseland, Coryndon developed into an even greater hunter and naturalist and rivaled Selous. He was not an exceptional shot but excelled in stalking and tracking game.[11] He shot many fine trophies, which he used to decorate Government House wherever he was posted. He filled out in physique and became stronger, even though he had several bouts with malaria. When European immigration to northwestern Rhodesia began, he shifted his residence in 1899 to Kalomo on the plateau, where he built the first brick house in the territory in 1903. He had laid out a small government township in attractive surroundings, with big game in abundance. Unfortunately, he was more interested in hunting than in the minutiae of sanitary administration. Malaria was rife in Kalomo; many Europeans died from disease; and Coryndon's successor in northwestern Rhodesia, Robert Codrington, shifted government headquarters from Kalomo to Livingstone.

Coryndon in 1907 accepted the post of British resident in Swaziland, a much troubled territory under the high commissioner's office. Lord Selborne had recommended him to the colonial office: "He strikes me as a man of strong character and possessed of excellent administrative qualities which have not been used to their full advantage in his present somewhat anomalous position."[12] Coryndon was eager to transfer to the imperial service,[13] and Selborne felt he would be admirably suited to the Swaziland post. Coryndon had gained a reputation for just and skilled handling of African problems. By 1907 northwest Rhodesia was no longer an African kingdom; settlers and prospectors had flocked in. Coryndon had grown tired of the work and longed to go where only "native problems would engage him."[14]

In his dealings with Africans, Coryndon seems to have been successful. He was kind but firm although he never became overly familiar with them. Lewanika regarded him as a trusted friend. Coryndon was tactful with him; he explained things to him, got his permission and views on major issues—the hut tax, land concessions, freeing slaves. Ten years after Coryndon had left Barotseland, he received a letter from the new paramount chief, Yeta III, announcing "the death of your great friend my father [Lewanika]."[15] Yeta wrote, "I still remember with great esteem the days you were administrator of this territory, and I can assure you that everyone who knew you in this country can never forget you."

Throughout his career Coryndon took a great interest in the welfare of Africans and supported missionary efforts to teach them modern agricultural methods, and to improve their health and morals. At this time he was not an advocate of literary education for them; he preferred industrial and agricultural learning. He hesitated from 1898 to 1906 before establishing the promised Barotse National School, which was founded in 1906 by using a percentage of the funds collected from the hut tax. Coryndon could have started the school to stop the influence of the African Methodist Episcopal church, whose school had attempted to meet the needs of those Barotse elite who wanted education. He was well known throughout Barotseland, although he made no effort to impress Africans with the dignity of his office. His usual way of getting around the country was on horseback with one mounted servant and a pack horse to carry their belongings, depending on his rifle to provide meat for the journey. This contrasted sharply with the way most district officers and officials traveled in Africa, accompanied as they were by long lines of porters and *askaris* and even being carried in hammocks or chairs.[16]

Coryndon's administration of Barotseland was a scratch one. He never got adequate financial support from the British South Africa Company. Housing and health conditions were poor. He had too few police and administrators to help him run the country. He was a more progressive economic planner than the company's directors; but, as elsewhere during his African career, he did not have the resources to put his ideas into practice. The colonial office also was to limit his funds to develop Swaziland, Basutoland, Uganda, and Kenya.

Yet Coryndon's record in Barotseland was good; he had matured into an able, firm administrator. He was still an imperialist and a believer in white settlement. He had assumed the natural paramountcy of settler interests, as did most officials of the Chartered Company, but his experiences in Barotseland, then in Swaziland and Basutoland, forced him to discard his earlier colonial prejudices and to look at problems more from the African point of view. He was not at this time an efficient, desk-bound administrator, but he had energy and good ideas about organization and economic growth. For the rest of his career he tried to reconcile the needs of African development against white settlement. He succeeded where others failed in at least partially protecting Africans from white greed.[17] His residency in Swaziland was to be his first major test in this regard.

The British had not wanted to take over Swaziland in the 1880s. They would not let the Transvaal incorporate it although after 1894 they did permit Pretoria to administer the area. Conditions grew chaotic. The Swazi repeatedly asked for British help in their struggle with the whites, but the Natal commissioner and native agent, Sir Theophilus Shepstone, refused, and sent his son "Offy" to live at the court of Mbandzeni as resident advisor and agent. Many of the concessions were granted during this period. King Mbandzeni (Mbandine Mbandzeno, Umbandine)—who liked greyhounds and champagne—gave away most of his country to white concessionaires, along with the rights to farm, to graze, and to mine its land.[18] By 1899 the Swazi were no longer independent, and in 1902 Britain reluctantly took over the territory. The concession claims unfortunately had been validated by a court, and high commissioner Milner had to decide what to do.

European concessionaires were not content to let the Swazi use the land; they wanted clear title; they wanted to stop indiscriminate cultivation and to displace any Africans whom they did not require for their own purposes. In 1904 Milner appointed a commission to decide which of these concessions were valid and to divide the land between the Swazi and the Europeans. Earlier he had requested Godfrey Lagden, a South African native official and anthropologist, to prepare a confidential memorandum for him regarding the problem.[19] Milner thought that if the Swazi were left unprotected and free to continue living on land they had given away, there would be bloody fighting over grazing, land, and water rights. His desire to protect the Swazi would lead to the formation of African reserves, for he saw safety for the African only in the separation of white rights from African rights. Lagden concurred; he suggested giving about one-third of the European concession area to the Swazi and putting this land in native reserves scattered about the country. Moreover, he thought the Swazi were in a rebellious mood because they feared losing their land and being forced to move into the reserves. He counseled against haste but felt the Swazi needed a firm hand; they had been "corrupted" for a long time by playing off white people against each other. The commission appointed by Milner finished its report in 1907, soon after Lord Selborne had replaced him as high commissioner, and its recommendations closely followed Lagden's memorandum.

Swaziland became a British protectorate in 1906, under the control of the high commissioner. Remarkably, no major clashes had resulted from the concessions issue; the Europeans had been prevented from acting on their grants by Lord Milner and the Boer war. As Selborne took office, he asked for Coryndon to be appointed resident, with George Grey as special commissioner to mark out the native reserves.[20]

Grey was born at Fallodon in Northumberland in 1866. His elder brother went on to become Sir Edward Grey, a member of Parliament, and secretary of state for foreign affairs. George Grey was a brilliant man. As a younger brother he did not inherit the family estate and so he went to Rhodesia, fought in the 1896 rebellion, and spent time prospecting and exploring in the Rhodesias and the Congo. He located some of the Congo's major copper deposits and managed mines there until 1906, when the Belgians took over. Then he went to Swaziland.

As special commissioner, Grey's job was to decide which third of the concession lands were to be cut off and joined to contiguous Swazi areas. He was boycotted by the Swazi queen regent (Gwamile) and most of the chiefs, who argued that King Mbandzeni had not sold the land but only loaned it. They insisted that the white man "had no land in Swaziland." Grey got some cooperation from them by pointing out that the demarcation of reserves would proceed anyway; if they wanted some voice in the choice of their reserves, they must work with him. For almost two years he covered the whole country by foot, horse, and wagon. It was as careful a survey as could have been made in those days and as fair as contemporary views allowed. As Grey said:

> The question of the preservation for all time of native rights without prejudicing the progress of European industry and civilization, from which the native has and will reap benefit, is very difficult. . . . I have been the instrument that has locked up much of the beautiful fertile country from which Whites are to be forever excluded. Let us hope that the Swazi will progress and be worthy of the benefits we ensure for him.[21]

His report was submitted December 5, 1908, and went into effect four weeks later, on January 1, 1909. To the Europeans went 976,558 hectares; to the Swazi, 687,635 hectares; to the crown, 63,549 hectares. The Europeans had lost about one-third of their holdings; the Swazi did not have to move for five years, after which they could arrive at agreements with European owners.

Selborne came personally to explain the settlement to the Swazi. The queen regent and the chiefs took the report well although they were overwhelmed by their losses. They said they had trusted the high commissioner to protect their interests. Selborne made no answer but ended the meeting by saying: "I have ordered two beasts to be killed for you. I now wish you all goodbye." In 1909 Coryndon was appointed special commissioner to carry out the partition.[22]

The high commissioner came to Mbabane in May 1909 to hear European appeals from Grey's report; only one was granted, a remarkable tribute to Grey's work.[23] The whites submitted a petition to Selborne calling for closer union with South Africa and objecting to Swaziland's being classed a native territory like Basutoland. Selborne promised them that it would not remain a native territory but would become part of the new union of South Africa to be formed in 1910.[24] In this he proved to be wrong. Coryndon himself did not work for Swaziland to be incorporated into South Africa, and he repeatedly reassured the Swazi on this point.[25]

Grey and Coryndon thus had adjudicated a messy and potentially dangerous situation. Whites received a large portion of their concessions; conflicting boundaries were adjusted and delimited. The Swazi lost their general rights to the whole of Swaziland but received exclusive use of large, demarcated, segregated areas of their country. In these reserves all concessionary rights were extinguished, and their areas were thought to be large enough to provide for future expansion. Coryndon and the high commissioner started the Swazi National Fund, which was to be used to buy back land and to start a school for princes. The Swazi were encouraged by Coryndon to buy crown and European held property, and gradually they acquired over half the territory.

While Grey was dealing with the land questions, Selborne had ordered Coryndon to impose a firm administration on Swaziland. Both men felt that its people needed "a benevolent despotism." There is no question that Coryndon at first was harsh to the Swazi—especially to the queen regent and the chiefs, whom he regarded as having wasted their people's heritage. He did not know where the money paid by the concessionaires had gone (the king had received £1,000 a month). He wanted to depose the queen regent and declare the young Sobhuza as paramount chief, but Selborne refused. Coryndon, however, was determined to make the Swazi "shape up," rule well, and be prudent.

He first met with the chiefs on May 23, 1907. He spoke politely but firmly, and his message was hard. He warned them against evil white advisors and assured them that he did not come to take away their powers but to increase them. He said that Lewanika, whom he had served, was stronger after he—Coryndon—had left than when he arrived, for he had stopped wars and slave raids and had united the nation. The high commissioner had rejected the Swazi petition to send a delegation to England, but Coryndon told them that he would try to get that changed.

With great reluctance, the colonial office assented in November 1907 to Coryndon's plea to let the Swazi delegation come to England on the understanding that nothing would be changed by talking to the king. The colonial office minute called for "a decently brief stay" and then an immediate departure; the minute writer noted haughtily, "We had a Swazi deputation here in 1895 and if they had been encouraged to go on talking they would probably be discussing still."[26] The Swazi delegation met the king, saw an army review, and had tea with a few problack groups and with Ramsay MacDonald, who promised to get the Labour party interested in their case. Because MacDonald lived in an ill-lit, third-floor apartment near Lincoln's Inn Field, the Swazi were not impressed with him or his promises. The group was followed, and reports were made on whom they visited. Some of them went to "a resort of fast women," and some drank whiskey.[27] The delegation accomplished nothing.

Meanwhile, Coryndon had toured the entire country he was supposed to rule. He then called a meeting of his officials to reorganize the government, stressing that they rule by virtue of their personal prestige and not by repressive legislation.[28] He rearranged districts and reorganized the judicial system and the police, who began to enforce the law. He had difficulties at first in collecting the hut tax and imposing a new system of registration. His efforts to set up an efficient administration were thwarted by Lord Selborne and the colonial office on the ground that Swaziland's revenue was limited; few changes could be made without expense to the government.[29]

Coryndon's administrative staff therefore remained small. He had a government secretary, 4 assistant commissioners, 24 men in the court system, and a police force of 25 whites and 161 Africans—this to govern 85,000 people in a mountainous area of 6,704 square miles. He and his police mounted 4,720 patrols and covered 315,491 miles in his first year as resident. In 1908 he was dealing more harshly with tax defaulters—fines and imprisonment, but no hut burning. As in Barotseland, Coryndon saw the tax not only as a source of revenue for government but also as a symbol of obedience and acceptance of a new colonial authority.

To the Swazi—in light of their previous history of sheep stealing, quarreling, witch-hunting, and fighting—this police presence was a great boon to peace and order in the territory. But they feared and resented Coryndon in those years. Not only did they lose their land under his residency but he also enforced new laws and collected taxes. The native police gave him the name the Swazi remembered him by—*Msindazwe*, signifying "he who weighs down, sits heavy upon the land." In the first years of his career, he appeared to them as a holy terror. To his servants he was known as *Mahagane* ("violent temper") for he fired the servants left by his predecessor. But it was the name *Msindazwe* that caught on throughout the land as Coryndon brought the Swazi to account. They thought him arrogant, stern, hard, unsympathetic, and inflexible. In 1909, when he sentenced a prince of royal blood (Njinjane) to death, his popularity was at its lowest.[30]

Coryndon and the Swazi came to understand one another better after 1909, and he earned their respect. He had established at Zombadi (Zombadze) a school for the sons of chiefs; he had protected the people from white adventurers; and he had restored to them some of their land. Even the Swazi queen mother said in 1913 that she no longer swore by the name of the former king, Mbandzine: "[Now] I swear by Coryndon."[31] He had kept pressure on the Swazi to buy back land from white concessionaires. He was loved, extolled, and respected as few Europeans ever were by the Swazis, and they called his firstborn son *Izwe Lake*— "His Land," or Swaziland.[32]

Development was limited during Coryndon's residency—1907 to 1914—for although he had ideas, the country was poor and mountainous with few resources to bring in revenue. He depended on the hut tax, mining concessions, rents, and import dues; in 1908, for example, his revenue was only £39,529. For three years in a row, disease and drought damaged cattle and crops. He could do little more than establish an administration, collect taxes, and run a court system. Yet Coryndon did a lot with few resources. He rebuilt the capital, Mbabane, put up new buildings, planted trees, and introduced mountain trout into local streams. He worked on a new road from Mbabane to the Transvaal. The land was too rough for wheeled vehicles but he built bridges and tracks throughout the country.

For his work in Swaziland, Coryndon was much praised and was made a commander of the Order of St. Michael and St. George in 1911. Selborne thought he showed great natural ability, common sense, and an imperturbable temperament. Coryndon had proven himself to be courageous, physically and morally. According to Selborne, he never hesitated to take a position, nor did he ever shirk his responsibility. Selborne felt that Coryndon had shown great sympathy for the black man as well as for white settlers. He knew a great deal about people and their problems. He aimed to secure justice for the black man yet throughout his life he maintained the confidence of white men.[33]

In 1910 Coryndon applied for promotion in the colonial service and asked to be considered for the governorship of the Bahamas, Barbados, Fiji, or the Leeward or Windward Islands; he said he would accept appointment in Gambia,

Uganda, or Sierra Leone but not in a settler colony. The then high commissioner, Gladstone, recommended him, citing Lord Selborne's high opinion of Coryndon as "a capable and experienced administrator possessing energy and initiative."[34] He applied again in 1913 for the position of governor—this time, of Nyasaland— but colonial office minutes show that he was low on the list; although he had manifested "considerable ability in dealing with natives," it was doubted "whether his financial capacity is as good." High commissioner Gladstone once again praised Coryndon and noted "his qualifications as excellent." One of his problems was that he had not learned the secret of writing a report to meet colonial office standards. Even when in 1908 he wrote one that drew praise for its fullness and plain, direct style, it still did not comply with colonial regulations. He did not properly complete a blue book until 1911.

Coryndon, moreover, had many ideas and plans for Swaziland's development that were unrealistic considering the available resources. He had trouble balancing his budget and received a £20,000 loan from Basutoland. He continued to need advances and loans. Still, it is hard to see what else he could have done; there was drought, East Coast fever attacked the cattle, and horses died under government officials. The colonial office minutes kept repeating that he did not recognize "the need for stringent economy." He did, but he also wanted to develop the Swazi. In 1911 he started the Swazi National Fund, to be raised by an additional two shilling tax on the £1 tax paid by Africans and a two shilling tax on each head of European owned cattle. The purpose of the fund was to provide good stud bulls and horses and to establish a small experimental farm and some schools—especially for technical education. Most of the fund had to be used to combat East Coast cattle fever. Previous to Coryndon's first development plan, which appeared in 1911, he had been encouraging cotton as a crop and giving out good corn and black wattle tree seed.[35]

When Coryndon left Swaziland in 1914, the country, in colonial parlance, "had been much improved." The territory was better policed and administered than before. The cash economy had spread further afield; more money became available through remittances sent home by migrant laborers and through the export of crops. Revenue had increased to £58,437, by the current standards a respectable sum for so backward a protectorate.

The colonial office appointed Coryndon in 1914 as chairman of a commission to report upon the native reserves of Southern Rhodesia. Its members were F. J. Newton, W. V. Atherstone, H. Marshall Hole, and E. C. T. Garraway; and its purpose, to determine whether the reserves were large enough to satisfy the present and future needs of Africans. Coryndon methodically set forth the way the commission was to travel, to act, and to question. In 1915 alone he spent seven months taking evidence, traveling about the countryside and deep into African areas where there were no roads or bridges. The members covered the colony on horse, on foot, and by wagon. Their routine of travel was hard: up at 4:30 A.M. for chocolate and a biscuit; trek from 5:00 to 11:00, when they stopped to wash and eat; work on the report; break camp at 3:00 P.M.; trek until 5:00 or 5:30 when they camped for the night; to bed by 8:30. Coryndon ordered that nothing be left around a campsite to mar the countryside; all litter and ashes were buried, and the site left as they had found it. Coryndon followed this practice all his life for he was a keen naturalist and environmentalist. Holland, the commission secretary, noted that "as it was with our camps, so it was with Coryndon—everything neat, clean and orderly, and without any fuss."[36]

The commission heard witnesses, white and black, throughout the country. Coryndon showed sympathy for the Africans and patiently listened to their views. His reputation among them was that of a great native commissioner, firm but just wherever he served. After two years of work, the commission's report was completed. It later served as the basis for the order in council of 1920 that rearranged the native reserves.[37] The report recommended reducing African holdings by a million acres; it also advised regrouping many smaller reserves to remove them from areas of white settlement. In order to use reserves to their fullest, the commission advised that wells and bores be sunk, roads built, and instruction given in improved agricultural methods. Native commissioners were to distribute seed and to counsel African farmers. Education, hitherto neglected, was to be emphasized. Finally, the commission suggested that local African self-government councils be started.

The report was attacked by the British South Africa Company, anxious to defend its stewardship, and by missionaries and the Aborigines' Protection Society, determined to safeguard African rights. The Sabi reserve suffered the largest loss of territory when a section twelve miles wide (291,800 acres) was taken from the Africans to provide for a railroad and for ranching and farming schemes by the British South Africa Company. The issue was debated in the British Parliament and in the *London Times*. Arthur S. Cripps, the local missionary, led the fight, together with J. H. Harris of the Aborigines' Protection Society. In 1920, however, the Southern Rhodesian missionary conference voted support of the commission's finding, asking only that some land be restored to the Sabi reserve.

There is no question that the British South Africa Company and the settlers wanted to pare down African reserves and that the commission was made up of men sympathetic to company and settler interests. It depended for much of its information upon data sent in by the commercial branch of the company. The object was to get all the land that might be usable for future settlement and company prospects. Company inspectors told the commission which land was valuable for white settlement; report after report repeated the same sentiments: "This land is good for whites; reserve it for future settlement," or "This land should be taken from the natives; whites could make better use of it."[38] Coryndon and the others believed in the benefits of white settlement and development. Areas "locked up" by backward African farmers should be put to better use, they felt. Since the Africans had plenty of land, the commission was not reluctant to assign some for future white settlement.[39]

Mistakes were inevitable, and some changes were made later; but the basic division of land in Rhodesia has remained as Coryndon and his commission laid it down. Certainly the whites had the skill and enterprise, and they did develop the country. Africans as yet did not suffer from lack of land, but they possessed insufficient physical or social capital to modernize the colony. The immigrants made improvements in a way Africans could not have done at that time. But not enough effort was made to improve African farming practices. Coryndon's hopes were not fully realized on that point although some improvements in the native reserves followed the commission's recommendations.[40]

From 1916 to 1918 Coryndon was resident of Basutoland. In 1917 he had a staff of thirty-eight men to rule an area almost as large as Belgium. Basuto chiefs were prone to take up arms and cause disturbances, a practice Coryndon quickly ended by punishing the guilty chiefs. He started building straight away—a new residence for himself, a new courtroom, and a water supply for Maseru. Road building, tree planting, and fencing changed the face of the capital. Coryndon handled the Basuto national council of chiefs well; he was impressed with the common sense and dignity shown by the council—and by their short speeches.[41] Not much could be accomplished in less than two years, but Coryndon's successor noted that he had left his mark and improved conditions. An editorial in the local paper, *Mochochonono Ts'Itoe*, said the Basutos were not sorry to see him go. They felt he was autocratic and severe. He imposed new laws and enforced old ones. His administration of the Basutos was strict, and this they were not used to.

Governor of Uganda

Eight years after he had first requested promotion Coryndon was appointed governor and commander in chief in Uganda. At forty-seven he was one of the youngest men ever appointed to a governorship. He was to face racial and economic problems in his new assignment, as well as difficulties caused by the war against the formidable German general Lettow-Vorbeck.

World War I had hurt Uganda's economy: the European plantations were deserted; about 200,000 cattle were lost to rinderpest; and over 60,000 African carriers had been recruited. There were few government officials to run the colony and Coryndon, as its governor and commander in chief, had taken part in the war. He was mentioned in a dispatch from Lieutenant general Deventer for gallant and distinguished services in the field, and he was made a commander of the Order of the Crown by the Belgian king.

War had also disrupted trade on Lake Victoria, and the railroad was congested with war materials. Demobilization brought further disorganization, and in 1918 the country suffered a severe drought. Postwar recovery was slow; there was a high incidence of rinderpest, influenza, and famine in some areas. Capital was not forthcoming from England, and colonial office schemes to encourage white settler emigration to develop the colony largely failed. In spite of these adversities, Coryndon's governorship must be regarded as successful.[42]

Uganda did without a grant-in-aid from London after 1915–1916. Coryndon kept pushing for greater expenditures and a larger staff. He asked for an increase in salaries and allowances in 1918, and the next year he pushed for better pay and working conditions for Africans in the civil service. He convinced the colonial office that Uganda—with 59 officials in comparison with 139 in the East African protectorate—was understaffed if he were to administer it more closely and to carry out economic development. London authorized the recruitment of nine additional district officers. The colonial office was pleased with Coryndon's reports following the war:

> Mr. Coryndon's dispatch seems to be most able and to be a good augury for the future administration of Uganda. He has got hold of the crucial points of the cotton

question and sees them very clearly, and I think his proposals may be accepted practically as they stand.[43]

The governor planned for growth; he pursued a policy of dual development of plantation enterprise by whites and of farming by blacks. He called for increased cotton production by Africans and for greater administrative supervision of the cotton industry. In his efforts at its regulation, he fell victim to the faulty economic reasoning of most colonial officials. He tried to reduce Indian control of ginning and to reduce their profits. He failed to see their productive economic role and opted instead for state control and economic paternalism. His efforts were restrictive and restrained trade. But in the rest of his plans he showed foresight and an excellent sense of how to develop Uganda's resources.

Coryndon increased government revenues by levying a £1 poll tax on non-Africans and by increasing the tax on Africans by fifty percent in 1918. In May 1919 he asked for a £1 million general purpose loan for a public works program in Uganda: new government buildings, telegraph and road extensions, lake transport, and water and electricity supply. His argument made little mention of European planters. He wrote that the future of Uganda rested with the Africans, who were intelligent and amiable. The colony's rainfall was good and constant, the soil rich and productive, and there was plenty of water power. Cotton was the major crop, he noted, but others should be encouraged: rubber, cocoa, sugar, castor, sim-sim (a food crop), and coffee.[44]

In 1919 he started to meet with chiefs to get their views and to inform them of his plans. He spoke frankly of the problem of venereal diseases and of the need to encourage their people to go to work. He told them of his projects to combat rinderpest, East Coast fever, trypanosomiasis, and sleeping sickness. Coryndon also informed the chiefs he intended to develop a comprehensive scheme of training African artisans, drivers, clerks, and interpreters. The chiefs expressed approval of what they heard, and the *Uganda Herald* reported that the meeting was informal and characterized by goodwill, with tea served at its conclusion.[45]

Coryndon was a major force in developing African education and health services during his governorship in Uganda. His 1919 request for a £1 million loan included funds for African education. He asked for funds to finance African training in technical and medical fields and to improve health care. He argued that the protectorate had a growing need for African artisans; car and truck drivers; inspectors and inoculators for sleeping sickness, venereal diseases, and veterinary work; mechanics for repair and engine control; clerks and interpreters; dispensers (medical assistants); agricultural instructors; and carpenters. Africans, he wrote, should be trained to replace Indian artisans (a suggestion that antedated a similar one he gave while governor of Kenya during the Indian crisis). He appointed a local committee to work on African education and conditions of service in government.[46]

In 1920 Lord Milner was to give Coryndon his £1 million development loan in four equal installments, starting in 1921–1922. Some reductions had to be made later on as the depression hit, but this loan was nevertheless a major factor in developing Uganda's infrastructure and its health and education systems. Coryndon had matured a great deal since his days as resident in Swaziland. He had become more than a developer; now he was a good manager as well. By the end of 1921 he had accumulated a budget surplus equal to six months' revenue.

Technical and industrial training for Africans was what Coryndon wanted. At first he set up technical schools under government departments: carpenters and masons were to be under the director of public works, motor drivers and engine drivers under the director of transport, agricultural instructors under the director of agriculture, and African dispensers (medical assistants), health inspectors, and inoculators under the principal medical officer. Later Coryndon argued for a range of schools within one college.

Churchill, as secretary of state for the colonies, had approved the establishment of a new technical school in Kampala in September 1920, and Coryndon selected the site on November 4 of that year. He planned to open a central technical school immediately. Experts from the technical departments would do the teaching. He wanted elementary, intermediate, and technical schools as well as a postgraduate institution. By March 1921 the Uganda Technical College had begun and by early 1922 fourteen boys were studying carpentry, building, and mechanics. In August 1922 the name was changed to Makerere College, and teacher training, clerical instruction, and courses in agriculture, medicine, and surveying were added to the curriculum. Coryndon, then, was the real founder of Makerere College, which he himself renamed in 1922. (Although he is listed first on the roster of founders, he did not have any college buildings named after him.)[47]

The 1923 Uganda budget estimates mentioned Makerere College for the first time. It was Coryndon's last budget in Uganda. He asked for lecturers in veterinary and agricultural science and in surveying to be drawn from government departments, but he budgeted for full-time staff as well—two instructors of carpentry, masonry, and bricklaying, one instructor of machines (to train drivers and mechanics), and a medical tutor. One of the main objectives of the college was to train Africans to take charge of the rural dispensaries.[48] This effort in Uganda of training clerical workers, teachers, African artisans, and medical assistants was in sharp contrast to the education policy in Kenya, where the settlers and the education department opposed African education and where there were few, if any, such programs and no government schools. Coryndon in effect created the Uganda public school system.

Once the war was over, Coryndon had pressured the colonial office for more funds to combat the grave medical problems of the colony. Uganda not only suffered from constant epidemics such as sleeping sickness but also had a high incidence of venereal diseases. Returning porters may have brought in and spread new diseases. In spite of the colony's financial exhaustion, Coryndon was able to get something done. A critical report in 1919 by Dr. Wiggins of the Uganda medical department attacked government medical services for Africans and gave Coryndon the ammunition he needed. London was agreeable to better health care and to supporting medical education for Africans, but funds were not forthcoming until 1920–1921. Coryndon had only eight doctors in 1920. He asked for more physicians and more African vaccinators; he also wanted medical training facilities for Africans. To build and run a school for training twenty-four certified African midwives each year, he used £1,000 from his 1920 development loan plus £3,000 raised by public subscription. The Lady Coryndon Maternity Training

School was opened in June 1921. Lady Coryndon, a gracious and active woman, had been instrumental in establishing African dispensaries (clinics) and maternity training schools throughout Uganda.

Coryndon had also launched a campaign against venereal diseases in 1919. Work began on a school for training Africans in medical work, and by 1921 several treatment centers were in operation. A venereal diseases hospital at Mulago was reopened in 1921, and the training of African nurses was resumed. Subdispensaries were being built throughout the colony. Before he left for Kenya in August 1922, Coryndon budgeted £8,000 to buy drugs to treat venereal diseases.[49] By 1923 he had established twenty-seven clinics throughout Uganda, which had treated 184,061 cases. In this field of health care and training, too, Coryndon was ahead of his fellow governors not only in Kenya but throughout much of Africa. His advice and encouragement gave Uganda midwifery schools, clinics, wayside clinics, and training schools for African medical assistants.

Coryndon was not as strong a supporter of settlers as the *History of East Africa* and other sources claim; nor did he wish to turn African producers primarily into wage laborers as in Kenya. Similarly, his efforts to change Uganda's land system did not stem from any plot to rob Africans of their holdings and to throw them open for sale to whites.[50] Coryndon was pro-economic development; he was not pro-white planter. Uganda had appeared to some people to be a more pleasant and prosperous place in which to live than Kenya. After the war, the colonial office under Milner and Churchill had encouraged veterans to go to the colony to help develop the land, but Coryndon was opposed to these efforts. Settlers were given 500- to 1,000-acre plots at a low price to plant rubber, coffee, cocoa, and sugar. But not many came. The white population grew slowly. In 1915–1916 there were 196 European plantation owners with 25,184 acres under cultivation, and 481 officials. By 1918 there were 847 whites—mostly officials—and 200 plantations. Europeans had the same amount of land in 1920 (188 square miles) that they had in 1918–1919, and the total white population in 1922 had grown only to 1,261 (it had reached a high of 1,269 in 1920).

In these pioneering days there was understandably much mismanagement and lack of technical knowledge. Workers were always in short supply and the government would not provide forced labor. Managers of local estates were appointed from local people who had no prior experience with tropical agriculture. Nor did the Africans have experience with coffee, and coffee failed as a crop. Europeans and Africans planted Arabica coffee, but the Buganda switched to robusta coffee. The planters rushed to pick their crop, dried it badly, and stored it. As a result, Uganda coffee got a bad name on the English market as musty in odor and poor in color. Then rubber planters were badly hurt by the fall in market prices of 1920–1921. Coffee, rubber, and cocoa plantations were all doing poorly, and by 1924 many planters had failed; those who stayed turned to cotton.[51]

In his first years Coryndon impressed the European community with his energy, drive, and planning. The *Uganda Herald* praised his practical and stimulating ideas, noting that it was a pleasant change after many years of comparatively little progress. He worked to improve railway administration and to develop a deepwater pier at Kilindini. Whenever Coryndon went to England he spoke with officials in the colonial office, with industrialists, and with members of the Empire Cotton Growing Association on the need to increase the production by

Africans of high-quality cotton. Since the price for cotton was high, he saw a future for Uganda but he needed to improve the internal transportation system—more roads, railways, bridges, vans, and a light railway had to be provided. Coryndon saw only limited scope for European plantations—in coffee and rubber. On a visit to London in 1920 he further explained his plans to the colonial office and asked their help in getting additional funds to carry out economic development.[52] He had already ordered fifteen new vans and a large ferry pontoon for the Nile at Jinja. He hoped also to harness Ripon Falls to provide electricity and water to Jinja, Kampala, and Entebbe if capital could be attracted.[53]

In 1921 Coryndon won approval of the secretary of state for the colonies to establish executive and legislative councils for Uganda. Although Africans were not represented in the councils until 1945, these still were useful bodies for helping the governor rule the colony and for granting some part in government to the nonofficial white (two) and Indian (one) representatives.[54] Coryndon did not push for a legislative council as part of his and the colonial office's plan to encourage European plantation settlement. He never thought of making Uganda a "Kenya-like" colony.[55] In 1918 he had opposed efforts to expand white settlement. Very early on he had made up his mind that Uganda was not an area for white settlers—"it is not possible for climatic reasons."[56] Not only did Coryndon oppose colonial office efforts to settle veterans there, but he offered protectorate funds to send them elsewhere. The colonial office, however, rejected this proposal.[57]

In a speech made in 1921, as the depression deepened in Uganda, Coryndon repeated his views that the colony was a "native" territory not like Kenya. His duty, he said, was to give full consideration to the rights and claims of Africans. It was, after all, revenue from the cotton produced by Africans that had provided the protectorate with a budget surplus for six years.[58]

As governor, Coryndon therefore did not neglect African interests to serve those of the Europeans. The opposite was true: he provided minimal service for the whites and concentrated his administration on developing the Africans' economy and improving services to them, especially transportation, health, and education. Several chapters in the *History of East Africa*, therefore, distort Coryndon's motives and record.[59]

He did not support European planters excessively and he did not let them dominate his administration and its technical services. Saddled with war veterans as settlers, Coryndon gave them modest help and assistance—two coffee experts and one veterinary officer. His development schemes were aimed largely at improving African output and African health. These efforts paid off; African exports provided the government with more revenue, which Coryndon then used to improve the services to all the colony's residents. Cotton was king in Uganda. The Europeans had a few good years in coffee and rubber, but their exports were only a small share of the colony's export trade. Cotton exports were the heart of the colony's wealth. The value of cotton exports jumped from £369,318 in 1914–1915 to £4,134,136 in 1920 and usually represented from seventy to ninety percent of the total value of Ugandan exports. In contrast, coffee exports amounted to only £90,362 in 1920; rubber, to £23,767. Even with the depressed prices of 1922, cotton still accounted for seventy-two percent of the value of all exports, or £877,625. As a builder and economic planner, Coryndon had seen Uganda's future in cotton grown by Africans and not Europeans; he did not risk his colony's future growth to serve European interests, as asserted by recent historians. His policy was dramatically shown in 1921 when he refused to give planters an advance to save their coffee and rubber plantations.

Economic conditions had worsened during 1921, and planters were going bankrupt. Local banks refused to give them an advance, so they appealed to the governor. Coryndon wrote to the colonial office advising against aiding the planters, as he did not think their failure would hurt the protectorate's finances. He recommended letting eighty percent of the Europeans' cultivated land revert to bush and repeated his long-held view that Europeans had no future in Uganda.[60] Later he relented somewhat and asked the colonial office to let him make loans to fourteen estates while allowing fifty-one others to go bankrupt. London refused.[61]

Although he would not intercede for the settlers he was supposed to be actively aiding, Coryndon did not hesitate to ask the colonial office for authority to buy up African-produced cotton for which there were no buyers. The colonial office authorized him to spend £100,000; half of this sum would probably have saved all the European planters.[62]

Cyril Ehrlich, in his otherwise excellent chapter in the *History of East Africa*, misinterprets the debate over land in Uganda and Coryndon's role in that debate. Contrary to what Ehrlich says, Coryndon did not agree with Morris Carter and Sir Frederick Jackson that "the African's main productive role would have to be as a wage labourer."[63] He cites as proof of this Coryndon's failure to set aside reserve land in four districts so that the Africans would just be used as wage laborers. It is true that Coryndon did not want to lock up land in "native reserves," but this does not mean that he wanted to reduce the Africans' role as farmers and to make more use of them as workers. There is no evidence that Coryndon planned extensive land alienation, and he did not resort to forced labor. Certainly many of the Uganda administrators opposed land alienation but not because they opposed European plantations.

The official, imperial view was that Uganda should develop like West Africa; that is, by peasant production and not by white plantations. The colonial office had rejected the Carter committee report in 1915 to push plantations. After the war, Milner and Churchill did strive for greater European settlement, but Coryndon and his provincial commissioners were not enthusiastic and growth was slow. The 1921 report of the land settlement committee, again chaired by Carter, encouraged white plantations in Uganda but not at the expense of African occupied land. In any case, as Ehrlich notes, Coryndon in 1922 got the colonial office to reverse the Carter proposals and to return to prior land policies. This was done in 1923, after Coryndon had left the country.

But the big issue in this debate was not really increased white settlement but rather the varied land policies of Uganda. The dispatches flowing between London and Kampala had little or nothing to say about increased European colonization. Kenya was reserved for that. Coryndon knew before 1922 that Uganda was not a planters' country. He did not change his land policy because settler plantations were failing—although they were—but because the spread of the freehold system of Buganda to the other protectorate provinces was causing tension and injustices.

In Buganda, under the Uganda agreement of 1900, certain official and private estates were set aside for the Kabaka and chiefs. The land settlement committee of

1920 had recommended the extension of freehold principles to all parts of Uganda, while guaranteeing all people sufficient land for their needs. Land was to be granted to nonnatives if enough were available after the needs of Africans had been met. The provincial commissioners did not like the spread of the freehold principle but Carter pushed for it as he had in the past. In 1922 the commissioners again protested the spread of the freehold principle; but they did not oppose alienation of land to non-Africans. Coryndon by now agreed with them and sent a lengthy memorandum to the colonial office. The entire debate and its supporting material deal with the spread of freehold tenure, not with the alienation of land to non-Africans.[64]

The issue of alienation came up only because the Buganda Lukiko (Assembly) passed a resolution forbidding the sale of land to non-Africans. Nowhere else was the question raised; the provincial commissioners were not opposing alienation of all land to whites but only of land granted to chiefs. The second provision of the new land settlement scheme would, in effect, have established native reserves for Africans and crown lands or alienated lands for non-Africans. In fact, the provincial commissioners wanted unoccupied areas surveyed and opened for settlement to Europeans.

Coryndon did not foresee, nor did he attempt to carry out, large settlement schemes for Uganda. He argued there was no need in Uganda to set aside native reserves or to segregate whites and blacks as had been done in Southern Rhodesia and South Africa. This was because Africans had plenty of land, and there was no need to lock land up in reserves and thus to forestall any future land alienation. His provincial commissioners disagreed with the land settlement committee of 1919; it was they who pushed for native reserves and a declaration of no alienation now or in the future. Their concern was not triggered by fear of large land alienation to settlers.[65] The land settlement report of 1920, however, argued against native reserves in order to preserve the land for future use by Africans with their backward technology. Africans were to be given enough land for their use; and all land alienated had to have the local provincial or district commissioner's approval. Churchill accepted this program.[66]

There was also controversy over the Africans' right to sell their land to non-Africans. The secretary of state had hesitated to give a final decision on this question but felt he had to consider it when Coryndon asked for permission in 1920. The Uganda agreement of 1900 had declared Africans to be "absolute owners"; therefore, the administration had no right to restrict their selling land if they wished. The intention was eventually to give freehold to all Uganda Africans whereby they could dispose of land as they wished. Previously, only Buganda chiefs had this right.

The colonial office therefore had to let Africans sell to non-Africans, for they already could sell to Africans. Although London wanted to prevent undue accumulation of land in the hands of Europeans, they were furthering such accumulation in the hands of Africans. Reluctantly, then, the colonial office agreed to Coryndon's request, and Africans became free to sell their land to anyone.

Arguments against this freedom seem paternalistic and devoid of economic sense. The denial of the right to sell land hurt development—Africans could not borrow money on their land for capital improvements if they could not alienate their holdings. Europeans were discouraged from coming to Uganda to develop plantations as they had been discouraged from going to West Africa (in the case of

Lever Brothers). Whereas Coryndon was not an advocate of large-scale white settlement, he did want further development, and Europeans had more capital and skills than Africans. Some plantations would obviously increase the territory's resources.

The governor and the provincial commissioners then called for nonprivate estates in Busoga and Bunyoro. They feared the creation of a landless peasantry if freehold tenure replaced communal tenure. They foresaw peasants' selling or losing their land to chiefs and others as had happened in Buganda. This was the main issue; all other questions were secondary. Now that the administration was proposing to abolish Africans' rights to alienate their land, the position changed. The administrators were not fighting the governor to prevent land alienation to Europeans; they just opposed the sale of occupied lands.

The change of attitude over freehold was occasioned, above all, by troubles in Buganda over the land distribution of 1900. Coryndon called a conference of provincial commissioners to draw up a memorandum. The meeting had little or nothing to do with European plantations or their failure. Coryndon changed his mind not because he gave up attempts to make Uganda a white plantation colony, as Ehrlich claims,[67] but because he was concerned with possible injustices and tension if freehold tenure spread beyond Buganda. He and his staff therefore recommended restricting freehold tenure to Buganda and, when necessary by agreement, Ankole and the Toro districts.

The administrators had always opposed the spread of freehold. They wavered in 1920–1921 because chiefs in Bunyoro and elsewhere were expecting to get freehold and not because Carter and Coryndon were trying to alienate more land to planters to make Uganda a settler colony. The prevailing philosophy asserted that tribal lands should be held communally and not individually; the feeling was that Africans had to be protected after the crown lands ordinance lapsed in 1922. There was no fear of land alienation to non-Africans. Large tracts would be available once the scheme for native reserves was marked out. The provincial commissioner opposition to the report of the land committee was based solely on its advocating the spread of freehold tenure. Coryndon wrote a memo to the colonial office supporting the commissioners, and a new ordinance was drawn up.

During the 1920s, Indians in Uganda—as in Kenya—began to agitate for reforms. An Indian deputation called on Coryndon on January 4, 1921, and made several demands. Though thankful that Indians were accorded one seat in the new legislative council, they called for equality with Europeans, who had two, and an end to government regulation of cotton ginning and of land ownership and to segregation.

Coryndon had had good relations with Indians, and they felt he was fair and reasonable. They accepted his plan for Indian areas in Kampala and for a new market in Jinja. The deputation concluded its meeting with Coryndon by stating that although relations with Indians were quite good in Uganda, they wished to have these matters on record since another governor might not treat the Indians as justly as Coryndon.[68] He refused, however, to give Indians two seats in the legislative council and the colonial office backed him. The council opened without the Indian representative, and Indians boycotted that body for five years.

The labor supply was a continual problem throughout colonial Africa. There never seemed enough workers for all government projects and private businesses. In Uganda it was especially difficult to find wage laborers because so many Africans were cotton growers and did not feel pressure to seek outside employment. Indeed, the Ugandan government had many projects for which it could not find workers. Yet Coryndon hesitated to use all his powers to get Africans to "come out" to work. He wrote to the colonial office, "I feel that the situation should be met by encouragement and education, and not by coercive legislation."[69] (This statement was made at the same time as the famous Governor Northey circular of 1919 in Kenya, which empowered district officers to force Africans to seek work.)

Coryndon had to defend himself against charges of planters that his administration was not helping them recruit labor. While governor, Coryndon refused to provide private businesses with labor on demand. He left it to the district and the provincial commissioner to cooperate (or not) with recruiters and let labor leave the district. He pointed out to the planters and the colonial office the difficulties the colony faced; there were many demands for manpower—railway and road building, government public works, private employers, plus competition with the East African protectorate. He reaffirmed his policy of not using force or undue pressure. Coryndon had tried to help the planters, but he would not restrict labor from going to Kenya, where wages were higher.[70] Many British governors were not so liberal and sought to keep labor in their colonies; Cameron in Tanganyika, for example, and Sharpe in Nyasaland refused to let Africans migrate to higher wage areas.

Various arrangements were tried during Coryndon's governorship to get workers for all the colony's needs. He attempted to eliminate traditional labor for the chief by letting people commute the corvée by a money payment. He had the district commissioners assist private employers to find labor; he established labor offices to supervise labor conditions and to help recruit workers. He gave permission to make tax defaulters work on projects such as road and bridge building in their own areas. Although the colonial office did not like tax labor, it could not refuse Coryndon because it had allowed the practice in Tanganyika.[71]

The labor supply remained a problem during Coryndon's rule of Uganda, but conditions improved slowly; and in contrast to other governors, Coryndon kept wages high even when labor was plentiful. He realized the relationship between high wage rates and the labor supply and sought to encourage Africans to keep working.

The labor question in East Africa was much debated in the 1920s. In 1921 J. H. Oldham, of the conference of missionary societies in Great Britain and Ireland, exchanged letters with the colonial office over the question of African labor in East Africa. Oldham objected to traditional unpaid labor in the reserves used to build roads and other public works. He also questioned the practice of government officials who put employers in touch with Africans. Oldham claimed this was a form of compulsion. That some compulsory paid labor was necessary, he accepted.[72]

Coryndon was in London at the time, and he helped the colonial office draft the reply to Oldham and to prepare corrective legislation. The reply to Oldham said that Churchill would change the draft proposal to remove the danger of officials' pressuring Africans to work for private employers but held firm on the need of using unpaid, forced labor for work in the reserves.

Relations between Uganda and the East African protectorate were usually strained. Although they shared the railway and port facilities, Kenya was the dominant colony. Coryndon began to complain in 1918 about the inefficient relationship between Uganda and the East African protectorate. He saw the need to rationalize the activities and relationships of the three East African territories, and he became the leading advocate for cooperation and planning in East Africa.

Uganda suffered especially from mismanagement of the railway and from surcharges imposed by Nairobi without consultation. Coryndon charged Nairobi with indifference to Uganda's interest: "We are in fact partners in East Africa and should combine to improve the whole conditions and develop the whole resources of the country between Ruwenzori and Mombasa."[73] He opposed the policy of independent consideration of problems and policies that affected both areas, such as the railway and port facilities at Kilindini.

In 1920 Coryndon argued for and secured an interprotectorate railway council, responsible for transporting all merchandise and for controlling the port of Kilindini, as was the custom in South Africa.[74] He decried the waste and inefficiency of the present system and called for the takeover of the Lake Albert marine service. He came to support administrative amalgamation but not under Northey of Kenya or Byatt of Tanganyika. Coryndon wanted to consolidate the three veterinary departments: one head would coordinate efforts to control and preserve the vast herds of African owned cattle in all the countries that bordered Lake Victoria. His goal was to establish a central veterinary research laboratory. He supported the reopening of the great German built Amani Agricultural Institute, to be paid for by the three territories. This was the beginning of Coryndon's dream of a single authority to control Lake Victoria and the land around it. The colonial office cautioned him to be patient.[75] Nevertheless, lecturing in 1921 Coryndon outspokenly advocated a coordinating machinery among the three governments of East Africa to organize, plan, and carry out policy for the region.[76]

Coryndon lamented both the delay in establishing the railway council and its purely advisory role. Such a council would be of no practical use unless it had full executive powers to run the railway system. The colonial office's response to his farsighted views was that he was trying to establish Uganda's equality with Kenya. But this was not the major reason for Coryndon's objections. More than the colonial office or any other governor, he saw the benefits of economically and administratively rationalizing operations in East Africa. Coryndon was right, but it was not until the 1950s that some of his ideas were put into effect.[77]

At this time, Coryndon was not for amalgamating the two territories; he saw each territory working out its own individual and social destiny. He felt Uganda would suffer if united with Kenya. He argued that a more efficient system would be to place the territories under an experienced high commissioner. This may have been the first time the idea was advanced to the colonial office since the memorandum of Tomkins in 1910 on the union of Uganda and the East African protectorate. (The customs department and the railway and marine system had been under a single administration since 1917.)

Coryndon, who had called for cooperation and for rationalizing common services, opposed amalgamation because he feared Uganda's special position under the 1900 agreement would be jeopardized by the more settler oriented control in Kenya. He felt the principles and practices of administration in Uganda differed too greatly from those in Kenya for the two colonies to be united. His opposition may have been based in part on fear for his own future; perhaps he suspected that Northey, not he, would be made high commissioner. By 1924 Coryndon had changed his mind. As governor of Kenya, he won Milner's support for the idea of a high commissioner for East Africa.[78]

We have a fine description of Coryndon in Uganda from T. S. Thomas, who served under him there as acting chief secretary; this account can serve as a summary of Coryndon's work in the colony.[79] They first met in Nairobi, where Coryndon stopped on his way to take up his post as governor. Thomas was impressed with how naturally and simply Coryndon spoke—a man who had lived with men, liked to be with them, and knew how to handle them. He had common sense, courtesy, and tolerance and was always ready to hear the views of others. In short, Thomas thought Coryndon the most human governor he had known. He liked to be in a small circle of friends, free of the formality of the governorship, and to talk of his years with Rhodes, of Swaziland, and of Basutoland.

As an administrator, Coryndon was sound and courageous and dealt carefully with the essentials—he might reread an important paper many times before making a decision. Once decided, he had no doubts, and issued clear orders so everyone knew his intention. He knew how to deal with his staff; he was kind but not blind to people's faults. When his trust was won it was given unconditionally. According to Thomas, Coryndon got on well with Africans. He devoted himself to improving their material and physical well-being, recognizing that the prosperity of Uganda depended on African farmers and their good health. He established the colony's system of midwifery schools and clinics. In education, he cooperated with the missionaries, established an education department, and set up the first government schools. He also arranged for labor inspection on plantations and tried to reform the system of customary labor for chiefs. In 1919 Coryndon was awarded a KCMG (Knight Commander of the Order of St. Michael and St. George).

In 1920 Coryndon secured a £1 million development loan from the colonial office and levied an excise duty that provided the government with money to expand cotton cultivation. He developed a fine road system, extended the Uganda railway, and planned an electric power system using the Ripon Falls. His 190-mile extension into Uganda of the Kenya railway had far-reaching effects on the cotton industry by linking the eastern province directly with the coast.

As governor, Coryndon had looked ahead and planned for a secure future; he especially pushed for regional cooperation. He served in Uganda from December 15, 1917, to August 30, 1922, when he became governor of Kenya and high commissioner of Zanzibar. Coryndon was to go to Kenya full of misgivings but determined to do his best.[80]

Governor of Kenya

After the war, white settler politicians in Kenya actively campaigned for more influence over local government.[81] They put strong pressure on the new governor, General Sir Edward Northey, who had led the Allied forces in East Africa. Settlers wanted to have European elections for the legislative council and to keep the Indians out of Kenya. The Indian issue was to dominate Kenyan politics for the next decade; Europeans feared being swamped by Indians and even being made a colony of India, as was suggested by some Indian politicians.[82]

Indians in Kenya were affected by nationalism in India, and after the Montagu reforms of 1917 the government of India began to champion the rights of Indians overseas. The controversy developed over the demand that the rights of citizenship of Indians be recognized throughout the British empire, a principle that had been approved at the imperial conference of 1921 by Canada, Australia, and New Zealand and by the crown colonies but had been rejected by the Union of South Africa. The European settlers of Kenya followed the lead of South Africa and threatened to resist if the claims of Indians were accepted by the government.

Kenya was the chief crown colony affected by the Indian problem. The settler population, which had been trying to make Kenya a white settler colony, temporarily put that issue into the background to deal with the question of Indian citizenship. The Indian community demanded citizenship, an end to segregation, and more political say in local councils—a right the Europeans had won earlier on, at first by nomination to the executive and legislative councils.

In Kenya, the debate heated up when, in 1919, only Europeans were allowed the right to be elected to the legislative council. White attitudes were complex. The Europeans distrusted Indian middlemen but nevertheless did business with Indian traders. The whites also feared competition from Africans. On the other hand, the more enlightened settlers—men like Lord Delamere—were also convinced that the European community would benefit from African prosperity; European farmers were eager to employ skilled African artisans; white producers of specialized cash crops did not disdain to purchase food from African producers. The whites, however, were determined to secure for themselves political paramountcy in the colony, a claim that seemed all the more justified to them at a time when imperial supremacy was challenged in countries as far afield as Ireland, Egypt, and India. Lord Milner, then colonial secretary, largely accepted white claims but, mindful of India's importance within the empire, proposed a special franchise for Indians. The whites secured an adult male franchise; the Indians were offered first two, then four nominated members for the legislative council. The first election was held in 1920, the second in 1922.

The colonial office was caught in the middle. The government of India demanded equal rights for Indians (although denying them this in India itself), and the settlers objected to having Indians on a common roll. Churchill, now colonial secretary, offered a solution based on equal rights for equal men—that is, voting rights for those Indians and Africans who could meet "European standards." At first he promised to limit Indian immigration, while reserving the white highlands for exclusive white settlement, but then he had to adopt a tougher line. Northey, who had been ruling Kenya with the settlers in a "government by agreement," was recalled and retired. Churchill and the colonial office chose Coryndon to replace him, and, essentially, to solve the Indian question.

Coryndon arrived on September 1, 1922. He had telegraphed a friend: "Have accepted Governorship of Kenya: no more peace." In this he was correct for his administration was much taken up with the Indian question; his plans for rationalizing the economies of East Africa and increasing African productivity had to be curtailed.

The settler community was shocked at the way the colonial office had treated Northey. They believed Northey had been recalled because he had refused to carry out Churchill's Indian proposals and that Coryndon was brought in to pass them. The Europeans waited distrustfully to see what kind of line the new man would take: "We imagine he has sealed orders in his pocket."[83]

Coryndon had no sealed orders; he did not even have copies of the basic published documents that had been issued and had to have his secretary request them from London. In effect, Coryndon had no private instruction, explanation, or advice from London. Soon after he arrived, he had to avoid Delamere's question as to what the new colonial secretary's views were because he did not know them. Here he was called upon to fight a very difficult battle; his only weapon was a statement in a secret dispatch to the effect that the British government considered the matter very serious.[84]

The Kenya papers reported that Coryndon was popular and successful in Uganda. The press looked to his South African background as a sign that he would side with the settlers. One settler politician put it more strongly:

[Coryndon] has a great reputation for being all out in the cause of the African native. We sincerely hope that this is the case. Our interests, i.e., the white settlers, and those of the said native are fairly identical and both dead against Indian domination. [85]

Later, in September, the Wood-Winterton report from the colonial office and the Indian office shattered settler hopes. There was to be no immigration restriction; segregation was to be ended; there was to be a common roll for Indian and European voters and elections to the legislative council with four seats reserved for Indians. The local whites planned their resistance, which included rebellion. A settler named Wheatley toured the country to organize armed resistance to the Indian question. The settlers refused to give Coryndon a pledge of secrecy if he negotiated with them. Military preparations were made; leaders were chosen; and a colonywide "convention of associations" organized settlers in each district. The people up-country wanted to seize power. Nairobi and Mombasa held back.

Devonshire wanted Coryndon and settler delegates to come to London to discuss the problem, but Coryndon was afraid of what the settlers might do in his absence. He got the white leaders to agree to an armistice: "The [colonial office] undertake not to attempt to force any measure on us whilst Coryndon is discussing the affair. We undertake not to take direct action until [Coryndon] returns, but reserve to ourselves at any time to terminate the armistice should either side break off the discussion."[86]

By the time a delegation left for London, the settlers had already made their military plans. They intended to capture the treasury, the railway, and the postal system. Senior officials were to be arrested, and the governor kidnapped and removed to a remote farm. Since many ex-soldiers had settled in Kenya—perhaps 1,000—they had a small trained army at hand and were ready to fight a Lettow-Vorbeck type of guerrilla war.[87] Some British naval forces were sent to Zanzibar when Coryndon left for London with a settler and Indian delegation early in 1923.

Devonshire had called the disputing parties to London, along with Coryndon, in March–April of 1923. Lord Delamere, leader of the settler faction, wanted to see Churchill's plan carried out. The *London Times* of April 25, 1923, agreed with settler demands for protection from being swamped by Indians.

Throughout the Indian controversy, Coryndon tried to maintain a balanced view, conclude an agreement, and avoid trouble. He played the aloof, impartial arbitrator. He tried to win concessions from the colonial office and asked that the government of India stop pressuring Kenya. He believed the settler threats to use violence and thought of resigning; but he stayed on and won enough concessions to get both sides to agree at least partially. Coryndon secretly negotiated with both settlers and Indians and got some missionary support for the settlers' position on restricted immigration. He clearly stood closer to the settlers' position than to the colonial office's, but he made only one statement that linked him to the settlers—at a public meeting he commented, "I am a South African." His efforts to frighten the colonial office into concessions failed (he had sent secret dispatches to London indicating the military buildup and expressing fears of not being able to defend the colony). The colonial office, however, backed down on the question of letting Indians on the common roll for fear of an armed rebellion and because of Coryndon's defense of the settlers' position.

The white paper issued in 1923[88] satisfied no one. The Indians did not get a common roll; the highlands remained white; and Indian leaders feared a bill would be passed to restrict Indian immigration. Still, Coryndon drafted a franchise bill for Indians that was more liberal than any prevailing in India. The whites had to accept five Indian seats on the legislative council and had to give up their voting monopoly and residential segregation in the towns. Furthermore, Europeans were told that they could not expect responsible government for a long time. This was an especially harsh blow to settler hopes: Southern Rhodesia had received responsible government in 1923 and Kenya whites expected no less. The Indians responded by a program of noncooperation. This failed, however, and Indians finally took their place on the council in 1924. A new constitution was issued, but the Indian problem continued to disturb Kenya.

Ironically, the presence of Indians in Kenya thwarted white ambitions and preserved Kenya as an African colony at a time when Africans had no direct voice or say in political decisions. Although the whites appeared to have won in their struggle with the Indians, they failed in their effort to dominate the 2.5 million Africans. Coryndon had gotten the settlers to accept a missionary, Dr. J.W. Arthur, on the delegation to London to represent African interests, and other missionary pressure groups bombarded the colonial office concerning the need to protect African interests. As a result, the 1923 white paper rediscovered the African, and henceforth London would seek to administer Kenya on behalf of Africans.

In their struggle against the Indians, the Europeans had also stressed African interests and rights and the need to develop African areas and to protect them against Indian competition. Coryndon was especially vocal along these lines for this position fit with his basic philosophy. When the colonial office declared, "Primarily Kenya is an African territory . . . the interests of the African nation must be paramount," the Europeans lost the struggle for paramountcy, but Coryndon obtained a freer hand to do more for Africans.

Imperial Trusteeship

After World War I, a sense of imperial trusteeship developed among the British and French. Colonial governance came to be seen as primarily for the benefit of the indigenous peoples. There were elements of fair play and guardianship in the term. Even local settler politicians in Kenya spoke of "native trusteeship." Previous governors such as Sir Charles Eliot and Sir Percy Girouard had talked only vaguely of protecting and developing Africans. The notions of protection and development blended with the so-called dual mandate developed by Lord Lugard, whose ideas were similar to Coryndon's own views of trusteeship while he was governor of Uganda. Since he was widely read and corresponded frequently with his fellow governors, he undoubtedly knew of Lugard's book, published in 1922, and used it to launch his own variation of the dual mandate—the "dual policy."

Coryndon governed a settler dominated colony; hence, he could not act as Lugard had acted. He had to overcome some settler resistance to African progress. First he won settler agreement to improve African conditions so as to make the colony less dependent on Indian artisans and traders. Then he called for the development of African reserves to make the colony wealthier. Coryndon's dual policy thus rested on the "complementary development of native and non-native production."

The transformation of Kenya from a settler colony thus came about during the Indian controversy. The white paper of 1923 announced the paramountcy of Africans and the need to protect and develop the "native races." This policy was a logical outgrowth of World War I idealism, the principle of self-determination, and the mandate system.

Heretofore, settlers had actively discouraged African economic advances. By orders in executive council in 1920, for example, administrative officers were discouraged from promoting the well-being of Africans in the reserves: "They were told that the proper place for the native to practice [sic] agriculture was on the farm as an employee of the settler."[89]

Before Coryndon's arrival, little had been spent on health or education projects or on programs to stimulate African production. One outstanding exception to this was the work of the administrator John Ainsworth, who considerably helped to improve African agriculture in the reserves. Ainsworth transformed Nyanza province into a leading producer of corn, sim-sim, and hides. The chief native commissioner of Kenya under Coryndon felt that Africans had not been fairly treated in the colony: they had been exploited; their economic development was repressed; they were overtaxed and they did not receive a fair proportion of the colony's expenditure on medical, educational, or other services.[90]

Once the Indian controversy seemed resolved, the white settlers became more willing to provide services to Africans. They felt that trained Africans would replace the Indians. Coryndon used this notion to promote African education, to develop their lands, and to improve their health. He announced his dual policy in 1924, but he had been acting on its principles from the beginning of his governorship, although without adequate funds. His economic and financial committee report (1922) called for the government to encourage the Africans to expand the production of export crops. Just as he had done in Uganda, Coryndon spoke of Kenya's Africans as the colony's greatest asset. More care must be given to the African's welfare, health, and productivity for he believed that a prosperous African population would benefit the whole colony. He called also for an education program suited to the needs of Africans.[91]

Coryndon had a wider interest in the African population than to use them against Indians or to stimulate their economy. His dual policy therefore evolved into a program to promote their economic development and their welfare at the same time that the Europeans were developing in their areas. Coryndon followed the pattern he had developed in Uganda: improve the infrastructure, then health and education facilities, while encouraging production for the market. Funds and motivation had previously been lacking, but after 1922 both motive and money became available. Railway expansion was pushed; roads were built into the reserves. Seeds were given out, a dairy school was opened for the Masai, and some Africans were trained as agricultural demonstrators in laboratories outside Nairobi. African suspicion and conservatism had to be overcome in many areas to get them to use ploughs instead of hoes, properly to treat their hides, to cull inferior animals from their herds, and to grow more food.

The key to improvement, the governor saw, was to give more power and resources to local authorities. In 1924 the legislative council passed a bill to establish a native council in every reserve. The native councils, which had limited powers of taxation and self-government, were long overdue in Kenya. For years, the rest of British Africa had followed a policy of indirect rule through indigenous institutions. In Kenya, insofar as the government ruled Africans, it ruled them directly. Coryndon's scheme was a compromise between direct and indirect rule for he made the district officer the chairman of the native council.

Native councils were seen as a link between the people and the government. They were to be the training ground for leaders and the key to developing the reserves. With direction from the district officer and funds from taxes, the council could improve sanitation and build clinics, roads, bridges, and schools. Government departments, especially the agricultural department, gave advice and instruction. Thus was begun a program of separate but parallel development. There were some initial objections from settlers who feared losing their black laborers, but Coryndon and his successor, Grigg, nevertheless pushed ahead.

In the dual policy program, Coryndon was helped by settler leaders such as Delamere, who had a pet scheme to set up a training college for African artisans in order to replace Indians. Delamere had no trouble in getting the governor to support his idea, and in 1924 an African industrial training center was built at Kabete.

In general, Kenya's educational system was far behind Uganda's. Since Indians and Goans were readily available for relatively low wages to work for the government or to provide skilled labor, the government had lacked incentive for educating Africans. Coryndon could do very little to rectify this situation in the short time remaining to him, but he did encourage government departments to train Africans and he gave increased subsidies to mission schools. He supported the Phelps-Stokes report, which called for more and better education for Africans, especially in teacher training and in industrial and agricultural skills.

Few Africans had been educated in the English language; hence, few were employed by the government as clerks, interpreters, or officials. In 1923 the governor issued a native civil services report that called for changes in government employment practices "to get rid of the expensive luxury it cannot afford of an alien clerical service both European and Asiatic."[92] Coryndon (as he had in Uganda) brought Africans into governmental service in Kenya for the first time.

Coryndon's plans are revealed in his 1924 and 1925 budgets. These provided for special African programs, above and beyond general funds for administrative, medical, and agricultural services. Though Coryndon could not do what he did in

Uganda—that is, create the educational and medical systems of the colony—he made specific improvements. He called for the printing department to add African apprentices; he equally encouraged Africans to become clerk-typists by providing night classes in Nairobi. Already the government was giving funds to the missions to train African attendants and orderlies, and a sum of £1,000 had been provided to missions for medical work.

The education department was expanded. Coryndon felt that he had failed to do very much before because of the opposition of the settlers and of his director of education. Coryndon wanted to speed up the industrial training of Africans. At Kabete, he was building a teacher training school for village schoolteachers, modeled on the famous Jeannes schools, to provide instruction in reading, writing, and arithmetic, along with Swahili, hygiene, and gardening. The subsidies to mission schools were greatly increased—to over £15,000. A training institute for carpentry and masonry was allotted 134,000 shillings; and women's education, £5,000.

Agriculture was not neglected. Forty more African field instructors were to be trained; the free seed program was continued; more experimental stations were established. New equipment was to be purchased for the veterinary department, and Africans were to be trained as inoculators.

To reassure the Africans, Coryndon promised to demarcate the reserves; the Carter commission was appointed to do this. (For the third time, Coryndon was involved in momentous land settlement commissions.) To help make the reserves more productive, Coryndon also tried to increase the number of traders and shops so that Africans would be induced to grow crops for sale. He felt the existing system penalized Africans and favored Indian traders. Kenya needed more feeder roads and trading centers so Africans could bring their goods to market. Coryndon wanted to establish corn production centers in the reserves to distribute seeds and to teach Africans improved methods of farming. These centers would also teach improved methods of dressing hides and would have clinics attached to them.[93] Unfortunately, few of these projects were adequately promoted after Coryndon's death.

Robert Coryndon made small beginnings and opened new perspectives for Kenya but not much more. After his death the well-being of the Africans was not promoted because the settlers' needs for labor transcended the government's interest in developing African peasant agriculture.

Coryndon and the East African Federation

Coryndon was a man who wanted to get things done; he was a builder and a developer. The tragedy of his Kenya governorship was that he had too little time and support to carry out his ideas. He died in 1925, having wrestled with the Indian problem and having struggled with settler resistance to African development. He was, however, a prime mover in the drive for a closer union of the three East African colonies.

Churchill accepted the idea of closer union in 1921, and a commission reported on this proposal in May of that year. Coryndon had been lobbying for various forms of cooperation when he was governor of Uganda. At that time he had opposed political union; he and his staff feared domination by Kenya. Kenya and

Tanganyika whites favored union but Governors Byatt and Cameron of Tanganyika opposed this plan. Cameron, who succeeded Byatt in 1925, also feared settler domination of the union.

Although he was a keen supporter of federation, Coryndon was convinced that an economic association should precede political union. During his governorships in Uganda and Kenya he called joint conferences on questions of customs, veterinary and shipping matters, and railway management. It was Coryndon who was the prime force urging a strengthening of the economic links among the three territories. By 1924 Kenya and Uganda had joint customs, telegraph, and railway systems. Coryndon and many Europeans felt that a complete customs union was the first step in an economic union. He wanted to unify railways, harbors, and the transport of the three territories under the existing intercolonial board, with himself as minister of transport. He felt that a unified postal, military, and police service would follow.

In September 1923, Coryndon wrote to the colonial office proposing that when Sir Horace Byatt retired from Tanganyika, a lieutenant governor should succeed him. Coryndon clearly saw himself as high commissioner of East Africa; he even studied the South African high commissioner system. In a letter to Sir Sidney Henn in 1924, he asked him to get the new Labour party's colonial secretary, J. H. Thomas, to defer appointing a governor to Tanganyika until the East African commission reported and to let Coryndon govern through a lieutenant governor. Thomas appeared to agree to wait, but then announced Cameron's appointment. (Thomas was a very close friend of Sir Hugh Clifford's, who had pushed for his chief secretary, Donald Cameron, to be made governor of Tanganyika.) Cameron's opposition helped block unification efforts. He simply did not understand the economics of cooperation and argued, on moral grounds, that Tanganyika enjoyed a special position as a League of Nations mandate.

At first, the drive for closer union came essentially from Coryndon and the colonial office; then the settlers under Lord Delamere came to support it. It made economic sense. They were aided by other groups. The imperial economic conference of 1923 studied the possibilities of cooperation in developing the resources of the empire and of strengthening economic relations among the constituent parts. Earlier, a Joint East African Board had been organized to encourage trade and investment in East Africa and to promote an East African federation. The chairman, a member of parliament, was Sidney Henn. He knew little about East Africa, but he worked closely with Coryndon, and it was through Henn that Coryndon placed his ideas before a wider audience.[94] Henn and the joint East African board put pressure on the colonial office and submitted recommendations to the secretary of state for the colonies. These reports embodied many of the ideas Coryndon had been pushing for and can stand as a summary of his views on closer union or federation.

The report called for fuller development of the indigenous African population, especially by improving medical services, sanitation and hygiene, and educational services. The board called for grouping of colonies under a high commissioner or governor-general in order to reduce government expenses by abolishing duplicate government departments and administrations. The railway system of East Africa should be under a central manager who would be responsible also for harbor facilities. An advisory board would assist the high commissioner and a full customs union was requested in order to reduce internal trade barriers. A customs union and the unification of tariffs would facilitate reciprocity and mutual preference among the East Africa group, the United Kingdom, and the rest of the empire. The final suggestion was that research be coordinated.[95]

In 1924 the joint East African board held a conference on East African federation, and Henn got a parliamentary commission appointed to study this matter. The Southborough commission advised in 1925 (Cmd. 2387) against political union but called for more economic cooperation and planning. A meeting of governors was suggested to plan further joint action. The major obstacles to closer union were the different financial positions of the territories and their different political outlooks. The economic depression of the 1930s ended these efforts, and political federation was to fail. But Coryndon's dream of practical cooperation in common services was to be achieved in time. The East African common services body stood for many years as a memorial to his vision and planning.

Coryndon, earlier than anyone else, saw the possibility of a common market for East Africa. He foresaw a free trade area, with a common external tariff, a common currency, linked to the British pound through an East African currency board. He had early on outlined the kinds of common services the area needed: ports, railways, statistics collection, telecommunications, customs, excise duties, and income tax. He had to win Delamere over to the side of federation, but Delamere then became a major force in pushing for closer union. Both men agreed that Nairobi should be the federal capital and that an imposing residence should be built. Delamere carried the battle for funds successfully through the legislative council and eventually two fine buildings were erected in Nairobi and Mombasa at a cost of £80,000. The governors conferences of 1926 and 1927 discussed matters of cooperation. A permanent secretariat was established in Nairobi.

Coryndon was dead by then, and his successor, Sir Edward Grigg, who believed he had a mandate from the colonial office to establish a political federation, pushed for that goal but to no avail. Had Grigg stressed economic cooperation rather than political federation, the East African common services might have been established in the 1930s instead of the 1950s. It was not until 1948, when control was given to an East African high commissioner, that Coryndon's plans began to be acted on. The common services superstructure was one of the most constructive achievements of British colonial rule, and Coryndon had been its originator.

Among the new organizations established after 1948 that had been foreseen by Coryndon were: The East African Customs and Excise Department, the East African Railways and Harbours Administration, the East African Agriculture and Forestry Research Organization, and the East African Statistical Department. In 1967 a Treaty for East African Cooperation established the East African Community, and it too embodied many of Coryndon's dreams: the East African Common Market, the East African Harbour Corporation, the East African Posts and Telecommunications Corporation, and the East African Railway Corporation.

Coryndon also had visions of a Lake Victoria authority. In November 1924 he took a journey around Lake Victoria and wrote a brilliant report to the colonial office about what should be done to develop the area.[96] He surveyed the lake districts for their economic potential and suggested ways they could be improved: more roads, encouragement from local officials, advice from government experts.

The area, he believed, was potentially very rich—it could grow more corn and cotton could be introduced to the Bukoba district. The lake area needed better transportation facilities, roads, railways, and ports. Coryndon suggested building a new line from Namirembi bay to the falls of the Kagora river to link up with the densely populated area of Ruanda-Burundi. He also called for government markets every twenty-five miles, with African market masters in charge. In each market there should be a clinic to treat venereal diseases and minor illnesses. Agricultural demonstration centers should also be established to show the people how to improve their crops, dry hides, and make ghee. An agricultural school would further stimulate production around the lake.

Coryndon concluded from his trip that the trade and traffic of the lake region were as yet an untapped resource. District officers should stimulate production, and a survey should determine where to build feeder roads to ports. The area would need more tugs, lighters, and ports in the lake—at least twenty-five additional landing places were needed.

There was a major need to coordinate the activities of Lake Victoria under one agency. At present, Coryndon wrote, the lake was dealt with inadequately by three governments. No one planned research on sleeping sickness and the tsetse fly in the area or cooperated in plague control. Although navigation on the lake came under the Uganda railway administration, this body had to deal with three governments on matters relating to crafts, piers, labor for unloading crafts, etc. There was no central authority to collect and register statistics on the ecology of the lake and its environs. Such a central authority could also study the agricultural potential of the basin, distribute seeds, and investigate pests and diseases. Fishing was another neglected industry. Africans had to go farther and farther into the lake to find fish. The government clearly had to know more about lake fish in order to keep up the yield and should develop the market for fresh and dried fish.

The solution was evident to Coryndon: a federation of the three governments to coordinate and plan the best use of the natural and human resources of the Lake Victoria basin. Nothing was ever done about this grand vision. As with his ideas on economic cooperation throughout East Africa, Coryndon's scheme for Lake Victoria would be proven right.

Coryndon as Developer

When Coryndon took over Kenya, the colony had suffered considerably from the postwar depression, and the government had been forced to make some retrenchments. Under Coryndon's guidance, however, the colony made a rapid recovery. More settlers arrived after 1922; more farmland was opened up; capital poured in; and exports increased. Port and railway traffic doubled. Felling, a South African, had been brought in by Coryndon to run the railway and had succeeded brilliantly. The railway showed a large profit. In 1924 Kenya and Uganda got a £3.5 million interest-free loan to build the Uasin-Gishu line into Uganda. Coryndon had put great pressure on the colonial office to get the loan approved. The joint East African board, under Henn, had carried the battle to Parliament, and the approval of the House was won largely because of concern over the empire's supply of cotton. By 1925 Coryndon had five rail lines under construction in

Kenya and two in Uganda. His work on railways in Uganda and Kenya alone would rank him as one of the greatest building governors in African history.

By 1924, then, Coryndon was pushing strongly for the colony's economic development. He planned to expand Mombasa and to make that city a great port. He talked Governor Byatt of Tanganyika into letting Kenya buy the Voi-Kahe line rather than close it. This meant that Mombasa, not Tanga, became a major port of East Africa because it was favored by Europeans from northern Tanganyika. Coryndon ordered refrigeration facilities to be built on the coast and tried to expand the meat export industry. African corn and cotton production was encouraged. Revenue became short again in 1925, and Coryndon had to put off some of his plans: loans for schools for all races, housing for African government employees, town planning, a water supply system for Mombasa, and corn-buying installations. Still, in three years he ended the colony's deficit and had a surplus of £149,723. Revenue exceeded expenditure during most of Coryndon's governorship and almost doubled between 1922 and 1925. He increased exports by 181 percent; the biggest gains were in corn, raw cotton, coffee, hides, skins, and sisal. Corn and cotton increases were partly the result of Coryndon's development work. He also helped to bring in other export oriented industries using local materials, such as the Magadi-Soda Company (1924) and tea factories (1925).

In summary, one can conclude that Kenya colony under Coryndon progressed steadily in spite of world depression in 1921–1922. He helped make Kenya a prosperous colony and, by his railway and port building and agricultural development work, laid the groundwork for Kenya's increased prosperity in the years to come. In both Uganda and Kenya Coryndon proved himself a great developer and fundraiser. He secured more loan funds than almost any other governor in African history up to 1925; by 1924 he had obtained loans of about £5 million, and in 1925 he began negotiations on a £5 million loan for Kenya. He put the colony's finances on a sound basis, while greatly expanding its trade. The position in 1925, at his death, was substantially better than it was when he took over in 1922. As the acting colonial treasurer, H. L. Bayles, noted in a review of the colony's position in 1926, "A genuine advance had taken place."

Coryndon's record as a builder ranks as high as, if not higher than, that of Governor Guggisberg of the Gold Coast (1919–1927). When Guggisberg first took office, he drew up a ten-year plan to lay the foundation of development in every direction. His achievements were great: constructing the harbor of Takoradi, founding Achimota college, and africanizing the government. But in many respects Coryndon achieved even more during his eight years in Uganda and Kenya. Both men had a great capacity for work, both were orderly and systematic in their approach to problems, and both had great drive and determination. Coryndon had greater vision: his dreams of an East African federation and of a Lake Victoria authority transcended the boundaries and problems of one colony.

Coryndon's Death

The Duke and Duchess of York paid a visit to East Africa over Christmas 1924. Coryndon had been ill and was advised by his doctor to rest; but he continued with his duties during the royal visit. In January the duke left for Uganda, and

Lady Coryndon left for England. Coryndon was to join her and their four children, but on February 9, 1925, he collapsed; he died after an emergency operation. Edward Denham acted as governor until Sir Edward Grigg arrived late in
1925.

Coryndon's funeral was a major ceremony. Letters and cables poured in from
the Arab, African, and European communities and from other colonies in which
he had served. The Duke of York returned to attend the funeral, and King George
and Queen Mary sent their condolences: "The Queen and I are grieved to hear of
the sudden and irreparable loss which has befallen you, a loss also to the colony of
Kenya and to the Empire."[97]

Coryndon was called a brilliant statesman who won the real affection of Ken-
yans for his fairness, impartiality, and sense of duty. In the House of Commons,
Lord Buxton eulogized Coryndon and said the colonial office had lost one of its
best men, who had done admirable service in Kenya and elsewhere. Sir Sidney
Henn wrote to Lady Coryndon, paying tribute to her husband: "He was an ideal
governor, and had he lived, I feel sure he would have become the first governor
general of East Africa, a post which I know he aspired to fill."[98]

The legislative council of Kenya voted Lady Coryndon and her four children a
compassionate allowance. Coryndon had not served the mandatory ten years as
governor to get death benefits at that rank. Delamere hinted that financial assistance was desperately needed, and the legislative council provided £500 per annum for Lady Coryndon, £200 for each of her sons, and £100 for her daughter.
Kenya colony and the Rhodes trust saw to the education of Coryndon's sons.

Coryndon had dreamed of a natural history museum and a central museum
and library for Nairobi. An appeal was made after his death to build such a museum in his memory, and the Coryndon Memorial was opened in Nairobi in September 1930 by Governor Grigg.

Coryndon had been a great governor, one of the greatest in African history.
Kipling was among those who appreciated his historical stature; some believe that
the governor served as one of Kipling's models for the poem "The Pro-consuls." In
many ways, Coryndon was the ideal imperialist of imperialist dreams—hunter,
athlete, man of action, diplomatist, pioneer administrator, advocate of native
trusteeship, and economic developer. The best tribute to his career may be found,
perhaps, in the now curiously dated language of the *East African Standard*, whose
columns had so often criticized him in the past:

> He was one of a line of Empire builders—a great connecting link between this
> country and her African neighbours—friend and companion of Rhodes, Smuts,
> Selous, and others who have made African history; he was one of a great band
> whose names will live forever in the annals of Africa. The gift of vision was his—he
> visualized a great confederation of the East African States with common objects
> and aspirations in which Kenya would not lose its individuality but rather would
> extend its influence. The Empire was to him a very live power carrying him inces-
> santly onward in its progress on the path of the development of African by British
> influence.[99]

It is a fitting epitaph.

Notes

1. This essay is based largely on the papers of Sir Robert Thorne Coryndon, Mss. Afr. S.633, Rhodes House Library, Oxford University (fifteen boxes), and the Colonial Office (hereinafter cited C.O.) series in the Public Record Office, London (hereinafter cited P.R.O.). For short sketches of Coryndon see the article by Frank Worthington, his brother-in-law, in the *Dictionary of National Biography* and the preface to the calendar of the Coryndon Papers prepared at Rhodes House Library. Box 10 of the Coryndon Papers contains reminiscences of people who knew and worked with Coryndon and forms the basis for much of what is written here. I wish to thank Christopher P. Youe of Dalhousie University for reading this chapter. Mr. Youe is writing a full-scale biography of Coryndon.

2. See Coryndon Papers, box 10, file 1, ff. 37–55, for Hole's reminiscences of Coryndon.

3. For details on this period see L. H. Gann, *A History of Southern Rhodesia: Early Days to 1934* (London, 1965).

4. Rhodes had a series of secretaries: Henry Currey, Gordon Le Sueur, Robert Coryndon, Philip Jourdan, and Jack Grimmer (who later served as Coryndon's private secretary). Rhodes was a difficult, demanding employer but a generous one.

5. L. H. Gann, *A History of Northern Rhodesia: Early Days to 1953* (London, 1964), p. 79; see also Marshall Hole, *The Making of Rhodesia* (London, 1926), pp. 399–401.

6. C. W. Macintosh, "The Life of Lewanika, Paramount Chief of the Barotse and Allied Tribes" (manuscript in Royal Commonwealth Society Library, Coillard Collection). Macintosh published a biography of Lewanika in 1944. See also Gervas Clay, "Lewanika and Coryndon," in *Your Friend Lewanika: The Life and Times of Lubosi Lewanika Letunga of Barotseland, 1842 to 1916* (London, 1968), Chap. 9; also Gerald Caplan, *The Elites of Barotseland, 1878–1969* (Berkeley, 1970).

7. Coryndon pressed the colonial office for a better boundary, but the colonial office refused.

8. For details see Colin Harding, *Far Bugles* (London, 1933).

9. Coryndon to High commissioner Selborne, 22 November 1905, P.R.O., C.O. 417/541.

10. Coryndon Papers, box 10, file 1, f. 31.

11. See ibid., f. 44.

12. Telegram, 9 January 1907, P.R.O., C.O. 417/440.

13. Perhaps seeing how Colin Harding was treated after years of Chartered Company service, Coryndon decided to seek the better conditions and greater security of the colonial service.

14. Coryndon Papers, box 10, file 1, ff. 30, 52.

15. Ibid., box 12, file 2, f. 8.

16. Ibid., ff. 52–53.

17. Ibid., ff. 54–55.

18. The Swazi spoke of his granting monopolies and concessions as "the documents that have killed us. We hold the feather and sign; we take money but we do not know what it is for." This is quoted in Margery Perham and Lionel Curtis, *The Protectorates of South Africa: The Question of Their Transfer to the Union* (London, 1935), p. 6.

19. See Godfrey Lagden Papers, Mss. Afr. S. 211, 2/4/ff. 45–60, Rhodes House Library, Oxford.

20. On the Swazis see Hilda Kuper, *The Swazi: A South African Kingdom* (New York, 1963). Coryndon's salary in Swaziland increased from £800 to £1,200 plus £380 in allowances.

21. See *Some Account of George Grey and His Work in Africa* (London [private printing], 1914), p. 8. While shooting lions from his horse, Grey was severely mauled; he died in 1911 in Nairobi, Kenya.

22. Coryndon was much impressed by Grey's work in marking out the reserves, and he was to use the same methods and rationale to demarcate the native reserve system in Southern Rhodesia in 1914–1916.

23. After the meeting with the Europeans, Coryndon was host that night at a dinner party for Lord Selborne. He feared for his future career when Selborne, making his way in the dark from the guest house to the residency for dinner, missed the path and fell down a steep bank into the tennis court.

24. C.O. 417/470/330.

25. The South African Act of Union (1910) called for the transfer at some future date of the high commission territories to the Union of South Africa.

26. Dispatch 752, C.O. 417/441.

27. Confidential dispatch 16, March 1908, C.O. 417/457.

28. See *Colonial Reports: Annual No. 559, Swaziland Report for 1906–07* (Cd. 3729), p. 15.

29. Dispatch 765, C.O. 417/441.

30. See account on origin of South African Native Congress, *Abantu-Batho*, (Maseru) 20 January 1916, in Rhodes House Library, Oxford.

31. See Coryndon Papers, box 10, file 1, ff. 27–29. The queen, by saying that she "swore by" Coryndon, meant that he had won her confidence and trust as well as that of the Swazi people.

32. Ibid. In 1909 Coryndon had married Phyllis Mary Worthington, the sister of his friend and private secretary in Barotseland, Frank Worthington. They were to have three sons and a daughter.

33. Coryndon Papers, box 10, file 1. Coryndon was made a CMG in 1911 to honor his work as resident in Swaziland, an unusual award for a nongovernor. He was to make KCMG (1919) when he was governor of Uganda and to be awarded the commander of the Order of the Crown by Albert of Belgium.

34. Dispatch 784, C.O. 417/487.

35. Dispatch 455, C.O. 417/502. The colonial office admitted that he had managed the Swazi National Fund well.

36. Coryndon Papers, box 10, file 1, ff. 57–66: reminiscences of Arthur Holland, secretary to the commission.

37. See Parliamentary Papers, Cd. 8674 (1917–1918), and Cmd. 1042 (1920).

38. Rhodesia, Archives, Salisbury ZAD s/2/2.

39. Africans in Rhodesia were given 51.55 acres per head of population, a higher figure by far than in South African or in the high commission territories, where the average was around 12 acres per person.

40. For example, two schools—Domboshawa and Tjolotjo—were started to teach agricultural and industrial skills.

41. C.O. 417/580.

42. For a different view of Coryndon in Uganda see *History of East Africa*, ed. Vincent Harlow and F. M. Chilvers (Oxford, 1965), vol. 2, esp. chap. 8.

43. C.O. 536/90/476.

44. C.O. 536/94/5 May 1919.

45. *Uganda Herald*, 26 September 1919.

46. Confidential dispatch, 6 September 1919, C.O. 536/95.

47. See Margaret Macpherson, *They Built for the Future: A Chronicle of Makerere University College, 1922–1962* (Cambridge, 1964), p. 2. Coryndon and Guggisberg (in the Gold Coast) rank as founders of two of the most important colleges for blacks in Africa.

48. C.O. 536/120/22 September 1922.

49. Confidential dispatch, C.O. 536/120. See also H. B. Thomas and Robert Scott, *Uganda* (Oxford, 1935), for some details on what was accomplished during Coryndon's governorship (but without explicit recognition of his contributions).

50. See *History of East Africa*, 2:424–429, 479, 481–482, 527–529, for these charges.

51. See Haarer Papers, Mss. Afr. S. 1144, Rhodes House Library, Oxford.

52. Coryndon was a good speaker and was always welcomed at the Royal Colonial Institute when on leave in London. The Royal Colonial Society reported he gave a most stimulating talk in March 1920.

53. See *Uganda Herald*, 16 July 1920, pp. 1–2.

54. Dispatch 16, C.O. 536/110. Coryndon designed all the furniture for the councils. The colonial office thought his designs were too expensive, but Churchill supported him and he even got his presidential chair and a Cuban mahogany table.

55. See this charge in *History of East Africa*, 2:527–529.

56. C.O. 536/91/236.

57. Ibid.

58. Coryndon Papers, box 1, file 2, ff. 61–63, typescript of speech made by Coryndon in reply to a toast by Lord Cranworth early in 1921.

59. See, for example, *History of East Africa*, 2:424, 527.

60. Telegram 5, 30 January 1921, C.O. 536/109.

61. Telegram, 22 March 1921, C.O. 536/109.

62. Telegram, 5 March 1921, C.O. 536/109.

63. See *History of East Africa*, 2:479.

64. Dispatch 524, C.O. 536/120.

65. Dispatches 14 and 45, C.O. 536/99.

66. Dispatch 520, C.O. 536/104.

67. Dispatch 524, C.O. 536/120.

68. Coryndon Papers, box 1, file 1/2, ff. 34–41.

69. Dispatch 411, C.O. 536/102.

70. Dispatch 314, 13 August 1919, C.O. 536/95.

71. Dispatch 307, C.O. 536/119.

72. Compulsory paid labor was allowed for emergencies and for clearly defined needs for public works but had to be approved by the secretary of state. Oldham and the missionaries were upset by the labor circulars of 1919 that Governor Northey had issued.

73. C.O. 536/91/private.

74. It was characteristic of Coryndon to draw on his South African experience in seeking personnel and solutions for the problems he faced in East Africa. He brought railway, agricultural, and veterinary experts from South Africa.

75. Dispatch 605, C.O. 536/104.

76. See Coryndon Papers, box 1, file 2, ff. 61–63.

77. Telegram, 10 April 1921, C.O. 536/110.

78. See Coryndon Papers, box 12, file 2, f. 106A. Milner, in a letter to Coryndon, said that it had always been his desire to create a high commissioner so as to treat the territories as a unit.

79. Ibid., box 10, file 1, ff. 72–75.

80. Before Coryndon left for Nairobi, he finished some important work: the regulations for an African civil service, which improved salaries and working conditions for the Africans. He wanted the regulations published by January 1, 1923, to coincide with the publication of the "Prospectus and Syllabus" of the new technical school, Makerere College. Dispatch 484, C.O. 536/120.

81. See George Bennett, "Settlers and Politics in Kenya," in *History of East Africa*, vol. 2, chap. 6. For Coryndon's governorship of Kenya see also Elspeth Huxley, *White Man's Country: Lord Delamere and the Making of Kenya* (London, 1935), vol. 2.

82. On the Indian question see Robert G. Gregory, *India and East Africa: A History of Race Relations within the British Empire, 1890–1939* (Oxford, 1971), chaps. 5–7. There were 10,000 whites and 23,000 Indians in Kenya in 1922.

83. Wheatley Papers, letter of 8 September 1922, Rhodes House Library, Oxford.

84. Coryndon Papers, box 3, file 3, ff. 34–39.

85. Wheatley Papers, letter of 22 August 1922, Rhodes House Library, Oxford.

86. Ibid., letter of 28 February 1923, Rhodes House Library, Oxford.

87. Nestor Papers, Mss. Afr. S. 1086, Rhodes House Library, Oxford.

88. *Indians in Kenya*, Cmd. 1922.

89. Coryndon Papers, box 4, f. 13, Morel correspondence.

90. Ibid. For 1922, Africans paid £725,314 in taxes; Indians, £143,000; and Europeans, £385,000.

91. *East African Standard*, 15 September 1923, p. 14.

92. Kenya, Legislative Council, *Proceedings*, November 1923, p. 66.
93. Coryndon Papers, box 5, file 2, 1924 discussions.
94. See Henn Papers, Mss. Afr. S. 715, 1/6/5–6, Rhodes House Library, Oxford.
95. Coryndon Papers, box 9, file 2, ff. 3–7.
96. See ibid., box 5, file 4, ff. 2–11.
97. Ibid., box 13, file 1, f. 4.
98. Henn Papers, box 1, file 6, f. 72.
99. *East African Standard*, 18 February 1925, p. 5.

Sir Andrew Cohen: Proconsul of African Nationalism (1909-1968)

Ronald Robinson

IF in some limbo of ruined empires all the British governors[1] of tropical Africa could be called together, they would probably form two mutually disagreeable companies: the old guard of indirect rulers, commissioned before 1947, would surely muster under the archetypal Lugard; the new guard of "democratizers" appointed after 1947, on the other hand, should assemble at the drumhead of the archetypal anti-Lugard Andrew Cohen: for he was most influential in dismissing the old guard in favor of the new to put an end to the long reign of indirect rule. As head of the African division in the colonial office from 1946 to 1951, he was the executive—as alter ego of his minister, Arthur Creech Jones, perhaps the moving spirit—behind a palace revolution in the African empire, which in democratizing its administration prepared the colonies for independence within the Commonwealth.

To attempt an objective account of that event while official archives are still closed might be premature; what follows is rather a biographical view of the great departure as Cohen saw it, based on his private papers and on personal knowledge of his part in it.[2]

Beginnings

During their feud of the time, the governor of Nigeria, Lord Milverton, derided Cohen as "the intellectual dreamer of Whitehall" who had appointed himself keeper of Creech Jones's conscience.[3] Insofar as Cohen was a planner with a moral vision, the charge was just. He was cut out to be a Platonic philosopher-king by education, temperament, and experience. Of giant stature and frenetic energy, he remained boyish in charm and enthusiasm.

Cohen was born in 1909. His father belonged to the anglicized, conservative *haute juiverie*, well connected with business and the professions; his mother came from the radical, Unitarian Cobbs. Andrew split the difference in becoming an agnostic, favoring Cohens perhaps in his passionate intellectuality and thirst for public recognition, and Cobbs in contempt for convention and zest for reform. On both sides his formation was elitist; but, unable to attend compulsory chapel, he was also unable to go to Eton. He was sent to school at Malvern and thence to Trinity College, Cambridge, where studies in ancient Greek and Roman classics taught him little of modern Africa. Under the influence of Carlyle and Euripides, nevertheless, Cohen fell in love with a heroic image of himself as the idea of the future in action. He went down from Cambridge in 1931 with a double first and quite enough intellectual snobbery to go with it. Being a younger son, he was bound for government employ; being a romantic, he dreamed of a foreign service post on a Greek island; according to the law of cussedness governing all large organizations, he was appointed to the home civil service in the inland revenue. In 1934 a friend of the family arranged for Cohen to escape and join the other classical scholars who monitored the dependent empire in the colonial office. Africa had become his life by chance.

Early Career, 1934–1939

For the next five years the junior official learned the ropes of African colonial organization and departmental tradition; decentralization was the governing principle of the one; moral posturing the ingrained habit of the other. The colonial secretary's department had never presumed to govern the colonies from Downing Street; the object rather had been to avoid doing so, in order to spare the home taxpayer the expense. Normally, each colonial administration was treated not as an extension of the United Kingdom government but as a separate, financially self-sufficient, and potentially autonomous entity. It was the business of the governor and his colonial service officials—a different breed from the home civil servants who manned the colonial office—to govern; it was for them to devise and execute policy locally, subject to the veto of the department, which was rarely used. The colonial office merely "supervised" them to insure that local revenue was not overspent, that vague standards of trusteeship were observed. In effect, the department enjoyed the right to preach and admonish but rarely the power to direct or execute. The practical politics of local colonial administration were thus the province of the governor; the somewhat philosophical empire of broad principle and ethics belonged to the colonial office.[4]

Cohen soon worked out his own eccentric balance between keeping the imperial conscience and being realistic. There were early signs of impatience with the remote ineffectuality of the system. For example, he had the temerity to suggest that colonial service men with experience in the field might make a better job of the colonial office than he and his colleagues ever could.[5] When he visited Africa for the first time in 1937, the credibility gap between imperial pretension and practice disturbed him. The shock of discovering what little the trustees had done for Northern Rhodesian Africans drove Cohen to propose the nationalization of British copper royalties to provide revenue for social services.[6] He was appalled also at the unofficial color bar, which, in spite of colonial office disapproval, still existed in Kenya and Rhodesia; he took a year off studying the black problem in the United States without finding the solution.[7] Even more actively than his colleagues, he took the obligations of trusteeship seriously; his sympathies lay with the black African rather than the white; he believed that colonial rule was morally unjustifiable except insofar as it advanced native interests above all others, including those of the United Kingdom itself.

The War Years

Into these youthful susceptibilities the war drove the necessary iron for a man of action. In 1940 Cohen was sent to organize civilian supplies at the siege of Malta, acting at times as lieutenant governor of the island at the age of thirty-three. It was his first taste of power, and the experience left a mark on him. Greatness had been thrust upon Cohen in an embattled government that had to reorganize a society to meet an emergency. Ever after a towering impatience to cut red tape and get things done possessed him, as if the siege was never lifted in his unconscious mind, and ever after he took a Fabian socialist view of the duty of the state to improve the social order. Cambridge, the colonial office, and Malta made him what he was: unflinchingly realistic in finding means to serve a passionately speculative vision of ultimate ends.

By the time Cohen returned to the office in 1943, the colonial organization was being jolted out of its arcane, laissez-faire tradition by the logistics of war. Centralized economic planning and control had been riveted on the colonies in the course of worldwide economic warfare; their administrators were intervening with a heavier hand to extract manpower and supplies from their African collaborators without requital in imports. Loyalty under strain was being bought with promissory notes on better living standards, social services, and political advance when victory was won. In planning the colonial economics of war, the office was already thinking about the economics of peace. Whitehall discovered that the African dependencies had become a vital asset to the United Kingdom. A swift expansion of their primary production would be necessary to redeem wartime pledges to subjects, to replenish the home economy after the ravages of war, and, more immediately, to appease anticolonial opinion in the United States.

Up to 1944 the state department in Washington seemed bent on making a Boston tea party of all colonial empires, with the prospective United Nations as host.[8] Nothing strengthened the case for colonial reform in Whitehall so much as this American "scare," for the British empire now hung to a large extent on the whim of the United States. At last, the vaults of the treasury, locked against colonial expenditure since Gladstone's day, opened to the necessity of gilding a more attractive image for British colonialism. In 1944 the colonial office squeezed £120 million out of the chancellor of the exchequer for postwar colonial development and welfare.[9] The sum, added to the British war debt to the colonies, assured colonial governments of considerable public capital to invest for the first time. Every window in the office rattled with excitement at the prospect of exporting to Africa the welfare state already blueprinted for home consumption.

Alongside these radical economic designs for the future, the department's political planning for peace seemed to Cohen out of step and out-of-date; its prescriptions up to 1946 were those of the septuagenarian ex-Indian governor and surveyor of Africa Lord Hailey. From 1940 to 1942, Hailey had visited every district in British colonial Africa to "investigate as a matter of high policy the important problem of future political advance for Africans in central government in its relation to the evolution of indirect rule."[10] Nationalists, he reported, were nowhere to be found, except "among a few sections of the Gold Coast and possibly the coastal areas of Nigeria"; even there the chiefs and moderate intelligentsia had them firmly by the throat. Accordingly, a policy of conservative political advance on the prewar perspectives of indirect rule was recommended. African representation in central government would be built up through indirect election from the chiefly membership of native authorities and provincial councils. All but a few representatives of the urban, educated Africans were to be excluded.[11] The formula was for continuing the prewar strategy of backing tribal leaders and institutions as bulwarks against nationalist agitation, while rewarding them with limited constitutional concessions at the center. So long as the traditional kings, chiefs, and notables kept the rural peasant majority loyal to the colonial regimes, there was no danger of urban nationalist minorities setting the grass roots of populism alight. The reformed constitutions that Sir Alan Burns introduced in the Gold Coast in 1946 and Milverton set up in Nigeria in 1947 embodied Hailey's backward looking formula. Along this cautious road, the colonial office expected that the African dependencies might be in sight of some form of self-government after some sixty to eighty years.

Postwar Developments in the Colonial Office

At the outbreak of peace—soon after Attlee's Labour party was swept into power in the euphoria over making all things better—Creech Jones became colonial secretary and Cohen was promoted to assistant undersecretary of state in charge of Africa. In effect, Hailey was deposed as mayor of the palace of planning. An old man with vast practical administrative wisdom from the past was succeeded by a young man in a hurry with a political vision of Africa's future. Cohen's rapport with the minister grew naturally; both men were connected with the Fabian colonial bureau, which championed the cause of the educated African in Britain; on socialist principles, both regarded indirect rule as a relic of reactionary imperialism. Late in 1946 an agreed minute, which Cohen may have inspired, opened the slaughter of the precedents that began the palace revolution. "Both the internal situation in the African territories themselves," the document declared, "and the state of international opinion [not to mention the public relations of the Labour party], demand a new approach to policy in Africa."[12] In order to keep pace with accelerated economic development, the argument ran, administrative and political advance must be speeded up. The question of transferring executive power was specifically included.[13]

Precisely what was the necessity for a new approach is not at all clear; the reasons given in the minute merely repeated a liturgy in official use since 1941 to justify costly social reform in the colonies, especially to the treasury. If in fact the pressure had arisen in the African territories, the initiative for a new course would have come from the colonial governors, not from the colonial office. Though provincial officials in some areas were disenchanted with the futility of indirect rule, the majority of governors were still devoted to it. African nationalism was as yet in its negligible infancy. Nor is it easy to discern pressures for a new approach either in international opinion (anticolonial fires were cooling in Washington at the beginning of the cold war) or in an anti-imperial spirit in the Labour party, which seemed to grow prouder of the tropical African empire the more colonial development and welfare was talked about.[14] Even so, a new approach might well have met the tactical and ideological requirements of the Labour ministry in relation to the trade unions and the party. A dramatic change of policy was expected of a Labour colonial secretary by the faithful. India was being liberated in bloody partition at this very moment; surely it was well to chart a new course for Africa that would be as distinctively "socialist" but would end in less bloodshed. Whatever occasioned the opportunity, Cohen and his official colleagues seized it with all the conviction of postwar utopianism. A departmental committee was set up to unroll a new map for Africa's political future. While Creech Jones was preoccupied with the crisis in Palestine, Cohen as co-chairman translated Labour's colonial shibboleths into terms of practical African administration.

What the colonial office was now doing was unprecedented: never before had the course of tropical African empire been drastically altered; never before had a policy for these territories as a whole been thought necessary or possible. Hitherto conventional wisdom had required a variety of local policies suited to the unique circumstances of each dependency. The colonial office had never initiated policy from the center, least of all in the constitutional and administrative fields, which had been the jealous preserve of the governor and his political officers. Yet Cohen was now drawing up a master plan of coordinated political and economic development for the next three decades without first consulting the governors.

By the middle of 1947 the breaking of precedents had led on to denunciation of the indirect rule doctrine of administration. Cohen nailed up his revolutionary theses in two classic manifestos. In February 1947 the first of these—Creech Jones's local government dispatch (which Cohen drafted)[15]—told the African governors that, so far as the colonial office was concerned, the household gods of indirect rule had been broken and cast out. Their very name and title was abolished; their covenants, by which neotraditional native authorities enjoyed a monopoly of administrative privilege and political representation, were to be scrapped; they were incapable of managing the local economic projects and social services required for rapid modernization. For this purpose, the rejected educated elite were to be brought in to provide the necessary leadership. "The modern conception of colonial administration," the colonial office insisted, required a "democratic system of local government" on English lines.[16]

Cohen and his men might not be quite sure what English local government was; town clerks and county treasurers were called in to advise; nor was the colonial office much better informed about the practice of native administration in Africa. Governors had rarely sent their district and provincial officers' reports home, and as a rule the office had not asked for them. What Whitehall did not know it could not interfere with; but if an administrative transformation was to be masterminded from the center, the colonial office had to know what was going on in the districts; new machinery was needed for exchanging information and reviewing progress in the field.

The local government dispatch announced for this purpose the setting up of the African studies branch[17] (next door to Cohen's office), a new *Journal of African Administration*,[18] and the first of a series of large conferences at which the new ideas were to be translated into practical field terms. Thus, a dispatch that began by laying down the democratic principle, which was not to be questioned, ended by implying that its authors lacked the systematic local knowledge to know whether democracy was feasible in Africa or not. How it was to be achieved in detail was to be worked out under Cohen's chairmanship at a Cambridge conference in August 1947 by a cross section of experienced colonial service officials.[19] Their report was to be submitted to a conference of African governors for approval in November. It was one more mark of a palace revolution that, in taking advice from junior officials before consulting the governors, the traditional sequence of policymaking had been reversed.

In May 1947 Cohen submitted the second manifesto in the form of the departmental committee's report.[20] This secret document showed a drastic alteration in colonial perspective, of which the local government dispatch was but the outward sign. If democratization from below was not hurried up, Cohen believed, it would soon be overtaken by democratization from above. What was radical about the committee's recommendations was the basic assumption that inevitably, "within a generation . . . the principal African territories will have attained . . . full responsibility for local affairs"[21]—in effect, this meant independence within the Commonwealth. The Gold Coast, it was foreseen, would lead the van. At a stroke of the pen, the official perspectives on African empire were foreshortened, cutting its life expectancy from eighty to twenty years.

Cohen's Plan for Decolonization. Cohen produced a blueprint for transferring power to colonial subjects similar to that recommended in Lord Durham's report for the British colonies of settlement a century earlier. Just as Durham had proposed responsible self-government for Canada, so Cohen now planned to bring it to Africa in four stages, as circumstances in each territory required. In the first stage, indirectly elected Africans would be granted a majority of seats on colonial legislative councils, one or two of them being brought into executive councils. Meanwhile, popularly selected councillors would be gaining executive experience in the reformed local authorities, and local electorates would be learning the art of popular control. University and training colleges were planned to multiply educated cadres capable of filling the higher ranks of the colonial services. In the second stage, African legislative councillors were to be made responsible to the governor as executive heads of domestic branches of central government. Cohen took it for granted that the more prolonged these first two stages were, the firmer the foundations for self-government would be. Ideally, therefore, universal franchises and directly elected majorities in legislative assemblies should be withheld until the third stage, when African "members" who enjoyed the confidence of the legislative majority would be made responsible to them for all branches of government except finance, security, and external affairs. Finally, African ministers representing the majority party would modulate into a cabinet with collective responsibility for the entire government on the Westminster model. For the first time in its history, the colonial office was taking seriously its pledges to prepare the African territories for independence.

It may seem strange for an empire to plan its own political demise precisely at the moment when, as a dollar earner and contributor to the home fat ration, its economic value was at its height. But Cohen insisted that without the transfer of power economic development was practically impossible for the following reasons. First, the cooperation of the African intelligentsia was required to execute modern economic and social projects; their price would be admission to more and more offices in government and it would have to be paid. As Cohen put it, "The increasing range and complexity of the matters in which the state has to take positive action" necessitated an accelerating transfer of power.[22] Second, he argued that imperial control could not be retained if modern elites were to be left out in the political cold to organize the popular discontent that the strains of modernization would inevitably stir up. "The pace of change," Cohen warned, "is still . . . under control, but the direction can hardly be altered";[23] the only alternative to controlled constitutional concession was anarchy. To avoid the risk of another India in Africa, it was better to concede too much too early than too little too late; more than that, magnanimity supposedly would strengthen "moderate" African collaborators against "extremist, anticolonial agitators" and put the brake on demand. By means of such paradoxical sophistry, each step forward to African self-government was justified as a step backward in the direction of prolonging colonial rule. The first three stages of reform, designed to win educated African collaboration, for example, were designed also to handicap the black elite's race for power at the center with the deadweight of the uneducated, communalistic, rural majority. Democratization, so-called, aimed "to bring together literates and illiterates in balanced and studied proportions" so that "the professional African politician's 'selfish' ambition" would be curbed for the commonweal.[24] Nor was power to be conceded stage by stage until those with pretensions to national leadership proved that they had united enough popular support behind them to insist upon it. To do so otherwise would not be to transfer authority but to see it dribble away. Third, Cohen justified his plan as the only solution with a constructive ending. Ethnically divided and locally oriented chiefs were incapable of uniting congeries of tribal communities on a national scale. For such tasks modern nationalists had to be brought in to transcend the ethnic divisions. If it was in the interest of Britain as well as Africa eventually to bring stable, cooperative nation-states into being favorable to the Commonwealth connection, there was no time to be lost in the building.

Reaction to the Plan.   There were many at the time who wished to turn colonies into welfare states; there were some who foresaw that the colonial age was expiring; but Cohen was one of the few to grasp the full implication. Not only did he realize that colonial administration would have to be nationalized but also he understood that it would be a race against time to lay sufficient foundations of stability for self-governing states. As the realist in him discerned that the imperial era was closing, the moralist hurried to end it constructively. In this sense a revolution had taken place in the perspectives and the social values of the policymakers. They were becoming less interested in governing Africa precisely because they had become interested in developing it. The revolution had swung the aim of the palace from one of jealously conserving imperial power in alliance with African kings and chiefs to one of nation building hand in hand with educated Africans.

To obtain recognition in the provinces is the palace revolutionary's difficulty in every age; Creech Jones and Cohen now faced schism and revolt among the satraps. Indirect rulers at the Cambridge and African governors' conferences protested that Africa was not ready for democracy. Milverton and Sir Philip Mitchell, governor of Kenya, objected that democratization at any level would undermine imperial authority because it would drive the loyal majority into the arms of the extreme nationalists. There were also rumblings among British officials in West Africa against africanization of colonial government. Creech Jones issued a ringing directive to recall them to their duty, drafted by the governor of the Gold Coast, Sir Alan Burns, and approved by "every official in the Colonial Office." British officials must now train Africans to take over their jobs and look forward to a merely advisory role. Diehards who objected to digging graves for their own careers should resign. "There was no prospect of the policy being changed," the directive continued, "except in the direction of still faster progress."[25] Once again British officials were called upon to act as proconsuls not of the empire but of self-governing states of the future. To this directive, Milverton objected from Nigeria that africanization like democratization would corrupt colonial government from top to bottom. He was thwacked back into line with Cohen's favorite campaign slogan: "Self-government is better than good colonial government." Corrupt and disloyal or not, Africans were to be pushed forward in all branches of colonial government. "It was the only chance of improving Afro-European relations on the West Coast."[26] The colonial office bided its time. No fewer than five African governors were due to retire by the end of 1947. Creech Jones and Cohen made sure that their successors were men of the new course. In fits and starts thereafter innovation spread from the palace to the provinces.

As early as 1947, evidently in the colonial office mind, the door to self-government had been unlocked for African nationalists to push open when they became able. It had been unlocked not in response to but in anticipation of nationalist pressure by a freakish concatenation of American anticolonialism, Indian nationalism, British economic need, and moral utopianism. Though by this time Dr. Azikiwe had formed his national council of Nigeria and the Cameroons, it was not yet a popular movement. Nkrumah had not returned to the Gold Coast yet; indeed, a missionary friend of his wrote to Cohen in October 1947 warning that Kwame was going out to "start some kind of nationalist movement." Ironically, Cohen was asked to see that the young man was gently treated so as not to embitter him.[27] These future leaders may have found more support in their own countries than the British credited them with, but they had yet to organize the elite and the people into mass movements.

African Independence

But more than all the debate at conferences, it was the scare of the Accra riots of 1948 that did most to swing West Africa onto the new course. On the lookout for—indeed, positively welcoming—the emergence of progressive national movements to energize development and integrate ethnic mosaics into unified states, Creech Jones and Cohen were ready to concede more to the first signs than they had intended. They took the riots as evidence that colonial control already had broken down and decided to regain it by granting dramatic constitutional advances to strengthen the hand of moderate chiefs and intelligentsia against extremists. In 1951 the colonial office introduced direct elections and a quasi-ministerial system into the Gold Coast. Four years after the Cohen report was submitted, the Gold Coast had advanced to stage three. What was more, the new constitution, which had been designed to give electoral victory to the collaborating moderates, by a psephological blunder handed it instead to Nkrumah's new party, which wanted independence at once. He had to be let out of jail and made leader of government business in the legislative assembly.[28] Inevitably this spectacular stroke of luck converted Nkrumah's following into a dynamic mass movement that was to finish the course to independence six years later.

What had been given to the Gold Coast soon could not be denied to Nigeria and Sierra Leone, and so the domino effect of vision and miscalculation spread through British West Africa. It was Cohen who planned these crucial initial transfers of power in the Gold Coast and Nigeria; his constitution mongering awoke the slumbering genius of nationalism there. He had hoped to educate the nationalists more gradually into their responsibilities, but the rising expectations that the beginnings of popular government unleashed had overtaken him. By 1951, nevertheless, Cohen was congratulating himself that West Africa had been set on course to self-government beyond recall.

Cohen's scheme for transferring power in Central Africa from 1948 to 1951 proved less fortunate. It is said that he naively believed better constitutions can improve human nature; if there is any truth in this claim, it is to be found in the bargains that his plan for federating the two Rhodesias and Nyasaland offered the settler leaders. By conceding considerable local authority to the white minority, he hoped at best to persuade them to share power with the black majority in a multiracial state; at worst, to stop the spread of apartheid from South Africa into the British dependencies. It seemed better to Cohen to make sure of half a loaf of political rights for Africans now than to wait for the settlers' repeatedly threatened unilateral declaration of independence, which would leave the Africans with none. Cohen converted Labour ministers to this plan,[29] but it was left to the succeeding Conservative government to carry out its principles in the British Central African federation of 1953. The anger of the African majority at the imposition of the new structure, however, was such that Kenneth Kaunda and Hastings Banda were able to organize nationalist parties strong enough to break the association ten years later.[30] In Central Africa as in the Gold Coast and Nigeria, Cohen's constitution mongering had made the nationalist cause popular. His vision, even when misconceived or misapplied, helped determine the nationalist shape of things to come.

A Governship and the End of Cohen's Career

In 1951 Creech Jones fell from office and Cohen was, as he felt, exiled from the colonial office, where his ambition lay, to Uganda, where a governor's boots might cool his radical heels. Though he disliked "the humbug" of the ceremonial, he practiced in the field what he had preached from the palace. Africans and Asians were invited to Government House and advanced in central government; Makerere was developed into a university to strengthen the educated cadres; local councils were democratized, which encouraged the formation of political parties and national consciousness. No governor ever tried so hard to manufacture a powerful national movement capable of uniting the dominant Baganda with the other communities in the protectorate. Eventually he deported the Kabaka of Buganda in order to remove the major obstacle to united self-rule, only to provoke a neotraditional reaction against the cause of national integration, which he had hoped to advance. Wittingly or unwittingly Cohen had succeeded in inducing national movements throughout West and Central Africa, but in Uganda, the only territory that he governed personally, he had failed.[31]

Cohen left Uganda in 1957 to represent the United Kingdom on the United Nations Trusteeship Council in New York. Returning to Whitehall in 1961 he became permanent head of a new department from which he directed the flow of British aid to independent Africa and the rest of the Third World until his death in 1968. Few African politicians had done as much as he had to build up nationalities under the scaffolding of a falling empire. A colleague, who had served Winston Churchill as private secretary during the war, wrote of Cohen's influence: "He seemed to make the history which we lived in and so affected all our work. He was a giant who towered above all of us of his generation at the Colonial Office."[32] Things were never quite the same again wherever he burst in, hands full of stuffed briefcases, his keys or the rim of his homburg clenched between his teeth.

As a result of Cohen's influence the governors appointed after 1947—the Arden-Clarkes, Macphersons, and Macdonalds—worked in an age apart not only from the earlier Cliffords and Camerons but also from their immediate wartime predecessors, the Mitchells and Milvertons. Cohen regarded himself as the pilot who steered the tropical African empire to the other side of the great divide. Before Cohen, the governor made policy; he was practically viceroy of an all-surveying monarchy. After Cohen he was more like a public servant negotiating between African demands and the tolerances of Whitehall. The direction of colonial government had changed hands. Before 1947 colonial administration had been noninterventionist and conservative: to keep order, to avoid revolt, and to preserve indigenous social organization were the overriding considerations; governors lacked the men and money to do otherwise. But after 1947 there came the time of plenty, when radical intervention became possible in the name of "social engineering" and "state building." The divide in the empire's perspectives on its own longevity and its choice of African collaborators went deeper still. Before 1947 the governor ruled in the serene assurance that colonies were forever; he was building an empire solidly on indigenous foundations. After 1947, sensing that his time was running out, he began to found self-governing states for nationalists who alone could complete the building. So, with Creech Jones and Cohen, the African empire came to the end of the beginning and the beginning of the end, where the rise toppled over into decline and fall.

Notes

1. For an analysis of their origins and education see I. F. Nicolson and C. A. Hughes, "A Provenance of Proconsuls: British Colonial Governors, 1900–1914," *Journal of Imperial and Commonwealth History* 4, no. 1 (1975):77–106.

2. This chapter is one of several sketches for a full-length biography that a generous research grant from the Ford Foundation has enabled me to undertake. I am greatly indebted to Lady Helen Cohen and Miss Ruth Cohen for access to Sir Andrew's private papers and for much other information.

   I was a friend of Cohen's, working under him as research officer in the African Studies Branch, British Colonial Office, 1947–1950, and as chairman of the Cambridge conferences on development problems, 1961–1970.

3. Milverton to Cohen, 4 October 1951; Cohen to Milverton, 10 October 1951, Cohen Papers.

4. Elgin to Lugard, 9 March 1906, Colonial Office (hereinafter cited C.O.) African 841, "Further Papers Relating to Administration of Tropical Colonies": "The Colonial Office should not attempt to administer but only supervise administration"; report of committee on appointments to colonial office and colonial services, April 1930, Parliamentary Command Paper, hereinafter cited Cmd. 3554, 43: "The details of administration are in the hands of the Colonial Governments, and subject to their being in conformity with the general policy outlined by the Colonial Office, the latter does not interfere"; Colonial Service, "Minutes on Proposed Re-Organisation," March 1900, C.O. Misc. 123, 15: "The whole tradition of this Department for at least a century has been to govern the Colonies, not as a whole, but as separate, local entities."

5. "Merging of the Colonial Office into the Colonial Service," memorandum, 15 September 1943, C.O. 850/194/20807.

6. Minute, 29 March 1938, on Young's confidential dispatch, 19 March 1938, C.O. 795/99/45105/7570.

7. Cohen caused a minor scandal by entertaining black friends in a white guest house in Louisiana. However, he returned home with a natural affinity for progressive and lively Americans, whom he much preferred to the "stuffy" British establishment. He was enthusiastic about Anglo-American cooperation in Africa from this time onward.

8. See W. R. Louis, *Imperialism at Bay: The United States and the Decolonisation of the British Empire, 1941–1945* (Oxford, 1977).

9. Oliver Stanley to Sir John Anderson, 21 September 1944, C.O. 852/588/19275; war cabinet (hereinafter cited Cab.) conclusion 152, 21 November 1944, Cab. 65/44.

10. Colonial secretary to African governors, telegrams of 18 December 1940 and 6 January 1941, C.O. 471001/39/11.

11. Note of discussion with Lord Hailey, 18 March 1941, C.O. 47100/1/41/8; Hailey, confidential report, "Native Administration and Political Development in British Tropical Africa, 1940–1942," Rhodes House Library.

12. Ivor Thomas, minute, (?) November 1946, note in Cohen Papers.

13. Committee report, 22 May 1947, notes in Cohen Papers.

14. See Partha S. Gupta, *Imperialism and the British Labour Movement, 1914–1964* (New York, 1975), chaps. 9, 10. However, there was Fabian pressure for a new course as there had been in 1929–1930; Hinden to Creech Jones, 21 October 1946, Cohen Papers.

15. Circular Dispatch to African governors, 25 February 1947, C. 60539.

16. Ibid., para. 1. See also A. Creech Jones, "The Place of African Local Administration in Colonial Policy," *Journal of African Administration* 1 (January 1949):1; Lord Listowel, "The Modern Conception of Government in British Africa," address to Royal Empire and African societies, ibid., p. 3.

17. George Barrington Cartland was the first chief of this think tank. He was followed by Rowland Hudson and then Claud Wallis.

18. See R. Robinson, "The Journal and the Transfer of Power," *Journal of Administration Overseas* 13 (January 1974):1.

19. Circular Dispatch, 25 February 1947, paras. 5–6, C. 60539; "African Local Government, Report of Cambridge Summer School" (1947), C.O. African 1173; conference of African governors, 1947, paper "Local Government in Africa," A.G.C. 12, enclosed in colonial secretary's circular dispatch, 13 January 1948.

20. Committee report, 22 May 1947, notes in Cohen Papers.

21. Ibid.

22. Ibid.

23. Ibid.

24. Minutes by F. Pedler and G. B. Cartland, n.d., Cohen Papers.

25. Burns to Lloyd, 11 February 1947, minutes, Cohen Papers.

26. Note of meeting of West African governors, 10 March 1947, Cohen Papers.

27. Rev. H. M. Grace to Cohen, 22 October 1947, Cohen Papers.

28. Cohen drafted and afterward claimed as personal declarations of faith the government white papers that granted the constitutional advances recommended for the Gold Coast first by the Watson and then by the Coussey commissions, Colonial No. 232 (1948) and 250 (1949). Cohen to A. Gaitskell, 31 August 1955, Cohen Papers: "The principle on which I stand is this. Our policy is African advancement; our only justification for being in Africa is to guide the Africans towards self-government."

29. Cohen to P. C. Gordon-Walker (secretary of state, Commonwealth affairs), 11 January 1952, Cohen Papers.

30. See R. I. Rotberg, *The Rise of Nationalism in Central Africa, 1873–1964* (London, 1966); D. C. Mulford, *Zambia: The Politics of Independence, 1957–1964* (London, 1967); Philip Mason, *The Year of Decision: Rhodesia and Nyasaland in 1960* (London, 1960); J. Barber, *Rhodesia: The Road to Rebellion* (London, 1967).

31. For an account of his governorship in Uganda see C. Gertzel, "Kingdoms, Districts, and the Unitary State: Uganda, 1945–1962," in D. A. Low and A. Smith, eds., *History of East Africa* (Oxford, 1967)3:65–108; D. A. Low, *Buganda in Modern History* (London, 1971).

32. Sir J. Martin to Lady Cohen, June 1968, Cohen Papers.

Belgium

Belgian Administration in the Congo: An Overview

L.H. Gann

WHEN Leopold II began to build his African empire, the Belgian stake in Africa was negligible. Africa played little part in the calculations of Belgian businessmen. There was no Belgian entrepôt trade on the shores of the Congo. There was no Belgian merchant marine looking for African cargoes. Belgian missionaries at first had but little interest in the so-called dark continent. The foundation of the Congo Free State, therefore, owed little to Belgium's bourgeoisie and even less to public opinion. The Congo Free State was the creation of the king, a royal speculator determined to establish his own private fief in Central Africa. His main support came from the army, from a few intellectuals interested in the colonial cause, and from a small group of financiers with personal links to the court and a penchant for risky speculations that was alien to the rank and file of their colleagues on the stock exchange. The king also skillfully benefited from humanitarian propaganda that he half believed himself, propaganda of the kind that allowed him to obtain considerable support in foreign countries.

King Leopold II, in certain respects, resembled Cecil John Rhodes. But Leopold's personal powers in the Congo were immensely greater than Rhodes's in the Rhodesias. The British Parliament, the British colonial office, and British public opinion all served to restrain Rhodes in some measure. The Belgian monarch was under no such disabilities. He looked upon the Congo as a personal estate to be exploited with a minimum of capital. This object was achieved by gaining a monopoly in the extraction of wild rubber and ivory through a crude form of *Raubwirtschaft* designed to benefit the king as well as a small clique of privileged concessionaires.

367

Leopold became absolute sovereign of the Congo Free State; his rule was autocratic in theory as well as in practice. The liberal and Catholic bourgeois were little inclined to send their sons to serve in a colony beset by scandals, plagued by diseases, supposedly overrun by foreigners, and inhabited, according to the metropolitan stereotypes, by bloodthirsty cannibals. When Leopold first began to look for administrators, he thus had to draw on army officers for volunteers, both Belgian and foreign. The spirit of the pioneer administration was therefore military and royalist.

In formal terms, administration was, and remained, highly centralized. The metropolitan organization in Brussels was headed by several secretaries-general, each in charge of a department, each in practice an agent of the king. The link between this central structure and the Free State's administrative headquarters in Boma was the governor-general (known originally as the administrator-general). The governor-general was assisted by an advisory committee consisting of senior civil servants whom the governor-general might or might not consult before acting on a matter of general policy. Under the governor-general there was an elaborate district administration. This form of governance was expensive. The administration employed many more Europeans than the neighboring British and German territories, and as the king tried to turn conquest into cash the European personnel increased in numbers. By 1906, the Congo Free State consisted of fourteen provinces, each headed by a commissioner general and subdivided into districts that were split further into sectors.

This autocratic system depended on a large colonial army, the Force publique, more numerous in relation to the population than the armed forces in the neighboring British and German colonies. The Belgian system was, however, somewhat softened by the operation of an independent judicature and by the work of the so-called state inspectors, an elite group of senior civil servants with far-reaching power. The Free State magistry—like the state inspectors—turned out to be a reservoir of liberal theory and reformist practice. Royal despotism was limited in its operation by broad powers exercised by local dignitaries, such as the vice-governor-general in charge of outlying provinces like Katanga, whose day-to-day administration could not easily be controlled from the center.

Free State governance rested on a system of concessionary regimes that linked state capitalism with private monopolies in a manner that had no exact parallel in any other European colonial empire; this system made the Congo Free State a prototype of the corporate state. The ruthless methods by which wild rubber and ivory were extracted from the population made the words "Congo Free State" a byword of brutal rapacity. But *Raubwirtschaft* of the concessionary kind did not, in the end, prove profitable. Wild rubber could not compete against cultivated rubber. Elephant herds were soon decimated, so that the importance of ivory lessened. The conquest and governance of the Congo proved far more expensive than the king had anticipated. The exploitative methods employed by the concession companies aroused widespread African resistance. In any case, the arbitrary nature of the "Red Rubber" regime would have proved incompatible with the needs of a modern mining economy, which the Free State was eager to promote, both for fiscal reasons and for profit.

In order to mine the newly discovered copper of the Katanga, the Belgians in 1906 set up the Union Minière du Haut-Katanga, a powerful trust linked to the

Société Générale, Belgium's most important financial institution. The Union Minière began to produce copper on a commercial scale. Elisabethville, the capital of Katanga, turned into a new center of power. Even before this economic revolution had been accomplished, the Belgian king found himself under powerful attack from a variety of groups, both foreign and domestic, that called for an end to the Free State regime on the ground that the king had violated a sacred trust. The Congo Free State initiated a number of reforms, but these—in the opinion of its critics—did not go far enough. And in 1908, Belgium assumed direct control over the Congo.

The king ceased to be absolute sovereign of the Congo. Instead, the framers of the Charte coloniale, the colony's fundamental law, created a system that was designed to exercise centralized rule from Brussels so as to stamp out abuses and limit the powers of the monarchy. At the same time, the new regime took steps to "belgianize" the administration in two senses. Foreigners gradually disappeared from the army and the administration, eliminating the Congo's "international flavor." The Belgians consolidated their power against British influence in Katanga; Anglo-Saxon influence weakened within the Union Minière, and workers of Belgian origin came to form the majority in the white labor force employed by the companies.

Under the new dispensation, the colonial minister formed the linchpin of government. He was the connecting link between the metropolitan and the colonial administrations. The colonial minister represented his fief in both branches of the legislature. He drew up the budgets of both the Congo and the colonial ministry in Brussels; he drafted the legislation to be presented to the Belgian Parliament. If he received the king's assent, he could provide for taxes and tariffs; he presided over the *conseil colonial*[1] (colonial council), an advisory body set up under the Charte coloniale. He more or less inherited the powers once possessed by the secretary of state of the former Free State. He issued all general instructions to the governor-general and he countersigned all executive decisions made in the king's name.

The crown continued to exercise considerable powers, at least in the formal sense. The monarch could issue executive orders and could legislate on a great variety of subjects in the form of decrees—provided the latter did not countermand the laws enacted by Parliament. The decrees had to be submitted to the colonial council, eight of whose members were appointed by the king, three by the Senate, and three by the Chamber. But under the new dispensation, Parliament was supreme. Parliamentarians had the right of interpellation, by which a minister could be called upon to defend a policy he had endorsed. Unlike its counterpart in Great Britain and France, the Belgian Parliament was also able to vote the annual colonial budget. This provision enabled Belgian parliamentarians to debate general questions concerning the Congo; hence Congolese affairs continued to be intertwined with intra-Belgian parliamentary disputes among Catholics, Liberals, and Socialists. Thus, an extra check was placed upon the administration in the Congo, but at the price of burdensome delays with regard to the colony's ability to frame its financial policy.

This elaborate system of checks and balances had less importance in practice than in theory. The Belgian Parliament rarely made use of its powers; within the space of a half-century the legislature passed only about a dozen laws, apart from technical matters concerned with loans, budgets, and such matters. Belgian sovereigns did not interfere in the work of administration. The colonial council painstakingly scrutinized the draft decrees placed before it in accordance with the Charte coloniale but did not provide the administration with new ideas.

Power centered principally on the local administration. The Germans unwittingly assisted this process of colonial devolution when, in 1914 and again in 1940, they invaded Belgium itself; the men on the spot in the Congo were left largely to their own devices. They ran the country in an empirical fashion—concerned, above all, that the economy should be solvent, that the budget should balance, and that no scandal should besmirch the colony's good name. The state machinery increasingly came to be interlocked with the great mining companies in a manner unknown to every other European colony in Africa. State and mining corporations formed two legs of the Congolese tripod of power; the Catholic church was the third. The power of the state was much more absolute than it was, say, in the British African colonies. There was no local legislature with lawmaking powers comparable to those of the British colonial legislative councils—only advisory bodies with limited functions. The settlers had no parliamentary representation within the Congo, much less the Africans. Colonial absolutism was, however, softened by a real sense of trusteeship, expressed in Governor Pierre Ryckmans's famous slogan *dominer pour servir*. The new spirit was fostered by colonial training and by an extensive body of colonial research. The new approach was far removed from the crude notions of exploitation widely accepted in the pioneering days and found almost universal intellectual acceptance.

The new attitude was symbolized by men like Charles Lemaire. Lemaire, a pioneer official, had seen the oldtime abuses firsthand. He returned to Belgium, convinced that Belgium had been guilty of many grave abuses, that Africans were capable of achieving great things, and that Belgian rule was justified only if the rulers helped the ruled. In 1920, Lemaire became the first director of the newly established Ecole coloniale supérieure, set up in Antwerp for the purpose of training Belgian colonial administrators. The Ecole coloniale was run as a boarding school, on British public school lines. Students were required to acquire manual as well as academic skills; their training emphasized a sense of personal responsibility, duty, and conscience. In economic terms, the Belgians increasingly came to value Africans as skilled workers and as customers of manufactured goods; the Belgians realized—in other words—that they could not develop a modern economy with unwilling conscripts. "Development" increasingly became a secular religion.

As concerns the formal structure of power, the governor-general formed the apex of the official hierarchy. He headed the civil service; he served as the ceremonial head of government; he played a major part in shaping the social tone of the bureaucracy. He was extremely well paid; his remuneration was greater than that of a high-ranking judge or a lieutenant general in the army in Belgium. A provincial governor stood at about the same level as the head of a department in Belgium or a university professor. Most governors-general, moreover, were drawn from the ranks of the administration itself. After 1912, no more soldiers were appointed; the military flavor had gradually disappeared from the administration by the 1930s. A few governors-general, such as Lippens, a leading industrialist, came from the business community, and a few were politicians.

Within the administration as a whole, the ambitious subalterns, who had risen from humble circumstances by hard work, initiative, and the ability to pass examinations, were replaced in time by diploma-bearing specialists. The colonial service continued to provide a ladder for advancement to those young men who managed to obtain scholarships to the Ecole coloniale but its ethos and social composition began to change. Service in the Congo gradually became a respectable occupation, one that appealed to sons of the provincial bourgeoisie. The Ardennes region—francophone, poverty-stricken, but relatively well supplied with schools—furnished many applicants for the colonial service; so did rural Flanders, where jobs for educated men were equally hard to find. Catholics came to look upon a colonial career as a form of secular mission work, a means of serving God by uplifting the heathens and protecting them against the real or supposed exactions of capitalists. Unbelievers, common in the Free State period, lost pride of place.

The average governor-general was a Catholic. He was well educated. He was also likely to be city-bred. Of the ten governors-general who were in office between 1887 and 1960, five came from larger cities—Brussels, Ghent, Antwerp, and Liège; three were born in medium-sized towns like Ostend. The majority, at least six, retired to Brussels and died there. Seven of the ten were lawyers by training; only three had begun their careers as professional soldiers. Of all the Congo viceroys, only Stanley was of working class origin. Three were sons of professional soldiers; the remainder were sons of merchants, lawyers, or civil servants. Their family background ranged from lower middle-class (Félix Fuchs's father was a park superintendent) to upper middle-class (Maurice-August Lippens, governor-general from 1921 to 1923, was the son of a burgomaster and senator of Ghent). On retirement, several governors-general obtained high positions in industry and finance. Lippens, for instance, became president of various great concerns. But unlike the British governors, Belgian governors-general were not normally raised to the nobility. The exception was the administrator elevated to a barony by reason of his military achievements: Lippens became a *comte*—but more because of his service as cabinet minister than because of his Congolese governor-generalship.

Without exception, the senior officials in the Congo spoke French at home. Their tenures of office ranged from two to as many as twelve years, or an average of about five. Their religious affiliation was overwhelmingly Catholic. Wahis was a staunch adherent of the church; so were most of his successors, as well as most of the senior officials in the colonial ministry and in the government-general. Of the ten governors-general who served between 1908 and 1960, seven were Catholic; the exceptions were Lippens, an anticlerical Liberal who served under the Franck ministry (1918–1924), Eugène Jungers, a man devoid of any religious affiliation, and Henri Cornelis, a Socialist and the last of the governors-general. In the lower echelons of the service anticlericals continued to be well represented but their influence did not become predominant until the final stage of the Belgian regime.

To recapitulate, the spirit of Belgian administration in the Congo was pedantic, bureaucratic, and rigidly empirical. In material terms, the Belgians achieved astonishing progress. The Congo, once a poverty-stricken, strife-torn backwater, turned into a major producer of tropical crops and of minerals (especially copper, uranium, and industrial diamonds). The Belgians created an infrastructure of medical, educational, and other social services. Hence, technicians and specialists played an increasingly important part in the operation of government. The Belgians in the Congo did far more than the British in Northern Rhodesia in teaching industrial skills to the Africans. They also pioneered the employment of a "stabilized labor force" for the mines—workers lived with their families. Ideally, the Belgians would have liked to have created a contented and loyal petty bourgeoisie composed of African artisans, farmers, and employees, whose rise would be unimpeded by white settler influence.

But even in its own terms, Belgian colonialism suffered from weaknesses additional to those that beset colonial governance in the British and French colonies. Colonial activity appealed only to a small group of missionaries, civil servants, intellectuals, and investors. The metropole as a whole remained indifferent to the so-called colonial task. Even within the professional ranks of the colonial service, a high proportion of officials thought of their work as a job rather than as a mission. André van Iseghem was a well-qualified man, a doctor of laws who had reached high office in the Congo; his observations, which may be trusted, were surprising, dating as they did from just after the end of World War I, long before anticolonialism of the academic kind had come into fashion. About fifty percent of the ex-colonials, according to van Iseghem, were indifferent to the colonial ideal. On returning to Belgium they wanted to forget their careers in the colonies, regarding it as no more than an interlude in their lives. Forty percent of them returned as convinced opponents of the colonial system. Their Congolese reminiscences, which they recounted in offices, clubs, and bars, destroyed the effects of colonial propaganda. Of the 3,400 ex-colonials in Belgium, mostly former officials, only about ten percent believed in the colonial cause. According to van Iseghem, colonial civil servants had all manner of grievances regarding their living conditions and pay. Above all, they suffered from a feeling of frustration. They resented their lack of prestige; they objected to the authoritarian structure of governance and the way they were treated. Having returned to Belgium they became men without a country (*dépaysés*).[1]

After World War II, Belgium's colonial position worsened even though the colony's economic development proceeded apace. The Belgians at first tried to hold on to the Congo and voted considerable funds for development programs. But dissension within the ranks of the rulers became increasingly acute as the political, social, and religious struggles within the metropole extended into the Congo. By 1958, the alliance between church and state had broken down. Even the union between state and trusts was shaken by an unpopular government decision to call in American capital to develop the hydroelectric resources of the lower Congo and by similar measures. The Belgians had failed to integrate educated Africans (*évolués*) within the colonial system. The Belgians equally failed to maintain adequate discipline within the Force publique, which could not, as a body, be shielded from wider discontent within the country. Faced with rising demands from educated African nationalists, faced also with the pressures set up by decolonization in the British and even more so in the French African territories, Belgian authority weakened further. The language of African demands became increasingly uncompromising. By 1959, the Belgian administration faced riots in the cities and a gradual breakdown of government. The Belgians could have restored their hold on the Congo only by the massive deployment of metropolitan troops (an expedient forbidden under Belgian law), by repression of all political activity, and by removing Congolese affairs from the influence of the Belgian Parliament.

But Belgium had itself undergone profound political and social changes. The bulk of the Belgian bourgeoisie and the petty bourgeoisie had become unwilling to have their sons serve in either a military or a civilian capacity in the Congo at a time when metropolitan careers were much more attractive. The political, constitutional, and social conditions for a successful colonial Belgian counterrevolution did not exist, and Belgian governance collapsed in bloodshed.

Note

1. L. H. Gann and Peter Duignan, *The Rulers of Belgian Africa, 1884–1914* (Princeton: Princeton University Press 1978).

Martin Rutten
(1876–1944)

Bruce Fetter

MARTIN Rutten, who served as governor-general of the Belgian Congo from 1923 to 1927, brought to that office many of the finest qualities of the Belgian provincial bourgeoisie. English-speaking readers, accustomed to considering the word "bourgeois" a term of opprobrium, may not understand that to most Belgians the word has lost none of its favorable connotations. To them "bourgeois" means a person living in a town or city, who is wealthy, highly cultivated, and follows a carefully structured code of conduct.

Background and Education

A man of this background was something of a rarity in the Belgian colonial administration. Most of the early governors-general and almost all of their subordinates were military men of relatively humble origins who had worked up through the ranks. This situation began to change after the first world war with the creation of the Ecole coloniale at Antwerp and the appointment in 1918 of the aristocratic Maurice Lippens as governor-general, but military men dominated the administration until the 1930s.

Rutten was molded for his unconventional career by his family and by his father, René. The elder Rutten was born in the Flemish province of Limburg, a poverty-stricken area that sent many emigrants to seek work in other parts of Belgium; he had moved at the time of his marriage to a Walloon girl to the province of Liège, where he settled in the village of Clermont-sur-Berwinne on the outskirts of the industrial city of Verviers. But he did not remain long with his young family. As a devout Catholic, he heeded the appeals of Pius IX and joined the papal army as a Zouave in the wars against the Italian nationalists. After several campaigns in defense of the faith he returned to Clermont, where he was soon elected burgomaster and a member of the provincial assembly, serving until his death in 1918.

Other members of the Rutten family followed an even more rigorously Catholic vocation. Martin's uncle served as bishop of Liège, and an elder brother became superior general of the Scheut order after some time as a missionary in Mongolia, China, and the Congo. The young Martin thus was brought up in a profoundly Catholic environment and in the company of family members who were successful and respectable.

The Ruttens, however, carefully separated their public careers from their private lives, which they guarded beyond the limits of ordinary discretion. Martin left a scanty public record of his early years. He was born in 1876 and was a good student, graduating with honors in law from the University of Liège in 1897. A distant man throughout his life, he wrote little about his personal relations; he did not marry until he had reached the summit of his career, at age forty-seven.[1]

African Career

After graduation, Rutten briefly went into private law practice with a well-known firm in Liège but found the work unattractive and turned to the magistracy. This was a popular outlet for young Belgian lawyers who normally took jobs with the ministry of justice, which controlled the appointments of both prosecutors and judges. Rutten, however, chose to sign on as a magistrate for the Congo Free State.

In 1901, when he departed for his first tour of duty, few reputable Belgians of any description—let alone a member of the respectable bourgeoisie—would even consider working in King Leopold's African empire. The Congo service had not yet acquired a reputation for cruelty and dishonesty, but it was considered a graveyard. Most Free State employees were not Belgians but foreigners attracted to the colonial service by the prospects of high salaries and rapid advancement. Such attractions, however, had little effect on conservative Belgian lawyers. Only a bare majority of the thirty-two members of the Free State magistracy in 1905 were Belgian citizens.

Why Rutten chose to join is difficult to determine because of the future governor-general's habitual discretion, but his background and later behavior provide some clues. Like his father, the younger Rutten had a strong sense of duty. Service in the Congo satisfied both a religious and a patriotic motivation; he would be bringing European law to the heathens, and he would be helping to build a Belgian colonial patrimony, for Leopold's domains had been willed to the Belgian people. Thus Rutten, like his father before him, enrolled as a young man in pursuit of his highest ideals.[2]

In the Congo, Martin Rutten served in two separate branches of the Belgian colonial government. From 1901 until 1918 he was a magistrate; from 1918 until the end of his African career in 1927 he was an administrator. Like his choice of the colonial service, this pattern was rare. Few magistrates left the judiciary for another branch of government, and few lawyers joined the territorial service—although possession of a law degree was one of the possible qualifications for entry. During Rutten's early years in Africa most territorial officials had come from the army; later the majority were graduates of the Ecole coloniale. Thus, his entire career was unusual: a member of the provincial bourgeoisie in the colonial magistracy, and a lawyer in the territorial service.

Rutten passed most of his African career in three very different locales: in rural, southeastern Katanga (Shaba); in the new town of Elisabethville, which he helped found in 1911; and in the hot, humid colonial capital of Boma on the estuary of the Congo river. Of the three he preferred Elisabethville not only because of its climate but also because he felt that the city—as the center of the new copper industry as well as of the provincial administration—best exemplified the achievements of Belgian colonization. Even though he left the copper city more or less definitively in 1923 after under a decade of residence there, he was known for the rest of his life as a Katangan and considered Elisabethville his second home.

Early Responsibilities.   The new post of Lukafu in rural Katanga, to which Rutten was assigned in 1901, was absolutely vital to the Belgian effort to maintain control against the British. Located on the Luvira river at the foot of the Kundelungu mountains, Lukafu had the British on two sides. One hundred miles to the east was the Luapula river, which served as the boundary between British and Belgian territory; 100 miles to the west and south lay the copperbelt, then honeycombed with British prospectors under the direction of a well-placed Briton, George Grey, whose brother would become foreign secretary in 1905.

The question of which European power should own the Katanga copperbelt was almost as old as the Congo Free State itself. The Brussels agreement of 1890 had enunciated the principle that European claims to lands in the interior of Africa could be validated only by physical occupation of the disputed territory. Both the British, through Cecil Rhodes's British South Africa Company, and the Belgians, under the banner of Leopold's Congo Free State, sought to gain possession of Katanga. Rhodes's highly capitalized company at first had the advantage over the Belgian monarch, who was on the verge of personal and public bankruptcy, but in 1891 the king managed to throw together a series of six expeditions to Katanga. Free State claims to the territory were temporarily established.

Between 1892 and 1900, however, the Belgian hold on Katanga was extremely precarious. The legal right to govern the region had devolved to a hastily organized chartered company, the Compagnie du Katanga, whose founders had agreed to govern the area in exchange for title to one-third of the land. Unfortunately for the king—and themselves—the company's agents, after successfully scaring off the British, reported that the region had no immediate value; it was too far from practical means of communication with the coast for the profitable export of any local products. The company thus refused to maintain more than a symbolic force in Katanga, and had the British entered the area they would have been able to prove that the Belgians were not effectively occupying it.

When the Scottish engineer Robert Williams obtained a royal charter for a new company to explore the resources on the British side of the Katanga frontier, the Belgians feared that the superficiality of their occupation would be made public and that they would lose the territory. To avert this possibility, Leopold forced a reorganization of the Compagnie du Katanga late in 1900, depriving it of governmental authority over the area. He then delegated that authority to a new parastatal organization, the Comité spécial du Katanga (CSK), backed by his own replenished coffers. This added capital enabled the CSK to send out the troops necessary to forestall the new British threat to the Belgian title although the danger was by no means completely eliminated. In the process of the negotiations that resulted in the CSK, Leopold had been forced to allow British prospectors into Katanga. They would serve as witnesses to the extent of Belgian occupation of the territory; if the Belgians did not control the region adequately, the prospectors could report this fact to the British government and undermine the Belgian claim.

The assumed British threat made it imperative to establish a permanent administration. Although Leopold had confidence in the ability of the CSK to guard Katanga's borders and to subdue its African population, he did not allow the new company to create its own legal system. Katanga was still part of the Congo Free State and subject to that entity's laws. Thus, he insisted that the Free State judiciary be extended to Katanga even though the territory was legally administered by the CSK. Free State magistrates, among them young Rutten, therefore worked alongside CSK officers to protect Belgian rights.[3]

Rutten's job in Lukafu had a modest title; as a substitute district attorney he was on the lowest rung of the magisterial ladder. But the post gave him the enormous responsibility of demonstrating to the British that Free State law was supreme in Katanga. He undertook his work with determination and within a few months of his arrival was actively protesting the British failure to keep their troops on their own side of the Luapula. In this he had the full support of the CSK administration. British prospectors were harder to handle than colonial administrators, and dealing with them became more difficult as time went on. Many of them were toughened veterans of the Boer war and had little regard for the claim of other Europeans in Africa. Unable to understand French, they frequently ignored the young magistrate's orders. To complicate matters further, between 1905 and 1908—during the infamous rubber scandals—their boss, Robert Williams, became one of the most active defenders of the Congo Free State, and Belgian officials were loathe to offend the agents of a friendly Briton. Rutten thus had to put up with considerable insubordination from Williams's prospectors, who were now employed by the newly formed Anglo-Belgian copper company, the Union Minière du Haut-Katanga (UMHK).

The few hundred resident Britons gave Rutten more trouble than did the tens of thousands of local Africans. In general, he dealt with the Africans only after their defeat by CSK military forces. Belgian demands on Africans in his part of Katanga during the early 1900s were relatively light. Unlike the situation in other parts of the Congo, there was almost no collection of rubber, and a hut tax in money was not collected there until 1914. Most local Africans thus were able to satisfy the Belgians with minimal tributes of grain and meat; Zambians from the Luapula valley did the undesirable heavy work of porterage as wage labor in order to pay the British hut taxes.

Freed from enforcing these less pleasant aspects of colonial rule, Rutten could approach the Africans more dispassionately than most of his colleagues. He was by no means an admirer of African culture, but he tried to learn as much as possible about African law in order to facilitate the application of Belgian laws. Africans spoke to him relatively freely, and he supplemented his personal knowledge with information supplied by local Catholic missionaries, with whom he had a deep affinity. Rutten learned less from the English-speaking Protestants, keeping them at a respectable distance.

Within a few years Rutten acquired a considerable reputation as defender of his faith and nation and as one who was knowledgeable about African customs. He was transferred in 1907 to the colonial capital of Boma, where he further added to his prestige through capable handling of legal matters as acting prosecuting attorney and attorney general. Boma was not to his liking, however, and in 1911 he was glad to accept the post of attorney general at the new appeals court in Elisabethville.

Elisabethville.   The Katanga that he found in 1911 was quite different from the region he had left four years earlier. During Rutten's tour in Boma, the Belgian copperbelt had grown enormously in population as a result of the completion of the railway linking Katanga to South Africa. Most of the new inhabitants lived in the mushroom town of Elisabethville, located where the rail line crossed the first exploitable copper deposits. Every train brought dozens of new settlers from the south, and within a single year more than 1,000 Europeans—most of them English-speakers—had come to the new European settlement. These settlers bid against each other for available African labor, thus precipitating a large-scale migration of Africans to the new town in search of relatively well-paying jobs. By the end of 1911 Elisabethville had a total population of more than 7,000.

Such rapid growth would have created problems for any administration, but the Belgians in Elisabethville were particularly taxed. It was three years since Belgium had formally annexed the Congo, thereby averting appropriation of the colony by some other European power, but the colonial administration still lacked the means to govern the territory effectively. Many areas remained outside of any European control, and the colonial government, recognizing its inability to conquer the entire country, was obliged to deploy its forces with great selectivity. Fortunately for the Belgians in Elisabethville, Katanga was high on the list of colonial priorities because of the perceived dangers of a British takeover, and in 1910 the colonial ministry had ordered 1,000 troops to the new city. Their presence made life somewhat easier for the administrators, but there still was an English-speaking sector of the population that was by no means sympathetic to Belgian laws and customs. Belgian officials who had already served in rural Katanga and dealt with the British there, were the best prepared to cope with this group, and Rutten had no trouble rising to the occasion. Any Englishman under his jurisdiction who was disrespectful of Belgian authority soon found himself afoul of the law and shortly thereafter on a southbound train.[4]

The new attorney general became a substantial member of the Belgian community. Off the job he could be found at the Belgians' social club, the Cercle Albert-Elisabeth, of which he was a charter member, or—on Sundays and holy days—at mass. Long deprived of church ceremonies during his stay in the bush, he was soon the leading Catholic layman in Elisabethville. As a result of his influence with the church, in 1913 Colonial minister Jules Renkin called upon him to patch up relations between the Scheut fathers and government officials. Rutten concluded that the missionaries, who had long been accustomed to ruling their domains without reference to the territorial administration, would have to submit to colonial authorities; but he wrote his opinion with so much tact that the missionaries accepted it without dispute.

Rutten's ability as a counselor also brought him into a jurisdictional dispute between the vice–governor-general of Katanga, Emile Wangermée, and the Belgian colonial ministry. Wangermée had been in charge of the CSK's African operations before the Belgian annexation of Katanga and had become that region's first chief executive under direct Belgian rule. He was thus the undisputed head of Belgian operations in southeastern Congo. Because of the supposed danger of a British invasion in 1910, the ministry had granted him wider powers than those of any other Belgian official except the governor-general in Boma. But the pressure was removed with British official recognition of the annexation of the Belgian Congo in 1913, however, and Katanga's special status was being reconsidered. In July 1914 Colonial minister Renkin decreed that the vice–governor-general should henceforth communicate with Brussels through the governor-general in Boma rather than act as an independent agent.

This subordination of Elisabethville to Boma infuriated Wangermée, who consulted Rutten before taking further action. Rutten advised him to live with the new administrative arrangement, but Wangermée tendered his resignation. Rutten's judgment was vindicated by the events that followed: the outbreak of the first world war made it impossible for the administration in Boma to exercise effective control over the provincial government in Elisabethville, and had Wangermée remained he would have enjoyed as much independence as before. But he had left the colonial administration in a huff and he never regained a position of power.[5]

From Rutten's perspective, however, Wangermée's departure left the attorney general the de facto head of the Belgian community in Elisabethville. During the war the vice–governor-generalship was filled on a short-term, acting basis by a series of men who knew Katanga far less well than he: Charles (later Baron) Tombeur, Adolphe de Meulemeester, and Baron de Rennette de Villers Perwin. All three relied heavily upon Rutten for advice. It was he, rather than they, who masterminded the most important policy implemented in Elisabethville during the war—the expulsion of the English-speakers.

In the early days of World War I nothing seemed less likely than a diminution of British influence in Katanga. The British government had declared war on Germany to protect Belgian neutrality. When the metropole was invaded many Belgians with colonial interests fled to London; there the colonial ministry established temporary offices, and the city became the seat of the Union Minière, by then the Congo's biggest industry. Belgium's rule of the Congo literally depended on British goodwill.

Not surprisingly, there were strains in the relationship between the Allies, and major troubles emanated from the conduct of the war in Africa. There were disputes over shortages of goods since colonial governments in Southern Africa strictly limited the exportation of food and clothing to Katanga in order to preserve adequate supplies for British expeditionary forces fighting the Germans in East Africa. It was the conduct of this campaign that was to be the greatest source of friction. In 1914 and 1915 Belgian military officers wanted to invade German

East Africa, but they were held back by British officials who felt that the Belgian plans were premature and ill-devised. In 1916 the Allies finally invaded the territory, while Belgian troops under Charles Tombeur, onetime acting vice–governor-general of Katanga, succeeded in capturing the German East African center, Tabora. To the chagrin of the colonial Belgians, however, the Belgian government was obliged to turn over most of their conquests to the British forces.

These differences of opinion were exacerbated by Anglo-Belgian rivalry, which had existed in Elisabethville since the city's creation. English-speaking shopkeepers had always competed with the agents of Belgian trading companies; Protestant missionaries had vied with Catholic priests for the souls of African workers; most important, English-speakers and French-speakers within the management of the Union Minière had quarreled almost continuously. Before the war the Belgians had nearly succeeded in forcing Robert Williams and his associates from the company's board of directors and in replacing Britons with Belgians on the company's Katanga staff. When war broke out these related processes had come to a halt; company headquarters was moved to London, and the proportion of Belgians on the UMHK African staff fell from fifty-three percent in 1914 to twenty-two percent in 1917. Those who remained in the company's employ in Elisabethville feared that they, too, would soon be forced out of their jobs. That these fears were not realized was in large part the work of Martin Rutten.

In the dispute for dominance of the Union Minière, Rutten changed the course of Katanga's history. His first target was not a Briton but an American, Preston K. Horner, director of the UMHK African operations. Rutten knew that Horner was not an agent of British imperialism but simply a man who was insensitive to Belgian feelings. He spoke little French and hired South Africans because there were no Belgians available on the local job market. Rutten felt, however, that by attacking Horner he could strengthen the Belgian hold on the copperbelt. At the very least, with Horner out, Rutten could occasion the appointment of a Belgian director in Elisabethville and ultimately persuade the Belgian government to send its nationals to the copper mines to prevent the industry's falling into British hands.

His major weapon in the campaign against Horner was his position as attorney general. In that capacity he was in charge of the small judicial police force that operated the inspectorate of health and safety. According to law, Rutten's inspectors were responsible for overseeing the UMHK mines—whose unsanitary conditions had long been a cause of complaint, particularly by British officials in Northern Rhodesia (from where most of the labor force came). In 1916 the British finally threatened to forbid recruitment from their territory, and Rutten personally took over the inspectorate. Early in 1917 he visited the Kambove mining camp, then in the throes of an epidemic. Conditions were so bad that Rutten threatened to withdraw the UMHK license to dig for copper in all of Katanga. Although his action was justified on the ground of public hygiene, he also had a political goal in mind: he wanted to get rid of Horner and his English-speaking cronies.

Rutten's action caused consternation among directors of the Union Minière and among permanent officials of the Belgian colonial ministry. The company promptly sent out an investigating team under Edgar Sengier, a patriotic Belgian who had already been party to an earlier attempt to force the British out of the Union Minière. On arrival in Elisabethville in January 1918, he immediately fired

Horner and promoted Belgians to responsible positions in the company's African operations, thus fulfilling Rutten's desire to remove the English-speakers from the direction of local UMHK offices.

The colonial ministry also implemented Rutten's objectives, but with mixed feelings. It authorized the recruitment of additional Belgians in London for the Union Minière staff, enabling the company to arrest the drift toward anglicization. Officials at the ministry sympathized with Rutten's goals although they were afraid to praise him openly; the Belgian government was too dependent upon Great Britain to reward his anti-British behavior so they hit upon the solution of a timely transfer. Shortly after Horner's dismissal, Rutten was abruptly moved from the judiciary to the territorial service and sent 1,200 miles across the continent to the Congo's capital at Boma. Although little was said at the moment to avoid further offense to the British, Rutten was not punished—he became vice–governor-general of the entire colony.[6]

Congo Administrator.   For the four years beginning in 1918, Rutten served an apprenticeship in the territorial administration. At first he was administrative assistant to Governor-general Eugène Henry, a job that he learned so well that he served as Henry's replacement during the governor-general's absences from Boma. Upon Henry's retirement Rutten was named vice–governor-general of Katanga, a clear promotion. His tenure as chief executive in Elisabethville in 1922–1923 was short. He returned to the city to find Belgians in control of the Union Minière and the country in full prosperity. He did not have time, however, to place the seal of his personality on the local administration. Newly appointed Governor-general Maurice Lippens resigned unexpectedly and Rutten returned to Boma as his successor in January 1923.

Numerous problems had arisen during Lippens's brief term of office, the most serious concerning a communications system, the missions, and the African labor supply. During Rutten's four years in office he accomplished a good deal toward solving all three. His experience during ten years of service in Katanga convinced the new governor-general of the need to connect that province with the rest of the Congo. Other parts of the colony were linked together by the Congo river and its tributaries, but even though the river rose in Katanga its waters there were not navigable. This geographical disadvantage was at the heart of Belgian concern for the military security of the province since the existing communications network would not permit rapid troop transfer between Katanga and the rest of the Congo.

In spite of improvements made during the first decade after Belgian annexation of the Congo Free State, communications were inadequate. By 1918 the Katanga railway had reached Bukama on the Lualaba (upper Congo) river, but from there the voyage to the lower Congo was arduous. To reach the coast by the existing rail and water network required five transshipments and 1,000 miles of superfluous travel owing to the shape of the river. Rutten gave highest priority to this problem during his governor-generalship. When he was appointed in 1923 he insisted that colonial officials use the existing rail and water route to the Atlantic coast for their trips to Europe rather than travel by rail to South Africa. Two years later he demonstrated the increased efficiency of Belgian communications by traveling from Boma to Elisabethville in six weeks. More important in the long run, however, was the construction of the Bas-Congo–Katanga (BCK) railway, which ran from the terminus of the Katanga railway on the upper Congo to the port of Ilebo on the Kasai river. Rutten spared nothing to see that its construction crews received needed supplies and labor, then in extremely short supply. The railway was completed a few months after he left office in 1928, and he considered it his most important achievement.[7]

More delicate than the task of improving communications was that of making peace with the Catholic missions. As Rutten had found a decade earlier, the problem lay in a disagreement between the missionaries and the territorial service over the Catholic fathers' legal and political powers over Africans. Few administrators questioned the right of the missionaries—or, for that matter, of any Europeans—to give orders to Africans; the dispute concerned how they were to rule them. Colonial minister Franck and other defenders of indirect rule felt that wherever possible Africans should be ruled by their own chiefs through their own laws. Early in the Belgian occupation, however, many missionaries had undermined the powers of the chiefs by surrounding the missions with Christian villages that were subject neither to chiefs nor to African law. Furthermore, missionaries frequently gave refuge to polygamous wives—even though they had been married according to local custom—on the ground that the marriages were contrary to Christian law. Chiefs and husbands who had lost their people to the missions complained to territorial officials, who frequently ruled that the missionaries had overstepped colonial law.

As governor-general, Maurice Lippens had taken a particularly strong stand against the missionaries. But the latter had influential friends, particularly among devoutly Catholic civil servants in the colonial ministry, who felt that the missionaries were being persecuted by Lippens—a well-known anticlerical. In an unprecedented manner, ministry officials attacked his policy in their semi-official journal, *Congo*. Although these attacks were not directly responsible for Lippens's resignation, they were certainly a contributing factor.

It was up to Martin Rutten to reestablish good relations between the office of the governor-general and the missions—and, for that matter, the higher echelons of the colonial ministry. Within weeks of his appointment, he issued a circular defining the rights of African Christians, missionaries, and territorial agents. Although recognizing the prerogative of African Christians to live in separate villages, Rutten insisted that these villages be subject to local chiefs wherever possible. He left the final word in all disputes to the territorial service but suggested that administrators maintain close contact with missionaries of all denominations. Thus, Rutten clearly defined legal priorities: Africans were subordinate to Europeans and missionaries to administrators.

At the same time, he wanted to protect the African legal system from unnecessary erosion. In cases in which a Christian wife refused to return to her polygamous husband, he therefore insisted that the bride price be returned (as in cases of divorce). It was an equitable solution. Rutten did not support African institutions when they conflicted directly with European ones, but he recognized the validity of African laws. To him Africans, though subordinate, were entitled to a certain respect from their colonizers.[8]

In dealing with the thorniest problem of his term of office, labor recruitment, he took the same attitude. He had no doubts about the need to subordinate Africans to European authority; the local population should provide labor for the economic and cultural development of the colony. But there should be strict rules concerning the number of men forced to leave their villages to take European jobs and the conditions under which they should live while employed. These restrictions angered European employers who wanted to spend as little money as possible on local labor, but Rutten enforced the rules in spite of their objections.

Labor allocation was another disputed area. His governor-generalship came at the time when many Belgians were beginning to gain confidence in colonial investment, and new companies proliferated in the Belgian Congo while existing companies expanded their activities. All were asking for African labor, so Rutten's first problem was to decide which employers should get the available workers. He had early established the principle that government projects of strategic importance, such as the construction of the BCK railway and of motor roads, had priority over private needs. In the corporate sector, he sought a way to regulate the competition between large and small firms. Highly capitalized enterprises such as the Union Minière, he reasoned, would be able to deprive smaller organizations by outbidding them on the labor market. His solution was to partition the colony, granting labor reserves to the large companies while allotting other territories to lesser employers.

Reaching a working arrangement with European employers proved to be easier than protecting African employees, but Rutten did not ignore the welfare of African recruits. He first established a special branch of the colonial administration to deal with African welfare and labor recruitment, the Service affaires indigènes et main d'oeuvre (AIMO), assigning certain administrators full time to this task. Next was the question of how many workers a village could afford to give to the recruiters. Shortly after Rutten left Katanga in 1918, a government committee led by the magistrate Antoine Sohier had investigated conditions in the Tanganyika-Moero district, an area that had been ravaged by the East African campaign. The committee set a limit of twenty-five percent on the number of able-bodied adult men who should be encouraged to leave their village at one time. In 1925 a special commission appointed by the colonial minister, Henri Carton de Tournai, suggested that this quota be lowered to ten percent of able-bodied men, and Rutten tried to stick to this figure.[9]

His concern with the welfare of Africans in the cities began when he was attorney general of Katanga (before the first world war). Rutten had then written the Congo's first local statutes calling for compensation to Africans injured on the job; as governor-general he broadened the coverage of these statutes and extended them to the entire colony. He also took an active role in drafting and implementing government decrees that created an urban government for Africans. These relatively small steps were important at that time. Partly because of this legislation, conditions in the cities for many Africans soon became superior to those in the countryside.[10]

When Rutten returned permanently to Belgium at the end of 1927, he believed that he had made substantial contributions toward solving the major problems he had faced as governor-general. He had stimulated growth of the colony's communications network, cemented good relations with the missions, and found at least a temporary solution to the recruitment problem. By modern standards he had not been a particularly progressive governor-general, but he had done a good job according to the standards of the time. During his administration the Africans of Léopoldville gained representation in a new municipal government, and those of Elisabethville obtained special courts that administered a form of African law especially adapted to local urban conditions.

Influence on Social and Economic History

Martin Rutten helped to make colonial careers respectable in Belgium, but he did not precipitate a rush of men of his social class to the Congo. Although other members of the provincial bourgeoisie—most notably, Pierre Ryckmans—followed in his footsteps, the majority were too comfortable in the metropole to risk their lives and health in tropical Africa. Only after the second world war, when transportation and public health facilities were improved, did a Congo career become attractive to men from good families.

In this respect, Belgians differed sharply from the British. At the time Rutten joined the Belgian administration, dozens of Britons of similar background and university education were entering the colonial service. The French, too, were recruiting large numbers of bourgeois—albeit largely from Corsica, Brittany, and the West Indies rather than from Paris. Thus, far more men of Rutten's standing were attracted to British and French colonial careers during his lifetime than were Belgians.[11]

Rutten's influence was greater on men of his region than on those of his class. As an alumnus of the University of Liège, he worked to recruit young Walloons for the colonial service, and with some success at the university level; he encouraged various members of the distinguished juridical family, the Sohiers, to enter the magistracy. His example, however, more frequently encouraged young men from less privileged backgrounds. Rutten and men like him became models for poor boys from the Ardennes who could not afford to go on to a university. Before the first world war they tended to rise through the ranks of the Force publique; after the war they received scholarships to the newly created Ecole coloniale at Antwerp, which attracted a large number of men who were intelligent but relatively impoverished.

Rutten also set an example for devout Catholics who wanted to serve their faith but did not have a priestly vocation. Before 1914 deeply religious Belgians who went to Africa usually did so as missionaries. For laymen, however, the Congo offered few contacts with the church; many of the early administrators were Freemasons or other anticlericals—a major cause of friction between the administration and the missionaries. Rutten's role in 1913 and 1923, when he mediated the disputes between these two factions, dispelled the notion that the Congo was an area of nonbelief and cleared the way for the devout from the Ardennes and rural Flanders. As a result, relations between colonial officials and Catholic missionaries improved considerably.

For most of his life, the governor-general set an example of economic disinterest on the part of the administrator. He never took bribes or enriched himself through his political connections. In this his deportment departed markedly from the norm for officials recruited by the Congo Free State. The Katanga magistracy, which Rutten dominated in the second decade of the twentieth century, had a reputation for honesty unparalleled in Belgian colonial administration, and he maintained nearly a clean record in avoiding colonial business connections. Unlike many of his colleagues, Rutten placed his loyalties with the government, to the exclusion of his business interests.[12]

It was this neutrality toward business that enabled Rutten to leave his special mark on the economic history of the Congo. He believed in capitalist development of the Belgian colony, but he also thought that the government had an obligation to protect its subjects from cruel forms of exploitation. During his service in Katanga he did not hesitate to attack the Union Minière for mistreatment of its workers, even though that company was the largest in the colony. Before 1918 he had viewed the copper company as a British enterprise potentially destructive of Belgian rule, and he continued in this course after the Belgians assumed control. Throughout his career Rutten placed national interest above company profits and colonial revenues, and he never treated the Union Minière with the deference shown by many of his colleagues. In the labor crisis of the middle twenties he considered the mining company to be so prosperous that it could find labor at the expense of other employers; thus, he remained healthily skeptical of the powerful firm's demands, even when the Union Minière was providing a large proportion of colonial revenues. Nor was this attitude simply a justification for favoring small settlers at the expense of larger ones. Rutten was unwilling to commit Africans to the unsupervised care of any private employer.

He believed that the government should protect Africans from undue exploitation; the condition of those in cash employment should be supervised during their entire absence from their villages, from the moment of recruitment to the moment of return. This attitude accounts for his concern for the rights of urban Africans, whose welfare he regarded as a government trust. It was no accident that legislation concerning municipal government in Léopoldville and urban courts in Elisabethville was enacted during his term of office.

Rutten's greatest impact on both Europeans and Africans was as an agent of the colonial government. To poor but talented young men from rural Wallonie he showed the way to colonial careers and was a model of propriety in office. To Africans obliged to accept European employment he offered government protection. By today's standards this protection was small, but it was greater than that offered by any previous Belgian administrator.

Influence on Governmental and Administrative History

In the development of colonial institutions, Martin Rutten was a bureaucratizer. This term has fallen into disrepute, like the term "bourgeois" applied to his social origins; but bureaucratizers performed an essential function in the establishment of colonial governments. Early administrators dealt with situations as they arose rather than applying the laws and regulations brought from the mother country —a style appropriate to the conditions of initial conquest, but no base on which to build a permanent administration. "Frontier justice" ultimately gave way to a more stable form of govermnent, and Martin Rutten was an important agent of that transformation.

At twenty-five, he did not enter the Congo with clear ideas of how the colony should be administered. Neither was his mind tabula rasa; it was colored by his legal training. Belgian law is a supremely logical discipline. In addition to the constitution, statutes, and administrative ordinances, it incorporates a single Napoleonic code to deal with all manner of legal problems. Unlike Anglo-American common law, which has developed out of a series of frequently conflicting legal decisions, Belgian law stresses order and self-consistency. Rutten's problem as a young man was to transfer this logical system to the frontier conditions of rural Katanga.

During his early service from 1901 to 1911 his main task was to make both Africans and Europeans aware of colonial law. The court system was extremely primitive, and cases were rarely appealed from district courts to the appeals court in Boma. His major responsibility was to apply existing law wherever possible. When a second appeals court was established in Elisabethville in 1911, he was free to deal with the structure as well as the delivery of Belgian colonial justice. This involved the development of new institutions, so as attorney general Rutten fostered the growth of the judicial police to the point that they became his main weapon when he attacked the Union Minière in 1917. He was also instrumental in extending Belgian authority through the administration of African law. He advocated recognition of the chiefs' judicial authority so long as their decisions did not conflict with colonial law, a policy that amounted to incorporating Africans into the Belgian judicial hierarchy—at the bottom, of course.

Rutten was willing to expand the colonial administration, but he was not willing to disobey his superiors. Thus, in 1914, when Emile Wangermée as vice-governor-general of Katanga ran afoul of the colonial ministry over the termination of Katanga's special status, he urged Wangermée to submit to orders from Brussels. He was willing to sacrifice the rights of Katangan officials in the interest of a uniform legal system.[13]

Rutten did not abandon his devotion to hierarchical principles when he joined the territorial administration, but he was not rigid in their application. Rather, he believed in the clear definition of the functions of each office and of the lines of authority. In creating the Service affaires indigènes et main d'oeuvre in 1925, he carefully assigned that agency a special place in the colonial administration and stipulated that the provincial directors of the service should be subordinate to the local vice-governors-general and serve on a par with district commissioners in the territorial service. He thus adapted the military model of a line and staff organization to the territorial service, in which specialists would serve in positions independent of the administrative chain of command, their relationship to the hierarchy nonetheless clearly defined.

In the territorial service as in the magistracy, Rutten held to the principle that one could manipulate bureaucracy but that one could not be disloyal. He was extremely discreet in his public remarks concerning other members of the administration. Although he disagreed with his predecessor, Maurice Lippens, on a number of vital issues, he steadfastly refused to condemn his actions. Instead, he publicly defended Lippens while he was in the process of fundamentally altering the latter's programs. As in Weber's bureaucratic ideal, the office was more important to Rutten than the individual who held it. He moved from agency to agency and from province to province without a word of complaint. He was his own best exemplar, bearing an air of stability wherever he went and imparting it to the local administration.[14]

Major Achievements

Rutten's contributions to the development of Katanga and of the central administration were enormous. More than any other man, he marked the region's colonial history. His career in Boma as the Congo's chief officer was a little less innovative, although in that post he guided the colony through an extremely difficult phase of its history—the boom that occurred when the first substantial Belgian investments began to flow into the colony.

Rutten's greatest achievement in Katanga was the expulsion of the British. From his arrival he was acutely conscious of the military dangers posed to the uncertain Belgian hold on the region by the number of British settlers, and it took him fifteen years to acquire the personal power to act against them; but during this period he carefully observed the situation, devising the tactics that he and his successors successfully employed at the end of the first world war. As a Belgian patriot, his first concern was for military security even at the expense of economic gain. His own initiative against the Union Minière was followed by other members of the administration in attacks against South African trade unionists, British shopkeepers, and even Zambian laborers.

He strengthened Belgian rule in Katanga less directly through his advocacy of improved working conditions for Africans. As industrial Katanga became a better place to live, African laborers were more willing to work there. When Elisabethville was first established, the laborers sought to leave it as quickly as possible because of the prevailing high mortality rate; by the end of Rutten's governorship in 1927, many Africans were finding the city more agreeable than their own villages. This was as much Rutten's achievement as that of any other Belgian official. He played a major part in establishing a Belgian policy that limited recruitment and set minimum standards for the treatment of African workers, and he facilitated their adaptation to urban conditions. It was during his regime as governor-general that the colonial ministry began to establish a legal system for urban Africans that differed from the rural legal structure.

Beyond the military and industrial concerns emanating from his experience in Katanga, the broader problem of mobilizing all available Belgian resources for the administration of the Congo preoccupied Governor-general Rutten. By settling the conflict between officials and missionaries, for example, he hoped to bring them together into a common Belgian team. It is noteworthy, although not publicly admitted by Rutten, that this team as it came into existence in the 1920s excluded English-speaking Protestants. Belgium's civilizing mission in Africa was increasingly a Belgian project.

The nationalist element in Rutten's thinking is most clearly seen in the priority he gave to strategic considerations that were economically unproductive or even counterproductive. The BCK railway, built largely during his governor-generalship, was neither the cheapest nor the quickest means of exporting copper from Katanga to Europe. Its importance was in binding the colony together. Soldiers could now be moved from one part of the colony to another in order to put down African resistance or to protect the colony from foreign attack. In the back of Rutten's mind—perhaps unconsciously, owing to his experience in 1911 and 1917—was the supposed danger of a British invasion.

To summarize his achievements, the jurist governor-general was a Belgian nationalist whose career was dedicated to strengthening his country's hold on its colony and to providing a rationalized administration and judicial system to maintain that control. He was not unmindful of African welfare but subordinated that goal to Belgian interests. His dealings with the Union Minière tended indirectly to benefit African welfare because Rutten used this issue as a weapon against the British. In constructing the BCK, however, their welfare suffered because he was willing to subject Africans to forced labor in order to speed completion of a project that he considered to be in the highest national interest.

In keeping with Rutten's early training and magisterial vocation, he considered the law a vital tool in the promotion of that national interest. He avoided short-term measures that would have bypassed legal procedures. Everything had to be legally correct not just to satisfy some inner compulsion for order but also to create a legal system that would support Belgian rule. To be effective, such a system had to take into account African as well as European law. Thus Rutten recognized the importance of African law just as he had recognized that of African welfare. Unfortunately for the colonized Africans, neither received highest priority under the colonial system.

Career upon Retirement

Rutten completed his term as governor-general at the end of 1927, when he was fifty-one years old and still in good health. He intended to continue playing an active role in colonial decision-making, and like many good ex-colonials he settled in Brussels, where he could keep in close touch with the colonial ministry. In October 1928 he was named to the Colonial Council, a body that edited the texts of proposed decrees to be promulgated by the colonial minister and countersigned by the king. The Council was the only organization independent of the colonial ministry that had any input into the colonial lawmaking process. Most of its work was done by ad hoc subcommittees assigned to investigate particular law proposals. Rutten assumed his seat as a junior member, an unaccustomed position for the ex-governor-general but one dictated by the practices of the council. During his four years of service he remained a junior member and chaired few of the subcommittees on which he sat.

The only major piece of colonial legislation that Rutten helped draft was the statute of 1931 on African municipal government. This decree created a local governmental institution for certain urban neighborhoods called Centres extracoutumiers (CECs), districts that already had been given special African courts. The new law provided that all designated districts have an appointed African chief, an assistant chief, and an African council. This African urban government originally was the project of Rutten's onetime subordinate, Gaston Heenen, now vice-governor-general of Katanga. Though Rutten was basically receptive to the proposal, the records of the colonial council, however, show that he played little role in altering the decree's final form.[15]

Unfortunately for the Congolese lawmaking process, Rutten never advanced beyond this relatively minor role. His career was cut short before he had served on the council long enough to attain the seniority necessary to give him a strong voice. Rutten's problem was a conflict of interest, the sole spot of tarnish on his record.

It was taken for granted that officials either maintain their places on the boards of colonial companies during the time of their service or become board members after retirement. Belgium's first colonial minister, Jules Renkin, actively promoted the interests of the colonial railroad on whose board he served while in office, and Rutten's immediate predecessor as governor-general, Maurice Lippens, was closely associated with the first Belgian colonial holding company, the Compagnie congolaise pour le commerce et l'industrie.[16] Rutten, in contrast, had joined no board of directors upon retirement.

While serving on the Colonial Council, however, he became involved with the Comité national du Kivu, organized to promote development of Kivu province. In 1930 his association with the company was denounced by a colonial journalist and he resigned from his government job rather than be accused of serving two masters. In March 1932 he accepted nomination to the Kivu company's highly paid board of directors but soon grew disillusioned with the company's operations and resigned in August 1934. He was unable to regain his position on the council and retired from colonial activities, except for his membership in the scholarly Royal Academy of Colonial Sciences, which he held from 1929 until his death in 1944.

Conclusion

Martin Rutten's role in Belgian colonial history was enhanced by his social position and restricted by his personality. Because of his family's status in Belgian society, Rutten—more than almost any other official who served in the Congo—was able to get his policies approved by the colonial ministry in Brussels. He resembled the permanent members of the ministry more than his colonial colleagues. Like the Brussels officials, he was French-speaking although of Flemish ancestry, Catholic, and educated in the law. Like the civil servants, too, he preferred to work behind the scenes rather than in the light of public scrutiny.

The quiet nature of his personality eventually limited his effectiveness as a leader. Even Rutten's most admiring colleagues characterized him as aloof. In keeping with this reticence, he was by no means an enthusiast and did not acquire a large following. He once described himself as a smiling skeptic. When he left the office of governor-general in 1927 he lost most of the influence he had formerly wielded.

In the long run, Rutten was not so much concerned with day-to-day politics as with the construction of permanent political institutions for the Congo. And he did play an important role in the formation of the colony's legal and administrative structure. He hoped that these institutions would endure for centuries and would have been appalled at the disintegration that began in 1960.

Nonetheless, Rutten's work would have lasted longer had he and his Belgian colleagues been more respectful of the rights of the Africans whom they administered.

Notes

1. *Tribune congolaise*, 10 October 1918, 30 April 1923, 23 January 1924; A. Engels, "Eloge funèbre de M. M. Rutten," *Institut royal colonial belge, Bulletin de séances* 16 (1945):12–15; F. Dellicour, "M. Rutten," *Biographie belge d'outre-mer* 6:714-720.

2. Dellicour, "Rutten," p. 715; H. W. Wack, *The Story of the Congo Free State* (New York, 1905), pp. 231-232; J. Stengers, *Belgique et Congo: L'Elaboration de la Charte coloniale* (Brussels, 1963), pp. 32–33.

3. These arguments are summarized in Bruce Fetter, *The Creation of Elisabethville, 1910–1940* (Stanford 1976), pp. 12–27.

4. Dellicour, "Rutten," p. 716; Major August Weyns, representative of the Comité spécial du Katanga to administrator, northeastern Rhodesia, 12 August 1902, Zambian National Archives, ZA BS 1/86 I; Charles Terlinden et al., *Comité spécial du Katanga, 1900–1950* (Brussels, 1950), pp. 31–69.

5. Fetter, *Elisabethville*, pp. 28–55; Léon Dieu, *Dans la brousse congolaise (les origines des missions de Scheut au Congo)* (Liège, 1946), pp. 277-279.

6. Fetter, *Elisabethville*, pp. 56–71; idem, "Central Africa 1914: German Schemes and British Designs," *Académie royale des sciences d'outre-mer, Bulletin des séances* (1972), pp. 541-549.

7. *Tribune congolaise*, 31 March, 31 May, 31 August 1923.

8. David M. Markovitz, *Cross and Sword: The Political Role of Christian Missions in the Congo, 1908–1961* (Stanford 1973); "Circulaire du gouverneur général sur les relations avec les missions," *Congo* 2 (1923):711-716.

9. Rutten to Carton de Tournai, 13 July 1925, 25 January 1926, Archives de service des affaires politiques, Lubumbashi, A 17.

10. V[ictor] D[evaux?], "Accidents de travail," *Revue juridique du Congo belge* 16 (1940):81; *Tribune congolaise*, 15 July 1924.

11. See William B. Cohen, *Rulers of Empire: The French Colonial Service in Africa*. Stanford: Hoover Institution Press, 1971.

12. A. E. L. Oudenne, "Un touche-à-tout," *L'Africaine*, 1 March 1930; Engels, "Eloge funèbre,"p. 14.

13. Dellicour, "Rutten," p. 17; Fetter, *Elisabethville*, pp. 28–55.

14. *Tribune congolaise*, 31 May 1923.

15. Conseil colonial du Katanga, Comptes rendus analytiques, 1929–1932.

16. S. H. Frankel, *Capital Investment in Africa* (London, 1938), p. 409; E. van der Straeten, "M. Lippens," *Biographie belge d'outre-mer* 6:664-672.

Pierre Ryckmans (1891–1959)

William B. Norton

WHEN Pierre Ryckmans was born, the Belgian Congo, which was to absorb his interest and energies for most of his adult life, did not yet exist. There was the Etat indépendant du Congo (Congo Free State) whose unlimited sovereign was Leopold II, constitutional king of the Belgians. Leopold had just made public in 1890—the sixtieth year of Belgian independence and the twenty-fifth anniversary of his accession[1]—his will bequeathing the Free State to Belgium; this really meant he had every intention of clinging to this colony until death.

Leopold, the Belgians, and the Congo, 1890–1927

For many years Leopold had worked to obtain for himself this vast African territory. He employed the Anglo-American explorer Henry Morton Stanley and others to negotiate treaties with several hundred indigenous chiefs in the name of the Association internationale africaine, organized under the king's patronage in 1876. The king secretly manipulated the Berlin conference on African affairs to grant him the title of sovereign of the Congo Free State. Few delegates of the thirteen European nations and the United States at that meeting (November 1884–February 1885) were aware that his officers already occupied the Congo basin and that other Belgian representatives were playing Franco-German territorial rivalry in Africa against threatened British encroachment to insure Leopold's total personal control.

In Belgium, only a small minority was conscious of the financial and moral responsibilities inherent in the king's bequest. This group included members of the oligarchy surrounding the throne and the king's trusted officers who were handling the details of exploration and international maneuvering. Some Belgians outside of government knew of the Congo Free State through their membership in geographical societies, and others had read of it in translations of Stanley's books or in missionary journals. But they and foreign observers were generally skeptical of Belgium's ability to found and develop a colonial empire eighty times its own size located in equatorial Africa. Nor could they imagine where the newborn state would find either manpower or money to open a million square miles of the upper Congo basin "to civilization and commerce and Christianity."

Belgium was not yet a democracy. Its limited monarchy was virtually unchanged from the time of its independence in 1830. The constitution of February 7, 1831, gave the country a bicameral Parliament and a cabinet of ministers chosen by whichever of the two established political parties was in power, Catholic or Liberal. Because of preoccupation with internal problems, there was little opposition either in April 1885 to letting him use the title of sovereign or in July 1889, when the nation subscribed 10 million francs at 3.5 percent interest to buy stock in the proposed 250-mile railway from Matadi to Léopoldville, bypassing waterfalls that made the lower river unnavigable. Another objective was to liberate the Congo's interior from the slave trade, which supplied East African markets; slavery had already been eradicated along the Atlantic coast. So in 1890 a still greater parliamentary commitment to the Congo state was required: an interest-free loan of 25 million francs, 5 million to be paid immediately and the remainder at a rate of 2 million annually over the next ten years. The Socialists derided the King for attempting to emancipate and civilize black Congolese while neglecting worse oppression of white Belgians at home. But Leopold obtained what he wanted.

The average Belgian knew nothing of the Congo. If its name had been heard, its location was vague. Farmers were concerned with crops and prices. Mine and factory workers suffered under low wages and poor working conditions; they were forbidden to strike or even to demonstrate against government restrictions and the recurrent threat of unemployment. Those who sought political remedies in the early 1890s demanded constitutional revision to permit universal instead of narrowly restricted suffrage.

Only 120,000 Belgians—less than eight percent of the adult male citizenry—were able to vote. These were the *censitaires*, those who could meet property and tax-paying requirements. Heading the move to enfranchise all men over twenty-one years of age were the Socialists, organized since 1885 as the Parti ouvrier belge but unable at first to elect a single deputy or senator to parliament. The Socialists turned to verbal and physical violence, and the turbulence became so great that the two older parties agreed on the compromise of 1893, which enlarged the voting population to 1.4 million men; but in an effort to foil labor's bid for power, the age limit was raised to twenty-five and a "plural vote" was permitted. This gave 900,000 of the new voters a single vote each; property or educational qualifications of the other 500,000 allowed them one or even two extra ballots, enabling this group to cast more than half of the country's 2.2 million votes. This arrangement was denounced as a clerical-bourgeois trick to rob the common man of his political rights, but in the election of 1894 the Socialists captured twenty-eight seats in the Chamber of Representatives and outnumbered the twenty

Liberals. The Catholics were left in a clear majority—for the moment—with 104 members. Such was the first installment of democracy in a cloudy and sometimes stormy political Belgium. Concern with internal problems was so intense that the various social classes and regional and economic interests awakened only gradually to colonial imperialism as either a promise or a threat to themselves and to the peoples with whom they were becoming involved as colonizers and colonized.

During the next decade the Congo Free State sank to a low level in Belgian and world esteem. The Free State still belonged to an aging Leopold II, its constitutionally uncontrolled sovereign, but he was on the verge of losing it. Reports of atrocities inflicted on the Congolese in certain rubber and ivory producing areas caused the king to send a commission (a Belgian, a Swiss, an Italian, and two secretaries) to investigate. Some halfhearted reforms based on the commission's 1906 report failed to convince either Belgian or international opinion that Leopold intended seriously to discourage exploitation of the region, and the legislature took action. As the Belgians' constitutional monarch, Leopold had to concur with the parliamentary majority but he was bitter at having to relinquish the Congo before his death. In 1908 the Parliament voted the *reprise*—the decision to annex the Congo as a Belgian colony and make its regime respectable. The powers that had taken part in the Berlin conference were not organized to create an explicit mandate or trusteeship system, and they now preferred that the Belgians run the Congo as an implied mandate. They could not permit a major colonial power to acquire so large and valuable a prize, nor could they risk dividing it among themselves—as among the neighboring Germans, British, and French.[2]

Belgian hopes began to revive. Before Leopold's death in December 1909, Crown prince Albert and Minister of colonies Jules Renkin each toured the area for several months. But it was not until most of Belgium east of the Yser river had been lost to the Germans in 1914 that many Belgians still able to fight found their way to Africa, where they helped the French drive German forces from the Cameroons before joining the British in expelling them from German East Africa. By the November 1918 armistice, the Belgians held a large part of East Africa, including the two small kingdoms of Ruanda and Urundi.

Belgium narrowly missed being left out at the Paris peace conference when Germany's former colonies were distributed as mandates under the League of Nations. Belgium did not need several million more African subjects in a remote, undeveloped, interior region nearly twice as large as the metropole. But it would gladly have traded the new territory for one that would widen Belgium's constricted access from the Atlantic coast along both sides of the Congo river, particularly the south bank, where the port of Matadi and the beginning of the railway were located. No such solution being feasible, Belgium accepted the Ruanda-Urundi mandate. With it came more explicit responsibilities than those implied in the *reprise* of the Congo, along with years of conspicuous representation on the Permanent Mandates Commission and then on the Trusteeship Council of the United Nations.[3]

The first annual report—written largely by Pierre Ryckmans as a junior colonial officer in 1921—indicates that most basic services and materials for the area would have to be supplied by the Belgians.[4] Roads and railways did not exist; reforestation of the cut and burned areas would take years to achieve; mineral deposits were unverified. The population, more dense than elsewhere in Africa, suffered chronic undernourishment and recurrent famines; soil exhaustion and erosion, insects, erratic rainfall, lack of crop diversification, and the social prestige of cattle raising had ruined food production. "After the king," said a native proverb, "nothing is superior to the cow"—but the herds were infected by pests. Modern medical doctors and veterinarians were a prime necessity. So were teachers. The sudden departure of the Germans had closed or disrupted Protestant and Catholic prewar mission schools, but reopening them would not fill the educational requirements of the mandate. A new type of secular school was needed. One such institution already was training African medical assistants to diagnose and treat diseases prevalent among their own people; another was teaching veterinary medicine. The report ended with the statement, "It is our first duty to improve living conditions for those indigenous to the colony . . . because in their welfare lies its importance and value to the colonizing country."[5]

Belgium could not colonize in the sense of profiting at the expense of the mandate, nor could Ruandi-Urundi be annexed to the Congo. The annual reports Belgium made to the Geneva commission were scrutinized to make sure that "a sacred trust of civilization" was being maintained; and the reactions of two totally dissimilar types of government had to be considered—the *bami* (kings) of Ruanda and Urundi, each at the apex of his pyramid of feudal chiefs and subchiefs, and the Weimar republic of Germany. The *bami* were less of a problem than the Germans.

In 1925 the Belgian legislature proposed to "unite Ruanda-Urundi administratively to the Belgian Congo"; this would make the vice–governor-general of the mandated area responsible to the governor-general of the Congo and through him to the minister of colonies. It was questioned whether this arrangement was compatible with article 22 of the League of Nations Covenant and with the Council's interpretation of the terms of the mandate.[6] Germany sent a sharp diplomatic protest; Belgium rejected it. The press on both sides added heat to the argument. Parliament refused to pass a different bill placing Ruanda-Urundi under an official who was not responsible to the colonial administration. The Belgians argued that "administrative union" between mandate and colony did not constitute "veiled annexation" and that measures already in existence coordinated the mandated British Cameroons with Nigeria and British Togoland with the Gold Coast, thus setting a precedent. Such a union would make available to Ruanda-Urundi many developmental services already operating in the Congo and avoid their costly duplication. The Permanent Mandates Commission agreed. So did the League Council.

Two years later the Belgians were not so successful. Germany, now admitted to the League with a seat on the Council, insisted on being represented on the mandates commission. Pierre Orts of Belgium was in the minority opposing such an increase in membership. He balked at working with the proposed German delegate, Heinrich Schnee, the last governor of German East Africa and one of the most strident "revisionists" seeking to regain Germany's "stolen" or "lost" colonies: "Such a man would only enter this organization with intent to ruin it."[7] The Council compromised by appointing the more congenial Ludwig Kastl.

The mandates commission lasted through its thirty-seventh session in December 1939. It maintained the principle of international trusteeship toward non-self-governing peoples and was reduced in number and effectiveness only by the withdrawal between 1933 and 1939 of one totalitarian dictatorship after another—Germany, Italy, Japan, and Spain.

Ryckmans and Africa, 1891–1934

Pierre Ryckmans was born in Antwerp in November 1891 to an upper middle-class family whose men were in business or the professions. Jacques Ryckmans, his grandfather, belonged to a prominent family in Malines, where he served for years as *secrétaire communal*. His son, Alphonse (1857–1931), followed his father into the law, completing his doctorate at Louvain in 1879; he was admitted to the Antwerp bar and served as a councillor in the city government (1899–1911) and as a senator in the national legislature from 1912 until his death.[8] He married Clémence van Ryn; the two had eight children; Pierre was the sixth. The three daughters married, two to doctors and the third to a businessman; two sons entered the Catholic clergy to teach, another went into business, and Pierre and his youngest brother chose the law.

Pierre spent six years at the University of Louvain and earned the degrees of bachelor of Thomist philosophy and doctor of law "with greatest distinction" in 1913, the year he was admitted to the bar at Antwerp. He volunteered for military service in 1914 and after Germany had overrun Belgium was sent to Africa, where he continued to fight and earned a promotion to lieutenant. After the armistice he remained in Africa for ten years, helping to build his country's administrative structure and policy. It was Ryckmans's work as a civilian official in Ruanda-Urundi that led to his writing the first report on that area to the mandates commission in 1921.

Ryckmans was fascinated with Belgian Africa, with its languages and with the indigenous people. His eagerness to discuss their problems with Africans in their own tongue lessened their diffidence. One of his duties was that of *conseiller*—guardian or tutor—to the child-king Mwambutsa, who had reached the shaky throne of Urundi in 1915, when he was little more than two years old.[9]

> When you feel the hand of a boy-king tremble in your own while you review a parade and the native musicians are murdering a European march tune; when you accept hospitality in an isolated hut on a stormy night, sharing your host's meal and a dry mat beside the fire; when a fierce warrior begs your help in recovering his stolen goat or errant wife; when a taciturn chief on his deathbed confides to you his lands and family, and when your promise to look after his son has perhaps eased his agony—then you no longer feel lonely among savages but rediscover yourself a man among men.[10]

He advanced from administrator of a small region through commissioner in charge of larger and more important districts, until he became commissioner general. With resolution of the 1925 diplomatic crisis in Belgium's favor, Alfred Marzorati became the new vice–governor-general of Ruanda-Urundi, and Ryckmans took over as Urundi's resident-general. In Marzorati's absence he acted in his place.

Ryckmans's return to Belgium in 1928 caused speculation that there was a policy difference between him and his superiors or that one of them stood in the way of his further advancement.[11] The ostensible reason was his family. He had married Madeleine Nève in 1921, a niece of Paul Nève's (1851–1881) (the latter had become a legend in the Congo by keeping Stanley's steamboat in working condition on the navigable stretches of the lower Congo; he died of dysentery before reaching the site where Léopoldville was to be built). The Ryckmans children adapted well to Africa; but their parents were concerned with their formal education. Ryckmans was also intent on developing his training and talents to their full capacity, while getting a perspective on his preoccupation with Africa.

His activities during the next six years were varied, but they continued to focus on the Belgian colonies. He practiced law, taught, wrote for publication, and served on a governmental commission that in 1930 sent him with a group of experts to investigate problems of the indigenous labor supply in the Congo. He joined the Institut royal colonial belge, the Institut colonial international (Paris), the Institute of African Languages and Civilisations (London), and the Institut national pour l'étude agronomique du Congo (INEAC). The last was headed by the Duc de Brabant, who visited the Congo in 1933 and was seriously interested in its problems; he became Leopold III when his father, King Albert, was killed in a climbing accident in 1934, and Ryckmans succeeded him in the presidency of INEAC.

Ryckmans brought Africa alive to others by his flexible style in lecturing and writing at the University of Louvain and the Ecole coloniale in Antwerp and even more through books, articles, and a five-month series of radio talks.[12] In 1931 he turned forty, still unsure of his professional orientation. Law seemed to offer the most promise were he to remain in Belgium; he was readmitted to the bar and went into partnership in Brussels for two years with his youngest brother, Xavier (Bob): "Pedro always did beautifully in whatever task he undertook," Bob commented, "but one could tell that his heart was not in our office but in Africa."

In Ryckmans's writings he attempted to gain converts to the ideology of *dominer pour servir*—men who would go out and practice it. His *Politique coloniale* asks in its first chapter whether "the occupation of colonial territories was morally justified." The book is cautiously affirmative: "Modern colonization is not without abuses, but it represents an immense improvement over that of the three preceding centuries." Regarding Belgian commitment in the Congo, he wrote that "it is the business of all Belgians, not the monopoly of those who have gone to settle there or who have invested their capital in it."[13]

Ryckmans criticized the apportionment of legislative powers by the Charte coloniale of 1908: the Belgian Parliament passed laws; the king issued decrees on the advice of the minister of colonies and after consultation with the colonial council; and the governor-general in an emergency could issue ordinances valid for not more than six months unless approved by a decree. Ryckmans believed that since the governor-general was in immediate touch with the colony, he should possess the initiative and at least share in the framing of decrees. In his conclusion he returned to the initial question of moral justification:

> If colonization was an injustice, we must redress it. If, as we believe, it was a generous promise, we must keep our word. Reparation or debt of honor, it matters little: payment is necessary.

We are in the Congo and intend to remain there . . . but only on condition of paying our debts so well that we become creditors in our turn . . . to the Blacks.

May our own young people, in going there, assume . . . the heavy and magnificent "white man's burden." And in our Congo may the balance between the benefits and evils of civilization always lean to the side of the benefits![14]

Ryckmans, Belgium, and the Congo, 1934–1946

Ryckmans was genuinely surprised in 1934 when he was offered the governor-generalship of the Congo. The post at Léopoldville had been ably filled since 1927 by Lieutanant general Tilkens, who was now due to retire,[15] and if Marzorati had been the obstacle to Ryckmans's previous advancement, he was no longer a contender.[16] Three major developments had altered the Congo's future prospects during Ryckmans's years in Europe: the Great Depression, the rise of Hitler and the Nazis in Germany, and Belgium's territorial and administrative colonial reforms of 1932–1933. The Belgian reforms offered the best chance of coping with the other two problems, but they had aroused opposition and needed to be proven by longer application in the colony itself.

Administrative Structure. Administrators of the Congo originally were personally chosen by Leopold II, who put Stanley "in charge of the project" late in 1878; he was followed in 1884 by another Briton, Colonel Sir Francis de Winton, who bore the title of administrator general. A Belgian, Camille Janssen, in 1887 became the first governor-general and after his resignation in 1890 it was a year before the king appointed Major (later General) Wahis as vice–governor-general (1891). He was raised to full rank in 1892 and remained in office until 1912. Five more Belgians preceded Ryckmans, and three succeeded him.[17]

At the time of the *reprise* in 1908, the Charte coloniale removed the governor-general from the king's personal authority. He became responsible to the complex balance of powers represented by the crown, Parliament, the cabinet, and the newly created colonial council; and his immediate superior was the colonial minister, who presided over sessions of the new council. This administrative structure remained intact from 1908 to 1960, interrupted temporarily only in 1914–1918 and 1940–1945 by wartime occupations of the metropole.

In the Congo itself, the governor-general delegated authority to several administrative levels, each with more numerous agents. Small adjustments could be made, but broad reforms like those of 1932–1933 needed a parliamentary law or a royal executive order.[18] Such changes were aimed at economy and efficiency; they redefined boundaries of the provinces, districts, and territories, downgraded former provincial governors, and reactivated councils at the central and provincial levels. To conserve manpower and money, 180 territories were reduced to 104 and 22 districts to 15. Provinces were increased from four to six with the creation of Kasai and Kivu; but they could be governed more economically by commissioners than by the former provincial vice–governors-general and this change eliminated confusion with the only two vice–governors-general who were retained: one for the Congo and one for Ruanda-Urundi.

Figure 1. The Congo Administration, 1908–1960

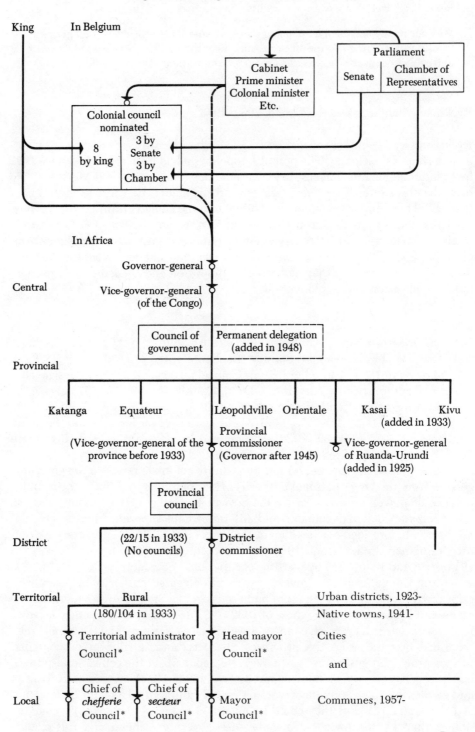

* See note 38 to this chapter.

The departing Tilkens had absorbed the harsh criticism aroused by some of the reforms that lowered rank or reduced salary without lessening responsibilities or the size of the area administered. The earlier central and provincial councils, first convened in 1915, had steadied the colonial regime during the first world war and until normal lines of authority were reestablished with the metropole; after 1920 they were discontinued. Their reactivation as consultative, nonelective bodies may have been the result of the 1932 meeting between Tilkens and Colonial minister Tschoffen at Léopoldville, attended by the four provincial governors. The meeting was followed by a council of government in 1934 under Tilkens, a gathering that Ryckmans and his successors were expected to reconvene each year. Despite the council's all-white complexion and its authoritarian bent, Ryckmans used the occasions for his annual opening address, delivered publicly at the first session and printed for wider distribution. In times of crisis or strain, these speeches served to rally support and bolster public morale.[19]

During the rest of 1934 Governor-general Ryckmans was ready to handle each problem, foreseen or unexpected, as it arose. He had to communicate, to see and be seen, to decide between alternative courses of action, and to commemorate. He was responsible for all official correspondence, reading reports from those subordinate to him and writing his own to the ministry. He made special visits around the Congo, traveling occasionally to Belgium and foreign countries. In Léopoldville he received innumerable visitors, ceremonial and informal. After mature reflection and impartial decision, he had to handle colonial officials by appointments, transfers, advancements, or dismissals. Memorable occasions were observed with suitable ceremony.

Ryckmans's skill enabled him to *dominer et servir* the Congo for twelve crucial years. The first half of his term was preoccupied with economic recovery from depression and escape from recession; the remainder focused more strenuously on turning near defeat into victory in a second world war. In his last regular prewar address (June 1939) he told the council that because of the hard lessons of the 1930s "the Congo economy has become healthy and now stands on . . . more solid and broad foundations.[20]

World War II. Twenty months elapsed before the government council again could be convened. During this period Ryckmans's war messages—three- to five-minute radio broadcasts—began with his announcement of the Nazi invasions of Poland and of Belgium;[21] on May 28, 1940, he broadcast twice to tell of the surrender by Leopold III of the Belgian army and of Colonial minister De Vleeschauwer's telegram from Paris advising all Belgians—especially those in the Congo—to continue to fight.[22] The messages showed Ryckmans's confidence in ultimate victory over the Axis powers and stressed the need for a strong colonial war effort to help drive the enemy from occupied Belgium and free the king. They culminated in 1944 with the Allied landings in Normandy, the liberation of Paris and Brussels, and the restoration of the monarchy with Leopold's brother—Prince Charles—as regent.[23]

At the irregular wartime meetings of the council of government in February 1941, December 1942, and November 1943, Ryckmans's addresses showed the accumulating strain and weariness throughout the colony before the tide began to

turn. Colonial minister De Vleeschauwer—after many delays and following a de-
vious route that touched Paris, Lisbon, London, Gambia, Sierra Leone, and
Nigeria—managed to reach Léopoldville and participate in the 1941 session. He
and three other Belgian cabinet members—Hubert Pierlot (prime minister),
Camille Gutt (finance minister), and Paul-Henri Spaak (foreign affairs minister)—had set up the government in exile in London and secured its recognition
by the free world. With Belgium's king, colonial council, and Parliament out of
action, it was vital to colonial morale that Ryckmans and the minister be in personal agreement and be seen and heard together in public. De Vleeschauwer's
remarks to the opening and closing sessions of the council of government
(February 4 and 8) set the tone for the governor- general and the work to be done
by the members.

Ryckmans contrasted present assets and liabilities to find a "dismal balance":

> Our country totally occupied; our king a prisoner with all his army; all our fellow
> citizens in the mother country under the invader's domination; . . . therefore no
> replacements for our colonial army or administrative or labor force; no harbor at
> Antwerp to take, as it normally would, three-quarters of our exports—that's the
> minus side. On the plus side we have, thank God, Great Britain's guarantee, its
> power, resolution, and fidelity to its given word. Actual resources? About twenty
> thousand Belgian refugees in England; a few thousand more scattered over the
> globe; a fraction of the National Bank's gold in safe custody; four cabinet members
> representing governmental continuity on free soil. That's all—*except the Congo*,
> where we are fifteen thousand citizens, the population of a very modest town, faced
> with governing fifteen million blacks while putting our vast natural resources to
> work. . . .
>
> We must not . . . simply survive, waiting to be saved. We must wage active war,
> hasten victory, liberate the homeland. Nor must we forget the tutelage we owe to
> the natives, our social and educational programs, our scientific research, our long-
> range encouragement of agriculture. For postwar Belgium will need more than
> ever a healthy and loyal people in a prosperous colony, equipped to export great
> quantities of high-quality products.[24]

Minerals from the Congo made a major contribution to the war effort. Between 1914 and 1918 the copper mines in the Katanga region had produced a total
of 85,000 tons, a modest showing since the 27,500 tons mined in 1917—the year of
highest production—did not even quadruple the 1913 rate. The worldwide mining crisis of the early 1920s, precipitated by falling prices, nearly closed down the
Union Minière du Haut-Katanga (UMHK), threatening its 1,000 European and
12,000 Congolese employees with unemployment. A young investigator, Edgar
Sengier, who was sent from Brussels, persuaded the management to double its
output in order to reduce its unit cost of production. As a result, the company continued to prosper despite a further price decline and became one of the world's
largest copper producers. It supplied more than 800,000 tons of copper during
World War II, with corresponding increases in tin, zinc, and especially cobalt.

The Congo's uranium, however, made the most dramatic impact on the war's
outcome. A vein of rich uranium ore had been discovered in 1915 at Shinkolobwe
in Katanga and supplied some of the scientific world's needs in the preatomic age.
In 1939 Sengier, now a Union Minière director, was alerted to its potential im-

portance by hearing through British channels about German experiments in nuclear fission. He secretly began shipments of uranium ore to New York for warehouse storage. An American colonel working on the Manhattan Project looked Sengier up in New York City shortly after Pearl Harbor to ask his help in obtaining a supply of uranium from the Congo. "When do you want it?" replied the Belgian. "We need it at once—but realize that's impossible." "On the contrary, you can have 1,000 tons immediately. It's here in New York. I've been expecting your request for the past year."[25] A few reliable helpers in Ryckmans's office in Léopoldville had been instructed to decode certain symbols in secret messages as "crude minerals." Only later did they learn that these related to the Allied supply of uranium—and to the first atomic bomb.

The greatest threat to the stability of the Belgian regime in the Congo came from divergent ideas about Ryckmans's priorities and methods. His cabinet head, Léo Pétillon, was well aware that the governor-general was blamed for being too hard—"imposing on the Congolese an excessive war effort, which, it was insinuated, served European interests principally"—and for appearing too soft, afraid to use his authority, when he tried to reason and persuade instead of command.[26] Ryckmans's dealings with members of the Belgian government in London—especially with the minister of colonies—and then with Monseigneur de Hemptinne, vicar apostolic of Katanga, are cases in point. He refused to yield entirely to what either of them wanted yet narrowly averted breaks with both.

Relations were not always smooth between Léopoldville and London. There is no doubt that both Ryckmans and the Belgian war cabinet were stimulated in 1941 by De Vleeschauwer's visit to the colony and his participation in the government council meeting. But the minister's four-month journey to the Congo with his wife in 1942 (June 20–October 28), though beneficial, had its turbulent moments. He and Ryckmans were joined by Prime minister Pierlot from July 26 to August 22, and the three held frequent, long, and sometimes heated sessions over finances, security, labor problems, production schedules, and the like. A crisis occurred on August 20, after hours of discussion, when Ryckmans handed his resignation to the colonial minister. But an agreement was worked out over dinner and the resignation was provisionally withdrawn. Ryckmans enjoyed relative peace while the minister, escorted by Pétillon, departed on September 3 to inspect the upper Congo around Stanleyville, returning on the fifteenth. Eventually De Vleeschauwer left his wife in the colony, remote from Nazi air raids, and returned alone to London.

Ryckmans had refrained from convening the government council during the minister's visit but managed to hold a meeting before the year ended. In his December 1942 speech, the reference to "our incalculable fatigue" because "the burden is heavy and the road long" may have been directed as much at these visits from members of the Belgian cabinet as at colonial tribulations. But Ryckmans wanted to remind everyone in the Congo that "this war will be won by tired out people."[27]

The so-called de Hemptinne affair showed that—as in every country dedicated to halting and eradicating Hitlerism—there were Belgians and Congolese who in varying degrees opposed their government's policy. Early in the long career (1876–1958) of this belligerent missionary bishop "he showed the ultra-Catholic and therefore anti-Protestant aspects of his Belgian nationalism and royalism," to quote *Pourquoi Pas? Congo.*[28] During 1943 his condemnation of the country's war policy as "too subservient to England" was published in *L'Essor du Congo* (Elisabethville). Pierlot's government in London, calling the protest "at least in-opportune" and fearing it might mean the development of a dangerous antiwar minority, sent ex–Minister of colonies Paul Tschoffen to investigate. To Tschof-fen's advice that de Hemptinne "moderate his political transports" and limit himself "to his religious duties," the irascible prelate retorted by branding the war effort "inconsidéré, imprudent, disproportionné, et stérile" and the consequent "vassalage to London humiliating to our national honor." De Hemptinne's "worst réquisitiore," in a letter to Pierlot and De Vleeschauwer dated December 15, 1943, virulently attacked Tschoffen's "intrusion into the colony," repeated his previous complaints, and added that "besides working the *indigènes* too hard we are postponing the fulfillment of duties that we owe them."[29]

Ryckmans took the situation seriously, especially the additional rebuke,[30] but he had no reason to panic. The guiding principle of his career was well known: the ruler's right to dominate the colony must be justified by his desire and ability to serve its people's real needs and interests. In his 1941 address to the government council and De Vleeschauwer, he had coupled his summons to "wage active war, hasten victory, and liberate the homeland" with the warning not to "forget the tutelage we owe to the natives" in such areas as education, agriculture, social im-provement, and scientific research.

Three times in 1943 Ryckmans had toured the interior provinces of Belgian Africa to sound out as only he could the feelings of the people. The longest of his absences from Léopoldville was from February 3 to April 1, when he flew to Co-quilhatville and Stanleyville and traveled to some of the smaller towns and villages in Equateur and Orientale provinces by boat, train, and automobile. In May he went through Kasai on the way to an intensive look at Katanga, with stops at Elisabethville and Jadotville. In October he flew to Usumbura and back with brief stops at all the provincial capitals, spending two weeks driving through the towns and countryside of Ruanda-Urundi, so full of associations with the early phases of his career. The symbolic climax doubtless occurred on the seventeenth when Ryckmans witnessed the baptism of Mwami (King) Charles Mutara Ruda-higwa, preceded and followed by dancing in colorful Ruandan panoply.

Within ten days of Ryckmans's return to Léopoldville from the third of his tours, the terse notation "Commencé discours Conseil" (November 3) showed that he was writing his address for the upcoming government council meeting of November 23–29, 1943, which turned out to be the last before his tenure in office ended. "Though by ourselves we have not enough power to rescue the homeland, we do not want it rescued without us," he asserted. He concluded: "When ac-counts are settled, we shall proudly present ourselves . . . [as] free Belgians on free Belgian soil, who have represented the nation and held aloft the flag during these years of struggle."[31]

This was not a direct reproach to the French defeatists and collaborationists like some in the French Congo who preferred to follow Governor-general Boisson along the Vichy-Pétain-Laval line.[32] Nor was it an explicit labeling as neutralists of de Hemptinne and people like him in Belgian Africa. Ryckmans appreciated the importance to the Belgian Congo in having an energetic, anti-Axis partner as a neighbor along hundreds of miles of river boundary to the west and north. He had gone to Brazzaville on July 14, 1943, to join Governor-general Eboué in celebrating Bastille Day,[33] and he went again on January 30, 1944, to meet General de Gaulle and René Pleven[34] and to observe the opening of the conference on postwar French colonial policy.

As the number and power of such active allies continued to grow, de Hemptinne's complaint about Belgian "vassalage to London" lost its force. Ryckmans was not so weary as to give up the initiative, having spent a large part of 1943 in mastering neutralism in the colony by defensive measures and by counteroffensive sweeps through every province. On February 10, 1944, he went overseas on a long and hazardous trip, leaving Vice–governor-general Ermens to decide whether any new measures were needed to counteract neutralism. In so doing, Ryckmans was convinced that relatively few of the "overworked" Congolese would join with de Hemptinne and risk precipitating such a shortage of jobs as they had endured in the depression. His absence would test the soundness of the Congo administration, which could be managed by subordinates for two to three months at a time, and Ryckmans learned to play a new international role, exchanging Belgo-American assurances regarding their respective war efforts when he visited the United States.

On leaving the colony Ryckmans may not have expected to return by way of North and South America, but a summary of his calendar reveals what his stamina, ability, and determination could accomplish:

10-20 February 1944: First leg of triangle, Léopoldville to London. Flying time 41 hours 15 minutes, with landings and takeoffs at ten intermediate stops—one at Accra for five days, partly on business, partly because of a failure at takeoff. Reached London on a Sunday in time for tea, after all-night flight from Casablanca to Bristol and a daylight train ride; 9:30 P.M. driven by air raid sirens to underground shelter, like everyone else.

20 February-15 April: London. Numerous sessions with members of Belgian war cabinet, singly or in council, and various Allied representatives such as Lord Hailey, British authority on Africa, and American Ambassador Winant. Many air raid alerts; some very violent. Encouraged by evidence of pre-Normandy invasion preparations.

15-17 April: Second leg of itinerary, London-New York-Washington. A three-day zigzag course with stops at Prestwick, the Azores, and Newfoundland.

17 April-4 May: United States. Crowded schedule of interviews, luncheons, dinners, with such people as Assistant secretary of state Dean Acheson, war production board chief Donald Nelson, and Sulzberger, proprietor of the *New York Times*. Visits to war industries in New Jersey, New England, Detroit, and Pittsburgh. Press conference and prepared radio broadcast publicizing the Belgian contribution toward defeat of the Axis. [The word "uranium" was not mentioned, but Ryckmans's travel notes include the name of Sengier among the Belgians with whom he dined and talked on his first full day in New York.]

4-11 May: Completion of triangular itinerary in 48 hours 18 minutes flying time New York to Léopoldville; stops at Miami, Puerto Rico, British Guiana, Bélem and Natal in Brazil, Ascension Island, British Gold Coast and Nigeria, French Cameroons and Gabon.[35]

Resuming his routine responsibilities in the Congo, Ryckmans became increasingly conscious over the next ten months of the approaching end of hostilities and the beginning of new relationships among the powers and between the metropole and its colony. Belgium was liberated in September 1944 and was spared reconquest during Hitler's last offensive gamble in the Ardennes by his defeat at the battle of the Bulge in December. The government was again in Brussels, and the familiar succession of ministerial changes geared to political party power was taking place. A change affecting the Congo—the replacement of De Vleeschauwer by de Bruyne as minister of colonies—reached Ryckmans's attention on February 12, 1945; in March he flew to Brussels.

For more than five weeks he pursued colonial business and attended reunions with relatives and friends long separated by the occupation. As a means to help impress upon Belgium its enormous debt to the Congo,[36] he arranged to have his council speeches and wartime broadcasts published and sat for his portrait and for a bronze victory medallion by Dupagne—the sculptor who did the lifesize Stanley statue erected in 1954 in Léopoldville. Ryckmans was not stressing his own importance but rather that of Belgian Africa. He took part in numerous discussions with politicians and officials who valued his experience and whose help enabled him to assess recent and impending changes in policy. On May 7, 1945, news of Germany's capitulation reached him and two days later he started back to Africa, stopping long enough in Paris to visit de Gaulle.

Postwar Congo Policy. During the fourteen months between his return to Léopoldville and his departure from the colony in mid-July 1946, Ryckmans was increasingly preoccupied with the future. He knew that postwar development of the Congo would be precarious unless guided and assisted by Belgium. The course of the colony's relations with the metropole, judging by crises facing other European colonial administrations, could become very rough. And there were scores of career decisions—his own included—facing those whose loyalty to the Belgian administration had pulled the colony through the double ordeal of depression and war. Some had reached or passed retirement age; others should be advanced or transferred within the colonial service; still others might do better in a different career.

In the summer of 1945 two decisions were made in Brussels concerning the Congo. Godding, a Liberal politician who had lived on his African plantations during the war, learned in Léopoldville on August 1 that he had been named minister of colonies. On the ninth he flew back to Europe with knowledge of the Congo scene and good relationships with the leading administrators. The other change was so basic that its impact would be more gradual. It was a royal order dated July 31, 1945, that reorganized the central and provincial councils.[37] Its intent was to enlarge and diversify membership in those councils over which the governor-general and provincial governors presided annually, thereby beginning the process of africanizing and democratizing them.[38] But Ryckmans expected soon to be relieved of his office and felt that such an important operation should be the responsibility of the next incumbent.[39]

In August Ryckmans returned to Europe. He and his wife took their first real vacation in many years, walking and bicycling together in Switzerland during the autumn. But now that he had reached the age of fifty-four and held the highest position in the colony, the question of his subsequent career was still unanswered.

The Ryckmans returned to Africa in the midst of a labor crisis late in December. A strike scheduled for January 7, 1946, was called off on the fourth but disagreement arose between Brussels and Léopoldville as to restricting Congolese workers from forming unions, associations, or committees of their leaders. The dispute reached a climax in late April and early May. Ryckmans offered to resign on May 6 unless Colonial minister Godding changed his position; having no one with whom to replace him, Godding telephoned on the eighth agreeing to some "modifications." Ryckmans remained. But when he learned of the ministry's decision to name Eugène Jungers as acting governor-general—transferring him to Léopoldville from Ruanda-Urundi, where he had been in charge since 1932— Ryckmans resumed writing the address for his official farewell. Entitled "Vers l'avenir," the speech was delivered on July 5 to a local audience in the Salle Albert I.[40]

The Ryckmans left Léopoldville on July 15, after Jungers had been in office a week. All elements of the population joined in an hour-long demonstration before their governor-general's flight—hundreds of Belgians and foreigners but also exuberant Congolese by the thousands, showing the naive faith that Ryckmans was truly "their own." Not even the announcement by the American consul on behalf of President Truman, naming Ryckmans to receive the United States Medal of Merit for his services to freedom, touched him more deeply.[41]

Ryckmans, the United Nations, and the Congo, 1946–1958

Within three months Ryckmans had another job—or rather, a periodic mission. On October 12 he was a dinner guest of Paul-Henri Spaak at the ministry of foreign affairs in honor of South Africa's visiting prime minister, Jan Smuts. Spaak told someone near him of the unexpected withdrawal of a member of the delegation he was about to lead to the United Nations General Assembly in New York. His companion, indicating the former governor-general, asked, "Why not Ryckmans?" There followed eight hectic weeks for Ryckmans and his co-representatives of meetings at the General Assembly's temporary Lake Success quarters on Long Island.

Ryckmans served on Commission IV—out of which grew the United Nations Trusteeship Council—and its subcommittees. These bodies were concerned with hammering into shape the trusteeship accords needed to replace old agreements between the League of Nations and each mandate holding country and making them acceptable to the General Assembly. "And here I am," he noted, "four years later, unable to escape, to give up my salary without upsetting my budget, or to find a different job while away from Belgium." What had been described as "a matter of at most two six-week sessions annually" sometimes required three or four round trips a year to New York; in the summer of 1947 Ryckmans traveled around the world with a subcommittee of the Trusteeship Council to inspect the Samoan Islands.[42]

Until 1957 Ryckmans and a few others—notably Ambassador Fernand van Langenhove—defended the *thèse belge*, the justification at the United Nations of

Belgium's handling of its colonial mission. It was a necessary and often thankless task. This feeling is apparent in his 1946 farewell address to the Congo and more directly expressed in the revised edition of *Dominer pour servir*.[43] Ryckmans decided not to change the title of the revised book though the word "dominer" might "smell of the imperialism of bygone days" now that colonies were becoming nations and the "right of self-determination" seemed to matter to so many people. "No, I'll keep the title. It corresponds to reality. Domination is a fact; so is and must also be service—until the work is finished and domination has become unnecessary."[44] At that time, all Belgians who had contributed to the Congo's adulthood would "merit the gratitude of a people who, after having ceased to be our pupil, will remain our friend."[45]

Ryckmans warned that Belgium was in a dwindling minority of colonial powers. Major empires were held by Belgium, Britain, France, and the Netherlands; the United States, Australia, New Zealand, South Africa, and Denmark administered less important external dependencies; Spain and Portugal, though long-standing colonial powers, were not then among the fifty-seven U.N. members. The aggressive majority was convinced that the colonial system was obsolete and should be eliminated.[46] In these debates, the Belgian thesis was more than a defensive stance against an anticolonialist majority. Ryckmans's strategy, while maintaining the Belgian position, was to exploit the weaknesses of his opponents in order to counterattack. If, in the process, the time was lengthened before the inevitable end of the parent-child or teacher-pupil relationship, the metropole could accomplish still more toward a smooth separation and a secure future for the ex-colony.

The Belgian defense rested on the distinction in the U.N. Charter between chapters XII–XIII, which set up the trusteeship system to replace the mandates, and chapter XI, which applied more generally to all dependent or non-self-governing peoples. The Belgians deplored the anticolonialists' evident objective of applying to the colonies—in their case, the Congo—the stringent international controls in chapters XII–XIII, which Belgium accepted for its trust territory, Ruanda-Urundi. They emphasized the general promise in chapter XI to "recognize the primacy of the people's interests in dependent territories" and to "assure their political, economic, and social progress."[47] More direct U.N. intervention between a mother country and its colony, they claimed, would violate the Charter's promise that the U.N. itself would not interfere with a member nation's "internal affairs"—hitherto understood to include sovereignty over colonies.

Ryckmans and van Langenhove realized that the anticolonialist tide would not stop once colonies and trust territories became indiscriminately subject to international regulation but would roll on as a flood of rising nationalist aspirations. They devised a counteroffensive. Chapter XI should be interpreted to include *all* non-self-governing or dependent peoples, not simply those in the colonies or external dependencies of a few advanced nations. Many member nations, some of which were loudly anticolonial, had underprivileged subjects who formed important minorities—in some instances numerical majorities, as in parts of Latin America. These people needed development, enfranchisement, relief from discrimination, and the opportunity to live more productive lives. Thus did the Belgian approach change from a defense of the few colonial powers into a challenge on behalf of the unemancipated millions who needed the protection of chapter XI.[48]

Belgium's contention that it was fulfilling the provisions of chapters XI–XIII depended on the quality of Belgian administration in Africa after Ryckmans's departure in 1946. His influence continued to be strong because of projects traceable to what he had said or done as governor-general and because of co-workers and successors who believed in him. Two ten-year plans—one for the Congo, ready by 1949 for implementation, and one for Ruanda-Urundi, which started to operate two years later—grew from Ryckmans's farewell speech. He had urged Belgium's long-range, planned development of its dependencies as a payment for their help in winning the war.[49] Eighteen months later he cautioned against tiring the Africans by "excessive zeal" or letting the Europeans "monopolize the show."

> There's a limit to the effort we can ask of the *indigènes*, even if it's work aimed entirely at benefiting them. . . . Yet instead of confining participation of the blacks to what the whites cannot accomplish without them, we must leave to them everything that they *can* do and restrict European intervention to the minimum . . . such as furnishing capital, equipment, and technical direction.[50]

Credit for the plans belongs not so much to the colonial ministers—Wigny or Dequae—who signed the preface to each ten-year plan when published, or to Jungers, during whose governor-generalship both plans appeared. While he was vice-governor-general, Pétillon worked for years with a number of specialists—in the Congo, in Belgium, and in Ruanda-Urundi—to formulate them. It was intended that each ten-year plan be followed by a second one based on the experience of the first—had not the unexpectedly rapid spread through Africa of national independence overshadowed this and other projects.

In November 1947 Pétillon presided over the first post-Ryckmans meeting of the government council in Léopoldville. He believed in transforming the system of government by bringing more Africans into the councils at every level and having most members democratically elected; this was to form the political basis for the communauté belgo-congolaise, which was the objective of his own term as governor-general from late 1951 to mid-1958.[51] In this manner Pétillon was eminently Ryckmans's disciple.

In the Belgian political overturn of June–July 1958, when the Liberal-Socialist coalition fell and the Catholics tried to establish a one-party government, their leaders urged the colonial ministry first on Ryckmans and then on Pétillon. Neither felt capable of coping with the partisan politics involved though Pétillon would have been glad to remain in Léopoldville under Ryckmans as minister—a relief from four years of an unsympathetic Buisseret. But Ryckmans had a graver reason for his refusal: symptoms of an illness later diagnosed as terminal. Pétillon accepted the post on the promise of immunity from partisan politics. He formed a working party whose report would recommend a colonial policy satisfactory to Congolese aspirations, to all three Belgian parties, and to world opinion. Ryckmans became chairman of the working party, but soon was too ill to continue. It devolved on Pétillon to finish the report just before Christmas, six weeks after party pressure had forced him out of the colonial ministry.

During the last seven years of his active career, Ryckmans added to his United Nations duties those of Belgium's atomic energy commissioner. His objective was to expend for economically constructive purposes the ingenuity and resources already being squandered on nuclear devices in fighting the cold war.

Pierre Ryckmans is today in Geneva, heading the Belgian delegation to the international conference on peaceful uses of atomic energy. . . . He has already negotiated a Belgian-American agreement on atomic energy and its sources. . . . Many Belgians do not know his position because its holder is extremely modest. But if you speak of plutonium, reactor, neutron, enriched uranium, or cyclotron, he will listen attentively and respond point by point with evident command of his subject. . . . Enthusiast, idealist, but also a realist, he is harnessed to his task with the faith that moves mountains.[52]

Having turned over to others his United Nations responsibilities, Ryckmans made what proved to be his last transatlantic round trip (January 18–February 3, 1958) in order to attend the installation of Brazil's first atomic reactor. The Brussels World's Fair was due to open that April, and during its planning Ryckmans was consulted on matters such as the radiation hazard to the public from exhibiting an operating reactor and the choice of the exposition's emblem. Such a reactor was displayed, after reassurance as to its safety, and later was sent to the new University of Lovanium just outside Léopoldville for its physics department.

Postscript

In mid-October, after Ryckmans had undergone surgery and six weeks of hospitalization, he declined the offer of the title of baron. He was able to see a few relatives and friends through the Christmas season; then the entries in his journal cease, just short of the Léopoldville riots of January 4–7 and the king's announcement on the thirteenth that Belgium would lead the Congo to independence "without fatal delays, but without thoughtless haste." He died on February 18, 1959.

Before the Congo's independence on June 30, 1960, two of Ryckmans's sons were active territorial administrators—Jean-Pierre at thirty-three in Ruanda-Urundi and André, thirty-one, in the lower Congo. Much as their father had done a generation earlier, they were learning at close range the needs and feelings of ordinary people rather than judging by the words of a few elite leaders. André was aware that the new Congo republic—convulsed from birth by the power struggle among its president, prime minister, and others—would lack the means to govern effectively at the territorial level; so he and another Belgian administrator decided some weeks before the deadline to hand authority to the most able local black, remaining to help and advise as long as they were needed. When the July mutiny of the Force publique (renamed Armée nationale congolaise) spread to his region, André was one of the Europeans mistakenly gunned down. King Baudouin expressed the national sense of bereavement by conferring the posthumous title of count simultaneously on both father and son.[53]

Belgium no longer wields sovereignty over the Congo (Zaire since 1971) or trusteeship over Rwanda and Burundi. Hence Ryckmans's legacy cannot be summarized by pointing out his contributions to an operating colonial system. This is not to deplore the waste of his talents on a cause with so little future—though such was implied by two writers who claimed that Belgian colonialists, being subservient to capitalist corporations, always kept African laborers overworked and underpaid; they cited Ryckmans to "prove" their contention.[54] Today, more than thirty years after thousands of people bade him an affectionate farewell, in Zaire he is still spoken of as their friend. On November 30, 1973, in a speech not generally marked by gratitude to Belgians or their institutions, General Mobutu praised Ryckmans as "a voice in the desert" because he tried after the war to persuade Belgium to repay the colony adequately for its contribution to that victory.[55]

A biography of Ryckmans should evaluate his career less on the basis of the transitory nature of what he accomplished and more in terms of his character. His patriotism grew from a love for the Belgian land of his birth, through an intense emotional tie with Belgian Africa as his adopted country, to his eventual identification with all humanity. What he said and wrote was the sincere expression of what he thought and was; the tenets of his faith, experience, and reason inspired his day-to-day conduct. Ryckmans was without pretense, a man *tout d'une pièce*. He had integrity.[56]

Notes

1. In 1830 the Belgians rebelled against their post-Napoleonic union with the Dutch. A convention chosen by 30,000 electors wrote a constitution and then named Leopold I (1831–1865) of Saxe-Coburg-Gotha as king. He swore to observe, defend, and transmit the constitution to his heirs: Leopold II (1865–1909), Albert (1909–1934), Leopold III (1934–1940; still living), and Baudouin (1951 to date).

2. See Jean Stengers, "The Congo Free State and the Belgian Congo before 1914," in L. H. Gann and Peter Duignan, eds., *Colonialism in Africa* (Cambridge, 1969), 1:261-292; Jean Stengers, "Quand Léopold II s'est-il rallié à l'annexion du Congo par la Belgique?" *Bulletin de l'Institut royal colonial belge* 23 (1952):783-824; A Stenmans, *La Reprise du Congo par la Belgique: Essai d'histoire parlementaire et diplomatique* (Brussels, 1949); W. B. Norton, *A Belgian Socialist Critic of Colonialism: Louis Bertrand, 1856-1943* (Brussels, 1965).

3. For Ruanda-Urundi history in the long view see Wm. Roger Louis, *Ruanda-Urundi, 1884-1919* (Oxford, 1963); W. B. Norton, "Belgium's Mandate for Ruanda-Urundi," *Boston University Graduate Journal* 6 (December 1957):39-46, 55-59; René Lemarchand, *Rwanda and Burundi* (New York, 1970).

4. Ministre des colonies, *Rapport sur l'administration belge des terres occupées de l'Est africain allemand et spécialement du Ruanda et de l'Urundi* (Brussels, 1921); for its reception see Commission permanente des mandats, *Procès-verbal de la première session tenue à Genève du 4 au 8 octobre 1921* (Geneva, 1922), pp. 28-30.

5. The words "colonie" and "colonisateur" should not, strictly speaking, have been used. But here in embryo was the idea that a decade later Ryckmans was to publicize under the caption *dominer pour servir* as equally applicable to the Congo and the mandate. In 1921 "colonialism" had not yet become an epithet. It would be an anachronism to say that Belgium, in hoping to *share* the benefits that an improved colony *or* mandate might yield, was confessing some kind of guilt.

6. See Belgian Parliament, *Annales, session extraordinaire 1925* (Brussels, 1925), pp. 428-429 (Senate), 524-528, 584-585 (Chamber of Representatives); Commission permanente des mandats, *Procès- verbal, 7e session, octobre 1925* (Geneva, 1926), pp. 52-61, 215.

7. Commission permanente des mandats, *Procès-verbal, 11e session, juin–juillet 1927* (Geneva, 1928), pp. 11-200.

8. Information from the Ryckmans family, with dates verified from the members' handbook, *Le Parlement belge*, G. Pulings (1925 ed.), Léon Troclet (1930 ed.), Paul Van Molle (1972 ed.)

9. In Ruanda the only durable and satisfactory arrangement Belgium ever reached with Musinga, its king, was his "retirement" in 1931 in favor of his twenty-one-year-old son, Charles Mutara Rudahigwa, to the relief of the Permanent Mandates Commission.

10. Incidents condensed, partly from radio talks in Pierre Ryckmans, *Allo! Congo! Le Congo vous parle: Chroniques radiophoniques* (Brussels, 1934), pp. 67–68; partly from idem, *Dominer pour servir* (Brussels, 1931), p. 112.

11. Biographical sketch of Ryckmans by Léo Pétillon, *Biographie nationale* 34 (Brussels, 1968):693–710.

12. Ryckmans, *Dominer pour servir, La Politique coloniale* (Brussels, 1934), and *Allo! Congo!*

13. Idem, *Politique coloniale*, pp. 9, 17, 18–23.

14. Ibid., p. 117.

15. Twenty-two years older than Ryckmans, Tilkens had gone to the Congo during World War I as chief of staff to General Tombeur, hero of Belgium's campaign through Ruanda-Urundi to capture Tabora. Tilkens worked closely with Minister of colonies Tschoffen on a thorough reorganization of the Congo administration. *Biographie belge d'outre-mer* 6 (1967):1004–1011.

16. Marzorati survived a severe attack of typhoid in 1929 that ended his African career; he was active and influential in Belgian circles concerned with the Congo until his death in 1955.

17. Fuchs (1912–1916), Henry (1916–1921), Lippens (1921–1923), Rutten (1923–1927), and Tilkens (1927–1934). Jungers (1946–1951), Pétillon (1951–1958), and Cornélis (1958–1960). A total of thirteen viceroys, of whom Ryckmans was the tenth—eighth of the eleven Belgians.

18. Two royal orders—*arrêtés royaux*—one on the administrative and the other on the territorial reorganization of the colony, both dated 29 June 1933, are in Congo belge, *Bulletin officiel*, 1933, part 1, pp. 473–507; see Minister of colonies Tschoffen's summary of the reforms in *Rapport annuel*, 1933 (Brussels, 1933), pp. 5–6, and Tilkens's summary in his *Allocution* of July 1934, pp. 21–24.

19. The eight discourses of 1935–1939 and 1941–1943 were printed currently in Léopoldville; they were collected and published with Ryckmans's farewell speech, "Vers l'avenir" (5 July 1946), in Pierre Ryckmans, *Etapes et jalons* (Brussels, 1946).

20. Ibid., pp. 115–116.

21. Pierre Ryckmans, *Messages de guerre* (Brussels, 1945), pp. 9–12 (3 September 1939), 13–14 (10 May 1940).

22. Ibid., pp. 18–20.

23. Ibid., pp. 182 (7 June 1944), 189 (23 August 1944), 191 (4 September 1944), 193–194 (21 September 1944), 195 (15 November 1944).

24. Ryckmans, *Etapes et jalons*, pp. 145–146.

25. George Martelli, *Leopold to Lumumba: A History of the Belgian Congo, 1877–1960* (London, 1962), pp. 194–203; David E. Lilienthal, *The Journals of David E. Lilienthal*, vol. 2: *The Atomic Energy Years, 1945–1950* (New York, 1964):437–438.

26. Pétillon, who was a close colleague of Ryckmans's from early 1939 to 1946, called him "un homme bâti pour diriger et commander, beaucoup moins pour obéir, encore moins pour collaborer." Some found him "trop individualiste et aimant trop le paradoxe pour ne pas dévier parfois de la ligne qu'on s'attendait à le voir suivre. . . . Bienveillant . . . cependant un chef difficile qui . . . empêchait ses proches de sentir sur quel pied il leur fallait danser." Pétillon, *Biographie nationale*, pp. 703-708.

27. Ryckmans, *Etapes et jalons*, pp. 163-180.

28. "Monseigneur Jean Félix de Hemptinne, vicaire apostolique du Katanga, le plus combatif de nos prélats," *Pourquoi Pas? Congo* (Léopoldville), no. 76 (16 July 1951), pp. 1767-1768.

29. To quote *Pourquoi Pas? Congo*, in the two months before this letter reached London it was "leaked all around the Congo." A version was printed as "Le Congo belge pendant la guerre, un son de cloche assez pessimiste," in the Belgian *Bulletin des vétérans coloniaux* (August 1945), pp. 4-8.

30. In his journal Ryckmans made a dozen entries regarding the problem between mid-January and February 9, 1944; they showed him working alone or conferring with advisors on the average of three to four times a week.

31. Ryckmans, *Etapes et jalons*, pp. 183-184, 198.

32. Pierre-François Boisson, who had come to Brazzaville only the preceding year, in 1940 wavered before deciding to accept the post of French West African high commissioner offered by Vichy.

33. Félix Eboué, a black born in French Guiana, had been governor of Chad; in August 1940 he was the first administrator of such high rank in Africa to declare for de Gaulle and against Vichy, thus saving all four provinces of French Equatorial Africa for the Free or Fighting French movement.

34. Pleven was de Gaulle's principal advisor (1941–1944) on colonial policy and one of many French prime ministers of the Fourth Republic.

35. Extracted from Ryckmans's journal.

36. In 1946, after three colonial office changes, one of the ministers telephoned from Brussels to say that the Congo's participation in the victory parade then being organized "is reduced from the expected thirty to only six people."

37. Text of the royal order in Congo belge, *Bulletin officiel*, 1945, pp. 224–230.

38. See figure 1 for local as well as central and provincial councils. By 1957 this evolving political framework for a Belgo-Congolese community enabled Africans, by voting and running for office, to rise as high in government as their ability and dedication might carry them.

39. Ryckmans was succeeded by Eugène Jungers, three years his senior and vice–governor-general of Ruanda-Urundi from 1932 to 1946. The complex task was shared by Léo Pétillon, vice–governor-general under Jungers, who became governor-general himself late in 1951. Most provincial governors first met their reorganized councils in May or June of 1946 or 1947.

40. Ryckmans, *Etapes et jalons*, pp. 201–225.

41. Presentation of the medal was made on August 12, 1946, at the American embassy in Brussels by Ambassador Alan G. Kirk.

42. Pierre Ryckmans, *A l'autre bout du monde* (Brussels, 1948).

43. "Les Colonies dans le monde actuel," in idem, *Dominer pour servir*, rev. ed. (Brussels, 1948), pp. 11–74.

44. Ibid., p. 6.

45. Ibid., p. 65. In a later, concise exposition of the thesis, he hinted at "thirty years" as the period within which peaceful and constructive independence could be achieved; idem, "Belgian 'Colonialism,'" *Foreign Affairs* 34 (October 1955):89–101.

46. Idem, *Dominer pour servir*, rev. ed., pp. 11–12, 53–56.

47. United Nations Charter, article 73, the first of the two articles in chapter XI.

48. Pierre Ryckmans, "La Thèse belge devant l'ONU," *Société royale belge des ingénieurs et des industriels, Bulletin (mensuel)* (February 1954):78–85; *Institut royal colonial belge, Mémoires*, vol. 37, no. 4: Fernand van Langenhove, *La Question des aborigènes aux Nations unies: La Thèse belge* (Brussels, 1954); Joseph L. Kunz, "Chapter XI of the UN Charter in Action," *American Journal of International Law* 48 (1954):103–110.

49. Ryckmans, *Etapes et jalons*, pp. 203–215.

50. Idem, *Dominer pour servir*, rev. ed., p. 73.

51. Léo Pétillon, *Témoignage et réflexions* (Brussels, 1967), especially the essays on the Belgo-Congolese community, pp. 287–325, and on the report of the working group and its recommendations, pp. 92–102.

52. Condensed from an article by G. P. in *Le Phare de dimanche* (Brussels), 21 August 1955, pp. 1–2.

53. Jean Kestergat, *André Ryckmans* (Brussels, 1961); Pétillon, *Biographie nationale*, p. 709; A. Gille, *Biographie belge d'outre-mer* 7 (1974):426.

54. Pierre Joye and Rosina Lewin, *Les Trusts au Congo* (Brussels, 1961), pp. 56–301. Joye is identified as "a high official in the Belgian Communist party" by Crawford Young, *Politics in the Congo* (Princeton, 1965), p. 18.

55. See *Elima*, successor to *Courrier d'Afrique* (Léopoldville), 3 December 1973.

56. Jean M. Jadot, "Pierre Ryckmans," *Académie royale des sciences d'outre-mer, Bulletin des séances* 6 (1960):135-170; pp. 162–170 list all of Ryckmans's published writings.

Portugal

Portuguese Colonial Governors in Africa, 1870-1974

Douglas L. Wheeler

IN 1974 and 1975 independence came to Portuguese-speaking Africa. The new African governments of Angola and Mozambique pulled down and carted away the statues of Portugal's colonial governors and soldiers. A reappraisal of the place of these governors in history now seems appropriate.

Portuguese colonialism in the modern era was motivated largely by an intense nationalism. A small elite of colonialists sought national prestige for a tiny, weak, and insecure country whose era of world power had long passed. By 1870 Portugal feebly but persistently held coastal enclaves in West and East Africa. At the end of the nineteenth century Portugal extended its dominions into the interior, and patriots intended to attempt in Africa what could not be done in Europe: retribution against stronger powers such as neighboring Spain and against England for Britain's ultimatum of 1890. This was also a drive toward national revival during an insecure phase of Portuguese history. As one colonialist wrote in 1909, Portugal's colonies were responsible for "our autonomous existence."[1]

Colonialism, too, became increasingly intertwined with Portuguese domestic politics, highly personalistic and often intensely factional. Modern Portuguese colonialism began to assume its post-1930 features just at a time of great political crisis. The country was experiencing a painful and turbulent transition from constitutional monarchy to parliamentary republic. Though colonial activity was viewed by some as a cause for national pride, the credit for colonial work was ap-

415

propriated by individuals, by political factions and parties, and, indeed, by regimes and governments. In the 1870s African colonial questions first came to the fore in the rise and fall of governments on parliamentary votes and debates. In the press, colonial questions found more coverage. It is no coincidence, then, that colonial issues became deeply involved in each major turning point in modern Portuguese politics. This was manifest in the crises of 1820–1822, 1834, 1890, 1910, 1926, and, most recently, April 1974, when a military coup by returned "African" officers overthrew the so-called New State, then the West's oldest dictatorship.

Not only were colonial issues considered important, but they were manipulated in struggles for power. During the troubled reign of King Carlos I (1889–1908), the monarchy and its allies used colonial activity and the popular glory of military victories in the colonies in order to bolster a regime of waning prestige and cohesion. After the monarchy fell and the first republic (1910–1926) was established, republican politicians and politics fully appropriated colonialism and colonial issues as their own. Republican politicans, statesmen, and governors laid the foundations of the "institutionalized, nationalist" colonialism of the post-1926 New State dictatorship. The New State made great efforts to encourage participation in colonialism by the elite and the masses as leaders, soldiers, or settlers. By the early twentieth century it was clear that attention to colonial developments and the defense of the colonies had become essential to political survival, whether under a democratic republic, which ultimately collapsed, or under the more centralized, authoritarian New State.

Under Portuguese dictatorship from 1926 to 1974, especially in the first thirty years—the more vigorous years of the regime—the government officially appropriated colonialism as a political prop, a diversion for a divided elite and a backward mass, and a convenient if demanding rallying ground for factious groups and individuals. As an engine of homegrown national pride and nationalism, colonial programs were always defended as an essential—and traditional—means of national revival or survival. The colonial mission freely suggested in 1900 was in 1930 and 1940 centrally managed, organized, and staged as a national cause. Portugal's colonial heroes were carefully selected and cultivated. The institutionalization of free, amateur colonialism, as it were, was a major feature of the dictatorship and had important consequences in Africa.

Governorships and Power Sharing

As an institution, the colonial governorship was influenced by the evolution of domestic administration and political trends, by the situation in the colony involved, and by the hundreds of individuals who headed the administration of the African colonies over the centuries. Chief problems of the institution were the struggle between the remote Lisbon government and the perceived needs of the governor to solve problems and to carry out programs or plans and the lack of continuity in administration. These problems were never solved to the satisfaction of the parties involved and indeed they were exacerbated both by traditional political factors in Africa—factionalism and personalism (the allegiance to persons over ideas and institutions)—and by a rigid, sometimes hostile Lisbon bureaucracy that wished to centralize colonial government in the metropole.

The title "governor-general" replaced that of "captain-general" in 1836, and the Lisbon government allowed governors considerable freedom in political and legislative matters; in most cases they were given military command of local garrisons. Until the Organic Charter of December 1, 1869, there was no formal delineation of gubernatorial powers. The 1869 charter was intended to modernize colonial administration and to decentralize decisionmaking. Governors were to delegate judicial power to certain officials appointed in Lisbon and to listen to local opinion on a council or commission. Centralization of decisionmaking, not decentralization, resulted. By the 1880s the powers of the governors were hedged in by Lisbon regulations, especially in financial and economic matters. Although the distance between Lisbon and the colonies and communication problems favored governors' freedom to act in some cases, the ministry of marine and colonies during the years 1869–1894 consolidated effective power of decision in Lisbon. The Conselho Ultramarino, revived as a colonial advisory body in 1851, was renamed the Junta Consultiva do Ultramar in 1868 and given less power. In effect, the ministry, with strong naval traditions, retained power, while frustrated colonialists complained.

Governors had a difficult, dangerous, and exasperating job. In Angola, for example, they suffered from bad health brought on by the climate and diseases and were in danger from hostile Africans. Most governors between 1834 and 1910 did not complete their regular three-year terms and were replaced by interim officials or committees. Though the governor was the highest Portuguese official representative, pay was not attractive; there were sometimes dangerous military operations to command; and much time was spent on petty details. Angolan governors after the 1850s, for instance, spent a lot of time dealing with petitions from hordes of white convicts, the ubiquitous *degredado* population of felons transported from Portugal and the islands.[2] Time for pursuing colonial improvements was in short supply, as were funds.

The importance of governorship as an institution can be partially analyzed by determining the rank of persons who held this office. Until the late nineteenth century, eminent metropolitan Portuguese usually did not become colonial governors in Africa. Before the 1890s most such governors were professional military officers, some naval, some army, who made a certain sacrifice in changing jobs. Colonial governorships at that time were rarely a springboard to top positions in the government. It is true that one eminent colonial governor who served in both Angola and Mozambique in the 1850s and 1860s, Brigadier general José Coelho do Amaral, was briefly a minister of marine and colonies, but his was an unusual case.

After 1890 this situation began to change. Following the popular surge of renewed colonial fervor and the "pacification" campaigns in Mozambique and Angola, the colonial cause reached a fever pitch of publicity in Portugal; the monarchist cabinets at last began to take colonial administration more seriously. The ministry of marine was reorganized to give more attention to colonial problems, and a number of first-class soldiers and civilian officials were sent out to "save" the colonies from threats, both internal and foreign, and to lay the basis of a modern colonial system. In 1892 and again in 1894–1895 the government appointed an eminent intellectual and politician, António Ennes, to be royal commissioner of Mozambique. His appointment signaled the beginning of a new phase of colonial rule: a trend toward decentralization and official emphasis on colonial efforts.

What powers did the governors exercise and how did the balance of powers between the metropole and the African colonial heads change over time? Five chronological periods may be identified:

1822–1894: increasing centralization of Lisbon control in ministry of marine and overseas; governors' initiative reduced

1894–1920: transition era to greater power for colonial governors; decentralization of control from Lisbon

1920–1930: zenith of devolution of powers to newly created high commissioners in both Angola and Mozambique; local autonomy

1930–1963: New State dictatorship reasserts full powers of control; centralization in ministry of colonies (overseas after 1951); high commissionerships abolished

1963–1974: some devolution of powers and decisionmaking to local colonial officials and representative bodies; military garrisons under separate commanders; incipient colonial federalism, especially beginning with Caetano's constitutional revisions in 1971

In the first period, governors enjoyed the autonomy that distance and communication problems fostered. In Angola, for example, the turnaround time for correspondence between governors and the ministry was four months. Governors' initiatives were small, and Lisbon legislation treated all colonies as virtually identical. As pressures rose for action in the expansion of Portuguese control and administration, governors protested about the indifference, inefficiency, and ignorance of the remote Lisbon bureaucrats. A governor-general in Angola complained in a letter to the minister of marine and overseas in 1877: "Whoever has lived for a long time in these lands cannot have much faith in promises."[3]

The ministry of marine and overseas (known as the colonial ministry at various times before 1911, when a separate ministry of colonies was established) increasingly assumed tighter control over colonial administration until 1894. At that time, the Lisbon government appointed a royal Commissioner, with unusually wide powers of civil and military initiative, for Mozambique. This marked the beginning of a transition era; under the administration of António Ennes there developed a tendency to allow the governors greater local discretion. Still, the Lisbon government remained jealous of its control over the colonies in Africa, and the national hero, Major Joaquim Mousinho de Albuquerque, had his extraordinary powers as royal commissioner withdrawn in a disputed incident in 1898.

Under the first parliamentary republic (1910–1926), the institution of colonial governorship took on a new importance. This was a time of the more important military campaigns of pacification in the hinterland of the colonies and of combat against German forces that invaded Portuguese Africa from neighboring colonies. The republican regime and its politicians were pledged to allow greater decentralization of control in the colonies. Via 1914 and 1920 laws, following outlines in the 1911 constitution, the colonies were granted greater autonomy and governors more power and initiative. The zenith of this administrative trend came in 1920, when the Parliament established high commissionerships for both Angola and Mozambique, the major African territories. High commissioners were given unusually wide authority in finance and economics: they had total control over the colony's budget, with little or no involvement from the Lisbon ministry of colonies; moreover, they could appoint large numbers of colonial officials, sign commercial contracts of unlimited size without Lisbon's approval, and arrange for foreign loans in order to develop colonial economies. These prerogatives of the new colonial proconsuls were the historic ne plus ultra of the devolution of powers from Lisbon control.

After abolition of the high commissionerships by the Colonial Act of 1930, Portuguese colonial governors never again enjoyed the same autonomy. Economic and financial irregularities—in Portugal and in its major colonies—were both a cause and a symptom of the collapse of the parliamentary republic and the rise of a conservative, authoritarian regime, the New State. After 1930 colonial governors were allowed only the initiative of pre–1894 governors, including precedence over military commanders. Lisbon reassumed tight control over colonial budgets, financing, loans, and development. The bold concepts of the ephemeral high commissionerships were largely shelved until after World War II, when home finances were stronger and the regime felt more secure. In the fourth period, 1930–1963, the New State thus exercised very close control over the governors and the minister of colonies retained authority over vital decisions. Although the governor-generalship remained the highest colonial office (carrying a four-year tenure), few governors benefited from the continuity of more than one term and they were rarely instrumental in determining key directions of colonial administration, which were set by the central cabinet (council of ministers) and the ministry of colonies.

The wars of African insurgency, beginning in 1961 in Angola, had an impact upon the division of powers between the metropole and the colonies. Conflicting pressures influenced the Lisbon government. On the one hand, there was pressure from colonials, colonists, and officials on the spot to develop economies rapidly, to increase social services, and to allow the locals the say that Lisbon had denied them effectively since 1930. On the other, there were nationalist pressures to restrict local autonomy and the initiative of Lisbon's governors for fear of encouraging separatist or independence movements and the eventual breakdown of the empire.

After 1961 economic expansion in the colonies and nationalist insurgent warfare in rural areas combined to reduce the governors-generals' powers. Except for a few special appointments of high-powered military figures like generals Spínola in Guinea (1968–1973) and Kaúlza de Arriaga in Mozambique (1970–1973), there was a diminution of gubernatorial power and authority. Lisbon's plans for greater foreign investment, rural development, social welfare, and education created an increasingly large bureaucracy of officials who moved between Lisbon and the provinces. The overseas ministry made major policy decisions and tried to supervise and manage in the field by means of inspection and regulation. After the Caetano government had entered office and brought about a devolution of power to provincial and local bodies, the governors' prerogatives were further decreased. The final impact came from the counterinsurgency war and the growth of a Lisbon military establishment in each province. In Angola after 1962, for example, the governor-general was not the de facto commanding officer of the larger armed forces; a high-ranking officer—whose rank was usually much higher than that of

Figure 1

*Organization of a Portuguese Overseas Provincial
Administration in the Mid-1960s*

Appointed by

Movement of orders
information, advice

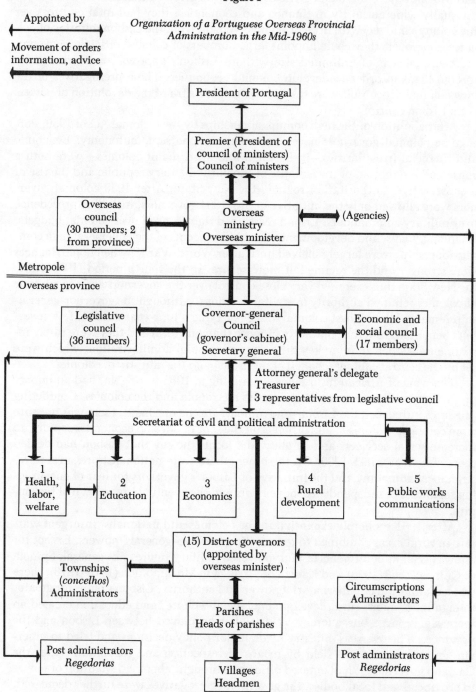

SOURCE: Adapted from Allison Butler Herrick et al., *Area Handbook for Angola* (no. 550–59)
(Washington, D.C., 1967), pp. 194–202, David M. Abshire and Michael A. Samuels,
eds., *Portuguese Africa: A Handbook* (New York, 1969), pp. 143–249.

the governor—commanded those forces. This commander was in fact responsible not to the overseas minister or to the governor-general but to the Lisbon minister of national defense. Thus, in various ways the governor's office lost ground (see Figure 1 and Table 1).

The regime responded to such pressures during 1963–1974 with measures designed to satisfy more than one group of discontents. Governors-general were en-

Table 1.   Survey of Overseas Administration

Overseas minister (appointed by premier in Lisbon)

General responsibility for overseas administration
Maintains inspectors and inspectorate of overseas
Maintains various overseas ministry agencies
Oversees all relations between metropole and overseas provinces
Appoints and manages overseas (general) civil service, legal system, and public works
Controls overseas budget
May cancel decisions of governors-general and/or legislative councils
Mediates disputes between provincial governments and metropole or between elements within provinces
Appoints (with premier's approval, president's signature) governors-general of overseas provinces who are responsible to minister; appoints district governors
Decisions have force of law, published in official bulletin of overseas province
Powers of decree law, as in 1961 crisis in Angola
Names about half of overseas advisory council

Governor-general (appointed by overseas minister, approved by council of ministers)

Responsible for general administration of his province
Chief representative of Portugal and of overseas minister
Highest official in province; highest salary (in mid-1960s roughly 50,000 escudos a month, or about $2,000)
Appoints overseas civil servants below district level
Carries out orders of overseas minister
Legislative powers during nine months when legislative council not in session
Presides over legislative council and economic and social council
Names heads of six secretariats in capital
Controls his government council or cabinet
May dissolve legislative council at any time
Extensive emergency powers; may not declare war, command armed forces (after 1962), or make peace and treaties (these prerogatives belong to president of Portugal and commander in chief of armed forces in province; in Angola, separate command after 1962).
Controls provincial budget, can make loans with legislative council approval, or not, but with overseas minister's oversight and advice
Chief diplomatic officer in province

Legislative council

Approves provisional budget
Authorizes contracts, loans
Elects two delegates to overseas council in Portugal
Holds sessions lasting three months, maximum
Introduces legislation but cannot submit bills that increase expenditures or decrease revenues

couraged to extend their terms of office beyond four years, but few of them were given actual command of the military garrisons that were fighting the wars. Lisbon allowed the introduction of larger, more representative organs in the colonial capitals—councils and later, in effect, mini-parliaments. But the ministry of overseas still exercised control over major decisions and plans. With the removal of colonially conservative Premier Salazar in the fall of 1968, the Caetano regime allowed a greater devolution of powers to governors and to local bodies. In a 1971 revision of the constitution, the regime attempted to satisfy some demands for colonial autonomy by expanding the representative organs and by holding larger provincial-but-managed elections.

The regime rarely appointed officers of rank higher than lieutenant colonel or colonel to be governors up to 1968, but after that date extraordinary civil and military powers were given to two governors. General António de Spínola in Guinea (Bissau, 1968–1973) and General Kaúlza de Arriaga in Mozambique (1970–1973) were in effect regime high commissioners with wide authority. These officials combined civil powers with command of the armed forces. In the fifth period under consideration, the government's allocation of powers appeared to alternate between an incipient colonial federalism and the backing of powerful executive representatives who, as both governors-general and commanding generals in Lisbon's full confidence, were sanctioned proconsuls. It was hoped that they would turn the tide of African insurgency in Portugal's favor and at the same time exploit the colonies' full economic potential in order to benefit the metropole. Portugal's African empire collapsed following a military coup d'état by junior officers in Lisbon on April 25, 1974. By the end of 1975 all of Portugal's African territories, including Angola (where a bloody civil war raged in 1976), had become independent in agreements that were negotiated under the aegis of a new military but anticolonial Lisbon government.

The Colonial Governors: Backgrounds and Relationships

Who were the governors? Whereas pre–1870 governors of the African colonies included a few politically appointed officials and titled aristocrats and notables sent out from Lisbon, the institution of governorship in Africa was dominated by professional military officers. A good number of them before the end of the 1870s were naval officers, but the requirements of the land based military campaigns of occupation and pacification during 1880–1920 solidified the army officer corps' claim to a monopoly of the office. And a law passed in 1922 required that governors of African colonies be "professional military men."[4] Of forty-seven regular governors-general who served in Angola from 1854 to 1974, only a handful were not from the military.

Nearly all the so-called heroes of Africa of the famous "generation of 1895," those who played a role in subduing Gungunyane's Gaza empire, were professional army officers. This included, of course, Portugal's most celebrated and decorated colonial soldier, Joaquim Mousinho de Albuquerque, appointed royal commissioner and governor-general of Mozambique in 1896. The central role of army officers was further entrenched during the military dictatorship (1926–1933) following the collapse of the first republic. The New State regime (1933–1974), although dominated by civilian administrators at top levels, found a key place for professional soldiers in the colonies.

Few civilians were appointed colonial governors. Among this small group were António Ennes, named in 1892 and again in 1894–1895 royal commissioner of Mozambique, and sometime politician-writer-physician Brito Camacho, who was high commissioner of Mozambique from 1921 to 1923. (Camacho was also, however, a reserve officer in the army medical corps.)

The quality of the officers named to governorships markedly improved beginning in the late nineteenth century, often in response to critical problems. Officers of higher quality and professional competence were appointed during crises such as the occupation and military pacification of 1885–1920, World War I, and the wars of African nationalist insurgency (1961–1974). Table 2 illustrates how army officers dominated the colonial governorships in Angola, Mozambique, and Guinea under the New State.

Table 2. Governors-general and Their Occupations in the Major African Colonies, 1926–1974[1]

Angola (1927–1974)			
Governors-general listed	17		
		Military officers	13
Governors for whom there		Army	8
are biographical data	15	Navy	4
		Air force	1
		Civilians	2
		Law	1
		Engineering	1
Mozambique (1926–1974)			
Governors-general listed	9		
		Military officers	5
Governors for whom there		Army	3
are biographical data	7	Navy	2
		Civilians	2
		Law	1
		Medicine	1
Guinea (Bissau, 1927–1974)			
Governors-general listed	13		
		Military officers	8
Governors for whom there		Army	7
are biographical data	8	Navy	1
		Civilians	0

[1]This list of governors-general excludes temporary, part-time, "interim" governors who served only briefly.

SOURCES: Governors' biographies in *Grande Enciclopedia Portuguesa e Brasileira* (Lisbon, 1900–1945, 40 vols.); Centro de Informação e Turismo de Angola *Enciclopedia Luso-Brasileira da Cultura*; *Governadores-Gerais e Outras Entidades de Função Governativa da Província de Angola* (Luanda, 1964); David P. Henige, *Colonial Governors from the Fifteenth Century to the Present: A Comprehensive List* (Madison, 1970), pp. 252–253; and notes by the author on governors under the Caetano regime, 1968–1974.

Despite their common military beginnings, governors differed in social and educational background. Many but not all of them were of middle-class origin, like most of the officer corps by the end of the nineteenth century. Some came from upper middle-class or upper class families and grew up on aristocratic rural family estates. A few, Mousinho de Albuquerque and Aires D'Ornellas, for example, were linked to old aristocratic, landed families; Aires D'Ornellas was, by birthright, a peer of the realm. Others like Norton de Matos (1867–1955) and Spínola (1910–) were sons of urban merchant families. A number of professional officers—sons of career officers or public functionaries based in Lisbon—were graduates of the secondary level military course in the Military Academy or Military College, and began to serve as novice soldiers in units between the ages of fourteen and seventeen.

In the last half century of the second empire (1920–1974) there were governors who had not graduated from a university but from army or navy service schools and special technical institutions. During the "generation of 1870" some officers attended Lisbon's technical college, Escola Politécnia. Officers of the "generation of 1895" who were appointed governors in Angola and Mozambique during the years 1896–1910 had been trained in the sciences, with special emphasis upon mathematics, navigation, astronomy for naval officers, surveying and geography, engineering, and hydrography for army officers. After 1911 and the establishment of regular universities in Lisbon and Oporto, there were governors who had attended or graduated from science programs at Coimbra University.

The educational preparation of the governors emphasized science, especially in the period before the first republic (1910–1926), when governors from more diverse social and educational backgrounds were appointed. A leading colonialist-geographer Ernesto Vasconcellos, permanent secretary of the Lisbon Geography Society, suggested in a 1911 newspaper interview on the colonial question that it was essential for colonial officials—in view of the need to develop, not just to pacify, the colonies—to be "real specialists."[5] Although the government established, with the aid of the Lisbon Geography Society, the Escola Colonial in 1906, its impact on the colonial governors was minimal. An increasing number of low- and middle-level colonial administrators, especially in the 1930s and 1940s, were graduates of this school, as were over a fourth of the colonial administrative cadre in the African territories by the mid-1960s.[6] Yet the top administrators were either civilians or military professional officers who had not been trained as colonial "specialists."

The New State dictatorship through legislation in the 1950s and 1960s attempted to upgrade the educational qualifications of the higher colonial officials by requiring, for example, that fifty percent of the district governorships be reserved for intendants and inspectors with university degrees. Nevertheless, most governors continued to be professional military men first and colonial experts second. Governors acquired their expertise through experience, as was traditional in the history of Portuguese Africa. Some of the twentieth-century governors were political appointees under the republic and under the early years of the dictatorship; most officers, however, were nominated by the ministry of colonies for their professional competence within their service or branch.

Except under crisis conditions, when the territorial or political integrity of the empire was imperiled, Lisbon ordinarily did not appoint the highest ranking officers to governorships. Thus, generals and colonels were sent to combat Germans or rebellious Africans in Angola and Mozambique between 1914 and 1920, but in peacetime the assignments went to run-of-the-mill majors and lieutenant colonels, the rank of most governors during the period 1930–1961.

The Salazar regime was reluctant to appoint the rare general officers who might become national heroes and challenge the home civilian hierarchy. After the political demise of the old premier, Lisbon made unusually high-level appointments and promotions. And several governors-general returned as potential contenders, jockeyed for political power, and launched political careers on the basis of their colonial records, among them Spínola and Kaúlza de Arriaga. Both officers were involved in efforts to overthrow Caetano and to assume high political posts. After the military coup of April 25, 1974, Spínola served as president of the republic for five months.

Yet, as I have already indicated, an African colonial governorship rarely was a steppingstone to high political office in the metropole. The Lisbon bureaucracy and not a few politicians—whether under the constitutional monarchy, the first parliamentary republic, or the dictatorship—traditionally resented, feared, and impeded colonial heroes of Africa in their careers. General Alves Roçadas and General Gomes da Costa, both veterans of the key colonial campaigns during 1895–1915, were candidates for heading military coups in 1926 (Gomes da Costa survived Roçadas to carry out the coup, only to be deposed weeks later by a younger general, Carmona). Others, such as Norton de Matos, were top officials in political parties and became cabinet ministers and candidates for the presidency.

The Colonial Governors in Perspective

The Portuguese governors in Africa had diverse beliefs and backgrounds but confronted similar problems as administrators. Many complained of lack of support in Lisbon, of lack of resources, and of hostility or indifference from local populations, both settlers and Africans.

The question of power sharing over time became complicated by the bureaucratic factor. The governors of the "generation of 1895" complained of an ignorant, remote, and inflexible Lisbon establishment; one law decreed that governors could not correspond with any Lisbon official other than the minister of colonies. The trend in the twentieth century was away from the individual governor's taking the initiative to his playing a role in the growing bureaucracy. A look at the numbers of functionaries in the ministry of colonies during the course of seventy years tells an important story: from a staff of 77 in the mid-1890s, the secretariat of overseas grew to over 40,000 in the late 1960s.[7]

As governors' jobs became more complex and their staffs larger, their power was less absolute. During most of the period of the constitutional monarchy (1834–1910), governors, by default, had considerable leeway in running the colonies, while the governments in Lisbon increasingly appropriated policymaking powers. Colonial autonomy, gubernatorial initiative, and decentralization of control were the holy grails of the colonialists of the "generation of 1895." During the era of the high commissioners (1920–1930), while Portugal was in transition from a turbulent parliamentary republic to a military backed dictatorship, governors enjoyed possibly the greatest measure of individual initiative and power in the history of Angola and Mozambique. But the New State abolished this policy and concentrated all significant powers in Lisbon in the council of ministers (cabinet) and in the ministry of colonies.

The final phase of the governors' roles came about after the April 25, 1974, coup that began the decolonization of the Portuguese territories in Africa.[8] On paper, the military dominated new regime in Lisbon increased the authority of the governors; the high commissionership was revived; and high-ranking officers filled these posts as chief representatives of the president of the republic. The high commissioners were commanders of the Portuguese forces in each colony and were empowered to guarantee peaceful, smooth transitions from colony to independent state. Except for relatively uneventful transitions in Guinea-Bissau (independent September 10, 1974) and in São Tomé–Príncipe (July 12, 1975), the changeover in the other states was fraught with violent conflict. The most costly and tragic episode was in Angola, which suffered the ravages of a bloody civil war among African nationalist movements during the period April 1975–February 1976.

The high commissioners' functions included a crucial military role. But these high-ranking officers discovered that their authority and capacity to influence the situation were limited by many factors during 1974–1975: lack of time to work out agreements; lack of support from the Lisbon government, which was preoccupied with a social and economic revolution at home; the politicization and fragmentation of the armed forces personnel under the high commissioners' commands and the refusal of troops to obey orders; fear among the European settlers; and conflict among rival African nationalist movements. In short, the high commissioners, despite their new rank, lacked the authority and power to contain the forces unleashed by the 1974 revolution.

Notes

1. Loureiro da Fonseca, "A Escola Colonial de Lisboa," *Portugal em Africa* 16, 204 (22 June 1909):177.

2. See Douglas L. Wheeler, "The Portuguese in Angola, 1836–1891: A Study in Expansion and Administration" (Ph.D. dissertation, Boston University, 1963), p. 125.

3. Governor-general Albuquerque to minister of marine, 19 October 1877, pasta 47, Angola, Arquivo Histórico Ultramarino (Lisbon).

4. JOSCIR (1886), p. 144, Law of 19 May 1882, cited)in João José da Silva, ed., *Repertório Alphabético e Chronológico ou Indice Remissivo da Legislação Ultramarina* (Macao, 1886).

5. Interview published in the Lisbon daily *O Século*, 10 April 1911.

6. Norman A. Bailey, "The Political Process and Interest Groups," in *Portuguese Africa: A Handbook*, ed. David M. Abshire and Michael A. Samuels (New York, 1969), p. 149.

7. Abshire and Samuels, *Portuguese Africa*, p. 144, n. 19.

8. For the role and powers of the high commissioners in the brief era of Portuguese decolonization, 1974–1975, see Carlos Benigno da Cruz, *S. Tomé e Príncipe: Do Colonialismo a independência* (Lisbon, 1975), pp. 101–159; Amadeu José de Freitas, *Angola: O Longo Caminho da Liberdade* (Lisbon, 1975), pp. 146–362; *Expresso*, 25 April 1974–11 November 1975; Douglas L. Wheeler, "Angola," *Issue* (African Studies Association) 5, 3 (Fall 1975):21.

Joaquim Mousinho de Albuquerque (1855-1902)

Douglas L. Wheeler

IN the age of Portugal's colonial revival in Africa, Joaquim Mousinho de Albuquerque was the unrivaled colonial soldier. In some respects, this charismatic figure was Portugal's most celebrated colonial soldier of modern times. He did not hold high political office,[1] his highest rank in the army was lieutenant colonel, and his governorship was limited to only two years in one colony. But his imprint upon Portuguese political, military, and colonial history was profound and enduring. He has been remembered chiefly for his role in the 1895 campaign in Mozambique and as a royal commissioner and governor-general of that colony from 1896 to 1898.

The legend of Mousinho de Albuquerque began in Mozambique in the 1890s among the soldier's friends and military companions. In the last years of the constitutional monarchy, following his dramatic suicide in 1902, key members of his Mozambique military staff began the cult of Mousinho. This cult or legend was kept alive by Portuguese monarchists, legitimists, and integralists[2] through the 1920s, when a younger generation of army officers revived interest in the colonial soldier's personality, deeds, and ideas. In the 1930s and 1940s the Portuguese dictatorship, the New State, completed the rehabilitation of the mystical colonial soldier and governor: Mousinho was adopted as the military patron saint, the secular saint, of the regime.

Background for a colonial career, 1855–1890

Joaquim Augusto Mousinho de Albuquerque was born on November 12, 1855, on the estate of Varzea, near Batalha, into a family of the landed upper middle class. His family was staunchly monarchist, religious, and traditional, their life-style austere but comfortable. They were traditionally soldiers, politicians, and writers. Mousinho, as he became known to his friends and to later generations of Portuguese, traced his genealogy back to medieval Portuguese kings and aristocrats. His paternal grandfather, an engineer, was the famous constitutionalist statesman and military officer Luís da Silva Mousinho de Albuquerque (d. 1846), one of Portugal's foremost nineteenth-century statesmen. His father, a professional military officer, José Diogo, was also an engineer of consequence in Portugal's second city, Oporto.

Joaquim, too, chose a military career. At age sixteen, in November 1871, he enrolled as a volunteer recruit in the Fourth Cavalry Regiment. In 1876 he completed the cavalry course at the army school and was commissioned a second lieutenant. From the beginning his great passion in life was the army and being a professional officer, a title he valued more than all his honors and decorations as a colonial hero. While he longed for adventure in Africa, he was a model family man; he married his first cousin; they had no children.

The young officer cut a stunning military figure, one rather unusual in Portugal, where officers tended quickly to become stout. Mousinho's charisma was founded in part upon his appearance—his slim, athletic figure, his military bearing, and his above average height for a Portuguese. In the many portraits and photographs made of Mousinho during his time of celebrity, one can see his thin, angular face, heavy mustache, and the monocle he often wore—in the style of monarchist high society.[3]

Unlike many of his generation of soldiers, Mousinho was able to attend a university, Coimbra, where from 1879 to 1882 he studied mathematics and philosophy. He did not receive a degree but his learning was ample and he was well read in a number of fields, which included the popular novels and essays of Eça de Queiroz, one of Portugal's greatest modern novelists. This background is revealed in his remarkable book *Moçambique, 1896–1898*, published in 1899, wherein he displays considerable literary ability. If Mousinho had not become a soldier, he later claimed, he might have been a writer.

Mousinho de Albuquerque, a "kind of posthumous son of the great Portuguese race of the 15th and 16th centuries,"[4] taught military cadets in Lisbon from 1884 to 1886, and in the latter year was given his first overseas assignment. He served in various posts in Portuguese India: as a superintendent on the Mormugão railroad in Goa and as the second highest official in the colony, secretary of the government-general. His years in Portuguese India, 1886–1890, helped to shape his later colonial career. In India he traveled and read extensively and studied British, Dutch, and French colonial literature. His contact with British colonial models had an impact upon his own later work in Mozambique and influenced his reform ideas and plans. He was widely read in the history of British administration in South Africa and was considered to be a Portuguese expert on South Africa.

Colonial career in Africa, 1890–1898

The Soldier, 1890–1895.   When Mousinho de Albuquerque first set foot in Africa in 1890, the year of the "English ultimatum," Portugal's position as a colonial power was weak and defensive. Though the British ultimatum created a new public and elite interest in the African colonies, Portugal had little effective control over the hinterlands or all of the coasts of present-day Angola and Mozambique. Portuguese patriots feared that Britain, Germany, and France had designs on its weakly held possessions. In East Africa the Portuguese held stubbornly to the coast of Mozambique. It was in the south at the town of Lourenço Marques that economic development and political activity were concentrated, but the capital of the colony was located then on Mozambique Island in the far north. Southern Mozambique was becoming more important because of the economic activity inland associated with the discovery of gold in Transvaal, South Africa, and with the beginning of British–South African colonization and occupation of Rhodesia. Mozambique's economic fortunes rode on the business and transportation coming through the port of Lourenço Marques. Even with this new stimulus many experts on African affairs at the time, and not a few of Portugal's colonial elite, believed that Portugal would sooner or later lose Mozambique to foreign interlopers.

Cavalry captain Mousinho de Albuquerque, fresh from service in Portuguese India, assumed the post of governor of the district of Lourenço Marques on October 25, 1890. Here he first experienced the frustration of the colonial soldier and official at odds with an inert and ineffective bureaucracy both in Africa and in Portugal. The thirty-five-year-old soldier wanted to administer his district in the spirit of those aspects of British colonial administration he admired: pragmatism, efficiency, and decentralization of powers and control, with attention to local needs, not metropolitan biases and interests.

His term as district governor was brief. Mousinho resigned after personal disagreements with the Governor-general Rafael de Andrade, on February 25, 1892, and returned to Portugal. In his first administrative post in Mozambique, however, he demonstrated his character and foreshadowed elements of his later behavior as a senior Portuguese official. As a soldier he was bold and aggressive; despite official cautiousness, Mousinho advocated putting pressure immediately on Chief Gungunyane of Gaza by a show of Portuguese military strength, and in early 1891 he encouraged a force of Portuguese volunteer-adventurers to attack Rhodes's British South Africa Company camps at Macequece. As an administrator he could not get along with his superior, the governor-general, deplored the impotence of the colonial administration, and showed that he could be patriotic, arrogant, and egotistical—but above all, dashing and daring.

In Portugal Mousinho resumed various garrison duties but longed to return to Africa to command, to fight, and to lead an administration. His opportunity came as an outbreak of African insurgency in southern Mozambique prompted the Portuguese government to mount an extraordinary colonial effort. After intensive debates and planning at high levels in Lisbon, the ministry of marine appointed the civilian António Ennes as royal commissioner, with special executive powers, in order to increase Portuguese control and sovereignty in East Africa. Ennes was instructed to deal with what the Portuguese considered to be a direct threat to their control: the African empire of Gungunyane of Gaza

A rising of Africans close to the town of Lourenço Marques aroused Portuguese fears. Some believed—probably wrongly—that Gungunyane was responsible for this rebellion and might attempt to expel Portugal from the areas south of his kingdom. It was already known that the British South Africa Company had signed an agreement with the African chief, was paying him a generous pension, and had attempted to arm him with modern rifles.[5] Portugal mounted a special overseas expedition, and elements of this force reached Lourenço Marques in April 1895. As part of this expedition, Mousinho de Albuquerque commanded a squadron of cavalry that would go into combat against the Shangana tribe of Gaza.

The course of the Gaza campaign of 1895 has been described and analyzed elsewhere in detail.[6] It became the most celebrated effort in Portuguese militarism and colonialism in Africa in modern times and created more colonial heroes and colonial mythology than any other. The importance here is the role of Mousinho de Albuquerque, who eagerly sought out the most perilous missions and actions. Over the months between April and December 1895 he became frustrated by delays in the campaign's course—delays blamed on tropical conditions, lack of communications, and inadequate transportation from the coast into the heart of Gazaland.

The cavalry under Mousinho fought in a number of actions in the first months after their arrival. But the expeditionary commander, Galhardo, was inexperienced in African fighting, feared a reverse, and was overcautious. Mousinho was irritated by his reluctance to advance rapidly toward the capital, Manjacaze. Armed with only a sword and a sidearm, Mousinho proposed bold dashes into the African heartland. His audacity and bravery won him notoriety among his comrades from the beginning.

The machine gun, not the cavalry charge, was the decisive element in the Gaza campaign. It was Portuguese modern weaponry, applied unsparingly to the masses of African warriors who fought for Gungunyane, that proved the ultimate answer to the control of southern Mozambique. The decisive battle came at Coolela on November 7, 1895. Mousinho had horses killed under him but persisted in charging the African lines. Oncoming regiments of Gungunyane's warriors were mowed down by Portuguese firepower and the Africans suffered thousands of casualties. Coolela broke the back of the Gaza domain under Gungunyane, who escaped capture by taking some of his possessions in a wagon about November 10 and deserting his kraal at Manjacaze. He fled north to Chaimite, a village associated with his African ancestors and with the traditional religion of his people. After Coolela his legions began to waver and to desert. Others declared a pragmatic neutrality before the increasingly aggressive Portuguese armed force.

From Portugal the government ordered termination of the Gaza campaign. The Galhardo expedition withdrew and boarded ships to return to Lisbon. On or about December 16, Royal commissioner Ennes departed for the metropole, convinced that the Gaza state was defeated. Its leader, Gungunyane, remained at large, the Portuguese knew not where. Some thought he had escaped into the Transvaal. It was believed that the famous chief would never surrender and that if he did not fight to the death he would escape to the north or west into areas not under Portuguese control or sovereignity. Authorities ordered that all operations in the hinterland cease until after the end of the rainy season in 1896.

On December 10 Mousinho, already recognized as one of the heroes of Coolela, was appointed military governor of Gaza district. Two days later Portuguese intelligence sources informed him that they had located Gungunyane at the small village of Chaimite north of Languene on the Limpopo river, and Mousinho decided on an expedition to capture or kill him. After weeks of preparation, the march began, and on December 28 the small Portuguese force, accompanied by thousands of loyal African auxiliary warriors, entered Chaimite. Mousinho walked up to the startled Gungunyane and arrested him in the name of the king of Portugal. The chief offered no resistance. The governor then ordered the summary execution of two other chiefs whom he blamed for instigating the war. At Lourenço Marques on January 6, 1896, Mousinho de Albuquerque officially handed over Gungunyane to the interim governor-general; the chief was soon sent by ship—a prisoner—to Lisbon, where he arrived on March 13 and was paraded in chains before Portuguese crowds to a prison.

The Chaimite affair had extraordinary aspects. Most observers had believed that Gungunyane—like Lobengula in Rhodesia to the northwest—would never allow himself to be captured even after military defeat and would escape or be killed. The collapse of African resistance after Coolela and the helplessness of Gungunyane before his bold captors astounded public opinion in Portugal and in countries that followed African affairs. Ironically, the capture was technically a case of insubordination on Mousinho's part, and he performed it with only a few European troops. Communications between the combat zone and the city of Lourenço Marques were uncertain and slow, and on December 31, 1895—three days after the Chaimite capture—the new governor-general repeated the order to cease all offensive operations until termination of the 1896 rainy season.

When the news of Gungunyane's defeat and capture reached Portugal, the public response was sensational and unprecedented celebrations broke out from the royal court of King Carlos I down to the street urchins of Lisbon and Oporto. In an age of colonial pessimism, defeatism, and national moral disillusionment, the 1895 military deeds of one rare officer galvanized public attention and aroused national imagination. In an age without heroes, Portugal now had a national hero of Africa who could match the deeds, so the Portuguese believed, of contemporary colonial heroes of Britain and France. Overnight the Portuguese public—encouraged by an excited press—made the name Mousinho a household word. Forty years later in the official Escola Colonial history text, the capture of Gungunyane was claimed to be a deed "without equal in celebrated history."[7]

The Hero-Soldier as Administrator, 1896–1898. Honors were heaped upon Mousinho de Albuquerque. The government awarded him a pension for life; he received important military medals and distinctions from foreign nations—from Germany, the Red Eagle Second Class; from Britain, commander of the Order of St. Michael and St. George; from France, officer of the Legion of Honor; etc. Because of his action in a war undertaken, the government claimed, "in defense of the national honor,"[8] Mousinho was promoted by distinction, not seniority, to the rank of major, and on March 13, 1896, he was named governor-general of Mozambique, a post he officially took up on May 21, 1896. In November of that year he was given additional power by Lisbon and appointed, as was Ennes before him, royal commissioner.

The new governor's first order of business was to gather an able and competent staff that he could trust to carry out his orders and to advance Portuguese national interests in Mozambique. He recruited the nucleus of Portugal's colonial elite during the years 1895–1920. To the brilliant staff officer—later governor of Angola—Eduardo Costa, Mousinho handed the governorship of Mozambique district; he selected an obscure captain, Pereira D'Eça (later a victor in Angola and a general) as the district governor of Lourenço Marques. The aristocratic staff officer Aires D'Ornellas (minister of marine and overseas in 1906–1908) was chosen to be Mousinho's chief of the military staff.[9] A young officer—later a general minister of war and important officer in the post-1926 dictatorship—Vieira da Rocha was named one of Mousinho's aides. With such a staff of luminaries, the hero believed that Portugal could make up for lost centuries in Mozambique.

Mousinho's term as supreme administrator can be divided into two major activities: military and nonmilitary. In military terms, a good bit of his time was spent on armed campaigns in various parts of the colony. His plan for the effective occupation and pacification of territories on the colony's borders was based upon the system used by one of his personal colonial heroes: Joseph Gallieni, the French general and governor in Southeast Asia and Madagascar. During February–March 1896 there were campaigns in the Maputo area from Lourenço Marques to the South African frontier. A great amount of time and effort was expended by the governor on the so-called Namarrais campaign in the north of Mozambique between October 1895 and March 1897 in an area adjacent to the capital at Mozambique Island. Mousinho was twice wounded in battle but he disdained fear. Nararrais country was more difficult terrain than that of the southern sections, and some believed these northern warriors were superior to the Shangana as unconventional guerrilla fighters.

In southern Mozambique, African resistance continued. Perhaps even more arduous and equally bloody as the campaign in the north was the "second Gaza campaign" of 1897. Governor-general Mousinho de Albuquerque commanded the Portuguese forces that responded to a rebellion by Gungunyane's former general, Maguiguana, who had escaped after Coolela. The governor was surprised by this resistance movement,[10] which he believed had causes similar to those responsible for the almost simultaneous African risings in Rhodesia. Africans responded to a set of grievances that included colonial maladministration, labor abuses, and natural disasters like drought, cattle disease, and a plague of locusts.

From June to September 1897 in Gaza Mousinho participated in the toughest pacification campaign of his career. He established his military headquarters at Chibuto, where, with Portuguese nuns from the order of St. Cluny, his wife organized and maintained a hospital for the Portuguese wounded. In September, after the African forces were defeated and dispersed and Maguiguana killed in battle, the campaign was concluded. A grateful government awarded the hero another medal, Portugal's Tower and Sword decoration. Though Mousinho de Albuquerque made great efforts to plan and carry out the decisive occupation and military pacification of the colony, African peoples resisted Portuguese rule both passively and violently long after this fiery governor resigned. As late as the 1920s, especially in northern Mozambique and in the Zambezi valley, there were serious African rebellions.

On a return trip to Portugal and a European tour from December 1897 to April 1898, Mousinho de Albuquerque, the soldier, was met with frenetic popular acclaim unprecedented in modern Portugal. As he landed in Lisbon, he was met and embraced by the king himself and hailed by huge crowds. The numerous celebrations were not staged by the government, as would be similar affairs for dignitaries of the New State in later decades. Loaded down with new medals and honors and named an aide-de-camp of the king, Mousinho undertook a tour of northern Portugal in January 1898. He was received ecstatically ("uma loucura" in the words of contemporary observers). The soldier was greeted as a secular saint, a modern miracle worker, perhaps a new Sebastian. Flowers were strewn in his path and students carried him on their shoulders. People believed that he represented "the old Portuguese heroism, heroic and triumphant!"[11]

The zenith of Mousinho's triumphs came on the northern tour. One observer speculated that the frenzied hero worship at that moment in time might have led to a personal dictatorship, that the opportunity for the "man on horseback" was his for the asking.

> If, in that moment, Mousinho would have raised his sword and uttered one word, all, all who were there, without distinction of class or of age, would have followed him blindly, dominated, hypnotized by his prestige, to carry out the most chimerical and absurd enterprise that he could have dreamed up.[12]

After a triumphant tour of France, England, and Germany, Mousinho stopped briefly in Portugal before returning to Mozambique. His reputation as a hero-soldier was established and his popularity at its peak. But even before he embarked for Mozambique in April 1898, he had disagreements over colonial policy with political leaders and with the ministry of marine and overseas.

As an administrator, Mousinho de Albuquerque was controversial. Although he experienced some contemporary popular criticism as a soldier who won fame by turning his sword against black Africans (*a cutilada*), the most voluminous debate concerned his actions as senior administrator in Mozambique. There are many pitfalls in the debate because of the intricacies of the politics of Portuguese colonialism in the context of the fin de siècle monarchy. A fair and balanced assessment of Mousinho de Albuquerque as administrator must take into account at least four factors: the politics of the metropole relative to colonial activity 1896–1902; Mousinho's reputation as a soldier; how the New State regime, a generation after the death of the colonial hero, adopted him as a keystone in its ideology and mythology; and his reform ideas and the imposing obstacles to success in 1896 Mozambique, which might have discouraged any administrator. These factors will be discussed along with the hero's record as an administrator. A study by R. J. Hammond[13] suggests that Mousinho was "no administrator." There is evidence, however, that as an administrator he has been misunderstood and underestimated.

The nature of politics in the metropole, very personal and factious, made this particular governor's crusade against "an exaggerated centralizing intervention of the government"[14] especially difficult. Even in the best of circumstances Mousinho was egotistical, but it is difficult to take very seriously the criticism that he flouted the constitution, acted illegally in Mozambique, and defied the colonial ministry.[15] It is inaccurate to infer from this criticism that government leaders obeyed the law; almost constant manipulation of the statutes for personal and party purposes was a key feature of the system under the late constitutional monarchy. The forced resignation of Mousinho de Albuquerque in 1898 was the result mainly of envy on the part of government leaders in Lisbon—the understandable attempt by an inert, corrupt, and remote bureaucracy to protect itself from the threat represented by the personality, reform ideas, and actions of Mousinho.

Although his ideas were not original, they undoubtedly influenced Portugal's gradual movement during 1898–1920 toward administrative decentralization and greater autonomy for local administrators. Mousinho recommended giving more power and authority to royal commissioners, colonial governors, and their subordinates, as well as adopting a legal system suited to conditions not in Lisbon but in Africa—a legal system that provided each of three groups; Europeans, "assimilated natives," and "natives," with separate court and penal systems. He was, in effect, a disciple of his predecessor António Ennes, but he wrote his own decrees to implement some of Ennes's ideas. In his *portaria* of instructions on a *regimento* (directive) dated April 8 and 12, 1898, may be found one of the colonial legal precedents for the so-called *indigenato* system, which matured after the New State legislation of 1926-1929.[16] This innovation was opposed at the time by the minister of marine and colonies, who argued that the measure was illegal.[17]

It is in the area of financial planning and control that the ideas of Mousinho de Albuquerque were most specific and probably most influential with later colonialists and colonial administrators, especially in Mozambique. The governor deemed the system he found in 1896–1898 inefficient, unwise, and even dangerous. His hands were tied since Lisbon had virtually full control of the colony's treasury by means of restrictive laws. A decree of 1888[18] forbade the governor to enter into any contracts to purchase, sell, or furnish materials valued at a certain price; a treasury inspector sent from Lisbon and a chief of the treasury department exercised actual control of finances, not the governor. Mousinho attacked such regulations as "absurd"[19] and deplored the already entrenched tradition that colonial administrators raise funds or increase income by inflating customs duties and taxes. He suggested, rather, that the colony might be better served by "development of the sources of wealth, by the economic improvement of the country." He urged that Lisbon allow him to raise loans for Mozambique projects, but he was refused permission to do so.[20]

Mousinho thought his ideas especially applicable in Mozambique, whose finances were of great importance to the imperial budget—in 1896–1897 the budgeted receipts of Mozambique amounted to some fifty-one percent of the total receipts from the empire. Six principal recommendations were outlined by Mousinho in his classic study *Moçambique* (1899):[21] (1) financial-economic matters should be accurately planned; (2) no financial subsidies should be forthcoming from the metropole; (3) loans should be raised for development projects but not for meeting budget requirements; (4) local colonial governments, districts, and—ideally—provinces should "live off their own resources"; (5) governors should be given the financial powers necessary to put Mozambique on what he considered to be the road to "economic regeneration"; and (6) governors should be allowed to raise loans. Note that although the 1920–1930 regime of high commissioners in Angola and Mozambique gave Lisbon's top official the power to raise loans, the post-1926 New State system returned to the centralizing colonial tradition. The New State system nevertheless matched to some degree the spirit of the other financial fundamentals outlined in Mousinho's defense of his two-year term as royal commissioner and governor-general of Mozambique.

In other areas of colonial thought and administration, Mousinho was more conservative. As regards the concept of a European "civilizing mission," he belonged to the mainstream of racist, ethnocentric, social Darwinists of his day. To Mousinho the Portuguese were a superior race; the Africans in general, savage and barbaric. He opposed "assimilation." A strict law-and-order man, he deplored the fact that capital punishment was illegal under Portuguese law and claimed that this was illogical and foolish in tropical African colonies; he insisted that the government apply the death penalty to Africans who had murdered whites. He also advocated corporal punishment for Africans in order to maintain Portuguese authority.

With regard to questions of white settlement and emigration, he wished to see implemented in Mozambique an official policy of discouraging the emigration from Portugal of both peasants and *degredados* (convicts and political prisoners), persons who, he believed, would prove liabilities rather than assets to prosperity. He urged that the metropole institute a directed, selective emigration program to encourage the settlement in Africa of skilled artisans and small businessmen with some capital.

Mousinho's analysis and his proposed solutions to the severe problems of Mozambique were strictly nationalist and conservative. A close student of British administration in South Africa and an administrator familiar with the British system then operating in the South African province of Natal, Mousinho admired the decentralization of the British empire. He believed that if Portugal gave some financial autonomy to Mozambique and, by extension, to other African colonies, this would greatly expedite their economic development.

A close reading of his major administrative study, *Moçambique*, suggests that Mousinho was much more than a narrow-minded nationalist who feared the loss of Portugal's African empire to foreign rivals. The more noteworthy sections of this work contain keen insights, logic, rationality, and many candid admissions. He admitted that he was no financial expert, that he broke the law, and that at times he did not follow imperial regulations. On one point Mousinho was admittedly unorthodox: he advocated keeping, the colony's capital on Mozambique Island in the far north and not transferring it to Lourenço Marques in the far south.[22] Keeping the capital in the north would, he reasoned, foster development and control north of the Zambezi river then outside the Portuguese sphere.

Mousinho's nationalistic and royalist feelings remained dominant. The lesson of his service in Mozambique, he claimed, was simply that if Portugal did not establish immediately an efficient and effective administration in Mozambique, the colonial powers in the surrounding territories—Germany to the north and Britain to the south and west—might take over the colony. He believed the loss of Mozambique would in effect spell Portugal's downfall. Mousinho marked well Spain's situation in 1898. He saw in Spain's recent loss of its American and Pacific empire a grim foreshadowing for the smaller and weaker Portugal. Mousinho suggested that this outcome could be prevented through the measures he advocated.

Among the projects he encouraged during his two years as chief executive in Mozambique were: the construction of railroads and telegraph lines; improvement of cargo and transit facilities in the key port of Lourenço Marques; establishment of military posts in the hinterland—especially north of the Zambezi river; improved collection of hut taxes from Africans; and reduction of foreign concessions.

Mousinho de Albuquerque's patriotism and nationalism were intensified by the non-Portuguese control of large sectors of the economy: the dominance of

(East) Indians in the retail trade of the hinterland, especially southern Mozambique; the predominance of Indian and Zanzibari rupees and English and Transvaal pounds as opposed to Portuguese currency; and the rights and concessions held especially by three chartered companies: Nyasa, Zambezia, and Moçambique. As royal commissioner Mousinho proposed to expel the Indian traders and to put greater restrictions on the chartered companies. Though he feared the entrance of powerful capitalist groups into Mozambique, he was more concerned with the fact that the benefits from these companies did not accrue to Mozambique or even to Portugal but to remote investors who did all they could to get their money out of the colony.

From his colonial writings, a new vision of a future Portuguese East Africa was formed. Mousinho envisioned a prosperous colony, supported mainly by agriculture, whose economy would be firmly in the hands of Portuguese citizens and of the government. His greatest hope was for what he termed the *nacionalização* of the economy of Mozambique, that is, the consolidation of Portuguese control; with a prosperous Mozambique, Portugal would enjoy "economic regeneration."[23] Mousinho's proposals to carry out this process were not impractical but would have been difficult to effect under the impoverished and unstable regimes of the years 1895–1926. It is probable that he would have preferred either the abolition of the privileged chartered companies or at least the requirement that they pay much more to the government for their concessions and rights. Mousinho recommended the occupation, pacification, and settlement by Portuguese with some independent means of lands outside the companies' sphere. One of his pet schemes was to apply the Zambezi valley estate system, the *regime dos prazos*, to lands south of the Save river.[24] Plantation schemes, not small farms, would have resulted. The historian can discern in this proposal, again, influence from the economics of the Natal province, a model Mousinho frequently mentioned in his colonial writings. His hopes for colonial profits for the Portuguese were expressed in his 1898 lecture to the Centro Comercial of Oporto, a group concerned with the economics of colonial expansion in Africa. He urged businessmen to invest in Portuguese Africa, and he saw great potential in growing cotton for export and selling Portuguese wines in South Africa, the Rhodesias, and British East Africa.

As royal commissioner of Mozambique for only two years, Mousinho was unable to work great changes. He initiated new schemes and he encouraged his staff and colleagues—later the so-called school of Mousinho—to make it possible for the colonies to be ruled from within and not from Lisbon. As indicated, the economy of Mozambique was largely in foreign hands in 1898, but Mousinho's concept of the nationalization of all sectors was influential in republican colonial circles and in the later dictatorship. He would have been pleased that the New State phased out the three great foreign chartered companies in Mozambique by the 1940s.

When his extraordinary powers as royal commissioner were suddenly withdrawn and his prerogatives drastically reduced by order of the ministry of marine and overseas in July 1898, Mousinho resigned. Despite official protests he left for Lisbon in August of that year, unemployed. His brief but notable career as a colonial administrator was finished. The royal commissioner was justifiably frustrated, as shown in this letter to his successor:

I have never had to regret being as conciliatory as possible, up to the point at which it was necessary to show firmness, and I have the consolation of never having failed to exercise [this firmness] and thus insulting the decorum of this post that I held and the national honor. I should not, however, hide from Your Exc. the fact that I have found myself at times placed in a very difficult position because of the ignorance in which the office [ministry] in Lisbon kept me concerning negotiations undertaken with foreign powers, promises made to some of them, and diplomatic relations with others, the full knowledge of which was indispensable in order to execute the policy of this govt.-general. On this point I can only hope that Your Exc. may be more fortunate than I have been and that you may obtain from the ministry all the information you may lack, and in time so that it can be useful, which never happened in my case. I went to learn of things in Lisbon that I could hardly believe that the ministry had not informed me about, so great was their importance for this province!

I believe that Your Exc. has only two paths to choose between: to be a simple executor of the orders of the ministry, furnishing it with the information necessary so that you will never clash with the opinions that are current there and with interests linked to its government, or, to speak the truth without concealment, to propose what seems to you best in your conscience and not to rest upon or flee from the reputation of being troublesome and obstinate as long as your proposals have not been approved or your requests satisfied.[25]

Soldier in the Wilderness, 1898–1902

The soldier-hero never returned to Africa, and the remainder of his life was brief. Discussion of his last years is essential to understanding his legend in later decades.

Mousinho remained popular with the royal court and with elements of the masses, but he was shunned by leading politicians in the monarchist parties. In the year following his return from Africa he published *Moçambique, 1896–1898*, which is both a defense of his colonial career and an attack on the politicians and bureaucrats of the Lisbon establishment. Mousinho suggested that Portugal might lose Mozambique to foreign rivals and that the colony's governance would collapse after his departure and the probable resignation of his carefully selected, loyal staff of army and navy officers. Those officers who had been his close associates in the 1895 campaign and later became high officials in both Mozambique and Angola did not in fact leave colonial service, and in subsequent years they tried to put some of his ideas into effect.

In November 1898, King Carlos appointed Mousinho de Albuquerque royal tutor and counselor to the heir apparent, Crown prince Luíz Filipe. Mousinho was asked to make the boy into a "man" who would one day serve as king.[26]

Mousinho instructed the young prince in military science, theory, and the martial arts and accompanied him on trips. Little of what passed between the teacher and student has survived in documents with the exception of a long letter to the prince dated 1900 or 1901; the letter also was meant to be a preface to a book. Although it was not published until 1908 (after the deaths of both Mousinho and the prince), the document became an extraordinarily popular piece of military-patriotic literature in later decades. Reprinted dozens of times from the 1930s to the 1960s, the letter is infused with mystical patriotism, royalism, and militarism, all essential elements of the post-1926 dictatorship's ideology. Worth quoting is one of its more important passages:

> It was Your Majesty who called me from the ranks of the army. You did not choose, it is certain, the bravest soldier, but simply one who, by a series of convenient but fortunate accidents, could show that, at whatever cost, he would obey what he was ordered to do. . . .
>
> In this age of depravity, in which the bonds of discipline are so weak, Your Majesty could understand that more than ever Portugal needed someone who has a firm will to rule, a strength to make him obeyed. And since no one can teach what he does not know, or what he has not experienced, it was the King who sought Your [aide] from the only class in which there are those who obey without reticence and who order without hesitation. For this reason, the first of my duties is to make Your Highness into a soldier. . . . You will learn how [to be a soldier] from your ancestors. This kingdom [Portugal] is the work of soldiers. . . . Those few brilliant and consoling pages in the history of contemporary Portugal were written by us, the soldiers, there in the backlands of Africa, with the points of our bayonets. . . . To be a soldier is to dedicate oneself completely to the public good, to work always for others.[27]

Despite his prestigious post as royal tutor and aide, Mousinho's last years were bitterly frustrating and empty. He pursued but never completed numerous schemes, some political, some military. The Lisbon establishment effectively shut him out; he was given no official posts or places on organizations concerned with colonial affairs. Under different circumstances, he might have been appointed to the policymaking body, the Junta Consultiva do Ultramar (Overseas Consulting Board), which advised the ministry of marine and overseas. Mousinho had made too many enemies to get such appointments. Although he was promoted to lieutenant colonel of cavalry in November 1901, accustomed adulation and honors were no longer forthcoming.

Longing for adventure and probably for death on a battlefield of imperial glory, Mousinho volunteered for several expeditions. He submitted requests to command a Portuguese unit in the multinational army opposing the Boxer rebellion in China in 1900 but was denied this post. After reading about the Anglo-Boer war in South Africa and realizing that the war's outcome might well influence the future of his beloved Mozambique, he asked that the king allow him to join a volunteer unit of Portuguese soldiers. Again, his request was refused.

The most important scheme of Mousinho's last years, however, concerned domestic politics and it remains shrouded in mystery. The frustrated soldier, the paladin of Africa, was a staunch royalist who feared that the unstable and ineffective constitutional parliamentary governments would destroy both the monarchy and Portugal. With a note of bitterness and perhaps more than a little irony, Mousinho had claimed in *Moçambique* that colonialists had never played key roles in domestic politics. What this colonial soldier intended was to establish a military regime backed by the army and led by a rightist politician such as the conservative João Franco.[28] Mousinho plotted with some of his aides, such as his chief of staff in Mozambique, the monarchist Aires D'Ornellas, to set up a government—with the king's backing—that would crush the rising republican party threat, suspend the troublesome and anarchic Cortes (Parliament), and set up a strong civilian statesman who would establish a rule of authority and law and order. To implement this scheme a military coup d'état was planned. The view among the small circle of African heroes inspired by the example and dashing figure of the major on horseback was that only an authoritarian, military government could remove the corruption of the monarchist parties, undermine the anticlerical republicans, and pursue a forward, aggressive policy in Africa. On large estates and in private homes Mousinho met with top leaders and consulted with officers from various units.

The plan failed.[29] King Carlos would not consent to unconstitutional acts and would not back—at least not before the demise of Mousinho—any such scheme. Mousinho soon became discouraged by the king's position and realized that as a colonial soldier he could not play a central role in Portuguese politics. Although he was not alone in considering the idea of a military dictatorship to "save" the monarchy (staunch monarchists harbored such a dream until the monarchy fell in 1910), Mousinho's impulsive, excitable personality lent a special style to the project. Even when the political party system began to disintegrate and a politician he admired, João Franco, seceded from a major party to form his own, Mousinho obstinately refused to join this group.[30]

There is abundant evidence that years before he had contemplated suicide or a quick death in battle. Among the various theories about his despondency are an unrequited love for Queen Amélia, rejection by the political establishment, inability to become a top leader himself, and worry that Portugal—especially after the rumored secret treaties between Britain and Germany in 1898—would fall victim to larger colonial powers and lose its independence. Whatever the reasons, Mousinho became seriously distressed. His last project was to research the history of his paternal grandfather, who sought a hero's death in battle in 1846. On the afternoon of January 8, 1902, Mousinho committed suicide on a Lisbon streetcar by shooting himself twice in the head. He was buried after a state funeral amid much pomp and national mourning. A popular cartoonist of the day insisted that the suicide aroused antigovernment anger in the common man.[31]

The Colonial Soldier Sanctified, 1926–1955

Mousinho de Albuquerque—his example and his ideas but particularly his legend—had a greater influence upon Portugal after his death than during his brief but passionate life. With the possible exception of the dictator Salazar, no Portuguese in modern times has so consistently aroused the imagination of his countrymen. Though this hero worship was at first restricted to a small elite of colonial and military men, the dictatorship systematically built Mousinho's legend into a national phenomenon. More has been written about Mousinho de Albuquerque than any other Portuguese military or colonial figure, again with the possible exception of Prince Henry the Navigator.

Symbols of this national cult include books, pamphlets, articles, memoirs, commemorative stamps, statues and booklets, and theses. In 1956 a colonial historian compiled a bibliography of books by or about Mousinho that listed hundreds of entries. There were statues erected to honor him in Portugal and Mozambique, streets named for him, and ships christened after him in the Portuguese navy and merchant fleets. In the 1960s and 1970s a type of armored car used by the Portuguese army was called the "Chaimite" (Mousinho's great triumph of 1895). In the standard Portuguese encyclopedia, carefully edited by censors of the dictatorship after 1930, Mousinho is the subject of perhaps the longest biographical article.[32]

The influence of Mousinho was most marked in two different eras: first in the years just before the fall of the parliamentary republic and later during the more vigorous years of the New State dictatorship, 1933–1945. In the first period, rightwing writers and politicians, mainly integralists, saw in him an exemplar who espoused many of their ideas of traditionalist conservatism, antiparliamentarianism, royalism, militarism, and colonialism. In the 1920s a group of young professional officers, writers, and students revived interest in Mousinho by means of speeches, writings, and discussions. Clearly his influence played a role in the increasing strength of rightist ideas among the Portuguese elite. His concept of the professional soldier as the ideal citizen and "savior" of the people from corrupt politicians found an echo among those conservatives who came to power in 1926, as did his idea that the army could save Portugal. The military dictatorship (1926–1933) thereafter attempted to set up Mousinho as a national hero.

What previous members of the cult of Mousinho had done in an ad hoc manner, the post-1933 New State dictatorship did deliberately and systematically. In the period 1933–1945, when elements of a Portuguese fascism were most in evidence among the new leaders and some of their followers, the cult of Mousinho reached its zenith of stage-managed popularity. The colonial soldier was adopted as the military patron saint of the dictatorship. As part of a general nostalgia and mystical patriotism, the worship of Mousinho was not unlike a modern version of the mass phenomenon known as Sebastianism, a messianism originating in the sixteenth century.

By various means the New State institutionalized the worship of Mousinho. Government bodies such as the Agência Geral das Colónias commissioned biographical studies of the soldier, reprinted his African writings, and encouraged elaborate commemorations of dates considered significant—December 28, the date of Gungunyane's arrest at Chaimite, and Mousinho's birthdate, November 12, were celebrated with considerable gusto on their fortieth and hundredth anniversaries, respectively. In the regime's rubber-stamp National Assembly, loyalist followers gave speeches of praise and some proposed that Mousinho's remains be removed to the medieval Batalha Abbey, a national shrine of heroes and burial place of Portugal's unknown soldier of World War I. The city of Lourenço Marques, which had already named streets and squares and erected statues in his memory, in 1955 instituted two prizes of ten contos each, one for the best essay on Mousinho and the other for the best children's book on his life and deeds.[33]

The New State made the cult of Mousinho a part of the indoctrination and training of the regime's major youth organization, Mocidade Portuguesa, originally modeled upon youth groups in fascist Italy and Germany. The intention was to instill in the future leaders of the regime the government's values and ideology. The cult of Mousinho, perpetuated through books, speeches, discussions, articles, and ceremonies, stressed "duty, service, and loyalty," virtues the regime contrived to associate with Mousinho, the colonial soldier sanctified. Portuguese youth leaders, including the future premier Marcello Caetano, endlessly praised Mousinho in speeches and in print. Caetano went so far as to maintain that the political thought of Mousinho was perfectly compatible with the New State's ideas. He went on to claim that "if [Mousinho] had not come too early," he would have been a "great statesman" in Salazar's regime.[34]

Colonial literature, especially in the 1930s and 1940s, also was alive with the cult of Mousinho. Writers extolled and exaggerated his virtues and ignored his flaws. In this colonial hagiography another cliché emerged: "the school of Mousinho," which referred to the so-called heroes of Africa on his staff in 1895–1896 in Mozambique, including Henrique Paiva Couceiro, Ayres D'Ornellas, Manuel Gomes da Costa, and Eduardo Costa. One writer suggested that in colonial legislation there was a "cycle of Mousinho." Mousinho's influence had been decisive, this writer argued, in inspiring the decentralization laws of 1906–1907 associated with Eduardo Costa and in inspiring the first republic's colonial legislation of 1914 and 1920.[35] There was an attempt to alter the unheroic, drab image of Salazar by making a flattering comparison between Mousinho, the colonial hero, and the mysterious professor from Coimbra University. In 1936 one source claimed that Salazar was in fact the natural heir of the great African soldier since one could observe in both men a "notable alliance of action and intelligence."[36]

There were other ways in which the Mousinho cult was used to influence public opinion under the New State. The secular worship of Mousinho nicely complemented an emphasis upon colonialism. Portuguese were diverted from harsh domestic realities; colonialism was a diversion from political conflict among personalities and factions in Portugal. In that authoritarian system, it was considered useful to trumpet repeatedly a well-selected, appropriate quotation from the sanctified colonial soldier: "In the metropole we can debate political questions, but in Africa we should be more Portuguese than [we are] here, and, as for politics . . . Portuguese, nothing more."[37]

The importance of Mousinho and his cult, then, was in part in the creation of a useful myth: by praising the colonial soldier with authoritarian-militarist tendencies, the regime was trying to promote Portuguese Africa as a unifying, nonpolitical cause, a rallying ground away from home.

Conclusion

Mousinho de Albuquerque was above all a man of action who, under different circumstances, might have played a decisive role in Portugal. In Mozambique he made more of an impact as a soldier than as governor, but his abilities and acts as an administrator and colonial thinker have been underestimated. His hopes for colonial development would have been hard to realize, since Portugal was a rural country with an estimated illiteracy rate of seventy percent or more. And whereas he was not a profoundly original colonial theoretician, many of his ideas did influence colleagues of his who later became governors, as well as subsequent governments.

Though his personality and background were claimed by his hagiographers to be "purely medieval,"[38] this characterization in fact is an oversimplification. Mousinho was a traditionalist but also an activist; in the French colonies he might have been a dashing cavalry officer. As a thinker he echoed the deep pessimism and racial prejudices common in his day among the Portuguese elite, but he was also justly critical of the political corruption of the system in Lisbon.

Whatever he may have been in life, in death he became the focus of a powerful cult. During the more active phase of Mousinho's posthumous myth, an English admirer of Salazarist Portugal went so far as to write:

> It is impossible to understand the Portugal of to-day without some acquaintance with the character and personality of this man who, as an inspiration, has contributed so largely to its foundation. He combined the deep religious feeling of a Gordon with the military and administrative capacity of a Lyautey, but he was, above all, a Portuguese. Not of the degenerate nineteenth century, but of the golden age when the Portuguese were imbued with a conviction of their nation's purpose.[39]

Mousinho de Albuquerque, in retrospect, was remolded to fit the ideas of a tradition-conscious political regime; if he had been alive, his individualism surely would have clashed with the collective suppression of rights, the grey bureaucrats, and the endless rhetoric and police terrorism that so characterized the New State. Ironically, the dictatorship used this cult to instill in citizens an aversion to several features of Mousinho's career: his quest for personal freedom of action; his attempt to increase significantly the powers of the colonial governors, to decentralize colonial rule, and to expand colonial financial autonomy. In this way Mousinho, the "eternal captain" of Portuguese youth, the soldier who killed himself in order to "die in time," became in death the victim of his own legend. His myth was relentlessly manipulated by the dictatorship that deliberately rehabilitated him.

To Africans in Mozambique, Mousinho de Albuquerque epitomized the most violent phase of Portuguese colonialism. Yet in some respects his style and fearsome reputation were not unlike those of certain traditional warrior-kings of Southern Africa. As a governor who was concerned with Mozambique's somewhat murky economic future, Mousinho called for sacrifices, hard work, and perseverance. That early call may find more than a faint echo in the new world of post-Portuguese Maputo.

Notes

1. Mousinho's only possible rival as a famous modern soldier in the colonies is another officer well known for his monacle, General António de Spínola (b. 1910), who was governor-general of Guinea (1968–1973), vice–chief of staff (January–March 1974), and briefly president of the Portuguese republic (May–September 1974).

2. Integralists were Portuguese monarchists who subscribed to the political views of the French writer Charles Maurras.

3. General Ernesto Vieira da Rocha, "Mousinho, Figura Imortal," *Boletim Geral das Colónias*, no. 128 (February 1936):37

4. From a biographical piece published in 1897 in the daily newspaper *Diário de Notícias* (Lisbon), cited in the obituary "Joaquim Mousinho de Albuquerque," *Portugal em Africa* 10, no. 109 (January 1903):27.

5. Philip R. Warhurst, *Anglo-Portuguese Relations in South-Central Africa, 1890–1900* (London, 1962); Eric Axelson, *Portugal and the Scramble for Africa, 1875–1891* (Johannesburg, 1967).

6. See Douglas L. Wheeler, "Gungunyana," in Norman R. Bennett, ed., *Leadership in Eastern Africa* (Boston, 1968), pp. 194–211; Douglas L. Wheeler, "Gungunyana, the Negotiator," *Journal of African History* 9, no. 4 (October 1968):585–602.

7. Gaspar do Couto Ribeiro Villas, *História Colonial* (Lisbon, 1938), 2:368.

8. General Ferreira Martins, *Mouzinho* (Lisbon, 1965), p. 105.

9. Miguel Pelágio Teixeira da Costa, "Ayres D'Ornellas e o Ultramar," *Boletim Geral do Ultramar,* nos. 499–500 (January–February 1967):28.

10. J. Mousinho de Albuquerque, *Moçambique, 1896–1898* (Lisbon, 1899), p. 87.

11. Luís de Magalhães, cited in Martins, *Mouzinho,* p. 155.

12. Ibid.

13. Richard J. Hammond, *Portugal and Africa, 1815–1910* (Stanford, 1966), pp. 272 ff. Much of the evidence Hammond uses on the judgments concerning Mousinho as an administrator is from British diplomatic records.

14. Martins, *Mouzinho,* p. 110.

15. Hammond, *Portugal and Africa,* pp. 273–276.

16. Perhaps the most definitive early precedent before the dictatorship is in Mozambique in 1917 laws, modified in 1919. For a pre–New State definition, for legal purposes, of *indigena* and *assimilado* see text in *Indices Alfabéticos e Cronológicos da Principal Legislacão de Moçambique Publicada Nos 'Boletins Oficiais da Colónia de Moçambique desde 1854 a 1920,* organized by Alberto Costa Mesquita (Lourenço Marques, 1941), p. 154, citing *Boletim Oficial de Moçambique,* no. 2, 1ª series, 1917.

17. Mousinho de Albuquerque, *Ofício Dirigido ao Conselheiro Alvaro da Costa Ferreira* (Lisbon, 1957), p. 26.

18. For the text of this decree (20 December 1888) see João José da Silva, *Repertório da Legislação Ultramarina (continuação) 1883–1892* (Nova Gao, 1896), p. 41.

19. Mousinho, *Moçambique,* p. 273.

20. Ibid., p. 295.

21. Ibid., pp. 263–295.

22. Ibid., pp. 192–194.

23. From a lecture delivered before the Centro Comercial at Oporto in 1898, as cited in "Dedicado ao 'Dia de Mousinho,'" *Boletim Geral das Colónias,* no. 128 (February 1936):27.

24. Mousinho, *Ofício Dirigido ao Conselheiro,* p. 30.

25. Ibid., pp. 8, 41.

26. Both King Carlos and Luíz Filipe were killed by assassins in Lisbon on February 1, 1908.

27. Passages as reprinted in José Carlos Amado, *História de Portugal* (Lisbon, 1966), 2:62, and in Carlos Vieira da Rocha, *João Teixeira Pinto* (Lisbon, 1971), on back cover of book.

28. Franco was "dictator," 1906–1908, backed by King Carlos, a political experiment that ended in the regicide.

29. Editorial "O Século," *História da República* (Lisbon, 1959), pp. 140–142.

30. See preface by Ayres d'Ornellas in Marshal Gomes da Costa, *Memórias* (Lisbon, 1930); passage also cited in anthology by Avila de Azevedo, *A Geração de Mousinho e o Pensamento da Revolução Nacional* (Lisbon, 1966), pp. 93–94.

31. The classic cartoon version of the Portuguese common man was and remains a character known as "Zé Povinho" (Joe Little People). José-Augusto França, *Zé Povinho na Obra de Rafael Bordalo Pinheiro, 1875–1904* (Lisbon, 1975), p. 13.

32. *Grande Enciclopédia Portuguesa e Brasileira,* Lisbon 18:45–51.

33. In Portuguese currency, a conto equals 1,000 escudos. In 1976 there were approximately twenty-eight escudos to the U.S. dollar; two decades earlier the value of these prizes was considerably greater. "Centenário de Mousinho de Albuquerque," *Boletim Geral do Ultramar,* no. 357 (March 1955):103–105.

34. Caetano cited in a book published during the commemoration of the centenary of Mousinho's birth, Luíz Filipe de Oliveira e Castro, *Mousinho: A Sua Vida e a Sua Morte* (Lisbon, 1955), p. 67.

35. Manuel Simões Alberto, "Mousinho e a Evolução das Normas de Administração Ultramarina (Análise do 'Ciclo Mousiniaho')," *Boletim da Sociedade de Estudos de Moçambique*, nos. 94–95 (1955):375–393.

36. "Crónica Colonial," *Boletim Geral das Colónias*, no. 128 (February 1936):116–119.

37. From a lecture by Mousinho de Albuquerque in January 1898 in Oporto, cited in ibid., p. 29.

38. João Ameal, *História de Portugal* (Oporto, 1958), p. 667.

39. F. C. C. Egerton, *Salazar: Rebuilder of Portugal* (London, 1943), p. 93.

José Norton
de Matos
(1867–1955)

Douglas L. Wheeler

GENERAL Norton de Matos was twice governor of Angola in Portugal's first republic: once as governor-general, 1912–1915, and again as high commissioner, 1921–1924. His last governorship was the most controversial colonial administration in modern Angolan history and as a cause célèbre it generated a debate that endured the course of the Portuguese dictatorship (1926–1974).

There are some interesting contrasts between Norton de Matos and Mousinho de Albuquerque. If Mousinho may be said to have died too soon, Norton, as he was known to his generation, lived perhaps too long. He lived thirty years after the abrupt end of his colonial career, and he spent much of that time as a colonial theoretician in the political wilderness and as a defender of his reputation as governor. If Mousinho was a soldier first and a colonialist second, the reverse was true of Norton. Mousinho devoted his efforts to Mozambique's future and Norton de Matos emphasized Angola. If Mousinho was a traditional monarchist who opposed republicanism, Norton de Matos was an ardent republican, a liberal, and a Masonic leader. High office eluded Mousinho, whereas Norton was twice a cabinet minister and reached for the office of head of state. If Mousinho's life and ideas were defended and adopted by the dictatorship, Norton de Matos was largely pushed aside and officially criticized, ostracized, and ignored for many years. Mousinho's legend grew after 1926, whereas Norton de Matos's record as senior administrator in Angola was officially condemned as the epitome of colonial error.

Yet in another sense Norton de Matos did not live quite long enough. In the 1960s colonial scholars began to rehabilitate his record in Angola. More important, the Portuguese colonial leadership, concentrated in the ministry of overseas, adopted and adapted several cf his key ideas on the governance and social and economic development of Portuguese Africa. Despite his role as a domestic political opponent of the dictatorship after 1926, in colonial affairs no single governor or colonial thinker did more to lay the basis for the development of Angola and for the dictatorship's fundamental policies in Africa.

Background, 1867–1912

José Maria Mendes Ribeiró Norton de Matos was born on March 23, 1867, at Ponte de Lima, in northern Portugal. He was the son of a rich merchant (at one time English consul in the town of Viana do Castelo) and a Portuguese lady. His family was able to send him to the University of Coimbra, where in 1888 he received a degree in mathematics and science. During 1888–1890 he completed the army staff course at the army school and was commissioned an officer. He later recalled that his "character" and interest in advancing the Portuguese empire were formed while a student at Coimbra and at the army school.[1] He was of that generation of officers that was greatly moved by the nationalistic feelings aroused in Portugal by the "English ultimatum" of 1890.

Norton de Matos became a staunch republican. Unlike the background of his older colleague, Mousinho, Norton's family traditions and his own early inclinations were liberal, antimonarchist, republican, anticlerical, and Freemason. To Norton, reviving traditions from Portugal's Golden Age would not resolve the country's great crisis. Rather, he prescribed republicanism as the cure for an increasingly arteriosclerotic monarchy; his great dream was a parliamentary, democratic republic.

Norton de Matos's education prepared him to be a staff officer in the regular army, and his extensive training as a civil engineer and surveyor served him well during and after his colonial career overseas. In 1890 he was commissioned a second lieutenant in the cavalry and was assigned to the Fourth Cavalry Regiment at Belém, outside Lisbon, the unit in which Mousinho de Albuquerque was serving. The young soldier came to know Portugal's future "hero of Chaimite" and admired his spirit of bravery and daring. But Norton de Matos himself inclined to practicality, pragmatism, and organization. During the years that immediately preceded his first work overseas, 1890–1898, Portugal was involved in a series of military campaigns in Angola and Mozambique. The young officer entertained severe misgivings: too much money was going into military activity and too little into "civil occupation and great works of development." If Portugal did not design a "coordinated plan," the nation was only "beating the air with its hands" in Africa.[2]

Norton de Matos was invited to join Mousinho's staff in Mozambique during 1896–1898, but he refused. His explanation is not entirely satisfactory. The young officer believed that Mousinho's mission in Mozambique would fail because of political opposition to, and personal jealousy of, Mousinho in Lisbon or through lack of a plan of postpacification development. Thus, Norton de Matos, though invited, was not to be a member of the "school of Mousinho."

Instead, he went to Portuguese India, where he spent a decade without returning to the metropole—investing enough time, in effect, for an entire colonial career. This experience was an important part of his preparation as chief Portuguese official in Angola. In India he was initially named director of the land survey department and he made and supervised scientific surveys of lands and properties, forests, and public works. Later, through study and travel, he thoroughly familiarized himself with British Indian administration, technical education, and civil surveying. Although he was already forty-one at the end of his Indian service and the spectacular military campaigns in Africa were over, Norton de Matos's time was well spent. The British had influenced his colonial theories and action and convinced him that Portugal could keep and develop its African empire progressively only by following British precepts: decentralization of control, pragmatism, rule of the colony largely from within. A look at the "Raj" inspired an early interest in civil public works and humanitarian reforms.

The British Indian model fails to explain, nevertheless, why Norton de Matos later became an advocate of planned, intensive European agrarian colonization in Africa. The British did not practice European settlement schemes in India as had the Romans two millennia before. Roman influence might have come through his reading and study and through the enduring imprint of some Roman traditions in Portugal.

After travel and an assignment to a Portuguese diplomatic mission to China in 1908–1910, Norton de Matos returned to Portugal to take up staff work in provincial military headquarters. By this time he was a leading republican among the minority of regular army officers who actively espoused republicanism and he was close to the leadership of the PRP (Portuguese Republican party). After the collapse of the monarchy in the revolution of October 5, 1910, Norton de Matos, now a major, was named chief of staff of the Fifth Military Division by republican General Correia Barreto, then minister of war in the republic's provisional government. At about the same time Norton was appointed professor of topography and geodesic surveying at Lisbon's Higher Technical Institute. In 1912 he became governor-general of Angola, his first African assignment, and he landed at Luanda in June of that year.

Governor-general of Angola, 1912–1915

Many observers hoped that the new republican administration would transform Angola and make Portugal's largest African territory into a progressive colony along the lines of some of those held by the wealthier and larger European powers. Norton de Matos attempted to provide in Angola elements generally missing from Portuguese rule: humanitarian reform, continuity of administration, a more professional colonial service, civil occupation, and economic development.

Conditions were lacking for significant change. Most of the vast territory was only nominally under Portuguese sovereignty, and large sectors of northern, eastern, and southern Angola were ruled by a variety of African chiefs. Portuguese military power was slight and white settlers few. In 1912 Angola had fewer than 15,000 Portuguese and many of these were transported convicts, *degredados*, or transient petty traders.[3] The economy was stagnant and the Luanda treasury bankrupt. Though some public works such as railroads and roads had been begun—in part by foreign capitalized companies—no development plan existed.

Norton de Matos attempted to build a professional colonial administration. He followed the organization of Portugal's first separate ministry of colonies in 1911 and—defying regulations—set up in Angola a department of native affairs to deal with the African population's problems. European racist attitudes in Angola were severe and forced labor still flourished, including transportation of Angolan blacks to work on the Portuguese cocoa islands of São Tomé and Príncipe, as well as some forms of African domestic slavery. He established the department of native affairs in order to "protect" Africans from labor abuses, to collect information on Africans, and to provide some forms of welfare. Despite the good intentions of the governor-general, the department proved ineffective.

The master plan was to bring effective civilian administration to the hinterlands of Angola. His instrument was to replace military commands and administrative units with civil administrative units. On April 17, 1913, he issued his famous "Regulamento das circunscrições Administrativas da Província de Angola,"[4] followed by an explanatory circular regulation.

The governor-general had ambitious plans for road, railroad, and telegraph line construction, white settlement, and the development of revenues through an efficient system of tax collection from the Africans. These efforts were obstructed by an African rebellion in the Congo district in 1913–1914, armed clashes with German forces in 1914, and lack of support from either the Portuguese in Angola or those in the metropole.

Norton de Matos's 1913 *regulamento* on circumscriptions was more than an administrative measure intended to create a civilian Portuguese government in the interior. It was an outline of the governor's colonial philosophy and doctrine and his plan for "civilizing" Angola. This document sketched what became known as Norton's *Política de atracção* ("policy of attraction" or appeal). As the governor explained the following year this program followed the most modern colonial policy in order to civilianize the administration, cut down on military campaigns, and employ justice and humanity instead of the traditional iron hand, the old "policy of war and campaign."[5]

There are eleven main points in the *regulamento:* (1) Military garrisons would be replaced with carefully selected corps of *sepoys* and the military improved by paying troops on time and with money instead of cloth. (2) The living quarters of European officials would be improved. (3) The quality of the colonial service would benefit by more careful recruitment and training. (4) African traditional authorities would be used in governance, with respect shown their laws and customs insofar as they did not conflict with the "laws of humanity" or with Portuguese law. (5) The Angolan African must be "civilized" and educated to be free and independent small farmers, craftsmen, or manual workers. (6) As in British India, governance of Angola must reconcile humane laws and respect for the land, persons, and property of Africans with law, order, and social discipline. (7) Racial mixture in Angola, "with which civilization gains nothing,"[6] must be avoided. (8) African and European employees who committed crimes would be dismissed immediately. (9) The government must increase the hut tax collected from Africans and explain to them the reasons behind the tax—that it would provide them with roads, schools, and medical facilities and that only Portuguese officials could collect the tax but not by force or in areas not yet "pacified." (10) Military operations could be carried out only when absolutely necessary since the policy of attraction sought to replace the warlike traditions of Portuguese rule in Angola. (11) The labor shortage in Angola could be solved by turning Africans in larger numbers into independent small farmers and craftsmen who could be employed later by large enterprises, both agrarian and industrial.

On paper the colonial theories and legislation of his first governorship are impressive. Though Norton did follow basic concepts of Henrique de Paiva Couceiro, governor of Angola from 1907 to 1909 and an important figure in the new era of colonial reform, Norton de Matos's contribution was to construct a coherent and consistent set of legislation and to act on important issues.

His ideas were not well received in Angola: white settlers opposed his attempts to abolish forced labor and to create a "free and independent" class of African farmers and manual workers; some professional military officers—including Major Gomes da Costa, one of the "school of Mousinho" in the Mozambique campaigns of 1895–1897—strongly opposed the governor's views on the reduced role of the military in Angola. Gomes da Costa was fired shortly after Norton assumed his post in 1912.[7] In attempting to reassert the prerogatives of the governor-general, who by law *was* commander of all armed forces in the colony, Norton decreed that any orders for military operations in the colony had to come only from the office of the governor-general. This was an important measure, which earned him criticism from officers in the garrison and from Portuguese merchants in the Huíla region of central Angola.[8] As he noted in his report to Lisbon, the conditions he encountered in Angola were discouraging, and all his years in India did not prepare him for the difficulties he confronted in tropical Africa.

Norton de Matos adopted the motto of the Brazilian republic as the touchstone of his first governorship—"Order and Progress"—but his administration was plagued by external events. The African rebellion in the Congo district was long and costly and required greater attention to military necessities than his colonial plan warranted. Norton de Matos was forced to return to Lisbon in 1914 in order to get the military support necessary to suppress the uprising; Lisbon refused him permission to raise a loan for needed revenue. Considerable time and energy were spent, too, on safeguarding the colony from German infiltration and armed aggression in central and southern Angola. It was the confrontation with German forces from German Southwest Africa beginning in late 1914 that led to the governor-general's decision to resign.

Norton de Matos declared a state of emergency in the colony beginning in October 1914 after an incident at Naulila (near the Kunene river) that involved Portuguese and German forces. On December 28, 1914, German troops attacked and inflicted heavy losses on a Portuguese garrison at Naulila. Portugal dispatched army reinforcements to Angola, and the Portuguese press expressed the often heard fear that Germany might conquer and annex Angola to German Southwest Africa. Under various pressures, Norton de Matos resigned his governorship in March 1915 and returned to Portugal.

Cabinet Minister and Politician, 1915–1921

During the years 1915–1917 Norton de Matos held high public offices: colonial minister in 1915 and then, for nearly two years (until the military coup of December 8, 1917), minister of war. Until his later appointment as high commissioner in Angola, his service as minister of war was the most politically controversial episode of his life. The decisions and acts of this office had profound importance for the economic and political future of the Portuguese republic and for Portugal itself. Although Germany was at war with Portugal in Southern Africa by late 1914, the two nations did not officially declare war on one another in Europe until March 1916. The political parties and groups of the parliamentary republic were sharply divided on the war question. Those backed by Norton de Matos, now known as the democrats, advocated all-out support for the Allied effort against the Germans in Europe as well as in Africa, and when the British required more aid from Portugal, such as confiscating German ships in the Lisbon harbor, they complied. This was, in effect, an act of war. Other parties were less enthusiastic about any policy that might oblige Portugal to commit its slender resources in a European campaign. When Portugal declared war on Germany in the spring of 1916, it was the democrats who worked to commit a Portuguese army to fight alongside the Allies in Europe.

As minister of war, Norton de Matos was among those republican leaders who believed an activist war policy in Europe not only would safeguard Portugal's African colonies after the war but also would symbolize its modernization and integration into progressive European civilization. Such a policy would follow the dictates of the ancient alliance with Britain. To some republican patriots, to commit a Portuguese army in Europe would be a great coup for the novice and struggling republic. The Portuguese elite looked to France as a second cultural home and even as a political model, and they believed that it would be splendid to be among the liberators of France from Germany.

At a converted engineering base in Tancos, Portugal, Norton de Matos was assigned the task of readying an expeditionary force to fight in France. His organization of this expedition, which eventually numbered 65,000 troops, is known in Portuguese republican history as "the miracle of Tancos."[9] Norton's organizing talents were prodigious; the Portuguese Expeditionary Corps began to reach France in early 1917. Despite Norton's efforts, they were largely ill-prepared to fight a modern war against Germany, even with Allied aid and support during 1916–1918. Portuguese forces suffered heavy losses from combat and disease and were routed by the Germans at the battle of Lys in April 1917.

Politically, some Portuguese troops never forgave Norton de Matos for his role in supporting the policy of Portuguese armed participation in the European theater of the Great War. In later years conservatives, including traditionalist monarchists (Miguelists), integralists, and sections of the Portuguese masses who were neither motivated nor prepared to support such an ambitious enterprise bitterly attacked the former minister of war. They argued that his policy was unnecessary, wasteful, and financially disastrous. One of the reasons why Norton was ostracized by the post-1926 Portuguese dictatorship lay precisely in his courageous if controversial deeds in World War I.[10]

In late 1917 a reversal of political fortunes threw Norton de Matos out of office and into exile in England. The military backed government of Sidónio Pais seized power in a coup and expelled Norton from the ministry of war; angry mobs sacked and burned his home and office. He escaped to England, where he remained until early 1919, when the fall of the Sidonista government led to the return of the democrats. Norton de Matos was then appointed to the Portuguese delegation to the Versailles peace conference, at which he worked toward restoring the prewar status quo in Portuguese Africa, returning the German annexed Kionga triangle to

Mozambique colony, and obtaining reparations from Germany to pay for war damages in Angola and Mozambique.

When Norton de Matos returned to Portugal in the fall of 1919, it appeared that his career in public life was finished. He was tired, disillusioned with the "moral" effects of the 1917 disasters and the years in exile, and his health was poor. He was fifty-two years old. In a newspaper interview he declared that he was leaving politics for good and that he desired only a peaceful retirement at his family home in Ponte de Lima.[11] Curiously, however, Norton remarked to the reporter that "perhaps" he could cap his career with service as the head of government in "some of our colonies of West Africa," especially Angola.

High Commissioner and Governor-General of Angola, 1921–1926

Following World War I there was a revival of colonial interest and activity in Portugal. Angola particularly received renewed attention in the press; colonial institutions became more active. The republican regime was pledged to decentralize power and governance in the colonies. The 1911 constitution pledged "decentralization," and in laws passed by Parliament in 1914 and 1920 the government instituted measures to allow more local autonomy in the African colonies, increase representative government, improve the colonial service, and allow greater decisionmaking and planning powers for high administrators. Some of the reforms that were presaged in Norton de Matos's 1913 *regulamento* in Angola and in the 1906–1907 administrative reforms under the late monarchy were written into republican legislation and approved by the Lisbon Parliament.

In 1920 the Parliament set up the so-called regime of the high commissioners. The purpose of allowing governors increased power was more economic than political. Colonial and political writers were convinced that Portugal's economic rejuvenation would be made possible by going beyond military occupation and pacification to develop the colonial economies. The economics of colonialism in Angola and Mozambique assumed supreme importance in the postwar years. Portuguese observers believed that the raw materials and resources of tropical Africa could make up for metropolitan weakness. A well-known academic in Oporto wrote in 1920: "In the colonies is the surest security of our national autonomy, the most solid guarantee of our prosperity."[12] There was a host of problems connected with this revived colonial thrust, and severe economic problems gripped Portugal at home: rising prices, runaway inflation, currency devaluation, widespread poverty, financial mismanagement, and increasing debt from the costs of Portuguese participation in World War I.

Colonial thinkers dreamed that by allowing governors in Africa new economic and financial powers, development and prosperity would result. Norton de Matos, an experienced colonialist and a veteran governor from Angola, was appointed the first high commissioner of Angola and he assumed his post in early 1921. He brought to his new job fresh energies and plans. He hoped to complete projects begun in his 1912–1915 governorship—roads, schools, railroads, and medical facilities—and to solve the ever present labor problem.

When Norton returned to Angola in 1921, he found conditions little changed from 1915. Though pacification was virtually complete in the interior and only one major military campaign was undertaken during his high commissionership,[13] in other areas of administration virtually everything remained to be done. The Angolan economy suffered from severe inflation, debt, and a long-standing budget deficit. Some foreign capital was working in Angola, but there was little Portuguese interest in investment there.

Traditionally the Portuguese feared foreign economic dominance. In the field of labor, Norton found that forced labor, corporal punishment of Africans, and the export of labor to the Portuguese cocoa islands continued almost unabated. Road building was lagging and minerals and soil resources remained to be developed. European settlers in the colony by 1921 (about 20,000) were too few to make much of an economic impact, and few Africans were being "assimilated" as independent small farmers and artisans.

In order to encourage his economic development program, the high commissioner issued a series of decrees designed to insure greater Portuguese control over land ownership, education, foreign missions and missionaries, various groups of European employees and officials, and the budding Angolan *assimilado* associations and their Luanda press. One of his earliest and most controversial measures was a decree dated December 9, 1921, seeking to "nationalize the foreign missions and to submit them to the complete will and control of the state."[14] The decree was motivated by Norton de Matos's fear that foreign missions, whose work he had so admired during his first governorship, were becoming predominant over Portuguese missions. By this decree the teaching of the Portuguese language was made compulsory in all missions; foreign languages could not be taught; and African language publications had to include a Portuguese translation. The measure, which had roots in regulations passed by previous administrations, was opposed by some foreign missions. Nevertheless, until the 1960s, it helped structure the Portuguese school curriculum.

Further laws were instituted to restrict land ownership by foreigners and to tighten passport and immigration control in order to discourage large-scale immigration of German settlers into south Angola. Several European organizations, including the Association of Public Functionaries, were banned in the interests of "order." Another highly controversial action of the high commissioner was his suppression of African associations and the African press. The history of the alleged Catete conspiracy, Norton de Matos's suppression of the *assimilado* associations, and his closing down of African publications is related in detail elsewhere.[15] In this account it is important only to determine the origins and consequences of this political episode.

The high commissioner's acts during 1922 strictly accorded with the law and those powers invested in his office by the republic's new policy of decentralized governance from within the colony. Norton de Matos rarely discussed these incidents publicly, and evidently he believed that the Liga Angolana and other groups in the colony threatened to undermine both Portuguese national control and his plans for rapid economic development. Ironically, opponents in Parliament of the pro-Norton, democratic governments appropriated the Catete affair as a hot political issue and attempted to use this and other matters to dismiss Norton de Matos and to overturn the politicians who supported him.

In economic questions, the high commissioner used his new powers to negotiate substantial loans for public works such as extending the Luanda railroad eastward and to support a scheme of Portuguese settlement. Most significantly, he negotiated a new contract in 1921 with a large diamond mining firm, the famous DIAMANG company; in return for extensive mining concessions in Lunda region, DIAMANG paid the Angolan government large tax and subsidy amounts. One estimate suggested that the diamond company paid into Angola's treasury during the years 1921–1923 some £1,233,247.[16] In effect, DIAMANG administered, ruled, and defended with its own police corps a large sector of eastern Angola—an arrangement that may have been "colonialism by proxy" but that for the time being allowed a penurious government to put more of its resources elsewhere.

Less controversially, Norton de Matos laid the foundation for the modern road network of Angola. He continued where he left off in 1915 and encouraged the expansion of various classes of automobile roads in order to open up the interior to white settlement and to complement the railroads that were penetrating the plateaus from the coast. An earlier measure (in 1913) had encouraged road building by rewarding each circumscription with an automobile as soon as it had constructed more than 100 kilometers of roads in its area.[17] During Norton's last term in office thousands of kilometers of new roads were begun or completed. They were intended for automobiles in order to facilitate commerce and communications and to eliminate the traditional African porterage.

He was not alone in viewing Angola as a potential El Dorado for a poor Portugal. Economic expansion was in the air at the time of his high commissionership. To a range of different groups in the metropole, Angola awaited development sooner rather than later. An editorial in one of Lisbon's most influential daily newspapers suggested in all seriousness that Angola would be the "economic redemption of the fatherland." Furthermore, "the very rich province could be the treasure chest and granary of Portugal."[18]

To the high commissioner himself, massive white settlement appeared to be the key to economic well-being. Rural white settlement, carefully planned and directed, would provide an impetus. With minor revisions—usually increasing the numbers of whites to be settled in Angola—this scheme was championed by Norton de Matos for the remainder of his active life. It called for intensive colonization on the healthier central plateaus of Angola by means of directing the emigration of Portuguese farmers and fishermen. The ultimate goal was to safeguard Angola for Portugal by means of more thorough occupation of the vast territory, development of the economy, and "integration" of foreigners, who "denationalize" the colony. Early outlines of this colonization plan[19] do not emphasize one of the later purposes of white settlement: to "assimilate" the majority of black Africans and integrate them into Portuguese civilization.

A careful study of this 1920 settlement scheme is more than an exercise in pure theory, one of the common pitfalls of the historian of Portuguese-speaking Africa, or an adventure in speculation after the fact. Norton de Matos's colonization plans and writings, in fact, laid the bases for the post-World War II *colonato*, direct rural settlement plans of the Portuguese government. According to the high commissioner's ideas, such settlements were to be founded upon: (1) Portuguese rural village structure and spirit; (2) Portuguese family life—families would comprise the villages; (3) elimination of African labor from Portuguese villages; (4) and "mixing" of African farm communities with Portuguese villages. In his plan for the years 1924–1927, Norton recommended that the government finance the settlement of some 600 villages, or a total of between 100,000 and 150,000 Portuguese from Portugal. In 1924 the white population of Angola could not have exceeded 25,000 persons. The government would subsidize these settlers by paying for their transportation and providing them with free land, tools, seed, and even housing. With his typical penchant for detail, Norton de Matos arranged for the shipping of some 133 "wooden houses" from England to Angola. In order to encourage Portuguese settlement the high commissioner himself established a new government agency, the Agência Geral de Angola, which, significantly, was the direct precursor of the New State's official colonial agency, the Agência Geral das Colónias, founded in 1924 but consolidated in the 1930s.

The immediate results of the colonization plan were meager: during the period April 1921–August 1923, only 761 Portuguese emigrated to Angola. Some came from Brazil and it is not clear how many of the total were part of the official scheme.

Finance, not white settlement, however, became the hot political issue and cause célèbre that effectively wrecked Norton de Matos's plans and ended his colonial career. Disputes over finances provided the material for a generation of controversy over his career, the high commissionership, and the origins of the authoritarian regime that was born with the promise of financial wizardry. The historian cannot be too cautious in plumbing the intricate depths of this financial episode because of the affair's relationship to the collapse of the parliamentary republic and to the rise of a dictatorship led by a financial expert. At the outset, at least two relatively safe facts are at hand: Angola's financial situation in 1924 was bad and after 1930 Finance minister Salazar managed—at least on paper[20]—to balance the budget of the colony although he did so at the expense of economic expansion or development as they were conceived by the forward-looking high commissioner.

If there is no need to defend the general's record in Angola, there is nevertheless a need to understand the conditions under which he acted. Mistakes were made and Norton's plans outstripped the resources available. In 1921 Angola had a debt of at least £500,000, and the plans for public works alone were beyond the means of the treasury in Luanda. Nevertheless, the republic had empowered the high commissioner to arrange for loans and to sign contracts without monetary restrictions; the high commissioner of Angola believed that if the capital was not to be had in Angola he could seek it elsewhere.

Portugal itself was crippled by severe economic problems: unprecedented debts, currency inflation and devaluation, and price rises. Both Portugal and Angola were plagued by entrepreneurs who launched get-rich-quick schemes while lacking most of the capital needed to back them.

In mid-1923 members of the Chamber of Deputies initiated a "campaign," as "personal as it was political,"[21] against the high commissioner and accused him of flagrant malfeasance in office. Norton de Matos responded by returning to Portugal in September 1923 and by writing reports that the government used to answer questions on the floor of Parliament. The campaign was led by a firebrand politician, Francisco da Cunha Leal, who was by no means a disinterested or objective bystander. Cunha Leal had many motives for attacking Norton de Matos. He was a leading member of the rightist Nationalist party, which was working to turn out of office the party of Norton de Matos; he harbored a ten-year-old grudge against the high commissioner that stemmed from a personal clash between them in Angola in 1912–1915;[22] he was backed by interest groups that wished to discredit Norton and by individuals—including some white settlers—who had been chastised and deported by the high commissioner for illegal activities in Angola.[23]

The glib Cunha Leal led the attack in Parliament and then published a vicious little volume entitled *Caligula em Angola* (Lisbon, 1924). Labeling Norton de Matos a "squanderer of other people's monies,"[24] Cunha Leal continued to accuse Norton of spending public money on personal needs, breaking the law, wasting funds, and doing nothing. His most potent arrow was nationalistic: Norton de Matos, he claimed, was guilty of attempting to build up Angola by tearing down Portugal and of encouraging Angola's separation or independence from Portugal.

Norton de Matos's defense against a host of such accusations was futile. He blamed many difficulties on Portugal's severe financial crisis: the escudo's value had fallen over twenty times since 1919, for instance. A number of banks had refused to make loans to the government. Norton's most critical comments were reserved for the powerful Banco Nacional Ultramarino, "a state within the state,"[25] he suggested, which in 1923 had helped to wreck his development plans. There were other factors that contributed to the large budget deficit: a stevedores' strike in Angolan ports, currency exchange difficulties between Portugal and Angola, and an annual low production of copper and diamonds.

The most telling attack on Norton de Matos centered on the civil rights issue of the suppression of *assimilado* associations and the African press in 1922;[26] despite the high commissioner's charges that there were (unproved) conspiracies to incite Africans to revolt by the Liga Angolana, and that national political and economic "unity" would suffer, rights guaranteed in the republic's 1911 constitution had been trampled upon.

In some respects, the high commissioner was exonerated of the accusation of financial malfeasance. Groups of settlers from Angola communicated their support for Norton de Matos, and some urged him to return to his post. In Parliament the debate went against the Cunha Leal faction; on March 10, 1924, the Chamber of Deputies passed a "motion of praise" for Norton de Matos's work in Angola.[27] Convinced that he could not count on government support and disillusioned by the personal attacks, Norton submitted his resignation in June 1924. He never returned to Angola. The government soon appointed him Portuguese minister to Britain. He spent the remaining months of the first republic, into the summer of 1926, in London.

In summarizing the accomplishments of Angola's most controversial high commissioner it is necessary to correct the erroneous and simplistic view that "bad administration" alone was to blame for the condition of both Portugal and Angola in 1926–1928 and for lack of foreign investment in Portuguese Africa. There were many other factors involved, not least of them Norton's attempt to mobilize the development processes in Angola and to plan ambitiously. Curiously, however, the high commissioner defended his policies with a financial rule of thumb that in effect served as the major financial principle of the Portuguese dictatorship until after 1961: the colonies must be self-supporting. In one of his last reports to the ministry of colonies in 1924, he emphasized his opposition to the seeking of foreign loans on principle: "We must develop our colonies almost exclusively by means of the nation's resources and, above all, by means of those of the colonies themselves."[28]

There was more Portuguese capital available than has been previously known but it had been withdrawn from the metropole. Norton de Matos's prescient plans for Angola went begging in part not because Portuguese capitalists absolutely lacked capital but because they refused to risk investing it under the conditions then prevailing in Portugal and in Angola. There was a vicious circle: unstable conditions caused a capital flight, which in turn helped prolong such instability. One Portuguese historian has determined that by 1925 the Portuguese capital flight abroad amounted to more than six times the total currency circulation in Portugal.[29]

Whatever the financial problems, the public works legacy of the Norton de Matos administration was significant. Between 1912 and 1924 Angola's railroad mileage increased from less than 1,000 kilometers to 1,500 kilometers. There were about 100 kilometers of roads in 1912; in 1924 there were about 25,000 kilometers. Norton de Matos's work laid the foundation on which the dictatorship constructed its programs of the next decades.

Senior Colonialist and Oppositionist

The first republic's collapse ended Norton de Matos's public career. In June 1926 the military dictatorship abruptly fired him as ambassador to London. He survived nearly twenty-nine years of the authoritarian regime but he never again held public office.

As a courageous oppositionist, as the surviving and still vigorous democrat and personal symbol of the "myth" of the first republic, the old general was by no means inactive. For his writings and his speaking out against the increasing repressiveness of the New State, he was persecuted and ostracized. After the failure of the revolution of February 1927 he was briefly exiled to the Azores but he continued to correspond with leading conspirators. On December 20, 1929, he was elected grand master of the Portuguese masons and led that besieged organization until the New State, in the law of May 21, 1935, dissolved it and confiscated its property.[30] At the same time the government dismissed Norton de Matos from his job as professor of civil engineering and surveying at the Higher Technical Institute in Lisbon. He was retired as a general in the Portuguese army.

Norton survived all his onetime colleagues. There was yet one more great role to play. In 1948 he became the opposition candidate for the presidency of the republic. The regime "allowed" one month's formal campaigning and the 1933 constitution provided for a presidential "election" with nominally universal suffrage. The election was scheduled for February 11, 1949, and Norton threw himself into the exhausting schedule. At age eighty-one, backed by the Movement for Democratic Union, Norton de Matos toured the country and received some popular acclaim. He inspired much younger political leaders of the opposition, including premier-to-be of the second republic (1974-   ) Mário Soares. For Norton de Matos, the 1948–1949 presidential campaign was "the culmination of his political career, a last service rendered to his country."[31] The regime applied familiar tactics of police terror, legal manipulation, and censorship, and the opposition never really had a chance. At the last moment, recognizing that the regime would not allow a free vote, Norton de Matos consented to withdraw his candidacy. One of the weaknesses of his candidacy had been that he was too closely identified with the flaws of the first republic, with the political past. Still, Norton's presidential aspirations had made the regime anxious.

Interest in colonial affairs dominated the general's last years. He became active for a time as an officer of a private colonial lobby, the União Portuguesa do Ultramar (1928–1931?). Consisting of colonial experts, businessmen, and settlers, this group mounted a campaign to alert the public and the government to the dangers of a monopoly by foreign chartered company capital in Mozambique, in the port of Beira, and, further afield, in Cabinda. They exhorted the government to "nationalize" the large chartered companies in Mozambique and to organize colonial studies more effectively. Norton de Matos ceased his work with the group when it was absorbed by another private but regime-sanctioned colonial lobby organization, Movimento Pró Colónias, dominated by Oporto businessmen.[32]

The dictatorship preferred its domestic and colonial heroes to be collaborators or at least to accept passively the regime's philosophy and policies. If colonial heroes were neither loyal nor cooptable, Norton found, then the New State system of "no-risk statism" preferred them dead, like Mousinho de Albuquerque, or senile, like some survivors of his so-called school. In 1929, when General Alfredo Freire de Andrade died, the regime paid tribute to him as "the dean of Portuguese colonialists."[33] Norton de Matos could have then informally assumed that title. Other colonialists, less closely identified with the first republic, cooperated with the regime and in return received official positions and recognition: Vicente Ferreira, for example, a younger and less acclaimed colonial governor than Norton, found himself vice-president of the main colonial advisory organ, the Conselho do Império; at his death he was honored in the regime's official colonial periodical.[34]

No such recognition or rewards for colonial service awaited General Norton de Matos. Despite his democratic principles and his feeling of personal superiority over the leaders of the dictatorship, Norton was hurt by the ostracism and he continually defended his record as governor and high commissioner. Drawing upon his years in India and his English roots and reading, the senior colonialist fancied himself a Portuguese Clive whose reputation was unfairly on trial.[35] It is significant that the official colonial periodical made no mention of the general after news came of his death in January 1955.

Ironically, the colonial writings of Norton de Matos from 1926 to 1953 were extremely influential. Although the regime ostracized Norton, many of his key ideas and plans were adopted, ideas and plans set forth in three books (1926, 1953, 1953)[36] and in a series of newspaper articles for the Oporto daily, *O Primeiro de Janeiro* (1931; 1952).

On the other hand, Norton's advocacy of liberal and humanitarian reform in Portuguese colonies went largely unheeded. As he wrote in *A Nação Una* (1953), a book he considered to be "an old man's [last] advice" to his country, Portugal had to end the "humiliations and exploitations" of Africans by white settlers and officials or else his colonial development plan would not work.

Without these conditions—the improvement of the lives of the natives, the indispensable adaptation of their mentality to ours, the absolute respect for their persons and for their interests, and the firm and continuous protection that we should give them—everything that we try to accomplish in the European sense, that is, by means of national unity, autonomy, and white colonization, will produce no appreciable advantage; it will be merely the erection of castles, apparently strong, with walls of rotten wood, upon quicksand.[37]

Norton de Matos's national plan was inspired by patriotism and an old-fashioned liberal paternalism. He defended his plan to transform Portuguese Africa and to save it from what he considered to be "extremes" of African nationalism or white settler apartheid by stating that his purpose was to build up Portugal. Of great concern to him were political developments in Africa: British West Africa was moving rapidly toward African independence, and in South Africa an Afrikaner dominated government was consolidating an apartheid policy. He entreated Portugal to beware and to prevent the influences from these developments from "infecting" Portuguese Africa.

From Norton's last writings we may select seven major doctrinal points or suggestions for the reform of Portuguese administration in Africa:

1. The central concept of a "Greater Portugal" (*Portugal Maior*), or a unified empire, in which all Portuguese territory was indivisible.
2. A massive, rural white colonization project
3. Liberal, humanitarian reforms for Africans
4. Administrative and political autonomy for the colonies
5. Economic autonomy
6. Massive assimilation of Africans into Portuguese life
7. Reinforcement of Portuguese military strength in Africa

To this senior colonialist, a unified, "happy" empire had to be founded upon the three pillars of his plan: autonomy, white rural colonization, and assimilation of Africans. The kernels of these ideas are to be found in Norton's colonial writings of 1924–1931; the projections for white settlement in Africa were merely revised upward. Here again was the familiar concept of a native Portuguese rural colonization; small farmers and tradesmen from Portugal, rendered "free and independent" by their possession of farmland and skills, would mix harmoniously with black farmers and tradesmen, also possessed of land and skills. The government of Salazar was urged to finance a massive white settlement project: to settle in Angola within thirty years (in theory, by 1982) some 1 million Portuguese from Portugal, or 200,000 rural farm families organized into 5,000 or 6,000 rural villages, Portuguese style. The same settlement project was advocated for Mozambique. The settlement in Africa of 2 million Portuguese would not, by itself, Norton suggested, preserve the empire's integrity. It would have to go hand in hand with effective mass assimilation of the African populations into Portuguese civilization. Criticizing the New State's post-1926 *indigenato* system, Norton de Matos proposed that the government abolish it.

The eradication of all forms of racial and social discrimination and injustice also had to be part of the reforms. In terms of new autonomy for colonies, the ex-high commissioner proposed that the economy of the empire be structured so that assets and liabilities would be shared equally by all in order that the metropole not exploit the colonial economies. Ending tariff barriers between the metropole and the colonies would be a crucial step. Finally, Norton de Matos proposed a significant strengthening of Portugal's armed forces in Africa to prevent "separatism," either white settler or black African. Increasing the metropolitan forces in Angola and Mozambique was part of his vision that "the white race will be the principal factor in the future of Africa."[38]

What was the estimated time scope of this plan? The general believed that his dream of *A Nação Una* ("the nation united") could be realized in 150 years. Whether Portugal followed this colonial plan, consciously or unconsciously, and its results at the time of the largely unforseen collapse of the empire in 1974, are questions worth examining.

Following the sternly nationalistic and centralizing Colonial Act of 1930, the New State opposed implementing the ideas that Norton so persistently advocated. The 1930s and 1940s, for economic and political reasons, were years of retrenchment, modest outlays, no overall development plans, and Salazar's pet "policy of balanced budgets" (*política dos saldos*). Massive white settlement schemes or assimilation plans requiring heavy expenses and large-scale educational reforms were out of the question.[39] After World War II, and especially in the early 1950s, however, Lisbon began to fund the rural settlement schemes known as *colonatos* and to plan development along modern lines. The 1950s, 1960s, and early 1970s saw committed, if cautious, development schemes and attempts to settle thousands of Portuguese in the valleys and on the plateaus of Angola and Mozambique. A younger generation of colonial civil servants and planners, to a degree following the spirit of Norton de Matos's plans of the 1920s for Angola, became more influential beginning in the early 1950s. Some of them, like Adriano Moreira, minister for overseas 1961–1962, reached the highest policymaking circles after the outbreak of war in Angola. The government, which was reluctant to spend anything on white settlement in the prewar years, now expended millions of dollars.

As is the case in so much of the history of Portuguese-speaking Africa, the verifiable facts were less impressive than the plans, the rhetoric, and the propaganda. In 1952, when Norton de Matos put his national plan in its final form, Angola had between 80,000 and 85,000 Portuguese settlers, and there were fewer than 50,000 in Mozambique. By 1974 Angola had perhaps 350,000 Portuguese and Mozambique about 250,000. Many of these settlers were recent. According to a 1975 study of Portuguese settlement in Angola,[40] over 50 percent had immigrated or were born in the territory *after 1961* and the outbreak of war.

Judged against the record of the past and Portugal's failure to divert the steady stream of its emigrants from Brazil and Europe to Africa, the total of approximately 600,000 in Africa in 1974 was extraordinary. But judged against the plans of Norton de Matos (an estimated total of 2 million whites by 1982), the reality was yet another shortfall. As for Portugal's record of assimilation by 1974, reliable figures simply do not exist. But even a generous estimate could not exceed two or three percent of the total of about 14 million Africans in both Angola and Mozambique. Despite the good intentions of some colonial theorists and governors, discrimination, exploitation, mob and personal violence, and repression of Africans were rule rather than exception by the time of the Lisbon coup of April 25, 1974.

The government had begun to implement virtually all of the major provisions of Norton de Matos's national plan but it lacked time and certain other resources or conditions that might have held Portugal's empire together or allowed it to evolve into a loosely structured Lusitanian commonwealth of states. The general's scheme was based upon his belief that most Africans would be willing to "become Portuguese." In this mistaken belief and in the notion of a broad time frame for his development and assimilation plan, the old colonial theorist was out of step with the winds of change blowing through the continent he had left a generation before.

Norton de Matos in Perspective

The career of Angola's first high commissioner was long and varied. As a colonialist Norton lived through three generations of modern Portuguese colonialism: 1890–1910, 1910–1930, and 1930–1950. Whatever the anachronistic, even naive, features of Norton de Matos's last plan to save the empire as he conceived of it, whatever his personal flaws of zealous ambition, egoism, and imperiousness, he made a contribution to Angola and Portuguese-speaking Africa. As his friend and anti-Salazarist colleague Egas Moniz, Portugal's 1949 Nobel Prize winner, noted in introducing the controversial *A Nação Una*,[41] Norton de Matos was "a giant in [Portugal's] colonial history."[42] His six-year career as senior administrator in Angola and his many years as a colonial writer gave him the knowledge and experience that few Africanists in Portugal of his day possessed. Norton de Matos's visions and grandiose plans were well thought out and logical, but too often they were beyond both his reach and the resources of his country. In the period 1948–1953, when few others dared speak out critically and realistically on either domestic or colonial problems, Norton de Matos staunchly stood against those who refused to acknowledge that Portugal's empire in Africa faced "tremendous dangers."[43]

One can only speculate about what might have occurred had Norton de Matos's colonial theories and plans been vigorously acted upon in 1952. Certainly, Portugal's hold on Angola and Mozambique would have been stronger and more formidable and, possibly, the forces of African assertion, disillusionment among the Portuguese armed forces, and African independence might have been postponed. More likely, massive white colonization might have produced briefly a Lusitanian version of a white settler secession state à la Rhodesia.

In assessing Norton de Matos as a governor, it is important to balance the obstacles he faced with his accomplishments. If he completed little of what he planned, the environment he confronted was notoriously hostile. If he was a democrat in Portugal, in Angola he brooked no opposition from Africans and *mestiços* who might thwart his plans for economic development. All in all, he did more than any other governor to bring to Angola a modern colonial administration that compared favorably with those of Britain and France in West Africa.

Norton de Matos did not live long enough to see his colonial reputation among the Portuguese rehabilitated. In Angola settlers erected a bronze statue in his honor in Nova Lisboa—but only in 1962. In Portugal a new generation of colonial scholars sang his praises as a leading colonial governor and thinker. In the official training school for colonial administrators, Norton de Matos's Angolan administration was carefully examined and commended; indeed, his rapid development doctrine became the latest colonial rage. Wheras liberal republican scholars reclaimed the general as a brave pioneer among oppositionists who stood up against the dictatorship during years of injustice, the judgment of a new generation of Africanists in Portugal was less certain.

In the last analysis it is clear that Norton's self-contradictions as an oppositionist at home and an old-fashioned paternalist in Africa must be weighed against his actual influence upon the course of Portuguese rule in Africa. No single modern governor and colonial theorist did more to construct the foundations of post-1920 colonial policy in Portuguese Africa. No colonialist was more influential in discussing and disseminating in their original form the concepts of a Greater Portugal, white colonization, and assimilation, which were later adopted and adapted by the New State: Despite his ignorance of the changes occurring in black Africa, Norton was ultimately correct in his striking disclaimer: Portugal, he wrote, could still see its empire collapse if, after following his advice, racial discrimination and dictatorial repression and exploitation endured.

To Africans of the pre-1961 generation of *assimilados*, the ex–high commissioner was the man who had suppressed their associations and press and had halted their advances in the Angolan civil service. To Africans of the post-1961 generation, Norton de Matos seemed to be just one more Portuguese colonialist. What was not clear to either group of Africans was that the Salazar regime in its preinsurgency phase used Norton de Matos, a domestic opponent, as a handy republican colonial scapegoat. Nevertheless, regime publicists later did not hesitate to quote freely from his more conservative writings—out of context—in order to unify the Portuguese behind the struggle to retain the empire.[44] Ironically, in independent Angola, new African leaders probably would support some of his general economic development goals, if not the means to achieve them.

Notes

1. José Norton de Matos, *A Provincia de Angola* (Oporto, 1926), p. 24.

2. Idem, *Memórias e Trabelhos da minha Vida*, 4 vols. (Lisbon, 1944–1946), 1:82.

3. Douglas L. Wheeler and René Pélissier, *Angola* (New York, 1971), p. 112.

4. The governor-general's circular of 17 April 1913, dispatched to district governors, the chief of staff, administrators of circumscriptions, and captains major, is reprinted in José Norton de Matos, *África Nossa* (Oporto, 1953), pp. 153–174; passages of the original *regulamento* are reprinted and discussed in ibid., pp. 174–184, and in idem, *Memórias e Trabalhos*, 3:181–190.

5. "Relatório," 28 June 1914, Norton de Matos to minister of colonies, *Arquivo Histórico Ultramarino*, Angola, Militar series, no. 999.

6. Norton de Matos, *África Nossa*, p. 164.

7. Idem, *Memórias e Trabalhos*, 3:168–171.

8. "Relatório," 28 June 1914.

9. For more detail on this era see Douglas L. Wheeler, *Republican Portugal: A Political History, 1910–1926* (Madison, 1978).

10. The Salazar government kept Portugal officially neutral throughout World War II although after mid-1943 Portugal gave the Allies special rights in the Azores.

11. Interview in *O Século* (Lisbon), 12 October 1919.

12. Bento Carqueja, *O Futuro de Portugal* (Oporto, 1920), p. 289, cited in Wheeler and Pélissier, *Angola*, p. 82.

13. The vast Lunda region of eastern Angola remained under African control, however, and in 1922–1923 a military operation was mounted against the Chokwe "rebel," Gunza. Perhaps the last "official" punitive expedition in this era took place in Lunda in 1926–1927, but pacification in the formal sense had been completed in the remainder of the colony. See René Pélissier, *Résistance et révoltes en Angola*, 3 vols. (Paris, 1975), 1:405–416.

14. Norton de Matos to ministry of colonies, "Relatório sobre a Situação . . . em Angola," 10 February 1924, Arquivo Histórico Ultramarino, sala 5, maço 1, pasta no. 604, processo no. 442c.

15. Wheeler and Pélissier, *Angola*, pp. 122–126.

16. Pélissier, *Résistance et révoltes*, 1:416 n.

17. Norton de Matos, *A Província de Angola*, pp. 153, 221.

18. Editorial, *O Século*, 1 January 1922.

19. José Norton de Matos, "Como Pretendi Povoar Angola," *Boletim Geral das Colónias*, no. 100 (October 1933).

20. Until Lisbon archives—government ministries—for this period are made available to the public, it is impossible to determine how honestly or dishonestly the finance minister balanced the budgets.

21. Renato Mascarenhas, "Norton de Matos" (dissertation for Higher Institute of Social Sciences and Overseas Policy, Lisbon, 1970), pp. 283–284.

22. Francisco da Cunha Leal, *As minhas Memórias*, 3 vols. (Lisbon, 1966–1968), 2:389–390.

23. Venâncio Guimarães, *A Situação de Angola: Para a História do Reinado de Norton; Factos e Depoimentos* (Lisbon, 1923).

24. Cunha Leal, *As Minhas Memórias*, 2:391.

25. Norton de Matos, "Relatório sobre a Situação . . . em Angola."

26. For a discussion of the politics of the high commissioner's suppression of the assimilados see Wheeler and Pélissier, *Angola*, pp. 122–126.

27. Mascarenhas, "Norton de Matos," p. 285.

28. Norton de Matos, "Relatório sobre a Situação . . . em Angola."

29. A. H. de Oliveira Marques, *A Primeira República Portuguesa* (Lisbon, 1972), p. 49.

30. Idem, *O General Sousa Dias e as Revoltas Contra a Ditadura, 1926–1931* (Lisbon, 1975), pp. 76–102; idem, ed., *A Maçonaria Portuguesa e o Estado Novo* (Lisbon, 1975), pp. 52–54.

31. Mário Soares, *Portugal's Struggle for Liberty* (London, 1975), p. 78; for an account of the 1948–1949 campaign and the role of Norton de Matos see pp. 75–83.

32. A. Gonçalves Pereira, *As Novas Tendências da Administração Colonial* (Lisbon, 1931), p. 37; "Movimento Pró-Colonias," *Boletim da Agência Geral das Colónias* 6, nos. 62–63 (August–September 1930):159–160.

33. "Informações e Notícias," *Boletim da Agência Geral das Colónias* 5, no. 50 (August 1929):375–376.

34. "Prof. Eng. A. Vicente Ferreira," *Boletim Geral do Ultramar*, no. 332 (February 1953).

35. Rodrigo Abreu, *Vida Preciosa: D. Ester N. Norton de Matos* (Viana do Castelo, 1958), pp. 254–255.

36. Norton de Matos, *A Província de Angola, África Nossa*, and *A Nação Una* (Lisbon, 1953).

37. Idem, *Nação Una*, p. 231.

38. Ibid., p. 219.

39. For the main outlines of policy in the 1930s and 1940s see the article by Minister of colonies Armindo Monteiro, "Directrizes duma Política Ultramarina," *Boletim Geral das Colónias*, no. 97 (July 1933).

40. Gerald J. Bender, "The Myth and Reality of Portuguese Rule in Angola: A Study of Racial Domination" (Ph.D. dissertation, UCLA, 1975), pp. 541 ff.

41. Norton de Matos, *A Nação Una*, was the subject of a debate in Portugal's prestigious Academy of Sciences; despite support from two eminent scholars, including Egas Moniz, the book was rejected as a candidate for a prize awarded for colonial administration writing.

42. Ibid., p. ix.
43. Ibid., p. 10.
44. A well-known quotation used by the regime from Norton de Matos, *A Nação Una*, was put on dust jackets of patriotic books: "If someone comes to your side and whispers to you words of disillusionment, trying to convince you that we cannot maintain such a large empire, expel them from the bosom of the nation."

Germany

German
Governors:
An Overview

L. H. Gann

IN terms of geographical extent, Germany's colonial empire was impressive in size. The dependencies included well over 900,000 square miles, considerably more than four times the area of the Reich, with about one-fifth of its population. This vast empire, however, was of marginal significance both to the German economy and to German capitalists. During the first two decades of Wilhelmian expansion overseas the Reich spent little money in colonial ventures. The pioneering companies rarely made money. Investment capital was hard to get at a time when the colonies were deficient in ports, roads, and railways; markets were scarce; agricultural experimentation was costly; and risks were high.

Table 1.   The German Colonial Empire, 1913

Colony	Capital	Estimated area (square miles)	European population	Estimated indigenous population
Togo	Lomé	33,700	368	1,031,978
German Cameroons	Buea	191,130	1,871	2,648,720
German Southwest Africa	Windhoek	322,450	14,830	79,556
German East Africa	Dar es Salaam	384,180	5,336	7,645,770
Kiaochow	Tsingtao	200	—	168,900
Pacific possessions	Rabaul and Apia	96,160	1,984	634,579
Total colonies		1,027,820	24,389	12,041,603
German Reich in Europe		208,780	64,925,993	

467

The pace of colonial lending picked up somewhat after the turn of the century. Even so, Germans did not invest a great deal of money outside the fatherland. Between 1900 and 1914 about one-tenth of current savings went abroad, and the bulk of this was placed in Europe; the Austro-Hungarian empire alone absorbed as much capital as the entire African and Asian continents. Only a tiny proportion of Germany's private funds was invested in its African colonies. By 1907 the reserves and share capital of a single great German bank such as the Dresdner Bank or the Diskonto-Gesellschaft amounted to more than the entire private capital invested in all of the empire's African holdings.

The colonial empire likewise counted for no more than a minuscule portion of Germany's overseas trade. Between 1891 and 1910 the colonial share of German exports rose, but the increase amounted to only 0.17–0.73 of the total. The colonies were equally insignificant from the German emigrants' standpoint. Millions of Germans had found new homes for themselves in the Americas, but the European population of the German colonies in 1913 was less than that of a small country town like Konstanz or Reutlingen.

The financial means available for colonial expansion was exiguous. Hence, the public treasury was forced to assume a considerable share of the burden. The total spent by German taxpayers on the colonies in the form of imperial subsidies and subventions between 1884 and 1914 amounted to 451 million marks, a sum considerably lower than the revenue received from Germany's post and telegraph services in the course of a single year. Even so, it exceeded by a considerable margin the total funds placed in the colonies by private companies (346.6 million marks). Seen in terms of German capitalism as a whole, colonialism was at best a speculative investment and at worst a form of conspicuous consumption at the general taxpayer's expense.

The German colonial empire was equally marginal to German society. There was no colonial tradition. There was no far-flung, British type "old boys' network" of men who wanted their sons to serve overseas. On the contrary, the German colonies were widely regarded as places for idlers and ne'er-do-wells. There was no separate colonial service with an esprit de corps of its own, and it was not until 1910 that the Germans acquired a uniform colonial civil service code with standardized conditions of service. During its initial period the service was besmirched by numerous scandals. A number of officials were convicted of atrocities, of rape, and of murder. Such scandals were amply ventilated in the Reichstag—more so than they would have been in the legislatures of other colonial powers such as France, Italy, or Portugal. The facts, bad as they were, lost nothing in the telling and were sometimes embroidered by hearsay evidence collected by veteran anticolonialists in the Social Democratic and Center parties. This impassioned publicity in turn worsened the public image of the colonial service and further discouraged suitable men from applying. The high cost of living in the colonies and the high rate of sickness did the rest—the German colonies were the stepchildren of metropolitan administration.

The marginal role played by the colonial establishment in German society was reflected in its central administration. Colonial affairs were managed by a section within the foreign ministry known as the Kolonialabteilung, its entire staff in 1897 consisting of a director, four senior officials, and a few clerks. In 1907 a separate colonial ministry came into existence, the Reichskolonialamt, headed by Bernhard

Dernburg—a successful banker and an energetic reformer determined to develop the economic potential of the colonies by applying science to agriculture, by developing railways and ports, and by increasing reliance on African peasant agriculture.

German Governors: Background and Functions

For all its disabilities, the German colonial establishment secured a number of able and competent officials. During the early era of conquest, a high proportion of applications for senior posts came from the ranks of the *Schutztruppenoffiziere*, a select group of officers tired of barracks routine at home and eager to acquire a professional reputation in the colonies. The *Schutztruppen*, though devoid of regimental prestige, contained a considerable proportion of aristocratic officers. They also served as an avenue of social promotion for bourgeois officers like Curt von Morgen, raised to the nobility by reason of his colonial exploits.

As the era of conquest drew to a close, an increasing number of senior officials were civilians. Generalizations with regard to their social origins are not easy to make: the civilians were drawn from several distinct strata—explorers and career bureaucrats, as well as technicians and professional men turned administrators. Their academic training, unlike that of British administrative officers, was standardized; it emphasized legal and administrative studies rather than the classics. The more senior German civil servants often were linked to the military through their reserve officer's commission, the passport to social acceptance in Germany. The Germans, moreover, never thought of employing a businessman in a gubernatorial capacity. The career of Sir Francis Chaplin (1866–1933)—ex-journalist, mine manager, head of the British South Africa Company's administration in Rhodesia, and finally a director of the company itself—had no equivalent in German colonial history.

Politically, German colonial administrators apparently held views very similar to those of their colleagues in other parts of the German administration. They ranged from the Catholic center to the extreme right; Social Democrats were excluded, and *Freisinnige* (liberal free traders) excluded themselves. There were considerable social differences among the various segments of the service. Aristo-

Table 2. Proportion of Nobles to Commoners among German Colonial Governors, 1884–1914

	Nobles	*Commoners*
German East Africa	6[1]	1
German Southwest Africa	3	3
German Cameroons	3	4
Togo	4	4
Total[2]	16	12

[1]Including two commoners raised to the nobility.
[2]Including one duke, two counts, and four barons.

crats continued to play a major part in the colonial administration at a time when the civil service in the Reich itself became increasingly bourgeois in nature; three-fourths of all German colonial governors were noblemen. Commoners, however, were not excluded—provided they held a reserve officer's commission and the "correct" political attitude. The proportion of untitled governors began to increase as administration became more complex, as bureaucratic routine increased, and as civilian problems came to the forefront.

The jobs done by colonial governors differed enormously, so much so that generalizations are hard to make. They were originally known as *Reichskommissare*; later they were upgraded to be *Landeshauptmann*, or resident. The title *Gouverneur*, whose incumbent was entitled to be called "Your Excellency," was granted only after a colony had attained a certain degree of development. The earliest representatives of German colonial power—such as Max Buchner in the Cameroons or Ernst Falkental in Togo—wielded little power. The military force at their disposal was negligible, and even a soldier like Curt von François in German Southwest Africa was looked upon by Africans as no more than one warlord among many.

The governor's office was modeled to some extent on that of a German *Regierungspräsident*, the chief administrator of a major Prussian territorial unit, the *Regierungsbezirk*. The actual *Regierungspräsident* supervised the entire administration, including the police, the local authorities, the public lands, forests, schools, and such; but the German governor's powers in fact went further. He headed the armed forces within his territory and thus exercised a privilege that seemed to most German professional officers anomalous at best and scandalous at worst. As a matter of fact, the *Schutztruppen* high command in Berlin was attached to the colonial ministry rather than to the army high command, an illustration of the low priority of colonial forces within the German military hierarchy. All important documents required the governor's signature. He was responsible for drawing up the territorial budget. He supervised the conduct of government—not as yet an excessively difficult task, given the weakness of Germany's colonial state machinery.

There was no British style executive council or any other collegial authority whose advice the governor was bound to seek. His *Referenten* (roughly equivalent to British heads of departments) were immediately subordinate to him. To a considerable extent, he was able to initiate policies—subject to the colonial office and the more remote threat of interference from the Reichstag. He also acted as the ceremonial head of government, and—like his opposite number in the British colonies—he stood at the apex of colonial society. But in social prestige, a German governor enjoyed nothing like that of his British confrère, who almost inevitably received a knighthood; they were gentry ex officio. A number of German soldiers were raised to the nobility by reason of their military exploits in the colonies, but no civilian administrator was ever rewarded with the coveted "von" for his services. Although they were well paid, German governors and their senior assistants did not do as well financially as their British colleagues. The governor of a large colony received an annual salary of around 50,000 marks—about as much as a minister-resident and plenipotentiary employed by the German foreign office in a capital of middling importance, or four or five times as much as a district commissioner, or *Bezirksamtmann*.

Table 3.   Comparative Gubernatorial Pay Scales, *c.* 1913

	Salary of governor (in marks)	Number of senior officials in receipt of the following (in marks)		
		20,000 and over	20,000	15,000
British East Africa	81,600	3	12	10
Gold Coast	81,600	10	12	11
German East Africa	50,000	—	2	9
German Cameroons	50,000	—	2	6

SOURCE: Germany, Reichstag, *Anlagen*, no. 1356, 13 (Legislatur-period I, session 1912–1914), "Die Kolonialverwaltung der europäischen Staaten," 9 February 1914, p. xii–xiv.

The legal powers enjoyed by the German governors were not quite as impressive as those exercised by the British. In the German dependencies there were no legislative councils on the British model over which the governor presided and in which he could pass ordinances. The *Gouvernementsrat* of a colony—composed of senior officials and, in settler colonies, of white representatives—had only advisory functions. A German governor had a fairly circumscribed competence with regard to the issue of local decrees (*Verordnungen*) and had to contend with more interference from the colonial ministry than his British colleague. The Reichstag also exercised much indirect power. Whereas the British Parliament could not directly interfere with the financial affairs of a colony, the German legislature had to approve all terrritorial budgets, an arrangment that gave it much latitude. Within the German administrative hierarchy as a whole, governors counted for much less than they did in Great Britain, and colonial governors never rose into the higher reaches of the German establishment, civil, military, commercial, or social.

Nevertheless, within their own sphere they were a force to be taken into consideration. Their appointments, unlike those of the French and Portuguese, were not purely political. Their tour of office was much longer than that of their French or, in many cases, of their British confrères. Rechenberg remained in office for six years, Zech for seven, and Theodor Leutwein in Southwest Africa for nine. The average tour was about five years; hence, the governor often remained for a period sufficient to give some administrative continuity to the territory he headed. Many governors were men of ability. Within his own territory, any German who was not a senior military or naval officer would be bold indeed openly to quarrel with the governor.

Nevertheless, the de facto authority in the hands of the German governors is hard to assess. Much depended on personal qualities and on local circumstances. On paper, the colonial empire was fairly centralized. In practice, the colonial ministry and its predecessor were geographically too remote and too understaffed to exercise effective control. A few colonial secretaries actually visited the colonies, including Dernburg and Solf, but such visitations were rare. Colonial administrators were apt to complain about metropolitan interference, especially about a pettifogging system of financial supervision, but the colonial ministry was ill-equipped to exercise effective supervision over the day-to-day conduct of government.

Within each territory, the governor's powers were again circumscribed by the size of the area to be governed. German East Africa alone was almost twice as large as the German Reich; Togo, the smallest German colony in Africa, was slightly bigger than Bavaria, a major German kingdom. The military and administrative machinery at a governor's disposal was negligible. In 1901 the German military establishment in all the African colonies combined amounted to just over 3,600 men. The four African territories under German sovereignty, extending over more than 1 million square miles, were administered by only thirty-five civilian and thirty-one military stations. The entire district staff of German East Africa, the most closely administered colony, amounted to forty-seven persons, as against twenty-three whites employed in the central administration at Dar es Salaam. The colonial establishments before World War I all partook in some measure of the administrative qualities of an ancien régime—absolute in theory but deficient in means of coercion.

Overall, Germany's gubernatorial establishment in the colonies was a pale reflection of the metropolitan establishment. In Germany, power rested in the hands of a coalition between the nobility and the upper ranks of the bourgeoisie. This alliance was cemented by protective tariffs that benefited both the landed and the manufacturing interests. In the political field, the arrangement depended on the exclusion from leading positions within the state of the so-called reichsfeindliche Elemente, groups supposedly hostile to the state, especially Social Democrats, ethnic minorities, pacifists, and unconverted Jews, with Catholics gradually finding acceptance. Governors, like their subordinates, voted for the establishment parties, especially the National Liberals (Heinrich Schnee and Theodor Seitz), also Conservatives or Free Conservatives; in addition, there was a small but influential group of reformers drawn from the conservative wing of the Center party (Julius von Zech, Albrecht von Rechenberg). This gubernatorial corps reflected both the strengths and weaknesses of Wilhelmian Germany, and as the Wilhelmian Reich collapsed in war, it dragged down Europe's most short-lived empire in Africa.

Julius Graf Zech auf Neuhofen (1868-1914)

Woodruff D. Smith

AMONG the territories that made up the short-lived German empire in Africa, Togo was known as the *Musterkolonie*, or "model colony." Its reputation must be understood in terms of the peculiar nature of German colonialism. Despite considerable propaganda to the contrary, Togo was not particularly valuable in an economic sense. The colony did generally export more than it imported, but the total amount of trade that Germany did with Togo was minuscule, certainly not enough to justify the continuance of German rule in purely economic terms.[1] Togo was instead a model colony because, uniquely among Germany's African territories, it regularly paid the costs of its own administration out of local taxes without requiring annual subventions from the imperial government. Despite the claims of the German government after the first world war, Togo was not held in complete peace and tranquility. The first fifteen years of German administration were marked by fairly constant military campaigns in the interior, although thereafter military action was comparatively rare. But the military campaigns usually were small enough to be paid for out of local revenues. Officials and colonialists therefore could point to at least one German colony that seemed to deserve praise; since few others were commendable, the colonialists naturally played Togo for all it was worth. Furthermore, since Togo was solvent and since it produced only a few official scandals, it caused little trouble for the colonial administration in the Reichstag and incurred little of the criticism to which the administration was inordinately sensitive.[2]

Togo's success rested upon an economic foundation that in most respects predated German control. Before 1885 the coast of Togo was already engaged in the production of palm oil and kola nuts for an international market. There existed a system of small-unit cultivation of oil palms and a local gathering and credit system centering around coastal merchant families who acted as the agents of European trading companies. Missionary societies had long been active, and there was an indigenous westernized elite among the coastal Ewe. It was upon this basis that the Germans built the successful part of Togo's colonial economy. The revenues that kept Togo solvent were export and import duties. As long as the Germans did not undertake major projects that involved unusually large expenditures, and as long as plans for economic development hinged on the existing economic system, the colony avoided financial difficulties. Any attempts to alter the country's economic basis would have required more money than Togo could provide for itself and more than the imperial German government was willing to spend.

According to German colonial propaganda after about 1900, and especially after the loss of the colonies in the first world war, Togo owed its success not so much to its environment and social structure but rather to the wisdom, benevolence, and efficiency of the German political administration in the colony.[3] There was, indeed, some reason for thinking that Togo was unusually well provided with competent officials, and it was their decision to develop the colony in accordance with the existing economy that contributed significantly to German success. French colonial administrators in Togo after 1918 appear to have had considerable respect for their German predecessors.[4] Nevertheless, the essential reason for solvency continued to be the profitable trade in palm products, which the Germans had not originated. Furthermore, the Togo administrative service was not as uniformly good as its press notices would have had it. Its reputation did, however, cause the Togolese government to be regarded as a model for German colonial policy in the period just before the first world war in a way that the limited size and profitability of Togo would not otherwise have justified.

The Togo administration benefited from the comparatively long periods that officials spent in the colony and from the relatively clear lines of authority within the administration. The geographical distances between the central authority at the capital, Lomé, and the individual *Bezirke* (the local units of German administration) were relatively short. Togo, moreover, alone among Germany's African colonies, did not possess a regular defense force but rather a paramilitary police force under civil control.[5] The long tenure of officials was probably most important; it was one of the keys to the success that the Germans had in devising means to govern through African political structures and with the assistance of Togolese elites.

Although officials in Togo do not appear to have possessed notably better educational credentials than the average civil servant in other colonies, they were better placed than their counterparts elsewhere to discover how African law and African political systems really worked. Not surprisingly, it was in Togo that the Germans first attempted to fuse German and African legal systems into a workable entity. Togo, on the other hand, was a promotional backwater. Only a few years after the colony had come into existence, civil servants from Togo largely ceased to be eligible for more responsible positions in other territories and had to be content with the fairly limited promotion opportunities available on the spot. A governor of Togo, therefore, always had to make a point of instilling some degree of élan into his small force of administrators.

Zech's Early Career

The public picture of Togo as Germany's efficiently governed *Musterkolonie* tended to merge after 1905 with that of Togo's most famous governor, Julius Graf Zech auf Neuhofen (acting governor from 1903 to 1905 and governor from 1905 to 1910). To some extent, the personification of Togo in Zech was an illusion fostered by propaganda, but it also possessed a certain amount of truth. What the public perceived was Zech's image of Togo, and this image indicated at least the direction of policy in the colony. Zech's reputation for success as a governor was the product partly of Togo's own economic and fiscal success and partly of the appeal to other German colonialists of his view of colonial policy.

Zech came from an old Bavarian noble family with a tradition of government service. His father was a high judicial officer in the Bavarian administration and the owner of an estate near Straubing, where Zech was born in 1868.[6] Zech's class background was one of the obvious constituents of his public image and also, to some extent, of his attitude toward colonial policy. An admirer described him as an obvious aristocrat, "from head to foot the count," whose naturally reserved demeanor was relieved by flashes of enthusiasm for projects that took his fancy.[7] Photographs of Zech show an intelligent and sensitive face whose most startling feature was a pair of large and extraordinarily alert eyes, which he used to great effect in holding people's attention. He seems to have been able to inspire among his subordinates a loyalty and respect notably absent elsewhere within the German colonial service. He was capable of lending to the routine activities of administrative life in a small, obscure colony a feeling that every ground breaking and bridge opening was of great significance to German colonialism. This facility was important both for morale within the colonial administration and for public relations at home. Zech was perhaps the kind of official of whom the journalist Paul Rohrbach wrote that Germany had too few, the class of "natural" colonial administrators, which was one of the strengths of the British empire.[8] Zech, incidentally, shared with Rohrbach and other German colonialists such as the later colonial secretary Wilhelm Solf a respect for British colonial methods and a desire to adapt them to German use. While governor he undertook an inspection tour of the British West African colonies for precisely that purpose. Zech was particularly interested in the concept of indirect rule and paid close attention to the policies of Lugard in Northern Nigeria and to British methods of governance in Yorubaland.

Zech's aristocratic background probably affected some of his most basic and important attitudes toward colonial administration; these, in turn, determined the direction that German policy took in Togo during his rule. To call Zech a paternalistic administrator in the German civil service tradition would be an understatement. From orders he issued as governor and from his own statements of purpose, there emerges the image of a progressive aristocratic landowner, interested in every aspect of the lives of "his" people, concerned both with exploiting them for greater profits and with protecting them against social dislocation and unnecessary physical abuse.[9] Within his mind these concerns were essentially linked. Ultimate economic efficiency was incompatible with excessive social disruption. His political style was also aristocratic, especially his attempt to involve himself personally in as many aspects of government as he could, rather than following the civil servant's or soldier's habit of "going through channels." He traveled constantly and worked an unusually long day for a German colonial governor.

Zech may also have been affected by contemporary liberal Catholic social thought, which was similarly directed toward protecting the social order at all levels while accommodating society to economic and social change. There is no direct evidence of such influence, but Zech and Freiherr von Rechenberg, the only other Catholic German colonial governor of importance, shared basic policy assumptions and aimed at preventing the establishment of African proletariats in their colonies.

Zech never tried to advertise himself; hence, not much information survives regarding his personality. Seldom in his official communications is there a personal note, and in his monographs on the ethnology and geography of northern Togo—which were based upon personal experience during interesting and exciting travels—he hardly ever expresses an opinion, much less describes what he himself did.[10] On the one hand, Zech was highly conscious of the importance of public images in his line of work—much more so than German officials generally. On the other, he displayed an extreme reticence about his personal life and feelings. He was unmarried and seems to have had little social life outside his official functions. He never wrote an autobiography. As far as one can tell, he did not participate in politics or act prominently for any interest group. He was a Catholic, but—unlike Rechenberg—not an active member of the Center party. Zech's thoughts on colonial policy and his conception of what he was doing in Togo must be drawn mainly from his official statements and those of other people, which means that it is sometimes difficult to differentiate between Zech the man and Zech the representative of German imperialism.

Despite his later reputation as a civilian administrator, Zech began his career as a military officer, and it was as a soldier that he first came to Togo. In 1886 Zech entered the Bavarian army as a subaltern and was appointed to a lieutenancy in an infantry regiment in 1888. Apparently he soon tired of army life in peacetime. He also may have felt, with some justice, that the opportunities for advancement and for the full employment of his very considerable talents in the military service of Bavaria were limited. His disenchantment happened to coincide with the discovery by the German government that running a colonial empire, even one of limited size, was a major undertaking that required a constant, and regrettably expensive, military presence. In the 1890s regular military formations called defense forces (*Schutztruppen*) or police forces were established in each of Germany's African colonies, thereby opening up opportunities for officers' commissions for service of a more active kind than was available in Europe. The new opportunities naturally attracted different kinds of people: misfits who could not expect advancement at home, officers of average ability who expected more rapid promotion in the colonies, and a few officers of outstanding ability, such as Zech. Zech in particular appears to have been attracted by the fact that a colonial officer could expect to exercise both civil and military authority since in many areas officers and NCOs were responsible for local government. In 1895 he received a commission in the Togo police force and transferred as first lieutenant from the Bavarian army to the service of the colonial department of the foreign office.

Zech arrived in Togo during a period in which the future of German enterprise in the colony was being determined through competition among British, French, and Germans for the interior of West Africa. Germany, with the narrowest of coastal holdings and the fewest resources to devote to the race, was almost bound to lose, but at the time of Zech's arrival it was still committed to the attempt. Expeditions were being sent frequently into the interior to explore and to sign agreements with indigenous political authorities in order to establish a claim to a connection between the Togolese coast and the Niger. Although it was not entirely clear what the value of such a connection might be, the Germans nevertheless assumed that the economic future of Togo lay in opening up the natural resources, markets, and labor reserves of the West African interior. The coastal region, small in size though economically successful, was looked upon merely as a base for interior operations—a base that fortunately was able to cover the costs of small military expeditions since adequate funds were not forthcoming from the Reichstag. It was not until the failure of the German push inland left Togo a small, hemmed-in colony that the German authorities began to see future economic development primarily in terms of the coastal region.

Zech's early career in Togo was bound up exclusively with the thrust into the hinterland. Upon his arrival in 1895 he was appointed chief of the new station at Kete-Krache (presently in Ghana), which had been established in the previous year as a point from which control over the Togo hinterland might be maintained and part of the interior trade of the Togo-Dahomey region might be taxed.[11] The Kete-Krache station was particularly useful in allowing the Germans to maintain continuous relations with the Dagomba, the most important of the peoples of northern Togo. Zech officially remained the station chief at Kete-Krache until 1900 although he had many other duties. The confluence of two trade routes, one to the northeast and the other to the northwest, made his station a convenient staging point for interior expeditions. Early in 1896 he led the first of many that he was to command to Sugu, to the northeast, in order to sign treaties and establish effective occupation vis-à-vis the French in Dahomey. With his sixteen soldiers he was able to overawe the local chiefs at Sugu, but his force was too small to leave a garrison when he retired to Kete-Krache. Shortly thereafter he led one of several small military forces sent into the northern interior to enforce German rule.

The inadequacy of German resources in the West African race for empire was demonstrated during Zech's second expedition to Sugu (1896–1897). He reached Sugu before a rival French force from Dahomey, but the French arrived in greater strength and Zech, knowing that he could not be supported by the Togo authorities, backed down and returned to Kete-Krache.[12] Zech's retirement from Sugu marked the end of Germany's hopes for interior penetration. All that remained was the firm establishment of the boundaries between Togo and the surrounding British and French colonies, and in this effort, too, Zech played a part. A treaty in 1897 set up the general boundary with Dahomey, and in 1899 another treaty created a neutral zone between Togo and the Gold Coast. A final border between Togo and the Gold Coast was surveyed in 1901–1902 by an Anglo-German commission, of which Zech was the senior German member.[13] German colonial authorities, having been disappointed in their hopes of developing the West African interior, naturally turned toward the comparatively flourishing coastal economy. Its exploitation had always been a part of German plans for Togo. Now, however, the coastal region became the focus of those plans. The northern half of the country was to be separated from the rest in the German governmental scheme and left essentially alone except for attempts to tax interior trade that crossed the colony's borders. Only gradually, and with the minimum possible risk to capital, would the coastal economy be extended into the interior—excepting, of course, the case of the mineral resources that it was always hoped would be found in the hinterland.

Having given up his military commission and become a civilian official, Zech in 1900 was promoted to the rank of district officer (*Bezirksamtsmann*) and assigned to head the Anecho district. Anecho was still the largest and most important town on the Togo coast although it was being overtaken by the new German capital at Lomé. Apparently by this time Zech had acquired the reputation of being the most competent of the junior officials in the Togolese service. He had done so in the face of comparatively stiff competition, including that of (lieutenant) Hans-Georg von Doering, an able officer who later headed the Togo police under Zech and succeeded him as acting governor.[14] Zech seems to have won out over his rivals not only by demonstrating military and gubernatorial ability at Kete-Krache but also by writing descriptive monographs of considerable value on northern Togo. Especially in the smaller colonies, the German colonial department placed great emphasis on scholarly attainments related to colonial administration in considering officials for promotion. Also, Togo was the only one of Germany's African territories in which civilian status benefited candidates for promotion. Zech did not do very much at Anecho; he took a year leave to travel in North Africa before assuming his duties in 1901 and then from December 1901 until quite late in 1902 worked on the Togo–Gold Coast border commission. In the latter capacity Zech once again distinguished himself and, equally important, received good press notices at home. In 1902, therefore, he was promoted once again, this time to *Kanzler* of the Togo administration, the second highest official in the colony.

Zech was named to his new job—in which he was responsible for the operation of the central governmental apparatus at Lomé—in the same year that a new governor, Waldemar Horn, arrived in Togo. Horn, however, soon became mixed up in a widely publicized scandal. Shortly after his arrival he ordered the whipping of an insubordinate chief, who subsequently died of his injuries.[15] Such events were not unusual in the history of the German overseas empire, where the standard theories of native administration emphasized corporal punishment as the most effective and economical sanction that could be taken against indigenous offenders. In most colonies the right to inflict corporal punishment was not restricted to government authorities but could be exercised by European employers against their nonwhite workers. The system was obviously susceptible to abuse, as the Horn affair and dozens of similar scandals demonstrated. Such incidents were accounted as unfortunate by German colonial officials for three reasons: they offended the sense of legal propriety that most officials had developed in the course of their training; they probably caused resistance from nonwhites that might otherwise have been avoided; most important of all, they created scandals that could be used by political parties in Germany to attack the colonial department.

The last of these considerations applied particularly to the Horn affair. Groups within the Reichstag that tended to be in opposition to the policies of German governments during the Wilhelmian era, especially the Social Democrats, the two left liberal parties, and the Catholic Center party, habitually used parliamentary review of colonial appropriations as a means of criticizing the government as a whole.[16] The colonial administration was particularly vulnerable because the individual colonies were perpetually in need of subsidies from the central government, and the Reichstag had insisted in the 1890s that the granting of subsidies be accompanied annually by an extremely detailed budget review that extended into every aspect of German colonial activity. This was one of the few avenues open to Reichstag parties to influence policymaking on a regular basis, and it was used to the fullest extent. The most effective criticisms, from the point of view of public opinion, were those that concentrated on clearly illegal or distasteful actions by colonial officials against nonwhites, and colonial rule produced many of these.

The Horn affair was used by the colonial opposition during 1903. The scandal struck the colonial department at a particularly bad time since there were several expensive projects, including a railroad system in East Africa, for which government interest guarantees were being sought. Horn was removed from office pending further investigation of the incident, and in 1903, as the second highest official in Togo, Zech was appointed acting governor. He was sufficiently impressive in this capacity to be made permanent governor in 1905.[17] Zech's promotion appears to have been the result of a deliberate effort by the colonial department to counter charges of amateurism by appointment of governors with impressive qualifications on paper and with previous colonial experience.

The Foundations of Zech's Policy, 1903–1910

On assuming office, Zech faced several important tasks. He tried to reform the administration of the colony, especially with respect to native relations; he also wanted to improve the image of the colony's administration after the Horn scandal. At the same time, the colonial department and the Togo administration had to respond to the interests of the organized colonial movement in Germany, especially the Colonial Society and smaller groups like the Colonial Economic Committee (KWK), an affiliate of the Colonial Society. Some of these lobbies were motivated mainly by political and ideological considerations and were satisfied with limited concessions on the government's part. Others represented economic pressure groups and called for policy decisions of a far-reaching and expensive nature. The latter became increasingly important as the colony tried to expand its profitable trade and to diversify agricultural production.

From about the mid-1890s world prices for tropical raw materials had begun a steady and—by the standards of the time—rapid increase, which was partly responsible for Togo's financial success. The buoyant tropical products market provided an incentive to diversify the Togolese coastal economy through the successful development of new products such as coffee and cocoa.[18] From about 1895 onward the focus of international attention shifted to cotton, the prime raw material for European textile industries. The worldwide price increase of raw cotton seemed to threaten the profitability of both the British and the German cotton industry; hence, organizations of cotton producers within these countries were set up in the 1890s to obtain government assistance in reducing cotton prices. In Germany it was the KWK that campaigned most vigorously for assistance to cotton producers. According to the KWK, the major reason for rising cotton prices was the monopolistic practices of raw cotton producers, particularly the cotton growers' associations in the United States. It proposed, therefore, that Germany grow cotton in its colonies, thereby lowering prices and creating a bargaining weapon to use in dealing with cotton producing countries.[19] In addition, government acceptance of the colonial cotton scheme would commit the state to generalized support of the cotton producers even if the scheme itself had little effect on prices. Colonial enthusiasts accepted this plan with great eagerness. It held out the possibility of making the colonies profitable and of obtaining more public funds for overall colonial development.

Togo, with its well-developed trading system, its apparent abundance of manpower, and its tropical climate, was selected by the KWK as the primary site for the cotton scheme, even though early experimentation in cotton growing had not been particularly successful.[20] The colonial department and the Togo administration backed the plan and used Togo's cotton prospects as a means of getting the Reichstag to vote funds for improving transportation facilities: a large pier was built at Lomé to permit cargo ships to load without the use of lighters, along with a system of roads and railroads to extend the coastal economic area into the interior. Implementation of the cotton scheme proved difficult. There was initially a debate as to the best method of organizing the project. In the Cameroons region economic development had been placed in the hands of large chartered companies with land concessions, and a similar procedure was proposed for Togo. The system in the Cameroons had not been particularly successful and had resulted in large-scale social dislocation. In Togo, experts feared that a labor exploitive plantation system might have disastrous consequences for indigenous forms of production and trade.[21]

In the debate over Togolese development, the advocates of plantation agriculture had been defeated by a coalition of merchants, missionaries, and government officials who proposed instead a form of cotton production by independent African farmers akin to the system whereby palm oil was produced. Reliance on indigenous cultivators was expected to promote the diversification of crops without incurring deleterious political and social consequences. A chartered company was formed to assist in this development, but the new body was limited in its scope and did not receive the vast land concessions granted in other German colonies. The company was intended rather to advance credit for individual planting enterprises and to handle the assembly and export of the cotton product.[22]

The cotton scheme got under way before Zech became governor and set the tone for much of the policymaking that occurred while he was in office. Zech apparently agreed with the approach to administration that the Togo development scheme implied; in any event the government was committed to it whether he liked it or not. The scheme's lack of potential became evident quite early in Zech's administration.[23] The KWK and the government sponsored experimental stations and training programs and imported workers from the United States to teach modern cotton farming techniques, but despite a brief period of heavy production, Togolese cotton was never of high quality and could not compete in the international market. By 1910, when Zech left Togo, the scheme had failed. It had served some puposes, however. It had encouraged capital expenditures in Togo that might not otherwise have occurred, and it had established a pattern for economic development that was followed more successfully with products other than cotton.

During the initial years of his administration, the governor's general policies tended to be determined by circumstances over which Zech had little control. This was the case, for example, with school policy. Along most of the West African coast the primary European language spoken and taught in mission schools was English. This was as true in Togo as in the Gold Coast. In 1903 the Colonial Society opened a campaign to accelerate the germanization of Togo. Zech moved with alacrity to respond. Although he presumably believed in the abstract advantages of germanization, he was most concerned with keeping the goodwill of the colonial movement at a rather difficult time and with turning events to his own advantage. He held a conference in Lomé in March 1904 at which representatives of all three missionary societies operating in Togo agreed to phase out English and replace it with German as the primary language of instruction. The incentive for doing so was the tying of government grants-in-aid to a certain number of effective hours of instruction in German per pupil. This was enough to satisfy the colonial movement, and Zech recèived the thanks of various colonialist organizations. But characteristically, Zech used the opportunity presented by the language reform to increase government control over the mission schools and to direct more closely their curricula. He was a firm believer in putting procedures into writing. He proceeded to draw up a standard course of studies for all schools in Togo and connected the grants-in-aid to evidence of following the prescribed curriculum. He heavily emphasized technical skills and the development of economic individualism.[24] This policy was to some extent in keeping with the majority view among German colonialists, who favored economic, rather than political, education on a large scale for Africans. It also was very much in line with Zech's intention of creating in Togo a society of peaceful, independent African farmers that could encompass both economic change and social stability, rather than permitting the formation of an African proletariat.

Economic Policy

Zech spent his first year in office working out the implications of existing policies and responding to various pressures upon him. But increasingly the governor came to assert his own views, especially with regard to economic questions, which he regarded as inseparable from social policy. He continued to support the extension of railways into the interior and also the construction of roads and bicycle paths away from railroad tracks. Initially he justified the expense of such schemes by reference to the needs of cotton production. But Zech increasingly considered the railroads as an instrument for slowly spreading a diversified form of commercial agriculture from the coast to the interior. Hence, he insisted that peasants should grow cotton only as one of several crops.[25] Unlike a great many other German colonial theorists, Zech did not look to improvements in transportation as the sole—or even the main—vehicle of economic change. The building of a railroad and an increase in the accessibility of markets could produce economic effects in themselves, but these would not necessarily be desirable.

Railroad building, for example, required large numbers of workers. According to some German theorists concerned mainly with the railroad projects in East Africa, a work force would automatically be created by the presence of the railroad, which could later be exploited by European employers as wage labor. Zech wanted to make sure that the employment of Africans on the railroads worked to the fulfillment of his overall plan for Togo and was therefore determined to exercise strong government control over the recruitment and use of laborers. The last thing he wanted was a black proletariat since he sought to make sure that European policy in Togo did not reproduce what he regarded as the failure of domestic European social development.

In addition to building a logistical infrastructure, Zech resolved to diversify farming and forestry. Together with the KWK, he established a program for developing Togo's wealth in timber. He recruited German foresters and set up a minuscule version of a German state forestry office. From his own estate in Bavaria he imported breeding hens, hoping to establish within Togo this standard Western form of subsidiary small-farm animal production. He also encouraged, both through government expenditures and through more informal means, experimentation with rubber, sisal, cocoa, coffee, and cotton. Despite the failure of the cotton scheme and despite the continued reliance of the Togolese economy upon palm products, Zech's policy did help to diversify Togo's exports; therefore, at least for a while, it protected Togo against some of the fluctuations of the early twentieth-century tropical commodities market. His aim of a peasant economy was not, however, fully realized, and there is some reason to believe that he never intended the whole Togolese economy to follow the small-farm pattern. For products such as rubber and sisal, Zech, together with most other German colonial officials, favored larger productive units, including European-run plantations. But even in the case of the latter, the manner in which native labor was to be used and the effect of the plantations on the existing structure of society were to be carefully regulated by the government so as not to obviate the aims of Zech's general policies.[26]

Zech looked upon education as yet another means of preparing the coastal peoples for a new social and economic order. We have seen how he manipulated the mission school issue so as to direct the school curriculum along lines of which he approved. He also continued the efforts of earlier governors to establish technical training schools in order to introduce skills important for economic development, and he used the cotton project as a vehicle for relating African training to his broad social aims. He established a school at Nuatja to teach advanced methods of cotton growing. In November 1908 Zech issued an order changing the curriculum of the Nuatja school and stating the real purpose of the school.[27] The students were to be selected from candidates aged twenty to twenty-three from all districts of southern Togo. They were to be chosen for their strength, health, intelligence, and goal consciousness and were to be given a three-year course of study in agriculture at Nuatja. The aim of the program was to create skilled farmers who could operate by themselves and who could teach and supervise others: in other words, people who would act as agents of social and economic change without threatening social stability.

Each student at Nuatja in his final year was to be assigned one hectare of land that he was to cultivate and from which he would receive the entire profit. Graduates received individual plots and settled in groups on newly developed land close to their home villages so that they might introduce new economic values to their kinsmen and neighbors. Zech's concept of the successful Nuatja graduate derived from the standard nineteenth-century image of the pioneer. Zech's pioneer, however, was not a German emigrant looking for new land overseas but a black man working to develop his own country. There was indeed a superficial similarity between Zech's Nuatja scheme and the German Colonial School at Witzenhausen (near Kassel), which was intended to produce white farmers who would settle in the highlands of the larger African colonies. The whole outlook of the Witzenhausen school, however, was tied to the radical right in politics, to which Zech's ideas of colonial rule based on an independent African peasantry were highly suspect.[28] The Nuatja project did not last long and did not live up to Zech's expectations; it did, however, symbolize Zech's thinking about colonial policy and his view of the means to achieve economic change without social dislocation.

Much of the rest of Zech's economic policy similarly involved government intervention to achieve social conditions conducive to development. For example, Zech continued a program (commenced before his governorship) to reduce the importation and use of alcohol in Togo. In this respect Zech both followed his own inclinations and responded to a certain amount of pressure from missionary societies and segments of the colonial movement. Zech saw alcoholism as one of the distressing by-products of Western civilization, one that sapped the initiative of workers and posed a threat to the social order in Togo. Not only did it have economically deleterious effects on workers but it acted to dissolve traditional social and personality structures, replacing them with the characteristic attitudes of the "degenerate" European proletariat. Liquor could not, however, be banned immediately in Togo. It was a major trade product and was in heavy demand within coastal and interior African economies. There was also a commercial lobby in favor of retaining trade in alcohol. Zech therefore moved slowly, using his authority as governor to increase gradually the customs duties on liquor and to ban, in 1909, the sale of spirits without a license in the northern half of the colony.[29]

Revenue in Togo was derived mostly from customs duties, which provided just enough to allow the government to function on a small scale. Zech, like other governors, tended to use his authority to fix tariffs as a means of carrying out more general policies, as in the case of the duties on alcohol. As government expenditures on transportation expanded, direct taxation became a necessity. The form of direct taxation adopted in Togo under Zech was not greatly different from that imposed in other German colonies, but Togolese taxes were part of an overall program for societal development and stability. For all areas except Lomé and Anecho, the tax was actually to be a labor service levy.[30] All adult males were required to work on public projects under government supervision for twelve days every year; alternatively, they could pay the equivalent of twelve days' wages at the prevailing rate. In the order establishing the forced labor system, Zech also regulated working conditions, including the provision of meals, etc., for workers sent a great distance from home. The intention of the order was that direct contributions to public welfare and development, such as labor services, should be controlled by the government and should not lead to the exploitation of Togolese workers by private industry. Although the labor tax in Togo was a form of forced labor and entailed many of the abuses associated with this system, Zech did insure that the labor service be used only for public purposes. The labor tax in Togo was normally not, as it was in other colonies, viewed as a means of monetizing the economy through payments in cash. Rather, the impost was seen as a means of raising revenue.

Zech's tendency to view government innovations both as responses to particular problems and as vehicles for achieving his broader social aims also found expression in a project that occasioned considerable comment: the creation of two punishment camps to which certain types of criminal could be sent and at which their labor could be employed for public purposes. Published descriptions of the camps show that they were not intended as ordinary forced labor centers but were designed to achieve multiple social goals.[31] According to the Germans, they served as places of detention for intractable chiefs whom the government found it expedient to remove from their offices and home villages and also for "work-shy" Africans—vagrants found wandering the roads. During the years of German rule, unemployment for the first time became a perennial problem. The process of economic change in southern Togo created aspirations among a large segment of the population toward entry into the cash economy without at the same time providing sufficient opportunities for employment. Togo became a labor exporting economy in the German period, a condition that continued to exist after the Anglo-French partition. Zech was clearly aware both of labor emigration and of unemployment. But apparently he believed that the development of a free peasant economy would itself create full employment and that the establishment of such an economy was essentially a matter of training the coastal population to farm efficiently and to open up "wasted" lands. Unemployment and vagrancy were therefore indications of deviation from both the traditional Togolese society and the ideal one that Zech visualized and were to be treated as social offenses and as signs that certain individuals needed "reeducating." Camps were set up in relatively remote districts. Zech and his supporters defended the penal settlements as humane means of instilling self-respect and economic virtue in recalcitrant Africans; the Germans, moreover, argued that conditions in the settlements were not those of a prison camp but, rather, duplicated life in a typical Togolese village. There is some reason to dispute the latter claim. Nevertheless, though Zech was clearly putting the best face on a penal arragement that had other advantages to him, there is no indication that he was insincere in his general conception of the nature of the penal settlements. Most comments concerning Zech's prison camps—based mostly upon published statements of the camps' purpose rather than actual observation—were highly favorable.

Political and Legal Reforms

Zech was an administrative reformer not so much because he sought to restructure the overall administration of Togo but because he liked to tinker with things. Many of the changes in administration that occurred under him were relatively unimportant. He did work very hard, however, to improve the morale of the Togo civil service through regularly—and, one suspects, often annoyingly—making himself a part of the activities of subordinates. Shortly after becoming governor he established a regular official periodical that was supposed to improve communications within the administration and, more important, to develop within the administration a clear allegiance to Zech's own conceptions of colonial administration.[32]

Zech was, as most previous governors of Togo had been, an advocate of indirect rule with respect to the coastal African population. (Direct rule in the interior was largely impossible anyway and did not even enter into discussion.) At least, Zech and his associates described the government system of Togo as indirect since most of the governance at the local level was intended to be performed by African chiefs who ruled their communities and who reported to the white district officers. The mere fact that Germans used blacks as intermediate officials did not, however, prove that German rule was indirect in any real sense. The Germans did rely on existing indigenous authorities to run the country. But as the Germans continued to encourage economic and social change and as the government shouldered an increasing number of tasks, chiefs increasingly came to resemble civil servants. This transformation was reflected in the changing standards of education and experience required of chiefs. The central administration, moreover, became ever more inclined to appoint and replace chiefs at will. Zech, like advocates of indirect rule in other parts of Africa, tried to improve "efficiency"; that is to say, he was forced to bureaucratize traditional political structures in order to accommodate them to changing economic needs. And he was careful to retain in his own hands the decisive voice not only on important issues but also on fairly trivial matters.[33]

Zech's most important role in the history of European colonialism in Africa—the only action he took that clearly transcended Togo and the German colonial empire in its effects—was his attempt to reconcile German civil and criminal law with African customary law. He was intent on avoiding scandals like the Horn affair. He believed that the development of a peasant economy necessitated both legal and administrative change designed to reduce social instability and facilitate economic development. He resolved also that the new laws should be intelligible both to whites and to blacks, all the more so since the administration of the law was, in the first place, the responsibility of African chiefs. German law formally applied throughout Togo, but unless German bureaucrats were willing to try all cases by themselves, they would have to accommodate to reality.

The first requirement was the codification of the existing customary law according to area and ethnic group. In 1906 Zech held a conference of district officers on African law and ordered each of them to compile statements of the law in their areas.[34] In January 1907 he directed a new member of his staff, Assessor Asmis, to begin a codification of the customary laws of Togo. Asmis's work, which was thereafter duplicated in the German Cameroons region, was one of the first systematic attempts to study African law from a social scientific as well as a legal and practical point of view. The assessor's reports were one of the main sources for Schultz-Ewerth's and Adam's *Das Eingeborenenrecht*, a study of native law in Togo, Cameroons, and East Africa, a landmark in legal anthropology.

Also in 1907, as part of his indigenous law project, Zech sent to all district officers a circular laying down guidelines for the administration of justice. This circular is frequently cited as evidence for the humane nature of German rule in Togo, and indeed the spirit reflected in it compares rather well with statements of native policy in other German colonies.[35] But above all, Zech's guidelines were meant to regularize the administration of the law so as to avoid past difficulties. Short of outright enforcement of German law through the direct exercise of overwhelming power, few other options were in fact open to him. Nevertheless, the clearheaded way in which Zech stated his policies and his eminent good sense speak well of him as an administrator; his philosophy had a fair amount of influence on the formulation of colonial policy in Germany. He acknowledged that imperial decrees had turned the German imperial criminal code into the basis for criminal law in the colonies. But according to Zech, the implementation of German law should be a long-term project. The German colonial administration should gradually advance the "civilization" of non-Europeans in the colonies, but this had to be done slowly and had to take into account the practices of indigenous societies. Until Asmis's project was completed and a full-scale legal code developed for Togo, district officers were to recognize as much of customary law as was consistent with the aims of the government and with German ethical and moral standards. The justification for so doing, even if it meant occasionally ignoring the imperial code, was the requirement in German law that a punishable offense involve criminal intent. It was argued by Zech, in an interesting recognition of cultural relativity, that criminal intent could not be found in an act that was contrary to German law but permissible or regarded as a minor offense in the offender's own culture and society. Presumably, with the success of Zech's educational policies, the number of cases in which this principle applied would diminish over time. Even in the long run, however, the implication is fairly clear that in those areas not specifically accounted for by German law, customary law—modified by the colonial government as necessary—would prevail.

In civil law, Zech had a somewhat freer hand. In matters of family law and other areas that did not impinge greatly on European activities in the colony, it was possible simply to allow the chiefs to administer customary law, locality by locality. Difficulties arose over matters such as land law. Regularization of land law was a thorny issue in almost every German colony, involving major economic interests and the confrontation of very different conceptions of land ownership. Zech's intention was to establish ultimately a system of individual land ownership by African farmers as the cornerstone of Togolese economic development. This required both a system for creating individual title to land and a means of legally protecting such title. At the same time, the economic prosperity of Togo for the present and the immediate future required the maintenance of traditional African communal systems of ownership, with only gradual modifications over time. Zech, in fact, appears to have thought that some kind of compromise between individual and group ownership of land could eventually be worked out.[36] But the requirements of economic development also necessitated a strong defense of the government's right of eminent domain; some provision also had to be made for larger European private enterprises, while simultaneously preventing such enterprises from dispossessing large numbers of Africans.

Zech's solution was to make the government the permanent guarantor of native rights and the controller of changes in land ownership. He established the principle for Togo that all land to which no individual or social entitiy had clear title belonged to the state.[37] This rule was different from that employed in other German colonies, such as Cameroons, where unowned land was open to private exploitation and the establishment of new ownership rights. If new land was to be developed and made into private property, Zech wanted it done with government sanction and under close government supervision. In the context of colonial issues of the period, the intention of his ruling was to prevent the de facto establishment of large land companies that would alter the course of Togolese economic development. Zech ordered a survey of all currently owned land in coastal Togo and an investigation of all land titles; the results were to be entered in an official land register. Adjudication of ownership disputes and appeals were handled by the government and ultimately decided by the governor. No African-held land could thereafter be alienated without permission of the governor. In one sense, the establishment of a system for registering land ownership and proving land titles made official expropriation easier. The main purpose, however, of Zech's reforms was to protect existing African titles from encroachment while insuring that new land would be developed in accordance with the small-farm, individual ownership model. It is clear from his description of what he believed to be legitimate land titles that he was doing his best to include within that category as many varieties of customary African land tenure as he could. Zech did not, in theory at least, intend his land reforms to be a vehicle for outright capitalist exploitation.[38]

As far as the actual administration of the law was concerned, Zech attempted to place a large amount of civil jurisdiction within the competence of native courts presided over by chiefs. Appeals from chiefs' decisions could be made to the district officers and to the governor. In criminal matters, offenses for which the assigned punishment was light could be tried in the first instance by the chiefs; for most major crimes, initial jurisdiction was exercised by the district officer. Certain penalties, especially capital and heavy corporal punishment, had to be reviewed by the governor before execution, an obvious response to previous colonial scandals.[39]

Zech's Place in Colonial History

Zech resigned the governorship in 1910 because of ill health. When he left office few of his policies had completely achieved their aims, but they had been successful enough to constitute a major influence on overall German colonial policy. Within Togo, Zech's legal and administrative reforms were in the process of being implemented, and the next four years saw their perpetuation under his successors. Togo continued to be advertised as one of Germany's most prosperous colonies. Between 1905 and 1911 the colony nearly doubled the volume of its exports despite the failure of the cotton scheme to live up to expectations.[40] Togo's economic success aroused interest in Zech's other ideas about colonial policy.

During the administration of colonial secretary Bernhard Dernburg (1906–1910), Zech had enjoyed a reputation as a competent official; since at least some of his conceptions of colonial government and development were similar to Dernburg's, no major conflicts arose between them.[41] But Dernburg was interested mainly in the large colonies, and it was not until after the secretary's resignation in 1910 and that of his conservative successor, Friedrich von Lindequist, in 1911 that Zech's conceptions became important. In 1912, a group appeared within the German colonial movement that attempted to recover Dernburg's reformist momentum and to redirect German colonial policy along "economic" and "humanitarian" lines. The reform movement was comparatively successful in the Reichstag and within the colonial administration. In 1914, for instance, the reformers succeeded in passing a parliamentary resolution that theoretically guaranteed the social and economic rights of indigenous colonial inhabitants to a far greater degree than any other colonial power did at the time.[42] The reformist position, although old in intellectual antecedents, drew inspiration from the policy followed in Togo, and both Togo and Zech himself were cited as the prime examples of enlightened reform. Zech, in fact, appears to have derived many of his policies from the tradition of "economic" colonialism that strongly influenced the reformists. The same elements were paramount in the reformist conception and in Zech's policy: the utility of a native peasant economy as the basis for economic development; the need to protect indigenous social structures and ownership rights; the overwhelming importance of education as the vehicle through which the government's economic and so-called civilizing missions were to be performed; a heavy emphasis on paternalistic humanitarianism; and the intervention of the colonial administration to prevent the creation of a black African proletariat.[43]

There is little evidence that German colonial reformism had much effect outside Germany. Zech, however, through his sponsorship of legal research and his program for the economic development of Togo, did have a certain amount of lasting international influence. The study of customary law directed by Zech was one of the foundations for legal anthropology and for subsequent work of great importance in colonial administration and in the construction of African legal systems after independence. Togolese economic development did not follow exactly the lines that Zech had desired, but he was responsible for the development of part of Togo's export economy. In addition, the German administration under Zech helped to create an effective educational system in Togo. He had intended education to be the basis of a strong domestic Togolese economy. Instead, the Togolese schools gave their graduates the ability to find clerical jobs outside Togo in the late colonial period, thereby accentuating the problem of labor emigration, with which Zech's policies and those of the French colonial governments in the 1920s and 1930s could not deal.

Zech as governor thought that he was laying the groundwork for a community of free peasant farmers in Togo, a community that would combine traditional social values with economic efficiency and allow a gradual infusion of Western culture. His policy derived from European concepts, favored in Germany both by conservatives and by some liberals as a domestic response to industrialization.[44] The society of coastal Togo seemed conducive to such development. However, Zech does not seem to have drawn his ideas initially from a consideration of the nature of that society but rather from European peasant agriculture, whose ideology was embodied among other things in the Togolese cotton scheme. His adherence to this particular set of social goals did have important and constructive side effects: it reinforced the policy of not opening Togo to big companies; it led to Zech's legal reforms; it strengthened his resolve to protect the ownership of African land; and it inspired his educational policy. But his basic economic and social program was in itself inadequate either for encouraging economic development or for protecting African societies.

The various economic development schemes that Zech helped institute were unable to generate sufficient capital to be self-sustaining. The peasant farmer model of development did not turn out to be practical, as it did in the Gold Coast, perhaps because of geographical factors. Control of the economic mechanism in

Togo passed into the hands of coastal traders and lenders, and the agricultural sector tended naturally toward subsistence crops. Even if the Germans had remained in control of Togo after 1919, it is difficult to see how things would have been much different. The problem of capital shortages in the 1920s would have confronted Togo at least as much under German rule as it did under the French, and the smaller scale of agricultural production would have made Togo just as unable to compete with the Gold Coast as it actually was under the French.

Zech's complementary aim of protecting traditional aspects of Togolese society was to a large extent self-defeating. Whatever he may have thought, even a free peasant society would have been something new in Togo and would have created social instability. Many of the mechanisms that he used to protect African social structures were themselves also agents of change. This was the case, for example, with the employment of African chiefs in the administrative system. Most significantly of all, Zech intended to create a society that would rest upon a class of people educated to make their own economic decisions; yet he assumed that such a society would remain politically quiescent. There is no indication in his policy statements of any plan to allow African political self-rule except to the extent that the chiefs—acting as agents of German authority—were to govern local communities in accordance with customary law. There seems to have been a basic contradiction in Zech's political thinking between his idea of an independent peasantry and his conception of an authoritarian, paternalistic government structure ultimately working to the advantage of Germany; this contradiction was not resolved by employing blacks in lower ranking government positions. The idea that a society of the sort that Zech envisioned would be difficult to create by authoritarian methods, no matter how "humane," seems not to have occurred to him.[45]

Zech's colonial thinking, therefore, is more important for its side effects, for its influence on late German colonial ideas and its assumptions about colonialism, than it is for the success and accuracy of its central tenets. Zech did not have the opportunity to reexamine his thinking in the light of later developments. After his retirement in 1910 he took little part in colonial or any other politics. He acted as Germany's representative at a conference in Paris on the Cameroons border and at an international conference on alcoholism in 1912; but he did not involve himself to a notable degree even in the 1912–1914 colonial reform movement. When war broke out he was called up as a reserve officer, and he was killed on the western front in 1914 at the head of an infantry battalion.[46]

Zech stands out in German colonial history as one of the most able and respected governors whom the German overseas empire produced. Despite the fact that much of what he attempted ultimately came to nothing and despite the considerable disparity between what has been reported about him in Togo and what he and the German administration actually accomplished, Zech was still an efficient and innovative administrator who made considerable contributions to applied social science and to the shaping of modern Togo.

Notes

1. In 1907 the total trade between Germany and Togo was a mere 7.5 million marks despite the fact that trade had nearly quadrupled in the previous decade. *Deutsches Kolonialblatt* (hereinafter cited D.K.B.), 1 August 1908, pp. 737–742.

2. In the Reichstag's annual budget review, Togo was usually passed through with little comment. See, for example, *Deutsche Kolonialzeitung* (hereinafter cited D.K.Z.), 8 February 1900, p. 52.

3. O. F. Metzger, *Unsere alte Kolonie Togo* (Neudamm, 1941), pp. 1, 26–30.

4. Robert Cornevin, *Histoire du Togo*, 3d ed. (Paris, 1969), pp. 167–169.

5. Georg Trierenberg, *Togo: Die Aufrichtung der deutschen Schutzherrschaft und die Erschliessung des Landes* (Berlin, 1914), pp. 43–75.

6. Heinrich Schnee, ed., *Deutsches Kolonial-Lexikon*, 3 vols. (Leipzig, 1920), 3:739.

7. Metzger, *Togo*, pp. 3–4.

8. Paul Rohrbach, *Der deutsche Gedanke in der Welt* (Leipzig, 1912), pp. 154–155.

9. Metzger, *Togo*, pp. 97–101; D.K.B., 15 December 1904, p. 751, and 1 March 1906, p. 140.

10. Julius Graf Zech, "Vermischte Notizen über Togo und das Togohinterland," *Mitteilungen aus den deutschen Schutzgebieten* 11 (1898):2; idem, "Land und Leute an der Nordwestgrenze von Togo," ibid. 17 (1904):3.

11. D.K.B., 1 March 1896, p. 130, and 15 November 1914, p. 836.

12. Trierenberg, *Togo*, pp. 93–99, 102–112.

13. See D.K.Z. of 6 February 1902, p. 58; 25 September 1902, p. 389; and 27 November 1902, p. 493; also see National Archives, Records of German Embassy in London (T-149), 139/1, 1605.

14. Trierenberg, *Togo*, pp. 6–7; Metzger, *Togo*, pp. 26–27.

15. *Stenographische Berichte über die Verhandlungen des deutschen Reichstages*, 19 March 1906, p. 2148.

16. Hans Spellmeyer, *Deutsche Kolonialpolitik im Reichstag* (Stuttgart, 1931).

17. D.K.Z., 27 May 1905, p. 206.

18. D.K.B., 15 December 1896, pp. 763–764, and 1 June 1902, pp. 1–2, 242–243.

19. George A. Schmidt, *Das Kolonial-Wirtschaftliche Komitee* (Berlin, 1934), pp. 5–14; D.K.B., 15 June 1908, pp. 582–588, and 1 July 1908, pp. 631–634.

20. D.K.B., 15 March 1892, p. 173.

21. J. K. von Vietor, *Wirtschaftliche und kulturelle Entwicklung unserer Schutzgebiete* (Berlin, 1913), pp. 61–95; Karin Hausen, *Deutsche Kolonialherrschaft in Afrika: Wirtschaftsinteressen und Kolonialverwaltung in Kamerun vor 1914* (Zurich, 1970), pp. 224–229, 274–290.

22. D.K.B. of 1 May 1904, pp. 294–295; 1 October 1906, p. 638; 15 September 1907, pp. 896–897; and 15 September 1909, pp. 866–867. See D.K.Z., 30 July 1903, p. 312.

23. August Full, *Fünfzig Jahre Togo* (Berlin, 1935), pp. 235–236; Arthur Joseph Knoll, "Togo under German Administration, 1884–1910" (Ph.D. dissertation, Yale University, 1964), pp. 104–112.

24. D.K.Z., 10 December 1903, pp. 501–502, and 24 December 1903, pp. 520–521. Also D.K.B. of 15 May 1904, pp. 325–326; 15 September 1904, p. 595; and 15 April 1906, pp. 220–222.

25. Comprehensive statements by Zech on his economic policy are found in D.K.B., 15 June 1904, p. 387, and D.K.Z., 13 May 1905, p. 185.

26. Metzger, *Togo*, pp. 3–5; D.K.B. of 15 October 1905, p. 616; 1 March 1906, p. 140; and 15 November 1908, pp. 1103–1105; also D.K.Z., 13 May 1905, p. 185.

27. D.K.B., 1 February 1909, pp. 88–89.

28. G. A. Fabarius, *Neue Wege der deutschen Kolonialpolitik nach dem Kriege* (Berlin, 1916), pp. 4–15.

29. Knoll, "Togo," pp. 187–195; D.K.B. of 1 January 1905, pp. 3–5; 1 August 1907, p. 707; and 1 October 1909, pp. 884–885; National Archives (T-149), 138/2, p. 1343.

30. D.K.B., 15 December 1907, pp. 185–186.

31. Metzger, *Togo*, pp. 105–108; Erich Schulz-Ewerth and Leonhard Adam, eds., *Das Eingeborenenrecht*, 2 vols. (Stuttgart, 1929–1930), 1:120; D.K.B., 1 June 1908, pp. 543–547.

32. D.K.B., 15 October 1905, p. 605.

33. Trierenberg, *Togo*, pp. 49–53; D.K.B., 1 January 1907, pp. 1–2, and 15 March 1910, pp. 209–216.

34. Schulz-Ewerth and Adam, *Das Eingeborenenrecht*, 1:10.

35. Ibid., 1:118–120; A. Schlettwein, "Kodifikation des Eingeborenenrechts in Togo," *Zeitschrift für vergleichende Rechtswissenschaft und Volkswirtschaftslehre* 43 (1927):248–252; D.K.B., 15 May 1908, pp. 467–468.

36. Full, *Fünfzig Jahre*, pp. 121–126; D.K.B., 15 October 1904, p. 631.

37. D.K.B., 15 May 1909, p. 481.

38. D.K.B., 1 September 1904, pp. 557–558, and 15 March 1910, pp. 218–219.

39. Full, *Fünfzig Jahre*, pp. 100–102.

40. Metzger, *Togo*, pp. 20–22. The total value of major exports increased from 12,712,000 marks in 1905 to 20,744,000 in 1911.

41. See Dernburg's statements of his policies in D.K.B., 15 December 1907, pp. 1195–1207, and 1 March 1908, pp. 216–231.

42. *Stenographische Berichte*, 7–9 March 1914, pp. 7897–7953.

43. Vietor, *Entwicklung*, pp. 96–144.

44. Woodruff D. Smith, "The Ideology of German Colonialism, 1840–1906," *Journal of Modern History* 46 (1974):641–662.

45. Zech's paternalistic position is clearly stated in D.K.Z., 13 May 1905, p. 185.

46. D.K.B., 15 November 1914, p. 836; Library of Congress, records on Franco-German relations, MAE 41, A12303, and MAE 42, A15532.

Heinrich Schnee (1871–1949)

L. H. Gann

ONE of the most characteristic representatives of German colonialism in its developed stage was Heinrich Schnee. He was born in 1871, the year in which Bismarck created the Hohenzollern Reich; he was a commoner by origin,[2] a National Liberal and imperial patriot by background, a civilian in outlook, a civil servant in training. Whereas the pioneers had ruled by the sword, Schnee stood for bureaucracy triumphant.

He was not a great governor. He lacked the romantic appeal of Hermann von Wissmann—a conqueror, pioneer, and subsequent drug addict. He was devoid of the literary and imaginative gifts possessed by Richard Kandt, a Jewish psychiatrist who advanced from the consulting office of a German lunatic asylum to the residency of Ruanda-Urundi. Schnee never deviated from the standards of his class as did General Berthold von Deimling—an erstwhile frontier fighter in Southwest Africa, a chauvinist and fire-eater who ended his career as a pacifist. In Schnee there was nothing of that deeply troubled religious streak, that uncompromising Lutheran piety that caused General Ludwig von Estorff, ex-commander of the *Schutztruppen* in Southwest Africa, to look back with anguish and repentance upon the German counterinsurgency campaign against the Nama and Herero in Southwest Africa.

Schnee, moreover, did not get a good press. Most military men did not like him. Paul von Lettow-Vorbeck, the supreme commander in German East Africa during World War I, considered him to be an interfering, bureaucratic busybody and studiously ignored Schnee in his own reminiscences. On the British side, Brigadier general C. P. Fendall, on meeting the German governor in captivity, described him as "a man of the less presentable lawyer class, full of cunning, by no means a fool but no gentleman."[3] Colonel Richard Meinertzhagen regarded

492

Schnee as a nice little chap, "weak, no character and rather typical of all second-rate civil servants."[4]

The general and colonels were mistaken. Schnee was a decent man—humane, well intentioned, hard working, cultured, personally honest, popular with his subordinates, conscientious, industrious, and literate. He was far from the nonentity described by Fendall. Only a reasonably strong-minded man would have been able to maintain his gubernatorial authority against a soldier as forceful and ruthless as Lettow-Vorbeck. In a minor way, Schnee was a reformer. Wilhelm Methner, his chief secretary in East Africa, who had seen service under three governors, considered him an "improver" in the tradition of Freiherr von Rechenberg, a conservative Catholic of negrophilist leanings and Schnee's predecessor as governor of East Africa. Schnee conformed to the stereotype of the Wilhelmian civil servant—competent, thorough, but devoid of vision. He was, in fact, far more characteristic of German colonialism in its developed stage than his more eccentric or colorful predecessors.

Origins and Training

Like most other German colonial administrators and soldiers, Schnee was in no way connected with those Hanseatic ports that actually made money from the trade conducted by the Reich with its overseas dependencies. His roots lay in Hanover. He was the citizen of a formerly independent kingdom that had reluctantly fallen under Prussian suzerainty as a result of the Prusso-Austrian war of 1866, five years before his birth. Schnee was born in Neuhaldesleben, a small town of the kind that seemed to produce the great majority of the civil servants who governed the German colonies. His grandfather was a Lutheran pastor, his father a *Landsgerichtsrat*, a respected member of the judicial bureaucracy in the small town of Nordhausen.

Heinrich Schnee grew up in a family where books were plentiful and education was taken for granted. The head of the family considered himself a liberal and delighted in describing the merits of Great Britain's constitutional monarchy and parliamentary system as expounded at the time by Rudolf Gneist, a distinguished legal scholar. "Conservative thought with its stress on authority and on the preservation of tradition," Schnee subsequently wrote in his private reminiscences, "stood worlds apart from my own."[5] He was educated at the local gymnasium, the kind of German secondary school that placed particular stress on the study of Latin and Greek; his report cards, carefully preserved among his papers, show an industrious boy whose conduct was "laudable" and whose academic accomplishments varied from "adequate" to "good."

As a peacetime soldier in the German army, Schnee did as creditably as he had as a schoolboy. He advanced to noncommissioned officer in the Eighty-fifth Infantry Regiment and was later commissioned as a reserve officer in the Sixth Grenadier Regiment in Posen, thereby attaining the social cachet that so many middle-class Germans of the Wilhelmian period valued more than academic distinction or even commercial success.

Schnee's academic education, like that of all senior German civil servants of the period, was heavily oriented toward legal subjects. He studied jurisprudence and constitutional law in Heidelberg, Kiel, and Berlin. Germany's leading philosopher at that time was Rudolf von Ihering, whose teaching profoundly affected university policy. Ihering rejected natural law; he insisted that the final object of the law was preservation of the state and that justice could be found only within the laws of individual states that provided the moral norms for society—a doctrine well suited to colonial conquerors determined to make their own legal notions prevail over those of their subjects. Again, Schnee did well. In 1893 he passed his examination as a *Referendar*, placing him on the lowest rung of the administrative hierarchy. A year later he qualified for a doctorate in law and subsequently mounted the second step on the official level by graduating as a *Regierungsassessor*.

In 1897 Schnee, now a promising young man of twenty-six, made the first unconventional move in his life. Entitled to call himself "Herr Doktor" and "Leutnant der Reserve" to boot, endowed with all the correct legal qualifications, he decided upon a colonial career. His father stood aghast. According to the elder Schnee, the colonies were places for *verkrachte Existenzen*—people who had failed in their profession or who had gotten into trouble at home. This attitude was then common in Germany. Wilhelm Methner and Theodor Seitz (subsequently one of Schnee's gubernatorial colleagues) record similar reactions on the part of their relations and friends.

Germany's economic interests in the colonies were still negligible. For all the talk of Wilhelmian *Weltpolitik*, of naval propaganda, and of colonial expansion (Germany added Kiaochow, China, to its empire in 1897 and Samoa a year later), the bulk of educated Germans still regarded the colonies as places where diseases were rife and scandals plentiful, where an ambitious youngster with talent was more likely to wreck his career than to make a name for himself. The Kolonialabteilung within the Auswärtiges Amt (the colonial department of the German foreign office) lacked administrative prestige and bureaucratic influence. Even socially, the mixed bunch of civil servants, military officers, agronomists, medical men, and technicians who served within the colonial department stood apart from their colleagues in the foreign service—accounted an altogether more aristocratic breed, superior to officials in the colonial or the consular branch.

From the vocational standpoint, a young man seemed indeed ill-advised to devote his life to the colonial office, first set up in 1890 as a separate branch within the foreign office and regarded as the Cinderella of government. It lacked bureaucratic prestige, parliamentary influence, and the social distinction associated with the diplomatic service. It was poorly run in the sense that incoming correspondence was hard to trace and senior civil servants were wont to commit that unpardonable bureaucratic sin of creating their own private files. Promotion prospects were poor in an office that numbered only a handful of administrators—the director of the department, who was answerable for most administrative matters directly to the Reich chancellor, four senior civil servants, and a handful of assistants and clerks, none of whom had ever visited any of the huge territories they were paid to supervise. The men in the field were also a varied bunch: army officers detached for colonial duties from their respective units (mostly infantry regiments), technicians, medical men, and officials from the various German states who served in the colonies for limited spells but were allowed to keep their seniority upon returning to the parent administrations.

Like the navy, the colonial service was truly German in the sense that it transcended the particularism of individual states like Prussia, Hesse, or Bavaria. But initially it had none of the efficiency or the social cachet that distinguished the German naval service. The system of colonial governance experienced by Schnee as a young official made for a maximum amount of instability; civil servants assigned to outstations were constantly shuffled around to meet the exigencies occasioned by frequent transfers to other services and by the high rate of sickness or death. Critics of the service were fond of belaboring its supposed penchant for *Assessorismus*, for those bureaucratic inanities that supposedly tied up able men with red tape, when in fact it contained at the time all too few trained assessors (*Assessoren*). When Schnee entered the service, there were not more than fourteen officials in Germany's entire colonial empire who possessed those higher academic and administrative qualifications acquired by Schnee in his university career. The service, moreover, did not possess a central training institution. To some extent this deficiency was made good by the Seminar für Orientalische Sprachen at the University of Berlin, where students like Schnee were able to take courses in African languages such as Swahili, Herero, Hausa, and Duala and also in more general subjects—geography, tropical hygiene, and colonial law.[6]

Within the colonial office Schnee was one of six new assessors who were groomed for service overseas. This group included Wilhelm Solf, later secretary of state in charge of colonial affairs and a man of considerable importance to Schnee's professional future. Their training consisted largely of learning to prepare memoranda, assisting in the compilation of colonial budgets, and occasionally attending discussions of the budget commission of the Reichstag, charged with examining the colonial budget prior to its being discussed, amended, and approved by the legislature.

During this period Schnee had to devote a great deal of time to the perusal of files on a medley of subjects, including justice, affairs of the South Sea islands, and especially personnel. The study of these records did not induce much respect for Germany's colonial statesmanship or its personnel. In a private letter to his friend Solf, Schnee wrote that the colonial office was not on good terms with its governors. There was a good deal of gubernatorial incompetence, and only Count von Götzen—then in charge of German East Africa—managed to enjoy good relations with headquarters in Berlin.[7]

Among the various bureaucratic entanglements was the case of Friedrich Freiherr von Schele, who sued the Reich for his return fare from East Africa, where he had served as governor during the early part of the 1890s. Schele had a prickly nature. A military man and an aristocrat, he resigned essentially over a matter of precedence. Instead of being allowed to communicate directly to the German chancellor he was expected to report to the colonial office director, Paul Kayser, a civilian, a commoner, a Jew, and—most demeaning of all from Schele's point of view—a personage not sufficiently advanced in the German official hierarchy to be addressed as "Your Excellency." Other files, Schnee recalled, illustrated the mixture of nonchalance and ignorance with which considerable areas of Africa—especially a portion of Ruanda—had been disposed of, not with a view toward the indigenous population or even toward German economic advantage but for the sake of not incommoding the great Bismarck with untimely memoranda on obscure subjects apt to arouse the prince's displeasure.[8]

German colonial policy in a wider sense, entailing a set of agreed principles regarding African destinies or African development, hardly existed before the turn of the century. When Schnee entered the colonial service the German colonial empire was only thirteen years old. Local governors and their subordinates adjusted themselves to differing local conditions and tried to enforce their authority as best they might. They were autocrats whose rule was tempered by a chronic insufficiency of funds, a pervasive lack of personnel—civilian and military—and sometimes by the attention of unsympathetic missionaries or a critical Reichstag ready to use scandalous or criminal proceedings in the colonies as a means of embarrassing the government of the day. The prevailing though by no means universal notion of economic development was represented by men like Gerhard von Buchka (colonial office director between 1898 and 1900), Jesco von Puttkamer (governor of the German Cameroons between 1895 and 1907), and Julius Scharlach, an influential financier who considered that Africans were born idlers and needed a good dose of German discipline.

Capital for the colonies was scarce. The great banks were as yet reluctant to risk their depositors' money in what appeared to be risky undertakings in faraway places. Funds, according to Scharlach, therefore had to be attracted to the colonies by the grant of far-reaching privileges to concessionary companies; only these bodies were capable of laying the foundations of civilization in "darkest Africa." Until 1902 these concessionary and plantation concerns held a commanding position within the Kolonialrat, an advisory body charged with giving expert counsel on colonial affairs to the German government. Schnee, like other assessors, sometimes had to attend the council's sessions for the purpose of recording its minutes. He was impressed by the way in which various companies used the Kolonialrat to support one another against public criticism and also by the element of showmanship that characterized some of the Kolonialrat's proceedings.

District Officer

Schnee had learned Swahili during his initial period of preparation in Berlin, hoping to secure a transfer to East Africa. But German East Africa was then the plum of the colonial service and no vacancy occurred. He therefore decided to accept a judgeship in the Bismarck archipelago in the South Seas, having heard wonderful tales from a colleague. At first sight reality exceeded expectations; as Schnee looked from the steamer upon his new domain, he was struck by its indescribable beauty—an endless ocean and a translucent sky, breakers, and a curving bay flanked by three extinct volcanos, whitewashed bungalows, and in the background the bluish-violet mountains of Neu Mecklenburg glowing in the morning sun.[9]

Colonial realities, however, differed sharply from first appearances. Germany's South Sea island possessions were then run by the Neuguinea-Compagnie. For the time being, the German government supplied the local *Landeshauptmann*, or resident, and also judges such as Schnee. All real power rested with Adolph von Hansemann, head of the great Diskonto-Gesellschaft and founder of the Neuguinea-Compagnie—a most successful banker, but a man little fitted to lead a colonial administration. Schnee records that Hansemann tried to rule the colony like a landed estate in Brandenburg; he poured a great deal of money into the enterprise but centralized power in the Berlin office to such an extent that little was achieved. Within its huge and scattered domain the company had to contend with difficult geographical conditions: mountains, tropical forests, a deadly climate, and a host of diseases that rendered inland penetration difficult. Lack of skill and experience on the part of local overseers, unforeseen agronomic difficulties, and a constant lack of labor made the planters' life hard. As a result, the administration on the whole operated at a heavy loss until 1899, when the German government took over the reigns of government.[10]

The most difficult problem of all, however, centered on the question of governance. There was nothing in Schnee's experience to acquaint him with the manners and customs of the Tolai, the Austronesian inhabitants of what is now New Britain. They were a matrilineal people, with a Stone Age culture, organized into small, stateless societies that depended on hunting, fishing, and a shifting form of agriculture, and engaged in blood feuds, ritual cannibalism, and endless, petty wars in which prisoners were apt to be tortured to death. The Tolai fought among themselves for plunder, honor, or vengeance—for instance, over offenses involving violations of sexual norms. They also had numerous quarrels with the Germans. There were disputes sparked by European traders unfamiliar with indigenous customs; there were affrays when the Tolai looted German stores or killed isolated settlers. The Germans avenged murders by shelling villages from warships or sometimes by sending out punitive expeditions that burned villages and killed the survivors. In their dealings with the Stone Age headhunters the Germans would not accept the simple *lex talionis*, the ancient law of an eye for an eye, but went far beyond the norms of retaliation accepted by the indigenous warriors and thereby added fuel to smouldering hatreds. They also tried to install a new form of governance by putting headmen known as *luluai* in charge of labor recruitment and tax collection, for which services they received a percentage of taxes collected.

German power did not, however, extend far beyond the fringe of white settlement. Away from government posts, plantations, and mission stations, the indigenous people continued to run their affairs in traditional fashion, very different from the desires of their overlords. The Germans wanted to buy copra; they also wished to recruit indigenous people as plantation laborers. But once the Tolai had satisfied their desire for guns, axes, and knives, they insisted on being paid in their own shell currency rather than in the white man's money, a preference that did not suit the needs of traders and plantation owners. Schnee himself disliked the Tolai with passionate intensity:

> I am among a people who raid one another, kill one another and eat one another. The Kanacks lack all those virtues that have been developed among more civilized peoples. There is, among them, no such thing as incorruptibility or honor. . . . Cowrie [shell money] can buy anything, merchandise, women, and help in war.[11]

Not surprisingly, Schnee's ideas on economic development conformed to the notions of the Scharlach-Puttkamer school in Africa. Progress must center on European planters producing copra and other tropical crops for the world market. The indigenous people were too backward to respond to economic incentives.

Labor for the plantations should be secured, if necessary, by the importation of indentured workmen from Java. European enterprise alone would put an end to aboriginal savagery.

Schnee's ability to put these ideas into practice was, however, strictly limited. His entire establishment consisted of a German court clerk, a police sergeant (a former merchant marine captain), and some thirty policemen recruited from a great variety of Melanesian communities. His work as judge involved an extensive amount of touring and a host of little campaigns, many of them seaborne and carried out with the aid of a single small vessel. Court cases often involved affairs never mentioned in those German law books that Schnee had studied with such assiduity as a *Referendar*. Some of the more difficult problems included adultery within the framework of polygamous marriage, incest as interpreted by the rules of the Tolai, and witchcraft accusations dependent on a philosophy far removed from the positivism of a German jurist.

Schnee, however, was an adaptable young man and a good linguist who rapidly improved his knowledge of the indigenous idiom. He came to enjoy his work and the powers of independent decision that went with it. He also acquired a good deal of ethnographic information later recorded in his *Bilder aus der Südsee* (1904), the first of many works from his pen. He used his knowledge to consolidate German influence by the appointment of local chiefs, approved of and supported by the government and willing to assist German authorities. This policy involved an entirely new departure within the context of stateless societies. But Schnee tried to pick influential clan heads, men of local power and reputation, whom he backed if necessary with his tiny force. He later extended this mode of governance to the island of Neu Mecklenburg. Within the limited means at their command, Schnee and his colleagues did a remarkably good job. Anthropologists such as A. L. Epstein, who surveyed the area in more recent times, were impressed by the scholarly work of the early German administrators and by the favorable image that they had left in the memories of the indigenous people.

Schnee's assignment did not last long, however. In 1900 he was transferred to the German portion of the Samoan islands, which had been acquired after twenty years of tripartite rule in concert with Great Britain and the United States. Samoa proved altogether more congenial than his previous station, and soon after arriving he found personal happiness by marrying Ada Woodhill, a beautiful actress from Sydney, who gave him love and perhaps an excessive degree of admiration until the day he died. He liked the local people with their love of ceremony, their exquisite manners, their physical beauty—especially their faces, so much more attractive to him than the features of the Bismarck islanders. Schnee found himself thrust into a society in which marriages between German men and local women were far from uncommon and in which the indigenous population had been converted to a Christianity of sorts. Also, local Samoan enterprise played a considerable part in an active economic life through the production of copra. Although he did not manage to secure the governorship, which he apparently coveted, Schnee was promoted to district commissioner (*Bezirksamtmann*) and served for a time as deputy governor.

Here Schnee again met Solf, his former colleague in the colonial office, who was now governor of Samoa. He was nine years older than Schnee and was also senior to him in official rank, and for a time Solf exerted considerable influence

upon the younger man. While Schnee was still a bachelor the two shared a bunga-
low; when one of them went home on leave they kept in touch by correspondence.
Solf even took it upon himself to secure his friend a decoration.[12]

Solf's social philosophy was very different from the views held by the Scharlach-Puttkamer school. Son of a Berlin industrialist, he was an anglophile in outlook and a liberal in politics, a highly educated man, a student of philology as well
as of law, and even something of an authority in Sanskrit. His views on colonial
development accorded with those of commercial men like Eduard Hernsheim, a
great South Sea trader of Jewish extraction, and J. K. Vietor, a distinguished Togo
trader. The latter, a humanitarian and a Calvinist strongly supported by Bremen
merchants, saw his influence gain ascendancy within the Kolonialrat from 1902
onward. According to Vietor, the future of Togo should not rest on the enterprise
of plantations but on a partnership between foreign merchants and native producers. Solf held similar convictions regarding Samoa. He argued that the colony
was too small to rely upon a solely European plantation economy. The indigenous
people should take an increasingly important part in economic life as agricultural
producers. Native land rights accordingly must be protected, and the government
should permit as few leases as possible to immigrant planters. Schnee fully agreed
with these ideas. He became convinced that the local land situation ought not to
be allowed to deteriorate further, and he began to offend German planters by disallowing a variety of applications for land.[13] After he left Samoa in 1903 the Solf
view prevailed, and further land alienation to whites was forbidden.

Metropolitan Bureaucrat

On returning from Samoa, Schnee was once again posted to the Colonial office
(known from 1907 as the Reichskolonialamt). He spent the greater part of his official career as a bureaucrat at Berlin headquarters rather than in the bush. Promotion came rapidly for a man without links to the nobility or special influence in
high places. His progress paralleled the expansion of the central colonial administration during a period of extensive change. It also reflected the process by which
administrative positions were rapidly being taken over by officials of bourgeois
origin.[14]

In 1905 Schnee was appointed colonial attaché (Kolonialbeirat) at the German
embassy in London. Here he and his British-born wife spent a pleasant year devoted mainly to social pursuits among high society. At only thirty-six he advanced
to be *Vortragender Rat*, a member of the German administrative elite, in 1906.
Schnee had a good training in law and had acquired a reputation for his ethnographic work in the South Seas. Thus, in 1907 he was called to serve on an official
commission set up to study indigenous legal systems in the colonies, a scheme proposed originally by Felix Meyer, the geographer, and then backed warmly by both
Bernhard Dernburg and Matthias Erzberger, a well-known Center politician and
critic of German colonialism.[15]

Schnee was an effective administrator. In 1911 he was promoted to head of the
political and administrative department (Politische und Verwaltungsabteilung),
the key section within the ministry as a whole. By now he had become a man of
some consequence. Well-spoken and dapper, with bushy eyebrows and a tooth-

brush moustache, he had good presence. Schnee conferred with ministers and parliamentarians. He obtained a foothold in the academic world when he received a part-time appointment in the Seminar für Orientalische Sprachen, where he lectured twice a week on colonial economics and policy to candidates for the colonial service. He published another book, a brief guide entitled *Die Deutschen Kolonien* (1908), reprinted in several editions. He was well off financially; to be precise, he had an income of between 14,000 and 17,000 marks as head of the political and administrative department, a salary equivalent to that of an *Erster Referent* (the most senior official next to the governor of a large German colony) and about fifteen times as much as that obtained by an industrial worker in Germany.[16] Schnee now moved in high social circles, though not in court society. He met financiers, industrialists, publishers, and parliamentarians and could entertain at some expense. Above all, he was still a relatively young man marked for further advancement.

While Schnee's career was advancing, the German colonial empire went through a far-reaching crisis. In the southern part of German East Africa there was a bloody revolt known as the Maji-Maji rising, a pantribal war of resistance occasioned by a great variety of German impositions—taxes, labor dues, and above all by the enforced cultivation of cotton. The Herero and subsequently the Nama peoples in Southwest Africa rose in protest against a policy that promoted white settlement at the expense of indigenous communities. A few intelligent *Schutztruppen* officers had an inkling of the war to come. But, as Schnee noted to his surprise, none of the recognized experts had anticipated that the Herero—supposedly a race of curs and cowards—would take up arms; much less that their erstwhile Nama enemies would join them.

In the end the Germans had to wage a grueling counterinsurgency campaign requiring the deployment of more than 17,000 volunteers from the German home army. All these men had to be incorporated into the *Schutztruppen* since neither the ministry of war nor the admiralty would take on such a difficult administrative task. The command of the *Schutztruppen*, a small section within the colonial office, had to organize and supply these forces, a task for which it was ill-prepared. The actual conduct of operations and of African policy was taken out of the hands of colonial authorities and entrusted to a military man, General Lothar von Trotha. A protégé of Schlieffen's and persona grata with the kaiser, Trotha won the war by wiping out a considerable portion of the Herero and their herds, leaving Southwest Africa in desperate economic straits.

These wars and the resultant financial expenditures, coming on top of individual scandals entailing corruption or cruelty, helped to give colonial issues a central place in German politics. Armed conflict speeded ongoing attempts at reform of the kind approved by bourgeois bureaucrats like Schnee and Solf and by bankers and merchants like Vietor and his missionary friends in the Deutsche Gesellschaft für Eingeborenenschutz, an association patterned on the British Aborigines' Rights Protection Society. Other supporters of reform included notables such as Julius Graf von Zech, who was in charge of Togo between 1903 and 1910—a Bavarian aristrocrat, a Catholic, and a convinced believer in the policy of developing the colonies through African peasant cultivation rather than through plantation companies.

In order to improve conditions, reformers such as Schnee agreed that the empire needed a proper logistic infrastructure, especially port and railway facilities. The colonies should be made more attractive to big investors. Administrators should be more carefully selected and more civilian in their approach than the military pioneers of old. Concessionary regimes should be revised; economic coercion should give way to a policy of encouraging African producers and workmen by means of economic incentives.

Within the colonial office the reform policy first was symbolized by Karl Helfferich, a protégé of Oscar Stübel's colonial office director between 1901 and 1905. Helfferich helped found the Deutsch-Ostafrikanische Bank; he reformed the East African currency (after World War I he helped to provide a similar service for the hopelessly inflated German mark); and he improved statistical services within the colonial office and recast its organization. Helfferich also tried to influence German capitalists to invest more heavily in the colonies at a time when the empire was the Cinderella of the stock exchange and when the entire capital placed in all German colonies did not greatly exceed the capital and reserves of just one major financial concern in Germany.[17] He left the colonial department in 1906 for a distinguished career in banking and politics.[18] His work, however, was continued with much greater political impact and financial effectiveness by Dernburg.

Schnee worked well with Dernburg as a senior advisor and clearly enjoyed the experience. The achievements of the new regime are fairly well known. Dernburg turned his office into an independent ministry with some political punch in the Reichstag. He strove for a more humane African labor regime in the colonies and tried to encourage peasant agriculture. He played a major part in pushing railway building in the German territories. Of even more immediate concern to Schnee as an expert in personnel questions was the creation of the Hamburgisches Kolonial-Institut to provide improved training for young officials, the passing of a major civil service ordinance in June 1910 that helped solidify the colonial bureaucracy, and the appointment of officials more in tune with the "new era"—including Theodor Seitz, a friend of Schnee's and close to him in background, bureaucratic training, political convictions, and age. Dernburg warmly supported Albrecht Freiherr von Rechenberg, the local governor in East Africa. A great nobleman like Zech, Rechenberg was a conservative-minded supporter of the Center party and one of the few Catholics to obtain a leading position within the German colonial hierarchy. He was also a convinced advocate of labor reform and of *Volkskultur* (African peasant agriculture).

Top of the Tree

In 1910 Dernburg was forced out of office by the rightward drift of German parliamentary politics and by his personal deficiencies as a statesman. After a brief interlude, the directorship of the colonial office was taken over by Solf in 1911. Smooth and adaptable, Solf was a man willing to compromise—willing to compromise with the settlers who detested Dernburg's supposed leanings toward negrophilism and autocracy, willing to compromise also with the shifting pressure groups within the Reichstag. Yet Solf in some fashion attempted to continue the

Dernburg tradition with its anglophile leanings and with its cautious advocacy of native trusteeship, along with his own personal belief in indirect rule of the Lugardian type. Solf, in fact, greatly admired Lugard, whom he visited in Nigeria and who supplied his guest, at Solf's request, with the confidential memoranda on native policy issued to British district officers in Northern Nigeria.[19]

Solf thought well of Schnee, and when the governorship of East Africa fell vacant, he offered the post to his former subordinate. Schnee had experience both in district work and in central decisionmaking. He had an excellent academic background and was also well qualified in Swahili, the administrative language of East Africa. In professional terms, Schnee, the son of a provincial bureaucrat, had now "arrived"; at the age of forty-one he headed Germany's most developed colony, known to colonial enthusiasts as "German India." In terms of German administrative sociology, his appointment marked yet another step in the progressive bourgeoisification of colonial leadership. For the first time in history, the highest gubernatorial position at the disposal of the colonial office went to a man who was neither a professional officer nor a nobleman. Schnee occupied a post that in earlier days would have gone to an exalted personage such as Adolf Friedrich Duke of Mecklenburg, a leading colonialist congenial to the kaiser for both political and social reasons.[20]

When Schnee arrived in his new capital in 1912, he found a modern city in embryo. Dar es Salaam was populated by some 22,000 people. Served by a railway into the interior, its maritime traffic was handled mainly by the Deutsch-Ostafrika Linie, a subsidiary of the Woermann-Linie in Hamburg. The town boasted a handsome railway station and an efficient electricity supply. There was a real hotel, the Kaiserhof, complete with private rooms and hot and cold running water. The Deutsch-Ostafrikanische Bank, with a monopoly on the issuance of bank notes, had opened its doors in 1909. There were pleasant streets lined with trees, and substantial, stone houses whose red-tiled roofs blended into the surrounding verdure. Architecturally the Germans had produced a pleasing variation of the Wilhelmian style, simplified and adapted to the tropical environment—quite different from the ugly spread of corrugated, iron-roofed bungalows that disfigured so many new colonial towns.

Nevertheless, Dar es Salaam had its shortcomings. Squeezed in between the pleasant European residential quarters in the east, the orderly commercial section in the southeast, and a new and well planned "native" township in the west, there was a labyrinthine slum wherein Indian shops and dwellings were interspersed with Arab and African huts, defying all efforts of proper municpial administration and sanitation, and adjacent swamps infected by mosquitoes. Even slum society, however, was changing.

In the old days, the town dwellers' chief occupation had been barter, agricultural enterprise, and trading in ivory and slaves. Land had been freely available; planters merely had to clear new plots. Profits had been used for expanding plantations by buying more slaves. In addition, there had existed a separate class of artisans, both slave and free. Under the new order, life was modified by the railway and the expansion of the cash economy. The old-style artisans found that their methods were too leisurely and too cumbersome to have much value; many were forced to learn their trade afresh and to work with new tools. New trades sprang up for which the young men acquired the necessary skills from foreigners. Hereditary apprenticeship decayed, and parental control over the young weakened. The traditional trading class was widely supplanted by Indians. Laborers and ex-slaves became accustomed to better paid work in the service of whites. The Germans ruled through salaried *akidas*, subordinate officials of Swahili background who enforced a host of new rules and regulations that superseded the laws of Islam. Westernization had come to stay.[21]

At the apex of this new society stood the whites. Their status was high. But the quality of their lives in Dar es Salaam left much to be desired. Unlike their compatriots in the bush, the denizens of the capital had no opportunity for hunting and fishing. There was as yet no motor transport; even senior officials got about by ricksha. Within the European community, women were still heavily outnumbered by men; in German East Africa of 1913 the white popluation comprised 3,536 men, only 1,075 women, and 725 children. The center of existence was the beer garden, a comfortable and shady place annexed to the brewery that stood at the corner of what later became Ingles Street and Ring Street. There was a club, but it was open only to the higher grade civil servants, the officers, and the cream of nonofficial society. Many residents complained of backbiting and petty squabbling and of bitter disputes over matters of precedence and ceremonial. These personal disputes envenomed local politics and were apt to make life miserable in a city whose intellectual attractions were limited to a small circulating library, an occasional musical soirée, or a military concert provided by a *Schutztruppen* band.

Nevertheless, Schnee and his wife enjoyed themselves. As governor, Schnee stood at the very top of the social pyramid. He was commander in chief, chief executive, and *arbiter elegantiarum* combined. He was entitled to be called *Wirklicher Geheimer Rat* (Truly Privy Councillor). According to the meticulous order of Wilhelmian precedence, he had to be addressed as "Your Excellency," but only "as long as he held his official position and only while residing outside Europe."[22] His annual salary was 50,000 marks, the kind of remuneration received by a minister plenipotentiary in the German diplomatic service.

The administrative machinery at Schnee's disposal, though more extensive than the bureaucracy of British East Africa, was rudimentary in modern terms (see Table 1). The total number of European officers was small. In Dar es Salaam the central administration included no more than a dozen senior officials (*Referenten*), and governance of the districts required only thirty European administrators and clerks. The *Referenten* were equivalent to heads of departments in British colonies; they dealt with specialized topics such as personnel, veterinary and medical problems, agriculture and forestry, mining, public works, etc. The task of supervising this bureaucracy was relatively simple. Schnee was assisted by Wilhelm Methner, a highly competent civil servant who carried out the duties of *Erster Referent*, a position similar to that of the chief secretary in a British colony. He supervised the work of the other *Referenten*, who had to communicate to the governor through Methner's office; in Schnee's absence Methner stood in for him. The governor headed the colony's slender military establishment, a defense force of fourteen *Schutztruppen* companies under their own commandant. In peacetime there were 2,500 men backed by an 1,800-man police force, a negligible number in relation to the country's vast size. Schnee also presided over the Gouvernementsrat, the advisory council composed of elected settler representatives and senior civil servants. Assuring the efficient governance of the districts was his responsibility.

Table 1.   East African Administrative Personnel: Comparative Figures for 1904

	German East Africa		British East Africa	
	Whites	Nonwhites	Whites	Nonwhites
Central administration	23	4	6	3
Justice	12	—	11	20
Finance and supplies	39	1	15	22
Customs	17	40	2	52
Medical and veterinary services	21	1	15	2
Central police administration	23	—	8	7
Ports and public works	52	—	13	23
Forestry	6	—	4	1
Surveys	5	—	2	3
Agriculture, botany, geology	11	3	3	—
District administration	47	—	46	38
Teachers	8	—	—	—
Postal services	16	2	10	46
Total	280	51	135	217

SOURCE: RM. 5, v. 5668 Verwaltung, German Naval Archives, Bundesarchiv, Freiburg.

Nothing would be more mistaken than to accept the stereotype of a tightly meshed administration, all-powerful and all-seeing, conveyed by some of the colonial literature of the period. By the time Schnee assumed office, German East Africa was divided into nineteen districts (*Bezirke*), each headed by a commissioner who ruled areas as large as European principalities with a staff fit for a parish council. Their white staff consisted of a police sergeant, a clerk, and a secretary. Larger districts might have one or two branch offices run by a subordinate official. In addition, there were three *Residenturen* wherein a German Resident acted as advisor to indigenous princes whose authority the Germans recognized. The judicial administration was divided along racial lines: "nonnatives"—that is to say, whites and minority groups regarded as equivalent in status to Europeans (Goans, Japanese, Syrians, Parsees)—were subject to the jurisdiction of courts known as *Bezirksgerichte*, of which there were only four in the entire territory. Appeals might be directed to the superior court (*Obergericht*) in Dar es Salaam, which acted in the governor's name.

Financially, the governor's position was far from easy. It is true that the revenue at his disposal had grown in an impressive fashion, but the imperial treasury was still called upon to meet an annual deficit. By 1913 revenues reached 19,321,000 marks; the Reich paid just under 3.5 million marks a year for the upkeep of the *Schutztruppen* in addition to other subsidies. In absolute terms the country's revenue was negligible—no more than the capital of a medium-sized corporation in the fatherland and practically nonexistent when compared to the resources available to a great metropolitan trust. At that time the share capital and reserves of the *Deutsche Bank* amounted to a total of 312.5 million marks, more than fifteen times the annual revenue of Germany's richest colony.

The country had made a certain amount of economic progress, and when Schnee assumed office, a good deal of the logistic infrastructure had been completed or was in the process of expansion. New port facilities had come into existence where few had existed before. Railway lines had been extended. European settlers had pioneered in augmenting the cash economy.[23] A few hundred white planters accounted for the greater part of the country's exports, particularly in sisal and cultivated rubber. Between 1903 and 1913 foreign trade increased more than fourfold, from 18,242,259 to 88,910,000 marks.[24]

But German East Africa still was far from prosperous. There was no mining industry. In terms of British currency, the colony's commerce was worth only about £4.5 million; it was of trifling value compared with that of British West Africa, estimated at £30 million a year. Little more than half the colony's exports went to Germany, the rest going mainly to Great Britain and India. Yet despite its slender resources, an ever growing number of Africans were being drawn into the cash economy. They worked as porters, soldiers, railway construction workers, and plantation hands. African cultivators sold increasing amounts of export goods such as hides and skins, cotton, and peanuts. Seen as a whole, the territory's economic future seemed secure. The initial wars of conquest were over, and no large-scale insurrections had followed the great Maji-Maji rising of 1905. In short, Schnee expected to guide the country through a period of peaceful construction.

Governor at Peace

When Schnee took office, the country's economic future was as yet far from settled. The Pan-Germans and their allies hoped to turn German East Africa into a "white man's country." On the other hand, Albrecht von Rechenberg, Schnee's predecessor, had tried to develop the colony through a policy of encouraging African agriculture. Rechenberg had no faith in European settlement. He felt that Germany's future lay in Eastern Europe, whereas the colonies were only an encumbrance to be governed as cheaply and as humanely as possible. In his opinion, the Maji-Maji revolt was not an irrational outbreak occasioned by superstitious witch doctors but a definite response to economic oppression. The future German East Africa should be developed through a partnership of German railway builders, Indian traders, and African cultivators. To the settlers, Rechenberg was very much a "coolie-and-groundnuts man."

Schnee's temperament was more sanguine than Rechenberg's. A National Liberal by inclination, he was convinced that European settlement and social reform were not mutually exclusive. He saw no necessary contradiction between *Volkskultur* and plantation agriculture; the two forms of enterprise complemented one another. Local agriculture, Schnee argued in *Unsere Kolonien* (1908), was bound to become increasingly important, a point of view that echoed the Dernburg-Rechenberg line. Africans were already important producers of crops like corn, millet, and bananas. By 1913 they also accounted for the greater part of German East Africa's cotton exports, a development assisted by the German authorities by means of agricultural research, the distribution of seeds, and similar measures. Despite the opposition of German farmers, Africans had also begun to cultivate coffee, and black farmers accounted for the bulk of German East Africa's exports of skins, hides, peanuts, and other related products (see Table 2). European planters, on the other hand, were particularly suited to produce more specialized crops like rubber and sisal, which by 1913 were German East Africa's most important exports. According to Schnee, however, there was no room in East Africa for German smallholders of the kind favored by "folkish" nationalists such as Eduard von Liebert (governor of German East Africa from 1896 to 1901, a militant Pan-German, and ultimately a member of the Nazi party). The greater part of the available land had already been alienated. Schnee wanted white settlement to be restricted to specific areas; white farmers ought to be men of means.[25]

Table 2.   German East Africa Exports in 1913

	Value in million marks
Animal products	
live beasts	0.079
hides and skins	5.490
ivory	0.230
beeswax	1.414
Crops	
rubber	6.568
peanuts	1.918
cotton	2.415
sisal	10.712
copra	2.348
coffee	0.931

SOURCE: Heinrich Schnee, ed., *Deutsches Kolonial-Lexikon*, 3 vols. (Leipzig, 1920).

Both black and white cultivators required better railways, extended agricultural services, improved research, as well as cattle dips, dams, and wells. Accordingly, Schnee ordered the foundation of a veterinary institution and encouraged agricultural research at centers such as the Agricultural Institute at Amani, whose work was designed to assist both European and African agriculture. The colony's agricultural department continued to promote cotton cultivation. Seeds and some equipment were distributed gratis, a minimum price was guaranteed to cotton growers, the coercive methods that had contributed to the Maji-Maji rising were relaxed, and the acreage of land under cotton cultivation increased.

Peaceful coexistence betweeen African peasant agriculture and European farming—as envisaged by Schnee—hinged above all on the labor question. In East Africa mechanical equipment as yet played very little part in farming, and agriculture still depended largely on human muscle power. Hence, there was constant competition for labor, both among different white enterprises and between the "white" and "black" sectors of the economy as a whole. The white population was numerically insignificant; in 1913 there were only 5,336 Europeans in the entire territory. But this small group formed a powerful lobby. They had introduced new crops, such as sisal and coffee, into the country; they had developed new marketing techniques; and they had imported new agricultural implements such as steam plows, as well as new farming techniques, including the scientific breeding of livestock and the method of cleansing cattle in cattle dips to protect them against ticks. They were influential in the local advisory council and in Germany itself. German nationalist organizations were always ready to take up the cause of overseas colonists. In addition, some of the larger East African enterprises such as banking were linked to powerful concerns in Germany; some of the plantation companies could pride themselves on stockholders' lists that read like extracts from the *Almanach de Gotha*.[26]

From the economic standpoint, however, these concerns operated mostly under conditions of great difficulty. The pioneers took great risks and lost a good deal of money at a time when marketing facilities and communications were deficient. The majority of the colonists, especially those least able to pay adequate wages or to provide their workmen with acceptable conditions, blamed an all-pervading labor shortage for their troubles. According to contemporary German estimates, the territory's population amounted to more than 7 million people; the actual number must have been a great deal lower. The settlers therefore could not understand why the country should be hard put to provide a labor force hardly in excess of 90,000 hands.[27] Smaller and less efficient employers preferred to rely on coercion and brutality rather than on economic incentives. In particular, they were apt to call for some kind of conscripted labor. Despite the efforts of Rechenberg and Dernburg, the conditions of labor migrants left much to be desired. Modeled to some extent on conditions in Mecklenburg—one of the most backward parts of Germany—German labor discipline was usually harsh, and corporal punishment appears to have been employed much more widely in German than in British East Africa.[28] In theory, the Germans prided themselves on being *streng aber gerecht* (severe but just); in practice, severity was apt to outweigh justice.

Schnee was determined to continue in the Rechenberg tradition. He opposed the notion that government should supply private firms with workmen. The administration ought not even to be required to furnish employers with voluntary labor, lest coercion reappear in another guise. These views accorded with the preference of many administrators who disliked the thankless job of having chiefs round up unwilling and inefficient conscripts. In addition, district officials stationed among the Nyamwezi and Sukuma, who supplied a substantial part of the country's wage labor force, were now voicing bitter complaints: the exodus of young men depleted the local economies; field work was being left to women and children; family life in the villages was disrupted; and African labor migrants— correctly likened to the *Sachsengänger* of East Germany—were bringing back disease and "evil notions" to the villages from their places of employment. According to Schnee, the country's economy could not do without migrant labor, but government should step in to regulate labor conditions in a more effective fashion. Above all, the unlicensed labor recruiter must disappear from the scene.[29]

On February 5, 1913, Schnee issued a far-reaching decree. In the future, all recruiters would have to be licensed by the government under strict conditions.

Women, children, the sickly, and the elderly could no longer be hired at all. All labor contracts had to be approved by local district officers. Employers were obliged to provide proper medical facilities for their workmen. A working day could not exceed ten hours, and a contract could not go beyond one year. This policy was in opposition to the views of the Deutsche Gesellschaft für Eingeborenenschutz, which would have preferred to see agricultural laborers permanently "stabilized" on European plantations and there assigned plots for their own use— a policy accepted by the Reichstag in a formal resolution on African control just before the outbreak of World War I.

As a financial administrator, Schnee contributed most to the colony's fiscal reform, replacing a graduated hut tax with a head tax. Under existing financial regulations, Africans resident in substantial houses built in the Arab style were penalized by a tax that imposed higher dues on dwellings of a more solid construction. In addition, missionaries complained, the hut tax encouraged families to crowd together in an unsanitary fashion in order to avoid higher taxes. By a decree dated August 23, 1912, the government abolished the hut tax and imposed a head tax that varied from three to five rupies according to the district (one mark equaled 0.75 rupies, or one British shilling). The new system increased territorial revenues; by 1912 taxes—which were essentially revenue contributed by Africans —accounted for 4,461,000 marks out of a total income of 12,475,000 marks. It also promoted administrative centralization: the *akidas* lost much of their financial power since revenue collection was more closely supervised by the European administration and opportunities for graft at the lower level were said to diminish.

Partly because his own brother served as a medical officer in the colonial service, Schnee took a keen interest in public health. In his opinion, the government ought to give first priority to the task of improving African health conditions. Measures designed to safeguard against disease were but the "biological aspect" of a successful labor policy in a country whose population was supposedly inadequate to deal with the requirements of an expanding economy. Schnee made some progress in cleaning up the swamps of Dar es Salaam and improving the city's sanitary conditions according to the precepts of an American physician who had previously worked in Panama. Considerable sums were allotted to fight yaws and smallpox. Robert Koch, who had discovered the tuberculosis bacillus, introduced Atoxyl as a tentative remedy against sleeping sickness. Paul Ehrlich, the first physician effectively to treat syphilis, contributed his drug ".606," a preparation against tick and blackwater fever. By 1914 the Germans had three sleeping-sickness stations and a research institute at Dar es Salaam. In a countrywide campaign against smallpox, sixteen medical stations were set up and vast numbers of Africans were vaccinated. The colony's hospital services were expanded with the help of the Hamburg Institute of Tropical Medicine, a program that had far-reaching results for the future.

Schnee was a touring governor. He liked hunting and enjoyed traveling through his new domain, which he got to know pretty thoroughly. He shared the average German—and British—administrator's preference for the "romantic" Masai and the "aristocratic" and "dignified" Tutsi, as against the Bantu-speaking farmers, whose demeanor appeared to Schnee more mundane than that of their pastoral neighbors. But he was a realist. He saw that the country's economic future depended on communities such as the Nyamwezi, who had increasingly turned from porterage to service in the German military and administrative establishments, and on former Bantu-speaking warrior peoples like the Ngoni, who were beginning to be important as hired hands on plantations. He also liked Africans as people:

> The character of the Bantu on the average has nothing of the grim, the sullen, and the treacherous that I had found among the Papuans and the Melanesians in the South Seas; the Bantu should rather be described as frank and cheerful. I have often talked in Swahili with servants and carriers . . . and sometimes listened to those campfire conversations that many a native graces by a great command of language and imagination in recounting stories, tales of animals, or personal reminiscences.[30]

As a civilian administrator, Schnee continued his predecessor's policy of promoting Swahili as the territorial language of administration. It was taught in all government schools and in many mission stations. The government continued to employ Swahili-speaking junior officials, and Schnee himself made a point of speaking Swahili to important chiefs and at major public occasions such as the inauguration of the Mittellandbahn[31]—the central railway line of East Africa built both for strategic reasons and to benefit African agriculture. The government's policy of creating an indigenous class of subordinate administrators depended on the joint educational effort of mission and state schools. By 1913 there were 465 mission stations in the field, of all faiths and sizes; between them, they provided some form of elementary education to about 100,000 pupils. The administration also maintained some schools of its own—ten "principal" and eighty-nine "subsidiary"—including industrial institutes that taught crafts, Swahili and German, and other skills. The total number of students in government schools in 1913 amounted to about 6,100, including many *askaris* and traders.

As an African administrator, Schnee continued to operate a mixed system whereby a small minority of the population—mainly the Swahili-speaking communities along the coast and in the cities—were governed by Muslim officials known as *akidas*. The greater part of East Africa's population was administered through indigenous chiefs whom the government attempted to use as auxiliaries. The powers of these dignitaries varied considerably. Minor chiefs might be little more than local constables, whereas the "sultans" of the great interlacustrine kingdoms retained a wide measure of independence, including the right to impose the death penalty upon their subjects.[32]

Regarding the broader question of interracial relations, Schnee tried to hold a balance that would benefit both blacks and whites. Actually, as John Iliffe shows in his excellent book quoted earlier, Schnee's measures were apt to favor the European community—more articulate than the Africans, better educated, and more closely in touch with officialdom. Though personally far from anti-Indian, Schnee restricted Indian immigration and the right of Indians to acquire township lands. He facilitated land alienation to whites by charging lower prices than before, and they strengthened their position in local government. The first district councils with European majorities were elected in 1913, and municipalities under European control were set up a year later. In 1912 the advisory council was reorganized so as to give it an elected European majority. White immigration continued, and shortages of land were felt in West Usumbara, around Korogwe, and in the Moshi districts.

In terms of overall policy, however, Schnee was untroubled. Concessions to the whites did not mean very much. The advisory council was in no wise a legislative body. Europeans remained negligible in numbers; their political power was heavily circumscribed. They were far from united among themselves and were mostly concerned with parochial issues. The planters were not strong enough to prevent African growers from competing with Europeans in the open market by selling coffee or other cash crops, and land shortages occasioned by white settlement were purely local in character. The period of armed African and Arab risings seemed to be over. Modern forms of political organization had not as yet taken root. And when the Germans had to take up arms against the British, there were no great African leaders to use Germany's hour of weakness to raise the banner of revolt.

Governor at War

When World War I broke out in Europe, the colonies were ill-prepared to cope with their predicament. German East Africa's armed forces—including white conscripts, local police and sailors, and *askaris*—amounted to little more than 5,000 men. Allied seapower largely cut off the German colonies from the fatherland; only scant supplies reached East Africa from the metropolis, and these in adventurous fashion. Like their compatriots at home, the Germans in East Africa assumed that hostilities would be over within a few months and that the fate of Africa would be determined on the Vistula and the Somme. They had made no preparations to meet the civil and economic problems that would beset them in wartime or to mobilize the German settlers. The relatively poor showing made by German marines untrained for tropical warfare in the Maji-Maji rising had convinced experts that whites could not fight in the bush without extensive supplies and extraordinary medical precautions. If the British were to attack in force, the experts argued, German East Africa would not be able to hold out for any length of time.[33]

Schnee did not get much backing from his distant home government in this predicament. In any case, the colonial office—like other civilian bodies in Germany—was ready to yield to the military in all matters of importance. If Schnee is to be believed, Solf would not oppose the military trend. Instead, he yielded to the establishment even in small matters—to such an extent that he did not dare present the emperor with a sample of the gold coins struck by the East African administration because a mere elephant appeared in place of the image of the "Supreme War Lord."

To make matters worse, German East Africa suffered from those very conflicts between civilian and military authority that beset German society as a whole. The *Schutztruppen* officers knew themselves to be members of a professional elite; they had been chosen with great care from a large body of applicants eager to further their careers in the colonies. But for all their ability, they were a status-conscious lot: Schnee records that military officers in charge of administrative posts were apt to experience deep crises of conscience when plagued with settler complaints because they were unable to respond by challenging the complainant to a duel. Even in peacetime, average *Schutztruppen* officers resented Schnee's gubernatorial privilege of exercising supreme power over the military. As a civilian and a mere reserve lieutenant, he enjoyed a privilege held by no civilian official in Germany itself, and to most professional German officers his position appeared an anomaly at best and an aberration at worst.

The personality of the military commandant was not the kind to lighten the governor's burden. Paul von Lettow-Vorbeck, the newly appointed commander of the *Schutztruppen*, conformed in many respects to the stereotype of the Prussian officer common in British history books. Descended from an old Pomeranian military family, he was removed from his parents' home at an early age to become an officer cadet. The army was his home, his career, and his life. Later he served in a variety of colonial appointments and—more important from the vocational point of view—he spent some time with the general staff, the core of the German army. Among his German colleagues and subordinates, Lettow-Vorbeck enjoyed a multifaceted reputation; he was the kind of man who was capable of inspiring love and loyalty among some and hatred among others. He was popular with his *askaris*—tough mercenaries who regarded themselves as members of an African elite, well paid by the standards then prevailing in Africa, highly disciplined, and proud to record even in their old age that they had served as an *askari M'daichi*, a German soldier.

Schnee regarded Lettow-Vorbeck as a brilliant officer, imaginative and aggressive, a first-class tactician, and certainly one of the best generals of World War I. But the governor considered his commander in chief to be an overbearing, ruthless, and self-centered man who took pleasure in humiliating those whom he disliked—a "psychological sadist," a martinet who would not easily brook interference from a mere civilian governor. The quarrel between Schnee and Lettow-Vorbeck was never allowed to come out into the open. After the war the colonial office asked Schnee to withdraw a secret report on Lettow-Vorbeck lest the story concerning the quarrels between them should become public, further depress German morale, and give comfort to the opponents of colonialism—especially the Social Democrats.

The charges and countercharges, the testimonials and countertestimonials that fill some of the files on the Schnee papers no longer interest the public. But irrespective of personalities, Schnee and Lettow-Vorbeck were divided from one another by profound differences in background and upbringing. Lettow-Vorbeck was constantly irritated at the governor's petty bureaucratic concerns. If the general's war diary is to be believed, Schnee insisted that the military not shoot game to make shoe leather and that they fill out forms for transporting men and materials by train. The governor would not even compel his district commissioners to hand over their modern arms to the *askaris*, who were armed with outmoded rifles.[34] Schnee and Lettow-Vorbeck also differed profoundly over wider questions of strategy and policy. Lettow-Vorbeck was a soldier. His strategy, like that of his colleagues on the German general staff at home, gave priority to military factors and was designed to produce the maximum effect with minimum delay.

The Germans rapidly increased the strength of their armed forces. Lettow-Vorbeck was rightly convinced that white soldiers, given proper training and acclimated to Africa, would fight as well in the tropics as anywhere else. Something like 3,000 settlers therefore were conscripted, men inured to local conditions and determined soldiers. The remainder carried on, maintaining the country's administration and economy. Whatever deficiencies Lettow-Vorbeck may have had in dealing with white officers, he had no problem in leading African "other ranks." The picture of the "ever faithful *askari*" beloved by old German history books is surely overdrawn; Schnee's wartime diaries record numerous cases of desertion, especially on the part of conscripted black soldiers and pressganged porters. But even when conditions were at their worst there were no mutinies, no mass indiscipline of the kind that occurred in the German armed forces in Europe toward the end of the war. Despite incredible hardships, the *askaris* stuck it out to the end.

As a military technician little concerned with the wider political and economic implications of his colonial strategy, Lettow-Vorbeck was determined to begin the war with a general offensive against British East Africa at a time when the territory was poorly defended. He wanted to tie down the maximum number of Allied soldiers in a subsidiary theater of war, away from Europe. Schnee, on the other hand, wanted nothing to do with this design. He would have preferred German East Africa to be neutral, holding much in common with Sir Henry Belfield —his opposite number in Kenya—who majestically declared in a speech in 1915 that British East Africa had no interest in the war except insofar as its unfortunate geographic position placed the territory in close proximity to the German colony.

Colonial administrators like Schnee and Belfield, however, did not get their way. The Allies would not consent to an arrangement that would have kept European hostilities out of Africa, convinced that only the Germans would benefit from such an agreement. Nevertheless, Schnee successfully resisted Lettow-Vorbeck's design for a blitzkrieg in the bush. He felt that this strategy of concentrating all available German forces against British East Africa would have left the remainder of the German colony undefended and might have entailed an uprising in the southern part of the German territory, where the Africans still remembered the Maji-Maji outbreak. Lettow-Vorbeck conducted some raids but was prevented from striking at the Uganda railway in force at a time when the British had no means of countering such an attack.[35] Schnee also vetoed a plan for a preventive assault on the northern portion of Portuguese East Africa while the Portuguese were still neutral.

The governor's general object was political; he meant to keep the German flag floating over East Africa—or at least some part of the colony—as long as possible. Once the combatants came to the conference table, as he believed they must, Germany would still have an African bargaining counter that would strengthen its hand in negotiating a peace treaty that would give neither side a complete victory. All in all, however, the discordant Schnee–Lettow-Vorbeck team worked surprisingly well. The Germans successfully defended their entire colony for nearly two years. In doing so, they managed to tie down a total of about 114,000 British troops drawn from many parts of the empire, as well as substantial Portuguese and Belgian forces.

The East African campaign was full of picturesque details of the kind that delight filmmakers and writers of adventure stories. The British employed a professional white hunter to track down a German cruiser hidden in the Rufiji delta, where its crew had so skillfully camouflaged the vessel that it looked like one more clump in the tangled, dark-green undergrowth. The Germans sent out a Zeppelin with supplies to their beleaguered army; the airship got as far as Khartoum, where the British, having broken the German wireless code, sent it back to its base in Bulgaria by forged signals.

The war in East Africa was exceptional in many other ways. The performance of the German troops was unexcelled in the history of war as a piece of footslogging. Lettow-Vorbeck and his Germano-African force—traversing some of the world's most inhospitable country—covered well over 2,300 miles, a distance greater than that between East Prussia and the Urals. The campaign was full of military firsts—the first use in the tropics of armor, observation planes, bombers, and airborne ambulances, all pioneered by the British.

The secret of the German superiority was successful adaptation to Africa. Their officers were carefully chosen. Many of them were of aristocratic birth and eager to prove their mettle in the field at a time when peace in Europe seemed as yet unclouded. For all their many prejudices, they had a tremendous respect for the fighting abilities of their African recruits. There is a world of difference between the enthusiastic descriptions contained in the official *Schutztruppen* field service manual concerning the Africans—their courage, resilience, marching power, and knowledge of the land—and the standard accounts provided in so many contemporary mission journals with regard to the Africans' assumed wickedness and sloth. As Charles Miller points out in an excellent and most readable study, the Germans not only trained their African soldiers but also learned from them how to lay an ambush in the forest, how to construct camouflaged pitfalls lined with bamboo stakes, and how to build tangled thorn *zaribas* that stopped an assault more effectively than barbed wire.[36] The Germans—like the African tacticians whose methods they studied—became masters in choosing defensive positions in difficult country from which their movements could not be seen or their strength assessed, in keeping open many safe lines of retreat, and in fading away into the bush only to reassemble at a given point to strike at the enemy again with sudden fury.

In terms of equipment and manpower they were far inferior to their opponents, who commanded the sea and prevented supplies and reinforcements from reaching the East African theater of war. The Germans mobilized something like 17,000 men—the Allies more than seven times this number. Unlike the British, the Germans lacked wagon transport, air support, trucks, cavalry, and armored cars. The standard weapon of the *askaris*, the Mauser M-71, was a museum piece; the single-shot, .450-caliber rifle gave off thundering reports and emitted clouds of black smoke, immediately disclosing the rifleman's position. But the Germans made excellent use of their machine guns. They had trained their soldiers to be marksmen.

Their forces were also more homogeneous than those of their opponents. The enemy troops arrayed against Lettow-Vorbeck included, at various times, Britons, Indians, Belgians, Portuguese, and men from what are now Malawi, Ghana, Nigeria, Kenya, Rhodesia, and South Africa. Lettow-Vorbeck relied principally on Africans. The *Schutztruppen* represented a variety of tribes such as the Nyamwezi, who had always been willing to serve the Germans as porters and fighters, as well as former enemies of the German establishment such as the Hehe. In addition, there were the conscripted German settlers, most of them well adjusted to the country and to local conditions and immune to tropical diseases. Originally these whites were formed into separate *Schützen* companies comparable to British settler units like the Northern Rhodesia Rifles. But with a view to achieving greater cohesion, Lettow-Vorbeck gradually assigned European enlisted men to African companies and placed blacks into the *Schützen* groups, so that the two became virtually indistinguishable. From military necessity rather than conviction, the general—a regular soldier whose political predilections seemed reactionary even to some of his colleagues—thus created the first racially integrated force in modern colonial warfare.

His basic tactical unit was the field company, a self-contained body, almost an army in miniature, more mobile than British colonial battalions; in appearance it was more like a band raised by an olden-day Swahili warlord than the Prussian formations in which Lettow-Vorbeck had been trained. When the uniforms wore out, the soldiers dressed in whatever they could buy or loot on the way. German columns were followed by the soldiers' own servants, by porters, and by the soldiers' wives who cooked their husbands' meals and looked after the sick. Their presence also added a touch of brightness to the bedraggled-looking formation owing to the women's passion for gaudy colors.

In the last stage of the war Lettow-Vorbeck relied entirely on captured enemy supplies. The entire German convoy looked like a carnival procession infused with a spirit of gaiety when an important depot had been looted. Arriving at a bivouac at the end of the day's march, porters and soldiers' servants cut branches to make frames for tents or grass-roofed huts; women crushed corn and got the campfires going, and hunting patrols brought in game. Command of interior lines enabled the *Schutztruppen* to fall back on food depots set up earlier along strategic routes, where the villagers had been set to grow food in advance of the army's need. If neighboring cultivators had to go short of supplies it mattered little to Lettow-Vorbeck, who gained not only increased mobility but denuded the countryside to hinder the pursuing British.

Adaptation to local conditions also marked the German war effort in the industrial sphere. The Germans created tropical ersatz industries,[37] such as the manufacture of a gasoline substitute from copra and dyestuffs from indigenous barks. They wove army blankets, put together boots, minted gold coins, and distilled *Schnaps*. Among other products yielded by local plants were a disinfectant, a quinine substitute, digitalis, and a benzine substitute; ointment bases were made from hippo and elephant fat. Thus, for example, though badly stricken by disease, the German army suffered less from malaria than their opponents, and their incidence of gangrene and tetanus remained extraordinarily low despite terrible jagged wounds and the ravages of a climate that encouraged putrefaction.

During the first two years of war the civilian sector performed a minor economic miracle. Farmers, white and black, intensified production to supply the army. The Germans built up small industries that turned out products such as soap made from local oils and blankets and uniforms woven from local cotton. They improved their repair facilities as well.

Schnee realized, as Lettow-Vorbeck did not, that the German war effort would collapse unless it enjoyed a considerable measure of passive support from the Africans. Faced as they were by vastly superior Allied forces, the Germans would have had no means to suppress large-scale indigenous revolts. Schnee prevented such outbreaks by curbing the military. Wherever he was in a position to do so, he quickly ended such practices as arresting local chiefs or *akidas* to serve as hostages for the good behavior of their communities or as sureties for the ready delivery of food. He refused to sanction the burning of villages suspected of being friendly to the enemy. As far as they were able, the Germans paid for their food. In order to meet their obligations, they struck their own gold and copper coins, which were accepted freely by Africans, who hoarded the money at a time when cash could no longer buy supplies imported from Europe.

Gradually, however, Allied military and economic superiority began to tell. During the latter part of 1916 the Germans were forced to withdraw to the southern and southwestern parts of the country, yet in the end the Germans descended upon the country a third time. By then, Schnee reported, no animals were left. Except for a few beans, no food was to be had. Even the game had largely been depleted by enemy troops. Most of the local African people had left in despair. But by this time the Germans had little choice. Their columns subsisted by requisitioning food and by "shooting game for the pot" where they could.

For transport, the Germans—like their opponents—depended on carriers, many of them unwilling conscripts.

> The escape or the attempted escape of prisoners of war and of Africans pressganged as porters had become a matter of common occurrence. . . . Shots rang out almost daily. At dusk or during the night sentries fired at would-be deserters. Unfortunately, innocent people have repeatedly been killed in this fashion, men whose only crime consisted in trying to escape from involuntary servitude as porters.[38]

By the latter part of 1918 the German forces had been reduced to a motley following meticulously recorded by Schnee as consisting of 30 officers, 125 white noncommissioned officers, 1,168 *askaris*, 130 prisoners of war, 1,516 porters, 482 locally conscripted carriers, 282 African servants, 13 craftsmen, and 819 women and boys. Given the small size of the German military establishment in East Africa, German losses had been enormous. Total casualties, including men killed, wounded, and captured, amounted to 552 officers, 3,731 European settlers, and 14,252 *askaris*—this not counting a much larger number of carriers. Lettow-Vorbeck, although wounded with his vision impaired, was still indomitable. Schnee was in low spirits. But between them they had brought off an astonishing feat.

The end came in November, when the Germans were apprised of the armistice in Europe and then agreed to lay down their arms. There was a stiff ceremonial parade at Fort Ablercorn in Northern Rhodesia. General Edwards, the British commander, shook hands with the German officers who were presented to him with military punctilio. In 1919 Schnee and his comrades in arms were repatriated. He came back to a defeated country, beset by hunger, class war, and despair. The German colonial empire had ceased to exist, and Schnee had to come to terms with political realities of the day. In more practical terms, he had to look for a new job.

Publicist and Politician

When Schnee returned to Germany he was only forty-eight years old. He had a distinguished record, some highly placed friends, and reasonable expectations of reaching high office under the republic. Some of the ex-colonials, soldiers for the most part, would not see eye to eye with the new order of things. Lettow-Vorbeck was mixed up in the right-wing Kapp putsch. Liebert became an early member of the Nazi party. But men like Solf, Seitz, and Schnee, adherents of the old National Liberal tradition, had no regrets for the Hohenzollerns. Solf—and also Dernburg —briefly reached ministerial office under the republic, and Schnee had high hopes that he might exchange his furnished room in Berlin for the ambassadorial residence in Washington. However, he never obtained the post for which he believed himself so eminently fitted. So he turned to politics and joined the moderate, right-of-center Deutsche Volkspartei, backed mainly by bankers, industrialists, and professional men in the cities. He approached the party's leader for a Reichstag candidacy and was advised to run for a Potsdam constituency—advice he accepted. In 1924 Schnee was elected to the Reichstag.

Schnee's main interest continued to center on the colonies. He became a member of the Interfraktionelle koloniale Ausschuss, an informal committee composed of Reichstag members from numerous parties of the center and right who were interested in the return of the German territories. He likewise joined the Interparlamentarische Union, most of whose German members derived from the Social Democratic and Center parties. The *Union* was designed to provide a common platform for parliamentarians of many different countries, and Schnee used it as a forum for pleading Germany's cause in the war-guilt debate that filled political journals and newspaper columns after World War I.

He also became a member of the Deutsche Kolonialgesellschaft, which continued to advocate colonial revisionism. At first he found the going hard. The Communists and the great majority of Social Democrats would have nothing to do with "the colonial idea." The parties of the extreme right, including the Nazis, were interested primarily in continental expansion. Their policy was designed to humble Poland, Czechoslovakia, and ultimately the Soviet Union, thereby providing Germany with a great Eastern European empire. Colonial revisionism was associated, however, with the traditional colonialists at the center and the moderate right. The Deutsche Kolonialgesellschaft, for its part, wanted to project a moderate image and to dispel the popular impression that the colonial cause was irretrievably linked with that of the militant chauvinists. In 1920 Seitz, Schnee's friend, assumed the society's presidency, replacing the Duke of Mecklenburg, a former governor of Togo and an ultranationalist.

By 1930 Seitz's health was apparently failing. Schnee took his place, heading an organization with some 20,000 members. In addition, he worked through a variety of other associations designed to provide a platform for the interests of German traders and industrialists and to strengthen the cause of German colonial revisionism by means of peaceful cooperation with the Western powers.

Schnee wielded a ready pen and wrote extensively on colonial questions. He coined the German phrase *Kolonialschuldlüge*—the "lie concerning Germany's supposed unfitness to rule backward races." And Schnee's *Die deutschen Kolonien unter fremder Mandatsherrschaft* was translated into English by his wife under the title *German Colonization Past and Future: The Truth about German Coloni-*

zation (published in England in 1926). It was introduced to British readers by William Harbutt Dawson, an English historian and one of many British intellectuals who believed that the Allies had bitterly wronged Germany by imposing a harsh peace upon the defeated Reich and by despoiling the Germans of their colonies.

Schnee's most substantial academic work was the *Deutsche Kolonial-Lexikon* (Leipzig, 1920), a three-volume set he edited under difficult circumstances. This monumental study was compiled by members of the defunct colonial establishment and represented the "official" Wilhelmian view; much of the information amassed by its contributors remains of great value. He also put together an interpretative study that attempted to deal with general questions of nationalism and imperialism. Schnee had read Lenin but argued that Lenin's theory did not go far enough. Imperialism, according to Schnee, was not simply an economic phenomenon but "the extension of the political or economic influence on the part of a great power over foreign countries and peoples and their forms of social organization."[39] The growth of capitalist monopolies had certainly exercised some influence on prewar imperialism. But imperialism was not solely economic in motivation, as Lenin had asserted. Lenin, Schnee continued, had also ignored the economically progressive function played by entrepreneurs in unlocking new sources of wealth and had likewise been mistaken in saying that colonialism necessarily led to war between the colonial powers. German colonialism had not occasioned serious clashes with foreign powers. The Anglo-German conflict derived above all from Germany's unwise decision to build a great fleet. Economic competition would not have entailed war by itself; otherwise, an Anglo-American war would have been inevitable given the fact that the United States represented a more serious threat to the British economy than did Germany.

According to Schnee, both the Western Allies and the Soviet Union were pursuing imperialist policies. Germany's own policies had been purely defensive—an argument that disingenuously ignored the designs for a vast German ruled Mittelafrika drawn up during the Great War by the senior civil servants of the colonial office at a time when the German colonial empire was already tottering to its fall.[40] Germany, he concluded, needed colonies in the interests of both world peace and domestic prosperity. The future would see further imperialist struggles over control of vital raw materials, including oil. The League of Nations by itself would not be able to avoid future wars. This objective could be accomplished only by agreements concluded between the great powers in their own enlightened self-interest. Provided Germany played its cards wisely, it might regain at least part of its former possessions by getting the League to transfer these territories to Germany under the guise of mandates.

Schnee's book essentially reproduced the arguments put forward by the Deutsche Kolonialgesellschaft and similar organizations. The revisionists believed in a policy of gradualism. Meetings of bankers, businessmen, and bureaucrats argued in private that Germany should aim initially at equal rights for German residents in mandated territories and colonies. Germany should extend its school system abroad. German missionaries should be allowed to work among colonial peoples on the same terms as clergymen of other nationalities. The Western powers should be prevented from annexing the mandated territories outright. Colonial propaganda should be intensified among the German workers, who unfortunately were taking very little interest in the question.[41]

For all the propaganda produced by the *Reichskolonialgesellschaft*, the colonialists were never able to gain mass support. None of the "promising men" of the colonial era—Solf, Dernburg, or Schnee—ever attained national prominence. Success went to the militant right-wingers who came to dominate the German political scene even before Hitler's formal coup. As the Republic foundered, Schnee, like so many of his class, became convinced that only a national coalition of all right-wing forces—including the Nazis—could save the day. A government of national union, he argued, would be able to "tame" Hitler and his militants. There was no point trying to exclude a large segment of the electorate from participation in power by constantly holding new elections. Germany needed an authoritarian government capable of resisting communism, of putting the unemployed back to work, and of restoring the economy.

In 1932 Schnee accordingly left the Deutsche Volkspartei. A year later he became a member of the Nazi party. At first he was a propagandist, using his international connections to argue that Germany's treatment of the Jews was an "internal matter"; foreigners had no right to meddle with the "Jewish question" in Germany on the ground that the German Jews were not a separate national group and therefore were not entitled to the special protection extended by the League of Nations to ethnic minorities. He soon became disillusioned with the regime, however, and for its duration he represented the party in the Reichstag by not opening his mouth.

As Schnee saw it, the Nazis turned out to be no more than demagogues. The government began to interfere with religious matters. Hitler's treatment of the Jews became "dubious." Above all, the Führer—by liquidating Roehm and his real or assumed adherents—had destroyed the cherished *Rechtsstaat*, the rule of law. Hitler's manner of dealing with the Roehm putsch profoundly shocked Schnee's convictions as a man trained in law. By proclaiming himself Germany's supreme judge, Schnee wrote in his private notes (probably in 1938), Hitler had pushed back his country a thousand years, for even a brutal mercenary like Roehm should have been entitled to a fair trial.[43]

The great majority of the Nazi party, moreover, remained indifferent to the colonial revisionism of the Deutsche Kolonialgesellschaft variety. Hitler and his followers had little patience with the colonial establishment inherited from the Wilhelmian era. The Führer's first priority was the east, where he looked for lebensraum. Africa was only a sideshow. The Nazis preferred to create their own colonial organization, and in 1936 the Deutsche Kolonialgesellschaft was dissolved. As far as Schnee and his friends were concerned, Hitler's attitude toward the colonial question was essentially "negative." In 1933, when Schnee still expected great things from the Führer, he had already been warned by Solf that Hitler opposed their colonial aspirations, condemned their past, and despised their future.[44] Solf turned out to be right. The Nazi revisionists had no need for superannuated governors. Nothing happened to Schnee personally, but he was attacked in *Der Stürmer* for once having associated with Jewish capitalists.

The story of Schnee's last years makes painful reading. He represented a vanished world, a nationalist upper class proud of its special role in society, its technical efficiency, and its general culture, but devoid of judgment and—in the last instance—unwilling to stand up for its principles. For all its talk of military honor and *Kameradschaft*, the great majority of these men and women would not live up to their professed principles—as, for instance, in publicly acknowledging the heavy losses suffered by German Jews in World War I or the sense of patriotism shown by Social Democratic soldiers.

By the time World War II was being waged, Schnee was in his seventies, an aging man, obtuse, and without even the critical sense that he had shown in his younger days. In 1943, for instance, he visited Poland at the invitation of the German army. He saw the smoldering ruins of the Warsaw ghetto. He heard pistol shots being fired while the last survivors were being rounded up. He was told of mass shootings carried out by the S.S. He listened to accounts purporting to demonstrate that bunkers had been built in the ghetto and that its defenders had included not only Jews but also "Bolsheviks and German deserters." He understood that Poland had been turned into a brutal police state. But in his private notes he still professed himself unable to get precise details concerning the treatment of Jews,[45] the kind of knowledge available to many a private soldier in the German army. He was even wider of the mark regarding the Pacific area, a region on which some considered him an expert by reason of his antiquated colonial experience. By the middle of 1944, when the Japanese empire was beginning to totter, Schnee still maintained in a lecture that the Allied strategy of "island hopping" was unsuccessful, that Allied "air terror" was bound to be ineffective, that the Allies had been unable to penetrate even into the periphery of the Japanese defenses, that Japan's economic position had improved by reason of its conquests, and that Japan could not be defeated by maritime means.[46]

For all his lack of comprehension, Schnee was what was known to German Jews of the period as a "decent Nazi." He tried to help former Jewish friends in a variety of ways. His "denazification file," compiled for the Allied Commission for Denazification in 1947, contains a number of genuinely moving letters from opponents of the regime who certified that he and his wife had assisted them and had taken some risk in so doing.[47]

World War II and its aftermath brought a series of further personal tragedies. The Schnees were bombed out. Franz Kempnerer, a half-Jewish friend and a former reserve officer in German East Africa, was hanged by the Gestapo. Other friends of Schnee's—von Lindequist, a former secretary of state of the colonial office, along with his wife—committed suicide when Russian troops occupied their estate at the end of hostilities in Europe. Schnee himself survived the war with all its terrors—only to be killed in 1949 in a Berlin traffic accident.

In retrospect Schnee's career seems meaningless. Nothing remains of the empire he helped to administer and to defend. Meaningless also seem his decorations and honors that once were a matter of pride—the Iron Cross of the First Class, the Iron Cross of the Second Class, the Order of the Red Eagle, the Golden Leibnitz Medal of the Prussian Academy of Sciences, or the Eagle's Shield of the German Reich. Bismarck's Germany has broken asunder. Foreign armies continue to stand on German soil. Yet by a strange twist of history the colonial territories created by the Germans from a mosaic of conflicting local polities—Tanzania, Togo, and Cameroon—survive as united and independent republics.

Schnee would not have appreciated the final irony.

Notes

1. This essay was written with financial assistance from the Historische Kommission in Berlin, whose help is gratefully acknowledged.

2. By 1912 the officers serving in the *Schutztruppen* of German East Africa, Cameroons, and South-west Africa contained 73 nobles as against 149 commoners. The total number of lieutenants comprised 55 nobles and 165 commoners; something like thirty-three percent of the total were noblemen. In the Prussian army the proportion of noble-born infantry lieutenants stood at twenty-two percent in 1908.

3. Charles Miller, *Battle for the Bundu: The First World War in East Africa* (New York, 1974), p. 328.

4. Cited by John Iliffe, *Tanganyika under German Rule, 1905–1912* (New York, 1969), pp. 201–202. Iliffe gives a fine sketch of Schnee's gubernatorial activities. An excellent account of local administration is given in Ralph A. Austen, *Northwest Tanzania under German and British Rule: Colonial Policy and Tribal Politics, 1889–1939* (New Haven, 1968).

5. Schnee reminiscences, folder 20, Schnee Papers, rep. 92, Preussisches Geheimes Staatsarchiv, Berlin, the Schnee Papers being a voluminous source.

6. Johannes Tesch, *Die Laufbahn der deutschen Kolonialbeamten: Ihre Pflichten und Rechte* (Berlin, 1902), pp. 1–24.

7. Schnee to Solf, 19 September 1901, Solf Papers, Bundesarchiv, Koblenz.

8. Heinrich Schnee, *Als letzter Gouverneur in Deutsch-Ostafrika* (Heidelberg, 1964), pp. 9–24.

9. Idem, *Bilder aus der Südsee: Unter den kannibalischen Stämmen des Bismarck Archipels* (Berlin, 1904), pp. 7–15. For a modern anthropological account see A. L. Epstein, *Matupit: Land, Labor, and Change among the Tolai of New Britain* (Berkeley, 1969).

10. Stephen Winsor Reed, *The Making of Modern New Guinea, with Special Reference to Culture Contacts in the Mandated Territories* (Philadelphia, 1943), pp. 111–152.

11. Schnee to his father, 13 August 1899, folder 2, Schnee Papers; idem, *Bilder aus der Südsee*, p. 92.

12. Solf to Schnee, 8 July 1902, no. 131, Solf Papers.

13. Schnee to Solf, 19 May 1902, and Solf to Schnee, 3 July 1902, no. 131, Schnee Papers. For the wider question of mercantile policy and trusteeship see especially Otto Diehn, "Kaufmannschaft und deutsche Eingeborenenpolitik in Togo und Kamerun von der Jahrhundertwende bis zum Ausbruch des Weltkrieges; Dargestellt unter besonderer Berücksichtigung des Bremer Afrikahauses J. K. Vietor" (Ph.D. dissertation, University of Hamburg, 1956), which throws much light on the internal shift of power within the Kolonialrat.

14. In 1899 the proportion of noblemen holding the most senior positions in the central administration (*Staatssekretäre, Vortragenderräte,* and *Dirigenten*) numbered two out of four; in 1906, two out of eleven; and in 1913, one out of fourteen.

15. The work of the commission ultimately resulted in the magisterial publication by Erich Schultz-Ewerth and Leonhard Adam, *Das Eingeborenenrecht: Sitten und Gewohnheitsrechte der Eingeborenen der ehemaligen deutschen Kolonien in Afrika und der Südsee,* 2 vols. (Stuttgart, 1929–1930).

16. For salaries see *Kürschners Staatschandbuch* (Munich, 1912); for comparative data within Germany as a whole see Nikolaus von Preradovich, *Die Führungsschichten in Österreich und Preussen, 1804–1918, mit einem Ausblick bis zum Jahre 1945* (Wiesbaden, 1955).

17. According to estimates supplied by Bernhard Dernburg, then minister for the colonies, in his *Koloniale Finanzprobleme* (Berlin, 1907), German capital invested in the colonies in 1907 amounted to about 300 million marks. At that time the share capital and reserves of the Dresdner Bank was valued at 231 million marks; the Diskonto-Gesellschaft, at 227 million marks. The Deutsch-Ostafrikanische Bank, founded in 1905 with the aid of the Deutsche Bank, the Diskonto-Gesellschaft, Von der Heydt und Co., and other concerns, was an economic dwarf, with a capital of 2 million marks.

18. For a detailed account of Helfferich's work within the colonial administration see a memorandum by Theodor Seitz (undated), no. 5, Seitz Papers, Bundesarchiv, Koblenz.

19. Lugard to Solf, 10 November 1913, no. 41, Solf Papers.

20. Of the seven governors who ruled in East Africa during the German period, four had been members of the higher nobility and two had been soldiers raised to the nobility. Only Schnee was a civilian pure and simple.

21. G. Gillman, "Dar es Salaam, 1860 to 1940: A Story of Growth and Change," *Tanganyika Notes and Records*, no. 20 (December 1945): 1–23.

22. Schnee to Solf, 26 February 1914, no. 31, Solf Papers.

23. In 1913 the white population stood at 5,336, about four-fifths of whom were German citizens: 551 were officials; 186 members of the armed forces; 498 missionaries and clergymen; 882 planters, farmers, and truck drivers; 352 engineers, technicians, and builders; 355 artisans and workmen; 523 traders; 19 physicians; and 169 in diverse professions. For further details see the relevant entries in Heinrich Schnee, ed., *Deutsches Kolonial-Lexikon* 3 vols. (Leipzig, 1920).

24. The country's ordinary revenue in 1913 amounted to 16,478,000 marks, of which 6,220 derived from taxes. The extraordinary income from loans and previous savings stood at 36.8 million marks. The ordinary income for 1904, the year before the outbreak of the Maji-Maji rising, was 5,938,000 marks, of which 1,128,000 derived from taxes. In 1904 there was no extraordinary revenue.

25. Schnee to Solf, 3 October 1912, no. 31, Solf Papers.

26. The Deutsch-Ostafrikanische Plantagengesellschaft, the first of the German East African plantations, had a distinguished list of stockholders who included, among others, the Grand Duchess of Saxe-Weimar, Prince von Hohenlohe-Langenburg, and Counts Henkel von Donnersmarck, Arnim-Muskau, Mirbach, and others; see F. Schroeder to A. Von Palézieux-Falconnet, 27 November 1892, 2 February 1888, and 9 December 1887, no. 7, Palézieux Papers, Bundesarchiv, Koblenz. The founders of the Deutsch-Ostafrikanische Bank, according to Von der Heydt, *Kolonialhandbuch; Jahrbuch der deutschen Kolonial- und Überseeunternehmungen* (Berlin, 1912), pp. 20–22, included the Deutsch-Ostafrikanische Gesellschaft, the Deutsche Bank, the Diskonto-Gesellschaft, S. Bleichröder, Delbrück, Leo und Co., Von der Heydt und Co., Mendelssohn und Co., Salo Oppenheimer, and Robert Warschauer.

27. According to Adalbert Bauer, "Der Arbeitszwang in Deutsch Ost-Afrika" (Ph.D. dissertation, University of Würzburg, 1919), p. 15, the total number of African workmen in employment, 1912–1913, was 91,892; of these about 50,000 were in the pay of European firms and about 25,000 were employed by other Africans. Bauer reports that the response of local firms to contemporary questionnaires concerning the labor question showed considerable variation. The majority were dissatisfied, but some—such as the Deutsche Holz-Gesellschaft für Ostafrika or the Ostafrikanische Plantagengesellschaft—were generally satisfied with the existing position.

28. After World War I, Major C. C. Dundas, later a British governor, compiled a "Report on German Administration" for the use of the British government. Dundas's unpublished report—a copy of which is to be found in no. 555, *Kleinere Erwerbungen*, Bundesarchiv, Koblenz—is probably the most scathing indictment of German judicial and labor practices to be found in contemporary literature. Dundas showed, among other things, that despite Dernburg's efforts, flogging continued to be widely used for economic as well as criminal offenses: in 1912 German courts imposed a total of 8,057 beatings, comprising 48 percent of all sentences; the corresponding figures for British East Africa were 380 and 4.2 percent (ibid., pp. 102–104).

29. Schnee to Solf, 26 February 1914, and 2 December 1912, no. 31, Solf Papers; see also Wilhelm Methner, *Unter drei Gouverneuren: 16 Jahre Dienst in den deutschen Tropen* (Breslau, 1938), pp. 322–323.

30. Schnee, *Als letzter Gouverneur*, p. 125.

31. Commander Walther of H.M.S. *Seeadler* to the Kaiser, 23 August 1912, RM 3, vol. 3043, Bundesarchiv, Freiburg.

32. According to the research of Theodor Gunzert, a former administrator, the number of "detribalized" persons administered directly by *akidas* amounted to no more than about 150,000, or 1.5 percent of the population. Village communities placed under the authority of the *akidas* comprised a population of about 1 million, or about 10.5 percent of the total population. Larger chieftainships under European supervision accounted for about 3.2 million people, or a third of the population. The large interlacustrine kingdoms were estimated to contain about 5.25 percent of the population, with some 5,250,000 people. See Gerhard Jacob, "Die deutschen Kulturleistungen in Ruanda-Urundi," n.d., no. 40, *Kleinere Erwerbungen*, Bundesarchiv, Koblenz.

33. For excellent summaries of the German military and especially the civil war effort in East Africa see reports by *Geheimer Baurat* Brandes (head of the German public works department) dated

———1917 and 25 February 1918, folder 26c, Schnee Papers. For Schnee's private notes (later used in an expurgated version by his wife in editing his posthumous *Als letzter Gouverneur*) see "Ostafrikanische Erinnerungen," folder 18, Schnee Papers. See also the unpublished wartime diary of Schnee covering the end of the war (in shorthand, with a typed transcript) in folder 19, Schnee Papers.

34. See Paul von Lettow-Vorbeck, "War Diary," Imperial War Museum, London (translation of the original held in the Bundesarchiv, Freiburg, to which access is restricted).

35. There is an extensive body of literature, British and German, on the war and related subjects. For a general bibliographical survey see Peter Duignan and L. H. Gann, *A Bibliographical Guide to Colonialism in Sub-Saharan Africa* (Cambridge, 1973), section on "German Africa"; Jon Bridgman and David E. Clarke, *German Africa: A Select and Annotated Bibliography* (Stanford, 1965).

36. Miller, *Battle for the Bundu*.

37. For details see the Brandes report of 1917, Schnee Papers; W. O. Henderson, "The War Economy of German East Africa," *Studies in German Colonial History* (London, 1962), pp. 87–95.

38. Schnee diary, 14 September 1918, Schnee Papers.

39. Heinrich Schnee, *Nationalismus und Imperialismus* (Berlin, 1928).

40. *Schlussprotokoll der Kommission [des Reichskolonialamtes]*, January 1916, no. 48, Solf Papers.

41. Schnee to Solf, 26 May 1930, no. 31, "Richtlinien für die Behandlung der deutschen Kolonialfrage," Solf Papers. Members present included Cohen-Reuss, a right-wing Social Democrat and a member of the Reichswirtschaftsrat; Kastl, director of the Reichsverband der deutschen Industrie; Kiehl of the Deutsche Bank und Diskontogesellshaft; Amsinck of the Woermann- und Deutsch-Ostafrika Linie; and ex-governors Shultz-Ewerth, Schnee, and Solf. Solf did not fully accept the committee's resolution; he questioned the committee's statement that colonial markets and raw materials were essential to the German economy.

42. Schnee to Dingeldey (leader of the Deutsche Volkspartei), 29 October 1932, no. 80, Schnee Papers.

43. Notes by Schnee (concerning events between 1932 and 1934), folder 28, Schnee Papers.

44. Solf to Schnee, 2 October 1933, no. 131, Solf Papers.

45. "Reisen im Generalgouvernement Polen," May to June 1943, folder 26, no. 107, Schnee Papers.

46. "Die Weitere Entwicklung in Ostasien und im Pazifik" (talk given to the Deutsche Wirtschaftsgesellschaft), 22 May 1944, Schnee Papers.

47. See, for instance, Heinrich F. Albert (a former cabinet minister in the Weimar republic) to Schnee, 1 April 1946, Schnee Papers; Walther Sternheim (a Jewish ex-judge who had won the Iron Cross First Class as a reserve officer in German East Africa) to Schnee, 20 December 1946, folder 10, Schnee Papers. For Schnee's own interpretation of the German debacle written after the end of the war see "Wie alles kam," folder 13, Schnee Papers.

Men of Two Continents: An African Interpretation

A. E. Afigbo

AMONG professional historians in Africa, biographies have not found great favor. The reasons for this trend in modern historiography on the continent are not very clear, as the matter has not yet been investigated. Pundits, engrossed with the debate over the relative roles of great men and "vast impersonal forces" in human history, are likely to put it down to the fact that until recently it was considered more fashionable, more liberal, and more profoundly academic to dismiss great men as the pawns of impersonal forces usually considered beyond human control and human comprehension. African scholars who are focused on the problem of sources for writing the Afrocentric history of African nationalist dreams are more likely to explain the attitude toward biography in terms of the scarcity of information vital to reconstruct meaningfully any sizable fraction of African history through this medium. For it has correctly been observed that the historian can probe the personality and achievements of great men successfully only if the latter "left behind them a generous volume of correspondence, autobiographical material and kindred records."[1]

There are, however, some of us who without advocating the investigation of African history through biography believe that great men and their doings are already tending to dominate works on African history to the extent of almost squeezing the masses out of the story. Much of African history deals with empires and kingdoms. When these are not about Ghana, Mali, Songhay, Asante, Oyo, Jukun, Buganda, or Monomotapa, they are about the British, the French, the German, the Portuguese, or the Belgian empires in Africa. In personal terms when they are not about the Mansa Musas, the Askia Muhammads, the Sonni Alis, the Idris Alomas, the Mutesas, the Chakas, the Usman Dan Fodios, the El-Hadj Omars, and so forth, they are about a monstrous regiment of European adventurers—Lugards, Rhodeses, Faidherbes, Bingers, Mousinhos, and so on. Nor is this surprising: a substantial body of data on precolonial Africa comes from king lists, royal chronicles, and songs of praise associated with the courts of kings and kinglets; whereas data on the colonial period come largely from records left behind by members of the ruling colonial elite.

Understandably, there is a growing feeling among African scholars that this dominant "heroic tradition," which sees African history in terms of empires and kingdoms, of emperors and kings, may well be part of the explanation for the egregious egotism and astounding performance of many an African ruler of today. In other words, it may have encouraged modern leaders to think that the man who is larger than life, be he a buffoon or a statesman, is of the very essence of African experience. Consequently, African scholars are increasingly drawing attention to the greater relevance of socioeconomic and cultural history, whose methods and approach appear to place more refreshing emphasis on those developments and processes that center around the common people. For similar reasons many Africans have developed an abiding suspicion of the kind of book entitled *Mr. X and the Making of Nation Y*. At the same time, many have tended to see the European colonization of Africa as an assault on, and the exploitation of, one people by another rather than as the movement of a few mavericks in nineteenth-century Europe; just as they regard the eclipse of direct European colonial rule in Africa as the rejection by African peoples of this system of subordination and exploitation rather than as the work of a few so-called detribalized, maladjusted, and self-centered men.

It is a fact, though, that there is no such thing as a vantage point that commands an exclusive view of reality. Bearing in mind this truism, one must concede that even the biographical approach has some contributions to make to our overall understanding of the evolution of African society in the precolonial and colonial periods. But the scholar who would approach the history of colonial Africa through the study of the careers of great men, especially of alien conquerors and rulers, must do so in the full knowledge of a number of related requirements.

The most fundamental of these demands arises from the fact that the colonial governors of concern to us here were men of two continents. They were born and nurtured in Europe, each bearing the cultural prejudices and presuppositions of his country, his social class, and his time. Each of them came to Africa in the service perhaps of his country, perhaps of himself, perhaps of Africans, perhaps of nobody in particular, or perhaps for want of what else to do for a living, or perhaps to meet a violent and dramatic early death. Of this question of motivation, we shall hear more later. But one consequence of the fact that the proconsuls bestrode two continents, or rather drifted forward and backward from the one to the other continent, is that we cannot claim to understand their role in the great events in which they participated until we can assess them from the two vantage points provided by Africa and Europe. The records they left behind in the form of either official correspondence or published books and autobiographies, the records that accumulated about them in the metropolitan press and the colonial ministries, and the comments and observations on them by men of their social class or by fellow officers of the colonial bureaucracy, give us the view from Europe.

These and other such sources may give us the details of their pedigree, their social class, their political opinions and alliances, their economic and social circumstances, their career and odyssey before attaining gubernatorial office, the dazzling splendor of their office, the problems they faced or thought they faced in the colonies, their approach to problems, of governance, and their sense of priorities and of personal achievement—yet all this constitutes only that part of the story that justifiably could be described as the beginning.

To grasp the fuller picture we must also view the governors from the vantage point provided by Africa, no matter how hazy and obscure our view from there may be compared with the view from Europe. The material for gaining such a view lies on the pages of the local colonial press and broadsheets, where such were permitted to exist, as well as in the private papers and memoirs of men like Herbert Macaulay and Nnamdi Azikiwe of Nigeria, Blaise Diagne of Senegal, Caseley-Hayford, J. B. Danquah, and Kwame Nkrumah of Ghana, Jomo Kenyatta and Tom Mboya of Kenya, and so on, writings yet to be published and studied. Finally, some of it lies in the remembered traditions of the royal personages and local officeholders whom these men fought, conquered, and used as tools.

It may be thought that the colonial governors were so elevated as to be beyond the ken of the average African. If the young district officer saw the governor so infrequently, if at all, how much less the average African, it could be argued. This may be a valid point to make, but it can be driven too far. While doing fieldwork on the warrant chiefs in 1962, I discovered there were many uneducated, ordinary folk who knew that 1914 was a landmark in Nigeria's political and administrative history because of the policies of Sir Frederick Lugard. One of them confidently informed my that Lugard abolished the warrant chiefs in 1914 because he argued that, just as the English gentleman knows the laws and customs of England, African rulers should know theirs and so should be given a freer hand than hitherto to rule their people. Lugard may not have abolished the warrant chiefs, but he sought to do so in order to discover the real chiefs and give them more powers. However, he failed. The colonial masses may, for the greater part of this period, have been "dumb," but they were neither unintelligent nor blind. Writing in 1903 Charles Partridge, who was then a district commissioner in Southern Nigeria, observed:

> The personality of the District Commissioner is an element of no small importance. His "subjects" are very human, very observant of numerous everyday forms . . . and very apt to form their own opinion of the white stranger and his policy.

There may not have been many Africans in a position to form opinions on gubernatorial officeholders during the early years of colonial rule, but their numbers must have increased as time went on and as they became more educated, or at least more sophisticated in other ways.

Without the view from this African vantage point we can hardly assess satisfactorily the importance of the colonial governors and the value of the achievements for which many scholars have come to consider them and their lieutenants justly deserving of immortalization by historians. As Plato rightly observed, it is not for the expert cook to say how tasty is the dish he prepared; it is for the hungry man whose lot it is to eat it. The delimitation of the boundaries of modern African states, the building of railways, the sinking of mines, the establishment of archives, and the opening of hospitals and schools may, no doubt, be "a good thing," indeed, "a very good thing," when judged from the perspective of Western Europe. However, they become less than good or even positively bad and dangerous if the African consumers of these imports do not appreciate or want them or find them unworkable. On this question of governors' achievements and the relevance of their work we shall hear more later.

My literature teacher in one of the colonial grammar schools that then abounded, a man who liked to reduce his lessons to mnemonics, taught us that a full appreciation of the personality and part of any character in a play or a novel can be attained only through a study of what he says about himself and what others say about him. This principle applies also to historical writing. In his study of the administration of Nigeria between 1900 and 1960 I. F. Nicolson faced certain dilemmas in trying to assess Lugard's career. He discovered that Lugard's biographer, Dame Margery Perham, had in her numerous works made exhaustive use of what Lugard said about himself in his private papers. "In these circumstances," writes Nicolson, "it seemed to the author both more fair and more important to base an examination of Lugard's life and public acts on publications and public records rather than on an examination of his private papers."[33] Here we are merely insisting that we should go further, and take into account the views of those on whose rights these men trod.

There is a fundamental sense in which the colonial era in African history, by which I mean the regimes set up and run by these governors, is obscure and difficult to understand, indeed more so than some other periods in African history. Thus, the governors and their aides were part and parcel of the system to such an extent that they could hardly be expected to have succeeded in abstracting themselves from it in order to achieve a fair account of how they came, saw, conquered, and ruled. What is more, for the greater part of the time most of them were under strong pressure from humanitarians, evangelists, greedy captains of industry or their superiors back home, or the Africans whom colonialism was brutalizing in order to civilize; accordingly, the governors had to be perpetually either on the defensive or on the offensive, negotiating their way perilously round the obstacles thrown up by these different interest groups. Their accounts of the situations and systems with which they had to cope in the colonies are thus most likely to be doctored reports of a partially perceived reality. The Africans on their part, we are justified to assume, were dazed by their defeat, their humiliation, and their exploitation to such a degree that by the time they were able to pull themselves together, or acquired the gift of recording in detail their experiences, the whole macabre drama had passed its climax.

The Europeans back home—that is, the bureaucrats who ran the colonial ministries, the merchants of sensational journalism who entertained their readers with stories of African whimsicalities, and the manipulators of religion who rejoiced in the opening of a "new" world for the practice of their trade—were in no position either to understand or correctly to assess what was happening in and to Africa. To illustrate this point I offer the example of the difficulty they must have had in understanding the office of the governor, which is the subject of this volume. This office carried with it considerable power and authority over the political, economic, social, and cultural life of millions of Africans. Yet, as Jacques Marquet has correctly pointed out, this considerable power came to the governor "from above,"

> He was accountable for it only to his superiors, and he exercised it in an authoritarian fashion over the people he administered. This political relationship had ceased to exist in its totality in Western Europe at the end of the nineteenth century.[4]

The problems of bridging the intellectual and emotional gulf that colonialism created between Africa and Europe appear insoluble. When in the colonial period some Africans pointed out, at the top of their voices, that colonialism was unjust, the creators and manipulators of the colonial bureaucratic apparatus considered "this resentment unfair," pointing out that they deserved gratitude instead of abuse "since they were bringing the only real civilization to a land where only savagery and barbarism had reigned."[5] Today when African scholars insist that European colonialism in Africa does not lend itself to easy and clear-cut judgments on its value and achievements, they are suspected of being blinded by nationalism. After all, was not the colonial regime the handiwork of brilliant men—conquerors, administrators, development planners, diplomats, and scholars?[6]

However, this timely collection of biographies helps to underline the fact that historians may underestimate the problems they face in dealing with this period of African history. To illustrate my point I shall turn to the assessment of gubernatorial performance and of the relevance of what these men achieved for the continent in which they spent, for most of them, the greater part of their working lives.

Each of the governors saw it as part of his assignment to promote the creation of what Sir Herbert Richmond Palmer described in pictureque terms as "a colourable counterfeit of the mother-country."[7] As in all cases of counterfeiting the resemblance proved to be superficial only—in this case, structural rather than functional. Describing the French system, Jean Suret-Canale has argued that

> it suppressed or ignored the political structures which were truly African and the African culture, replacing them by colonial structures and colonial education— which were indeed "French" but profoundly different from what existed at the same level in France itself.[8]

Taking the political and administrative system in British colonies in more detail, we find that the governor superficially resembled the king, the prime minister, and the speaker; his executive council looked like the cabinet; and his legislative council like Parliament. But in function and in the extent of powers entrusted to each, the governor was as unlike the king, the prime minister, and the speaker, his executive council as unlike a cabinet of responsible ministers, and his legislative council as unlike the House of Commons, made up of democratically elected representatives of the people, as anything could be. In the end, when the work of actually creating modern states in Africa was taken in hand, the post of governor was left to wither away; the executive and legislative councils had to be transformed so radically that it is often difficult to speak of these changes seriously in terms of constitutional evolution as is at times done by some historians. In other words, the political and administrative structures that obtained for most of the colonial period can be described as largely irrelevant from the viewpoint of the subsequent political and administrative structures of African states. In the case of the Belgian, French, and Portuguese territories, the difference between colonial political and administrative structures and practices and new systems that came with independence is probably more striking. Taking the French system, for instance, we discover that until the eve of the post-1945 changes, which in time led to independence and belated experimentation with democratic government, it rested on a tripartite despotism—the despotism of the president of the French Republic, the despotism of the governor and his white lieutenants, and the despotism of the chiefs whom the French retained or created.

The consequences of this situation are still with us today and may remain with us for a while yet. The fact is that leaders who were brought up by colonial governors and their aides under an authoritarian and illiberal regime were expected, almost overnight, to set in motion a liberal parliamentary system. It is no surprise that this expectation has for the most part been disappointed. Not only have most of the parliaments been sacked or reduced to parlous existence, but we are still engaged in basic debate as to whether this is really what we want—a debate that would have been concluded during the period of colonial tutelage if the political aim of colonialism had been the creation of viable democratic states.

Almost the same degree of ultimate irrelevance marked the performance of these governors in the area of local government—the level that touched on the lives of our people much more vitally than even the question of parliaments and cabinets. The British governors spent most of their time arguing in favor of basing local government on traditional rulers and actually attempting but never quite succeeding, to groom them for this vital role. The French, however, vacillated between reliance on traditional rulers and chiefs and reliance on the educated, new elite. By the time it became necessary to relinquish power, neither the British, nor the French, nor the Belgians, nor the Portuguese had succeeded in preparing either the traditional or the new elite for taking over the leadership of the new states that were precipitately brought into existence, in some cases through hastily conceived legal enactments. Here, again, the work of the governors during the high tide of colonialism had to be abandoned in favor of new experiments.

Meanwhile, some aspects of the colonial political and administrative style of life of the governors had borne fruits abundantly. The emphasis the governors placed on the form, style, and external brilliance of political and administrative power left its mark on those Africans whom fate, rather than the governors, had designated the heirs of the colonial apparatus of power. Recently, Africans have had openly to express disgust at the flamboyance and ostentation of their heads of governments. On this, Thomas Kanza has written:

> The entourage of African politicians presents a generally dismal spectacle. Presidents, ministers and political chiefs surround themselves with an assortment of upstarts, crooks and profiteers whose behaviour is bound . . . to bring national and international discredit.[9]

One cannot help seeing this situation as a carry-over from the days when the governor on tour had to be attended by outriders and a large retinue of high-ranking officials and prominent chiefs.

Similarly, the governors' use of such state institutions as the police and the army not for protecting citizens and defending national frontiers but for beating down opposition and dissent was noted and emulated by their successors. The fact is that at a time when, for instance, the strike was recognized as a legitimate means by which the European worker could draw public and official attention to his plight, the underpaid African worker or peasant oppressed by taxation had no such right. And if he dared appropriate it to himself, the army and the police were unleashed on him. The same forces were also on occasions unleashed on political agitators. The result was that the colonial police and army grew up with a tradition of periodic and decisive intervention in the internal politics of these territories. After independence they were not retrained for a new role and so have continued to intervene in politics—at times even against the rulers.

The governors, especially the earlier ones, usually have received the credit for drawing present-day national boundaries in Africa. It is in this sense, more than in any other, that some of them deserve the appellation "makers of modern Africa." Clear-cut boundaries are no doubt a good thing seen from the viewpoint of contemporary international relations, which owes a good deal to Western ideas. But just as they get the credit for this rationalization of the map of Africa, the governors must also take the blame for its untoward consequences. For one thing, many of the boundaries are not that rational, as a number of interstate imbroglios have shown. Much more important, the rigidity of these boundaries must be held responsible for the destruction of one of the immemorial rights of African peoples— the right to "walk" away from an oppressive and tyrannical state or community. The right to walk away (or to walk out) and the right to contradict oneself were among those that reformers pressed for inclusion in the Declaration of the Rights of Man during the French revolution. Yet the French in Africa went out of their way to suppress these rights. Those Africans who sought to exercise these freedoms were dubbed nomads and marked for liquidation. But for the destruction of this ancient right, many African peoples would have been spared the untold agonies of their recent history. Similar analyses of other "benefits" that colonial governors conferred on Africans would be instructive, too, but we must pass on to other issues.

Arising from the foregoing is the question of who served or saved whom? For some time it has been fashionable amongst our European colleagues to attempt to wish away the primacy of the economic motive in the European colonization of Africa in favor of other motives considered less culpable than cupidity. Thus, the experts of balance sheet and "official mind" history in recent years have been vigorously arguing that Europe's trade with Africa was negligible compared to its trade with the developed areas of the world at the time Europe decided to undertake the colonization of Africa. Similarly, it has been contended that the colonies themselves were not a paying concern. On the contrary, their budgets had to be supplemented and their development plans financed, at least in part, from imperial grants and loans. It may well be that this was so or it may well be that the history of imperial balance sheets is yet at too early a stage to support such clearcut conclusions. On the other hand, it may well be that if all the African human, agricultural, and mineral resources that were fed into the European economy had not been sold and bought in a market grossly unfavorable to Africa, the story told by the balance sheets would have been different. It may also be that the benefit Europe derived from Africa cannot be measured entirely in material terms.

This last observation pushes itself imperiously to the fore when an attempt is made to decide who served whom. Few will dispute the fact that from about 1875, at least, Africa offered boundless opportunities for young Europeans, at times even for socially and academically handicapped individuals like Binger, to achieve fame and to improve on their economic situation. They could do so by exploring, soldiering, governing, or speculating. Writing on this matter, especially with reference to the opportunities that African exploration offered, Henri Brunschwig has correctly observed:

> The aspiring explorer usually left on this first journey unknown and almost alone. . . . Either he foundered or he brought back to France a bundle of treaties and new scientific findings of value to humanity as a whole. Within a short time he was famous—the Legion of Honor, gold medals from geographical societies, receptions in the great hall of the Sorbonne. . . .[10]

Binger's career clearly illustrates the correctness of this observation. Africa raised him from obscurity and poverty to fame and prosperity. Lugard himself, after an indifferent earlier career as a soldier in India, came to Africa and discovered his prowess as a political journalist, a soldier, a merchant-company adventurer, and above all an administrator—a man on whom the League of Nations was subsequently to depend.

For some members of the African gubernatorial brigade, men like Mousinho de Albuquerque or even Lugard—frustrated and soured by heartless women—Africa appeared to offer the best opportunity for a dramatic, early death either at the hands of "murderous dervishes" or chieftains or from malaria, in any case, some obvious alternative to outright suicide. Unfortunately, this dark expectation was not always met. Consequently, Lugard rose to be a man of international renown, whereas Mousinho after dodging the issue for many years, eventually took his own life, later becoming a legend to be manipulated by the forces making for reaction in Portuguese political life.

The conclusion is thus in some respects inescapable that most of the colonial governors needed Africa more than Africa needed them. But for the opportunity that Africa offered, few, if any, of them would have earned an entire paragraph in a serious book of history. But today we are witnesses to insistent appeals for full-length biographies of most of them. Any other group of Europeans of the time could have drawn the boundaries, built the railways, the hospitals, and schools, and run the authoritarian regimes that made these innovations possible. After all, there was nothing in the colonial systems that required their being run by the men who actually ran them. "The similarity of British forms of administration," Anthony Kirk-Greene has correctly observed, "was such that it was not necessary to be completely familiar with the people, language, or custom of a territory."[11] It is understandable, then, that the governors were posted from one territory to another apparently without any consideration of whether Mr. A were fit to govern colony B. If there were really a colonial mission, clearly conceived and consistently pursued, would the governors for each colony have been chosen in such a way as to be so varied in their political, economic, and social ideologies? Would it not have been necessary to perform a kind of ideological screening that would insure that only men committed to the accepted mission got the opportunity to pilot the colonial ship?

The environment in which the governors sought to carry out their duties was a very complex one indeed. First, there were the rival demands of the two continents Europe and Africa. They most likely understood the European demands although some governors were alienated from Europe or at least from their social class or families, a fact that would help explain the reckless disregard with which they flung themselves into perilous adventures in a continent that was still popularly, but erroneously, believed to be the white man's grave. The real demands of Africa they probably never understood or bothered about even though there are many scholars of our time who would want us to believe the contrary.

Superimposed on the irreconcilable demands of the two continents, or at least existing side by side with them in some manner, was a third and even darker set of demands—the personal motivations of the governors. Some of these motivations, like the quest for personal fame and material success, were probably recognized by the governors. But thanks to the insights into personality recently provided by psychoanalysis, we now know that multiple forces must have been at work. And we are told that generally these unconscious forces, which powerfully influence men's lives, are hidden from awareness. All these issues raise the question of whether we are justified in believing that we can really understand the colonial governors, the systems they ran, and the part they played in recent African history through the process of conventional historical analysis.

For instance, there is enough evidence to suggest that many of the governors were restless souls, some of them fleeing from military life to exploration, to searching for precious metals, to colonial administration, and so on. Also significant is that they pursued these professions in a continent that at the time could be described as being on the fringe of civilization, where life was believed to be nasty, brutish, and short. Again, were the governors men who had properly adjusted themselves to Europe or to their class or to their families? If they were, why did they choose a precarious existence in Africa and/or Asia? Was it for fear of failure at home? Was it for the service of humanity and, if so, what humanity?

Also deserving of special notice is the fact (brought out in this volume) that the majority of the governors were of middle-class origin. Now this was the class whose emergence around the middle of the eighteenth century brought about far-reaching revolutionary changes in European society: in the political sphere the middle classes helped erase the last vestiges of feudalism and dynasticism and insure the triumph of modern parliamentary democracy; in the economic sphere they broke the shackles of mercantilism and ushered in the era of free trade; and socially they attained status by means of achievement rather than ascription.

Now it was largely representatives of this class who came to Africa and established one of the most illiberal regimes of modern times. Yet, in politics and administration these middle-class African governors were authoritarian, for the most part preferring to work with the members of the "feudal" aristocracy in place of the Western educated elite whom their enterprise had brought into existence. Generally, every one of them ran a police state in which the police and the army were used to protect not the people but the government. Economically they reverted to mercantilism and protectionism and at times went out of their way to deny African entrepeneurs the opportunity to compete with the large European commercial firms. Socially they favored status attained by ascription at the expense of achievement and generally assigned higher status, better jobs, and higher pay to white men simply on the ground of color. To Africans they assigned inferior status with all its attendant handicaps, again on the ground of color. The question is, why did representatives of a revolutionary class sponsor and pursue in Africa policies associated with the lordly class they overthrew or superseded?

The same question arises when we consider more seriously the personality of many of the governors. Two or three examples will be taken and examined here to round off this discussion. Mousinho de Albuquerque, for instance, must have been a very complex character. In him we had a soldier into whom discipline had been drilled and who therefore should have been used to taking orders and commands from his superiors without question. Yet this was precisely what Mousinho could not do. During his first tour of duty in Mozambique (October 1890–February 1892) he could not work with his superior, Rafael de Andrade; nor would he accept and implement loyally the policy defined and handed down by the authorities in Lisbon. This policy required that colonial governors avoid adventurist militarism in their relations with African states. But Mousinho pursued an aggressive policy that tended to bring Portugal into conflict not only with African chiefs but also with Rhodes's British South Africa Company. Because of these conflicts with the metropole Mousinho soon resigned his appointment and returned to Portugal.

Restless and still thirsting for fame deriving from achievements recorded in Africa, he accepted a new appointment in Mozambique. This time Mousinho was in supreme command in the colony, yet similar problems arose. He continued his commitment to rapid expansion by military force in place of the "go-slow" policy that Lisbon prescribed. What was more, he was too egotistical to submit to orders from Portugal. Rejecting Portuguese imperial policy, he wanted more and more powers devolved on him as governor. In particular he wanted greater control over the finances of the colony. Because Mousinho could not have his way, he again resigned about two years after taking office. Joaquim Mousinho de Albuquerque was thus a complex personality—an aggressively nationalistic patriot who lacked the humility to subordinate his personal ambitions for command and control to superior authority at home if only to advance the interests of the fatherland. Some years later—again thwarted in his personal schemes—he took his life.

Sir Frederick John Dealtry (later Lord) Lugard was another complex personality. We find in him the same preference for advance by military conquest over advance by peaceful negotiation and the same imperious temperament with its insatiable longing for command and control. On one occasion he confessed to his wife, "I love this turgid life of command when I can feel that the sole responsibility rests on me for everything." As a result, one of the really interesting features of Lugard's life is the running battle he had to fight throughout his career as colonial servant to assert his independence of his superiors and to establish undisputed control over those under him.

Lugard ranged ceaselessly from one service to another in Africa looking for an appointment that would give him supreme power over a piece of African territory. When eventually Joseph Chamberlain placed him on the road to such a post, Lugard insisted on carrying out his assignment in his own way rather than implementing the chessboard policy the secretary favored for dealing with the French threat to what later became Northern Nigeria. Again, when he became high commissioner for Northern Nigeria he did all he could to undermine the policy of advance by negotiation and diplomacy in order to convince the traditional rulers about the irresistible military might of the empire he served. In 1906 Lugard had to resign because the colonial office stood up to him over his scheme for "continuous administration," which would have made him an absentee governor for six months a year during which he would direct the affairs of the colony from London. An unforgiving and unrepentant enemy, he raised this issue once more when in 1912 he was being sent back to Nigeria in the higher office of governor-general. This time Lugard succeeded in wringing the concession from an unwilling colonial office. Beyond that the details of his administration reveal one long struggle in which, using his advantage of the so-called superior knowledge that came to him from being "the man on the spot," he blackmailed and blustered his way from one demand to another—at times with bloody consequences, as in Egbaland.

Meanwhile, as Lugard fought and cajoled his way into having almost a free hand in running the administration, he spared no effort to insure that he controlled every action of his subordinates, leaving them little initiative. Fellow Europeans who worked under Lugard were virtually reduced to ciphers by means of his subsequently famed "Political Memoranda", in which he sought to set down every detail of what a political officer was expected to do in the field. He gave his staff detailed instructions even on such matters as how to approach a local chief and when to burn down the houses of recalcitrant villagers. The local chiefs on their side were left in no doubt that the old order had changed and that they had to do the bidding of the new master to keep their position. They were not running a separate administration, he told them plainly. Instead, they and their institutions had been hitched once and for all to the remorseless wheels of the Lugardian juggernaut.

Also pointing to the existence in Lugard's personality of a darker side that conventional historical analysis may not sufficiently illuminate is his handling of evidence. This trait first came to light during the Anglo-French race for Borgu: Lugard produced a worthless piece of paper that he claimed was a treaty he had signed with the king of Nikki. To justify his preference for conquering the emirates instead of winning them over by diplomacy, he completely distorted the political and social picture of their rule in reports he sent to his superiors in London. The Fulani emirs were painted in lurid colors as alien conquerors and unrepentant slave raiders. Yet on the morrow of conquest, Lugard praised the same people as born rulers and the only hope for civilized administration in the central Sudan. Between this later picture and the earlier one he saw no contradiction.

Of this habit of playing hide and seek with objective facts, I. F. Nicolson has given us numerous other examples. Also, the local records relating to Southern Nigeria are full of evidence to the effect that Lugard knew, before he left Nigeria in 1919, that the reforms he introduced were not working smoothly. But in his report on the amalgamation of 1914 he assured the colonial office and other members of his metropolitan audience that he had set up in Nigeria an administration that would meet the requirements of that colony for years to come.[12]

From the point of view of unveiling the personality of each governor as a necessary step to understanding his motivation, his career, and his performance, one is bound to find Brunschwig's study of Binger very illuminating and intellectually stimulating. Here we have clearly presented the case of a deprived and poorly educated orphan determined to attain fame and wealth or die in the attempt. Without illusions or sentimentalism he picked on "darkest Africa" as the arena for this all-or-nothing quest for material and other successes. In the light of Binger's subsequent career there is no doubt that he chose wisely. And so we see him moving ruthlessly from nonentity to national fame as an explorer and from there to the governorship of an African colony, by which time his ambition was realized. With that, Africa began to mean less and less to Binger and he started regarding his post in the Ivory Coast as a kind of exile from glamorous Parisian society, where, probably, he was eager to flaunt his success like upstarts are wont to do. He was governor of the Ivory Coast from March 1893 to June 1897, a total of fifty months, but spent only nineteen months there.

To understand Binger's role in the colonization of Africa, it is thus both superfluous and misleading to place much emphasis on his patriotism as a Frenchman or on philosophical or other commitments on his part to the enlightenment of Africa. As Brunschwig has rightly concluded, "at a time when money rather than birth or knowledge meant power, he dreamt of becoming one of the great capitalists of his time."[13] In this ambition Binger saw and used Africa as his stepping-stone—and succeeded.

How many more of the governors who today are hailed in history books written by their countrymen and admirers as the saviors of the old and the makers of the modern Africa were motivated as was Binger? Indeed, one continues to have the nagging feeling that the men who held gubernatorial office in colonial Africa, and the regimes they set up and ran, constitute a theme more amenable to psychoanalysis than to conventional historical investigation.

Notes

1. William L. Langer, Foreword to *The Psychoanalytic Interpretation of History*, ed. Benjamin B. Woolman (New York, 1971), p. viii.
2. Charles Partridge, *Cross River Natives* (London, 1905), p. 13.
3. I. F. Nicolson, *The Administration of Nigeria, 1900–1960* (Oxford, 1969), p. 321.
4. Jacques Marquet, *Africanity* (New York, 1972), p. 37.
5. Ibid., p. 39.
6. See the introduction to this volume.
7. Herbert R. Palmer, "Some Observations on Captain R. S. Rattray's Paper: 'Present Tendencies of African Colonial Government,'" *Journal of the Royal African Society* 33, No. 130 (1934):37.
8. Jean Suret-Canale, *French Colonialism in Tropical Africa, 1900–1945* (London, 1971), p. 83.
9. Thomas R. Kanza, *Evolution and Revolution in Africa* (London, 1971), p. 116.
10. See p. 111 of this volume.
11. See p. 231 of this volume.
12. A. E. Afigbo, *The Warrant Chiefs: Indirect Rule in Southeastern Nigeria, 1891 to 1929* (London, 1972), chap. 5.
13. See p. 124 of this volume.

Index